Japan

a travel survival kit

Ian L McQueen

Japan – a travel survival kit
  3rd edition

Published by
  Lonely Planet Publications
  Head Office: PO Box 617, Hawthorn, Victoria 3122, Australia
  US Office: PO Box 2001A, Berkeley, CA 94702, USA

Printed by
  Colorcraft, Hong Kong

Photographs by
  Ian L McQueen (IMcQ), Alan Elliott (AE), Japan Information Service (JIS)
  Front cover: Bunraku (Puppet Theatre) (JIS)
  Back cover: Bronze Lanterns, Kasuga Taisha Shrine, Nara (AE)

First Published
  October 1981

This Edition
  February 1989

Although the author and publisher have tried to make the information as accurate as possible, they accept no responsibility for any loss, injury or inconvenience sustained by any person using this book.

National Library of Australia Cataloguing in Publication Data

McQueen, Ian L
  Japan, a travel survival kit.

  3rd ed.
  Includes index.
  ISBN 0 86442 045 5.

  1. Japan – Description and travel – 1945 – Guide-books. I. Title

  915.2'0448

© Copyright Ian L McQueen 1989

Ian L McQueen

Ian L McQueen is a Canadian who has been living in Tokyo for many years. He spent his earlier years in the port city of Saint John, New Brunswick, later graduating in chemical engineering from the University of New Brunswick (Fredericton).

Travels in South America, Europe and the Caribbean were followed by an extended stay in Japan during which he travelled from the north of Hokkaido to Okinawa. This was followed by a year and a half travelling through Korea, Taiwan, Hong Kong and most countries of South-East Asia.

Ian then spent nearly five years in Australia where he completed graduate studies in chemical engineering at Melbourne University. He returned to Japan in 1978 to research the first edition of *Japan – a travel survival kit* and remained there through the preparation of the second and third editions. He is also a co-author of Lonely Planet's *North-East Asia on a Shoestring*.

Lonely Planet Credits

Editors	Hugh Finlay
	Debbie Rossdale
Design, cover design	Valerie Tellini
Illustrations	Margaret Jung
Typesetting	Ann Jeffree

From the Author

Japan – a travel survival kit was written to provide all the information needed for planning independent travel through Japan. When I came back to Japan in 1978 to write the first edition, there was no other readily available book that gave this type of information for the economy traveller. I repeated the travels that I had made in 1970 to see which of my good experiences then could be repeated, and tried to gather all the practical, detailed, and useful information that other travellers in Japan would need to know. What I wrote was the book that I had wanted for my first travels in this interesting country.

Any book of this type reflects the views and judgments of its author. In this case they are based on appproximately 80,000 km of travel in Japan by motorcycle and car (and many more by train), from Hokkaido to Kyushu twice, and on comparisons with the culture and attractions of a good number of other countries.

While writing, I have tried to maintain an objective viewpoint, balancing my memories of the sense of wonder felt at times during my first visit in 1970 against the knowledge and realistic viewpoint gained after spending more than 10 years in the country.

Often I suggest obtaining certain information in Japan. The Japan National Tourist Organization (JNTO) has done a marvellous job of preparing large numbers of pamphlets and other types of printed information for the benefit of travellers. It is pointless to attempt to duplicate all the information that is thus available. A certain amount of reading between the lines is advisable when using literature from any official (or semi-official) source as such literature is always non-controversial.

I plan to remain in Tokyo for several years to come, and would welcome comments and suggestions regarding the book from travellers passing through. (I regretfully will not supply travel information; that is the purpose of the book! And the TIC is better for this in any case.) My telephone number is (03) 715-1353 (evenings and weekends only.)

Many individuals and organisations have given information or other forms of assistance in researching and producing this book.

The Japan National Tourist Organisation, through both its head office and its Tourist Information Centres in Tokyo and Kyoto, have provided invaluable assistance of many kinds. The staff at the TICs deserve special thanks for their friendly helpfulness.

Grateful acknowledgment is made to the Australia-Japan Foundation and the Japan National Tourist Organisation for supporting the research of the first edition.

I would like to thank Canon Inc for help in the preparation of the original manuscript and thank various colleagues on staff for their information and assistance, particularly K Sasaki, H Kawatsura and A Miyaji.

The following individuals deserve specific mention for their assistance: D Britton, D Green, T Kaihata, N J Kang, M Kira, K Matsumoto, R Morley, J Morris, N Nagayoshi, S Onda, J Pearce, D Petersen, H Suzuki, D Weber, W Wetherall, J Yamamoto, Dr G Zobel and Ian N Lynas.

Gilles Pineau was an invaluable source for most of the detailed information on Okinawa and other islands of southern Japan.

My apologies for not being able to single out everyone who has supplied useful information.

From the Publisher

Thanks must also go to all the travellers who wrote to Lonely Planet with information, comments and suggestions. These include: Mitsuhiro Adachi (Jap); David Adamian (USA); Dale Bay (Jap); Betsy M Blan (Nl); Carl Bloch (Dk); Paulette Chitwood (USA); Cathy Chivers (UK); Prof Jack M Cluntz (Jap); Linda Cole (Aus); Kinowhita Coop (Jap); A Corsi (UK); Rod Currie (UK); Richard Curtis (USA); Julie Delahanty (Can); Mike Diederich (USA); Mark Donohue (Aus); Robert Duncumb (Aus); D L Ebbels (UK); Stuart Farrow (Jap); Chris Fox (Jap); Ebe Fumagalli (It); Karen Gipson (USA); Richard Harold (UK); Clinton Hart (Aus); David Heath (UK); Ed Henderson (USA); Bertil Holmstrom (Sw); Louise Hope (USA); Jack Horger (USA); David Irwin (UK); English H Kyoto (Jap); Ralph Levenstein (Can); Chris Liebert (UK); Pauline Loiselle (Can); Mandy Ludlam (Jap); Maryann Maslan (USA); N. McGeachy (Jap); Peter Moorhouse (Aus); Sandy Moritz (Jap); T Munn (Can); Peter Okamoto (Jap); Ira Richmond (USA); G I Robertson (NZ); Tomas Rohlin (Jap); Corinna Maria Scheidies (D); Ed Henderson (USA); Stacy Nagaoka Shirouzu (USA); Asmund Skard (Nl); Doug Slaymaker (Jap); Masami Takahashi (Jap); The Kampung Inn (M); Steve & Carla Walters (Aus); F Scott (Aus); Takashi Watanabe (Jap); Elaine Williams (Aus); G Peter Witteveen (USA); Jacqueline Young (UK); Edi Rohrer (CH).

Aus – Australia, C – Can, CH – Switzerland, Dk – Denmark, – It – Italy, Jap – Japan, Nl – Netherlands, NZ – New Zealand, M – Malaysia, Sw – Sweden, UK – United Kingdom, USA – United States of America.

A Warning & a Request

Things change – prices go up, schedules change, good places go bad and bad places go bankrupt – nothing stays the same. So if you find things better or worse, recently opened or long since closed, please write and tell us and help make the next edition better! All information is greatly appreciated and the best letters will receive a free copy of the next edition, or any other Lonely Planet book of your choice.

Extracts from the best letters are also included in the *Lonely Planet Update*. The *Update* helps us make useful information available to you as soon as possible – it's like reading an up-to-date noticeboard or postcards from a friend. Each edition contains hundreds of useful tips, and advice from the best possible source of information – other travellers. The *Lonely Planet Update* is published quarterly in paperback and is available from bookshops and by subscription. Turn to the back pages of this book for more details.

Contents

Introduction

Japan is one of the world's most interesting countries to visit. It has a long history yet is possibly the most dynamic country on earth with an incredible amount of industrialisation – very much a mixed blessing. Its historic culture and society were completely different from anything known in the west, and many attitudes formed in the distant past affect life today. Festivals from centuries ago are still held, linking present with past. Despite the exotic element of the country, it is one of the most accessible in terms of good transport and accommodation, friendly people, and there's little risk of eating bad food.

Thousands of western travellers go to Japan every year (along with several times as many Asians from nearby countries), but only a relative few venture outside Tokyo, Kyoto and a couple of other well-visited tourist destinations. Of course there is nothing wrong in spending time in these places, as they do house many of the country's chief attractions, but those who venture a little off the beaten path will find that they are in country where foreigners are still quite a rare sight and the people are friendly. It is not like the outer reaches of a little-known Himalayan kingdom, for example, but an element of discovery is still possible.

It is sad but true that a considerable number of travellers arrive in Japan not really knowing where to go, what to see, where to stay, what to eat, when the weather is good, and how to see the most at the lowest cost. Japan is far from all western countries and expensive both to get to and to travel in, so few people can afford repeated trips to see what they missed the first time. This book was written to provide all the information needed for planning independent travel through this intriguing country.

To the foreign visitor depending only on official sources, Japan can be likened to the image on a rear-projection screen, with the visitor seeing only what it is desired that he see. It takes a while to be able to see around the screen to the full reality. Parts of the screen image – the cherry blossoms, Mt Fuji, *geisha*, the castles, temples and gardens – are certainly a part of Japan, but the reality also encompasses dreary, crowded cities, small houses, high-pressure education, social and employment systems, lack of care for wildlife and destruction of the natural environment.

I hope visitors following this book will be aware of the reality of Japan, enjoy the many good things, but go away with an objective picture of the country in its entirety.

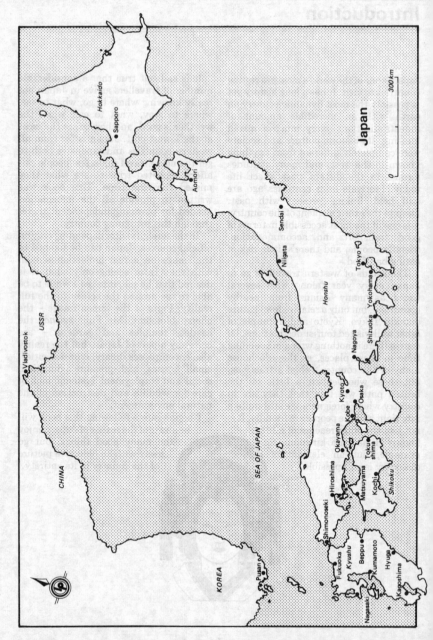

Japan

300 km

0

Hokkaido

Sapporo

Aomori

Sendai

Niigata

Tokyo

Yokohama

Shizuoka

Nagoya

Honshu

Kyoto

Kobe

Osaka

Okayama

Tokushima

Hiroshima

Matsuyama

Kochi

Shikoku

Shimonoseki

Fukuoka

Kyushu

Beppu

Kumamoto

Hyuga

Nagasaki

Kagoshima

USSR

Vladivostok

CHINA

SEA OF JAPAN

KOREA

Pusan

Facts about the Country

HISTORY

Because written Japanese records of history don't exist prior to the Nara era (600 to 784 AD), most knowledge of Japan before that time is based on Chinese records. Archaeological excavations have found traces of settlement from 100,000 years ago, but nothing further until a few thousand years ago.

The earliest civilization about which much is known has been named the Jomon period, tentatively dated up to the second century BC. There is some evidence of a Polynesian/Southeast Asian connection in these people and possible links between Japanese and Polynesian language structures may have been brought with them.

There were probably northern Asian elements present in Japan at this time as well. It has also been hypothesised that the Jomon were in fact the Ainu people. Jomon pottery has been found in many areas of the country, as far north as Hokkaido, and the Ainu once lived throughout much or all of Japan.

The next civilisation that has been assigned a name is the Yayoi, identified by a clearly different type of pottery. It is likely that these people were closely related to (or belonged to) the peoples of southern Korea and that there were close ties of trade between the islands of Japan and the Korean peninsula, the landmass nearest Japan.

Bronze and iron were introduced into Japan at this time, although the bronze age was short lived. Late in the 4th century settlements appear to have been conquered by warriors from Puyo (Korea); these were semi-nomadic, horse-riding people displaced from the Manchuria area who gradually conquered much of the Korean peninsula. Evidence for this is the sudden appearance of horses and armoured warriors (unknown in Japan in the 3rd century) and the commencement of the construction of large tomb mounds in many areas of Japan, a practice previously unknown in Japan but common in Korea.

These burial mounds are found from Kyushu through to the Tokyo area. Despite the light that the contents could probably throw on Japanese history, the authorities seem reluctant to excavate, reputedly on the grounds that the tombs are of the ancestors of the present royal family. Since it is very unlikely that the royal lineage extends back so far or so extensively, cynics suggest that excavations would show, as did Asuka tomb (near Nara) in 1972, a strong Korean connection. Since the Japanese hold Koreans in low regard, ties to the royal family just would not do. The academics amuse themselves by proposing their own theories and attacking those of others.

The native Japanese probably became dominant around the end of the sixth century and developed into a loosely joined nation governed from Yamato (near present-day Nara). Culture from Korea and China flowed into the country during this time, including Buddhist teachings, the Chinese writing system and many new arts and crafts. This leads to the dawn of the Nara era (Nara-jidai).

Nara Era (600 to 784)

The most famous organiser of the early Japanese state was Prince Shotoku (shown on the now-obsolete Y10,000 bill). In his lifetime (573 to 620) he introduced a constitution and concept of the state, promoted Buddhism as a state religion, greatly improved education and culture and set up an excellent system of state administration. Many temples were built in Nara under his direction, some of which (such as Horyuji temple in Nara) still exist. Subsequent rulers continued his programme of codification of laws and administration.

This period was the first time that the capital remained in the same location after the death of the ruler. It was a prosperous time and Nara grew to a large size, much greater than the present city. The Buddhist temples gained so much power and wealth that they were a threat to the ruler, so a later ruler (Kammu) moved the capital to Heiankyo (now Kyoto) in 794 where it remained until 1868.

The first four centuries of Kyoto rule are called the Heian period (794 to 1192). The early days were ones of achievement, with cultural delegations from China, conquest of the Ezo (Ainu aboriginal people) in northern Honshu, and the blending of Buddhist beliefs with those of Shinto to make the former more acceptable by representing Shinto gods as early manifestations of Buddhist incarnations.

During this time the Fujiwara family gained great power, members becoming prime minister, regent to the throne, and supreme advisor to the emperor. With their luxurious lifestyle and neglect of administration, corruption grew, civil war broke out between 1156 and 1160, and the Taira family rose to power. In turn, they repeated the luxurious extravagance of their predecessors. They were overthrown by the Minamoto (better known as the Genji) in 1185 after a string of battles along the south coast of the country, ending in the battle of Dannoura (Shimonoseki) when the Taira were obliterated. This led to the Kamakura period.

Kamakura Era (1192 to 1333)

The Genji made their government headquarters in Kamakura (near present-day Tokyo). It was the beginning of military government (or *bakufu*) under a *shogun* ('generalissimo'), which lasted with few breaks until 1868. Military outposts were set up throughout the country with the duties of maintaining order and collecting taxes.

The Minamoto lasted only 27 years, the last one being assassinated, then a Fujiwara was invited from Kyoto to fill the post of *shogun*, although control remained in the hands of the Hojo family. The imperial capital remained at Kyoto, but the emperor had become a mere figurehead, as he would for most of the period until 1868.

Twice during the Kamakura period the Mongols under Kublai Khan tried to land at Hakata (northern Kyushu). The first wave was fought off (barely), and defensive walls (traces of which may still be seen near Fukuoka) were built in preparation for the second attempt. The walls helped somewhat, but a destructive typhoon wrecked the Mongol fleet, decimating its 100,000 warriors. This typhoon was obviously a wind (*kaze*) sent by the gods (*kami*), or a *kamikaze*. This word was revived late in WW II, in a second attempt to save Japan from invasion, to describe the suicidal attacks made by 'kamikaze' pilots against American ships.

After the victory over the Mongols, the military could not reward the expectations of its soldiers, and emperor Godaigo took advantage of the unrest to regain power for the imperial throne in his own right.

Muromachi & Azuchi-Momoyama Periods (1336 to 1598)

Godaigo failed to reward his military commanders in proportion to their services, and indulged his courtiers, so forces under the Ashikaga clan drove Godaigo out of Kyoto into the mountains of Yoshino and a new military government was set up in Kyoto (1336). The result of this was that for the next 57 years there were two courts, after which they were united, with the military government dominant. This was the Kyoto *bakufu*, which lasted until 1573. The period 1336 to 1573 is the Muromachi era; the original

Emperor Godaigo

gold pavilion at Kinkakuji temple (Kyoto) dates from these times.

The luxury of Kyoto life led to poor administration, heavy taxes and civil war from 1467 until 1568 when Nobunaga Oda entered Kyoto, but he was assassinated in 1582. The struggle for control of the country was taken over and completed by Hideyoshi Toyotomi. The short period from 1573 to 1598 is the Azuchi-Momoyama era, named after the castles of Oda and Toyotomi. It is usually called only 'Momoyama'; the name symbolises a colourful, flamboyant decorative style, quite in contrast with the restrained style that is normally thought of as Japanese. The original Osaka castle, of which the immense foundation stones remain (with a modern superstructure), was built in this period.

Edo or Tokugawa Era (1603 to 1867)

The time of Hideyoshi Toyotomi led up to the beginning of the best-known period in Japanese history, the Edo (or Tokugawa) era. Ieyasu Tokugawa succeeded in subduing all rivals. He set up a *bakufu* government in Edo (now Tokyo); the emperor continued to reside in Kyoto, without power. The country was divided into nearly 270 fiefs, each under a *daimyo* (feudal lord) who owed their power and allegiance to the *shogun*, Tokugawa.

During this period contact with European traders and missionaries increased to the point where the government felt the foreign influences (particularly Christianity) were a threat to the stability of the country. Christianity was suppressed with the martyring of many thousands (especially in Kyushu, the centre of Catholicism). Only the Dutch were permitted to trade and only through Nagasaki on the southern island of Kyushu; the Portuguese were banned in 1639, and the English and Spanish had been excluded earlier. (The early days of the Tokugawa era is the period fictionalised in James Clavell's novel *Shogun*; the character 'Anjin' was patterned on an actual shipwrecked pilot, Will Adams.)

The following two centuries or so saw a Japan sealed as completely as possible from contact with the outside world. Many Japanese who left and returned were executed to prevent the introduction of outside ideas (although swearing to say nothing of what they saw while abroad was usually enough to spare their lives). Society was highly organised, with clearly defined classes (nobility, military, farmers and merchants) with little mobility between classes. Interestingly, the merchants were the lowest class. Incredibly detailed laws decreed every aspect of life, such as the type of clothing that might be worn, the kind of food one was allowed, place of residence, movement, even the position in which one might sleep! Orders of the military leaders were to be obeyed instantly; hesitation or expression of displeasure or question was likely to result in instant death. (This historic fact might give some explanation for the tendency to this day on the part of the Japanese to show relatively little expression and to follow orders without much question.)

The isolation was brought to an end with the arrival of the Black Ships of Commodore Perry (US Navy) in 1853 with a demand that Japan open its doors to trade. Yokohoma and other ports were opened within a few years. The entry of the foreign barbarians was not universally welcomed and the Choshu clan, controlling Shimonoseki Strait, then closed it, resulting in a three-day bombardment and the destruction of the shore installations by British, American, French and Dutch ships in 1864. The Choshu then realised that the country had to be modernised to overcome Japan's powerless position.

Emperor Meiji had begun his reign in 1852 but was as powerless as his predecessors in the face of the Tokugawa. The Choshu joined with the Satsuma clan

Emperor Meiji

of Kagoshima (southern Kyushu) to press for the end of the Tokugawa government and the restoration of the emperor to full power. In the ensuing period of fighting and confusion the *shogun* stepped down and Emperor Meiji began his amazing reign in 1868. Fighting by elements loyal to the Tokugawa continued in several parts of the country and had to be put down by force, but eventually the emperor was given full powers. This is called the Meiji Restoration, although a more apt word is 'revolution', and the period of turmoil was much more like civil war than is usually recognised.

Meiji Era (1868 to 1912)

During the Meiji era Japan went from being an isolated feudal agricultural nation to one of the world's most powerful and dynamic countries, with a modern navy and army (that defeated Russia in 1905), a network of railroads, industry of all kinds, and a parliament. Every effort was made to modernise all aspects of Japanese life. This resulted in some excesses as many relics of the past were intentionally destroyed, including many picturesque castles and traditional objects like bronze lanterns. (The collection in the British Museum was rescued from a scrapyard by a ship's captain.)

Taisho Era (1912 to 1926)

Meiji was succeeded in 1912 by Emperor Taisho, but there is little record of his rule. It seems he was mentally unstable – reportedly the result of inadvertent poisoning by a white lead compound while being suckled by a wet nurse. (The compound was commonly used by women to whiten their skin; its side effects, especially its effect on the brain, were not fully appreciated.)

Showa Era (1926 -)

The present emperor Hirohito, succeeded to the throne in 1926 and is now the longest reigning monarch in the world.

The awakened national spirit and expansion of the Meiji era had far-reaching effects beyond the Taisho era and well into the present Showa era of Emperor Hirohito. The need for raw materials and markets for the growing industrial machine led to wars with China in 1894 and 1937; the former resulted in the ceding of Taiwan to Japanese control. Korea was invaded in 1910, providing the foundation for national antipathy towards Japan that persists to this day.

The worldwide economic depression of the 1930s gave the military the ability to expand its control over the country, resulting in conquests of many Asian countries. It led, however, to the ultimate disaster of WW II and the devastation of Hiroshima and Nagasaki – the first and only cities ever to be atom-bombed – and the destruction of almost all the other major cities by fire and explosive bombing. It was also the first time in its recorded history that Japan had been conquered. Occupation by Allied forces (mainly American but including British, Australian and New Zealand) followed.

Post-war changes have been dramatic, with rejection of military values to such an extent that the armed forces are still held in low esteem. The right-wing militaristic mentality which promoted State Shinto as a national religion has largely disappeared. A small minority still supports it, and trucks laden with loudspeakers drive through the streets of the large cities (particularly Tokyo) blaring nationalistic and military (WW II era) music and slogans, but they are ignored by the general populace. One look at the immature young men or semi-thugs strutting on the truck roofs in their uniforms explains why.

Prior to WW II, the emperor had been revered as a living god by State Shinto. After Japan's defeat he renounced any claim to divinity. The present Emperor (Hirohito by name, but rarely referred to in this way by the Japanese) is a frail, bespectacled, kindly looking octogenarian whose main interest outside state duties is marine biology, about which he is knowledgeable and has written books. One has the impression that he played only a passive role during the pre-war period and that the military government carried out their actions in his name but without his active participation. Today he is a constitutional monarch, like the monarch of Great Britain. His present role is as a symbol of the Japanese state; although he is consulted and advised, he has no actual power in governing the country.

The use of war was renounced in the new constitution, although Japan is allowed a self-defence force, which today is, in fact, among the world's more powerful armed forces.

The country has an elected democratic government; the Diet has two chambers, the House of Representatives and the House of Councillors which enact laws, but the administrative arm (the civil service) is very powerful and controls many aspects of business, etc, with sufficient strength to go counter to the will of the legislative branches if it feels so inclined. The conservative Liberal-Democratic party has held power for nearly all the post-war period. It is a party in favour of free enterprise (though the government gives much financial assistance and 'administrative guidance' to important or new industries), and the country is firmly and reliably in the Western camp.

Interestingly, a peace treaty has never been signed with the USSR, partly because that country opportunistically seized four islands off Hokkaido that had long been Japanese, thereby joining WW II against Japan only a couple of weeks before the end.

GEOGRAPHY

Japan is made up of four main islands – Honshu, Hokkaido, Kyushu and Shikoku – plus hundreds of smaller ones. Together they stretch nearly 3000 km in the temperate and sub-tropical zones between latitudes 20° and 45°N. Equivalent locations are from Morocco to Lyons or Milan or from Miami to Montreal. Total land area is 377,435 square km, about 85% of which is considered mountainous.

Mountain ranges divide the country into four zones – the Japan Sea and Pacific Ocean sides of the northeast half, and the Japan Sea and Inland Sea sides of the southwest half – all of which have definite differences in patterns of both weather and customs of the people.

Japan is still geologically young and volcanic eruptions are not uncommon. The Pacific Plate (one of the huge areas of the earth's crust afloat on the mantle) is slowly forcing itself under the islands of Japan, causing frequent earthquakes, most of which are harmless. The volcanoes, 67 of which are considered active, are part of the 'Ring of Fire' that follows a fault line (a junction of two plates) around the earth.

Active volcanoes include Usu-zan on Hokkaido, and Aso-zan and Sakurajima, both on Kyushu. Other volcanoes on Honshu wake up from time to time; recently there was an eruption of one that had been thought dead. It is also theoretically possible for Mt Fuji to erupt again, although it hasn't since 1707 and shows no signs of doing so.

Administrative Divisions

Japan is divided into administrative units that for the most part follow natural boundaries. With the exception of Hokkaido and three other units (Tokyo, Kyoto, and Osaka), these smaller units are called *ken*. Modelled on the French prefectural system, there is a total of 43 of them in the country.

Hokkaido was only settled extensively late in the 19th century and still has a small population relative to its size. The entire island is a single *do* (district), evidenced in the last syllable of the name.

Tokyo is a *to* (metropolis), while Kyoto and Osaka and their surrounding areas are both *fu*; all three compare in size with the smaller ken. When writing the names of the latter cities in Japanese, they are Tokyo-to, Kyoto-fu and Osaka-fu.

Political Divisions

Politically, the country is divided up into the following regional groupings:

HOKKAIDO
TOHOKU: Aomori, Iwate, Miyagi, Akita, Yamagata, Fukushima
KANTO: Ibaraki, Tochigi, Gunma, Saitama, Chiba, Tokyo, Kanagawa
CHUBU: Toyama, Ishikawa, Niigata, Fukui, Yamanashi, Nagano, Gifu, Shizuoka, Aichi
KINKI: Mie, Shiga, Kyoto, Osaka, Hyogo, Nara, Wakayama
CHUGOKU: Tottori, Shimane, Okayama, Hiroshima, Yamaguchi
SHIKOKU: Tokushima, Kagawa, Ehime, Kochi
KYUSHU: Fukuoka, Saga, Nagasaki, Kumamoto, Oita, Miyazaki, Kagoshima
OKINAWA

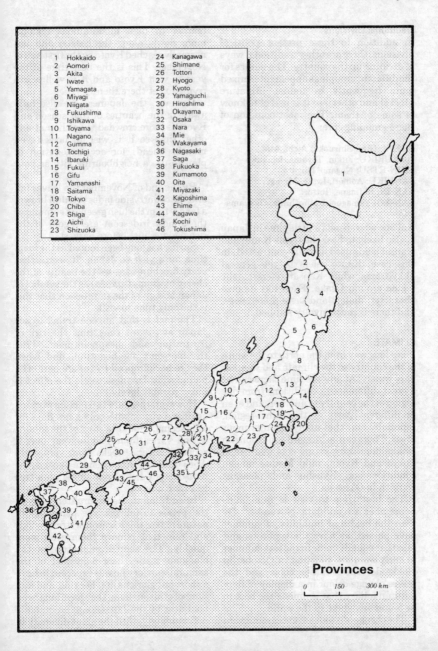

1	Hokkaido	24	Kanagawa
2	Aomori	25	Shimane
3	Akita	26	Tottori
4	Iwate	27	Hyogo
5	Yamagata	28	Kyoto
6	Miyagi	29	Yamaguchi
7	Niigata	30	Hiroshima
8	Fukushima	31	Okayama
9	Ishikawa	32	Osaka
10	Toyama	33	Nara
11	Nagano	34	Mie
12	Gumma	35	Wakayama
13	Tochigi	36	Nagasaki
14	Ibaruki	37	Saga
15	Fukui	38	Fukuoka
16	Gifu	39	Kumamoto
17	Yamanashi	40	Oita
18	Saitama	41	Miyazaki
19	Tokyo	42	Kagoshima
20	Chiba	43	Ehime
21	Shiga	44	Kagawa
22	Aichi	45	Kochi
23	Shizuoka	46	Tokushima

Provinces

0   150   300 km

Traditional Divisions

In addition to these present political divisions, there are other traditional ways of dividing up the country. The names for the different groupings appear intermixed quite frequently in tourist literature (JNTO and other), so it is useful to know of some of them. The most common of these groupings are:

TOKAI: Gifu, Shizuoka, Aichi, Mie
HOKURIKU: Fukui, Toyama, Ishikawa
SHIN-ETSU: Nagano, Niigata
SANRIKU: Aomori, Iwate, Miyagi
SAN-IN: Shimane, Tottori
SAN-YO: Yamaguchi, Hiroshima, Okayama

Anyone who spends a little time in Japan is also likely to hear the terms Kanto and Kansai being used, usually contrasted. In this case, Kanto refers to the general Tokyo area while Kansai refers to the region around Osaka. Each has its own character, dialect and taste preferences, and there is much rivalry implied.

CLIMATE

It is a long way from the north to the south of the country so the climate and weather vary widely. At any one time there can be a great difference in conditions from one region of the country to another, and even in different parts of the same region, especially in the many mountainous areas. There can be blizzard conditions on Hokkaido, sunny, crispy-cool weather in Tokyo and Kyoto, mild Mediterranean conditions on Kyushu and pleasant warmth in Okinawa.

The best time to visit is from mid-September to mid/late November. By then the heat and humidity of summer have passed, as have the typhoons and rain that usually come in the late summer to early autumn. Starting in October in Hokkaido, the weather cools and the leaves change colour in a display of fiery autumn foliage that is among the best to be found anywhere in the world.

The change of colour advances southward (earlier in high mountainous regions, more slowly along the coasts) and has normally reached Kyoto by the first half of November. This is the best time of the year to visit Kyoto and it is well worth trying to get there then.

However, the Japanese are also fully aware of the beauties of that season and Kyoto is more crowded then than at any other time so it is wise to book (even months ahead) for accommodation or plan to use a neighbouring city as your base.

By the end of November the leaves fall and the countryside fades to a dull brown; a far cry from the lush greens of summer or the almost iridescent green-gold of the rice paddies just before harvest.

Spring has long been touted as the ideal time for a visit to Japan. It seems that every brochure stresses the beauty of the cherry blossoms (*sakura*) as the symbol of Japan and gives the impression that this is the only time to visit.

The fact is that anyone trying to see Japan at *sakura* time runs the risk of frustration and disappointment. True the blossoms are beautiful, and when they're backdropped by (or are part of) a picturesque Japanese castle the effect is incomparably lovely.

However, there are two factors working against a visitor with only a few days for sightseeing. First, the start of the *sakura* season varies from year to year over a range of several weeks from very early April until late in the month. Second, the blossoms are fickle, remaining on a tree less than a week.

In addition to the natural tendency of the petals to fall off, the perversity of nature makes this a season of strong winds and rain that remove them even more quickly. The short-lived nature of the blossoms made them a symbol of the samurai warrior who was expected to have a short but glorious life. For this, and as a symbol of all our lives, they have long been held dear by the Japanese.

Fortunately, with the great diversity in

climate from north to south and from coast to mountain, the blossom season lasts for six to eight weeks nationwide, advancing in a wave of pink and white from Kyushu north to Hokkaido.

Since *sakura* are an early blossoming species (though not the earliest, as plums come out in February) their appearance is followed by a period of several weeks while the rest of nature catches up and other greenery appears. In general, spring begins chilly and clear in March and finishes hot and humid in June. On Hokkaido and in the highlands of Honshu the temperatures are considerably lower so that snow may remain on the ground as late as May or even June. There are some mountains where skiing is possible right into August.

Spring leads up to the rainy season, or *tsuyu* (also called *baiyu*), which normally begins around 10 June and continues until about 20 July, although it varies from region to region and year to year. During this period rain can be expected almost every day.

However, since 1978 there has been almost no rainy season, so don't be put off if this is only time that you can visit. It has been said (facetiously) that Japan actually has six seasons: winter, spring, rainy season, summer, typhoon season, and autumn.

Incidentally, it is a popular belief among the Japanese that there is no rainy season on Hokkaido but foreign residents report that a lot of water tends to fall out of the sky there at that time. Generally there is no rainy season along the Sanin-kaigan coast of western Honshu.

Summer is hot (around 32°C) and uncomfortably humid in the southern, coastal and lower regions, which includes most major cities. In Hokkaido and in the highlands everywhere this season is generally delightful with warm to hot temperatures and low to moderate humidity. Even in northern Honshu (the Tohoku region) it gets hot but there are often strong breezes to keep it all bearable.

A canteen of water is a good friend and it is not too hard to get through four to six litres of water a day. It is a good season for walking and enjoying the scenery; birds and fantastically beautiful butterflies flutter around the lush green countryside and the air is filled with the shrill chorus of cicadas.

The warm weather usually lasts well into October and it is still pleasant in early November. Despite the scorching temperatures in the southern cities, swimming pools automatically close on the first day of September and people abruptly cease going to the beach on the same date.

Travellers who plan to spend several months travelling around Japan would probably find the optimum route to be Hokkaido and northern Honshu through the hot season of July-August, the southern part of the country (Kyushu/Shikoku) between August and October, and the central part between September and November. For Kyoto, aim to be there in early to mid November; the period from from 10 to 20 November is generally the best for the autumn leaves, although this can vary by a week or more in either direction. At that time the temple area of Kyoto must rate as one of the most beautiful places in the world with its gorgeous combination of beautiful temples set among brilliantly colourful leaves.

Winter is generally a time of clear air, bright sun and cool or cold weather. Snow covers much of Hokkaido, northern Honshu and the mountain highlands, often to a depth of several metres. Houses in the snow country may have a separate door at roof level for access during the winter! In lower regions, snow doesn't become a permanent feature until 100 to 200 km north of Tokyo which, along with the other large southern cities, is usually snow-free except for the occasional light falls that usually melt by midday, though in 1983-4 there were 29 days when snow fell. On three of those days it was more than 150 mm deep and played havoc with traffic, and the snow stayed around for weeks. The following year it didn't snow once until March.

Overnight temperatures are rarely much below freezing in Tokyo (although in unheated apartments it may seem much lower!) and daytime temperatures are commonly in the 8 to 10°C range. Kyoto is higher up and is in mountains so is colder and somewhat snowier than, say, nearby Osaka.

For ordinary touring, winter cannot be recommended very highly. Remember that when visiting temples and many other old wooden-floored buildings, it is necessary to remove your shoes and pad around in slippers, so warm socks are a must! Houses are usually not centrally heated as fuel is expensive.

Youth Hostels are usually heated, especially in the colder regions, but an extra fee is levied to pay for the fuel. The large western-type hotels are invariably heated and comfortable, while public buildings, such as stores and offices, are generally overheated to the point of being unbearable.

It is said that Kyushu is semi-tropical. While the coastal areas (particularly Kagoshima) are a few degrees warmer than Honshu, it is still no tropical paradise – just pleasant. In the mountain areas it is also cold and snowy in winter. Okinawa and the other Ryukyu Islands are the warmest parts of Japan; their winter climate varies from cool to warm, but is not tropical.

For skiers, winter is, of course, a good time to be in the country. Conditions and facilities have been described as good although they are very crowded and not worth a special trip to Japan.

ECONOMY

The economic miracle that has taken place in Japan is well known and needs little review. It is incredible to the visitor of today to think that all the major cities (except Kyoto, which was spared because of its historic treasures) lay in ruins 40 years ago, and that the Japanese people were on the edge of starvation for several years after the war.

Now the country leads the world in many industries such as cars, steel, quality cameras and electronics, although it is facing severe economic problems because the NICs (Newly Industrialised Countries) like Korea and Taiwan have largely taken over the labour-intensive industries like textiles, have made disaster zones of the steel and ship-building industries, and Korea is now a major producer of automobiles. In addition, the phenomenal rise in value of the yen since early 1986 (engineered by the USA by a mechanism that I have yet to figure out) has made it difficult for even the most efficient industries to export and remain profitable.

PEOPLE

The origins of the Japanese people are not known with any certainty. There are elements in the language that hint at a Polynesian/Southeast Asian connection in very early times and it seems only logical to assume that various peoples immigrated across the relatively narrow Japan Sea from the Korean peninsula, from Siberia via Sakhalin Island, and from mainland Asia areas such as Manchuria and other parts of China. There are intriguing bits of evidence such as tribes in the northern hills of India with several types of food, like sushi, identical to that in Japan.

Recent research has also shown that certain factors in the blood that are similar in one racial group, but different from those of other groups, show an apparent close kinship between the Japanese and a group living in the Lake Baikal region of Siberia.

There are many dialects spoken in different regions of Japan. It can be proposed that the dialects developed by parallel immigration of numerous ethnic groups, each with its own language and distinctive rhythm and cadence, was carried over into the vocabulary and grammar of standard Japanese as it established itself throughout the country (in the same way that the English accents developed). There are many words in one dialect that are not used anywhere else, and many dialects of Japanese are totally unintelligible to people from other areas.

The people of one region often look quite distinct from those of another region; Kyushu people would not be mistaken for Tohoku people for example.

Although foreign visitors cannot identify accents, they can notice the great variety of facial and other features around the country (for example some have narrow eyes, while others are almost as round-eyed as westerners), and there is also a large variety of skin colouring from dark tan to whiter than a pale European (the women of Tohoku are known for white skin and rosy cheeks). The Japanese however, do not generally remark on these differences to each other because they want to believe they are all of the same group, something very important in Japanese society.

Many Japanese like to consider themselves as a unique race, different from other Asians, but the fact is there can be no such thing as an identifiable Japanese race. They have a national culture but the present inhabitants of the Japanese islands are a mixture of many peoples of Asian origin. In their physical appearance many Japanese *are* clearly identifiable as such, but as much as 30% to 50% of the population could be dropped into another country of the region (Korea, China, Philippines, Thailand, or even Indonesia, India or Nepal) and be indistinguishable from the local population.

In addition to the mainstream (Yamato) Japanese, there are also minority peoples. The Ainu (pronounced 'eye-noo') are now found only in Hokkaido, though once they lived at least as far south as the Tokyo area, and quite possibly much farther south and west than that. Formerly a hunting and fishing people with an animistic culture, their way of life was destroyed through the centuries by the ethnic Japanese and they now live much like other Japanese. No one knows the origin of the Ainu; their language seems unrelated to any other in the world, although native Siberian tribes have a similar bear cult. They are also said to be the most hirsute people on earth. There are about 15,000 Ainu in Japan at present.

Other lesser-known races or ethnic groups, each of only small numbers (Oroke, Gilyak, etc), are also found on Hokkaido. The people of Okinawa are also of a different ethnic group. It would seem that the Yamato Japanese are not very conscious of these different groups and believe firmly that Japan is solidly mono-ethnic. Former prime minister, Nakasone caught much flak from Ainu when he stated to the world that the Japanese have no ethnic minorities.

There is another group who are ethnically Japanese but who, for some reason in history, were made outcasts and have been treated as such ever since. They were formerly called *eta*, and are now called by the euphemism *burakumin* ('village people'). The government is taking steps to improve their lot in life, and progress is slowly being made, but they still find that they are discriminated against in housing, employment and marriage. Some organisations have actually prepared books listing the names of hamlets and towns where these people live, and many companies (even some big name ones) refuse to hire people from these places lest they sully the company. Many families of mainstream Japanese (the burakumin *are* Japanese) refuse to let their children marry one; prior to a marriage it is standard procedure to check the background of the future spouse.

Part of the belief still held regarding the uniqueness of the Japanese is a legacy of the pre-war government promotion of Shinto. Myths regarding the origins of the Japanese (such as that they were descendants of the

Sun Goddess Amaterasu-Omikami) were actually taught in schools. The purpose was to instill a feeling of nationalism. Japanese were encouraged to feel superior to, and separate from, other peoples. This served the ends of the militarists who were pushing Japan into conquest of other Asian countries. They have not been able to break the habit. Indeed, hundreds of books under the generic term *nihonjinron* ('study of the Japanese') perpetuate these feelings of separateness by describing (inventing is a better word) differences (never similarities) between the Japanese and other people.

In formal business situations, the Japanese may seem a stolid people with little spontaneity, personality, spark or dynamism. Various explanations can be offered for this reticent behaviour. One is that it has long been a virtue in Japanese society to be self-effacing and stoic. Another is that in the Tokugawa days a change in expression or hesitation of any kind when receiving an order could be grounds for death on the spot. Present-day Japan is still very hierarchical, so workers in offices, students in school, and others low on the organisational ladder, are still expected to jump when instructed by a superior. Indeed the entire language is based on preserving careful distinctions

of rank. The school system, the working environment and society in general act to inhibit spontaneity and individuality. The attitude is summed up by the old saying: 'The nail that sticks up gets hammered down'.

In relaxed surroundings, however, these people can be quite different. Japanese men become boisterous when drinking and the facade slips. (This is the only time they may voice their honest opinions without fear of retribution.) Anyone who has experienced a *karaoke* bar knows that the Japanese can put the reticence aside completely. In these places, where recorded music provides the accompaniment, well-lubricated customers almost fight each other to pick up the microphone and sing along with the music (for hours on end if given the chance), not shy in the least, and oblivious to any shortcomings in their crooning ability.

Women are expected to be shy and demure, and in the same formal circumstances of an office, etc, are rather quiet. Outside such circumstances, they are a little more outgoing, but still in much more of a shell than their western counterparts. It is only with a small group of close friends that they can be more natural.

The ideal for women is that they

remain as childlike and dependent as possible. A look at pop singers on TV will show the type, dressed in adolescent (or more juvenile) styles, and acting childishly. There is, incidentally, nothing genetically wrong with women's voices. The high-pitched PA and radio announcements that would give a dog an earache are only representative of what they are taught as being desirable. It can be very interesting for a foreigner who is talking with a Japanese woman in normal tones to hear her voice go up an octave when she addresses a Japanese.

Behaviour in Japan is mainly situational, not determined by a universally applicable set of standards. Whereas the average westerner is generally guided by Judaeo-Christian ethical values of correct behaviour (reflected in the concept of common courtesy), such over-riding principles do not exist in Japanese society. One knows how to behave in this or that situation, with people of higher, equal or lower rank, but there is no overall idea of doing right on principle or general notion of how to behave in unusual circumstances (such as encountering a foreigner for the first time in one's life in some remote part of the country!).

Within the business world, the Japanese exchange *meishi* (business cards) so that each person knows where he stands in relation to the other and can choose his behaviour and language accordingly. There are completely different verbs for use with people of different status.

This seeking of information about another person is a possible explanation for the usual litany of questions that a foreigner tends to be asked on first meeting a Japanese. Another explanation is that they have all learned the same list of questions in their English class. I encountered one student who read all the standard questions from a sheet of paper from school.

One of the great achievements of Japanese society is to have developed a social structure, with codified ways of interacting, that minimises interpersonal strife and gives the ability to live in crowded conditions without serious conflict. As one learns more about the country, one finds out that there *are* disputes among neighbours about all the petty matters that cause problems in any society, but those people involved usually keep their cool and remain relatively civil. This can lead to rather formalised, even stultified, conversations, with little or no spontaneity, but it does keep things moving along.

The system can cause problems when a foreign visitor is dealing with a Japanese who has had little contact with non-Japanese, for neither knows the ground-rules of the other. Tales of misunderstandings are rife. For example, Japanese have a trait of talking and acting in such a way as to maintain the greatest degree of harmony, even if it means not telling the truth. In the case of two Japanese, they both know it is not the truth but they see it as a way to avoid saying something unpleasant to each other, and both try to maintain the required harmony. This has been called mutually comprehensible deception. A foreigner encountering such actions would tend to interpret this as insincerity (or duplicity, or worse) but it could be a classic case of cross-cultural misunderstanding. Related to this system is the Japanese smile that can hide all real feelings.

Partly as a result of the system of personal relations, Japan is one of the safest countries in the world in which to live, and violence is quite uncommon. The average Japanese is easy-going, not fanatical about anything, just working hard to move up the promotional ladder and make a good life. However, there does exist a potential for violence.

In the past couple of decades student politics has flared up with occasional mayhem, mostly limited to radical leftist factions murdering each other. Even most student radicals appear to shed their views like a dirty shirt when they graduate and join a company to become a typical salaryman.

Under the surface, many Japanese are actually very emotional and highly strung. They rank by far the highest in the developed world in psychoses. If pushed beyond the breaking point, they can snap and become quite irrational. It doesn't happen often, but it is possible.

In addition to a live-and-let-live attitude, the Japanese have a self-indulgent, selfish side to their nature. This is recognised by the Japanese themselves. In one survey, they chose it as one category defining their nation. It is apparently an extension of the 'us' and 'them' mentality; everyone looks after one's own group and has little or no concern for others. Charities as known in the west are almost non-existent.

An offshoot of this touches on the oft-heard cliche about their oneness with nature. For the most part they have no more appreciation of nature than any westerner. The average Japanese thoughtlessly drops cigarette packets, wrappers, bottles and cans wherever he happens to be. A depressing number of beautiful gardens, temples and venerable tea houses have loudspeaker systems extolling at top volume the tranquillity of the place, which completely destroys the contemplative mood that each was intended to engender.

The Japanese are also the worst offenders against the endangered species of the world. While most other countries have virtually banned their import, pelts of rare animals and many other such natural products are imported without qualm, and ivory is easily obtainable. One tropical fish dealer caught with a specimen of a rare and endangered species stated that without selling them he couldn't make a living!

The Japanese are the last nation in the world to hunt whales on a large scale, defending the practice on the specious grounds that it is a needed source of protein, that the Japanese people have become accustomed to eating whale meat, and that many people would lose their jobs if it were abolished. At the time of writing, whaling has been banned internationally, but the Japanese are planning to kill several hundred whales nonetheless 'for scientific purposes', after which they will be made available for sale 'in order not to waste the carcass'. This is being portrayed as scientific whaling.

Almost any writings about Japan for foreign readers stress the cultural life of the Japanese. As a result, one gets the impression that everyone in Japan is adept in the arts, and spends every spare moment while not working indulging in one traditional art after another. This is not true. Many Japanese, particularly housewives, do spend much time and money studying the arts like *ikebana* (flower arrangement), and refine their mind through the tea ceremony, but the average Japanese probably has little more interest in such arts than a western counterpart.

One of the myths about Japanese behaviour that should be permanently laid to rest is their politeness. As anyone who has travelled by commuter train in Japan can aver, the Japanese are not an excessively polite people in public. Any hint of manners vanishes in the attempt to get into or out of the train. When I return to Canada and travel on the subways of Montreal or Toronto I am always struck by the overall courtesy of the populace in comparison to the supposedly polite Japanese. I am astounded to see that western men still give up seats to women, a practice unheard of in Japan unless the woman is faced with imminent collapse.

The best summation of Japanese politeness is that Japanese are polite only with their shoes off, meaning they are exceedingly polite to people they know well enough to be indoors with (where shoes are removed).

Bowing to show respect is largely a conditioned reflex. Mothers push their children's heads down in a bow before they can even talk. The depth of a bow is more an indication of the rank or business importance of the recipient than a genuine measure of the bower's esteem, and the observant person can learn much about the true feelings of the person doing the bowing by watching the expression on his face.

Attitudes to Foreigners

The Japanese word for foreigner is *gaijin*, a word heard often while travelling around the country, as one person points out the obvious to another, namely that there is a foreigner nearby. Japan is very much a 'them and us' country, and a fuss is constantly made about anyone out of the ordinary. The 'us' can be a family, a school, a company or a department. *Gai* means 'out' and *jin* is 'person', so literally: 'outside person'.

Although they generally regard themselves as superior to all other peoples, the Japanese are generally friendly and kind to foreign visitors. Foreigners of European extraction are generally given far better treatment than are fellow Japanese; non-Japanese Asians or those of non-white races, such as black Africans, may not receive such overwhelming good treatment.

Foreigners of Japanese ancestry fall into yet another category. They are expected to have inherited Japanese characteristics by birth (ability to speak the language as a birthright, be able to use chopsticks) yet are treated like other foreigners (semi-pariahs) when they are looking for an apartment, etc.

The Japanese are very much of two minds about foreigners, both not really liking them while simultaneously holding those of European origin in exaggeratedly high esteem (most of the time, anyway), because it was hundreds of experts from Europe and America who brought knowledge of the modern world to Japan during the Meiji era. Also it was people of European origin who defeated the Japanese during WW II, and the Japanese respect a winner. Not liking foreigners is a carry-over from the Tokugawa era when contact with the outside world was banned. One suspects that the propaganda from before and during the last war is still exerting an influence on the populace. (Many of those high in the ruling LDP party are rightists who had positions of influence during WW II.)

It is not uncommon to find that newspapers, magazines, films and TV present a distorted view of foreigners and foreign cultures. A repeated unfunny joke is the supposedly knowledgeable experts on radio and TV talking about this or that aspect of western culture, spouting nonsense that would draw guffaws if they could be understood by non-Japanese.

The written word is not necessarily any better at informing the populace of the outside world as there is virtually an industry producing books purporting to explain the Japanese (to the Japanese) in which some quite absurd assertions are made about the supposed uniqueness of the Japanese; they are absurd because they are often based on mythic perception of what Japan is and on very poor knowledge of what the rest of the world is really like. This type of pseudo-study is known as *nihonjinron*.

THE CYCLE OF LIFE

For the average Japanese, birth is most often in a hospital. Health standards are very high and infant mortality is perhaps the lowest in the world. However, the death rate of children up to the age of about 10 is the highest in the developed world, and higher than in many Third World countries, probably because of very low safety consciousness. Most children in the front seat of cars, for example, are almost universally not restrained in any way, and are thus at great risk in any sudden stop. Interestingly, Japanese babies are said to have a 10-month gestation because the counting begins at the end of the last monthly cycle, not from the time of the first missed one.

Infants are carried in close contact with

their mothers, who are rarely out of sight, so the child never has anxieties about affection or care. This feeling of security is believed to have many beneficial psychological results, though the spoiling causes problems later in life.

City mothers generally push their children much harder in the academic direction than those in the countryside or smaller centres, and the school standards are also generally better in larger cities, so an education gap does exist. There is not much perceived need for a highly educated farmer or fisherman, either by the educators or the people involved, although some children do escape the traditional life through education.

Sex roles are clearly defined. Boys are generally pampered by mothers and receive preference over female children, and the girls are expected to defer to any boys, although this (like so many other aspects of Japanese life) can vary from family to family.

This pampered treatment does, however, generate a feeling of dependence (amae in Japanese) among boys; a feeling that lasts a lifetime for many men. It is said that many look for a wife who will spoil them in the same way that their mothers did. (The term 'Peter Pan syndrome' pops up from time to time in description.) The sense of dependence is also felt towards school teachers, the boss or any other leader in the person's life and is one explanation for the lack of personal assertiveness remarked on by many.

There is also a seniority role, with the eldest boy being accorded priority over any other children. In the case of twins, the first-born is the more important. This boy will normally inherit the family property and will also be expected to take care of the parents in their old age.

The carefree childhood begins to be circumscribed early and competition in the academic stream begins as early as nursery school (age 3 or 4) when the parents aim to get the child onto the fast track that leads to the right kindergarten,

the right primary school, the right high school and finally to one of the top universities. Children of these families will be urged through all their formative years to study with the aim of passing the fiendishly difficult (and often tricky) entrance examinations of the top few universities. It is very common for the children to attend cram schools (juku) after regular school hours to have a few more facts pushed into their heads, or to have made clear what had been skimmed over rapidly in regular school. Children in regular school do not interrupt the teacher with questions or requests for elaboration and the teacher proceeds at his or her fixed pace. It is up to the child to clarify independently any information not understood in class.

The system right through to university is based on cramming in facts and having the students regurgitate them. There is little (if any) practice in analysis and drawing conclusions; a fact of life that becomes apparent after extended exposure to Japanese adults who have been through the system.

School is generally not a happy experience for a large percentage of students as the academic pressure is high (aimed at an academic elite) and most schools have a myriad of rules rivalling those of the military, right down to specifying the type of undershirts the boys should wear, and (at some schools) even compelling the boys to wear their hair close-cropped. Although physical punishment is nominally banned, some teachers are quite brutal physically, and every year a few students are assaulted so severely that they die. Not all is gloom and doom, but schools are not as free and interesting as they are in many other countries.

The first six years of school are primary school, followed by three years each of junior and senior high. Successive years bring on ever increasing study loads. Those who are not successful in passing university entrance exams may go on to a technical school, or may join the workforce in a factory, store, or other similar type of work. Some students who were unsuccessful with the exams one year may try again several times in successive years. Such long-term triers are nicknamed *ronin*, the word for masterless samurai who used to wander around the country looking for work.

The remarkable thing about the Japanese educational system is that the most difficult part is getting *into* university because of the very difficult entrance exams. Once in, most students have a second childhood, with very undemanding courses; few fail.

As with everything in Japan, there is a hierarchy of universities, with Tokyo and Kyoto national universities (Todai and Kyodai respectively) being at the top of the perceived ratings. Next comes a clutch of universities led by Keio and Waseda (both private institutions in Tokyo) and several other private and national universities, then local universities. The reason for the great popularity of the first two is that their graduates are almost certainly guaranteed offers of work with the prestigious public service, while those from any other university rarely succeed. This ensures that the public service has the academic elite, but it also makes for a very incestuous relationship between those two universities and the government.

The same type of relationship is very common within universities and within departments, so that a student normally does all his studies at one university (through to PhD) in one department (no cross-pollination), and universities normally hire only their own graduates for teaching posts. The result is a very insular world, designed largely to maintain the *sempai-kohai* relationship of leader and protégé. The protégé's role is, if he wants to advance (there are relatively few women post-grads), to promote the ideas of his benefactor, not to engage in his own independent research that might upset the applecart. The result is that not all research coming out of Japanese univer-sities is worthy of the name, and some would actually be laughed at if translated into a foreign language. However, the system has obviously produced the people needed to push the country forward, so something is working right – so far, anyway.

It is predominantly men who attend four-year universities, while the majority of female students opt for a two-year college programme. The reason is rooted in the same Confucian ideas that it is the men who should work, and that women should stay at home raising children and taking care of the man. In the past it has been the rare company that offered any senior position of any kind to a woman, no matter how much ability she had. This is still the general case, but slowly the barriers are coming down and women are being given more opportunities.

There is an element of circularity at work here. Traditionally women have been expected to marry after a few years in the company, so the company did not give them good jobs. The women, perceiving that career possibilities were limited, never tried to move much beyond filing, writing and tea-making activities, their role being regarded as assisting the men, who were the real doers. Two years at college is considered enough to give the women a final polish, a taste of higher education and a touch of exposure to foreign culture in the form of an English or French literature course (but not enough, heaven forbid, that she would become fluent in the foreign language or become really tainted by western thinking that would make her unacceptable in the still rather closed Japanese society). They have been perfect office workers, without the drawbacks of ambition, and prime candidates to be married off to the company's male employees.

Things are changing however, and the larger and most progressive companies are making it possible for some women to move into responsible positions, and a few have even given overseas postings to top women employees, something unthinkable in the most modern companies just a few years ago, although it should be noted that most of these jobs are of the translation and correspondence type. It is a time of change and moderate ferment, and an interesting time to observe the country in its evolution from rigid male dominance to one of greater equality. It isn't all that many years ago that women were kept out of responsible posts even in today's most socially progressive western countries, so credit should be given to Japanese companies for the progress made so far.

Once into a company after graduation, the new worker's world is also circumscribed. In the most rigid of companies, there may be a training programme lasting up to half a year and strongly resembling military training, with living in barrack-like quarters, early morning rising with calisthenics and exercises, training, singing the company song and being indoctrinated with the company way of doing things. Most companies will hire only new graduates, so that everyone joins at the same age. Until recently a person joined a company for life, and job hopping was almost unknown (largely because companies would not hire workers from another company) but this rigid structure is slowly giving way and some companies now hire specialists who have worked with other companies.

The men making up this group of workers, generally found only in large companies, are known in Japanese as 'salarymen', and are really the only people in Japan who have what is generally called lifetime employment. They will normally advance in parallel for several years, although the more able will have their chance to show their abilities and slowly pull ahead of the pack. If they do not do something rash or disgraceful, they can expect to remain on the payroll until retirement. However, these people make up only about 35% of the adult male population.

Factory workers do not have quite such security, although companies do their best to find alternative work for their employees in bad times rather than just laying them off. In large companies with on-going prosperity, a worker would expect steady employment, although his pay might not be as high as that of the higher administrative workers. The problem these days, with the high yen and shrinking rates of expansion, is that companies are running out of divisions to which they can shift unwanted personnel.

It is in the smaller companies that things are more uncertain. By lacking the prestige that goes with size, they cannot attract the better educated people who might help them move ahead, and they cannot pay the same wages that the large companies can afford.

There is a two-tier or multi-tier structure in business, with a small number of very large and prestigious companies (those involved in the manufacture of cars, electronics, optical goods, machinery, etc) that can afford to give the top conditions, and a large number of lesser companies that often take the brunt of economic slowdown. Most of the biggest companies do not make the components that go into their products, but merely assemble the myriad of smaller parts supplied by much smaller companies.

These small companies may be only a single family, and the pay that they receive for making these parts is only a fraction of what the major companies pay their own employees. The five-day work week and eight-hour day are unknown to these workers, and they may get only two days a month holiday and work 12-hour days to make a living. These are the workers not seen during the visits by foreigners to large factories, but they are contributing in no small way to the prosperity of the country. Without them, the large companies could not give such good conditions to their own armies of workers, and when there is a downturn in business, it is these small companies that get squeezed first for cost reductions.

The average salaryman will wait until he is in his mid to late-twenties before marrying, while the women are typically 23. Once over 25, many women begin to worry since the average man is looking for a sweet young thing who is going to pamper him as his mother did and have no strong views of her own – habits that diminish as the woman experiences more of life and the world.

In days gone by, marriage was as much a union between two families or clans as between two people, and it was not uncommon for the two families to get together and decide that their son and daughter were well suited to each other and would be married. The couple actually involved would have had no say in the matter. Nowadays such determining of matters by parents is so rare as to raise comment the few times it occurs.

What are called 'arranged marriages' in many English-language publications are actually marriages resulting from arranged introductions, *omiai* in Japanese. Such introductions may be arranged by relatives, friends, business acquaintances, a boss or professional matchmakers called *nakodo*. The parents are normally present at the first meeting (often in a coffee shop) if they live in the same city; independent offspring away from home may make their own arrangements. If the two young people feel that there is sufficient mutual interest, they will arrange to meet again. After only a couple of dates they might decide to marry, or they could meet several times and then call the whole thing off.

Roughly half the marriages are the result of arranged introductions. The others are known as 'love marriages', though better termed 'random introduction', for couples who meet by *omiai* usually also develop a sense of affection for the prospective partner before agreeing to marry. The arranged introduction system has the advantage that the couple will be from compatible backgrounds and serious about marriage, so they will be primed for acceptance with a suitable partner.

To westerners, reasons for getting married in Japan sometimes seem rather trivial or shallow, more financial than romantic; somewhat more akin to arranging a corporate merger than linking two lives. Although there are many marriages based on affection as strong as westerners know, many other couples seem content with an arrangement whereby the husband brings in an income and the wife tends the house, and bears and rears the children with little apparent affection between them. Probably for many couples a feeling of mutual respect is sufficient. Marriages resulting from *omiai* appear to be just as stable as those of a seemingly more romantic origin. It is certainly more and more common to see married couples holding hands and showing affection for each other in public than was true only five to ten years ago.

If a young salaryman has shown no inclination to get married by his late 20s, it is not uncommon for his boss to start making moves to introduce him to likely wife prospects. It is considered to be an unnatural condition not to be married, and indicates a lack of stability for a man. This is not good for his career prospects.

The marriage ceremony is usually Shinto, although some families prefer a Buddhist ceremony, and a growing number in the larger cities choose a Christian ceremony with white wedding gown because they like the 'mood'. In the case of the first two, only close family members attend the actual wedding, and all guests attend the reception banquet. Costs of weddings are generally astronomical.

When the couple marry, one of the two is taken in as a member of the other family. Usually the woman joins the man's family and takes his name, but if the girl's family has no son to carry on the name, it is not uncommon for the man to become part of her family and to take her family name.

It has traditionally been a worry for a woman to marry the oldest son in a family. In smaller cities and farm communities, the wife and the son live with his parents and, in the worst case, the wife may be treated virtually like a servant by the mother-in-law. With the media bringing new ideas into even the most remote communities, women are learning that this is not necessarily their lot in life.

In the early days of a salaryman's marriage, the couple will probably live in a small apartment in a multi-storey building, which is quite possibly owned by his company and the apartment rented at minimal cost.

This apartment would typically have three small rooms plus a bathroom. The large room is about six mats in size (one tatami straw mat is about one by two metres), the smaller room about 4½, and the kitchen about two. The large room serves as a living room during the day, and is a bedroom at night when the bedding is taken out of a closet and unrolled on the mats.

Instead of being the picture of Zen emptiness, the rooms are normally chock-a-block with a TV, video recorder, cabinets and low tables, air conditioner, a stack of magazines and photo albums, perhaps a miniature refrigerator, and usually an incredible jumble of other items. (I visited a home in which the smaller room was filled with a full-size grand piano!) The lack of storage space in which to put things away and the resulting untidiness is one reason for Japanese reluctance to entertain at home. Homes in the countryside are usually much bigger.

As the couple becomes better established, they may buy a small house or condominium. This is becoming progressively more difficult in the large cities because the huge amount of money awash in the country in recent years from overseas earnings has been put into real estate, with the result that already high land prices have risen as much as 50% in a year.

To afford the purchase, employees of large companies are often eligible for low-interest loans, but in worst cases it has not been unknown for not only the couple to pay off the mortgage, but their children may also be expected to continue for a number of years afterwards. Many couples have just resigned themselves to having to rent all their lives.

Life is no bed of roses for Mr Salaryman. He typically has to commute one to two hours each way every working day, and spends long hours at the office. Although the nominal working day is eight hours, it is not at all unusual for him to work another two to three hours as a matter of routine. He may grumble (outside the office) about this extra time, for he is slightly coerced into it by the fact that everyone else is doing it and he doesn't want to appear to be a shirker, since togetherness is the rule in offices. In addition, the extra pay that he earns may buy the luxuries that might otherwise be out of reach.

After work he might go out for an hour or two of drinking with his workmates. He might really enjoy this, or he might actually prefer to go home to his wife and children, for he often arrives home after they have gone to bed. The younger generation of salarymen is more and more likely to put family ahead of company whenever possible. Whether he actually accomplishes much during his overtime is not important; appearing to work hard is often the important criterion (form being generally more important than function in Japanese society).

Mr Salaryman usually hands over his entire pay to his wife who then pays the bills and gives him an allowance.

The average number of children is two and the national rate of population increase is very low, currently standing at less than 0.6% annually. Larger families would be too large for most houses, and their income is stretched if they are paying for a house. Most women are content with the role of mother to her children and comfort to her husband, although increasing numbers are returning to work after the children are old enough to be cared for by others.Child-minding centres are almost unknown. It has similarities to the pattern of movement out of the kitchen into the workforce that took place in the USA and elsewhere beginning about 20 years ago.

The pattern of marriage has undergone great change since WW II, with more couples doing activities together as families, rather than each partner having virtually a separate life. On the other hand, with the increased freedom offered by an independent income from a job, quite a few older women are separating from uncaring, demanding, domineering, or otherwise undesirable husbands whom they tolerated while the children were growing up. (The nickname for such men is *sodai gomi*, 'bulky trash', a category for garbage collection.) Divorce at any earlier stage is out of the question due to the small or non-existent settlement that they would typically receive. Sometimes women divorce their husbands just before he retires when they realise that he is soon going to be underfoot all the time.

Assuming that the couple has stayed together and put their children through university or otherwise seen them on their way, retirement for the man comes early, typically 60 (only recently increased from 55). After this, of course, he is still young and not at the end of his working life. The family probably needs a continuing income so he will usually have to find another job. This seems to be a waste of hard-earned experience and some companies are taking note and extending the retirement age.

The average lifespan for men is about 75, that for women about 81 (claimed to be the longest in the world), so she can expect to outlive him by some years. When the end does come, most Japanese have a funeral with Buddhist rites, although a few choose Shinto. This leads to the observation that people generally look to Shinto for happy events, and to Buddhism for the sad ones. (Buddhism has beliefs about the afterlife, whereas there is no body of scriptures for Shinto.) After the ceremony, the body is cremated and, after a period of time, the ashes are buried under a headstone. The memory of each person is preserved in the form of a small, vertical wooden tablet with the person's name written on it. These tablets are kept at the family altar (*Butsuden*). At various times these ancestors are venerated by the family, but they are not worshipped as some foreigners may believe. The veneration could be regarded as a type of on-going memorial service.

SEX

As it is in many other countries, sex is an entertainment commodity in Japan and men are the usual buyers.

Soaplands

A bath-house/brothel and not to be confused with *sento* (local public baths), *onsen* (hot-spring resorts) or *sauna* (which do have genuine massages) – all legitimate establishments.

Pink Saron

Obviously this is a mispronunciation of 'Pink Salon'. These are bars with hostesses. There is a flat fee for drinks and nibbles (say Y3000), but the tender ministrations of the hostess can become a lot more personal if extra money changes hands.

Pink Sarons are plentiful in large cities and elsewhere, usually near large railway stations and identifiable by garish pink signs and touts standing outside.

Hostesses

Hostesses in bars and clubs are there to please their male customers by boosting their frail egos with flattery and attention.

Although there are bars where the girls merely sit opposite their customers and do nothing more than pour drinks and make conversation, more usually the girls will allow the customer to become more physical and can often be induced to accompany him afterward.

Call Girls

In the large cities, small stickers with a provocative picture of a scantily clad woman, a phone number, a price and a time can be found in phone booths in many parts of the city.

Equal Opportunity

There are clubs for women where handsome young men give them total attention and offer similar services. However, they are reportedly very expensive.

Note

Many clubs and almost any activity involving commercial sex are under control of gangsters. Foreigners with little knowledge of the language are very susceptible to being suckered into exorbitant bar bills for which payment is extorted by violence if necessary.

THE ARTS

For times of current performances of the following consult the TIC or a publication like *Tour Companion* in Kyoto.

Kabuki

This is a very Japanese form of theatre with spectacular costumes, highly stylised actions and fantastic stage effects. Plots are often thin, or even incomprehensible, possibly based on a folk tale, but *kabuki* is worth seeing at least once for the visuals alone.

There are performances through much of the year at Kabukiza in Tokyo, which is

described in more detail in the Tokyo section.

Noh

This is another form of drama, more restrained and refined than *kabuki*. There are theatres in the large cities with performances at various times through the year.

Bunraku

The featured performers are not humans but life-like puppets, usually manipulated by three persons. The limbs, eyes and mouth all move and even though the puppeteers can be plainly seen, the dolls take on a life of their own.

This art form originated in Osaka and a new theatre was built just for these performances, but bunraku appears from time to time in Tokyo as well. (There is another puppet tradition in Japan, that of Awaji-shima island, one entrance to the Inland Sea area; it is described in the section covering that region.)

Traditional Dances

At various times through the year in Kyoto, there are performances of traditional dances, typically in the cherry blossom time and in the autumn.

Stage Shows

There are several stage shows in the large cities. One favourite for decades has been the Takarazuka Revue, a flashy all-woman stage show. There are theatres in Tokyo and the original site, Takarazuka (out of Osaka). It's totally innocent but well polished.

Rock Concerts

A large number of western rock and pop performers visit Japan but tickets are often expensive and can be very difficult to obtain.

Classical Concerts

There are several excellent symphony orchestras, chamber groups and other classical groups (either based in Tokyo and visiting form overseas) and a large number of very impressive concert halls. Unfortunately, prices are out of the range of the budget traveller.

Folk Dancing & Other Groups

This is more of interest to those staying a while in Japan but many Japanese are interested in the music and dances of other countries (as well as those of their own) and form groups to learn these dances and participate in the traditions. I saw a group practising Yugoslav dances in Yoyogi-koen park (Tokyo) one weekend and one of my more interesting friends made her living teaching flamenco dancing! Would you believe that Tokyo has a complete Japanese pipe band? Their members have the full Scottish regalia, including bearskin busbies, and they play and dance very well. There is even an annual Highland Gathering in Tokyo. A high-tech note: for perfect pitch, they were seen tuning their pipes with a portable digital frequency meter!

The large cities have little theatre groups (like the Tokyo International Players) and other foreign-community activities. These get good coverage in *Tokyo Weekender*.

RELIGION
Shinto

Shinto – 'Way of the Gods' – is the so-called native Japanese religion. It has no fixed ceremonies or scriptures and is basically an animistic belief largely concerned with obtaining the blessing of the gods for future events. Ceremonies are held to bless babies, children (Shichigosan festival), weddings and the start of new enterprises. Even large corporations take no chances and enlist the aid of a Shinto priest; it is not uncommon to see a Shinto ceremony for blessing a building site before construction begins.

Before WW II, Shinto was glorified by the state and used to bestow a blessing from the gods on the militaristic line that the government was following. State aid was given to shrines throughout the country. After the war, however, all such aid was cut and Shinto reverted to its earlier, simpler form, supported only by donations from the faithful.

Before Shinto existed there was a shamanistic folk faith similar to that in many other Asian countries. It still exists in isolated parts of Japan, such as Osorezan in the very north of Tohoku, and is known as Minkan-Shinko. (Judging by the ease with which charlatans can sell specially blessed items for curing ailments, it would appear that there are receptive elements for this type of religion in the psyche of many Japanese. But then, our own countries have the equivalents.)

When Shinto was first introduced, many existing shamanistic deities were given new Shinto names in a (largely successful) attempt to supplant the older religion by absorbing its gods and ceremonies. (In the same way, Christianity took over many ancient pagan festivals in Europe.)

Shinto shrines, called *jinja, taisha* or *jingu* (depending on the rank) are generally identifiable by a *torii* gate – two uprights and a double cross-bar. There is often a thick braided rope made of rice straw suspended between the uprights of the *torii*, a *shimenawa*, put up after the harvest season. There are normally carved stone *koma-inu* (guardian lions or dogs) at the entrance, similar to those seen at Chinese shrines. If portrayed correctly, the mouth of one lion is open, the other closed. This symbolises 'Ah' and 'Um', the sounds of birth and death, the Beginning and the End, from Hindu mythology. The distance between them is the Path of Life, a reminder to those walking between them of the shortness of their temporal existence. (Most Japanese however, are unaware of the significance.)

The shrine building is often very simple, although all incorporate customary design elements of symbolic importance. There is often a rope hanging down from a rattle suspended in the eaves. Worshippers shake it to wake up the gods and get their attention and then clap their hands together before praying. This is almost a reflex action with most Japanese, even those who claim to have no religious faith.

It is common for people to follow both Shinto and Buddhist beliefs without any conflict in their minds, as each covers certain aspects of life not touched by the other. Buddhism, with its many sects and voluminous literature, appeals more to the intellectual side of the religious nature while the simplicity of Shinto makes it instantly accessible to all.

Buddhism

Buddhism arrived in Japan from China in the middle of the 6th century. Through the centuries, the original teachings of the Buddha in India had already been modified by the Chinese to suit their temperament and culture, and this derivative form which reached Japan was further moulded so that foreign Buddhists scarcely recognise the Japanese faith as being part of their own. Numerous Buddhist sects have developed in Japan since its introduction; even in recent decades there have been new ones, such as Soka Gakkai.

Most Japanese families have some ties with Buddhism, if in no other way than through burial by a Buddhist priest on temple grounds. The eldest son of most families is guardian of the family altar, an ornately gilded wooden structure in the household place of honour. In it are tablets with the names of deceased family members. Regular ceremonies honour these ancestors – ceremonies which have led to the mistaken belief that the Japanese actually worship their ancestors. During the annual *Obon* season (around mid August; it varies with the lunar calendar) it is believed that the souls of the deceased return to visit. It is a happy time with group dancing in public places everywhere in the country.

To foreign visitors, the greatest manifestation of Buddhism in Japan is the beautiful temple buildings in Kyoto and some other parts of the country. The significance of the brilliantly gilded figures, altar fittings, etc, will be lost on those not familiar with Buddhist symbolism, but they can still be appreciated by a foreign onlooker as works of art. Another symbol of Buddhism and of Japan itself is the

Daibutsu, the great bronze statue of Buddha at Kamakura.

Others

Christians make up about 1% of the population although adherents are found in disproportionately larger numbers in public life. The fact that it is a 'foreign' faith militates against its greater acceptance along with the fact that the Japanese are generally not a religious people.

Many new religious sects have sprung up in this century, a large number just since WW II. Most are centered around their founder. (In the mid 1980s, one group of women committed mass suicide when their leader died.) The sects range from the weird to the wonderful, covering the full range of faith healing, shamanism and mysticism, and most are well removed from traditional Buddhism, Shinto, and even Christianity.

HOLIDAYS & FESTIVALS

It is useful to know the dates of Japanese holidays because these are the times when people often head back to their home towns so the trains are crowded and it is likely to be impossible to get reservations for any transport or rooms. Japanese office workers are renowned for not taking their annual holidays (possibly in order to appear keen and dedicated to the job) so they take full advantage of long holiday weekends.

There are 12 national holidays. The following Monday is taken as the holiday if the actual date is a Sunday, but not if it is Saturday, that being regarded as a working day, although a growing numbers of firms are working a five-day week. On national holidays most offices, factories and businesses are closed, although most stores and restaurants remain open.

National Holidays

1 Jan	New Year's Day
15 Jan	Coming-of-Age Day
11 Feb	National Foundation Day
21 Mar	Vernal Equinox Day (can vary)
29 Apr	Emperor's Birthday
1 May	May Day (semi holiday)
3 May	Constitution Memorial Day
5 May	Children's Day
15 Sept	Respect-for-the-Aged Day
24 Sept	Autumnal Equinox Day (can vary)
10 Oct	Physical Culture Day
3 Nov	Culture Day
23 Nov	Labour Thanksgiving Day

The three holiday periods to be really wary of are around New Year (roughly December 28 to January 5), the end of April through to early May, and mid August.

New Year is the biggest holiday season of the year and many people try to return to their family home. Nearly all businesses and many restaurants are closed; busy cities like Tokyo are nearly deserted for a couple of days and most shops are shuttered, so it is the least interesting time to visit except if you have personal connections. In recent years the degree of closure has been decreasing and the duration becoming shorter.

In the period from 29 April to 5 May there are no fewer than four holidays. It is known as Golden Week; many businesses give their employees the entire week off and, because the weather is usually fine, everyone travels – or tries to! It is very difficult to obtain reservations on trains and at hotels, and train passengers without reserved seats will have a high risk of having to stand up for the full journey. The most serious implication for the traveller, however, is that many youth hostels close during this period.

Although it is not a listed national holiday, be wary of the *Obon* season, a week in mid August when everyone tries to visit the graves of their ancestors. Again, transport is difficult to obtain but it is a lively and interesting time because there is dancing on the streets and in parks every night in almost every neighbourhood.

There are busy seasons also when school children go on excursions, but these mostly affect youth hostel accommodation in historic or nature areas and are mentioned in the youth hostel section.

Festivals

Japan has a huge number of festivals, many with a known history of hundreds or even thousands of years, with evidence of religious and folk rites.

The Tokyo Tourist Information Center (TIC) has free monthly handout listings of the festivals in Tokyo and the rest of the country, and they are posted for the Kyoto region on a bulletin board in the TIC in Kyoto. If you want an idea of what will be happening in a later month, staff can simply copy the info sheets of the previous year as many dates remain the same from year to year.

Festivals provide an insight into Japan that cannot be gained in any other way, and it is worthwhile planning an itinerary to take in as many as possible. With few exceptions they are occasions of joy and celebration. The men (and some of the older women) get gloriously drunk and happy, and often invite any foreigners present to join in the fun and sample the contents of the cask of sake just opened. (This can make taking pictures quite difficult after a while!)

A feature of nearly every festival, especially those in the country, is the drumming. The amazingly basic rhythm is executed with great skill and precision. The drumming is apparently a carry over from long-forgotten days of the earliest inhabitants of the islands.

For the visitor, there are two things worth knowing about festivals. The first is that they are one of the most enjoyable types of event that one can see while in Japan. The second is that the big ones are such attractions that they draw hundreds of thousands of people from all over the country and saturate all available accommodation. For this reason, the dates of the major festivals are given in the relevant sections in the book so that travellers can try to make advance reservations in that area, or know that it will be necessary to go elsewhere to find accommodation.

LANGUAGE

It is very useful to take at least an introductory course in spoken Japanese. Even in the big cities it can be difficult to communicate using only English, and it is that much more difficult outside the big cities. It *can* be done; thousands have managed before you!

If you have no time to take a course, the most valuable assistant during your travels will be the basic phrasebook, the *Tourist's Handbook*, available free from the Tourist Information Centers in Tokyo and Kyoto (and, presumably, by mail from overseas JNTO offices). It has the most frequently asked questions and a series of answers in both languages, so a Japanese person can point to the correct answer.

For self-study of the rudiments of the language, one of the best books is *Japanese Made Easy* by Monane, published by Tuttle. For a comprehensive study of Japanese, *Beginning Japanese* by Jorden can be recommended. It is published by Yale University Press.

The Japanese language is reputed to be difficult. The Japanese love to believe this, as they have a great psychological need to believe that everything about their ethnic make-up, society, culture, and language are unique and related to no other. Their academics are careful to avoid any line of research that might contradict this comfortable belief. Conveniently ignored is the fact that Korean and Japanese are (to quote R A Brown in the *Japan Times* while reviewing Roy Andrew Miller's *Nihongo: In Defence of Japanese*) 'as structurally isomorphic as any languages could be: for any Japanese morphological or syntactic pattern there is an identical pattern in Korean . . . . .'. He continues: ' . . . . and every educated Korean is well aware of this. Japanese tend to find it astonishing.'

However, while it is true that the writing system is probably the world's most convoluted, the language itself is relatively simple, at least in the earlier stages. Any language that has no gender, no singular or plural, no verb endings, no noun endings, no adjective endings and almost no irregular verbs, has certainly eliminated many of the complications of nearly all western languages.

Of course there are compensating complications, such as the lack of relative words (like 'that'), and the difference of most sentence structures from those we are familiar with, but the language is by no means as difficult structurally as it is made out to be. The biggest problem much of the time is that the major complexity of the language is knowing when to use what level of politeness, and *that* requires a detailed knowledge of the structure of Japanese society.

Much is made of the supposed vagueness of Japanese. However, it is not the language itself that is vague, but rather the way it is used. Japanese can be spoken just as precisely as English, but to do so would often be considered impolite; instead, the speaker alludes to or suggests a fact so as not to appear superior or presumptuous in suggesting he knows something the listener doesn't. Women use this suggestive form to a greater extent than men, which makes their statements less forceful or believable than a similar statement by a man.

The existence of 'women's language' and 'men's language' is clearly sexist by western thinking, but is an inescapable fact of Japanese life. Its function is partly to keep women in an inferior position; a woman using stronger forms of expression sounds masculine and quite undesirable. (The existence of 'women's language' is a problem for foreign men who learn Japanese from their girlfriends because they end up speaking like women.)

Actual meanings are traditionally conveyed as much by gesture and tone of voice as by the words themselves. Because of the circumlocutions often required to bypass a direct statement, misunderstandings can easily occur, with the result that the Japanese language is excellent for maintaining social distinctions but poor for imparting information and knowledge.

Younger Japanese today tend not to follow the older conventions of speech and are dropping many of the 'formula' phrases, the result being that the older people are complaining that young people are losing the ability to pick up these cues, and that they have to state everything exactly if they want to get their message through!

Certainly the language is not simple, due to the multitude of verb forms and the many words needed to indicate social distinctions, but it is not difficult to learn a major proportion (perhaps 70%) of the language in *romaji* (the romanised form). You have to learn the written form for the rest because each character (*kanji*) has at least two pronunciations, *on* (Chinese) and *kun* (Japanese). These multiple readings for *kanji* cause untold difficulty for travellers because names (especially place names) have many ways of being pronounced.

Incidentally, as far as possible, the correct local pronunciations of place names are used in this book; these may occasionally differ from names in literature printed in Tokyo, for they may use Tokyo readings of the *kanji*. Place names in Hokkaido are the worst example of this. It all sounds silly but it's true; the average Japanese cannot pronounce the names of a large number of places on a road map.

Important words are written in *kanji* (Chinese characters) while grammatical endings are written in *hiragana*, a syllabary of all the vowel and consonant-plus-vowel sound combinations in the language. Yet another complete syllabary is used to transliterate foreign words. Unfortunately they use this method initially for learning the pronunciation of English, so many learn incorrect pronunciations since the syllabary is deficient in l, f and some other letters.

Communicating with Japanese

Except with Japanese who have really mastered English, usually by living overseas, there will be problems with many questions requiring a 'yes' or 'no' answer. In Japanese a 'yes' answer will mean 'Yes, what you say is true', so it is essential to avoid asking negative questions, like 'Aren't you going?' A Japanese will answer 'yes' if he is *not* going, 'no' if he *is* going. It takes a while to get into the habit of asking unambiguous questions.

Another problem is an 'or' question. Even though Japanese has an exact equivalent, they seem to have insuperable difficulty recognising that there is a choice between A and B. The simplest way around the problem is to say 'Is it A?' or 'Is it B?' rather than 'Is it A or B?' The latter is almost sure to get 'yes' as a reply.

It is surprising that young Japanese do not speak English better than they do; most of them seem unable to put together more than one or two sentences of correct English. About 300 hours of instruction is given at junior high school level, nearly 500 hours in the senior school, and a further 300 to 600 hours at university is required to become an English teacher.

Unfortunately, a very large proportion of teachers at all levels cannot carry on a conversation in English and have learned English in the same way as they are teaching it – as a field of academic study. Another problem is that English is mostly taught using the Japanese *katakana* syllabary to represent English sounds, a purpose for which it is entirely inadequate, having no distinction between the letters 'r' and 'l', and misrepresenting several other sounds, which explains the frequent interchange of these letters. (Often quoted is the banner strung across the Ginza when General MacArthur was being proposed for US president: 'We play for MacArthur's erection'.)

The Japanese must have a sense of humour. Why else would the car manufacturers choose the names that they do. Nearly every model has a name which Japanese cannot pronounce correctly, with a copious mix of r's and l's, such as 'Gloria', 'Corolla', 'Tercel' or 'Starlet'.

Romanisation

As a courtesy to visitors to Japan, many signs are written in *romaji*. As well as names on road signs, some other Japanese words may appear on signs. Unfortunately there may be difficulty in knowing how to pronounce them because there is more than one system of romanisation.

The most common is the Hepburn system, devised more than a century ago and still useful as an aid to English speakers in pronouncing Japanese correctly but it is of negligible use to speakers of other languages. The other systems are useful in formal studies of Japanese but they are not very useful for general application because you have to learn the conventions of the system.

The Hepburn system, with few changes, is used throughout this book. Either it or the Ministry of Education system may be seen on signs in Japan, sometimes both in the same sentence.

The following is a list of the major differences between the two systems; the Hepburn is pronounced like normal English.

Hepburn	Min of Education
shi	si
sha	sya
shu	syu
sho	syo
chi	ti
cha	tya
chu	tyu
cho	tyo
tsu	tu
fu	hu
ji	zyi
ja	zya
ju	zyu
jo	zyo

The use of the two systems of romanisation (both of which Japanese know) leads to mistakes as a result of carelessness or

ignorance. One common mistake is interchanging 'a' and 'u' because they sound the same to the Japanese (compare the sounds of the vowels in 'a cup'). Because 'n' and 'm' are also interchangeable, the word 'damper' (meaning a shock absorber to British) gets written 'dunper'. Sometimes, also, one sees 'thu' instead of 'tsu', or 'tu'; this is a mistake as the 'th' sound doesn't exsist in Japanese.

Phrase List

Japanese is basically easy to pronounce. The consonants are pronounced much the same as in English (all 'hard' not soft), and the vowels are similar to those in Italian:

a	as the English indefinite article
e	as in the 'a' of ale
i	as in machine
o	as in oh
u	as in the 'oo' of hoot

The 'o' sound shifts when followed by 'n'. so the Japanese word *hon* rhymes with the English word *on*, not *own*.

Although there is a rhythm to the language, there is not nearly as much stress on individual syllables as in English, and each syllable is generally pronounced separately. Thus Hiroshima is 'hi-ro-shi-ma', not 'hi-rosh-i-ma'.

The following phrases may prove useful in daily travels. They are intended for survival, not as a language course. Therefore they are simplified and in some cases barely grammatical but should be understandable.

yes
  hai; ee
no
  iie; chigau (different); *nai/nai des* (not/it is not). All mean 'no' but most books only give *iie*; it is too abrupt and rude for use with friends (except as in 'No, you can't pay for this.') The other two forms are heard more often.

how much?	*i'kura?*	
how many?	*ikutsu?*	
where? (is)	*doko? (des'ka)*	
when?	*itsu?*	
which one/way?	*dochira?*	
where is . . .?	*. . . wa, doko des'ka?*	
this . . .(here)	*kono . . .*	
that . . .(near you)	*sono . . .*	
that . . .(over there)	*ano . . .*	
this (thing)	*kore*	
that (thing, near you)	*sore*	
that (thing, yonder)	*are*	
here	*koko*	
there (near you)	*soko*	
there (yonder)	*asoko*	
right	*migi*	
left	*hidari*	
beyond	*saki*	
this side of	*temae*	
far, beyond	*muko*	
in front of	*mae*	
next to	*tonari*	
straight ahead	*massugi; zuutto* (or *zuuuuuuto* when spoken by country people!)	
today	*kyo*	
tomorrow	*ash'ta*	
day after tomorrow	*asatte*	
yesterday	*kino*	

Numbers

For numbers up to 10, the Japanese have one set of words which can be used alone and another for use only with a 'counter'. A counter is one of many words, depending on the shape or nature of the object. The with-counter numbers are used to make composite numbers above 10, and in expressions of time. There are too many counters to mention here, so use counterless numbers or write the number down.

The number goes after the word for the things. When requesting something put 'o' between the word for the object and the number; eg *kore o futatsu kudasai* ('two of these, please').

	counterless	with-counter
0	*zero; re*	
1	*hitotsu*	*ichi*
2	*futatsu*	*ni*
3	*mittsu*	*san*
4	*yottsu*	*yon, shi (shi is a homonym of 'death', so is often avoided.)*
5	*itsutsu*	*go*
6	*muttsu*	*roku*
7	*nanatsu*	*nana, shichi*
8	*yattsu*	*hachi*
9	*kokonotsu*	*kyu*
10	*to*	*ju*
11		*ju-ichi*
12		*ju-ni*
20		*ni-ju*
30		*san-ju*
49		*yon-ju-kyu*
100		*hyaku*
200		*ni-hyaku*
1000		*sen*
5000		*go-sen*
10,000		*ichi-man* (Not *ju-sen*; Japanese count by ten-thousands.)
20,000		*ni-man*
25,000		*ni-man-go-sen*
100,000		*ju-man*
1,000,000		*hyaku-man*

Time

o'clock (one o'clock)	*-ji (ichi-ji)* (Use with-counter numbers for time.)
minute (for telling time)	*pun*
second (duration)	*byo*
hour (duration)	*jikan*
year (date)	*nen*
year (duration)	*nenkan*

Telephone

hello	*moshi moshi* (The caller usually says this first.)
may I speak with . . . ?	*. . . -san onegai shimasu? (-san = Mr, Mrs, Miss, etc)*
isn't here	*imasen*
extension (eg ext 153)	*naisen (ichi-go-san) (With counternumbers used here.)*

Post Office

post office	*yubin kyoku*
stamps	*kitte*
poste restante (general delivery)	*kyoku dome yubin tome oki*
registered	*kaki tome*
special delivery	*soku tatsu*
air mail	*kohku bin*
sea mail	*funa bin*
aerogramme	*kohku shokan*
money order	*yubin gawase*
stamped post card	*yubin hagaki*
parcel	*kozutsumi*
letter	*tegami*

Trains

ticket	*kippu*
one way	*katamichi*
return	*ohfuku, shuyuken*
express	*tokkyu*
limited express	*kyuko*
rapid (no surcharge)	*kaisoku*
local	*kaku eki teisha*
reserved (seat)	*shite, (seki)*

unreserved	*jyuseki*
What track for . . . station?	*. . . (eki) wa, nan ban sen (des' ka)?*
next train/ tram	*sugi no kisha/densha*
basic charge (all trains)	*unchin*
limited express charge	*tokkyu ryohkin*
green car (1st class) charge	*gurin ryokin*
excursion ticket	*shuyuken*

Youth Hostel

(I am a) member	*kai-in (des')*
membership card	*kai-in sho*
Are you a member?	*kai-in des'ka?*
Do you have a membership card?	*kai-in sho arimas' ka?*
Do you want meals?	*shokuji wa?*
evening meal	*yu-shoku*
breakfast	*cho-shoku*
Do you have a sleeping sheet?	*shiitsu arimas'ka?*
May I stay?	*tomare mas'ka?*
full	*ippai*
Is there a room available tomorrow/the day after tomorrow?	*ash'ta/asatte heya wa aitemas'ka?*

Facts for the Visitor

VISAS

Everyone entering Japan must have a valid passport or other travel document. In principle, everyone must also have a visa, although this requirement is waived in many cases.

There are two general categories of visa, short-stay and long-stay.

SHORT-STAY VISA

Short-stay visas are for visits of a touristic or cultural nature, and of a relatively short duration. Valid purposes include sightseeing, recreation, attending meetings or conventions, inspection or study tours, participation in contests (athletic and other), visiting relatives and friends, learning cultural arts, goodwill visits, and similar non-remunerative activities. Such visas must be obtained from a Japanese diplomatic mission prior to arrival in Japan.

Citizens of most English-speaking countries and western European countries (with the notable exceptions of Australia and South Africa) do not need to obtain a visa beforehand for tourist purposes, although they must obtain one for any other type of activity. As of December 1988 citizens of the United States of America do not require visas for 90 day visits.

Shore Pass

Although the name dates from the days of sea travel, a shore pass can be very useful to many travellers in the air age. It permits a stopover of up to 72 hours without visa, even for those who require visas to enter for longer periods of time. During this 72-hour period the holder is free to travel anywhere within the country, so it affords the opportunity for a quick look around.

To obtain a shore pass, one needs a confirmed onward flight leaving within the 72-hour period. One obtains a shore pass prior to passing the immigration inspector. At Narita Airport there is a small mobile desk (quite clearly marked) at the entrance to the hall where travellers line up for immigration procedures.

Transit Visa

Passengers on a cruise ship that will dock at two ports in Japan can get a transit visa on landing that is valid for up to 15 days of travel through Japan to rejoin the ship at the other port. Passengers are supposedly required to designate their route but there would be no further check of their whereabouts once they were on shore. The ship's agent makes the arrangements for a transit visa.

Be sure that your visa is actually stamped in your passport, not on the application form or elsewhere, even though the latter is legal. It has happened that people with multiple-entry visas have been refused a second entry because the visa was not stamped in the passport.

Period of Stay

On arrival the traveller is given a Period of Stay by the inspector at the point of entry. It varies; for citizens of a country without a visa-waiving agreement (including Australia and South Africa) this period is usually 60 days, normally extendable for two further 60-day periods for a total of 180 days. After that it is necessary to leave Japan, following which it is usually possible to return after obtaining another visa in the third country. Most people go to nearby Korea, Taiwan or Hong Kong.

For citizens of a country with a visa-waiving agreement, the period of stay is as follows: 30 days for New Zealanders, 90 days for citizens of Canada, Denmark, France, Sweden (and many others), and 180 days for citizens of West Germany, UK, Switzerland, and some others. The

enforcement can be haphazard at times; some Kiwis have been known to be given 60 days because the inspector didn't have a 30-day stamp, and Americans have occasionally been given 90 days.

The number of extensions possible depends on the status of residence, as described later. When the last extension has expired, such persons can also go to a nearby country, then enter Japan again, starting the process all over. Beyond a certain number of such re-entries, one can expect to encounter reluctance or refusal.

Status of Residence
In addition to the period of stay, visitors are also issued with a status of residence on arrival. There are several categories of status of residence, most of which are of the long-stay type and are detailed in the later section on that topic.

The two status categories normally given for tourism purposes are either 4-1-4 ('tourist/cultural'), or 4-1-16(3), which is a catch-all that is also given for a wide variety of other activities such as working, teaching and long-term cultural study. Note that this latter stamp, the 4-1-16(3), must be endorsed with a second stamp to be valid for anything other than touristic purposes.

Nationals of a country that does not have a reciprocal visa-waiving agreement (or one with such an agreement but only for less than 90 days period of stay) will automatically receive 4-1-4 status valid for 60 days, with the likelihood of two 60-day extensions.

Extension of Period of Stay
The 4-1-16(3) status, if obtainable, is vastly preferable for anyone who plans to travel extensively in Japan. A 90-day period of stay is usually given with it and this is theoretically renewable for up to three years (although any period over a year is usually given only when the visa has been endorsed for employment, etc).

In addition to giving the potential for remaining in Japan longer than the 180-day maximum allowed under the 4-1-4 category, it also allows an extra 30 days of travel each time before it is necessary to seek out an immigration office and apply for an extension.

Although extensions are usually given on the spot these days, the immigration department has the right of only accepting the application of the traveller, and then deciding whether to give the extension and advising the applicant by postcard that the application had been granted – a time-consuming process that could keep you stuck in that city while the wheels turn. Better to have a few extra days up your sleeve by having the 90-day period rather than the 60-day one. A similar delay is likely to occur if you obtain the extension in one city and try to extend it in another.

The proper term to use, by the way, is 'extension of period of stay', not 'extension of visa'.

Beyond the first extension, there is the possibility that a Letter of Guarantee will be required. In such cases, the authorities prefer a Japanese as guarantor, but a settled foreign resident is acceptable. See page 46 for an example of such a letter.

Potential Problems

Keep in mind that even if you have a visa, or your country has a visa-waiving agreement, you are not automatically entitled to enter Japan when you arrive. The inspector at the port of entry is king and can refuse entry, compelling the would-be visitor to fly back out of Japan at his own expense.

Visas are issued abroad by the Ministry of Foreign Affairs (Gaimusho) at Japanese diplomatic missions but actual permission to land is granted at the port of entry by inspectors who are under the jurisdiction of the Ministry of Justice. They have the right to demand to be shown an outward ticket, proof of adequate funds, etc.

Although most inspectors are reasonable, there have been many cases of totally unreasonable behaviour. In one case, a traveller had arranged for money to be waiting for him in Japan, but because he had little in hand at the port of entry, he was refused entry. Anyone who has had dealings with banks, particularly Japanese ones, can only sympathise with the person's problems in having the funds transferred to another country.

Even having money in hand is not necessarily enough, however. One American man (perhaps not coincidentally, black) married to a Japanese woman but unable to get permanent residence and thus depending on repeated tourist visas to enter and stay in Japan, arrived at Fukuoka to meet her. Despite having US$2000 in cash in his pocket, he was held in a small room for six hours and not allowed to enter the country until his wife had managed to buy a $40 air ticket for him to fly to Pusan (Korea) – and all this on a weekend night.

Immigration inspectors can also be arbitrary in the Status of Residence that they grant, as I can aver from personal experience. Being Canadian, I am nominally entitled to a 4-1-16(3) status with a 90-day period of stay, by bilateral agreement. When I arrived in Tokyo in early 1978 I was given the desired 4-1-16(3) as requested on my landing card. Several months later, after a visit to Korea, I flew into Fukuoka, requested the same status, but was given only a 4-1-4. When I protested (politely), I was told that I was entering as a tourist and would be given a tourist stamp (4-1-4). When I protested that I was Canadian, and entitled to 4-1-16(3) status, I was told brusquely that I had the choice of accepting the tourist visa or going back to Korea.

You really have little choice if this happens to you. There is an appeal process if you are actually refused entry, but it is not for protesting the type of status given. I would suggest sending a note to your embassy giving details of the incident and request that they make a protest. If enough people protest, possibly the capriciousness of inspectors can be limited. A note to the Ministry of Justice might also do some good; there is always the *remote* possibility that the ministry in Tokyo is unaware of what is happening at the smaller ports of entry.

The Japanese authorities can refuse entry to any of the following:

Persons with contagious diseases or leprosy.

The mentally disturbed.

Those with insufficient funds.

Drug addicts and users.

Ex-convicts who were sentenced to more than one year in prison.

Prostitutes.

Anyone deported from Japan less than a year earlier.

Anyone who may cause harm to the interests and security of Japan.

The last is a wonderful catch-all and can be interpreted as the authorities wish. In 1979 a New Zealand member of the Indian religious sect Ananda Marga was turned back at Narita even though he had a proper visa and there is no law prohibiting this group in Japan. As for prostitutes, this is a bit of a joke because hundreds of women from South-East Asia arrive and are met at the airport by gangsters who cart them off for their sordid work, and nothing is ever done to stop them.

Note

All foreigners staying in Japan for more than 90 days must register with the authorities and obtain an Alien Registration Card (ARC). *This includes tourists!* See the section on Alien Registration further on.

LONG-STAY VISAS

There are two groups of people who will be applying for a long-stay visa: those who are in Japan already on a Tourist or similar short-stay visa, have used up all permitted time and wish to stay longer, and those going to Japan for the first time with the intention of participating in an activity that would require staying longer than the time permitted by a tourist-type visa, or to engage in an activity not allowed under a tourist-type visa.

The simplest way around the problem of continuing a stay in Japan for an extended period when you only have a short-stay visa is to take up an activity that can provide a valid reason for a longer stay. Two common types are cultural (study of the Japanese language, traditional arts like the tea ceremony, flower arrangement, music, dancing, traditional games (*I-go*), martial arts, etc), and student (academic or non-academic). While it is generally possible to obtain permission to work part-time on a cultural or student visa, if the primary intention is full-time employment, it is generally better to get a working or teaching visa. All these types of visa are detailed in this section.

Except for people going for a university-type study programme, or those who are being transferred to Japan by a company, it is usually difficult to set up the foundation for a long-stay visa without actually going to Japan and making the necessary arrangements in person. The usual procedure is to go to Japan, giving 'travel and sightseeing' as the purpose of

entry, thus obtaining either 4-1-4 or 4-1-16(3) status, then finding a job and making the arrangements for a visa.

Complete information on the requirements for obtaining any type of visa can be obtained in Tokyo from the visa section of the Ministry of Foreign Affairs (Gaimusho). Immigration bureau offices are only for extensions of the period of stay and change of status.

Staff at the visa section are helpful and speak sufficient English. Just remember the rule for talking with nearly all Japanese: speak slowly and clearly and avoid slang that cannot readily be understood. There is no need to fear asking questions regarding visas. They will give out photocopied sheets that list the exact documentation that is required when applying for any kind of visa at a Japanese representation overseas, and they can check the documents that you have collected to be sure that you have everything that is required.

Study & Working/Commercial Visas

For the most part, the only type of visa that can be obtained easily before going to Japan is for a recognised course of study, especially at university level where standards are recognised internationally and entry is based on the applicant's academic record. In such cases, the student's home university can normally provide the required documentation.

Other people who can obtain a visa without first going to Japan include employees being transferred by a company to Japan, or someone who is hired by a Japanese company (usually an English school).

Working Holiday Visa

In 1980 an agreement was signed between the Japanese and Australian governments setting up a plan whereby young citizens (18 to 25, sometimes up to 30) could arrange a working holiday for a period of up to a year, with extension at the discretion of the authorities. This is the first such agreement of the type entered into by Japan. Australians should obtain further information from Japanese diplomatic representatives. There is a similar plan for New Zealand, and it may become open to youths of other countries as well.

Information on documentation required for these types of long-stay visa should be available at any Japanese diplomatic representation overseas and the same office will accept the application and issue the visa. In general, an application will consist of an application form in duplicate (Form 1C), a photo 45 x 45 mm, a Letter of Guarantee, documents showing the reason for wishing to go to Japan, school records or company documents, documentation on the institution where you will study/teach or details on your company's activities in Japan.

Student & Cultural Visas
For language or cultural study, one first finds a suitable school and then gets them to provide letters of guarantee and other documents to satisfy the authorities. In past years it was invariably necessary to leave the country and submit the documents to a Japanese diplomatic mission overseas. There is now the possibility that the visa status can be changed (even from a tourist visa) within Japan. Consult the immigration office in the city where you wish to study. The TIC offices can probably give some guidance as to current practice.

If it is necessary to go abroad to apply, the Japanese embassy in Seoul is the most popular for this purpose. So many foreigners make similar applications that it handles them as a matter of routine. If all papers are in order, a study or cultural visa will usually be granted in one working day.

It is usually possible to get permission to work when one has a study/cultural visa. This is typically good for up to twenty hours a week. However, if the course you are taking is given only at

night, it is sometimes possible to get permission to work full-time during the day, as long as there is proof that you are actually carrying on with the activity for which the visa was granted.

Working & Teaching Visas
In the case of working/teaching visas, it is usually very difficult to arrange employment with a school or Japanese company from outside Japan unless you are being transferred by your company from another country. The exception is that some English schools do recruit overseas, but not infrequently they are located in relatively out-of-the-way towns where the school finds it difficult to attract teachers from within Japan. The usual procedure is to go to Japan, giving 'travel and sightseeing' as the purpose of entry. (Do not give work as the reason for entry, for that is a prohibited activity and you would likely be turned back at the port of entry.) Once in the country, make the necessary arrangements in person.

When you have found a job and obtained the required documents, go to Korea and apply for the working visa. This takes about six to eight weeks. During this time you could travel around Korea or return to Japan on a tourist visa.

The embassy in Seoul will give you a receipt to acknowledge receipt of your application, but they will not routinely inform you whether your application has been approved. However, personnel are usually agreeable to sending a self-addressed card, or to sending a cable if the cost is prepaid. Otherwise you must check regularly on the current status. If you remain in Korea, this means checking at the embassy from time to time. If you return to Japan, you can inquire at the visa section of the Ministry of Foreign Affairs (Gaimusho), either in person or by phone (tel (03) 580-3311). With the receipt issued in Seoul, find out the file number being used in Japan (it will be different from the one used in Korea); this can make enquiries much easier. When making enquiries it helps to have the assistance of a Japanese person as the staff speak little English and it is difficult for a foreigner to speak in the expected polite manner.

It does no harm to inquire regularly after a few weeks have passed. When I applied for a working visa, I began to get impatient after more than eight weeks of waiting. I finally went into the Visa Section and asked about its progress. While I watched, the clerk searched through a tall pile of papers on his desk. Finally he located my application, at the very bottom of the pile. The approval came two days later.

Note

Anyone who is leaving Japan to apply for status 4-1-6 (student), 4-1-7 (teaching), 4-1-12 (technical), or 4-1-13 (skilled labour) can speed up the procedure abroad by obtaining a 'Certificate of Eligibility for Status of Residence' from an immigration office in Japan. This procedure might also be useful for an application for a cultural visa as well.

When you have received your visa, check carefully what has been stamped and written in your passport. Unfortunately, there have been cases of incompetence at such offices. One Australian businessman, for example, applied for a multiple-entry business visa, submitted all the necessary documents, waited a period of time, then received his passport back with a visa stamped in it. When he flew to Japan, he found that he had been given a single-entry tourist visa! Also, check to see that your visa is stamped in your passport, not on the application form or anywhere else.

Alien Registration

All aliens, with the exception of diplomats and US military personnel, must register with the authorities and obtain an Alien Registration Card (ARC) if they remain in

Japan for 90 days or more. *This includes tourists!*

You must also carry this ARC (or passport) with you at all times as you can be asked by police or other authorities to produce either one at any time. It is not unknown for a person walking innocently down the street to be challenged. Failure to be able to show either document will most likely lead to several unpleasant hours in custody while someone else fetches it. Contrary to logic, the offender is usually not allowed to go and get it, even in the company of an officer and even if the card is in a building nearby. If there is no one else who can get it, an impasse is reached. It is a needless annoyance bordering on idiocy in many cases, but one that could befall any foreigner. Although a challenge is not a regular occurrence, it happens often enough to be a concern. It is difficult to say if it is done out of perversity, or as a show of authority. It is doubtful that they catch many criminals this way.

Obtaining an ARC is simple and costs nothing but does require three photographs – about 5 x 5 cm. It is issued by the municipal office of the city, town or ward (ku) in which you are living. In the case of travellers, the address of a lodging place is acceptable.

An ARC is surrendered when you leave Japan (except long-term residents).

A change of residence within the district must be recorded at the original issuing office. A move to another district requires re-registration in the new district within 14 days.

Fingerprinting Persons over 16 years of age who are granted a total stay of more than one year must be fingerprinted.

Protest against this requirement is on the increase and much unfavourable comment has been made over the years, observing (probably accurately) that Japan's control and treatment of aliens reflects an element of xenophobia that has existed in the country since it was first opened to foreigners in the 19th century, and probably much further back than that.

The ARC system was set up after WW II to keep control of Koreans and Taiwanese who had been forced to go to Japan before and during the war, and it is widely believed that the card system is kept in effect to keep these minorities in a subordinate position. Each year there are more and more protests about the system, with some protesters going on hunger strikes to make their point.

However, rather than easing up on the system and joining the rest of the world, the Justice ministry has actually tightened up regulations and has forced at least one Korean protester to leave the country with his Japanese wife because he refused to be fingerprinted. Previously, refusal was punishable only by a fine, and there is no written regulation calling for deportation. This was a good example of the power of the bureaucracy to make their own regulations not covered by law.

The regulations requiring registration are said to be the strictest (and the most bothersome) in the free world. Japan is the only country that requires fingerprinting of aliens but not its own citizens. (Some require it of both.) In Japan, only criminals are fingerprinted, and this fact, say some, indicates how highly the Japanese regard foreigners. (The fingerprints are of no practical use, for it is the photographs in documents that provide identification.) Several people, including the Reverend Jesse Jackson, have compared the ARC with South Africa's pass laws. (*Those* were finally repealed). The Japanese requirements certainly emphasise the meaning of the Japanese word for foreigner, *gaijin*, which literally means 'outside person', and the omnipresent sense of 'us' and 'them' that prevails in Japanese society.

In 1979 Japan signed an international agreement that may eventually result in the abolition of the Alien Registration

procedures, but at the time of publication of this book, this has not occurred.

Letter of Guarantee

For any type of long-stay visa, and often for an extension of stay as a tourist, a Letter of Guarantee is required. An acceptable form of letter is shown below.

If possible the guarantor should be a Japanese citizen who has the financial resources to take on this obligation. To demonstrate this capability, the guarantor is usually required to supply a certificate of employment and recent certificate of tax payment.

For a working or teaching visa, the company or school can provide the letter, and for a press or commercial visa, the guarantee letter would of course be provided by the person's organisation.

The Japanese authorities always prefer to have a Japanese guarantor. In one case, a foreign employee of a very large multinational corporation presented a letter of guarantee from his company, but was asked if he couldn't find a Japanese guarantor. So he asked his secretary if she would write a letter of guarantee for him. She did and it was accepted!

Form Letter of Guarantee

To: Consul-General (Ambassador) of Japan
Letter of Guarantee

In connection with the application by . . . for a (teaching/working) visa, I hereby guarantee the following:

1. Logistic support while he/she is in Japan.
2. Transportation fee for repatriation.
3. Any other information concerning . . . will be given gladly.

Signature

Guarantor: Name:
Nationality:
Address:
Tel:
Status of residence:
Occupation:
Relationship to applicant:

Letter of Credit

If you have time to make preparations before leaving home base, a way that can sometimes get around the problem of finding a guarantor is to arrange a line of credit with a bank where you are known, and have it issue a 'to whom it may concern' letter with a message to the effect: 'This is to certify that (name) has arranged a line of credit with this institution valid until (date) for an amount sufficient to guarantee his/her repatriation from Japan.' I obtained such a letter once and it was accepted at the Tokyo immigration office for extending a tourist-type visa. The letter is kept on file and can be referred to again for subsequent applications for extension.

Status of Residence

The following table lists the main statuses and the nominal period of stay for each.

4-1-4	tourist – 60 days
4-1-5	commercial/management of business – 3 years
4-1-6	student (junior college level and up) – 1 year
4-1-7	lecturers/professors (academic) – 3 years
4-1-8	cultural/artistic/scientific – 1 year
4-1-9	entertainers – 60 days
4-1-10	missionary/religious – 3 years
4-1-11	journalist (radio/press) – 3 years
4-1-12	specialised skills/technicians – 3 years
4-1-13	specialised labour (eg specialty cooks) – 1 year
4-1-14	permanent resident – permanent
4-1-15	spouses and children of person in category 4-1-5/6/7/8/9/10/11/ 12/13 – same as spouse/parent
4-1-16(1)	short-term version of 4-1-5/10/11/ 12 – 180 days
4-1-16(3)	short-term version of all statuses – up to 3 years (case by case)

Periods of stay listed as more than one year usually have to be renewed annually, although recently the authorities were giving extensions for three years if the person had worked for one company for several years.

The 4-1-16(3) category is a catch-all. It is given to the citizens of many countries as a tourist visa (and much to be valued, as described in the section on short-term visas). It can also be the category given for a working visa. However, there must be a second stamp validating it to make it a working visa.

Change of Status

A person entering Japan may engage in only the activity allowed under his or her status. Permission must be obtained from an immigration office to change activity – or even to engage in the same activity in a different place – or to change status.

For example, permission would be needed for a person with a student status (eg 4-1-6 or 4-1-16(3)) who wanted to teach English; for a teacher who wanted to change to a different school; for a person on a cultural visa (4-1-8) studying pottery who wanted to take up lacquer-making; or a person wanting to change status from teaching (4-1-7 or 4-1-16(3)) to commercial (4-1-5 or 4-1-16(3)) so as to engage in business.

The good news is that the authorities seem to grant such requests in most cases. In all cases, though, it is necessary to check before taking on the new activity. There is always the chance that the authorities will check whether the change has already been made, in which case a letter of apology might be needed. Failure to obtain prior permission may result in unfavourable consideration of a future request for an extension, or possibly even outright deportation.

If one is working for one employer and changes to another, one is supposed to obtain a letter of release from the first. Sometimes, however, the departure is unfriendly, and the first employer will do nothing whatever to help. This is not a problem, for the letter is not an absolute requirement. When requesting a change of status to transfer to the new employer, it is sufficient to put 'personal difficulties' or 'better pay' as reasons for the change.

Change of status can be obtained in Japan without leaving the country by those with status 4-1-5/6/7/8 and 4-1-10/11/12. In the past, a person holding 4-1-4 status could not change status within Japan, but the authorities have eased the regulations in recent times, and it might be possible to change to a Cultural visa while still in Japan on a Tourist visa. Inquire as to the current situation at the TIC.

Re-entry Permit

If you have long-term status and wish to leave Japan for a short time and then return to take up the same activity, you should obtain a re-entry permit before leaving. This is not a landing permit (entry is not guaranteed), and you must still satisfy the immigration inspector at the port of entry, but it does facilitate re-entry and preserves the original status. Failure to obtain the permit will almost certainly result in cancellation of the original status.

There are two types of re-entry permit: single-entry (Y3000), and multiple-entry (Y6000). Either is valid for up to one year; it will be less if the balance of the permitted period is less. It must be used within six months of issue and its period of validity (and that of the original visa) cannot be extended outside Japan; if it (or the visa) expires while the holder is abroad, a new visa must be obtained before the holder can return.

Letter of Apology

When dealing with government authorities at any level in Japan, people frequently fall foul of some regulation or other. The standard practice is to write a letter of apology, stating something to the effect that the event was an oversight, that it was unintended, that the person humbly hopes that he/she has not caused inconvenience to the department/person/whatever, etc. If the infraction was not serious, the letter is generally accepted and the matter overlooked.

Whether anyone gives the slightest credence to the sincerity of the letter or the writer is yet to be determined. If it becomes necessary to write one, just regard it as a quirk of the system, part of the charm of the country. Just remember the advice: always show sincerity, even if you have to fake it. It seems that a letter of apology goes a long way toward getting one off the hook for a wide range of misdemeanors, but it would not be wise to explore the outer limits of this process!

Further Information

There are two books that give more detailed information on immigration procedures; one is comprehensive, while the other abridges the information and is more easily understood.

The more detailed of the two is *Immigration – A Guide to Alien Residence Procedures in Japan*. It is published by the *Japan Times* in cooperation with the Ministry of Justice. It is available at a number of bookstores in Tokyo such as Kinokuniya and Maruzen. The cost is Y300 and it can be obtained by mail from: The Japan Times, 5-4 4-chome Shibaura, Minato-ku, Tokyo 108. The cost for surface postage is an additional Y200 in Japan, or Y300 to any other country. The main shortcomings of this book are due to the fact that the Ministry was involved with producing it and so it is vague in many areas where one would like to know the exact regulations. (Generally there are none; this is the land of case-by-case.) The book is stronger on changing status within Japan than obtaining a status (visa) to begin with.

Another source of information about immigration regulations is the booklet *Now You Live in Japan*.

IMMIGRATION OFFICES

Tokyo	(03)	471-5111 or 986-2271
Sapporo	(011)	261-9211
Sendai	(0222)	56-6076
Narita	(0476)	32-6771
Yokohama	(045)	681-6801

Nagoya	(052)	951-2391
Osaka	(06)	941-0771
Kobe	(078)	391-6377
Takamatsu	(0878)	61-2555
Hiroshima	(0822)	21-4412
Shimonoseki	(0832)	23-1431
Fukuoka	(092)	281-7431
Kagoshima	(0992)	22-5658
Naha	(0988)	32-4185

CUSTOMS

Japanese customs laws are quite generous in their allowances, especially for liquor. You can bring in three 760 ml bottles of alcoholic beverages. Other limits are: 400 cigarettes or 100 cigars or 500 g of tobacco, with a maximum combined weight of 500 g; two ounces of perfume; two watches valued no higher than Y30,000 each (including any in current use); and other goods with a total value of not more than Y100,000. Inspectors are generally lenient, allowing in anything that could be considered reasonable for a person's stay in Japan. Luggage often isn't opened unless they are suspicious of the contents.

Even if you don't smoke, it might be worth bringing in foreign cigarettes (US or British are the best). They are very welcome gifts to Japanese smokers, and are a nice thank you for assistance or when hitch-hiking. They are also appreciated by foreigners in Japan because the Japanese tobacco from which the local cigarettes are made is rather low in quality.

As for booze, it is expensive so bring your limit if you like spirits or if you'll be visiting friends. Do not bother to bring in liquor with the intention of selling it. The days when anyone could sell it at a high profit by walking into a bar are long gone. It might still be possible to unload it at a small profit but it is not worth the bother. The Japanese themselves go overseas in droves these days; the reselling racket dates back to times when the Japanese couldn't afford to go out of the country or were virtually banned from doing so.

On arrival, a verbal declaration is usually sufficient if you have no unaccompanied baggage. If you have sent belongings separately (eg, by mail), declare them upon arrival on the form provided. You show this form to customs when the packages arrive. It is unlikely that any duty will be charged on the contents. Parcels arriving without such a customs declaration are subject to duty although the inspectors are usually not too harsh. Packages of food and low-value items or gifts usually come through without trouble.

The Japanese authorities are very down on narcotics, marijuana and stimulant drugs (amphetamines). Anyone caught bringing any of these products into Japan can expect no sympathy from the law and Japanese prisons are few steps from Dark-ages conditions. Even suspects are treated like prisoners before they are tried and the remand process can go on for weeks.

Firearms are very tightly controlled in Japan; anyone caught smuggling them or ammunition can expect an unpaid vacation.

Pornography is frowned on in Japan, but what constitutes porn is laughable by western standards. The main determinant is whether any pubic hair can be seen. Western films showing this pernicious substance are defaced by little blobs that only serve to bring more attention to what is being concealed than if it were shown. The portrayal of pubic hair in any form has traditionally been a complete no-no, although camera magazines are showing ever more. This domestic relaxation will probably have no effect on the practice of defacing imported magazines to the extent that the offending parts are blacked out or even abraded down to bare paper.

One could be sympathetic to official attempts to keep the morals of the country pure if it weren't for the huge amount of blatant commercial sexuality permeating the country and the countless Japanese comic books (*manga*) portraying incredible scenes of rape, torture, disfigurement and degradation of women, and these are on sale everywhere.

WORKING IN JAPAN

With the exception of a small number of jobs that use a particular technical, financial or other special skill (computer designer or cook, for example), the work available to foreigners generally is related to English or other foreign languages. This work includes teaching, translating, copywriting and technical writing and rewriting; the latter two usually involves translating from Japanese.

Teaching

Private Schools The Japanese are eager for English lessons and there is a continuing need for teachers. Most work is at small, private schools, the quality of which varies from those dedicated to doing a good job, through to being a purely money-making scheme with no regard for the students whatever. Since it is easy to start a school and it can be lucrative, the average school would tend toward the latter end of the scale.

The better schools demand some credentials, such as a degree in English or a TOEFL (Teaching of English as a Foreign Language) certificate, while the worst of the down-market places will take anyone who walks in the door and can make themselves understood in English, no matter how bad the accent, pronunciation or grammatical knowledge.

The up-market schools want only teachers of North American or British origins (and accent), so Aussies and Kiwis, for example, have a rough time unless they can pass themselves off as Brits. It is also difficult for native speakers of English who are not of European appearance, even if their speech is flawless. The schools (and presumably the students) want the total experience of being taught English only by a lily-white face, preferably accompanied by blonde hair and blue eyes. Thus, those of Japanese, African or Indian-subcontinent

ancestry, for example, would have much more difficulty landing a job, no matter how good their accent and ability.

The better schools also require that teachers have a working visa. Strange things can happen in trying to do things correctly, however. In one case, a couple of South Africans of English background applied for a working visa to teach English. They were turned down because an official found in a reference book that the official language of their country was Afrikaans, so they, therefore, could not be qualified native speakers of English!

The less prestigious schools will hire anybody, no questions asked about visas or any other qualifications, and thus these organisations provide expense money for large numbers of travellers on tourist visas. That's not to say that these amateur teachers are totally ineffective. Many make an honest effort to try to teach their pupils, and may actually be more enthusiastic and effective than the better qualified ones.

Although it is not guaranteed, it seems that the immigration officials do not go out of their way to catch schools that are hiring non-documented foreigners.

Pay is typically Y3000 per hour of working time at schools but it can be difficult to get more than a couple of consecutive hours at one school, so large numbers of teachers are continually travelling by train from one school to another. A deduction for income tax of 10% is usually made, although the actual rate can be higher when the tax return is filed. Pay for private lessons can be substantially higher (and payment of income tax depends on the honesty of the teacher) but it takes a long time to become established giving private lessons.

Teaching *can* be fun, if you are fortunate enough to have an advanced student or a free-conversation class able to speak fairly fluent English. It can be a great way to learn about Japan and the people. The Japanese can be remarkably outspoken when using a foreign language and teachers with private students may find themselves acting also as confidant and hearing more about private Japanese matters than they ever dreamed possible.

The very way that Japanese must be spoken has an inhibiting effect in Japanese conversation, to say nothing of the restrictions imposed by social rules. Women in class will even discuss matters forcefully, and argue (politely) with men, much to the astonishment of the latter! Unfortunately, these jobs in advanced classes are the plums of the profession and the most in demand, so the veteran teachers will usually get them. Someone must lay the groundwork to get the students up to this level and this is the position that new teachers are normally given.

Trying to coax a response out of terminally shy teenage girls (*any* response!), overcoming the insidious effect of years of exposure to basic English and English words incorrectly used in Japanese, or trying for the hundredth time that day to get a class to remember that a plural subject requires a plural verb, can be very trying. Most teachers earn their pay.

Finding a job is a combination of combing the ads in the newspapers (the Monday *Japan Times* is the best single place to look, but then everyone else is chasing the same jobs), going around to schools, being given unwanted classes by other teachers, personal introductions, self-promotion (ads on notice boards and even on utility poles) and good luck. The best time of the year is in September and January when new terms are beginning. The summer is the slackest time because many students are on vacation.

Teaching positions are more easily found in Tokyo than in other large cities because it is both the commercial and political capital of the country. They are difficult to find in Kyoto because so many foreigners want to live in this historic and cultured city that there is usually an over-supply of willing teachers. Those who do live in Kyoto often have to commute to Osaka, an hour away by train, or even Kobe, two hours away.

On the other hand, schools in smaller cities outside the metropolitan areas advertise fairly regularly. Since relatively few foreigners want to live in such places, away from the bright city lights, anyone who enjoys slower-paced provincial cities will have a much higher chance of landing a job, with the associated probability of lower living costs. Some schools do recruit overseas and some of these are good institutions, but people have arrived in Japan only to find that the school was second rate or that they were far out in the sticks.

Some people who are working in other fields regard teaching English as (pardon the borrowing) 'the last refuge of a scoundrel', but the fact that there are also well-qualified people doing it brings up the tone of the work.

Teaching Assistant (National Programme) In recent years, a joint programme of the Home Affairs, Education and Foreign ministries has brought sizeable numbers of young foreigners (usually recent university graduates) to Japan to help teach English at junior and senior high schools of the national school system. In 1986 the teachers were drawn from the USA, Britain, Australia and New Zealand. The intake that year was 851, a large increase over 122 previously participating in the scheme.

Pay was a quite respectable Y300,000 per month and positions were available in all parts of the country. No special training in teaching English was required, just a degree from a recognised university.

The scheme is not all gravy and easy sailing for the teachers, as my conversations with a couple have revealed. It seems that most teachers rarely see any single class more than once a month, so they are doing little more than presenting a foreign face and spouting a few sentences. It is not uncommon, moreover, for the class homeroom teacher to carefully unteach the native-speaker's correct pronunciation, even while the foreigner is still in the room! A good tolerance for frustration is recommended as one qualification for any prospective applicant.

Still, the programme is a brave beginning toward teaching English as a practical means of communication, rather than solely as yet another subject for examinations, and should be encouraged. The discouraging side is that high school students have only three hours of English classes per week and that nearly all of this is boring grammar and translation drill.

On a more positive note, the programme does give an excellent opportunity to live among the Japanese and experience Japanese daily life.

Teaching Assistant (Municipal) Tokyo (and probably some of the other large cities) have English teaching programmes that hire foreigners as teaching assistants. The work is similar to that of the other teaching assistants – that of providing a living example of English speech.

In some schools the foreigners are given wide scope to talk, teach and motivate, while in others they may do nothing more than read a passage, one line at a time, while the teacher discusses each in turn. The pay is good, although the number of hours may be limited per day. Qualifications in the past have been a university degree, though not necessarily in education. It is necessary to inquire from the municipal board of education as these jobs are not advertised.

School Teaching There are several international schools in the large cities (particularly Tokyo) that have been set up to teach the children of foreign residents and Japanese children whose parents want them to be able to speak English. Vacancies occur from time to time for qualified teachers of a regular western school curriculum. Pay and conditions are considered quite reasonable and the school can be the sponsor for a visa. Qualified

American teachers can also make inquiries about teaching at Department of Defence Schools at various military bases around Japan.

Non-teaching Jobs
Various opportunities arise for persons with skills in written English.

Copywriting Those with a bent for catch-phrases may be able to find a niche with one of the advertising agencies or smaller outfits that prepare the text for promotional literature, pamphlets and catalogues. The largest agencies usually fill such positions by people with a proven track record whom they bring in from overseas. They are the ones who get the perks such as an apartment.

There are many small agencies, sometimes associated with translation companies, that try to get this work from large companies. These positions may be advertised in newspapers (Monday *Japan Times*, especially) but it can be productive to target companies in the field for direct inquiries.

Translating There is a crying need for competent native speakers of English to do technical translation. As I can aver from experience in correcting and rewriting translations of service manuals for a large and well-known Japanese company, there is a great scarcity of competent technical translators. Few people who have technical knowledge learn Japanese to the level required for translating, and those who study Japanese usually have no technical training.

Objectively though, it must be said that despite the actual need, there is no guarantee that employment prospects are plentiful because very few people working in companies requiring translation work seem able to recognise that any problem exists. The common attitude is that because a text has been sent to someone called a translator, it will automatically be exactly correct. Very few Japanese are

当用漢字

competent to judge if text in English is correct; in fact, the more that it sounds like Japanese written in English words, the better many think it is. Because of this virtually universal attitude and mentality, there is no guarantee that the truly competent translator would be any better able to get work than an abysmally bad one would, especially if the latter were Japanese.

There are several frustrations that can be expected in translation work that the prospective translator should be aware of. One is the fact that the Japanese generally write their language very poorly (often with abominably bad organisation of information), omit incidental information like subjects and verbs, sometimes use incorrect *kanji*, and generally create a product that can take up to ten times as long to translate as an equivalent document from another European language into English would. In addition to the frustrations that this engenders, it has an even more serious side effect: the fact that

the pay per hour tends to be quite poor (especially considering the expertise and study required) due to low throughput.

A second problem is that the Japanese cannot recognise good English and, moreover, believe that their few years of study at the rate of two to three hours per week has equipped them to understand any nuance of English and to write it as well as any native speaker.

It is not at all uncommon, therefore, for a translation by a competent native speaker to be edited by a junior Japanese staff member (with no special training in English) into a hopeless garble. This is a common occurrence. A translator must be prepared for frustration and long hours, especially as everything is always needed yesterday.

Rewriting & Technical Writing Japan is probably the only country where most translators translate from their own language into the target language. The knowledge of any foreign language by Japanese is generally rather imperfect with predictable results. Thus, it is standard practice for any translation to go next to a native-speaker rewriter to be put into correct English.

If the original translator has a good technical knowledge, this may require nothing more than putting the result into grammatically correct form, but this is the rare case.

In addition to having problems with poor knowledge of English, many translators seem not to understand what they are reading in Japanese, either because they do not understand the technicalities of the subject, or simply because the original Japanese is so poorly written that they cannot understand what it says. It is not at all uncommon that one Japanese cannot understand the meaning of what another has written!

A good rewriter must draw on prior technical knowledge of the subject and supply missing information. The work process is much like a combination of doing a crossword puzzle and playing a game of Trivial Pursuit. Most Japanese are not aware of this need for careful examination of the translated product, assuming that because it has come from a translator it must be correct, so the work of a good rewriter is not generally appreciated.

This type of work is a natural for someone with a technical background and who can write correct English (often mutually incompatible abilities, unfortunately). The work of this type most often available best suits a background in electrical engineering or computer science because of the huge volume of computer documentation cranked out every year. There is a lesser demand for people familiar with the technology and terminology of the chemical, medical, pharmaceutical, construction, nuclear, electrical and electronic, machinery and other high technology industries. Some rewriters work on a freelance basis; others work full-time for one company. Each arrangement has its advantages and shortcomings.

Full-timers working for one company (not a translation agency) have the chance for greater job satisfaction than do freelancers because they can go back to the source of the original material and straighten matters out completely. However, it takes a while on the job (and perhaps a few tantrums) before the rewriter manages to gain some authority to specify what should and should not be allowed to pass, and to be able to keep out of finished work the little fingers that would otherwise make corrections.

The rewriter working full-time in a Japanese company will find that the Japanese employees do unexplainable things, like preparing glossaries of English words that correspond to Japanese technical words used in the company and inserting meanings that are not correct, without ever checking the meanings with the native speaker before printing it for use as the translation bible.

Working with the product of Japanese printing companies will give numerous opportunities for amazement at the way a typesetter can look at a correctly typed manuscript, read an 'a', and type a 'u', or similarly substitute an 'r' for a clearly typed 'l'. (There is the making of a psychology PhD in this!) In fact, working in almost any Japanese company leads foreigners to wonder how the Japanese have been so successful, for they seem to do so many things in a way that defies logic and appears counterproductive. Every foreigner working in Japan has tales to tell.

Full-timers do well to get much over Y2500 per hour, but there is the advantage that every working hour of the day is being paid for. Larger companies can sponsor rewriters for a working visa because they are offering full-time work (the normal requirement for a contract acceptable for a visa). Such jobs do not appear frequently, but tend to be advertised in the newspapers.

Some full-timers have a contract whereby the company pays all taxes, so the negotiations are on a net basis. In such cases, it is wise to establish that this means full payment of taxes and is not limited to the 10% deducted from each pay.

For freelancers there is work from the many translation agencies. Sometimes they advertise in the newspapers (Monday *JT*, again) but many jobs come up through word of mouth, or by finding the names of translation agencies and approaching them directly.

There can be a good deal of flexibility in freelance work, and some rewriters have a nominal contract with an agency as a full-timer but actually do work for that company only as it comes available, picking up any other assignments that come up in the meantime. This type of work is a favourite with those on cultural and similar visas because it can be done on a spare-time basis.

In reality, however, anyone doing this work must take any assignment that comes along lest he/she lose future work with that agency. Since these people have their names with a number of agencies, they commonly find that they have no free time at all! Pay can be on a per-page basis, or by the hour in the agency office. In an office, pay can range from Y2500 per hour for beginners to over Y4000 for people who have proved their knowledge and ability, so it can prove lucrative if the person does not need to have much free time.

Other Jobs
Cook A category that qualifies a foreigner for a working visa is as cook in a specialty restaurant (French, etc) although it would be necessary to show credentials and certificates.

Modelling One of the fields in which a westerner can offer a skill or ability that a Japanese cannot is modelling. Western models, especially girls with blonde hair, are widely used for modelling clothes, promoting shampoo and appearing in all manner of advertising work. Judging by billboards visible everywhere in the cities, exceptional beauty is often not necessary for such work.

There are many agencies in this field in big cities like Tokyo. Sometimes they advertise but most prospective models find the names of the agencies and make the rounds one after another. There is strong competition for jobs, so there can be long periods without an assignment, although the pay when one does score is very good. Some models are hired overseas and have their fare and living expenses paid, in addition to salary, in return for a fixed and exclusive contract.

When a job has been secured however, there may be a long wait for pay to be received, for the agency does not get paid until at least a month later, and they may try to stall. Anyone who intends to leave the country soon after a particular job should let it be known that they expect to be paid on the spot.

Film Extras Sometimes jobs come up as extras in films. This is one place to demand cash payment at the end of the shooting, for these companies are often under financed and neglect to pay.

Hostessing & Related Activities Another type of work, best suited to attractive blonde women, is working as a hostess in clubs or nightclubs. They can make a good income just from their official duties of talking with customers, but girls who have been hostesses uniformly remark that it is boring. They have to make small talk with men, mostly Japanese men who speak next to no English, and it is a continual battle to keep the wandering hands off. A major problem with this type of work is that the famous nightclubs, like the Copacabana and the Mikado, have all closed, and there is not the number of opportunities once available.

Paying Taxes
Income taxes are generally lower than in most western countries, but are still not inconsiderable. In addition, there is ward (ku) tax, about 50% of national tax. Full-time employees may be eligible for national health insurance; this depends on the area. If one is eligible for the insurance plan, there is also the obligation to pay into the national pension plan (unless you are over 40). Unless you stay in Japan after retirement, you will not be able to get any benefit from this, but it is not possible to get out of paying for it once you have enrolled for health insurance.

STUDYING IN JAPAN
Studying in Japan can be broken into three broad categories: academic, cultural and religious.

Academic
Studies at Japanese universities leading to undergraduate or postgraduate degrees, or studies on an exchange basis at accredited educational institutions, are usually arranged between the Japanese

and foreign university. With the assistance of your home institution it will be possible to obtain a student visa prior to arriving in Japan.

A very useful source of information in Japan is the Information Centre, Association of International Education, 4-5-29 Komaba, Meguro-ku, Tokyo 153. Their book *ABC's of Study in Japan* has answers to most questions regarding study in the country.

Cultural

To study various aspects of Japanese society and culture, such as the tea ceremony, flower arrangement, the Japanese language, the game of I-go, etc, it is usually difficult to arrange a course and obtain a visa prior to arriving in Japan. The normal practice is to go to Japan and make arrangements while in the country, then arrange the visa.

Studying the traditional arts, particularly flower arrangement and tea ceremony, is regarded by many Japanese virtually as a way of life. (The name for the tea ceremony is *cha-do*, literally 'the way of tea'.) Both are regarded as suitable activities for housewives to practise to improve themselves, to introduce an element of traditional Japanese culture into their lives, and thus to make them better Japanese. Because of this, neither is intended as something to be studied for a few weeks before moving on to another interest. A Japanese taking up one of these arts expects to take expensive lessons for years.

Masters of tea ceremony and flower arrangement schools are very rich people and have been able to construct very impressive buildings on some of the world's most expensive real estate.

The system has several grades through which the student passes, with each graduation costing large amounts of money. I attended one such party put on by a student advancing to a teacher's certificate; the display and demonstration that she had to give, plus a 'gift' to the teacher, came to more than US$20,000. An outsider should not be tempted to call it a racket, but it certainly does see the students parting with a great deal of their money, although it does so *gracefully*.

In the larger cities there are a few organisations that are prepared to give a short course in flower arrangement, in English, at costs more in line with what foreigners regard as acceptable for a course of study. It is also possible to see the tea ceremony being performed on a daily basis.

For information on any of these activities, talk with the knowledgeable personnel at the TICs in Tokyo or Kyoto.

Martial Arts There are many martial arts being taught in Japan and within each there are likely to be several schools, each with a different emphasis, degree of physical contact (and consequent danger of injury), etc. The best way to find a suitable art and school is to join the Japan Martial Arts Society – a group founded in 1983 by experienced foreign practitioners. Membership within Japan costs Y4000, plus a Y1000 registration fee. Overseas residents may join and receive the society's newsletter by remitting US$35 (including the $US5 registration fee) by cheque or international money order payable in US dollars to JMAS, CPO Box 270, Tokyo 100. Members are entitled to tap the vast knowledge of the old hands.

Religious (Zen Study & Meditation)

One of the few things regarding Japan that most people outside the country seem to know about is Zen Buddhism. Contrary to popular belief, however, the general Japanese populace does not spend large amounts of time silently contemplating gardens or the sound of one hand clapping. Zen is a little too esoteric for the average Japanese. As a result, foreign visitors who wish to investigate Zen will not have a huge number of options open to

Zen in Tokyo By far the best place to begin delving into Zen is Tokyo, as facilities are available for learning – in English – the fundamentals of belief, practice and zazen meditation. Two people to contact for further information are: Ann Sargent (tel (03) 940-0979), and Gaynor Sekinori (tel (03) 891-8469), both of whom can advise on classes and lectures, etc. Both are associated with the Soto sect.

Elsewhere in Japan Eiheiji temple is one of the two main temples of the Soto sect in Japan and is famous throughout the country. It is near Fukui, which is on the east shore of Biwa-ko lake, not too far from Kyoto. Its magnificent historic buildings and mountainside setting make it a target of thousands of sightseers each year, along with the many who wish to study Zen.

Foreigners are invited to participate in the activities of the temple and may arrange accommodation there. It is necessary to organise this well in advance of a proposed visit so that arrangements can be made. Contact: Sanzenkei, Eiheiji, Eiheiji-cho, Yoshida-gun, Fukui-ken.

Jofukuji temple on Shikoku is a small local temple that also functions as a youth hostel (No 7404 in the YH Handbook). The young priest is friendly and speaks good English. He welcomes visitors who wish to join him informally in meditation. It is a family-type temple and no advance arrangements are needed for Zen participation although, like any hostel, it may be booked up at any time, so it might be advisable to check first. The temple is on the side of a valley, peaceful at any time and very pretty in November when the leaves change colour. The address is: Jofukuji, Awafu 158, Otoyo-machi, Nagaoka-gun, Kochi-ken; telephone (0887) 74-0301.

There are no temples in Kyoto where foreigners can receive instruction in English. Several temples used to let foreigners join in but too many people became restless and disturbed others. An introduction from another priest would

them, and will have to actively seek out places to study.

Most temples and instruction centres in Japan will accept those who speak Japanese or who are already familiar with the practices of Zen meditation. Otherwise, foreigners are generally not welcomed unless they have an introduction from a responsible Zen teacher (with the exception of the Tokyo instruction set-up).

Zen Sects There are two main Zen sects in Japan, Soto and Rinzai. Differences between them are minor. In *zazen*, Soto practitioners face a wall, while in Rinzai they face the room; Rinzai uses more *koan* (riddles) than Soto; and Soto sessions last longer, typically 40 to 50 minutes against 20 or so for Rinzai.

The Rinzai sect is more active in giving classes for laymen, but these are almost exclusively in Japanese; the Soto sect seems to have more programmes in English.

probably be the only way to obtain admission to temples in Kyoto. For further information contact the TIC in Kyoto; they may be able to help.

A good introduction to Zen is *Zen Mind, Beginner's Mind*, by Shunryo Suzuki, a Soto priest. You'll find a very large selection of Zen books at English bookstores in Japan, especially in Tokyo (Kinokuniya, Maruzen, etc).

MEETING THE JAPANESE

It is unfortunate that most visitors to a foreign country such as Japan have little opportunity to meet the people who live there. They are always on the move and there is often a language barrier. Yet it is only through such contact that a visitor has a chance to learn of their daily life, work, pleasures and problems. Leaving Japan without meeting any of its people, other than hotel employees, etc, is like wearing earplugs to Carnegie Hall or a blindfold to the Louvre.

Because of the education system inflicted on the Japanese (they study to pass exams, not to learn), most of them have little ability to speak English despite untold hours of instruction at school. The emphasis is all on written rather than spoken work with the effect that contact with most people in Japan can be difficult.

There are, however, a variety of programmes aimed at introducing visitors to Japanese people who do speak foreign languages. Because English is the most widely spoken language in the world, it is the one that most Japanese learn. (This is a source of annoyance for many Europeans who encounter Japanese who think that everyone with 'white' skin speaks English.)

Through several independent programmes in operation around the country, you can visit a Japanese home for a couple of hours in the evening, meet Japanese people who are willing to act as guides and escorts at no charge, simply chat over a cup of coffee, or even stay with Japanese families in their homes around Japan.

Etiquette

My suggestion if you are meeting a Japanese person for the first time in formal circumstances is to incline your head slightly, in a semi-bow, and to use normal western courtesy. Don't try to mimic Japanese bowing because it is an art in itself, and don't attempt to shake hands unless the Japanese person offers a hand first, as they are generally not accustomed to the habit. Interestingly, however, it is not unknown for Japanese businessmen and politicians to shake hands among each other these days, even when no foreigner is involved.

Meeting a foreigner is stressful for many Japanese who have not had much contact with outside people, and they are likely to be very nervous. Conversation is likely to be a bit strained. Don't worry about it, and try to find some topic of common interest. Don't ask really personal questions unless the Japanese person has relaxed and seems willing to talk about his/her family and personal life. Sometimes such chats never rise above being a game of verbal patty-cake, exchanging words but little more.

Most Japanese who participate in this sort of programme have a genuine interest in meeting people from overseas and are quite open in their conversation. The most extreme of the latter are some Japanese who have had plenty of contact with foreigners and who speak English very well. They may tend to adopt what they have observed as being western ways of talking and behaving, requesting that you call them by their first names (unimaginable within Japanese society!), etc. Play it by ear in this case, but it is still better not to be too personal.

In homes, one usually sits on the floor, often an uncomfortable position for foreigners for extended periods. If you are invited to a home, try to keep your legs under you as long as possible; if it is necessary to stretch out, avoid pointing your feet at anyone as this is very rude. Most Japanese will realise that foreigners become uncomfortable and will make allowances for deviation from ideal Japanese manners.

Blowing your nose at the table is a class A social gaffe.

Home Visit System

This is a voluntary programme through which Japanese families in several cities receive foreign visitors into their homes. The system is semi-official in that it is publicised in a brochure issued by the semi-government Japan National Tourist Organisation (JNTO). Visits are normally arranged for a couple of hours in the evening. Food is not served but green tea and sweets will usually be part of the evening. Hosts will show guests around the house if desired, perhaps showing the finer points of Japanese house design (if it is not a modern western type!) and the garden, if there is space for one; Japanese houses are usually rather small.

The homes open under this programme are often those of well-to-do Japanese, so they will tend to be more spacious and elegant than average. The Japanese usually do not invite guests into their homes because they consider their houses to be too small and humble.

There is no charge for a visit. It is customary among Japanese to take a small gift to the host or hostess whenever visiting, even among close friends. Flowers, fruit or candy are suggestions. The Japanese participate in the programme just for the pleasure it gives the guests and the international contact it gives them.

The programme is operating in Tokyo, Yokohama, Nagoya, Kyoto, Otsu (near Kyoto), Osaka, Kobe and Kagoshima. Details about arranging visits are given in the sections covering each city. If possible, obtain a copy of the JNTO publication *Home Visit System*, which contains more information and useful tips. Most hosts speak English, but in each city there are some who speak other languages.

Almost every visitor who has made such a visit has spoken very warmly of the experience.

Clubs & Organisations

Several international organisations like Toastmasters and Lions International have affiliates in Japan. With prior preparation it should be possible to arrange to meet Japanese members who speak English.

If you have a hobby or special interest, it is possible to arrange a meeting with Japanese with the same interest. In the case of more obscure activities, one might get a Japanese person to see what specialty magazines are published in the field, and then contact the editorial office to see if they could help make contact.

Conversation Lounges

In Tokyo (and possibly the other large cities) there are several conversation lounges. Their purpose is to give an opportunity for Japanese (and other residents) to meet and talk in English. Most have coffee and light snacks at low (or no) charge. Those in Tokyo are advertised in *Tokyo Journal*.

Servas

Anyone travelling around Japan who really wants to get to know the Japanese should look into the international organisation Servas. If accepted as members of Servas, travellers may stay at the homes of Japanese families in many parts of the country, both rural and urban, for up to three days at no charge, sharing the family's home and life. Anyone looking for a free ride should read no further. Servas travellers staying with Japanese families are expected to spend much of their time talking with their hosts and otherwise participating in their lives. Only people who have a sincere interest in learning about Japanese family life and exchanging views and experiences would be interested.

Servas was founded in 1948 as a private venture in international relations. Reasoning that person-to-person contact by people from countries around the world is a worthwhile goal, a network of volunteer hosts was put together. In addition to Japan, there are hosts in at least 70 other countries. If it is possible, travelling members are expected to act as hosts on their return to a settled life, although this is not compulsory. Many hosts have never travelled themselves, but open their doors to travellers as their contribution to world understanding, and as a way to bring a little of the outside world to them.

It is preferable to join Servas in your home country. This entails filling in an application form and appearing for a personal interview in order to ensure that you are sincere in your interest in Servas and its ideals.

Regional staff are volunteers, but there are staff and administrative expenses at the local, national and international level; for this reason a contribution of about US$30 (it varies from country to country) is required. For the address of the national offices in your country, write to the international president, Mr Graham Thomas, Servas International Peace Secretary, 80 Bushwood, London E11; send an international reply coupon (or stamps if in the UK).

Those who are unable to join Servas before reaching Japan can make contact in Tokyo. The latest contact is Mr Inuma (tel (03) 710-0223), though it would be better to check with the TIC to find out the current coordinator. This programme is best suited to people who will be in Japan for a while, because an interview is necessary and there may be other delays.

Communes

Few outsiders are aware of the existence of several communes in Japan. They have a long history; Itto-en commune in the Kansai area (near Kyoto) dates back to 1905. Several welcome foreign visitors, usually on a paying basis, although it is often possible to reduce or eliminate the charge by working at commune tasks.

To write ahead for information, contact: Moshe Matsuba, Kibbutz Akan, Shin Shizen Juku, Nakasetsuri, Tsurui-mura, Akan-gun, Hokkaido 085-12, Japan. This is one of the communes that welcomes visitors.

If you arrive in the country without the opportunity to write ahead, telephone the head office of the Japanese Commune Movement at (0288) 26-2038. They speak enough English to be able to give verbal information, but do not correspond in any language other than Japanese. The address is: The Japanese Commune Movement, Head Office, 2083 Sakae-cho, Imaichi-shi 321-12, Tochigi-ken, Japan.

Various publications in English have been produced by the Movement. Contact Moshe Matsuba for details of what is currently available. Enclose a couple of US dollar bills or the approximate equivalent in other convertible currencies to cover their postage costs. (Do not send a bank draft or similar as the greedy banks will take it all!)

Free Guides

In some cities, like Nara, local organisations organise a free guide service, so Japanese people who can speak some English and who are interested in meeting foreigners are willing to act as unpaid guides for sightseeing in the city. Make inquiries at the TIC offices in Tokyo and Kyoto.

Teaching

One of the best ways to meet a cross-section of Japanese people is by teaching English. The system of teaching English in schools is so poor in Japan that private schools are necessary to provide an opportunity to learn from native speakers. Teaching without a proper visa is not legal of course, but it seems the immigration bureau does not waste too much of its time tracking down illegal teachers.

The only problem with teaching is that you may get any level of student. It is difficult to carry on conversations about Japanese society and culture with beginners who have trouble just putting five words together correctly. However, in conversation classes with advanced students it is possible to learn a great deal about Japan that doesn't appear in books. It is interesting that Japanese people will express very open and candid opinions in English (or another foreign language) that they will not say in Japanese; there are many constraints on behaviour in Japanese society which are reinforced by the very structure of the language.

Through teaching you also have an opportunity to experience every type of personality, from very open (and contrary to the stereotyped image of the Japanese) to girls who are so painfully shy that they refuse to answer questions for fear of making a mistake.

Casual Meetings

During your stay in Japan, some of the most pleasant memories will probably result from meeting various Japanese people. They can give you information about the country and insights into the society and customs. Many warm friendships have developed from such casual conversations. It is interesting that a Japanese who can speak English reasonably well, and who has overcome the initial fear of talking with foreigners, will often be more friendly and relaxed with a foreigner than with his own people. This is because the foreigner will not expect the social niceties that one Japanese person is supposed to display when first meeting another.

If you are busy with personal affairs, or are not free or otherwise inclined to talk at that moment, then do not feel obliged to do so. It is not uncommon for Japanese, particularly males of university age, to have the attitude that any foreigner they encounter has nothing better to do than provide them with free English practice. Some are rude enough to cut into the middle of a conversation. Many foreigners, particularly those who have been in the country only a short time, are still operating under the myth of 'exquisite Japanese politeness' and feel that they would mortally insult any Japanese by refusing such a wish. Forget this brain-washing! Good manners are good manners in any country. If you do not welcome an intrusion, by a Japanese or anyone else, you need not be put upon. You may politely inform the person that you are busy, wish to carry on your conversation with the other person, etc. For the average person this should be a sufficient hint. If the person then persists, you are free to be more firm as the circumstances require. This is not a recommendation to rudeness in general social situations, for most Japanese are very nice and conversations can be interesting, but you do not have to inconvenience yourself to accommodate someone else's bad manners.

Foreigners have a curiosity value to most Japanese. At places popular with tourists, many Japanese (especially children on a school excursion) will be outgoing and may even want your autograph. (Star for a day!) Even though westerners are common in large cities like Tokyo, we are still a rare sight in some places and most residents from these areas may well never have seen a foreigner. Keep this in mind if bombarded with a constant chorus of *Aro* (Hello) and try to keep smiling. If it happens in larger centres, you have the right to be annoyed, for they should have outgrown such behaviour.

The AIDS Factor

There is a certain element within the Japanese press that takes particular delight in finding any fault (real or otherwise) in western products, society, behaviour, culture, morals, etc. This gives them an opportunity to attack the west and, by implication, show the inherent superiority of the Japanese way. The AIDS epidemic of recent years has provided a splendid opportunity to stir up anti-foreign feeling, an aspect never too far below the surface of many Japanese anyway.

Numerous attacks against westerners, particularly Americans (and, most particularly, American blacks) have been printed in these publications with the effect that some of the less-alert members of the Japanese public (they do exist, despite what has been put out about the higher IQ of the Japanese) have been induced to make the pavlovian association: foreigner equals AIDS. On a TV AIDS information phone-in show, for example, one caller asked if he was at risk because he had held the train handstrap just used by a foreigner, and a black Canadian woman was temporarily banned from using a local public bath (until she protested vociferously). Another wrote that some well-dressed office types had pointed at him on the train and said very clearly 'AIDS'.

Such attitudes are quite likely to affect a number of foreign travellers in Japan in the form of remarks or even unkind treatment. There is a risk that such incidents will become more common over the next few years, for it is no certain thing that the Japanese public will become any better informed about the facts, and there seems to be a growing feeling of arrogance among some of the public now that Japan has become so successful economically.

Ironically, there is a very good chance that any increase in the prevalence of AIDS in Japan will be due to sex tours made by large numbers of the male population to the fleshpots of neighbouring countries.

Socialising & Dating

One of the characteristics of the upbringing of Japanese women is subordination to males, beginning with her brothers. In a relationship, she generally looks after her man. Conversely Japanese males tend to be spoiled from childhood, so the result is that Japanese men and western women tend not to be very compatible. This is reflected by the ratio of only one marriage of a Japanese male to a western female to every 10 of Japanese women to western men, and a high rate of divorce by western women who have married Japanese men, particularly those who married overseas, and found the man reverting to Japanese behaviour upon their return to Japan.

For some Japanese men there is prestige in dating a western woman. While this is not the general rule, some foreign women tend to wonder if they are being asked out for their company or for the prestige they bring. One American woman had this experience: her date took her to a restaurant – with 10 of his male friends – and then asked her to pay for the meal!

Many Japanese men have a very distorted view of western women, especially their moral standards, and expect them to leap into bed upon request. Any woman who suspects this attitude in her Japanese friend and wishes to dispel it should easily be able to give a suitable hint in conversation.

There are various ways to meet Japanese of the opposite sex. In Tokyo, there are coffee shops where people go to chat in English (conversation lounges), and several places where people gather for drinks and conversation; in Tokyo, Berni Inn, Henry Africa and Charleston are examples. (Such places tend to come and go in popularity, so it is necessary to ask around and find the current 'in' place.) There are also many discos in the large cities; the Roppongi area of Tokyo has several. They are not cheap, generally about Y3000 to Y4000 entrance charge, which includes some drinks and eats. Their main drawback as meeting places is that the sound levels are so high it is almost impossible to talk, and many discos and clubs admit only couples.

After meeting a suitably charming young man or woman, there comes the matter of future meetings. Some families are open-minded and have no objections if their daughter or son has an 'appointment' (date) with a foreigner, but others (especially the wealthy and upper-class families) object strongly. Suspicion and dislike of other races is universal. (One American friend who only delivered a message to a Japanese girl living in a university residence learned later that the keepers of the place had phoned her parents in Kyushu to inform them of this horrific occurrence. Nevertheless, many girls do play around during their college days.)

Couples in Japan who want privacy but who have no place of their own to go to be alone have a great range of facilities. Many coffee shops have inky-dark rooms (often downstairs) with two-people booths, high partitions between booths and discreet waiters. These offer a modicum of privacy for nothing more than the cost of a coffee, and reportedly quite amazing activities have been carried out in the cramped quarters. The next step up the ladder is also a type of coffee shop, but it has individual rooms with a couch and table in each and a door (unlocked). For a moderate fee, couples can stay until five am, and the table can be moved to block the door. Beyond this comes the love hotel – described in the Places to Stay section.

Marriage

Foreign men and women marrying Japanese are affected differently by Japanese law.

When two Japanese marry, the wife's name is removed from her family's register and transferred to that of her husband's family. Because registry is tantamount to citizenship, foreign spouses may not be put in family registers. A foreign wife may remain in Japan as long as her husband resides there and sends a letter to immigration authorities whenever her period of stay is due for renewal, stating that he wants her to remain. A foreign husband has no right of residence just because he is married to a Japanese woman. By Japanese law a wife is expected to reside in her husband's country. A foreign man must have an independent reason for remaining in Japan (work, study, etc, with appropriate visa), or else he can be deported with his children, who must take on his nationality by Japanese law. This unequal treatment is in conflict with a constitutional provision of sexual equality and is currently under legal challenge. For up-to-date information, refer to the publication *Now You Live in Japan*.

Children of mixed marriages often have a difficult time because their foreign blood sets them apart from the rest of the population in a society which values sameness and uniformity. They may also have difficulty deciding which society they belong to, Japanese or foreign; it is a problem trying to be both, and such children often fail to fit in completely with either, not learning either language perfectly. The pressure to be the same as everyone else is so severe that even Japanese children who have lived for some time overseas are often picked on when they return to Japan because they are different.

Anyone considering marriage to a Japanese and remaining in Japan (particularly foreign men marrying a Japanese woman) should have the prospective partner read the following two books (which are written in Japanese): *Sugao no Kokusai Kekkon* The Japan Times (Y1200); and *Kokusai Kekkon*

Handbook Akashi Shoten, Tokyo (Y1600). They describe both procedures and the potential problems.

THE FOREIGNER IN JAPAN

Japan can be an interesting and enjoyable country in which to spend an extended time. It is definitely foreign, very Asian, offering a new culture, society and personal relationships to explore, yet it is generally a comfortable place to live because the basic services that foreigners want or need are generally available and it has absorbed sufficient of the west that it is approachable.

Always keep in mind that although many aspects of western life have been borrowed, the background on which they are based is often unknown or imperfectly understood and has often been absorbed only superficially. This characteristic has manifested itself for centuries, as evidenced in religion for example. Buddhism in Japan bears almost no resemblance to that in any other country. The Japanese have taken certain tenets of the faith (often remote from the core), discarded the central parts, and then built an entire new structure around this new centre to suit the Japanese nature and history. The tradition continues today.

Most foreigners who remain in one place in Japan for an extended period of time typically go through a number of identifiable stages in their outlook on Japan. Writers commenting on the phenomenon (usually in a humourous manner) have identified up to four or five stages, but they can be summarised adequately by three:
- the wonderland (or rosy-coloured glasses) phase.
- the disillusionment phase.
- the acceptance of reality phase.

The first phase is characterised by adoration of everything Japanese, when everything is new and superficially so much better than in any other country in culture - politeness, arts, design, social organisation, social relationships, et cetera, et cetera, ad nauseam.

More than a few people are so enamoured that they try to live a totally Japanese lifestyle, eating only Japanese food, socialising only with Japanese, striving to learn the language, and endeavouring to become part of Japanese society.

The second phase comes from the often-acute disappointment of finding that the gushing reports read overseas were inaccurate, incomplete, biased, misleading, simplified or misguided and the crowded reality and ugliness of the cities and the difference in behaviour of the people from what had been expected becomes over-whelming. The most serious cases are those who have tried to become Japanese in every aspect of life, only to find that the Japanese don't *want* them to be part of Japanese society. Like a pendulum released from one side, their emotions swing to the far extreme in over-reaction, to dislike (often extreme) of the country and every aspect of it.

The third phase is where the pendulum comes to rest, balanced by the realisation that on one hand there *are* many aspects of Japan that are very interesting and worthwhile (some of which *are* worth copying in other countries), and that on the other there are many serious short-comings in the country that should be put right. It is at this stage that one can enjoy and accept the many good experiences that Japan offers, while keeping a balanced overall view.

The usual reaction by visitors given information like the above after only a few days in Japan is to express disbelief, telling of the great treatment that they have received, how wonderful the Japanese people are, and so on.

Yes, the people *are* wonderful - while the foreigner is perceived as a guest who is just passing through for a short time, then leaving. Those in Japan for only a short time will receive this guest treatment during their entire visit. The attitude

Top: Shamisen players at Takanawa Prince Hotel's annual cherry blossom festival, Tokyo (IMcQ)
Left: A pilgrim at Asakusa Kannon temple, Tokyo (IMcQ)
Right: Traditional Japanese archery at Ueno, Tokyo (IMcQ)

Top: Sweeping temple steps, Amonohashidate (AE)
Left: Nodate (outdoor tea ceremony), Kanazawa (AE)
Right: Old woman, Noto-hanto peninsula (AE)

becomes much less warm when the foreigner lets it be known that he/she has been in the country for a long time, or plans to be. Generally this change is not to hostility, only to neutrality, with special benefits no longer conferred. One sometimes begins to wonder if there is a government department instructing the populace to give such excellent treatment to visitors, since it is so uniform throughout the country; many foreign travel writers visiting Japan seem never to get beyond it.

The major cause for disappointment with the realities of Japan and the Japanese is that much of the information about Japan available overseas is inaccurate, distorted, superficial, or incomplete and foreigners may come to Japan with unrealistic expectations. There are several reasons for this.

Information from Japanese sources presents only a Japanese point of view. While the writers have the advantage of knowing the language perfectly and have the ability to ferret out facts that we outsiders cannot, working against objectivity is the fact that the Japanese try at all times to present only the positive where Japan is concerned. Negative aspects of any issue are normally kept from view. This is an aspect encountered throughout Japanese society, so it is not necessarily an attempt to mislead non-Japanese, although it may seem so.

This sort of thing is encountered in many ways in society. The Japanese are very adept at seeing only what they want to see and ignoring the rest (or pretending that it doesn't exist). Thus they are able to isolate and admire the one beautiful element in a scene and ignore the gas stations, fast-food shops, old and shabby buildings and litter surrounding it. The principle of the Japanese garden is based on this ability to concentrate one's attention on the beauty of only a small area.

One way to look on information about Japan from Japanese sources is to think of

Japan as an image on a projection screen, with only pictures favourable to Japan being shown. These images are generated by publications prepared in Japan that are aimed at overseas readers, and by foreign writers under the Japanese influences. Only those who stay in the country long enough will 'get around the screen' and have the chance to see the good, the bad, and (thanks, Clint) the ugly. One will then find that these good but cliched aspects of Japan *do* exist, and are definitely a part of the country and its society (and very much worth seeing), but that they are only a part of the overall picture. This is the point of view that many foreigners living in Japan come to: appreciation of the good, but awareness of the shortcomings.

MONEY

The name of the Japanese currency is the yen – which is about as much as anyone can say about it with any certainty. In the past few years the value of the yen in relation to one US dollar has ranged from below Y135 up to Y260. The Japanese economy is one of the most successful in the world today and the yen is increasingly becoming an international currency quoted in all major currency markets.

$$US\$1 = Y126$$
$$£1 = Y223$$
$$A\$1 = Y103$$

There are coins of 1, 5, 10, 50, 100 and 500 yen, and notes of 500, 1000, 5000 and 10,000 yen. The designs of the latter three denominations were changed in late 1984, and although they have disappeared, they are still legal tender. There is speculation that the Y500 banknote (already uncommon) will be phased out and that a larger denomination note – Y50,000 or Y100,000 – will be introduced.

The banknotes all have arabic numerals and can easily be identified; they are also of different sizes. The Y1 coin is aluminium, the Y5 is brass with a hole.

The brown solid coin is Y10 and the Y50 coin is nickel and also has a hole. The Y100 and Y500 are nickel and solid, the latter physically larger and marked 500.

In terms of actual purchasing power in Japan, compared with what a US dollar will buy in the US, the true exchange rate is closer to Y350 to Y800 to the dollar. Its official value is pushed up by continuing demand for the products of Japan's few really competitive and efficient industries, such as electronics, cars, motorcycles and optical goods. Steel and shipbuilding, both very important in the past, have lost ground as the result of overseas competition and the high yen.

Most other products, including food, are very expensive – the result of small-scale and inefficient production. Rice, for example, could be bought in the US or Australia for a about a sixth the price charged in Japan. Japanese families spend about 25% of their income on food compared with about 15% in the USA.

Changing Money

Only yen may be spent in Japan and it is illegal for foreign currencies to be used. Unlike in some other countries in Asia, the US greenback is not a second currency and the average shopkeeper would not recognise one.

Foreign currencies can be changed only at banks which have the sign 'Authorised Foreign Exchange Bank' on them, or at a few authorised stores that have a large tourist trade; they will have a similar sign posted. Both cash and travellers' cheques may be exchanged. In metropolitan areas, authorised banks are thick on the ground but don't get caught short of yen out in remoter areas as it can be a real hassle exchanging money.

The currencies of the following countries may be exchanged in Japan: Australia, Austria, Belgium, Canada, Denmark, Netherlands, France, Germany, Hong Kong, Italy, Norway, UK, Portugal, Sweden, Switzerland and the USA. Travellers' cheques in the currency of the following countries can be exchanged: Australia, Canada, France, Germany, India, Italy, UK, Switzerland and the USA.

While these currencies may be exchanged for yen, don't walk into a bank in a small city and hope to exchange Canadian notes, for example. The bank will only accept them for clearance and send them to its head office, a process that would take at least several days.

The currency of Taiwan is worthless in Japan and the currency of Korea is almost in the same boat as it cannot be exchanged at the usual banks in Japan. However, if you have Korean won and have exchange certificates proving the money was changed through an authorised Korean bank, you can convert them to yen at one of the three offices of the Korea Exchange Bank. They are in Tokyo (in the Marunouchi financial district, quite close to the TIC), Osaka and Fukuoka.

If you are going to Korea, convert your yen to US dollars; they receive a high rate on the black market, which is quite open in Seoul, whereas Japanese money is worth little more than the official rate.

Yen travellers' cheques are of little more use in Japan than foreign currency and there are many stories of clerks in bank branches outside the major cities who don't know what to do with yen travellers' cheques issued by their own bank. Banks are even more unwilling to cash the 'paper' of another bank, accepting them only for collection, so unless there is a branch of the bank that issued the yen cheques, you may have trouble trying to cash them. Also, the major banks that issue travellers' cheques often don't have branches in the smaller cities, so check carefully where they can be cashed.

Banks

There are two ways to avoid carrying large amounts of cash. The first, and probably the simplest, is to open a post office savings account. With such an account you can withdraw money from almost every post office in Japan during normal business hours and they also use a cash dispenser system. Since there are far more post offices than banks, this method is most useful. An account can be opened at any but the smallest post office; certainly there is no problem at the central post office in Tokyo (near Tokyo station). The

magic words are *Yubin chokin-o hajimetai*. That should be enough to open an account.

The other way to keep money in Japan is to open a passbook savings account with a large bank, preferably one that has branches nationwide, such as Mitsubishi, Mitsui and Dai-ichi Kangyo, and obtain a cash card for the account. You will be able to withdraw funds at any branch of the bank with the passbook by the invisible signature system, or from cash dispensing machines at almost any bank throughout the country using the cash card. (There is a Y50 charge if the machine at a different bank is used).

A cash card gets around the problem that many large banks, like Mitsubishi, have few branches outside the largest cities. Of the banks, the Dai-Ichi Kangyo has the largest number of branches through the country. I opened my account with the Mitsubishi Bank at the Tokyo head office (near Tokyo station) and found that staff spoke enough English to do this without difficulty.

It is also possible to open a US dollars savings account. This is probably of greater use to residents rather than visitors. It allows easy transfer of money in and out of Japan without having to exchange it each time. Banks might be unwilling to open an account for a stranger but by looking around there should be no trouble finding a branch willing to help.

Interest rates paid on dollar accounts are usually higher than for yen accounts (which are laughably low in any case) but a tax may be imposed and some banks deduct a handling fee of 0.1 of 1% per transaction (or a minimum charge of Y750 to Y1000, whichever is greater.)

Hanko Japanese bank customers must use a small seal, or stamp (*hanko*), on documents for all their financial transactions. They are not permitted to use a signature. However, non-Japanese are not subject to this restriction and so a signature is acceptable.

This requirement for using a *hanko* is one of the many aspects of Japan that foreigners find truly strange. If someone else gets hold of your *hanko*, they can withdraw all your money, sell your house and do a great amount of other mischief as long as it can be kept secret from you until the transaction is complete.

Cheques It is possible to open a cheque account and write cheques but the use of cheques is so uncommon that it would be difficult having them accepted. The universal use of cheques as we know it in western countries is totally foreign here. Instead, to pay a debt or account, the Japanese arrange a transfer to the account of the creditor at the cost of Y600 per transaction, or else send cash by registered mail at the cost of Y350 plus postage. The cheapest way to remit money within the country is by a postal money order (*yubin gawase*).

Transferring Money If there is no rush to have money transferred, the simplest way is to have a yen money order or draft (issued by a bank or a post office) sent by mail to the address that you specify. You could also carry a draft payable to yourself when coming to Japan. This is a cheap way of transferring money to Japan without carrying a large amount of cash. It also saves the 1% commission charged for travellers' cheques, although possible different exchange rates for travellers' cheques and drafts might affect the saving. A money order can be cashed only at the bank or post office listed on the order itself. Although *most* mail gets through in Japan, it would be safer to send a draft by registered mail, especially if it is to a Poste Restante (General Delivery) address.

Money can be sent directly from an overseas bank to its correspondent bank (or branch, if it has one), by mail transfer, which is slower but cheaper than the alternative method of cable transfer. It would be a good idea to talk with someone in your home bank before setting out, asking their advice on the best method of transferring money. Be sure that the sending bank understands *very* clearly *exactly* where the money is to be sent to: city, bank name, and branch. One payment that should have been sent to me from Australia was to go to the Mitsubishi Bank in Kyoto, and actually went to the Sanwa Bank in Tokyo!

Despite the use of computers and other technology, the Japanese banking system is slow and inefficient in some fields. Transferring money to and from Japan is more expensive than in many other countries and service charges seem to pop up out of nowhere. For example, you will lose a couple of thousand yen out of a draft received from overseas as a 'cashing charge', even though the draft was drawn on the very branch at which you are cashing it. Not without reason are the Japanese banks the largest in the world.

If remitting money out of the country, banks charge Y2500 to Y3000 per draft and preparing it will take several days unless you get it at the bank's main branch. Remittances to the USA may be somewhat less costly at an American bank, and to the UK, the charge by Standard Chartered Bank for a draft is somewhat lower than that of the Japanese banks.

If you have an account with the Bank of America in the USA, you can deposit dollars into the USA account by paying yen into the Tokyo branch. There is no transfer charge if you supply an encoded deposit slip for your account. Other foreign banks have a similar system.

In recent years the foreign exchange regulations have been relaxed greatly. For the amount of money that most travellers are likely to be dealing with, there are effectively no restrictions in changing money in either direction. An exchange receipt is given with each transaction. Up to Y3,000,000 may be exchanged without documentation, but if your exchange dealings are in this range, it is wise to hold on to the receipts.

American dollars may be purchased over the counter (though with the inevitable wait) as long as the bank has them in stock. A bank in Shinjuku (Tokyo) operates a machine that accepts yen and gives out US dollars. This may be the forerunner of such devices nationwide. For paying small amounts of money overseas, it is probably cheaper to buy US dollars and send them by registered mail.

Bank Hours Banks are open Monday to Friday between 9 am and 3 pm. They are closed on the second and third Saturdays of the month, and open the others from 9 am to midday.

Cash dispensers are open from 8.45 am to 6 pm on weekdays and from 9 am to 2 pm on Saturdays. Unlike in other countries, the cash dispensers are *not* open 24 hours, when they could be most useful. The banks got together and decided the hours. Excessive competition is bad, you know.

Bank Service The first time that you use a Japanese bank, you will wonder how this country has advanced so far. Service is incredibly slow. Nothing is ever finalised by one trip to the counter; one gives the withdrawal slip or whatever the document is to the teller, receives a numbered token, then waits five to 15 minutes for the number or name to be called. Take something to read.

Credit Cards

Several international credit cards can be used in Japan. These include Diner's Club, American Express, Master Charge and Visa Card. Enquire before leaving home about the usefulness of any other card if you have one from another large credit organisation.

Establishments accepting credit cards have signs prominently displayed. Usually the places that accept them are expensive

and are aimed at the wealthy or expense-account traveller. When using a credit card you are unlikely to obtain a discount of any size because the shops must pay a commission to the card company.

TIPPING

Japan has the distinction of being one of the few developed countries where tipping is not generally expected. If a service charge is expected, it will automatically be added to your bill (another way of saying it is compulsory). Quite separate from the service charge is the 10% tax incurred if restaurant or bar bills exceed Y1200.

Only at expensive nightclubs, which are a western type of import and which have largely disappeared in recent years, is tipping of waiters normal. Even nightclub hostesses do not expect tips if you pay the hostess charge and buy their drinks, although this will amount to plenty in any case!

TOURIST INFORMATION
Japan National Tourist Organisation

The best single source of information is the JNTO. This is a semi-official body set up to distribute tourist information and otherwise encourage travel to Japan.

The JNTO has prepared a large number of excellent pamphlets and other publications that provide a great deal of useful information for travel in Japan, including info specially slanted for the budget traveller. JNTO publications are available by mail from their many overseas offices although not all offices will be able to supply all publications.

Within Japan, the JNTO operates three Tourist Information Centers; two are in Tokyo (in Yurakucho district and at Narita Airport) and one is in Kyoto. In addition to the JNTO publications, the TIC have a large number of typewritten information sheets about various topics. These can be photocopied for anyone who is interested in a specific subject. Each TIC has an index of sheets available. Staff at the TICs are also goldmines of information.

While TICs can provide information on any aspect of travel in any region of Japan, they do not make bookings or reservations. These services are provided by travel agencies, the best known of which is the Japan Travel Bureau (another semi-official organisation) which has offices in every major city throughout the country, and branch offices overseas.

Unfortunately, these three Tourist Information Centers are the only places in Japan that are equipped to give a full range of travel information in foreign languages. Information offices in other cities are there to provide details on the local area only and there is usually no one who can speak any language but Japanese.

Japan Travel-Phone
As a courtesy to foreign visitors, the JNTO has organised Japan Travel-Phone, a toll-free, telephone travel information service. You can call from anywhere in Japan at no cost to make inquiries of a tourist nature (transport schedules, sightseeing advice, etc). It could also be useful if you were having trouble making yourself understood in some out-of-the-way place (or in a big city, for that matter!).

The service operates daily throughout the year from 9 am to 5 pm. East and north of Tokyo, dial 0120-222-800; west and south, dial 0120-444-800. Within the Tokyo area, dial (03) 502-1461; within the Kyoto area, dial (075) 371-5649. The last two are local calls charged at Y10 for every three minutes.

Publications The following are useful general information booklets or other publications offered by the JNTO/TIC. The number in brackets is the JNTO code number and the letter is the initial letter of the languages in which it is available: English, French, German, Spanish, Portuguese, Italian and Chinese.

Your Guide to Japan A 24-page booklet containing a wealth of general information about Japan – history, weather, geography, accommodation, transport, culture and the arts, and sightseeing. (101; E,F,G,S,P,I,C)

Japan Traveller's Companion A 24-page booklet containing more specific information than the above publication, with info on transport, accommodation, sports and embassies. (105; E)

The Tourist's Handbook A booklet of useful phrases along with the most frequently asked questions (printed in English and Japanese) that can be shown to a Japanese person, who can then choose the most appropriate answer from a list.

Tokyo (2222; E,F,G,S,P,C)
Kyoto-Nara (224; E,F,G,S,P)
Nikko (221; E,F,G,S)
Northern Japan (Hokkaido & Tohoku) (211; E)
Fuji-Hakone-Izu (223; E,F,G,S)
Central Japan (Kanto, Chubu, Kinki) (214; E)
Western Japan (Chugoku, Shikoku) (212; E)
Southern Japan (Kyushu, Okinawa) (213; E)
Hokuriku (Toyama, Ishikawa & Fukui)
Shizuoka
Tokyo, Kyoto/Nara maps

The JNTO-issued *Tourist Map of Japan* is useful for overall itinerary planning. It also has large scale maps of many cities in Japan.

The TICs usually have additional brochures and pamphlets of particular areas, such as Sado island and various prefectures. If you are thinking of going to one of these areas, ask what is currently available. These brochures are not printed by JNTO and so are not necessarily in stock.

The commercial publication *Japan Visitor's Guide* has some information and maps that may be useful supplements to those mentioned in this guide but it is best to wait until you get to Japan before obtaining a copy. It is distributed free at the Tokyo TIC and possibly at other tourist centres.

The publication *Japan Travel-Phone*

has the excellent Tokyo subway and Tokyo-area transportation maps that are also printed in the JNTO map of Tokyo, in addition to an excellent transportation map of the whole area Kyoto-Nara-Yoshinoguchi/Yoshino-Wakayama-Osaka-Kobe. All the maps show the station names in both *kanji* and *romaji*.

JNTO Offices Overseas

USA
45 Rockefeller Plaza, New York, NY 10020; tel (212) Plaza 7-5640.
333 North Michigan Ave, Chicago, Illinois 60601; tel (312) 32-3975.
1420 Commerce St, Dallas, Texas 75201; tel (214) 741-4931.
1737 Post St, San Francisco, CA 94115; tel (415) 931-0700.
624 South Grand Ave, Los Angeles, CA 90017; tel (213) 623-1952.
2270 Kalakaua Ave, Honolulu, Hawaii 96815; tel (808) 923-7631.
Canada
165 University Ave, Toronto, Ontario M5H 3B8; tel (416) 366-7140.
England
1676 Regent St, London W1; tel (01) 734-9638
Australia
115 Pitt St, Sydney, NSW 2000; tel (02) 232-4522.
Hong Kong
Peter Bldg, 58 Queen's Rd, Central; tel 5-227913.
Thailand
56 Suriwong Rd, Bangkok; tel 233-5108.
Switzerland
Rue de Berne 13, Geneva; tel 318140.
Germany
Biebergasse 6-10, 6000 Frankfurt; tel 292792.

GENERAL INFORMATION
Post

The Japanese postal system is generally reliable and efficient, though its rates are probably the highest in the world, and it has been known to lose letters. Post offices keep quite long hours and district post offices are open 8 am to 7 pm on weekdays, from 8 am to 3 pm on Saturdays, and 9 am

to 12.30 pm on Sundays and national holidays. 'District post office' means the main post office of the ward (*ku*).

Local post offices keep shorter hours: 9 am to 5 pm on weekdays, 9 am to 1 pm on Saturdays; closed on Sundays and holidays. Local post offices can accept letters for overseas destinations (air and surface) but registered mail, small packets and parcels can be sent overseas only from the district offices.

The central post offices of Tokyo and Kyoto (and possibly other large cities, like Osaka, Nagoya, etc) have some counters which are open 24 hours a day, so you can send letters and parcels, and collect poste restante and registered mail.

Mail can be addressed into, out of, and within Japan in *romaji*. To avoid letters going astray, write or print clearly as mail sorters and carriers are not linguists.

In Tokyo there is a special post office for overseas mail, Tokyo International Post Office (Kok'sai Yubin-kyoku). They know all regulations regarding foreign mail and can give information in English. It is in Otemachi (near Tokyo station) and is shown on the TIC's Tokyo guide map. In theory you can obtain information in English by telephoning 241-4877.

For wrapping parcels, most post offices supply free twine. If you need cardboard boxes, try any one of the pharmacies, grocery stores and many other shops which discard them every day.

Airmail envelopes should not be used for domestic mail. There may be a surcharge for coloured envelopes as they require special handling. Stickers may be attached to postcards as long as they don't add appreciably to the weight or thickness.

Philatelists may be interested to know that Japan, like every other country, regularly issues commemorative stamps (*kinen kitte*). These are sold at every post office in the country on the day of issue, but usually they disappear quickly the same day. After that they can be purchased (until sold out) at Tokyo CPO, near Tokyo station, Marunouchi side. The

philatelic counter is near the centre of the long counter on the ground floor. Stamps available are displayed on a board and the way of filling out an order slip is easy to figure out.

Receiving Mail Mail can be sent to Poste Restante (General Delivery) to any post office in Japan but preferably to the Central Post Office of the city, which is usually very close to the main railway station. Things to note are firstly that letters are usually held for only 30 days before being returned to the sender; and secondly that the Japanese seldom use the service and most people don't know that it exists. Postal clerks in smaller post offices may even be unsure where to put such letters so there is a risk that they will go astray.

At the post office, ask for either *tome oki* or *kyoku dome* and have your passport or other identification ready.

American Express offices hold mail for customers. They may ask for proof that you are a customer, but this can simply mean someone who has bought their travellers' cheques. Mail is normally held for 30 days but they will hold it longer if it is marked 'Please hold for arrival'.

The addresses of branches that hold mail are:

Tokyo
American Express, Halifax Building, 16-26 Roppongi 3-chome, Minato-ku, Tokyo 106.
Osaka
American Express, Kita Hankyu Building 3rd floor, 1-4-8 Shibata, Kita-ku, Osaka.
Okinawa
American Express, Awase Shopping Centre, 241 Aza Yamazoto, Okinawa-shi 904.

To reach the Tokyo office, take the subway to Roppongi and leave the station via the east end of the platform (the end at the rear of trains from the Ginza direction). Turn left after passing the ticket taker, exit the station, and turn right at street level. Walk past the Almond coffee shop (a well-known rendezvous), across the little street that goes downhill, and turn right at the main thoroughfare. After a five to 10-minute walk, the large American Express sign is visible on the left side of the street.

In Osaka, the office is near Osaka station.

Some embassies will hold mail for their citizens but they may normally return it after 30 days unless it is marked 'Please hold for arrival'. The embassies of Australia, Canada, South Africa, New Zealand and USA will hold mail, but the UK embassy will not.

Some banks will hold mail for their customers. For example the Royal Bank of Canada will, but First National City Bank won't.

Hotels and youth hostels will hold mail for their guests. Hotels are usually quite safe addresses for mail but the hostels vary. In my own experience I had mail arrive safely but a friend who had her mail sent to one YH found that every one had been opened (though nothing was missing). This is not typical however.

Postal Rates Very few employees at post offices speak any English, making it difficult to obtain information on postal rates.

Airmail letters up to 10 g cost Y110 to Australia, Y130 to the USA and Y150 to Europe. Small airmail packets up to 80 g cost Y200, Y240 and Y280 to the same regions respectively. Aerogrammes to all regions cost Y110 and postcards cost Y80/Y90/Y100 for the same regions.

Surface-mail letters up to 20 g cost Y70 to Asia and Australia, Y110 to Europe and the USA. Letters can weigh up to two kg and then cost Y1760 and Y2930 for the two regions respectively.

Surface parcel post to Australia costs Y1800 for the first 500 g and Y400 for each additional 500 g. For the USA it costs Y1750 plus Y600, and for Europe it is Y2100 and Y750.

To send a letter within the country costs Y60 for 25 g up to Y2800 for four kg.

Telephones
The telephone system in Japan is very well developed and it is easy to phone anywhere in the country or the world.

Local calls cost Y10 for three minutes. If no more coins are put in, the call will be terminated at the end of that time. Extra coins can be inserted in advance; some phones accept only Y10 coins while others take both Y10 and Y100 coins.

There are a number of different types of phone and most suffer from the lack of English instructions. The most common type is red, sometimes with a gold band, which can be used for local or inter-city calls. It can hold six Y10 coins, takes them one at a time as the time period expires and returns any unused coins. They are found in many shops, stations, etc. There is also a smaller sort of red phone, only for local calls, which takes one coin and cuts off after three minutes.

Pink pay phones are found in private homes and operate exactly the same as large red ones.

Yellow phones are the same in function as large red ones, except that they can hold up to ten Y10 coins and nine Y100 coins. They are one of the most useful type of phone for inter-city direct-dial calls. Blue phones are identical in function to large red phones, although rare examples also take Y100 coins.

Olive-green phones are the newest type. There are two types: those which accept Y10 and Y100 coins plus 'phone cards', and the others which accept only the cards. The phone card is a type of credit card for a fixed amount (Y500, Y1000, etc) purchased at tobacconists and other shops. The card is put into a slot and the cost is deducted during the call from the credit value contained in a microchip on the card. The amount of credit remaining is shown by an indicator on the phone and the card can then be used for subsequent calls until its initial value is used up. New in 1984, these phones are being installed all around the country.

Emergency numbers for use anywhere in Japan are: Police 110; Ambulance 119, however, the person answering will probably only speak Japanese. Yellow and blue phones can be used for making emergency calls without coins.

A full Japanese phone number has nine or ten digits, usually in three groups. The first group is the area code and is used only when dialling from another zone; usually only the second two groups are written. If, however, all three are shown, for some peculiar reason brackets are often written around the second group, not around the area code as is usually done in other countries. The latter method is sometimes used in Japan and is used in this book.

Long-distance calls (more than 60 km) within Japan are about 40% cheaper on Saturdays, Sundays and national holidays, and between 7 pm and 8 am. For information on these calls telephone 0120-019019 (toll free).

Telephone number information is available in English in Tokyo by phoning 201-1010.

International Calls Calls can be made through an operator or by dialling directly. To call the overseas operator, dial 0051 from anywhere in Japan. For information about overseas calls, ring (03) 270-5111. Rates are quite high; a call to the USA being at least 30% higher than the equivalent from the USA.

Collect (reverse charge) calls can be made to Canada, USA, South Korea, Hong Kong, Taiwan, Australia and western Europe.

International Subscriber Dialling (ISD) calls can be made from any private telephone not specifically disabled, from hotels and from some pay phones. Calls are billed in units of six seconds.

Any yellow pay phone can be used for ISD calls (just have a good supply of Y100 coins), as can any green phone with a gold front plate and a symbol of a globe and

telephone. The latter phones accept a telephone card as well as Y100 coins, which is very convenient. To begin a direct dialled overseas call from one of these phones, first dial 001, then the country code and the number. These phones are not uncommon in airports, major hotels and some train stations and shopping areas, but may be rather thin on the ground in country areas.

Telegrams

Within Japan, telegrams can be sent in roman letters from major post offices and offices of the telegraph company, NTT.

Overseas telegrams can be sent to most countries of the world and are accepted in roman letters at telegraph, telephone or post offices. Hotels catering to foreign customers can also help.

Any group of 10 letters is accepted as one word, so words may be run together to economise as long as the recipient can successfully separate them.

Addresses

Visitors to Japan should know from the outset that it is almost impossible to find a place just from the address; even Japanese find it very difficult.

Addresses are not by street and in fact, most streets have no name at all. Only the most major avenues have names, and even then, some Japanese may not be familiar with these. Addresses are by district, not by street.

The smallest district is the *chome*, usually only a few blocks in area. Within the chome, each building has a one-digit or hyphenated two-digit number, eg 4-4. What makes the system interesting is that until 1955, the numbers were assigned by chronological order of construction, not by location.

The next larger unit may may be called a *cho* or *machi* or have no name at all. Next comes a *ku* which is the equivalent of a ward. In Tokyo, well-known ward names are Chiyoda-ku, Chuo-ku (Central Ward), Minato-ku (Harbour Ward) and Shinjuku-ku. For example, an address of the type 1-2-3 Nishi Meguro means the same as 2-3 Nishi Meguro 1-chome; the 2-3 is the building number.

Japanese addresses are often written in *romaji* with commas in the middle of a line, such as '1-2-3, Nishi Meguro'. When the whole address is printed on a single line this can be confusing to a reader who is unfamiliar with the system.

Published maps are available that show the breakdown of every *chome*, building by building, but few foreigners bother with them. It is almost universal practice, however, for any business or store to print a small map on its business card or advertisements, showing the location relative to the nearest railway or subway station.

There was an effort during the Occupation to assign numbers and letters to the major thoroughfares of Tokyo but this attempt to rationalise a non-system was definitely not appreciated and was dropped when the Japanese were given full control of their own affairs in 1953.

The names of cities are properly followed by the suffix *shi*, as in Yokohama-shi. The word means city and is tagged on to distinguish between cities and prefectures (*ken*) of the same name; there is an Okayama-shi and Okayama-ken, for example. The cities of Kyoto and Osaka are special administrative districts known as *fu*, and Tokyo is a *to* (capital); they are not *shi*.

In the countryside there are many *mura* (villages). Another word found often in addresses in the countryside is *gun*, which corresponds to 'county', one step smaller than *ken*.

Electricity

Electricity service everywhere in Japan is 100 volts AC, an odd voltage used nowhere else in the world except Korea, and they're changing to 220 V. Northeast of an imaginary east-west line just southwest of Tokyo, the frequency is 50 Hz; southwest of the line it is 60 Hz. Most 117 volt

equipment (such as shavers and hair dryers) designed for use in North America, will work satisfactorily, if a little slowly or with reduced heat output. The plug is identical to that used in Canada and the USA; it has two flat pins.

Time

All of Japan is in the same time zone, nine hours ahead of GMT. Because of its eastward position, day begins in Japan ahead of nearly all major populated areas except New Zealand and Australia. In mid-summer, sunrise is excessively early at around 4.30 and the evenings are very short. As daylight saving is associated with the reforms introduced during the Occupation, it is not utilised.

When it is 12 noon in Tokyo, the time in other places is:

Hong Kong	11 am
London	3 am
America, east coast	10 pm*
America, west coast	7 pm*
Hawaii, Alaska	5 pm*
Sydney, Melbourne	1 pm
New Zealand	3 pm

(* denotes previous day)

The 24-hour system is used for writing nearly all times in Japan, whether it is railway timetables or notices in restaurant windows.

Laundry

Anyone staying at hotels or ryokan can have their laundry done by the hotel. Dry cleaning shops and depots are common in every suburban area. Travellers using youth hostels will have to do their own washing, in many cases in a wash basin or sink using cold water which is not very pleasant in unheated washrooms in mid-winter!. A manicure brush is useful for scrubbing.

The coin-operated washing machine reached Japan several years ago and can be found in conjunction with *sento* (neighbourhood public baths), in the larger cities at least. Many youth hostels have washing machines for visitors' use.

MEDIA
Newspapers & Magazines

There are four English-language daily papers: The *Japan Times* is the oldest English paper in Japan and the only independent; the others are all off-shoots of parent Japanese-language papers. The *Japan Times* has arguably the best general coverage and has become quite a good paper in recent years. It is much smaller than big-city papers in foreign countries but it has relatively few advertisements and has good coverage of world news.

The *Mainichi Daily News* is a morning paper competing with the *Japan Times*. It has many of the same articles and differs mainly in its coverage of local events. The name means 'every day daily news'.

The *Asahi Evening News* is virtually the same as the Mainichi, except that it is an evening paper available from noon. The name means 'sunrise evening news.'

The *Daily Yomiuri* is not quite in the same league as the others, being smaller and less pretentious, although its cost is much lower. Its coverage of stories can be as much as a day or two later than that in the other papers so it is not the paper for the news freak.

Prices of all papers except the Yomiuri are in the Y120 to Y140 range. They are sold in the large hotels in the major cities and at many news-stands at the larger stations and at many bookstores. Outside the main cities it can be difficult to find any of them and even then they may be a day or two old.

All the major foreign magazines, like *Time, Newsweek* and the *Economist*, as well as several European-language magazines, are available at large hotel bookstores in the big cities. There are several magazines produced in Japan that are worth reading for a feeling of life in Japan. These include *Tokyo Journal*

(Tokyo), *Kansai Time Out* (Kobe-Osaka-Kyoto area), *The Magazine* (Tokyo) and *Intersect* (national).

There are other magazines available that cover various aspects of Japanese society or history. These can be interesting and informative. However, it is necessary to have a certain amount of scepticism when reading such magazines. Some are not to be taken entirely seriously as they are seemingly products of the *nihonjinron* establishment and are published to promote the 'unique Japan'. Occasionally their writers get so carried away with the everything-Japanese-is-better theme that they can be unwittingly funny.

One example: the *East* (one of the seeming propaganda outlets) had an article describing some additions to the list of 1,945 standard *kanji* that must be learned in order to be literate in Japanese and which are combined in compounds of two, three and more to make up the words of the language, all of which must all be learned individually, including pronunciation. It had the memorable quote: 'Thus those who have mastered the 1,945 characters have finished learning the Japanese writing system. Once again, it is easier to learn Japanese than it is to learn English, which consists of hundreds of thousands of words.'

There are so many magazines now competing in a limited field that it is difficult to predict how many will survive, although it seems that many of these are put out even at a financial loss just for the prestige or publicity gained by the publisher.

Radio

The only regular broadcasts in English are those of the Far East Network (FEN) for the American armed forces. While they are slanted towards the interests and tastes of people in the services (very heavy on pop music and sport) they also have hourly news broadcasts and an hour-long news, sports and commentary segment between 6 and 7 pm on week nights.

Those people who missed out on (or who want to relive) the golden days of radio can hear broadcasts of 1940s and '50s programmes such as the Whistler and Amos 'n' Andy. Listening areas and frequencies (kHz) are: Tokyo (810); Sasebo, Kyushu (1566); Iwakuni, near Hiroshima (1575); Misawa, Northern Honshu (1575); and Okinawa (650). Tokyo-area programmes are listed daily in the *Japan Times*.

There are a few minutes of news in English each day on NHK, the government broadcasting organisation.

The Japanese AM stations are heavily biased toward pop music, Japanese style, although there is a substantial amount of the western variety as well. Programme notes are published in the English-language dailies.

FM fans will be astounded to find that for all the electronic entertainment equipment produced in Japan, there is a miniscule number of FM stations in the large cities like Tokyo and Osaka which have only two stations each (although one in Yokohama can be heard in Tokyo).

The nationally owned NHK station broadcasts several hours of classical, pop, jazz and easy-listening music each day. The others are very heavily into pop.

The FM frequencies used in Japan are 76-90 MHz, below the international standard FM band 88-108 MHz found on most radios, so a special radio tuned to the local bands, or a converter, is necessary to pick up the broadcasts. If you want to buy good Japanese hi fi gear to take home, buy the foreign-frequency model and use a converter while in Japan, or look for a model that covers both bands.

TELEVISION

Most programming in Japan is in Japanese only. Imported programmes and films are dubbed, but a new development in the electronics field is multiplex broadcasting of TV soundtracks. This often allows hearing the original soundtrack of the film or programme instead of the dubbed version, by use of an adaptor, although there may be some lack of continuity if segments have been cut. Films on cable TV to some apartment buildings and most hotels catering to foreigners usually have their original soundtracks.

Watching the Japanese programmes, even if you can't understand a word of the dialogue, can give many insights into modern Japanese life. The role of women is clearly seen on one programme after another – they are usually there only to provide a little scenery and to say *hai* (yes!) in obsequious agreement with every statement of the male who is, by definition, the most important and intelligent person on the screen.

SPORTS
Sumo

Not well known to foreigners except for its fat wrestlers, Sumo is a Japanese sport which is interesting to watch. Two men face each other in an earth circle and grapple when they both feel ready. The loser is the first one pushed or thrown out of the circle or who touches the ground with any part of his body other than his feet. The action lasts from a second to a couple of minutes.

There are six *basho* (tournaments) per year at the following times and locations: early January (Tokyo); mid-March (Osaka); early May (Tokyo); early July (Nagoya); mid-September (Tokyo); mid-November (Fukuoka).

Seats cost from hundreds to thousands of yen but the best view is that on TV, broadcast live from 4 to 6 pm with a summary of all 15 bouts late in the evening.

Baseball

The Japanese are as baseball-mad as the Americans and fans of the sport might enjoy seeing a game while in Japan. The players are good although it is admitted that the US leagues are at a higher level.

Sumo Wrestlers

Skiing

Japan offers good skiing if you live here but it would not be worth making a special trip. Information on ski areas and resorts is available from the tourist information center. Some are mentioned in general descriptions of the areas, later in the book.

HEALTH
Food & Water

It is very unlikely that anyone will become ill in Japan as the result of eating or drinking. Food sold is of high standard, milk sold everywhere is pasteurised (UHT method), and tap water can be drunk anywhere in the country. The digestive troubles that you expect in most of Asia are virtually unknown. Food from mobile stalls, often seen at night near railway stations, is safe to eat.

Consumption of water in another manner, however, *can* be harmful. Swimming cannot be recommended in most populated areas of Japan, even at beaches rated as 'suitable' or 'very suitable' by the Environment Agency.

A few years ago, doctors at the US Navy base at Yokosuka made their own assessments, using American standards, of 32 beaches in the Shonan and Miura-hanto peninsula areas near Tokyo that were given the above two ratings and warned base personnel against swimming at 25 of them. Several of the 'very suitable' beaches were rated as 'particularly bad'.

In addition to polluted water, beaches are usually covered with rubbish abandoned to the elements by the thousands of daily holiday-makers. Oneness with nature in action.

Medical

The standards of health care in Japan are good, as reflected in longevity. According to government statistics, the average life expectancy is 74.84 years for men, 80.46 for women, which is the highest in the world. Medical personnel are generally trained to high standards and many Japanese doctors would rate high in any country. Likewise, there are many good hospitals with up-to-date equipment and facilities.

The other side of the coin is that Japan has its full share of quacks and unqualified practitioners who, if they got through medical school at all, did so more through money and influence than by merit. So if any serious procedure, like an operation, is suggested, be sure to get a second opinion even if the first doctor complains about losing face. Better his face than your health and wealth. More than a few foreign residents plan to go home if serious medical attention is required.

After a while, most residents hear of hospital horror stories. One that I can trace to the source involved a foreign resident who was operated on for a ruptured appendix with only a local anaesthetic. Half way through the operation, while his innards were literally laid on the table beside him, his wife was taken into the operating room and greeted by the horrific sight. He lived. On another occasion, the victim of a stabbing was taken by ambulance from one hospital to another over a period of two hours and was rejected at each because it was 'busy'. He died.

On balance, several people have written to the English-language papers praising the staff of various hospitals for the excellent service during treatment.

Hospital charges tend to be very high and there is a tendency to keep patients longer than necessary by western standards in order to increase the hospital's income, especially at hospitals that are privately owned by doctors. There are several hospitals in the large cities that were founded by various Christian groups. Their approach to medical care would be more familiar to westerners, so anyone needing hospital care should try to contact

them. Also in the larger cities there are several western doctors with whom foreigners will be able to talk more easily. The Tokyo TIC can give more information on these doctors and hospitals.

The common types of shots normally required for overseas travel can be obtained conveniently at the Kotsu Kaikan ('Travel Building') not far from the Tokyo TIC in Yurakucho. Slotted into this building along with travel agents, *minshuku* and *ryokan* booking offices and other travel-related businesses, is an office where qualified personnel spend every working day jabbing or zapping (pressure spray injections). Costs are reasonable and they issue you with a card recording the shots.

A cheaper but less convenient alternative for shots is the Tokyo Port Authority or the health facility at Narita Airport although for the more obscure shots, these may be the only places.

Dental

Japanese dentists are equipped with the most modern instruments and facilities in the world, and much dental research is carried out in universities. Dental care is covered by national health insurance so the standard is good. What makes Japanese teeth look bad (apart from older people in the country who have had their teeth replaced almost totally with gold) is hereditary malocclusion, so very large numbers of people have crooked teeth. Orthodontics is not covered by the health insurance, and the snaggle-tooth look is regarded as cute.

Dental work for foreigners visiting Japan will not be cheap and even getting an appointment can be a problem. There are dentists in large international hotels who take casual patients. In Tokyo and Kyoto, the TICs can give further advice.

Costs

It is advisable to take out a medical insurance policy before coming to Japan because costs are extremely high. To be a doctor or dentist is to be in one of the most lucrative professions in the country. This is reflected in the fact that prospective students at some medical schools must make a 'gift' to the college of up to Y40 million before they are admitted, and the average total cost for six years of study is Y19 million. This of course means that only the children of wealthy parents get into these schools, and it is the patients who have to ultimately pay off that scandalous bribe for entry. Being Japan, this practice will probably continue ad infinitum; service for the general good is not a generally admired concept.

Contraceptives

The main methods of contraception in Japan are the condom, pessaries (two such brands are CCC and Sampoon), gels and foams, and the diaphragm; the latter is the least popular. The message is that contraception is the responsibility of the male.

Abortions are readily available at moderate cost and with no difficulty for both Japanese and foreign women.

The Pill is not generally available to Japanese women, so foreign women using it should make sure that they have their own supply. Foreign brands are not sold in Japan and the only type sold is a very high dosage type intended for cycle regularising, not contraception.

The Pill is not available in Japan because of lobbying by gynaecologists who would lose a lucrative business if the number of abortions that they performed were reduced. Because the number of these specialists is decreasing anyway, there will be less opposition to selling the Pill in Japan (the country has a huge export trade in them), and there is talk of allowing their use from about 1990.

Familiar brands of sanitary protection are found only at pharmacies like the American Pharmacy that cater to foreign clientele; Tampax is the only internationally known brand distributed nationwide.

Mental Health

If you get the 'coming unstuck' feeling, need advice or help in personal matters, or just need someone to talk to for any reason, there is a small choice of agencies who can help.

Tokyo English Lifeline (TELL) (tel (03) 403-7106) offers confidential and anonymous counselling by telephone; they can also refer callers to other agencies that might be able to help.

Another useful organisation is Tokyo Community Counselling Service (tel (03) 403-7106); it refers callers to professional counsellors in a variety of fields.

Tokyo Tapes (tel (03) 262-0224) offers an extremely useful and comprehensive range of tape recorded information. Callers phone and request one or more tapes by number. For a listing of tapes by number, ask for tape 302. The listing is also available from Tokyo Tapes, 610 Homat Commodore, 5-13-28 Roppongi, Minato-ku, Tokyo 106; and from the sponsoring organisations, the Franciscan Chapel Centre, St Alban's, St Paul's Lutheran, Tokyo Baptist or Tokyo Union churches.

Toilets

Most toilets in Japan are the Asian squat type. These are supposedly physiologically the best kind and are hygienic because no part of the body comes in contact with it. Whether the squatting position is as advantageous as purported is difficult to say. Many westerners find them uncomfortable and undignified, but unless you continually travel first class, you will face the need to use one at some time. Face the raised part and be careful not to let anything fall out of your pockets; some people completely remove their trousers to avoid such an occurrence.

Most public toilets have no paper so it is wise to have your own when travelling away from familiar territory. There are often vending machines for tissues at the entrance. Where paper is provided, it is almost always of extremely poor quality.

All western-style hotels, some *ryokan* and most large and modern office buildings and department stores have clean, western-style facilities.

In private homes, youth hostels, *ryokans*, *minshuku* and other residential places, there will be a separate pair of slippers at the entrance to the toilet area. Take off the house slippers and change into the toilet ones. Don't forget to change back again when leaving, and never wear the house slippers into the toilet – both are major social gaffes. It all becomes instinctive after a while.

Don't be surprised or shocked at the sight of men urinating in public, especially at night after coming out of a bar after an evening of hard drinking. Even in daylight it is not unknown to see a man pissing against a wall.

Smoking

About 66% of Japanese males smoke, the highest percentage in the world, although this is down from 80% in 1966. Not unexpectedly, the number of deaths due to lung cancer has quadrupled since 1950.

As with smoke everywhere, the problem does not end with the smoker, but the pollution affects everyone in the vicinity. Japan is about 20 years behind the more advanced western countries in making public areas smoke-free, although some progress has been made.

DANGERS & ANNOYANCES

Japan is a relatively benign country but there are several hazards that can threaten one's safety.

Wildlife

Snakes There are two kinds of poisonous land snake: the *mamushi* and the *habu*, both potentially deadly. All the main islands are the habitat of the *mamushi*, while the *habu* is found only on the islands south of Kyushu, between Kagoshima and Okinawa.

Like most snakes, they will usually try

to escape from people if they are not cornered or startled. Snakes are deaf and although they can feel vibrations in the ground, they cannot hear people's approach in advance, so it's quite easy to be upon one before it has a chance to hide.

The *mamushi* usually grows to a length of 700 mm or so and has a diamond-shaped head and a moderately thick body covered with a pattern of dark circles with lighter centres; it can be found in any grassy area.

The *habu* is larger, up to two metres long, and has the stronger venom of the two. It has a diamond-shaped head and a pattern of diamonds on its body. It is found in both trees and grass and is always present in pineapple fields.

Bite victims can be saved if they can receive anti-venin in time. The limb should have a tourniquet of sufficient tightness to minimise circulation of the venom without cutting off all circulation. The larger islands have treatment centres for *habu* bites.

Bears Bears kill a few people every year, almost always intruders in the animals' habitat. Most bears, and most attacks, occur in Hokkaido. Attacks are most frequent when the mother has a cub.

Foxes In recent years, many tourist promoters have been publicising the Hokkaido fox (*kita-kitsune*) as a symbol (read 'gimmick', cute sub-variety) of Hokkaido because of its friendly nature. For example, a farm for the foxes opened at Rubeshibe in April 1983 and quickly became popular. Anything 'cute' is sure-fire in Japan.

If you go there, do not touch any of the foxes. The majority carry the parasitic worm echinococcus that causes a serious disease of the liver in humans, and it can be transferred just by contact. The promoters are doubtless aware of this but commerce comes before health.

Wasps As if any other worries were needed, there can be a danger from wasps in wild areas, particularly in the period from mid-August to early September when they are breeding and protecting the queen. In 1986, four persons died in Hokkaido of shock or other effects related to wasp stings. This was described as very rare by the police, but the newspaper report continued with the news that 31 people had died in 1985 after being stung by wasps and horntails. Persons with allergies are most susceptible to ill effects from the venom. Beware of nests.

Mosquitoes Like most countries of the world, Japan has mosquitoes; not in huge swarms, but enough to make it advisable to use insect repellent. Their bites are relatively innocuous, but you can find mosquitoes (or more precisely, they can find you) from summer to at least November.

Beaches

Lifesaving is very much lacking at public beaches and there are often 50 or more drownings every summer weekend. Many of these are due to swimming after drinking but many of Japan's popular swimming beaches have dangerous undertows. If you get caught in one, swim with it into deeper water and work your way back to shore at a calmer place. Never try to swim against it. If you go into the water, be sure that you are with someone else who can swim well.

Sea Snakes All sea snakes are deadly poisonous. Fortunately, they are found only in tropical waters and they usually do not bother people who do not bother them. Nearly all are brilliantly coloured and easy to see.

Jellyfish A seasonal ocean hazard is jellyfish. In June 1987 about 300 persons were treated for stings on one weekend.

Sharks Sharks are not regarded as a hazard in Japanese waters, although one unfortunate girl was killed by one in the early '80s while being pulled behind a boat off the south coast of Kyushu. The southern islands are close enough to the tropics that they are within the ambit of several species.

Earthquakes

Earthquakes are common throughout the country. Most are very mild; nothing more than a feeble tremble (the vast majority only show up on instruments) and are strong not enough to cause any damage.

The most famous disaster was the Kanto earthquake of 1923 when about 40,000 people were killed in the Tokyo and Kanto area. Buildings of that day were mostly flimsy wooden structures and many of the deaths were the result of fires that followed the quake.

All buildings in the Tokyo area must now be built to resist earthquake damage, so an equally strong quake today would probably cause a lower death toll despite the vast increase in population.

If you are caught in a strong quake, get outside if at all possible. If you are stuck inside, do not to use elevators. Stand near a supporting pillar or in a doorway, and far from the centre of the room. Ducking under a desk or table is a good second-best and is better than no protection at all from falling debris.

Fire

Hotels Modern hotels in Japan meet good standards of fire safety. There are stringent statutes on the books and most hotels meet the requirements. Any of the large international hotels can be expected to meet high standards, as can the majority of hotels aimed more at domestic travellers. However, tragic fires, with large loss of life, have shown that not all is perfect.

A fire in the Hotel New Japan (Tokyo) in 1982 took 33 lives because there were no sprinklers nor fire-blocking doors. For several years the manager had ignored repeated instructions by the fire department to install sprinklers and take other measures to improve fire safety.

A fire at one elderly *onsen* (hot-spring resort) inn in Atagawa (Shizuoka-ken) in February 1986 took 24 lives. In this case the building was old and constructed of wood, a left-over from the ticky-tacky era of construction in Japan, and a classic firetrap.

Another *onsen* hotel fire at Kawazu later killed 57. As it turns out, hostelries older than a certain age (and thus the most hazardous) are exempted from the law requiring them to install sprinklers 'because of the high costs that would result'. In addition, in the case stated, the fire alarm system had been disabled by the staff (because it had gone off several times, giving a false alarm), the emergency doors were locked, and the only staff members with keys for the doors had fled as soon as the fire was discovered.

Hotels in *onsen* and other resort areas should be regarded as particularly hazardous in general because the main aim of most of the male visitors is revelry, which invariably involves large volumes of alcohol. In view of the very heavy smoking by the male population, the use of *tatami* (grass) mats in the rooms, and general carelessness when having a good time (true in any country), the potential for a blaze is higher than in most other places in the country.

Cinemas Movie theatres are a potential hazard in Japan, and it is surprising that there has not been at least one disastrous fire in one in recent years. It is common practice of theatre managers to allow in up to twice as many patrons as there are seats, to the point that every aisle is packed with people. Despite signs prohibiting smoking, people light up with seeming impunity. If you are faced with the prospect of a jammed cinema, it might be wiser to pass up that performance.

Doors & Tables

Causing all the above to pale into insignificance as a hazard is the warning that anyone taller than 175 cm must be on constant guard for low doorways. Until recently the Japanese were a very short people and doorways were made to suit. The frames for doors and sliding room dividers (*shoji*) seem to have a uniform height of 180 cm. Train entrances are also low.

It sounds facetious, but tables in restaurants and other public places are also a hazard to all long-legged foreigners. There is a crossbar or shelf under just about every table, positioned exactly where any tall person will crack his or her kneecap on it. Slide in slowly! This never seems to bother the Japanese, obviously because of their shorter legs.

Hazards From Your Fellow Man

Japan is one of the safest countries in the world. Most visitors will not likely encounter any trouble or problem during a visit. However, like so many other aspects of Japan, safety in the country has been exaggerated and distorted by a succession of articles in the foreign press and just possibly abetted by domestic sources.

Theft For theft of personal belongings such as cameras, Japan is one of the lowest-risk countries in the world. Probably the riskiest places are those with large numbers of tourists, such as the airports. A sign at the Tokyo City Air Terminal warns of pickpockets; though not stated, these pickpockets are most likely to be from third-world countries rather than Japan.

Generally though, particularly away from the large cities, you could leave a suitcase unattended for hours almost anywhere and find it still there and untampered with when you returned. There are even tales of absent-minded people leaving cameras on park benches and returning hours later to find them still there, but it isn't recommended to try it.

The average Japanese is just very honest.

Lost goods will more than likely be turned into the police or transport authority, so if you leave something valuable behind on a train, don't give up as there is a good chance it has been handed in. Umbrellas seem to be an exception and will disappear if left in an unlocked drip tray on a rainy day.

Bicycles and motorcycles should be locked whenever left unattended. My Honda 550 was wheeled away from in front of my house one night and was found some days later minus some rather costly parts. There are professional motorcycle thieves in operation who just load parked bikes into their truck and take off in a minute or two. They are most interested in the newest, flashiest models. Bicycles are also liable to disappear.

Your belongings are usually safe in your room in a youth hostel if you are sharing with Japanese. They leave their belongings unattended in a way that would horrify most westerners. It is usually more necessary to be wary of other foreigners than of Japanese.

Burglaries are quite common in the big cities, although they are rarely reported in the English-language papers. Readers planning to reside a while should take all the usual precautions applicable in any western city. In small towns you may find that the locals don't bother locking their doors very much, but don't be insulted if they do start locking up when a foreigner moves into the neighbourhood.

Assault & Rape Japan is one of the safest countries in the world for foreigners and locals alike. In general it is safe to walk on *most* streets of any city or town without risk of assault, mugging or worse.

The best thing to do if you get flashed at, or touched up on a train, is to try to ignore the incident. In other circumstances, it might be necessary to run, in which case yell and make as much fuss as possible. Depending on the circumstances, here are

some appropriate words for the occasion:
chikan (pervert)
omawari-san! (police!)

However, advice often given is that it is better for a woman to scream *kaji!*. This means 'fire', and the word is more likely to get attention than any other as the Japanese are disinclined to getting involved with other people's problems.

FILM & PHOTOGRAPHY

Japan is the land of photographers. Whatever the occasion, the Japanese take a photograph of it, with themselves or family or friends in it – front and centre. Taking photos is part of the social process, as the participants in the occasion almost invariably get together a few weeks later and show/exchange photos. If they then photograph the reunion as avidly, they have the makings of an infinitely long chain of social gatherings.

The upshot of this is that film is used in huge amounts and is available everywhere in the country. Prices are reasonable, probably comparable with those in the USA, a bit higher than Hong Kong and Singapore and lower than in many other countries.

The three major film companies are the great yellow father (Kodak) and the two Japanese companies, Fuji and Sakura (Konica). Polaroid film for newer cameras is also available. Film is also still sold for Kodak instant cameras, a commodity no longer available in the USA due to the judgment of a patent suit by Polaroid against Kodak.

Kodak films are a known quantity around the world, with a well-deserved reputation for quality products. Colour print films of both Fuji and Sakura are both well regarded, giving good colour and grain in all speed types.

Colour slide films from Fuji have been building up a good reputation overseas but Sakura colour slide film has not yet established itself as being in the same league as the other two.

The vast majority of film sold for the amateur market is for colour prints. Colour slides are not popular (no prints to share with others!) and represent only about 10% of film sales. This means that slide film can be difficult to find outside the big cities.

Processing

Prints Because of the vast number of colour prints made every year, processing is available everywhere and at reasonable cost; colour prints cost as little as Y20 each. Films left at local camera shops will usually be processed and returned in one to two days.

There are depots around the larger cities where film may be left in the morning and picked up the same day, perhaps later in the day, perhaps in an hour. There is one such seven-hour-service depot in the Mitsukoshi department store facing the Ginza and there are others around the city, some near the major hotels frequented by overseas visitors.

Slides All slide films can be sent for processing by any camera shop in the country. The seven-hour developing depots can get Ektachrome and the Japanese slide films developed in three to four days. For faster service of Kodak slide films (Kodachrome typically takes six to eight days), take your film to the Kodak depot in the Ginza and ask for fast processing. They can have the films back in two days.

Kodachrome, with prepaid processing, is not available in Japan. For developing Kodachrome film sold with development included in the price, send it to: Far East Laboratories Ltd, 14-1 Higashi-Gotanda 2-chome, Shinagawa-ku, Tokyo. They could also be left at the Kodak depots in the Ginza or Aoyama.

If you are carrying undeveloped film on an overseas flight, you should carry it by hand and request a hand inspection of films and cameras. Signs on X-ray machines that they do not affect film cannot be trusted. ISO 100 film can probably be exposed up to four times before the effect is noticeable but high speed films in the ISO 800-1600 range are likely to show effects such as random colouration or streaks after a single exposure.

ACCOMMODATION

The travel industry is well established in Japan and there is accommodation ranging from acceptable to excellent throughout the country. In the big cities there are hotels that match the world's best, plus a variety of alternatives down the price scale. In provincial cities there are usually some facilities with a claim to being of a type that is familiar to westerners and virtually everywhere there is Japanese-style accommodation of reasonable quality.

For budget travellers the sad word is that there is absolutely no dirt-cheap accommodation of the kind found in most of the rest of Asia, such as the Chinese hotels or losmen. The cheapest room anywhere will be from about Y1500 per person per night.

For the most part, in this book there are no listings of places to stay in the individual city sections. There are several reasons for this. Japan is a country of many cities, few of which would be of interest to a foreign visitor, so there is no sense listing accommodation in such places.

All the youth hostels are listed in an easily obtained publication, and there are hand-out publications listing reasonably low-priced hotels – ryokan (inns) and minshuku (private homes) – in nearly every area of the country. It is not practical to repeat all this information.

Another factor is the fact that Japan is the land of the clone and the location and types of accommodation are quite similar from one end of the country to the other. Once you have learned minshuku-spotting, for example, the rules of the game are much the same everywhere.

Information is included for locating several youth hostels, *ryokan* and *minshuku* in areas of greatest interest to overseas visitors. The phone number is given for at least one youth hostel in or near every port of entry into Japan, along with instructions for reaching it. After a traveller has been in Japan for a few days, the system of finding a place to stay becomes more familiar.

The Japan National Tourist Organisation (JNTO) has prepared several booklets and brochures on accommodation. These are available from the TICs and should be available by mail as well. One of these publications that has been available in the past is *Reasonable Accommodations in Japan* which has listings of economical places to stay in 26 cities around Japan. Check if it is still offered. Reasonable in this case means Y3500 and up per person. Accommodation charges quoted in Japan nearly always mean per person.

If you arrive in a fairly large city without having booked accommodation, you can usually get assistance at the main railway station. Most have an office (*an nai jo*) that can help you find a place, although the office may close soon after 9 pm and their listings may not include the least expensive places available.

Hotels

Hotels as they are known in the west, with beds, familiar furniture and amenities, can be found in the major cities (especially ones frequented by foreign business people), as well as in popular resort and tourist areas. In smaller centres a hotel is likely to have a mixture of western and Japanese style rooms, with an equal confusion about what is expected in service.

The quality of facilities and service in Japan can vary from internationally accepted levels in the major centres to something much less pretentious but nearly as expensive in more remote areas. Prices at hotels in Tokyo range from Y5500 to Y23,000 for a single.

A listing of the 359 government-registered hotels of the Japan Hotel Association (generally good quality and international standard) is contained in the JNTO publication *Hotels in Japan*. The places listed usually have air conditioning or central heating and other modern facilities.

Note that the word 'hotel' in Japan refers more often to a special type of accommodation that lets rooms for one to two hours to couples visiting with negligible luggage. If you are seeking the respectable type of establishment, you may have to make this clear, for the seedier type of place is what you are more likely to encounter in smaller cities and local neighbourhoods. Actually, this short-term type of establishment can be useful to the ordinary traveller for overnight accommodation, and is described under Love Hotels.

Business Hotels

This type of accommodation has appeared in Japan in recent years. It is intended primarily for travelling businessmen who want respectable and clean accommodation without the high cost of luxury hotels. It achieves economy by eliminating frills like room service – each floor has vending machines for drinks and the like.

The rooms vary widely in size but generally tend to be on the small side, with the worst ones being ridiculously cramped. It is worth asking to have a look at the room in advance if you suffer from claustrophobia. Costs vary from Y2000 to Y5000 for a single; doubles cost somewhat more.

At least two books that list business hotels around Japan are available at bookshops. The larger is called *Zenkoku Business Hotel* and the smaller *Mini-mini Zenkoku Business Hotel*. The former lists 1600 business hotels around Japan, the latter nearly 620, with 68 in the Tokyo area alone. Both are written only in Japanese so a little work is involved in using it, but it is not difficult to match the *kanji* of place names on a map with those in the books. Organisation is by *ken* (prefecture).

Ryokan

To sample the best of Japanese life, try to spend at least one night at a *ryokan*. At its best, the *ryokan* embodies the finest Japanese hospitality and elegance, providing a simple but flawless traditional room with high quality furnishings and the best in food and service.

The senses should be pleased or soothed in all ways so a good *ryokan* should have a beautiful garden, not necessarily large but definitely elegant. Unfortunately, there are many places called *ryokan* that do not live up to such expectations, but if the facilities are of high standard then the time spent there can provide some of the best memories of Japan.

There are 80,000 or so *ryokan* scattered around Japan. However there are many where foreigners would not particularly want to stay, and others where a foreigner would not be allowed to stay. There are a few reasons why a good *ryokan* might refuse to accept a foreigner. It is not (necessarily) because of racism, but simply because they are very exclusive – even Japanese cannot book into them unless introduced by someone of high enough position and who is able to give assurance that the visitor is worthy of being allowed to stay there.

Other *ryokan* do not want foreigners to stay because of bad experiences in the past with overseas visitors who didn't know how to behave, didn't understand the system or made demands that the staff were not able to meet. In general, Japanese are convinced that their way of life is completely beyond the understanding of foreigners and that foreigners of any kind will just not fit in. If you can make yourself understood in Japanese, many more *ryokan* will be open to you.

The JNTO has prepared a booklet containing listings of *ryokan* that are accustomed to, or prepared to accept, foreign visitors. Titled *Japan Ryokan Guide*, it is available from JNTO offices and the TICs in Tokyo and Kyoto. Prices for various types of accommodation are listed along with the contact address and the means of getting there. The prices are considerably higher than those listed for hotels in the companion JNTO hotel booklet, rarely under Y10,000 per person with two meals.

The Japanese Inn Group comprises about 65 *ryokan* that are prepared to accept foreigners. Their rates are in the range of Y3000 to Y4500 for a single and Y5000 to Y9000 double. Its publication, *Japanese Inn Group*, has access maps, phone numbers, etc. This booklet is usually available at the TICs, or can be requested by mail from: Japanese Inn Group, c/o Hiraiwa Ryokan, 314 Hayaocho, Kaminoguchi-agaru, Ninomiyachodori, Shimogyo-ku, Kyoto 600.

Bookings for *ryokan* and *minshuku* can be made in every part of the country at any travel agent, especially JTB. Also, every railway station of any size has an information office (*ryoko an nai jo*) that has listings of all accommodation in the surrounding vicinity. They can make reservations on the spot but it is rare to find anyone who can speak English at these offices, and remember that they don't always list the lowest priced places.

There are usually many *ryokan* in the vicinity of any major station so if you want to find your own try walking around the area. Look for large numbers of shoes at the entrance, or entrances that are wide and open, as distinct from the rather secluded entrances to the average private house. People at small tobacco shops or other local businesses can often help in finding a *ryokan*.

Excursion Fares There are combined train and accommodation 'specials' for travel to Kyoto (and other places) from the Tokyo area, in which the costs of the train and *ryokan*/hotel are combined into a reduced price package. The combined cost of Tokyo-Kyoto Shinkansen fare plus one night in an economy *ryokan* of reasonable quality on a trip that I made was less than the cost of the normal return Shinkansen fare. Individual travel agents make their own arrangements; the best known to contact for such packages is JTB (Japan Travel Bureau).

Minshuku

Short-time visitors to Japan usually have little opportunity to see the inside of a Japanese house; even fewer stay overnight in one. However it is a simple matter to arrange to stay at a *minshuku*, a family home that takes guests. There are *minshuku* (pronounced 'minsh'ku') in every area with tourist attractions, such as historic towns, coastal villages, hot-spring resorts and ski areas and they are operated by local people.

Some *minshuku* are interesting in themselves and are an actual attraction for visitors. At Shirakawa (Gifu-ken) there are many huge old thatched-roof houses in an isolated valley. Many of them are *minshuku* and afford the opportunity to spend the night in a very unusual farmhouse, even by Japanese standards, and one that may even be a couple of hundred years old.

For travellers not on an absolutely minimal (ie, youth hostels only) budget, *minshuku* are the best places to stay to gain an impression of what part of everyday Japan is like.

In a *minshuku* a guest is made to feel like part of the family and it is a unique way to experience the warmth of ordinary Japanese. Foreigners staying at *minshuku*, especially those in out-of-the-way places, are quite rare. You might actually be the first ever to stay at a particular home.

The hosts may have a few misgivings at first because many Japanese have never met or seen a foreigner, but if you can reassure them that you won't use soap in the bathtub, or wear the *benjo* slippers in the house, then they will relax and there

should be no problems beyond the usual ones of trying to make yourself understood in a foreign language in a foreign country. But that's what makes it all fun! The *minshuku* owners whom I have encountered have ranged between accepting and very good natured. The big problem may be that they are too kind – there are many stories of hosts pouring drinks all evening (at no charge) because of the honour of the visit.

Minshuku are not hotels, so there is minimal maid service. Guests may have to make their own beds at night and put the bedding away in the morning, provide their own towels, etc, although I have found that the hosts have done all these things as a matter of course. Perhaps it is special treatment that Japanese travellers do not get.

Charges are relatively uniform throughout Japan; in the range Y3500 to Y5000 per person per night including supper and breakfast. It is possible to negotiate a reduction if meals are not needed, but they are often local delicacies and it may be one of the few opportunities to sample typical Japanese cooking.

As with *ryokan*, you can usually find a *minshuku* from a railway station of any size. There is usually an information office with listings of *minshuku* in the surrounding area. They will phone ahead and make bookings, also giving warning that a foreigner is on the way.

Travellers who begin their excursion from Tokyo can make reservations by computer. There are several offices in Tokyo that can do this, but the most convenient is Travel Nippon (tel (03) 572-1461), on the fifth floor of the Yurakucho Building (near the TIC), because they speak English. The address is: Travel Nippon, 2-2-1 Yurakucho, Chiyoda-ku, Tokyo; open Monday to Saturday from 9 am to 5 pm.

A very good leaflet in English describing *minshuku* and how to behave at one (folding bedding, eating, etc) is available from: Japan Minshuku Association (tel

371-8120), New Pearl Building, Room 201, 10-8 Hyakunincho 2-chome, Shinjuku. Accompanying it is a listing of a large number of *minshuku* in nearly all regions of the country that are better prepared than average to take foreign guests; a map shows their general location.

Youth Hostels

Budget travellers in Japan usually stay in youth hostels. There are about 520 of them scattered throughout the country. They are clean, respectable and reasonably priced – by Japanese standards anyway; typically Y1600 to Y2100. The cheapest is in Gifu – a true bargain at Y300; a typical price in 1970! There is usually no other accommodation with such low prices. The cheapest *ryokan* and *minshuku* are approximately double the YH cost.

To stay at most youth hostels you need a valid membership card issued by a youth hostel association belonging to the International Youth Hostel Federation (IYHF). It is best to buy a membership card in your home country, but if this isn't possible then an International Guest Card (IGC) can be purchased from national headquarters in Tokyo or from the prefectural head office. The price is approximately US$9. Some hostels do not require a YH membership card; a foreign passport is adequate.

The International Guest Card is also available as a replacement in case a card is lost. The purchase price (less Y100) will be refunded, within Japan, after a replacement card has been received from the original issuing office and shown at the Tokyo head office.

Despite the name, there is no age limit on who may use the hostels. There are, however, more regulations than at other types of accommodation. Until recently there was curfew at 9 pm, hostels were closed between 10 am and 3 pm, and hostellers were segregated by sex. Some of these restrictions have now been eased at some hostels, but it is still case-by-case

which rules are relaxed, and at which hostels.

A regulation sleeping sheet is required at nearly every hostel. These can be rented but the cost soon mounts up, so its better to have your own, and only a few hostels allow sleeping bags to be used.

The best listing of hostels by far is the *(Japan) Youth Hostel Handbook*. Anyone planning to stay at more than a couple of hostels would be well advised to obtain one, either by mail or on arrival in the country. It used to cost Y350, but I was given the 1987 edition free at the office in Sogo department store in Tokyo. (It appears to be paid for by advertisements in it.) It is written mostly in Japanese, but there is adequate explanation in English and profuse use of symbols so that foreigners can use it easily. It lists every hostel in Japan by district, with maps at the front guiding you to the page on which to look. On the appropriate page there is a short write-up for the hostel, with a small map, telephone number and various details (the number of beds, costs of meals and heating, dates when open and the type of hostel). The name is given in *romaji* but the address is only in Japanese. This is a retrograde step – previous editions had the address in *romaji* as well; it is now very difficult to locate a hostel without help in reading *kanji*.

The Handbook is available at the national headquarters in Tokyo (a 10-minute walk from Ichigaya), at the branch office in the basement of the Sogo department store near the Ginza area of Tokyo (not far from the TIC), and at many hostels around the country. Hours are 9 am to 5.30 pm on weekdays; and 9 am to 4 pm on Saturdays. It can also be ordered and sent by mail within Japan or overseas.

The national HQ also has a free booklet *Hostelling Way in Japan*. It has much more info on hostel rules, rail fares, a list of hostels with bicycle rentals, distances between cities and much more, but its prices might be out of date.

The second, and less satisfactory, listing of hostels is the *IYHF Handbook Vol II* which lists hostels in Africa, America, Asia and Australasia. This booklet, Y600 in Japan, lists less than half the hostels in Japan, gives no instructions in Japanese and is not detailed in its description of locations. For travel in Japan it is a waste of money but it might be useful in the other countries it covers.

There are eight types of hostel in Japan: those built and managed by the JYHA (51); those built privately (107); those built with government subsidy (75); those managed by other youth organisations (55); private houses (61); temples (76); shrines (7); and *ryokan* (144).

As a general rule it is best to avoid JYHA hostels. While they may have the best facilities, too often the staff tend to be unfriendly, officious, or even rude, apparently having the attitude that they are doing a favour to the hostellers. No doubt there are good JYHA hostels and perhaps it is unfair to judge them by a few, but given the opportunity it is preferable to stay at other types, especially the temples, shrines, private homes and *ryokan*. Staff there are usually friendly and the atmosphere relaxed.

Hostellers staying at Buddhist temple hostels may be wakened abruptly at 6.30 am by drumming. This happens at Jofuku-ji, a Zen temple in a particularly beautiful valley on Shikoku island. The priest there speaks English and invites visitors to join in *zazen* meditation.

As a general rule visitors may use the 75 municipal hostels without having a YH card – a passport is adequate. Useful ones to know about are Hinoyama YH at Shimonoseki (the port for the ferry from Pusan, Korea), Tokyo International (Kokusai) YH, the hostel at Narita, and both Nagai YH and Hatttori-Ryokuchi YH at Osaka.

Generally very little English is spoken at any of the hostels or at the head office. If corresponding with the head office,

always send International Postage Reply Coupons for the return postage. YH associations everywhere operate on tight budgets and cannot afford to pay return postage.

During the busy seasons (New Year holidays, March, late April to mid-May, July and August) it is advisable to make advance bookings. This is most easily done by computer in Tokyo and Osaka. In Tokyo, booking offices are located at: Keio Dept Store (6th floor), Shinjuku, and Sogo Dept Store (2nd basement), Yurakucho (near the TIC). In Osaka you can book at the Sogo Dept Store near Osaka station. It is necessary to pay a Y200 deposit (credited to the cost of the room) per person per night plus a booking fee of Y50. The offices in Tokyo are open daily, except Thursday, from 10 am to 6 pm.

An alternative to computer booking is the use of return postage-paid postcards. Blank ones are available from post offices for Y80 each (Y40 for sending and Y40 for the return portion), but it is much simpler to use pre-printed ones that have spaces for all the required information. These are available from the YH head office and cost Y80 for ten (plus postage if they are ordered by mail). Each of these cards will require two Y40 stamps.

If you cannot book ahead, you can take comfort in the fact that it is usually possible to get a bed at most hostels throughout the year, with the exception of those in the most popular areas during the school holidays. Such areas are around Kyoto/Nara and the resorts, especially those in the mountains. To check on vacancies, the simplest way is to telephone a day or two in advance and make a booking. Japanese hostellers usually don't mind making the call for you to get you over the language hurdle.

Another reason for planning ahead is that some hostels inconveniently take holidays that are not listed in the Handbook, as I have found out – more than once I have showed up at the door after dark only to find the building deserted.

If you are planning to eat the hostel supper on the first night it is essential to phone ahead, or arrive early enough to permit the cook to prepare the extra food. Hostel meals are nutritionally adequate but very few are gastronomic delights. A typical meal consists of: a crumbed pork cutlet (fatty), a portion of shredded cabbage, a piece of fish sausage, miso soup, three slices of cucumber, a slice of tomato, eight french fries, 1/3 of a banana, one mandarin orange, 14 pieces of cold macaroni with mayonnaise and as much rice as you can eat.

Many hostels have *jisui* (members' cooking), which means that hostellers can have the use of a gas cooker and pots and pans. The gas is usually metered, so it can be a contest to try to finish cooking the meal with one Y10 coin. There is a small charge (Y20 to Y30) for the use of the kitchen.

Staying at youth hostels offers other advantages in addition to the relatively low cost, in particular the opportunity to observe what Japanese homes and people are like. Although the hostels are institutional in nature, and many buildings are modern structures with not a hint of Japanese tradition in them, many others are like enlargements of the traditional Japanese house.

In a traditional-building type of hostel, there are soft *tatami* mat floors, sliding *shoji* doors, and many other typical architectural details. The bath will be like that of an average home (though probably larger), and hostellers sleep on mats laid out on the *tatami*. The modern buildings usually have furniture to match and western-style bunk beds. The photo with the description of the hostel in the Handbook shows the building and this can often give a good clue as to its type.

Staying at hostels also provides the chance to meet a number of young Japanese and find out what makes them tick. While few can converse in depth in foreign languages, it is usually possible to have simple conversations.

One feature immediately noticeable to westerners is the general lack of social mingling of the sexes. To overcome this shyness there may be 'Meeting', the Japanese word used to describe an hour-long get together in the evening. This typically takes the form of a talk about the attractions of the nearby area, transport facilities, etc, followed by party games which serve the purpose of breaking down the barriers of shyness. Most westerners opt out after their first experience, unless dragged into attending, as it is all in Japanese and often childish.

During the summer there are often unscheduled and informal activities like bonfires, fireworks, playing traditional games, or dancing to the music of a portable cassette player.

Most hostels are goldmines of information on attractions in the surrounding area. There are usually bulletin boards covered with train, bus and boat schedules and other useful info. Usually it's all in Japanese but you should be able to get some help in deciphering it.

Virtually all hostels have posted rules and hours for eating, bathing, lights out and getting up. At busy hostels these are usually rigidly adhered to, but during the off-season or when there are few people staying there, the rules may be greatly relaxed, especially for foreigners, who often receive deferential treatment everywhere in Japan.

In recent years several rules have been relaxed at the 75 or so municipal hostels: curfew has been extended from 9 pm to 10.30 pm, with lights out at 11 pm. A radical departure from the past is that alcohol is allowed in some hostels as long as the drinkers don't disturb other guests. Whenever possible, married couples will be given rooms together in these hostels. Except in large metropolitan areas, the curfew is no hardship as most Japanese towns close up soon after dark.

Bathing usually has its rules too. At some hostels you can take a bath at any time during the evening, while at others you may not use the bath outside the prescribed hours even though the tub is sitting unused and full of water that will go to waste. It is almost impossible to take a bath or shower in the morning. To do so would run counter to centuries of tradition.

Being public institutions, municipally owned hostels often have magnificent locations on prime real estate. Hinoyama YH at Shimonoseki commands a superb view of the Kanmon Strait, which separates Honshu from Kyushu, and the graceful suspension bridge which spans the gap. Ura-Bandai YH (No 1606-Tohoku) is only a short distance from an emerald-green lake and numerous other smaller ponds of similar intense colour. It also features a good view of the jagged top of Mt Bandai. There are many other hostels around the country with equally fine settings.

If you stay in a hostel where you must share a room with Japanese hostellers you may find you have to fight a guerrilla action to get a window open for fresh air during the night, even in mid-summer. There seems to be a perpetuation of the idea held in medieval Europe that night air is somehow dangerous and must be shut out at all costs, even on a hot night in a small eight-bunk room. The modern hostels with solid concrete walls and close-fitting doors and windows are the worst in this respect. The older, more traditional buildings are sufficiently draughty that this is not so much of a problem (though they're also cooler in winter!).

Another possible inconvenience is the noise of other hostellers which may keep you awake at night or wake you very early in the morning. The polite way to ask them to be quiet is to say *Shizuka-ni sh'te kudasai*. For a much stronger effect, say *Shizuka-ni shiro!* in a firm tone.

Pensions

The word 'pension' has been borrowed from the French but has acquired the connotation in Japan of accommodation in a somewhat rustic lodge-type building with a strong association with sports, such as tennis, which are prohibitively expensive in urban areas.

They are usually located in fairly remote country areas, many situated near ski slopes. Other sporting facilities typically include boating, swimming, walking trails, table tennis and cycling.

Pensions are generally operated by younger people so the spirit is more open and unrestricted than youth hostels, while the facilities are more elaborate and luxurious than those of a *minshuku* and more homey than a hotel. Prices are higher than those of a *minshuku*; the cheapest are about Y3400/5400/7900 for single/double/triple plus Y1500 for dinner, while more expensive ones run up to Y5200/7200/9700.

The pension idea has been operating in Japan only since about 1973, but there are already more than 200 around the country, from southern Kyushu to Tohoku. The pensions are not especially set up for foreign guests but anyone with a sense of fun and adaptability will be able to get by and enjoy the features offered.

Pensions are listed, often with photos or sketches, in a regularly updated book called *Japan Pension Guide* which is available at bookshops for about Y700. It is written only in Japanese but you should be able to understand the important features such as price. In addition, the TICs in Tokyo and Kyoto can give further information and assistance. Bookings can be made by calling the following offices (although the help of a Japanese speaker will probably be needed): Tokyo (03) 295-6333; Osaka (06) 448-2641; Sendai (0222) 65-0534; Fukuoka (092) 471-7555.

Temples

Many Buddhist temples can accommodate visitors overnight and at some of these you may participate in prayer and religious observations such as *zazen* meditation. At others the accommodation can be regarded

just as a room (usually traditional *tatami* style) that happens to be on temple grounds. Most temples are very graceful structures, representative of what foreigners think of as the traditional Japan, so it is a good idea to stay at a temple at least once during a visit to Japan.

It is easy to find a temple that accepts guests; at least 75 function as youth hostels (along with their religious purposes of course) and they're all listed in the YH Handbook with a symbol. A few temples are modern concrete structures, but most are traditional wooden buildings that embody the finest skills in Japanese woodworking. The temples below with numbers in brackets are those in the YH Handbook.

Many temples are quite historic. Zuiryuji (No 3207, Takaoka) is about 350 years old and has several large buildings, although it is being reconstructed at the moment. Other temples are set in beautiful surroundings, such as Jofukuji

on Shikoku (No 7404) which is on a hillside overlooking a valley. Jofukuji is a Zen temple and one of the young priests speaks good English and invites his guests to join in zazen meditation. Because it is a family temple it is small and no advance arrangements need to be made to stay overnight, though a phone call in advance would be prudent, as with any hostel.

There are five temples in the Kyoto area that accept lodgers. They are: Enryaku-ji (on Mt Hei – the number one temple of the Tendai sect, with a history of 1200 years); Myoren-ji (noted for its beautiful garden); Komyo-ji Shukubo, Daishin-in (a former detached palace of the emperor Hanazono that was later rebuilt as a Zen temple); and Inari Taisha Sanshuden. The last named is actually a shrine, not a temple, and is the most important of the many Inari shrines in Japan. It is noted for its more than 1400 *torii* gates that have been placed along paths that wind up the mountain.

The prices for accommodation only range from Y1500 to Y3500. Some offer meals as well. To stay at any of these temples, it is best to make arrangements through the TIC in Kyoto. They will also give any information that may be necessary so that you will know what is expected of you.

In the area around Koya-san (reasonably close to Nara) there are more than 50 temple lodgings available, virtually covering the mountain. Koya-san is very important in the Buddhist history of Japan and is very popular with pilgrims so accommodation may be hard to obtain. Costs are Y4500 and up, with two meals. Reservations can be made through the JTB, or through the Koyasan Tourist Association (tel (07365) 6-2616). The address is: Koyasan, Koya-machi, Into-gun, Wakayama-ken.

Cycling Inns

There is a small network of cycling inns which have been set up specifically for bicycle travellers, both those on their own bikes and those who rent bikes at the inns. The facilities and costs are similar to those at the youth hostels, except that there is usually a workshop for bike repairs as well. The buildings have all been built in the last few years and the aim is to eventually have one every 100 km or so; at the moment there are about 20 of them.

The inns are built in regions of natural beauty that invite exploration by bike; often there are specially constructed cycle paths that are separate from regular highways. In many cases it would be worth a trip to the area for sightseeing. Rental charges are reasonable, from as low as Y200 for four hours plus Y50 per additional hour, to a maximum of Y250 per hour.

Information about locations and bike rentals can be obtained from a booklet issued by the Japan Cycling Association called *saikuringu teminaru* ('cycling terminal'). Although it is in Japanese only, approximate locations of inns are shown on a sketch map at the front. Detailed addresses and specific information on how to get there from the nearest railway station is given with the description of each inn and its facilities. Copies can be obtained from the JCA.

It may be easier to contact the Japan Bicycle Promotion Institute first as they have English-speaking staff who can give info and assistance. Write to: Mr H Konno or Mr H Ise, Japan Bicycle Promotion Institute (tel 583-5444), Nihon Jitensha Kaikan Building, 9-3 Akasaka 1-chome, Minato-ku, Tokyo.

Kokumin Shukusha (People's Lodgings)

People's Lodgings are accommodation and recreation facilities in a number of popular resort and natural park areas throughout Japan. They have been built by local authorities under the guidance of the Ministry of Health and Welfare as a means of bringing a vacation in attractive surroundings within the reach of most Japanese. The room charge of about Y3400 a night with two meals is lower than that of most *ryokan*.

The lodgings are open to anyone, Japanese or foreigners, and no membership in any organisation is required. During the summer and busy travel seasons, they tend to be fully booked, or it may be necessary to share a room. Otherwise, anyone showing up at the door will be given a room and couples will be put together if possible.

Bookings are most easily made through JTB which issues vouchers for reserved rooms, but this system is in effect for only about 70% of the lodgings and it takes about a week. Bookings can also be made privately by mail or phone, provided you can speak or write Japanese. The TICs have a complete listing of all lodgings in Japan; it runs to several pages and is not a published booklet, so it is necessary to inquire in person.

Kokumin Kyukamura (Vacation Villages)

These vacation villages are intended

mainly for stays of several days for workers who want a quiet, relaxing rest. They are primarily in quiet locations, sometimes near famous resort or sightseeing areas, sometimes in rather remote regions. There are 27 throughout Japan; 19 have camping grounds with good facilities and about half have sporting facilities. Rates run from Y1500 per person for room only. Usually two or more different menus are available at different prices.

The villages haven't been used much by foreigners and there is no quick booking system available. There is an office in Tokyo, but the simplest way is to go to the Tokyo TIC, explain your travel plans, and ask their advice.

Seishonen Ryokamura (Youth Village)

This youth village programme, which began in the late 1960s, provides a good way to see Japanese life in the more remote areas as all 50 or so villages are in fairly isolated parts of the country. They are situated in actual villages or towns that have a negative population growth and are in danger of becoming ghost towns.

Often there is a central lodge plus a very simple camping ground. Rates are similar to those of *minshuku*, Y3500 to Y4000 with two meals.

As with vacation villages it would be best for any foreigner who is interested in staying at a youth village to contact the TIC in Tokyo and discuss travel plans. They can make suitable recommendations and suggestions. Staff at the TIC warn that hosts at the youth villages are not familiar with foreigners, so a little knowledge of Japanese would be useful.

Camping

Camping has not caught on in Japan to the same extent that it has in western countries, mainly because there isn't the same reliance on car transport, but the number of camping grounds is increasing yearly. The JNTO publication *Camping*

in Japan is an excellent list of camping grounds and is available from the TICs in Tokyo and Kyoto.

Camping facilities vary from spartan to ultra-elaborate, with prices to match. Some have only tent sites and a source of fresh water, while others have bungalows and cottages as well. Most grounds are open only in July and August. In Japan summer is, by definition, only those two months, even though the weather is warm through June, much of September and is pleasant well into October.

Many young Japanese set up their tents in almost any open space in the country. This is forbidden in national parks and the intensive cultivation of land makes it difficult to find open and flat space in many areas but tents in vacant fields are a common sight. Probably the campers ask permission before setting up camp. This could be a problem for someone not able to speak Japanese although I have met foreigners doing the same thing and they had encountered no hostility.

Love Hotels

There is one other type of public accommodation available throughout Japan, but due to its very nature it gets much less promotion as a place to stay than the more socially acceptable *ryokan* and *minshuku*, etc. This is the Love Hotel. The Japanese usually refer to it as *Abec Hoteru*, 'abec' being the closest pronunciation possible to 'avec' (the French word for 'with'). These places rent rooms for short periods (as little as 30 minutes) and post rates for one hour, two hours and longer periods. However, they may be used purely as overnight accommodation, as long as you are aware of their peculiarities.

The busy period is during the day and the early evening; business generally begins to slacken off in the later evening, and they will usually rent rooms for the night for little more than the short-term charge of earlier in the day. So if you can wait until quite late in the evening you can obtain quarters that are usually comfortable, clean (though perhaps decorated in a rather garish style, with lots of red, pink and purple) and more spacious than most other accommodation in Japan, at a cost of about Y5000 to Y5500 a night. You will probably have to vacate the room quite early in the morning though, otherwise it may be necessary to pay the hourly rate for every hour of extra sleep-in.

Many love hotels have facilities rather out of the ordinary, such as floor-to-ceiling mirrors, often with a mirrored ceiling too, for good measure. The decor may resemble the harem of a sultan or other equally lush and plush places. A common feature is a colour videotape recorder for instant replay of the action.

Once you learn to recognise the word 'hoteru' in Japanese you will find them everywhere. Outside a sign usually shows two prices – one for a 'rest' (*gokyukei*, about one hour), the other for a 'stay' (*goshukuhaku*), which normally means a longer period and is usually the rate applied to an overnight stay. The price is quoted for one room, not per person as is the case at most other types of accommodation, so it can be an economical type of place to stay if you don't mind the inconvenience of having to wait till quite late before you check in.

Entry to the 'hoteru' is the ultimate in discretion. After passing through a narrow entrance (or driving into an underground garage) the customers can no longer be seen from the street. Usually the person admitting them is out of sight behind a curtain. After the use of the room, the fee is paid to an anonymous hand. One never sees the staff and supposedly vice-versa. Customers never see each other either by the way, as each room has a separate entrance for maximum privacy. Outside the cities there are also 'moteru' for the motorised trade. While Japan does have motels of the kind found in western countries, the majority are of the variety just described. There is usually no mistaking the two types as the exteriors of

love hotels and motels are often the ultimate in bad taste, with garish pink neon signs bordering the roof, flashing signs and outlandish architecture. There is one in the shape of a ship, while another in the Gotanda section of Tokyo is known throughout the country for its pseudo-feudal castle architecture, complete with turrets and other gewgaws.

Servas

Travellers who are genuinely interested in meeting Japanese families have the opportunity to stay in Japanese homes free of charge, through the international organisation Servas. This organisation is described along with other ways of meeting Japanese. The programme should not be looked on as a cheap way to travel, for people who stay with families are expected to participate in some aspects of daily life.

Communes

There are several communes scattered around Japan, some of which welcome guests. These are also described in the section Meeting the Japanese.

Long-term Accommodation

Costs Housing in Tokyo and other metropolitan areas is very expensive; in smaller places prices are considerably lower. In the metropolitan areas a single room of about three square metres may be found for less than Y20,000 a month, but any reasonable single accommodation with a minimum of facilities (kitchen with sink, gas outlet, bath/shower, toilet) and close to central Tokyo, will usually cost at least Y40,000; more like Y50,000 to Y80,000.

Places with a shared toilet and bath are less expensive, and there are some bargains to be found if you can spend a long time looking. These prices refer to normal, everyday Japanese accommodation; for apartments and houses comparable in size and facilities to those found in the USA, Canada or Australia, the rents are

Top: Young men carry a mikoshi (portable shrine) through a city street, Tokyo (AE)
Left: Commuting in Tokyo's rush hour, note the gloves (IMcQ)
Right: Signs in Tokyo's Akihabara area (IMcQ)

Top: A tea ceremony teacher gives thanks after a lifetime of service, Tokyo (AE)
Bottom: Shinto priests' wooden clogs, Meiji shrine, Tokyo (AE)

astronomical – from Y250,000 up to Y2 million a month.

Room sizes are measured by the number of *tatami* (reed) mats that do or could fit. There are actually at least three standard sizes of *tatami* in use in Japan, but one mat is roughly a metre wide and two metres long.

A small room is three mats (*sanjo*), a medium one 4½ mats (*yonjo han*) and a large one six mats (*rokujo*). Larger rooms do exist but are not common. Room types are listed as either Japanese-style (*wa*) with *tatami*, or western-style (*yo*) with a concrete or wooden floor, probably carpeted. In Japanese-language listings, it is common to see abbreviations such as 2LD, 3LDK, etc. The digit is the number of rooms, 'L' is living room, 'D' is dining room and 'K' is kitchen.

Apartment buildings and concrete houses have higher rentals than wooden buildings because of the greater comfort, strength, and fire and earthquake resistance.

It is usually necessary to have a bundle of money on hand before moving into your own apartment. First, there is one (or more) months' rent in advance (*maekin*); second, there is a deposit (*shikikin*) of one to four months' rent, refundable when leaving – minus the cost of any repairs; third, there is 'key money' (*reikin*), which is nothing but a bribe to get the place. Reikin is commonly two months' rent, occasionally one, rarely none, and is non-refundable; fourth, there is the agent's commission, one month's rent; fifth, there is frequently a maintenance fee, which may vary from a reasonable Y1000 to Y3000 per month to Y10,000 at the more ritzy addresses.

Finally there are separate charges for gas, water, electricity and telephone – all of which are expensive. Telephone installation charges are high compared with North American rates and it is necessary to buy a telephone bond (which can be resold immediately for negligible loss).

Location Tokyo is a huge city and despite quick train service, commuting long distances can waste a lot of time. Remember though, that express service can make a place that is farther out of the city a better choice than one closer to the centre of town.

After settling into a job or routine and stabilising your activities, ask others about the best or preferable residential areas so as to make the most of your position. In Tokyo for example, long-term residents want to live in Roppongi/Azabu because they are close to downtown and the area has the brightest of night lights. There is little housing at reasonable cost in these areas. The Hiroo and Shibuya areas are well regarded, while Ebisu, Gotanda and other areas can be equally convenient and less expensive, even if they're not quite as fashionable.

Check access to subways, JR lines or bus lines (but remember that buses don't run after 9 pm). The farther away from a train or subway line, the lower the rent.

Finding a Place There is more than one way to find accommodation for more than a few months. One choice is to follow up advertisements in newspapers, on bulletin boards and leads received by word of mouth, but one is then at the whim of chance as to location. The alternative is to choose one or two areas that seem interesting and then look for listings of places available in that area via a rental agency.

Near almost every railway station, and elsewhere in most districts, are rental agencies (*fudosanya*) with listings of apartments, houses and rooms for rent in that district. The agent (*fudosanya-san*) will ask about the type of accommodation required, number and sizes of rooms, and any other feature desired, then will prepare a list of places that might be suitable, taking clients to see them until one is found that is satisfactory. His charge for each placement is usually one months' rent. Add this to all the other charges listed earlier and you may have to lay out seven months' rent before moving in.

Fudosanya-san rarely speak much English except for the ones who look like used car salesmen and specialise in the horrendously expensive rental market catering to foreign executives on large living allowances. To overcome the language problems it is highly advisable to go with a Japanese friend when looking for any type of accommodation.

Newspaper advertisements for accommodation are usually for high-priced executive-style places, but occasionally there are reasonably priced ones. Newspaper ads appear daily but the *Japan Times* on Friday has the most comprehensive Tokyo listings.

Bulletin boards may have ads for apartments, houses, rooms, sub-lets, 'house-sitting' arrangements or shared accommodation. Look for them at supermarkets in areas with a large foreign population, or at the Tokyo TIC, Com'inn and other 'conversation lounges'.

In large cities there are usually regular English-language publications that carry classified ads. In Tokyo, the *Tokyo Weekender* (weekly) and *Tokyo Journal* (monthly) have sizeable sections of classified ads, including accommodation. Occasionally there are some moderately priced apartments listed privately so there is no agent's fee.

Warning Looking for accommodation is usually a sure way to see an unpleasant side of the Japanese. Many agencies have refused to deal with foreigners who walk in through their doors or speak to the house seeker in a rude manner, even if they speak Japanese fluently . If one gets past this barrier, it is similarly not uncommon for the house owner to refuse to rent to a foreigner. On the other hand, the people who own the building may be very pleasant, undemanding, friendly and very easy to get along with, but this is a rare minority.

To avoid problems as much as possible, the best advice is to take a Japanese friend along who can act as spokesman and reassure the agent/owner that you are trustworthy, honourable, solvent, reliable, able to fit in with Japanese customs, and are clean, unlikely to pee on the *tatami*, bring disrepute on the neighbourhood, or otherwise disgrace the owner and his/her descendants.

A recent development is agencies that specialise in finding reasonably priced housing for foreigners. They advertise in the *Tokyo Journal* and probably in *Kansai Time Out*.

FOOD

Travellers in Japan will encounter few difficulties in finding palatable food, although finding it at a suitable cost is more difficult, mainly because of the great rise in the value of the yen.

There has been some criticism of earlier editions of this book because there have been no specific recommendations as to restaurants. There is more than one reason for this. First, Japan is the land of the clone. Once you have identified one type of food, you will be able to find it from one end of the country to the other, and prices will be much the same everywhere. Next, the sanitation standards are more than adequate in virtually any place you will go, so there is no need to recommend specific places just because they will not give you food poisoning. Such dangers do not normally exist. And there are restaurants in just about every part of every town or city, so finding one will be no problem. There are tens of thousands.

Western restaurant-type food is available at the large tourist hotels and restaurants in the larger cities, but it will be very expensive and cannot be considered when travelling on a budget. If you want to eat at moderate cost you must eat as the locals do.

Typical Japanese cooking centres on a bowl of rice (*gohan*), usually with a bowl of *miso shiru* soup (based on soybeans, a good source of protein), and features one or more kinds of vegetable, plus a small portion of fish or meat.

More economical dishes are based on noodles, either *soba* (greyish; buckwheat), *ramen* (yellow), or *udon* (white; wheat).

Semi-western food can be found in most centres of population of any size. Typical offerings are hamburger steak, macaroni and spaghetti dishes, pilaffs, dorias and gratins, usually with a choice of bread or rice. Interestingly, rice served with such dishes comes on a flat plate and is called *raisu* not *gohan*.

Japanese food is not spicy, so there is no problem for delicate taste buds or stomachs. The weird foods that you may have read about, such as grasshoppers or chocolate-covered ants, are just as strange to the average Japanese as they are to foreigners. Yes, the Japanese do eat raw fish (*sashimi*), but it must be fresh to be eaten this way. If it seems a strange practice just remember how westerners eat oysters. Good sashimi has a weak flavour with no fish smell or taste. *Sushi* (raw fish or other ingredient with rice), on the other hand, has more flavour.

The only other common food that foreigners may find revulsive is *natto* – fermented soybeans that look, smell, taste and feel like something moist that was forgotten on a back shelf for too long. But don't let any Japanese make you feel inadequate if you can't eat it; approximately half the Japanese population find it just as unappealing.

Fish is the major source of protein. Beef is outrageously expensive – the result of deliberate and scandalous government policy to protect small and inefficient domestic producers who raise only one or two animals on miniscule plots of land. This also protects the farmers' votes on which the government has remained in power for more than 30 years. Imported beef is sold and resold among dealers (often without it leaving the freezer) until it sells in the shops for the going rate, which is approximately ten times the

original purchase price. Similarly, the price of rice is about six times the world level because the government buys everything produced at a fixed and high price.

Along these lines, if you wonder why bread is so expensive, it is because the government buys large amounts of wheat overseas at less than Y30,000 a ton, sells it to local mills for Y84,000 a ton, and uses the surplus to buy wheat from Japanese farmers at Y147,000 a ton.

Beef is not a traditional item of the Japanese diet. Until the country was opened to the western barbarians in the 1860s, the Buddhist Japanese would have been horrified at the thought of killing an animal so that it could be eaten. The famous Kobe and Matsuzaka beef are a relatively recent innovation in the diet. The meat is tasty and tender (and very, very expensive) but to the eyes of a lean-meat eater it is very fatty.

All dishes of a Japanese meal should be served at the same time so that you have a full choice at any one time, and they should not arrive in dribs and drabs. In a good restaurant this will be true, but more than one diner at less illustrious restaurants has found his dishes arriving at long intervals. This is only really likely to happen in western-style Japanese restaurants.

Those who have sampled Japanese cooking in restaurants in a western country, particularly the USA, may be surprised to find that there is no similarity to what they find in Japan. The fancy, flashy 'Japanese steak house' is an American invention. Food served at a good (expensive) restaurant in Japan is as much a treat for the eye as the tongue, but the service is very restrained and elegant. Vegetables are sliced in intricate shapes, and everything is decoratively arranged. Of course less pretentious restaurants for budget eaters are much more basic and utilitarian and likely to be quite noisy, as much from the staff as the customers. Basically, you get what you pay for – if you're lucky.

Some typical Japanese dishes are:

Sashimi: slices of raw fish of various kinds. Prices vary with type of fish; usually not cheap.

Sushi: raw or cooked fish, vegetables, egg, etc, on or in rice. Varying prices; many types reasonable in cost.

Tempura: batter-dipped and deep-fried fish and vegetables; of Portuguese origin. The accent is on the first syllable. Many types reasonable in cost.

Sukiyaki: vegetables, thinly sliced beef, *shirataki* (like vermicelli), *tofu* (soy bean curd), all cooked together at the table in a broth of water, sake, sugar and soya sauce. A winter dish; up-market prices.

Jingis Khan: similar to sukiyaki, but the pot has a dome in the centre surrounded by a trough; the vegetables are cooked in the broth while the meat (mutton) is cooking on the dome. A Hokkaido dish; up-market.

Shabu-shabu: similar to sukiyaki except that ingredients are cooked in water and get most of their flavour from spice dips. A winter dish; up-market.

Domburi: a bowl of rice with added chicken, egg, meat, etc. Not expensive.

Okonomiyaki: a type of pancake usually cooked on a griddle at the table by the diners themselves; various ingredients are mixed into the batter, eg, shrimp, squid, beef. Not expensive; best in cold weather because of heat from griddle at table.

There are many kinds of specialty restaurants in Japan. Typical is a *robatayaki*. Generally rustic in decor, they display the raw materials that are available, like whole fish, potatoes, etc; customers pick out the one they want, and it is cooked for them. If you want to visit such a restaurant, it is invaluable to have a Japanese companion.

Drinks

Just about every type of restaurant offers beer to drink with meals. Depending on the type of place, *sake* will usually also be readily available, as will whiskey which is usually drunk with water (*mizuwari*) or a mixer.

Restaurants serving western-type food will usually have wine as well. Japanese wine is generally unremarkable, especially that served in ordinary restaurants. Gastronomers will be delighted to learn that the average Japanese restauranteur believes that red wine, as well as white, should be served cold. (It probably makes the Japanese brands more palatable.) If you are fussy about this, you should ask to feel the bottle before it is opened. The various alcoholic beverages available in Japan are discussed in the Alcohol section.

Menus

One of the biggest problems can be understanding what food is available. Little hole-in-the-wall eateries will have vertical strips of cardboard listing items and prices posted on the wall, while better establishments will have a conventional menu, but usually only covered with *kanji*. However, a good number of restaurants in metropolitan areas will have menus with sufficient English to be understandable (though invariably with large numbers of strange spellings, but at least they're trying).

Choosing a meal is no great problem, however, even though staff rarely understand English. Most restaurants have very realistic wax replicas of various dishes on display, usually in the front window for inspection by passers-by, so you can point at what looks good.

Chopsticks

Western cutlery is available at most restaurants, but it is advisable to know how to use chopsticks, for these are what Japanese food is intended to be eaten with. Japanese chopsticks (*hashi*) are shorter than the Chinese variety and are easier to manipulate. Most inexpensive restaurants provide disposable chopsticks that are used once and then thrown away. The two sticks are still one piece of wood, and are split apart before use. The use of some 80 million of these chopsticks per day is coming under fire from conservationists because of the waste of precious wood.

While you are eating with chopsticks, there are certain happenings that you can reliably expect to occur. Any Japanese nearby who can speak some English is almost sure to compliment you with a phrase like: 'You can use chopsticks very well.' This is often said with wonderment, because it is one of the fondly held Japanese beliefs that only Japanese (and maybe some other Asians as well) can use chopsticks, as if the ability were an inherited trait.

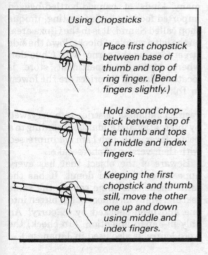

Using Chopsticks

Place first chopstick between base of thumb and top of ring finger. (Bend fingers slightly.)

Hold second chopstick between top of the thumb and tops of middle and index fingers.

Keeping the first chopstick and thumb still, move the other one up and down using middle and index fingers.

If this happens to you, and you wish to reply, you are free to confront him with the fact that a survey in the mid-60s of 10,000 people showed that younger Japanese are becoming progressively less proficient in their use, the early-20 group scoring only about 50%, and the early-30s about 63%. The less proficient get them crossed, drop things (well-known phenomena to foreign users!), hold them in their fist, and even use them to spear their food. This seems to be partly the result of using spoons with school lunches.

Economy Eating

For simple meals and lunches while on the move, some suggestions include *tempura* and *onigiri*. In most towns there is a *tempuraya* (tempura shop) with freshly cooked pieces of fish, vegetables, meat (called *katsu*, a corruption of the word cutlet) and *koroke* (croquets; potato cakes) on display on trays in the window. They are cheap, tasty and filling if a bit calorie-laden because of the deep frying.

A traditional food for lunches is *onigiri*, basically a ball of rice with a piece of fish or vegetable in the centre; the outside is wrapped in a sheet of crisp seaweed. The tastiest is *sake* (pronounced 'shake') which is made with salmon.

Nearly all department stores and office buildings have restaurants in the basement which offer reasonably priced meals, especially at lunchtime. You can order individual items, but the cheapest way is to order *teishoku*, the day's set lunch; it will usually be on display. A typical *teishoku* will have a bowl of rice, miso shiru soup, a plate of vegetables, meat or fish, salad and dessert.

Near most railway and subway stations, there are usually restaurants of many types such as simple noodle shops (where everyone stands), Korean barbecues, semi-western style restaurants, *sushi* shops, coffee shops (*kisaten*) and others. Simple meals begin at around Y500 to Y600. Places catering mainly to drinkers often prove more costly because each item ordered, such as a skewer of meat, is served and charged for separately, and is regarded more as a snack to accompany drinks than as a meal in itself.

The pizza chains *Shakey's* and *Pizza Hut* offer a real bargain between 11 am and 2 pm every day except Sundays and holidays – all the pizza you can eat for a fixed price; usually about Y500. The nutritional value is suspect, but it is certainly very filling and there's lots of cheese.

For familiar, filling, inexpensive food, there are hundreds of *McDonald's* hamburger shops around the country, at least one in almost every city of any size. The food is identical with that served in every *McDonald's* anywhere in the world. Other familiar chains of American origin (though operated under Japanese franchise) are *Wendy's Hamburgers* and *Kentucky Fried Chicken*. These places, particularly the hamburger shops, are probably the most economical places to eat in Japan, particularly for beef.

Visitors are always shocked at the price of a cup of coffee at coffee shops (Y250 to Y600). The usual excuse for the high cost is that you are paying for the space and the congenial surroundings. You can stay all day for the price of a single cup, and young people often have coffee-shop dates. For just a coffee without the luxurious surroundings, chains like *Lotteria* can be suggested. Their offering, however, will probably not be as tasty as the selection in the good coffee shops. Many Japanese coffee shops are true coffee-gourmet heavens.

Many coffee shops also offer a real bargain for breakfast (called morning service) which includes toast (and sometimes an egg) for the usual price of a cup of coffee alone.

Cooking at Youth Hostels If you have cooking facilities where you're staying, you can economise. Residential neighbourhoods have vegetable, fruit and meat shops, and supermarkets have spread widely since their introduction in the late 1960s.

As well as eggs, meat, fish, chicken, vegetables, cheese and milk, you can get a large variety of instant *ramen* (dried bundles of noodles) that cook in a few minutes. After cooking the noodles until they separate and soften, add the provided seasonings to make a broth. Served with a couple of boiled eggs, one has a reasonably filling meal not totally devoid of nutrition. Supermarkets also usually offer a good selection of prepared food such as *sushi*, *tempura* (meat, fish, squid, vegetables,

etc) and croquets (potato with or without corn, curry, etc).

Super-economy Tip For those on a super tight budget, bakeries slice the crusts (*pan no mimi*) off loaves of bread and you can get a bag of them at little or no cost. Peanut butter and jam are available. Jam from Romania and Bulgaria is probably the best in Japan and widely available. Much of the domestic product lacks fruit.

For more detailed information, a good inexpensive book is *Eating Cheap in Japan*.

Tokyo residents can save money on many kinds of canned/bottled/bagged imported foods at an interesting, unique shop called Sanmi. It is in the Ginza area, on the left a couple of blocks down the side street forming the corner with Chuo dori where Matsuya department store is located. Many of its prices are the lowest in Tokyo.

Pastries Japanese pastries rate very well by international standards, according to a pastry lover, although I am not impressed with their version of cheesecake.

Beware of the object that has every appearance of a jam donut. It has the same shape, the same colour, the same texture. Many an innocent has bitten into one and been shocked by......curry! An only-in-Japan invention. (To check, the word 'curry' is also used in Japanese.)

Etiquette
It is polite to slurp noodles; the attitude is that it makes them taste better. Otherwise Japanese table manners are not so different from those in the west. Observe other diners and follow their lead, especially when drinking. Details on drinking etiquette appear in the Alcohol section.

Dietary Problems
If you are not supposed to eat certain foods (especially meat), you have the potential

for a large problem. The Japanese are generally incapable of understanding that some people have dietary preferences or taboos. It all begins at school when the pupils are compelled to eat everything put in their school lunches, whether they detest a food or not.

Even if you request that the cook leave out all meat, for example, there is still the chance of finding some in the finished dish. Any complaint will be met by the equivalent of a cheerful, 'Well, it's only a bit of pork!', with the intimation that it won't hurt you.

Monosodium glutamate is widely used, so if you have a reaction to it, you must be careful of what you eat. The only really safe food is fresh vegetables, fish or fruit. Even raw meat seems to give the same reaction; apparently chemicals are put in to tenderise it. The worst foods for MSG are soups and sauces, and any food in Chinese-type restaurants is especially suspect. Even the salt in shakers is not to be trusted. Asking the waitress if food contains MSG will do no good, for she will automatically say that it doesn't and requesting that the cook not use any will have no effect. In addition, canned food does not need to be labelled to show the ingredients as it is in some other countries (although it has been announced that this will be a requirement around 1990).

Japanese cooking has traditionally used a large amount of salt. Stroke has also been the second most common cause of death. The word is now getting out among the population of the effect of excessive consumption of salt, and people are cutting down, but prepared food of all kinds (canned and in restaurants) still contains more than is healthy. Those on a low-salt diet must be careful.

ALCOHOL
Alcoholic drinks of all kinds are readily available everywhere in Japan but may be rather expensive compared with many western countries. They are sold in local shops virtually without restrictions and are generally available at any hour from vending machines.

Beer, sake and whiskey are usually available at almost any eating establishment. Imported whiskeys and wines are available, especially in larger cities, but there are few bargains.

Beer
Beer is the favourite alcoholic drink. Japanese beers are well regarded by beer connoisseurs and are generally brewed in a German or Czech style. Well-known brands are *Kirin, Sapporo, Suntory* and *Asahi*. A typical price for a large bottle (633 ml) in a restaurant is Y500, while it is about Y215 at neighbourhood shops, and a 500 ml can is about Y200 from a vending machine.

Traditional Drinks
Sake (pronounced 'sah-kay', not 'sah-key') is the traditional Japanese drink. It is a very pleasant accompaniment with Japanese food or on its own. Sake is brewed by fermenting a mash of rice that has been cooked with water, and thus is more like beer than wine, except that the alcohol content goes as high as 17% (considerably more than the typical 12% in wines). It is certainly possible to get very drunk on it, but it is not quite as potent as much folklore would lead one to believe. Such tales probably date back to Occupation days and are based on mistaking *sake* for much more powerful *shochu*.

Sake is served hot in small 180 ml flasks, from which it is poured into tiny cups. The flask is called a *tokkuri* and is usually a decorative item made of pottery; it makes a good memento of Japan, along with a set of cups (*sakazuki*).

There are several grades and types of *sake*. The highest grade (*shu*) is *tokkyu*; next comes *ikkyu*, then *nikyu*. *Sake* from different regions of Japan has different characteristics and tastes, so these designations do not indicate the flavour, only the quality. In addition to the standard types of *sake*, there are many specialty or regional types. Two of these are *amazake* (sweet *sake*) and *otoso* (*sake* with suspended rice solids).

In shops, *sake* is sold in large 1800 ml bottles, as well as in smaller sizes. The size is a traditional measure called *issho*. At festivals a common sight is a large wooden keg of *sake*, opened by simply smashing in the lid; the contents are handed out freely in a square wooden box with neatly dove-tailed leakproof joints. These boxes (*masu*) are of 180 ml capacity and were the traditional way of measuring granulated solids, like rice, as well as liquids. They make good souvenirs of Japan; the 180 ml size is called *ichi-go*.

Shochu Another Japanese alcholic drink popular these days is *shochu*. It is a distilled liquor made from rice, wheat, sweet potatoes, sugar cane – anything containing sugar that can be fermented. The Kagoshima area of Kyushu is the *shochu* capital of Japan, though it is also made in many other areas.

The distillation process is a copy of brandy-making that was introduced by foreign missionaries in the late 1500s, and *shochu* was once the beverage of feudal lords and the upper classes.

Earlier this century, *shochu* was popular throughout Japan. However, at the end of WW II, materials for high quality *shochu* were not available and bootleggers blended it with anything on hand, including highly poisonous methyl alcohol. From then on it gained a bad reputation as a low-class drink associated with *jikitabi* (manual labourers nick-named for their split-toed boots) who get blotto on it regularly.

In recent years new processing methods have been introduced that eliminate most of the impurities that cause bad hangovers. Good *shochu* is little more than alcohol and water, 25-35% alcohol content (50-70 proof); the strength will be marked somewhere on the label. The leading brand is Jun ('purity'). It is cheap at Y590 for a 720 ml bottle, a fraction the cost of

whiskey. It substitutes well for vodka in any mixed drink.

A popular home-made drink that visitors lucky enough to be invited into a private home may be offered is *umeshu*, which translates as 'plum wine'. It is made by soaking green, sour plums in *shochu* to which has been added lots of sugar. The process is started in late June or early July and lasts at least three months. The result is a delicious but very sweet and potent drink.

Wine
Because of the lack of experience with wine, the Japanese public is generally not demanding as to quality and as there is no long history of making it, Japanese wines have not reached the high levels of quality achieved in beer and whiskey. Most of the best known and widely advertised brands are very ordinary. Because of high costs in Japan, there is no incentive to make the necessary investments for improved processing facilities; it is cheaper to import wine from other countries.

As for Japanese wine, the Austrian tainted-wine scandal had interesting ramifications locally. Soon after the news about this scandal came in from abroad, a government agency, with simply amazing promptness, went around putting stickers on Japanese wine with the Japanese word equivalent to 'Safe'. A little later it became known that wine sold in Japan needs to contain only 5% locally made wine to be called Japanese wine, and many companies import low-cost bulk wines from a variety of countries, like Chile, Bulgaria...... and Austria. One company, Manns, had actually sold bottles containing the glycol-tainted wine. When news came out of Europe about such wine, company representatives in Japan secretly went around to stores and took all these bottles off the shelves, then the company advertised that people who drank their wines were safe from glycol! (Company executives were fined a total of Y30,000. By comparison, one old gent who made home-brew *sake* was fined Y300,000 for his crime.)

There is a fairly good selection of imported wines from many countries on sale in the metropolitan areas, particularly in some of the large department stores. Even local stores in many neighbourhoods often have a number of wines from countries like France, Australia and the USA. Prices are sometimes as low as Y900, but this is unusual; the typical range for inexpensive but good wines is Y1200 to Y1500. (With the high yen, some reasonably good wine may be available at special sales for under Y600 a bottle.) The Australian wines selling in this range have been the standard lines of good and reliable quality and sell for about double their home price – for Japan, a remarkably small mark-up.

Whiskey & Other Spirits

Imported whiskeys are available, especially in larger cities, so you should be able to find your favorite if you want it. Unfortunately, there are few bargains. Johnnie Walker Black Label (760 ml bottle) sells for Y5800 and up, nearly always more; Red Label costs Y2900 or more. Due to the prestige accorded to imported liquors, the price of foreign whiskeys has scarcely changed despite the near-doubling in value of the yen. Rather than being something for drinking oneself, they are regarded more as something you give someone as a gift. If the price were to be cut, the value as a gift would also be devalued. When the price of one imported scotch *was* cut, the sales actually fell! (The Japanese mentality gives foreign marketing people nightmares.)

The government also does its bit by having different grades of liquor for taxation purposes and, by pure coincidence, imported scotch is virtually the only high-grade liquor and attracts a much higher rate than any Japanese product. Fortunately for those who like whiskey, some of the local products are good. Suntory Black Label is said to compare well with

imported Scotch and costs less. Other Suntory products are also well regarded.

Brandy and cognac are incredibly expensive in Japan. The prices have no relationship to their price in country of origin nor taxes, but purely what the market will bear. If you like them, or have a Japanese friend who does, be sure to bring your limit in duty free.

Drinking Customs

When drinking beer, *sake*, etc, with a Japanese person, the proper etiquette is to fill his glass or cup after he has filled yours. While he is pouring, hold your cup or glass up so that he can fill it more easily. If you don't want any more, put your hand over the glass. If you are new at the game, a Japanese may think you're unfamiliar with the rules and may fill his own glass. This is normally considered bad manners and the Japanese say *te jyaku* which means 'who fills his glass with one hand, drains it with the other'; in other words, an alcoholic. Before he can pour anything into his glass, take the bottle from him, and fill it for him. This may result in a mock fight, but the gesture will be appreciated.

When drinking with Japanese people, particularly those who are on a good salary, it will be difficult to pay any share of the bill. Customarily one person, often the most senior, will pick up the tab and pay everything. It is necessary to think up some way to repay the favour at a later date. (Among friends, they will divide the bill later; they may do so at the table if they know each other well.)

With students and other people who are not very wealthy, the bill is usually split up according to who had what. As a foreigner you may sometimes have trouble paying for your share, but if you are drinking among friends they will not put up a fuss – it is only strangers who want to give the foreigner a good impression who will insist on paying for the whole lot.

Getting drunk is one of the few safety

valves open to Japanese to escape the manifold duties and obligations they must continually observe. Because of this, almost any behaviour while drunk is excused. Consequently, hordes of faceless salary men, who show little individuality or personality during working hours, get quite thoroughly smashed quite frequently, sometimes nightly. They sing loudly, sometimes perform dances that can only be described as bawdy, and carry on in a manner quite un-Japanese. Getting drunk is a very popular activity in Japan, and doing it with a group is almost a ritual, helping to cement interpersonal relations with co-workers, etc. Records in China mention that the Japanese were much given to drink at festivals 2000 years ago, so the process has a long history.

Virtually the only ill-effect of this excess drinking is that many drinkers don't know their limit and cannot hold their liquor (literally). The results of their overindulgence, known locally as 'platform pizzas', may be seen on streets, railway platforms and even inside railway cars, especially on Friday and Saturday nights.

Drinking Places

There are two main types of drinking establishments in Japan: those strictly for drinking (usually with music and comfortable surroundings), and those for drinking with pleasant female companionship, ie, hostesses.

Bars, pubs and other drinking places range in price from reasonable to astronomical. The appearance of the place does not necessarily give an accurate indication of the prices to be paid. A place that looks expensive probably will be; nightclubs and similar places are guaranteed to take a huge bite out of a wallet. However, even a place that looks modest or run down is no guarantee that it will be cheap; some simple looking places are extremely expensive, either because of special service, atmosphere, or whatever appeals

to Japanese on huge expense accounts. There are stories of innocent *gaijin* walking into such joints, ordering a single beer, and being presented with a bill for Y38,000!

To avoid such over-charging, stand bars are the answer. Many are operated by large companies in the liquor business, like Suntory and Nikka. Otherwise the safest course as soon as you enter an unknown bar is to ask the price of a drink and check if there is a cover charge; some places charge a couple of thousand yen as soon as a customer sits down. A favourite lurk of even better quality places is a dish of peanuts or other nibbles (called a 'charm' in Japanese) that the customer is obliged to pay for at a price equal to a couple of drinks. Foreigners can sometimes get away from this racket by politely indicating that they don't want it and feigning lack of understanding about the system.

Places with hostesses are always going to be much more expensive than those for drinking only. Customers are charged for the time that girls sit with them. Anyone going in only to drink, without benefit of hostess, would probably be unwelcome.

Hostesses are part of the Japanese system of male ego-boosting; they flatter and flirt and act as a listening post for the man's frustrations in life. (The sweet words that they speak are accepted by the man as completely true and his proper due.) Often these women are available for other outside activities, usually on a paid basis, but sometimes on a purely friendly basis if she likes the customer. Boye de Mente's book *Bachelor's Japan* gives some specific advice on this topic. Though the book is long in the tooth, its message is still valid.

Beer halls are popular and relatively inexpensive places for a drink (and for eating). They can be recognised partly by the prominent jugs and bottles of beer in the window, although many restaurants also offer beer and have similar window displays; there is often a rather thin line between a restaurant and a beer hall, as both serve food as well as drinks.

Almost any restaurant of any size will offer alcoholic drinks with the meal, particularly beer and sake.

The words for large, medium and small mugs of beer are *dai, chu* and *sho*.

During the warm months many department stores open beer gardens on the roof, often with live entertainment. Prices are reasonable, the height of the buildings gives relief from the hot air at ground level, and it's a good place to see Japanese having a good time.

For economical drinking, with a simple list of drinks such as *sake* and beer, and simple decor (sometimes scruffy), investigate the 'workingman's nightclub' or *aka chochin*. These are found in many places and almost invariably near stations. The name literally means 'red lantern' which is what will be found outside the establishment to identify it.

BOOKS

There is a large number of books about Japan on the market inside the country although distribution overseas is likely to be patchy and not all books listed here may be readily available.

A revolution has taken place in books about Japan in recent years. In the past virtually all books on the country, people, and culture have been praising, describing them with nothing but enthusiasm. In recent years, however, several have taken a more neutral stance or have even been openly critical of various aspects once considered beyond reproach.

Most of the 'old school' books are translations from Japanese and were often written by Japanese specifically for the edification of foreigners. However, a disconcerting number of such books fall into the grouping *nihonjinron* ('theory of the Japanese'). The name sounds academic and commendable but their main purpose is to convince the Japanese populace of their uniqueness compared with all other peoples of the world, or to persuade non-Japanese of the truth of these views.

If these works could be understood by foreign readers they would be laughed at, but the difficulty of reading Japanese has made the numbers of non-Japanese readers negligible and the risk of refutation (or of becoming widely known about in other countries) has been small. However, books in English appearing recently have taken this genre of Japanese literature to task, one giving an excellent analysis of the reality of Japanese life and society, another cutting the ground out from under the theoretical grounds on which *nihonjinron* is based, and others giving anecdotal recounting of realities.

One book by a quack named Tsunoda has been translated into English and provides an example of the type of nonsense that is being published in Japanese. It tries to show that the Japanese brain is organised and processes information in a way different from that of all other peoples. It is hard going but can be ploughed through by those who enjoy off-beat humour. Keep in mind however that it was not written to be amusing.

The sad aspect of all this is that a sizeable amount of the work is being cranked out by people with impressive academic credentials and who work at some of the country's top universities. Part of the reason is that within the university system one must support the work and theories of one's superior if one wishes to advance; original thinking is discouraged, and attacking the theories of others, no matter how ridiculous, is anathema. It would seem that there is little criticism in Japan in almost any field.

People & Society

The Japanese, Jack Seward (Lotus Press, Tokyo).

More about the Japanese, Jack Seward (Lotus Press, Tokyo).

The Tourist & the Real Japan, Boye de Mente (Charles E Tuttle). All three books are getting on a bit in years but their comments are still valid, except for costs and economic commentary.

The Land of the Rising Yen, George Mikes (Penguin Books). Although published in 1970, this book (if it can be found) gives a witty and perceptive look at the country and people – better than any five sociology and history books combined.

A Look Into Japan (Japan Travel Bureau). This pocket-size book answers all those 'What is that?' questions asked by most travellers in Japan. Want to know the symbolism of the various positions of hands or feet on Buddhist statues; the names of the buildings in a temple/shrine; the parts making up the buildings; the parts of a room; the construction and movement of *bunraku* puppets? This book has the answers.

Shadows of the Rising Sun, Jared Taylor. This book gives a very good overview of the country, the people and the culture in a very objective and incisive manner. Taylor grew up in Japan and speaks the language so his observations are reliable.

The Japanese Mind: The Goliath Explained, R C Christopher (Simon & Schuster). A good book covering most aspects of Japan, though criticised from one quarter from having borrowed too liberally from the writings of others.

The Roads to Sata, Alan Booth (Weatherhill). Alan Booth walked from the north of Hokkaido to the south of Kyushu then wrote about his experiences and the people he met. For anyone contemplating travel in more remote areas this is a good introduction to the behaviour and reactions of typical Japanese when a non-Japanese face shows up on their turf. It is realistic and candid, portraying both the great kindness and the subtle (and not-so-subtle) discrimination against a non-Japanese.

The Myth of Japanese Uniqueness, Peter Dale, Croom Helm, (Nissan Institute for Japanese Studies, UK). For anyone really interested in Japan in depth, this book is of great interest as it provides an objective look at Japan while totally demolishing

Japanese calligraphy

the writings of the *nihonjinron* which have for years influenced most works written on Japan by non-Japanese. It might be a bit deep for the casual visitor but is invaluable to anyone truly interested in Japan. It is, unfortunately, *very* expensive at over Y10,000, so would best be borrowed (if available).

Japanese Society, Chie Nakane (Penguin Books). Rather turgid and exhausting at times, it gives a thorough examination of the social structure of Japan but should be approached with a little scepticism for not a few of the supposedly unique Japanese characteristics sound surprisingly like aspects of western countries.

The Chrysanthemum & the Sword, Ruth Benedict. This book is regarded as a classic but its conclusions are not accepted wholeheartedly these days. It was put together during WW II by interviewing Japanese immigrants (interned under the shameful US programme during the war) as an attempt to understand the thinking of the Japanese in Japan. It is remarkable in what it accomplished but its observations should be taken with a little reservation.

Any books by Takeo Doi should be regarded with great scepticism.

Economy

Japan: The Coming Economic Crisis, Jon Woronoff (Lotus Press). An excellent dissection of the Japanese economy, how it works and potential problems. Woronoff has written several other books on politics, society, and economics, several of which overlap somewhat, but all are worth reading.

History

Japan from Prehistory to Modern Times, John Whitney Hall (Charles E Tuttle). *The Japanese*, Reischauer.

Language

Japanese Made Easy, T A Monane (Charles E Tuttle).
Beginning Japanese (Parts 1 & 2), Eleanor Harz Jorden (Yale University Press).

The former is a paperback giving adequate instruction for basic conversation as used for travel. The latter is a pair of paperbacks in a choice of two sizes. These two have much more detail in vocabulary and explanations of usage, so are better suited to a formal course of study.

Japanese in Action, Jack Seward. This is a perennial best-seller for understanding the language and the people.

Action Japanese, N Kuratani (Gakken) and *Japanese for International Businessmen*, K Butler (ALC Press) have both had favourable reviews and may be worth investigating. Don't let the name of the latter put you off; it is useful for any visitor. Both books relate usage to the social situation.

Bookshops

Tokyo has by far the largest number of stores selling foreign-language books (mainly English) although at least one store in every major city should have a small selection. Two well-known chains of stores stocking foreign books are Kinokuniya and Maruzen. In Tokyo, the main Kinokuniya store is a landmark for rendezvous in Shinjuku.

The biggest problem is the high cost of both imported and locally produced books.

MAPS

Road maps are given out free by some service stations but generally they have to be purchased at no small cost. There are no maps that are labelled extensively in *romaji*; the best you can look for is maps with key cities, and perhaps some lesser ones, marked in both scripts. A further complication is that the city names are printed in *kanji* (characters) while railway stations are shown in *hiragana* (phonetic symbols representing syllables) so that one cannot be used to locate the name of a place written in the other script. (See the note in *Jikokuhyo* about *hiragana* spellings for names in *kanji*.)

Maps are available from several sources. You can check if gas stations have maps of the immediate and surrounding areas. Maps of the whole country (by region) are available at the head offices (or travel advisory offices) of some of the oil companies. It would be best to check with the TIC as to which companies still have this service.

The JAF sells a book of maps that cover the entire country. The maps are to a suitable scale and have many places identified in *romaji* as well as *kanji*. Being in a single book and relatively small, they are convenient to use, although it can be difficult to follow a route that extends over several pages. The books cost Y2000 (less 10% for members of JAF or any the nine affiliated foreign associations). JAF also sells a series of individual regional maps at Y450 each.

I use the Routiere series for my travels. These have enough names in *romaji* to be useful and are printed on paper-like plastic that is not affected by periodic soakings. They are many times the size of the maps in the JAF book, so each map covers a larger area. This makes them more convenient for planning longer trips but a set of nine to cover the entire country becomes quite costly at Y800 each.

There is another series of maps also printed on plastic under the brand name of Area, but these have no *romaji* whatever. The same company has another set of maps, one for each prefecture but don't get them – you'd have to buy 46!

If a set of maps is too pricy, you can get by adequately with one map of the entire country (Y800), but it lacks small details. This is number 10 of the Routiere series. (Ask for 'Zenkoku no chizu.') Maps are available at any large bookstore.

A hint on map reading: The legend that explains the meanings of the symbols is in Japanese only. Roads marked in pale pink or pale green are unpaved, usually high in the mountains, and their surface is usually rough (or muddy) and treacherous for motorcyclists. It is difficult to go even 10 kmh on these roads.

If you ever have to use a hand-out map (of a regional tourist attraction for example) and it has lots of cute little illustrations of buildings, animals, etc, do not trust it to be true to scale, or even correct as to the number of streets and their relationship to each other.

See also the section on bicycling as there are maps published for cyclists that are equally suited to motorists. The only drawback is that they cover only the central part of the country.

WHERE TO GO

Deciding where to go depends largely on personal interests but it is probably a good bet that most people who come to Japan have an impression of the country based to a large extent on its history and wish to see what remains from the days of the samurai, plus social arts and folkloric items that have developed through the centuries.

Even though the book has been canned by the critics for historical inaccuracies, James Clavell's *Shogun* has probably done more to make the world aware of Japan and had more influence on overseas perceptions of the country than any other single source.

Cities of Interest

A few cities and clearly defined small areas are on almost every visitor's itinerary – places such as Kyoto (and nearby attractions) and Nikko. Time permitting, many people also wish to see either Hiroshima or Nagasaki for their unfortunate relationship with the A-bomb.

Kyoto, near the centre of the main island of Honshu and itself less than three hours from Tokyo by Shinkansen express train, was the imperial capital for just over 1000 years. The centuries of refined and elegant living of the people of the court combined with the construction of magnificent temples and other structures mean that Kyoto now has the greatest concentration of worthwhile attractions in the country. In addition, it is possible to see a number of traditional crafts still being performed.

Only an hour to the south of Kyoto, Nara is the site of a capital even older than Kyoto; and two of the country's finest castles are closeby: Himeji, less than two hours westward; and Hikone, one hour eastward. The pearl-culture area of Ise is also only about two hours away.

Nikko, less than two hours north from Tokyo by train, combines the man-made beauty of two incredibly colourful mausoleums dating back more than three centuries, with the natural attraction of a lake backdropped by mountains and a high waterfall.

Hiroshima and Nagasaki both have excellent museums showing the chilling effect of the A-bombs that were dropped. Hiroshima is easily reached by Shinkansen from both Tokyo and Kyoto, and those people with a Japan Rail Pass can even make a long day trip there out of Kyoto (or a *very* long one out of Tokyo). Nagasaki, with a more scenic setting, is on the south coast of the main southern island, Kyushu, and cannot be reached quickly by train.

Tokyo, Osaka and Nagoya have little in the way of conventional tourist attractions because all three cities were levelled during WW II. However, each (and particularly the first two) has some modern attractions and there are interesting places within easy reach of all three.

From Tokyo one can make day trips to Kamakura (the great bronze Buddha), Nikko, Matsumoto (one of Japan's finest castles), Yokohama (the very fine Sankei-en garden and some lesser attractions), Kawasaki (excellent collection of traditional farmhouses in a park setting) and the area around Mt Fuji and the Izu-hanto peninsula.

Regional Attractions

To find the 'real' Japan it is necessary to get out of the cities and into the countryside, mountains, or smaller towns. Although there are many interesting regions in Japan, the two that I would choose if I had only a limited time would be Tohoku and Chubu. The reason is because of their concentration of things to see and large areas of attractive scenery. The former is the northern part of Honshu, the latter the inland region roughly between the Mt Fuji area and north of Nagoya; the western coast of this region, plus nearby Noto-hanto peninsula, can be added to the attractions.

Tohoku This area has Mt Bandai and a cluster of scenic lakes around its northern base, other nearby mountain scenery (some of clearly volcanic appearance), the scenic bay of Matsushima, many scenic views along the east coast, picturesque views around lakes Tazawa-ko and Towada-ko, the towns of Kitakata and Kakunodate with many old buildings,

and a valley with more thatch-roof houses than any other area in Japan. There are also many interesting festivals which take place at the beginning of August.

Chubu The Chubu area takes in ample mountain scenery, with terraced paddy fields and traditional farmhouses along many roads. Journeys that are recommended are from Matsumoto (home of one of the country's oldest and finest original castles) through to Takayama, an old town with many historic buildings still standing, and a reconstructed village of traditional farmhouses moved there from the surrounding countryside and arranged to give the appearance of a functioning village of olden times.

En route between the two cities is the beautiful scenery of Kamikochi, and beyond can be found the rustic scene of the Shirokawa-go area with its clusters of huge three-and four-level thatch-roofed farmhouses. To the north of this area (but still inland, accessible via Toyama) is the scenic beauty of the Tatayama mountain region. Stretching into the waters of the Sea of Japan north of there is the picturesque Noto-hanto peninsula, and near its western base is the old city of Kanazawa with its many interesting remnants from the past two centuries. (It was not bombed during WW II.)

Heading south from Matsumoto via a different route are three towns that have survived relatively unchanged from a century ago when they offered a rest stop along the main land route between Tokyo and Osaka, while a parallel valley offers some pleasant gorge and mountain scenery. It is possible to make a loop out of the Matsumoto area taking in all these attractions.

Hokkaido The northern main island has little historic background, having only been seriously settled by the Yamato Japanese (as distinguished from the indigenous Ainu) in the last century. Its strongest point is its abundance of spectacular scenery which includes two regions of mountain terrain – one in the east around Mashu-ko lake, and the other in the west near lakes Toya-ko and Shikotsu-ko.

Other attractions include several stretches of coastal scenery, such as the Shiretoko-hanto peninsula to the east, and the Shakotan-hanto peninsula to the west.

Kyushu The southernmost main island has some places of historic interest and is regarded as the cradle of Japanese civilisation. Despite this, it is notable more for its natural scenery, like Mt Aso and the surrounding valley that constitute the remains of the largest volcanic crater on earth – the continually erupting Sakurajima across from Kagoshima (itself a city of some interest).

The Kirishima plateau and the interesting coast along the southeast side are worth visiting, while the city of Nagasaki is of note for both the A-bombing and historic remains, as well as its favorable appearance. Kagoshima also offers some attractions.

West of Kyoto The south coast (San-yo kaigan) is very heavily built up and offers little sightseeing despite bordering the Inland Sea.

Cities with some attractions are Okayama, Kurashiki, Onomichi, Hiroshima and Iwakuni. The north coast (San-in kaigan) has only a small number of attractions, but it is one of the least built-up of the settled areas of the country and for that reason is very pleasant to travel through. It is comparatively flat and would be one of the most enjoyable areas for bicycling (along with the coast near Kanazawa).

As a brief summary, here are the locations of some of the best castles and gardens in the country – always popular attractions.

Castles: Himeji (Kyoto region), Matsumoto (Tokyo region), Hikone (Kyoto region), Matsuyama (Shikoku), Inuyama (Nagoya region) and Matsue (San-in kaigan).

Gardens: Yokohama, Takamatsu (Shikoku), Hikone (Kyoto region), Okayama, and Kanazawa.

Note that the last two gardens have been assigned ratings (as have many things in the country, ranging from companies to universities to scenic places). These appear to have been handed down from on high some time in the distant past, never to be questioned. Thus the top gardens, to the Japanese, are at Kanazawa, Okayama and Mito. Personally, I found Mito to be a total disappointment as it was mostly open lawn. The one at Okayama was nice in the garden section, but again was largely lawn, and the one at Kanazawa was large and good, but was fitted with loudspeakers to extol at high volume the wonderfully peaceful atmosphere of the place and tell how it encourages contemplation, etc.

THINGS TO BUY

Even back in the good old days when a US dollar was worth vastly more yen and yen price tags were lower, there were relatively few bargains in Japan. The only good buys were in cameras and other optical goods, electronic products, watches, motorcycles, cars and oil tankers.

Well you can forget about the oil tankers now – the Koreans are building them cheaper. As for the other goods, prices have gone up with inflation (as they have everywhere) and the value of the yen has skyrocketed so that there are even fewer bargains today. However, the quality of Japanese goods has been excellent for years and has continued to improve. There are features undreamed of only a few years ago so you are paying more but getting value for money.

It comes as a surprise to most westerners to find that many Japanese goods cost more in Japan than they do at home. There is more than one reason. One (and the one heard always from Japanese sources) is that the distribution system in Japan is notoriously long and complex, with many links in the chain, each of which tacks on its mark-up. Foreign importers can usually buy in huge volume and distribute the goods more efficiently and therefore more cheaply.

Another reason is that large Japanese companies selling overseas always go for market share, even at the expense of profits, so they are willing to sell abroad at negligible profit (if necessary) in order to keep a foothold. There are suspicions that they are selling many products in the US market (and probably others) at a loss, but this is denied, for that practice is known as 'dumping' and is illegal in the USA. Where the truth lies is not certain, but the fact is that even where import duties are applied, prices are often lower overseas than in Japan.

Japan's distribution system is actually a form of social welfare. Many of the people employed in sales and distribution have relatively few skills, do not work for companies that can pay large retirement pensions and are actually surplus to the task of distributing the goods, but are supported by the system as a type of tax.

Something to keep in mind when looking for Japanese products is that a large number of Japanese goods sold overseas are made for export only and are never seen on the domestic market. An example is the miniature cast-iron grill called a *hibachi*. This item has never been used in Japan and can be found only in stores selling to US service people. (A true *hibachi* is a large ceramic pot that holds burning charcoal for heating purposes.)

One of the big surprises about Japan is that much of its industry is small and inefficient. In 1986, over 81% of the country's exports were accounted for by only three categories of industry: steel (now actually a money loser), automobiles

and high technology goods. The large assemblers of components, like the car manufacturers, buy many of their parts from very small companies (usually family workshops) that may have only a few pieces of machinery and depend on long working hours by family members to survive.

There are many hand-made artistic and decorative items still being made with the exquisite attention to detail for which Japan has long been famous. They exhibit the best workmanship imaginable – flawless lacquerware, hand-forged swords and knives, incredibly beautiful hand-woven fabrics and textiles; the list goes on and on. Naturally, the prices for time consuming hand labour will make these items costly but the quality of the work justifies the price. The coexistence of the finest centuries-old artistry with some of the world's most modern mass produced goods is one of the fascinations of Japan.

While Japanese stores are usually very competitive with each other, especially for items like cameras and electronic goods, there is very little bargaining, and certainly none of the camel-market haggling of some countries. The Japanese regard this with contempt and consider it bad manners.

The way to try for a discount is simply to ask politely if they can make it a little cheaper. Often the quoted price is the lowest that they can offer although I have had one go down when I mentioned that another competing store already was selling for less than that. If the clerk can not do better on price, there is the chance that he can throw in an accessory to sweeten the deal.

When shopping for a camera or other expensive item, it is generally not a good idea to go with a Japanese friend. Because the Japanese have little tradition of bargaining, they tend to pay the first price asked. If you are with a Japanese friend and the price you are offered with him is not as good as you've seen elsewhere, just politely postpone the purchase. Don't bluntly say you can get it cheaper somewhere else as things aren't done that way in Japan; say you'd like to think it over.

Customs Inspection at Home

You should determine in advance what you are allowed to take back to your home country without incurring duties. Check with your embassy if you are in doubt.

Americans should take note of US trademark regulations. In addition to the dollar limit on what can be brought back duty-free (now $300), many goods of foreign origin are registered with the US customs service by trademark. These companies have the right to limit the volume of private imports of goods bearing that trademark; some companies totally ban private imports, while others place no restrictions on such activities. Items made in Japan that fall into this category include cameras, binoculars, lenses and hi fi gear. The booklet *Trademark Information* can be picked up at the US embassy in Tokyo, or ordered by mail from: Department of the Treasury, US Customs Service, Washington DC 20229, or the US Government Printing Office, Washington DC 20402.

Tax-free Buying

Most goods sold in Japan have a national sales tax of between 10% and 35% imposed on them; list prices and price tags in most shops include this tax.

Foreign tourists can purchase many types of goods free of this tax. A card is stapled into your passport at the time of the purchase and is removed by a customs official at the port of departure. You may be asked to show that you have the item in your possession so as to ensure that the goods are taken out of the country.

Only some stores, generally located in popular tourist areas, offer goods on a tax-free (*menzei*) basis; many of these, such as camera shops, will have a prominent 'Tax Free' sign. An individual item (serial number) must have been registered with

the tax office to allow its sale tax-free. Thus, a shop selling to the domestic market would not stock tax-free items.

The tax-free price is not the lowest possible price; it is only the starting point for negotiations. For items such as cameras, you can obtain a further discount of between 5% and 25%, depending on the brand and the store.

Some sharper operators trade on the gullibility of tourists and sell 'Tax Free' but with no discount from list prices. (Shops at Narita Airport tend to operate on this system.) Most shops though, in a competitive environment, will give good discounts, especially in Shinjuku (Tokyo) where competition is cut-throat.

Something to keep in mind is that the final price available from some shops selling at domestic (with tax, *kazei*) prices can actually be lower than the final price at tax-free stores (especially for cameras). The sales tax is levied on the manufacturer's price, not the selling price, and the manufacturer may offer a large lot of merchandise at a special low price to increase sales volume, with the result that the final price is cheaper than what the tax-free stores can offer. You must check around for the best price.

Although tax-free purchasing is intended for tourists and other short-term visitors, those on working visas may be able to buy tax-free during the first six months or when planning to leave Japan.

Cameras

Cameras and lenses are among Japan's best known products, with a reputation for quality at reasonable prices. Before the rise in the value of the yen, the industry had virtually eliminated all international competition in 35 mm cameras and it dominates most of the other camera markets as well.

Although prices have risen in recent years, they are lower than what could be expected purely in terms of the exchange rates.

Japanese cameras are often cheaper (10

to 20%) in Hong Kong and Singapore so it is worth buying at one of those places if you are going through there.

The lowest prices in Japan can be found in Tokyo, especially in Shinjuku, a sub-city with many large stores of all kinds. Some shops in the Ginza area sell at very reasonable prices but others are fully aware that many well-heeled foreign tourists pass by their doors and feel no need to reduce their prices excessively.

The Yodobashi and Sakuraya stores in Shinjuku are close to the Takano Building and are easy to find from the station (JR Yamanote line or Marunouchi subway line) once you are above ground on the east side. Both are brightly lit and the store jingles are repetitious, incessant and loud. There are other branches of these two stores, plus those of Doi Camera, on both the east and west side of Shinjuku station.

As with most purchases, you should compare prices carefully if you want a bargain. Make sure you are comparing identical equipment, ie, the same model with the same lens. Sometimes you can get a better price on a camera by buying only the body at one store and the lens at another. If you have time to check around, you should compare the prices of buying both as a unit and separately.

Keep in mind that some stores offer lower prices by selling a camera body by a famous manufacturer along with a lens that is not made by the camera manufacturer. Unless you know the brand name of the lens, it is better not to accept it. There are several independent companies that manufacture excellent lenses but there are some smaller companies that make lenses of unknown quality. If you spend the money for a good camera, be sure that the lens matches it in quality.

Many brands of Japanese photographic equipment are not available in Japan. For example, one company may make the lenses sold under several different names overseas; the only brand lenses normally available in Japan are Komura, Sigma,

Tamron and Tokina. Some companies put different nameplates on the same model of camera in different markets and some models are never sold at all in Japan.

If you buy a camera, it is wise to check immediately that it is giving correct exposure and is functioning properly. Servicing is faster and much easier in Japan than elsewhere. The best way to check it (other than the simple test of operating the shutter on all speeds at the store) is to run a roll of colour slide film through the camera (Kodachrome 25 or 64 films can be recommended; don't use print film) and check if the pictures are satisfactorily exposed.

Test pictures should be taken of normal subjects that are evenly lighted and that do not contain large areas that are very bright or very dark. If the camera has shutter speeds that can be varied manually, use the full range of them and make a record of the setting for each shot to match them to the pictures later. If only the aperture can be varied, use the full range available. If you buy extra lenses, test them all, using the full method just described. For information regarding quick processing of the film, see the Photography section.

For years there have been stories circulating about where manufacturers 'dump' their substandard cameras. This is one of those old myths that never die. No reputable manufacturer allows a defective piece of equipment out of the factory door – they have too much to lose.

Electronics & Hi Fi

Hi fi stores in Japan, especially in Tokyo, are a gadget-lover's paradise, but there are pitfalls.

First, electronic products, like many other Japanese goods, are often cheaper in other countries, whether it's US discount stores, duty-free stores, Hong Kong or Singapore. In other words, know your prices. Admittedly, the very latest models may not be available elsewhere.

Next, remember that most electronic goodies are either heavy, bulky or both. This makes them prohibitive as checked air luggage. The weight limit for parcel post is only 10 kg and sea freight or express charges are not cheap. (Sea freight charges just for having something crated, hauling it to the docks and customs inspection amount to about Y20,000; then there are the actual shipping costs, documentation charges and customs duties at the other end. The cheapest way to send an item, in most cases, ends up being air freight.)

If you still want to buy, you'll find that many items on display are made for Japan only. Japan's electrical supply is 100 volts with a frequency of 50 or 60 Hz, depending on the region. Low-power equipment may work satisfactorily on 117 V (as in North America) but with no guarantee against damage. The frequency affects motor speeds. (In Australia, UK, Europe and most other countries, supplies are 230-240 V at 50 Hz.)

Japanese TV channels and some other specifications are different from those of most other countries, as is their FM radio band (76-90 MHz), so the Japanese domestic models are unusable elsewhere. Many portable radios now have an FM band covering both domestic and foreign bands, 76-108 MHz.

Because the local models are not usually exported, getting service and parts could be a problem. Many Japan-only models have export equivalents with adjustable settings.

If you are buying FM stereo equipment, note there is a specification called the 'stereo de-emphasis time constant'. In Australia, UK and Europe it is 50 microseconds; in North America it is 75. The modification is simple but would cost a serviceman's time to change. It would be simpler to buy the right model in the first place. Some have a switch at the back that allows selection between the two.

Some 'Tax Free' shops specialise in selling the export models. Several shops in the Ginza area (along the main streets, and in the International Arcade) stock a few types of electronic equipment, especially portable items like tape recorders and radios, along with camera gear, but the range is usually limited and the higher quality models may be a little rare. Prices tend to be higher than in the discount areas because Ginza real estate is the most expensive in the world. In recent years, export models have become available from some of the stores in the Akihabara area.

The best place in Tokyo to buy domestic models of electronic equipment is Akihabara (the name means 'Autumn Leaf Field'). The station of the JR Yamanote and Keihin-Tohoku lines exits directly into the midst of the activity. Akihabara station of the Hibiya subway line exits onto a street parallel to (and one long block away from) the electrical area, passing under the JR tracks en route. In this district there are hundreds of shops of all sizes selling everything electrical that is made in Japan. Among the stores selling tax-free goods are Laox and Yamagiwa.

LP Records

The music of a country you visit is always a good souvenir. Some Japanese music is very much an acquired taste, particularly the screechy *gagaku*, but other types can be appreciated by almost any western ear for its often haunting beauty.

Most pleasing is the music of the *koto*, a long, board-like stringed instrument played while seated on the floor, and the *shakuhachi*, or bamboo Japanese flute. These two instruments are often combined and complement each other.

One of the most beautiful of all Japanese compositions is *Ko jo no tsuki* or 'Moon over Castle ruins'; and another is *Sakura Sakura*. Both should be enjoyable for any listener and are included on almost every disc of traditional Japanese music.

Japanese phonograph records are very

expensive by world standards but the quality is also among the best in the world. As in other countries, the CD (Compact Disc) format of recording is increasing in popularity because of its high sound quality.

Clothes

Japan is not a place where you would normally look for clothes, although residents can find some good buys when they become familiar with the market. The main problem is that most off-the-rack clothes do not fit well because the physique of the average Japanese is quite different from that of most westerners (long torso and short legs relative to height).

With women's clothes, the fashions in Japan are quite different from what most foreign women would want to wear. The good news is, though, that if you do manage to find something that you like and that fits, it will be of good quality and well made.

Finding shoes to fit the average large western foot is also a problem in Japan. If you do need to buy shoes while in Japan you could try Big Shoes Akasaka, 3-21-18 Akasaka, near Akasaka-Mitsuke subway station; Ginza Washington Shoe Store, Ginza 5-chome, diagonally opposite Matsuzakaya department store in Ginza; branches of the Isetan department store; and Ten Shoe Store, Shinjuku west side, north of the big intersection.

If you're coming through Korea, or planning a trip there from Japan, you will find that you can have clothes and shoes custom-made there cheaper than most off-the-rack clothing in Japan.

Antiques

The post-war days when Japanese antiques were sold for a song are long gone. The song has become an operatic chorus with full orchestral backing and prices for almost anything really good range from high to astronomical. They are high enough that Japanese buyers have been

going overseas for a number of years and buying back Japanese items at foreign auctions.

If you don't know your Japanese antiques it is best to avoid spending large sums. If you see something that you really like, then buy it, but remember that Japanese dealers know the value of their merchandise. Prices vary depending on how the dealer sizes up the customer.

There are regular flea markets in Tokyo and Kyoto where stallholders set up for business. The chances of finding a treasure are quite remote, as these people are not as naive as they might let on.

If you wish to examine a piece of pottery or glassware, ask the stallholder to hand it to you. The occasional unscrupulous operator carefully assembles the pieces of a broken item so that it collapses as soon as anyone touches it, so the customer has to pay for it.

Spectacles

Glasses are expensive in Japan. It is better to get them in Hong Kong, Singapore or Korea, but if this is not possible, cheap glasses are available at a type of self-service glasses supermarket. The company, Megane no Drug, has several branches in Tokyo; phone (03) 735-0022 for information.

Computers

There are many microcomputers made in Japan but this a product in which the Japanese have (uncharacteristically) largely missed the boat. There are no bargains compared with what is available in the market in most western countries (especially the USA). Until recently, floppy disks made in Japan were selling in the USA at about one-fifth the price in Japan. (But there is no dumping, they assure us.)

The only type of computer that an overseas visitor might want would be a laptop model but even these would most likely be much more expensive in Japan than elsewhere. The best places for computer goodies in eastern Asia are Hong Kong and Singapore.

Watches

The electronics revolution has struck the timepiece industry as well. There is an amazing variety of electronic watches and they are on sale everywhere.

The cheapest models are sold in simple and inexpensive blister-pack packaging hung on display racks. Names that have established themselves in this field are Casio and Alba. Cheapie types sell at back-street discount shops for as little as Y500, while the advertised brand models begin in the Y1800 range and models with stopwatch start from around Y2500. More expensive digital and analog style electronic watches are also available.

Conventional mechanical watches are also manufactured in large numbers and varieties of design and price. These tend to be prestige models and those made by Seiko and Citizen sell generally for rather high prices.

The best single area for watch shopping is Shinjuku, both in the camera stores and in some specialist timepiece shops (on both sides of the tracks). Reasonable prices may also be found in the Akihabara area and even the up-market Ginza area.

Books

The Japanese printing industry produces some of the finest quality colour printing in the world. Many books are published in English every year, including collections of photographs of Japan and works on other subjects related to the country. They make excellent souvenirs of a visit to Japan.

Actually, without being facetious, probably the best way to see the beauty of Japan is through the pages of these often-gorgeous picture books. First, the photographer takes the viewer into parts of the country inaccessible to most travellers. Second, the everyday reality of Japan is that the once-large expanses of physical beauty of the last century have been whittled away by decades of development, so it is usually necessary when sightseeing to concentrate one's view on a particular small part of the overall scene in order to see only the beautiful part and exclude the ugly. The Japanese in general are adept at this and the photographers do the selecting and screening job for the viewers of their books. This selective vision process partially explains also the aesthetic sense of the Japanese and their ability to enjoy small, concentrated areas of beauty, such as the stereotyped Japanese garden.

Maruzen and Kinokuniya sell English-language books in a number of cities. In Tokyo there are also Jena, Kitazawa and Yaesu stores, the Tuttle shop (which sells titles of that publishing company), plus stores in the arcades of most of the large international hotels. The arcade in the Imperial Hotel probably offers the greatest selection.

Books imported from overseas are very expensive. The bookstores are still converting overseas prices to yen at a rate of about Y300 to the US dollar, a rate last seen in the early '70s.

Lacquer (Makie)

Japanese lacquerware is one of the most beautiful things you can buy in Japan.

Every region produces many different objects – bowls, vases, plates, wall plaques, trays – so the variety is enormous. Some cities known for lacquerware are Kyoto, Kanazawa, Wajima and Kamakura.

Quality objects can be found in most large department stores as well as in specialty shops. Prices of the finest pieces, with flawlessly smooth finish, gold designs and so on, can run into hundreds of thousands of yen, but smaller and less pretentious pieces can be bought for a couple of thousand.

It is better not to buy extremely expensive pieces unless they will be taken to an area of relatively high humidity. In dry climates, the lacquer, or underlying wood, may crack.

Cloisonne

This is produced by soldering fine wire to a metal base to trace the outline of a pattern, then filling in the spaces with material that is fired to a glassy finish. It is a popular purchase in Japan.

Dolls

Delicate Japanese dolls make a beautiful decoration in any home. There are several styles of doll made in Japan, such as Hakata clay figurines, and the more familiar kimono-clad dolls with fine porcelain faces and hands. The latter vary in quality, so it is wise to compare.

They are sold by department, specialty and tourist shops. The few that I have bought have all come from Takashimaya department store, Nihombashi (Tokyo), they seem to have the best selection.

Pearls

The process for culturing pearls was developed by a Japanese (Mikimoto) and they remain one of the favourite purchases in Japan. Mikimoto is still the world leader in fine pearls but many other companies also produce good quality pearls.

In the Ise area (accessible as a day trip from Kyoto/Nara) you can see how the oysters are induced to produce pearls, as well as seeing the largest number of these gems that you are ever likely to encounter in your life. It is a good opportunity to get an idea of the range of colours available before buying: gold, silver, grey, black and white. It wouldn't hurt to check prices in Tokyo in advance to see if they are better at the source, but be sure you have exactly the same specifications of size, number, colour, etc, so the comparison is valid. The value of the pearls varies with rarity, of course, so large pearls and some colours are worth more.

Because of increasing pollution off the coast of Japan, producers are now harvesting the pearls earlier, so many pearls are being produced with a thinner coating of nacre on the irritant that is placed inside the oyster.

Americans buying pearls should note a quirk in the US customs law that sets a 2½% duty rate on unknotted strings of pearls, but 27½% for knotted strings.

Cars, Motorcycles & Bicycles

Information regarding the purchase of vehicles is given in the Getting Around chapter.

Swords (Katana)

Japanese swords are the finest weapons of their kind ever made anywhere in the world. Because of the great skill and workmanship involved in making these 'jewels of steel', good swords have very high prices, often millions of yen.

Few foreigners can appreciate the fine details of a good sword, such as the pattern in the grain of the steel of the blade. Consequently they do not attach the mystique to a sword that the Japanese do and would not wish to pay the high prices demanded. Swords selling for Y10,000 or so are nothing but toys – pieces of ordinary steel shaped like a sword and chrome-plated to give the outward appearance of the mirror-like side of a real sword.

Though not quite the same in purpose

or construction, a good Japanese kitchen knife employs some of the features of sword-making in its manufacture and can be an interesting, functional and cheaper souvenir than a sword. The most useful type is intended for cutting *sushi* and has a blade 250 to 300 mm long. Better ones are made of two pieces of steel forged together, one hard but somewhat brittle for the cutting edge, the other softer and more flexible for the rest of the blade. This is the same type of construction used for a sword blade (except that swords are usually made of at least four separate pieces of steel) and the border between the two types of steel can be seen on close inspection.

Prices of good knives run from about Y4500 upward. Knives of all qualities made of ordinary carbon steel (the traditional material) have some tendency to rust and may impart a slight metallic taste if used to cut acidic foods. Blades with sufficient alloying to make them rust resistant do not cost much more and can be more strongly recommended. One of these knives should last a lifetime if not abused and can be sharpened to razor sharpness. Knives are sold by both specialty shops and department stores.

Kimono

Although the kimono (pronounced ki-mo-no, with equal stress on all syllables) looks beautiful on Japanese women, it does not adapt well to being worn by taller western women. Even Japanese women must take many hours of lessons to learn how to put on and wear a kimono correctly.

So-called kimono sold in tourist shops have only a passing resemblance to the real thing. If one is emblazoned with images of Mt Fuji, shrines, temples, cherry blossoms or Tokyo Tower, you can be sure it is not authentic.

Unfortunately, the beautiful cloth for kimono is too narrow to make into western-style clothing but it could usefully be employed for wall hangings or the like and would get more exposure in

this way than if worn. Good kimono cloth is extremely expensive. It may be seen in any large department store and some smaller shops sell nothing but cloth and accessories.

Another material to consider for wall hangings is the sash (*obi*); some of them are also very attractive and costly.

Incidentally, although all kimono tend to look much alike to untrained eyes, there are several styles for various occasions. The length of the sleeves is one style difference; formal kimono have very long sleeves. Other differences are the colouring and the type of pattern.

Wedding kimono, the most spectacularly brilliant of all, may be bought in stores in Tokyo and Kyoto at very reasonable prices. These are rental kimono that are no longer usable in business (although they appear perfect to the unknowing eye). They have no other application in Japanese life, so a kimono that might have cost a million yen new can be purchased typically for Y10,000.

Ask at the TIC offices for information on stores that stock them. Residents should keep their eyes open for occasional advertisements in the newspapers by department stores (in Tokyo, usually Takashimaya, Nihombashi store) for sales of these garments.

Model Equipment

For the model enthusiast there is a great variety of Japanese equipment, including engines, radio control sets, kits, etc. Most popular in recent years have been the 1/12th and 1/10th scale electric-powered, radio-controlled car and buggy kits, as they are quiet and clean and can be run almost anywhere.

Engine-powered vehicles are also popular but are more of a specialty item because of the greater skill required to start and adjust the engine.

The more advanced models of these vehicles are far past the toy stage and in fact are well-engineered miniatures with tiny ball bearings, die-cast aluminium all-independent suspension systems with functioning shock absorbers, etc.

There is also a huge variety of aircraft and model boat kits, engines, and fittings available, far more than any one shop would have in stock. A catalogue is printed every year illustrating every kit and much of the equipment available; any store should have a copy. Japanese balsa model airplane kits have a very good reputation for quality, with perfect die-cutting, sawing, etc.

Most of the radio-control sets sold are for Japanese frequencies (40MHz), plus simple sets on the six international 27 MHz frequencies (usable for model cars and boats only, in most countries), but most shops can normally obtain export models of the most famous brands (Futaba, JR, Sanwa) in a few days.

Be sure that the model you choose can be used legally in your country (some models sold in Japan don't meet requirements of countries like the USA, and the allowable frequencies are different

from one country to another), and check the prices against those at home to make sure that you are not paying the same or more; many Japanese sets sell for substantially less in the USA, for example, than in Japan.

Japanese engines have built up a reputation for quality around the world. The best known brands, with models of almost every size, are Enya and OS. The most exotic (and expensive) of these are a five-cylinder radial and a four-cylinder opposed engine, both masterpieces of the machinist's art.

For smaller sports-type engines, Fuji and G-Mark can be recommended. Saito specialises only in four-stroke engines, and also has a good reputation. Their first model product was, and is, live steam equipment for boats, boilers and engines of various sizes and configurations.

Of the many hobby shops in the Tokyo area, some with staff who speak some English are: Aile Ken 4, across from the Sweden Centre (near Roppongi station; tel 402-0004), Futaba Sangyo in Akihabara (in the building just before Mansei-bashi bridge, across Chuo-dori from the police station), and Tenshodo in the Ginza area (on the north side of Harumi-dori, above the jewellery shop of the same name, almost opposite the Jena bookstore).

Exquisitely detailed miniature railroad equipment is also sold in Japan, particularly HO and N scale. Some locomotives sell for as much as Y950,000 each and are masterpieces of the model maker's art. More reasonably priced model equipment is also available. Three places to look are; Tenshodo; Itoya, also in the Ginza area but on Chuo-dori north of, and on the same side of the street as, Mitsukoshi department store; and Tokyu Hands, in Shibuya, a famous emporium selling handicraft materials of every imaginable sort, and an experience in its own right. (Itoya is basically a stationery store but always has an amazing number of specialty items rarely seen elsewhere.)

Novelties

Although Japan no longer produces the cheap toys that it was once known for during the Occupation era, several gewgaws of various types can still be found.

Many visitors want to know where they can buy the plastic models of food that are seen in the window of nearly every restaurant. One place where they are sold is the Kappabashi area of Tokyo. Details are given in the Tokyo section.

Toys

A large variety of toys is made in Japan. In addition to local stores serving nearby residents and the toy department of large department stores, there are specialist toy stores in Tokyo (and probably in the other large cities).

In Tokyo, there is one in the Ginza area, a block or so south on Chuo-dori (toward Shimbashi) and on the right from Ginza crossing. (This is in the general vicinity of the TIC, so you can get directions during a visit.) Another store is on Omote-sando, near Harajuku, so it can be visited along with Meiju-jingu.

Getting There

AIR

Japan has seven international airports: Tokyo, Niigata, Nagoya, Osaka, Fukuoka, Kumamoto, Kagoshima and Naha. The first four are on Honshu (the main island), the last is on Okinawa (far to the south of the main islands) and the rest are on Kyushu, the southernmost of the four major islands.

Tokyo

Tokyo has the largest number of international flights but nearly all go to Narita Airport, nearly 60 km out in the country. Getting into central Tokyo from there takes an absolute minimum of 1½ hours.

The only international airline to fly into convenient Haneda Airport is China Airlines. Most domestic flights also use Haneda.

Niigata

Niigata, on the north coast almost due north of Tokyo, is the port of entry from Khabarovsk (USSR) for travellers using the Trans-Siberian railway or Aeroflot route from Europe. Only about a third of the passengers from Europe are able to get bookings on the ship from Nakhodka to Yokohama and the rest must fly into Niigata. The city is easily reached by bus from the airport.

Niigata is linked to Tokyo in as little as 113 minutes by Shinkansen train (the most expensive way), or in about 4½ hours by a regular express.

Nagoya

Nagoya, near the middle of the country, is connected with Hong Kong, Seoul and Manila. The airport is about half an hour away from Nagoya station by regular airport bus. The station is a stop for all Shinkansen (bullet) and other JR trains,

and there are bus services east to Tokyo and west to Kyoto and Osaka.

Nagoya itself is a commercial city with little of interest to tourists, but there are many attractions within easy reach, so it is a starting point worth considering.

Osaka

Osaka is a good starting point for travel in Japan as it is close to Kyoto (the premier tourist city in the country) and the trip from the airport is short and simple.

Buses from the airport go to various destinations including Kyoto and the Osaka station area; from Osaka station it is a short trip to Shin-Osaka station, one of the major stations of the Shinkansen, which offers rapid connections well to the north of Tokyo and as far west as Fukuoka in northern Kyushu.

There are flights to Osaka from Los Angeles, Hong Kong, Singapore, Bangkok, Seoul, Manila, Kuala Lumpur and Taipei.

Fukuoka

Travellers from Antwerp, Brussels, Hong Kong, Seoul, Pusan and Taipei can use Fukuoka (in Kyushu) as a convenient entry point. From there it is easy to circle around Kyushu, then carry on through western Japan to Kyoto, Tokyo, etc.

Fukuoka is the western terminus of the Shinkansen. There is a frequent bus service between the airport and Hakata station. (The station is named Hakata after the city where it is located, across a river from Fukuoka.)

Kumamoto

The rather provincial city of Kumamoto is linked to points in Korea. It is a gateway to the Mt Aso volcano and Nagasaki is not far away in the opposite direction. A circle around the rest of Kyushu can easily be arranged.

Kagoshima
This is the southernmost city in the main islands and has several places of interest in and around it.

There is regular bus service between the airport and Nishi-Kagoshima, the main station of the city. From here you can travel north through Kyushu, seeing virtually everything of interest without backtracking.

Flights link Kagoshima with Hong Kong, Nauru, Ponape, Seoul and Singapore.

Naha
The major city of Okinawa, Naha is a good starting point for exploring the numerous islands to the south of Kyushu. There are many flights from Naha to a number of cities on the main islands, as well as boat connections to several cities such as Tokyo, Osaka, Kobe, Kagoshima and Hakata.

Air Fares
From Europe From London you can fly to Tokyo for £295/580 one-way/return, but try to check this against the cost of a cheap flight to Hong Kong with a separate ticket on to Tokyo. The London to Hong Kong route is very competitive with tickets from as low as £100 standby.

From elsewhere in Europe there are discount fares from various airlines. From Amsterdam for example, the cheapest fare to Tokyo is about £180/320 one-way/return with Biman Bangladesh Airlines. You can fly there with Pakistan Airlines for about £210/320, or with Air India for about £245/445. The same fares with Pakistan Airlines and Air India are also available from Frankfurt.

From North America The cheapest trans-Pacific flight, Los Angeles or San Francisco to Tokyo, is US$559 to US$599 with Canadian Pacific via Vancouver; the one-way fare is US$315. Malaysian Airlines have a similar fare.

The regular return economy fare from Los Angeles to Tokyo is US$851 to US$951, depending on the season.

From Australia Japan was one of the last major destinations from Australia to get any sort of discount fares. Even so the only 'cheap' fare is an Apex (advance-purchase excursion) return ticket from Sydney with JAL or Qantas. You must pay at least 30 days before departure and must stay away for between 14 and 120 days; no stopovers are permitted. The fare is A$998 return.

The normal one-way economy fare is A$660 to A$710, depending on the season.

If you plan to visit Singapore, Hong Kong or Bangkok the best deal would be an Apex ticket to one of these destinations and a separate return ticket from there to Japan. China Airlines are popular with travel agents for this. You can buy the ticket in Australia or wait until you reach your stopover point. The total fare is more than the Apex fare to Tokyo but it's the cheapest way to get a stopover.

Around the World
Japan Airlines is about the only airline to offer an ATW deal through Japan. The ticket costs US$1500 but the big disadvantage is that it takes you through Alaska rather than the lower 48 states in the USA.

For about the same price a travel agent could probably fix you up with a ticket using other airlines which would go through the States.

Circle Pacific
Circle Pacific fares offer much better value if you want to travel only in the Pacific area. For A$1600 you can fly with Thai International from Australia to Bangkok, then through Hong Kong, Taipei, Tokyo, Hawaii, Los Angeles, New Zealand and back to Australia.

SEA

There are no longer any regular passenger services between Japan and countries of Europe and North America, although there are regular services to the neighbouring countries of Taiwan, South Korea and China.

Cruise ships stop occasionally but even these have been coming less frequently in recent years. The main ports for them are Yokohama and Kobe and visitors on ships that stop at both can leave the vessel at one and rejoin it at the other.

For cruise passengers with one or two nights in the Yokohama-Tokyo area, suggested places to visit are Nikko, Kamakura and Tokyo. If your ship calls at Kobe next, you can travel from Tokyo to Kyoto by Shinkansen train, catching a glimpse of Mt Fuji en route (atmospherics permitting), tour Kyoto for a while, then go on to Kobe to rejoin your ship.

Apart from cruise ships there are a few cargo ships sailing the Pacific that take passengers. Most prefer to take passengers for the entire trip, so it may be harder to get a booking to Japan on a ship going on to other countries. The best advice is to find a capable travel agent who can find a freighter that will be going to Japan. Fares vary enormously but usually even the cheapest will be considerably more expensive than flying.

Nakhodka & the Trans-Siberian

The only regular passenger service to Japan (except ferry services to and from Korea and China), operated by the Soviet-owned Far East Shipping Line, operates between Nakhodka (east coast of the USSR) and Yokohama (near Tokyo). The frequency of service has decreased considerably over the past few years and a single ship is now used for virtually all sailings.

The schedule of sailings is two per month in April and October; two or three in September; weekly from May through August; and an extra sailing by a second ship in July over the route Nakhodka

– Yokohama – Hong Kong – Yokohama – Nakhoda. Ships take 51 hours from Nakhodka to Yokohama, 54 hours the other way. The bad news is that less than a third of the passengers reaching Nakhodka by rail or air are able to obtain bookings on the ship; the rest must fly to Niigata.

The Trans-Siberian sector is typically nine days travelling between Moscow and Nakhodka with a break at Khabarovsk and Irkutsk.

Almost all travellers have had good comments on the ship service and most have been satisfied by the Trans-Siberian rail trip, though there have been some stories of being unable even to obtain the meals that they had paid for – but this is another story altogether. For a full run down of the whole Trans-Siberian adventure, check out Robert Strauss' *Tran-Siberian Rail Guide* (Bradt, 1987).

The representatives of the shipping company are United Orient Shipping and Agency Co in Tokyo (tel 475-2841/3). Information is also available from the Japan-Soviet Tourist Bureau (tel 432-6161) in Tokyo or Osaka (tel 531-7416). The Tokyo TIC usually has a leaflet giving more details and directions for getting to the Tokyo representative office.

To/from Korea

Shimonoseki There is a daily ferry service between Shimonoseki (at the far west of Honshu) and Pusan in Korea. The Kampu ferry is the least expensive way of getting from Korea to Japan; the lowest fare is Y9600. Further details of the ferry are given in the section on Shimonoseki and the TIC in Tokyo has a handout information sheet with complete details.

Many people want to go between Tokyo and Seoul to renew visas. The cheapest way to do this is by a lengthy trip by train or train and boat to Shimonoseki, ferry to Pusan and train or bus from there to Seoul and back. Unless you are desperate to save every last yen, you should consider flying directly between Tokyo and Seoul; the three-day excursion fare is only about

Y10,000 more than the combined surface fares and is one heck of a lot more convenient. In addition, the horror stories of immigration officials in Shimonoseki make it advisable to bypass that as a point of entry unless you have lots of money on hand when entering Japan.

Osaka There is also twice-weekly service from Osaka to Pusan taking 22 hours; minimum fare is Y18,000. The contact phone number in Japan is (06) 263-0200.

To/from Taiwan

There is a weekly boat service between Naha (Okinawa) and Taiwan, alternating week-by-week between Keelung, in northern Taiwan, and Kaoshung, farther south. The boats also stop briefly at the islands of Miyako and Ishigaki en route

from Naha to Taiwan (both trips) but do not stop on the return trip.

The shipping company is Arimura Sangyo; telephone numbers are: Naha (0988) 68-2191; Tokyo (03) 562-2091. The lowest fare is Y12,480 Naha-Keelung, Y14,400 Naha-Kaoshung. The TIC in Tokyo has a handout detailing the current schedules, fares, visa information, etc.

To/from China

There is a weekly service in each direction between China (Shanghai) and Japan (alternating week-by-week between Osaka and Kobe). The trip takes two days. Minimum fare (*tatami* class, which is often noisy and smoky) is Y23,000 one way, Y43,700 return, including two breakfasts. The office is in Kobe (tel (078) 392-1021).

Getting Around

Japan has an excellent public transport system in most areas of the country. It is beyond the scope of this book to give a full run-down as there are more than 28,000 trains a day throughout the country!

INFORMATION

The single most useful book for travel in Japan by public transport is the *Jikokuhyo*, or 'book of timetables'. This invaluable publication runs to well over 900 pages, with timetables for every form of scheduled transport in Japan – trains, buses, planes, ferries, even cable cars. If there were scheduled stage coaches, they'd be listed too.

There are several editions of various sizes and coverage. I recommend the largest (*oki-jikokuhyo*) because its maps are more detailed and because it has information on bus lines and ferries which the small ones do not. It is issued monthly, costs about Y700 and is available from any news-stand or bookstore.

The entire book is written only in Japanese but even if you can't read a single Japanese character you can still use it quite easily.

There is a version with some English, identified on the cover as *JTB'S Mini-Timetable* but apart from the major train services it lists only long-distance ferries (and no local services between adjacent islands), the few expressway buses (but none of the large number of local services found through so much of the country), express train services (but no local trains), and airlines. The English extends basically to the romanisation of the names of major places on the maps and the major cities shown in the timetables. For short or simple journeys it should be adequate, but for extensive independent travels you should learn how to use the large Japanese version.

The secret to using the all-Japanese version lies in the maps at the front of the book which show the entire country region by region. One peculiarity of the maps is that they are distorted to fit the pages and that north is somewhere off to the right. All but the last map show surface transportation; the last shows air connections.

JR Shinkansen (super express) trains are shown by a red line of alternating solid and hollow sections while main JR lines are shown in solid black and JR local lines are solid light blue. Private railway lines are shown by a narrow black line with crossbars; expressway buses are shown by a hollow red line; JR bus routes on ordinary roads are shown as hollow blue lines and private bus services are represented by a narrow blue line. A cable car or funicular railway looks like a stretched coil spring and a ferry is indicated by a thin red line in the water areas.

The availability of rental cars near a station is shown by a red car symbol. A cable car system, with gondolas suspended from cables, is known as a 'ropeway' and a funicular railway is a *keburu* (cable).

Areas of interest to tourists are shaded green and have a number in green that corresponds to a brief description (in Japanese) at the top and bottom of the page. However, many of the places listed would be of interest only to Japanese tourists.

The key to using these maps is the number (sometimes with a letter) written in red beside the transportation line. The number refers to the page which has the timetable for that service; the letter, if any, refers to the section of the page – it's that simple.

Although all place names are written only in *kanji*, it is easy to match the names of large cities with the names printed in *romaji* on another map, such as one of the road maps suggested elsewhere in this book. With a little practice it should be possible to compensate for *Jikokuhyo* map distortions and use the free JNTO map of Japan for this purpose. Also, there is a commercial railway map available in bookstores with the name of every major station printed in *romaji*.

Following the pages of maps of the various sections of the country are maps detailing the transport facilities in and around Kobe/Osaka/Kyoto, Nagoya and Tokyo/Yokohama/Kawasaki. Insets on the appropriate pages show the subway systems of Fukuoka, Sendai and Sapporo.

The final map represents all air services within Japan. The system has a hub-and-spoke organisation, the hubs being Sapporo, Tokyo, Nagoya, Osaka, Fukuoka and Naha (Okinawa). The colour of the lines representing the spokes corresponds to the airline, the names of which are all in Roman letters (eg JAL, ANA, etc). Beside the name of the linked city is a number that corresponds to the sub-section of the airlines section of the book (located at the very end of the final timetable section). City names are in *kanji* only.

The book is broken up into about 20 sections (the first 19 of which are JR train services) with bits of information and advertisements scattered among them. In a typical issue the first section gives schedules for Shinkansen, 'L' Limited Express (*tokkyu*) and sleeper services.

The second section shows the most convenient connections for the fastest non-Shinkansen service over long distances, such as Tokyo-Nagasaki or Sapporo-Tokyo. Sections 3 to 18 give the schedule of all intercity JR services, line by line. Section 19 gives the schedule of all JR lines operating in the Tokyo-Kawasaki-Yokohama and Osaka-Kyoto-Kobe metropolitan areas.

Section 20 is a great catch-all of everything else – JR fare information, JR highway (express) buses, private transport of all types (trains, buses, ferries, cable cars) region by region, boat services to and around Okinawa and other southern islands and bus services on the islands, long-distance ferry connections – including those to Pusan (Korea), Keelung (Taiwan), and Shanghai (China) – all international air services (with the city names also in *romaji*), excursion and sightseeing bus tours, and domestic airlines.

In summer issues there may be an extra section of excursion train and airline services appearing before the Shinkansen section.

Kanji characters all have two or more pronunciations. In addition to the readings listed in dictionaries, place and family names can have their own individual pronunciation found nowhere else which means that many place names just cannot be pronounced by a Japanese person unless he/she happens to know that place.

However, a helpful hint if you are diligent enough to be using a *Jikokuhyo* and map with romanised place names to plan your travels is that the pronunciation of all station names on JR train lines is shown in the timetables of those services. With a table of the pronunciation of *hiragana* characters, it is possible to read out the name of the place.

AIR

There are five airlines operating on domestic routes in Japan.

JAL (Japan Air Lines – Nippon Koku) operates only among Tokyo, Osaka, Sapporo, Okayama and Okinawa.

ANA (All Nippon Airways – Zen Nippon Koku) and TDA (Toa Domestic Airlines – Toa Koku Nai Koku) link a large number of smaller centres with the largest cities. ANA also serves the same trunk routes as JAL; and TDA serves a couple of them.

SWAL (Southwest Air Lines – Nansei Koku) is a regional carrier serving a number of small islands around Okinawa.

NKA (Nippon Kinkyo-ri Koku) serves some areas of Hokkaido.

Domestic air services radiate from large cities such as Tokyo, Osaka, Sapporo, Nagoya, Okayama and Naha (Okinawa).

Thus travel between regional cities is not possible without passing through one of the large airports.

At Tokyo, Haneda Airport is used for all domestic flights except for about 10 a day which link Narita Airport with Sapporo, Osaka, Fukuoka and Nagoya.

Listed below are sample one-way air fares. Return fares are 10% cheaper than two one-way fares.

Tokyo to:	
Sapporo	Y25,500
Nagoya	Y12,400
Osaka	Y15,600
Hiroshima	Y23,100
Fukuoka	Y27,100
Kagoshima	Y31,500
Naha	Y37,300
Nagasaki	Y31,100
Sendai to:	
Sapporo	Y20,600
Nagoya to:	
Sapporo	Y33,200
Sendai	Y20,600
Nagasaki	Y23,000
Kagoshima	Y23,100
Naha	Y35,000
Osaka to:	
Sendai	Y25,000
Nagasaki	Y19,000
Kagoshima	Y19,700
Hiroshima to:	
Kagoshima	Y18,500
Kagoshima to:	
Naha	Y22,500

TRAIN

The railway network in Japan is by far the best in Asia and can be ranked among the most comprehensive in the world. Trains in Japan are punctual, range in frequency from adequate to amazing, and in speed from pokey to phenomenal. They include the famed Shinkansen super-expresses ('bullet trains', although the Japanese do not use this term), among the fastest scheduled trains in the world. Fares are not cheap, particularly in times of the high yen.

Nominally, all the railways in Japan are privately operated. For 115 years up to 1987, the largest system was the government-operated Japan National Railways (JNR). By that time it had accumulated a debt of approximately Y5,200,000,000,000 (about US$37 billion) and the government decided that it was time to do something about it.

What they did was to divide the system into eight private lines, each of which is to theoretically become more efficient and shake off the bureaucratic handicap that got it into the original mess. One wishes them luck but as each of the new companies has carried over its share of the debt and a huge number of recently retired bureaucrats got parachuted into the new companies just before they started, one wonders if anything will improve.

The new lines are still coordinated and you can buy through-tickets that are valid for all regions of the country, so it is to be hoped that the overseas visitor will see no real difference from the old JNR days.

The JR system provides long-distance service throughout the country as well as services around the cities of Tokyo and Osaka. The true private lines usually run only comparatively short distances – up to 100 km or so – and are usually regarded as commuter lines.

Exceptions to this short-haul rule are some lines that run appreciable distances to resort areas near the major city on which they are centred, and the private lines in the Kinki district which provide the fastest, cheapest and most convenient services among the major cities of that area (Nagoya, Osaka, Kobe, Kyoto and Nara).

The main station of a JR line is almost invariably near the centre of the city. For private lines this may or may not be true.

In Tokyo, for example, all the private lines end at various points at some distance from the centre of the city and are connected by the Yamanote loop line.

Japanese Railways (JR)

The national railway is called JR in English, but most Japanese know it only as *kokutetsu*; *koku* means 'country' or 'national' and *tetsu* means 'line'.

An interesting sidelight, with no relevance to timetables, is that someone noticed at the time of the break-up that the radicals making up the *kanji* character for 'railway' separately meant 'lose money'. (The Japanese learn the characters as a whole, without knowing their origin or derivation.) To get around this problem, the authorities found another character almost identical – minus a tiny stroke – with the same sound and meaning 'arrow'.

Fares are calculated by distance and the class of service. There is a base fare from point A to point B to which is added surcharges for the various types of express trains, seat reservation charges, 'Green-sha' (1st class) and sleeper/roomette.

The JNTO booklet *The Tourist's Handbook* can be useful for buying tickets as it has English and Japanese phrases written in the format of an order form.

There are more than 28,000 trains every day throughout Japan; in *Jikokuhyo*, JR train schedules fill more than 400 pages! There is a summary of services printed in English which is given out free by the JNTO and is called *Condensed Railway Timetable* (407-E). It gives the schedule of all Shinkansen services, *tokkyu* and *kyuko* (express) JR trains (but no locals), and many of the most important private lines. It also explains the various discounts and surcharges.

The TICs in Tokyo, Kyoto and Narita give out photocopied sheets of the schedule (and required changes of train) for travelling between Tokyo and Kyoto/Osaka by Tokaido line (non-Shinkansen trains).

These trains take about 10 hours, compared with less than four by Shinkansen, but the fare is less than half.

Other sheets from the TIC cover JR services to and from northern Honshu. The TIC offices are the best sources of information for most travel inquiries but they do not sell tickets.

There are travel information centres at all major JR stations. At Tokyo station (Yaesu side), the Travel Information Service is clearly labelled in English and as long as you speak slowly, some staff members speak sufficient English to be helpful. Travel agencies like those listed for reserved ticket sales can also supply information, though they may not have anyone who can speak English.

If you are travelling in the spring, be warned that for many years there has been a nationwide strike of JR services during this busy time. It has usually lasted only a few days but can be a great interruption. Private railways and subways may be struck at the same time.

JR Services

There are several levels (speeds) of JR service which correspond largely to the total length of the particular journey. All trains have both regular and 'Green Car' (1st class) coaches; the only difference is softer seats and a little more room in the latter. For most travellers, the regular seats are entirely adequate.

The basic level is called *futsu* (also *kaku eki teisha* or *kakutei*) and these trains stop at every station. It is the slowest service and is usually limited to relatively short runs of about 100 km. Around major cities the quality of coaches on such service is good; some country lines tend to be the dumping ground for older coaches. In the backwoods the local trains are called *donko*, a folksy word with a descriptive sound, but a foreigner who uses it will find that the Japanese are amused.

Kyuko is translated as 'ordinary express' and refers to trains that make only a limited number of stops, skipping a number of stations en route. They run moderately long distances.

With the exception of a very small number of *kaisoku* services (translated as 'rapid' on timetables and notices), there is a surcharge for *kyuko* trains. The surcharges are:

Up to (km)	Yen
50	500
100	700
150	900
200	1000
200 +	1200

Reserved seats are available for a further Y500 surcharge.

The *kaisoku* services most likely to be encountered by foreign visitors are the Tokaido-sen and Yokosuka-sen lines between Tokyo and Yokohama; the Chuo-Honsen line from Tokyo and Shinjuku west to Takao and Tachikawa; and the Shin-Kaisoku service on the Tokaido Hon-sen line from Kyoto to Osaka, Kobe and Himeji.

Tokkyu is translated as 'limited express' and such trains stop only at major cities. They are the fastest trains (other than the Shinkansen) and are used for long-distance travel. Surcharges for these trains are:

Up to (km)	Yen
50	700
100	1100
150	1700
200	2000
300	2200
400	2400
600	2700
600 +	3000

Reserved seats are an extra Y500.

Overnight Sleepers

For long distance travel, an alternative to the super-express Shinkansen trains is one of the overnight sleeper trains.

The main services are from Tokyo and Osaka, with stops at stations near the starting point to pick up more passengers and at several stations prior to the terminus. The most important of these services are:

Tokyo to:	Nagasaki (Kyushu)
	Kagoshima (Kyushu)
	Kumamoto (Kyushu)
	Miyazaki (Kyushu)
	Hakata (Kyushu)
	Shimonoseki
	(western Honshu)
	Hamada (San-in coast)
	Hiroshima
	Okayama
	Takamatsu (Shikoku)
Tokyo (Ueno) to	Kanazawa (Hokuriku)
	Aomori (Tohoku; via Akita, via Morioka)
	Sapporo (Hokkaido)
Nagoya to	Kagoshima
Osaka to	Aomori (via Akita)
	Nagasaki
	Kagoshima
	Miyazaki
	Matsue (San-in coast)
	Hakodate (Hokkaido)
Hakata to	Kagoshima

The list of surcharges for the sleeping car is quite long because of the several types of accommodation (private compartments, upper/lower bunk, etc); plus the distance, plus whether it is a *kyuko* or *tokkyu* train.

The maximum surcharge (for a *tokkyu* trip of over 600 km) ranges from Y5700 to Y17,000, depending on whether it is a bunk, compartment, etc. These surcharges must also be paid by the holders of a Japan Rail Pass.

Shinkansen

The fastest services in Japan are the three Shinkansen super-express train lines: the Tokaido/Sanyo line running west from Tokyo to Nagoya, Kyoto, Osaka, Hiroshima and Hakata; the Tohoku line running northeast from Tokyo to Sendai and Morioka; and the Joetsu line running north from Tokyo to Niigata.

The trains hit a maximum of 240 kmh but the rails are continuously welded and mounted on a concrete bed so there is no sway and no clickety-clack. It is necessary to look at the speedometer in the buffet car to believe the speed at which it is travelling.

With more than two billion passengers carried without a single fatality, it has an incredible safety record. A ride on one is something that should be experienced at least once. They are known to foreigners as 'bullet trains' but in Japan they are just 'Shinkansen', which translates to the prosaic 'new trunk line'.

The original plan for the line was for it to link Sapporo (Hokkaido) with Hakata (Kyushu) and construction began on the 54-km tunnel under the Tsugara strait between Honshu and Hokkaido. After many years and Y690 billion, it was finally finished in 1985 but by then air travel had developed as a major means of getting to distant parts of the country and the future of the tunnel was put in doubt as it could never pay for itself. There were estimates that it would cost more to lay the tracks in it than it could hope to earn back and there were semi-facetious suggestions that the tunnel would better be converted to the world's largest mushroom farm.

In March 1988 the first trains started to use the tunnel and the JR ferry services across the strait were discontinued. However, the Hokkaido part of the Shinkansen was never built and the Honshu line was terminated at Morioka instead of running all the way to Aomori.

There are both reserved and unreserved Shinkansen seats. It is advisable to get reservations if possible, especially during the holiday periods when huge numbers of Japanese are on the move. At these times the unreserved coaches will be filled with people standing who may well have to make an entire trip of more than six hours

without a seat. Reservations can be made at any JR station with a Green Window.

As with ordinary JR trains, there are both regular and Green Car coaches. Usually only the first coach of a train is a non-smoker. The Japanese have not yet heard of the practice of dividing coaches into smoking and non-smoking sections and they are years behind the western world regarding non-smokers' rights.

Don't look for the gourmet meals and high-class dining facilities that one usually gets on such trains in Europe. One Japanese newspaper columnist has complained of 'awful' coffee, 'the world's worst sandwiches' and dining facilities that are 'a step below most lower class slum eateries'. This is an exaggeration but the food is no more than adequate. Women also go through the train from time to time selling boxed lunches (*bento*). The best bet is to buy a *bento* before leaving the station, where there is a better choice.

A Japan Rail Pass is valid for use on all Shinkansen lines and it is feasible to use it for lengthy day trips. One traveller used one to go from Kyoto to Hiroshima for a couple of hours before taking another train almost to Tokyo the same day.

All Shinkansen train schedules are listed in the JNTO publication *Condensed Railway Timetable* (available in the TIC offices in Tokyo, Narita Airport and Kyoto) and are also listed in *Jikokuhyo* (though only in Japanese). Trains begin running at about 6 am and all have arrived at their destination before midnight.

Tokaido/Sanyo Line The Tokaido line runs from Tokyo to Osaka (Shin-Osaka station) and the Sanyo line from there to Hakata. It is possible to go from Tokyo to Hakata in as little as six hours. There are two services on the Tokkaido/Sanyo line, *hikari* ('light') and *kodama* ('echo'). The fare is the same for both.

Hikari trains are the fastest, stopping only at Nagoya and Kyoto between Tokyo and Osaka taking three hours and ten minutes (three hours to Kyoto).

From Tokyo, nearly all *hikari* trains continue beyond Osaka but there are several patterns of stops by these trains so be sure to check a timetable to get the best train for your destination.

Kodama trains stop at every station along their route and run shorter distances, typically Tokyo-Osaka (a few through to Okayama), Osaka-Hakata, Hiroshima-Hakata, or Osaka-Hiroshima west-bound. The Tokyo-Kyoto trip takes three hours and 35 minutes.

There is a similar mixture of *hikari* and *kodama* trains east-bound, some *hikari* going only to Osaka from Hakata, many continuing to Tokyo, and many *kodama* running from Osaka to Tokyo; fewer from points farther west.

Trains leave Tokyo every four to 10 minutes typically (maximum wait 16 minutes), with comparable frequency from Osaka, and somewhat less frequently from Hakata. The first through-trains leave Tokyo and Osaka at 6 am, and from Hakata at about 6.30 am.

On a clear day, the Tokaido Shinkansen affords a superb view of Mt Fuji as it passes the region of Fuji city – one of the best views available.

Tohoku Line The Tohoku line runs northeast from Tokyo (Ueno station) through Fukushima and Sendai to Morioka. It was originally planned to go to Aomori and thence to Sapporo on Hokkaido but construction was suspended due to costs.

There are two types of service: *Yamabiko* (the express), and *Aoba* (the local). As with Tokaido/Sanyo trains, there is a number of patterns of stops.

Yamabiko trains generally skip four stations between Tokyo and Sendai (about two hours). There are about 18 of these per day, all but three of which continue to Morioka, stopping at every station (about three hours, 20 minutes). Also there are about six per day that

skip almost all stations between Tokyo and Sendai (about 1 hour 53 minutes), and also skip all stations from there to Morioka (2 hours 45 minutes total).

The *Aoba* trains (about 13 per day) make all stops between Tokyo and Sendai (the terminus), taking about 2½ hours.

The pattern and frequencies are about the same in the opposite direction for both types of service. There are also many extra trains on weekends in the summer, mostly between Tokyo and Sendai.

The view from the train on the Tohoku line is not nearly as good as that along the Tokaido/Sanyo lines. The tracks run through flat valley terrain quite distant from any hills of note (at least as far as Sendai), and where the track passes near built-up areas there are shields built onto the track structure to deflect train noises upward, and these impede the view.

Joetsu Line The Joetsu line is regarded by many to be a triumph of politics over economics. Niigata is not a particularly important city by Japanese standards but it is the home town and power base of the amazing former prime minister Kakuei Tanaka (the one found guilty of accepting a two-million-dollar bribe from the Lockheed Aircraft Company and now out of active politics as the result of a crippling stroke).

For this reason it is not surprising that it was favoured to be linked to Tokyo by Shinkansen line, despite the likelihood that it would never make money since about half the distance is through tunnels and would be very expensive to build and the traffic is not that heavy.

As with the other lines, there are two types of service. *Asahi* ('Sunrise', the express), and *Toki* ('Crane', the local); and like the others, there are several patterns of stops.

Asahi trains (about 16 per day plus extras on some weekends) make the Tokyo (Ueno station) – Niigata trip in about two hours. *Toki* trains stop at all stations and take two hours, twenty minutes.

This is the line least likely to be used by foreigners because of the lack of interesting attractions in the Niigata area. Niigata is the port of entry for flights from Khabarovsk (USSR), so it does provide a quick way to reach Tokyo.

Buying Tickets

Tickets to any station in Japan can be bought at any JR station. For short distances there are usually ticket vending machines and for longer distances they can be bought at the ticket window.

There are no reserved seats on *futsu* trains. There are both reserved and unreserved seats on *kyuko, tokkyu* and Shinkansen trains. Reserved tickets can be bought any time between a month in advance and a few minutes before departure. Seats on any of these trains can be reserved at any station with a Green Window (*midori-no-madoguchi*), which means all major stations in the country including most stations in Tokyo. The name refers to the green over the window or the green band around glassed-in offices.

Reserved-seat tickets may also be bought at offices of Japan Travel Bureau (JTB), Kinki Nippon Tourist Corp, and Nippon Travel Agency.

Seats on the Shinkansen can be reserved in Canada and the USA through JAL offices by passengers who will be flying by JAL to Japan.

JR Fares

Train fares are calculated from a base fare plus added surcharges, and these rise with monotonous regularity; increases are virtually an annual occurrence. Shinkansen fares are now almost as high as air fares.

For complete up-to-date fares refer to the JNTO publication *Condensed Railway Timetable*. For journeys over 100 km, student fares are available which give a 20% discount off the regular fares.

For a return JR train/ferry trip exceeding 600 km one way there is a 20% discount on the return section. One of the booking or travel agents would be able to help.

Some JR fares include:

Tokyo to:	Futsu	Shinkansen
Fukushima	3900	7200
Sendai	4900	8900
Morioka	7000	11,700
Shizuoka	3100	5900
Nagoya	5800	10,100
Kyoto	7600	12,600
Osaka	8100	13,100
Hiroshima	10,800	17,400
Shimonoseki	12,200	19,600
Hakata	12,800	20,700
Niigata	5200	9600

Japan Rail Pass

A definite travel bargain in this country largely bereft of bargains is the Japan Rail Pass, which is exactly the same in concept as the Eurail pass.

A JRP entitles the holder to use all JR train, bus and ferry services (including *kyuko, tokkyu* and the Shinkansen) without surcharge, for a period of seven, 14 or 21 days for Y27,000, Y43,000 and Y55,000 respectively. There is 50% reduction for children under 12 and a surcharge of about 40% for 1st class 'Green Car' service. Since the Shinkansen return fare between Tokyo and Kyoto is Y25,200, the potential of the JRP is obvious.

The JR network covers most parts of the country that visitors would want to see. Note, however, that the pass is not valid on private railway lines so there may be occasions when a pass holder has to pay separate fares.

A JRP cannot be purchased in Japan; it must be bought in a foreign country through an office or agent of Japan Air Lines, the Japan Travel Bureau or Nippon Travel Agency. Almost any travel agent should be able to arrange this.

The pass is open dated and you have it validated to start any time after you arrive in Japan. The pass can be validated at a major station, such as Tokyo, or at the JR counter at Narita Airport, but only do this at the latter if you know your travel plans exactly and are willing at that time to commit yourself to start on a particular date.

Technically, foreign residents of Japan are not permitted to use a JRP. Some residents wonder if a friend could purchase one overseas and bring it in with them. The validation procedure is supposed to require checking the passport of the pass holder for the date of entry and the status of residence to prevent residents from using the pass. The office at Narita reportedly follows the procedure scrupulously; other offices might be less diligent. It would be the purchaser's gamble. If contemplating this it would be wise to inquire of the travel agent when purchasing the pass if it is refundable if unused.

Excursion Tickets

JR also has excursion tickets (*shuyuken*). There are four different types: *ippan shuyuken, route shuyuken, mini shuyuken* and *wide shuyuken*.

Wide shuyuken is an all-inclusive ticket for direct travel (no stopover en route) from any place to a distant point, unlimited travel on JR train and bus services within the designated area, and direct travel back to the starting point.

In the north of Japan there are two 20-day schemes for travel in Hokkaido (one for all points on Hokkaido, one for the southern part only, and a variation of the first that includes an air flight in one direction), and another route in Tohoku (northern Honshu) for 10 days.

In the south of Japan there is a *wide shuyuken* for travel anywhere in Kyushu for 20 days by JR train and bus, with the option of a boat trip in one direction from Beppu (Kyushu) to Kobe/Osaka, or from Beppu to Takamatsu (Shikoku). Others offer unlimited travel within Shikoku for 20 days or unlimited travel in the San-in area (the north coast of western Honshu).

Mini shuyuken is similar to the *wide*

shuyuken but covers a smaller area and has a shorter period of validity.

Route shuyuken is for travel along certain designated routes that take in a number of places considered worth seeing. It is valid for 30 days and gives a 10% discount over regular fares.

Ippan shuyuken is an excursion ticket over a route chosen by the traveller. It must take in two or more designated areas with travel of more than 201 km (train, bus, boat) before returning to the starting point. It is good for 30 days and gives a 10% discount.

There are numerous options resulting from the number of schemes. It is advisable to obtain copies of the photocopied info sheets from the TICs in Tokyo or Kyoto. The same information is available at any JR or JTB office or travel agents but few of the staff at these places speak English as they do in the TICs.

Excursion tickets can be purchased at any JR station in Japan with a Green Window office or from any travel agency.

Groups of 15 people or more receive a discount of about 10%. Economy coupons are available for JR trains plus hotels and sightseeing on approved JR routes.

Special Trains

Special steam locomotive ('SL' in Japanese!) train excursions can be enjoyed at two places in Japan. JR phased out its last SL in December 1975 but the clamour of Japanese steam fanatics led them to revive some services on the Yamaguchi line in western Honshu – the only line where the water towers still remained.

The service commences in late July and runs daily except Tuesday and Friday. From September through to the end of November it runs on weekends and national holidays.

Trains make one daily round trip, leaving Ogori (one stop on the Shinkansen from Shin-Shimonoseki) at 10 am and arriving at Tsuwano (65 km inland toward Masuda on the north coast) at 12.16 pm, travelling at speeds of up to 65 km/h and stopping at eight stations on the way. The return trip leaves Tsuwano at 2.25 pm.

Trains have five coaches with a seating capacity of 400 but it is advisable to reserve ahead as the trip is very popular. The one-way fare is about Y1100 and a reserved seat is an extra Y500. Tickets can be bought at the Green Window of any JR station.

The only line in Japan where steam locomotives were never completely phased out is the short private Oikawa line in Shizuoka-ken. It runs from Kanaya (about 190 km southwest of Tokyo and 12 km west of Shizuoka city) to Senzu.

The basic SL service is the *Kawaneji* train, leaving Kanaya at 11.45 am, reaching Senzu at 1.02 pm and returning at 2.45 pm. During the off season it runs only on weekends but operates regularly during the week through July and August. The schedule is printed in *Jikokuhyo* and the Tokyo TIC or any travel agent can give more info. For the 40 km trip, either by steam or diesel, the one-way fare is Y1400.

In 1979 a C-56 type locomotive, built in Japan between 1935 and 1939, was brought back from Thailand where it had been used during WW II to haul war supplies on the infamous Burma railway. It will be used on the Oikawa line.

BUS
Express Services
Japan has been developing more and more of an intercity express bus system in recent years, partly as the result of completing the expressway system from northern Honshu to southern Kyushu, partly as some little-used railway lines are phased out, and (one supposes) because they can offer service at lower cost than the railways. Still, most long-distance travel is by train (especially the super-fast Shinkansen) or by air.

Working against buses is the fact that most ordinary highways are narrow and crowded, cities and towns are incessant and the maximum speed limit is 60 km/h. Thus, intercity buses mostly operate on expressways where the speed limit is 100 km/h and traffic usually moves smoothly.

In addition to the express buses, which make few stops, there are feeder (or local) bus lines that give access to nearly every place of interest. The maps in *Jikokuhyo* show a blue web of services in most areas. It will be useful to peruse the appropriate pages of *Jikokuhyo* for the possible routes if you plan to use public buses.

The main run is Tokyo-Nagoya-Kyoto-Osaka. From early morning buses run from Tokyo along the Tomei *kosokudoro* (expressway) to Nagoya and from there to Osaka/Kyoto along the Meishin *kosokudoro*, stopping at pull-offs on the highway that are within walking distance of a connection with the transport system of the city being served; the buses do not exit from the expressway. During the day it is necessary to change buses at Nagoya (see later for details of direct night buses).

Transfers are not particularly well coordinated, with buses leaving Nagoya just before the arrival of most buses from Tokyo, but the wait for the next one is usually less than 30 minutes. The last bus from Tokyo to connect for the trip to Osaka leaves Tokyo station at 11 am and to connect for Kyoto at 12.20 pm although buses continue to depart from Tokyo until 3.30 pm for Nagoya and later for closer cities like Shizuoka.

The same change at Nagoya is required when going from Osaka/Kyoto to Tokyo. The last connecting buses leave Osaka and Kyoto at 12.10 pm and 12.30 pm respectively. Fares are Y4500 for Tokyo-Nagoya and Y2000/2400 for Nagoya-Kyoto/Osaka.

The only direct buses between Tokyo and Kyoto/Osaka run at night, leaving late in the evening and arriving early next morning. There is only a single departure time for the night bus on each route, although several buses may leave at once. The night bus is popular so it is wise to make a reservation (a costly Y1500 fee) as far in advance as possible. They can be made up to eight days in advance at any JTB office or at the Green Window of large JR stations.

The buses are quite comfortable, with reclining seats, so sleeping on them is not too difficult and they are definitely more comfortable than sitting up on a night train over the same distance. If available, the preferred seat for longest legroom is the one immediately in front of the toilet. The cost, including reservation charge, is a bit over half the one-way Shinkansen fare (Y7800 Tokyo-Kyoto; Y1500 less without reservation), and it saves on a night's accommodation.

Since these buses are operated by JR, a Japan Rail Pass is valid on them. Information in English for Tokyo-Nagoya-Osaka/Kyoto services is available in handout literature from the Tokyo and Kyoto TICs and they can give information on any others. Large travel agencies can also give assistance, though there is the likelihood of language problem.

Northeast from Tokyo there are several express bus routes. Night buses go to the Sendai/Yamagata area, leaving Tokyo station at 10 pm for Sendai and 10.30 pm for Yamagata, arriving early the next morning; both cost Y5300. The return buses leave from Sendai at 9.30 and Yamgata at 10pm. Another night bus runs from Tokyo (Shinagawa station) to Hirosaki (farther north than Sendai) at 10.00 pm (same time from Hirosaki) and arrives the next day at 7.15 am; Y9500.

From Hirosaki, connections can be made to Aomori, Morioka, Miyako, Kamaishi and Ofunato (the latter three on the scenic east coast). In addition to these express services, the area is well blanketed with lesser bus routes that go to all places of interest.

An extensive system of buses runs in Hokkaido. A night bus leaves both Hakodate and Sapporo at 11.55 pm and reaches the other city at 6.30 am (Y4500). There are several express buses through the day from Sapporo to Noboribetsu (Y1500) and to Asahikawa (Y1700) and other cities from which other express and local buses give good service to every place of interest.

Several express buses run from terminals in Tokyo to places of interest to the north and west. From Ikebukuro (Sunshine 60 building, stopping also at Ikebukuro station east exit), buses run northward through Nagaoka to Niigata (Y5000; Y9000 return). From Shinjuku (some originating at Hamamatsucho station) buses run to a number of places in the Mt Fuji area. This is the easiest way to begin climbing the mountain (from the fifth station up the mountain; Y2100). Other buses go to Hakone, Yamanakako and Kawaguchiko lakes, Kofu, Iida and other places.

Of the many local bus lines in this area, one deserving special attention runs from Shin Shima Shima (near Matsumoto) through mountain scenery to Takayama and beyond; see the Central Honshu section.

From Nagoya there is express bus service to Kanazawa, Ina and Iida, the latter two being in the scenic Ina valley. As with other areas of the country, there are many local bus lines that cover the area extensively.

From Osaka there is express bus service west through the middle of the country along the Chugoku *kosokudoro* expressway and highway, mostly terminating at Miyoshi, although the 2.30 pm bus goes through to Kabe (arriving at 8.35 pm, Y4300, departure at 5.55 am for Osaka), from where it is possible to change to buses to go to Hamada on the north (San-in kaigan) coast (departing at 8.40 pm, arriving at 10.15 pm).

Although Kabe is less than two hours from Hiroshima to the south, there is no bus until the following day. From Hiroshima there is bus service to

Hamada, and to Masuda (also on the San-in kaigan coast) via both Hamada and Iwakuni.

For a straight-through run westward from Osaka, there is an overnight bus from Osaka (Osaka Umeda station, 10 pm) to northern Kyushu, stopping at Moji, Kokura (station), and terminating at Hakata (Fukuoka, 8 am, Y9000).

From Fukuoka there are express buses to Kumamoto and other places in northern Kyushu, and from Kumamoto to Oita on the east coast via a scenic highway, Nagasaki, Miyasaki and Kagoshima. In addition to these trunk routes, there are local bus services to all places of interest.

FERRY

There are many ferries linking the outer reaches of Japan. The word may conjure up the image of a short trip on a small boat across placid and sheltered waters, but in actual fact many Japanese ferries are large ocean-going ships of 10,000 tonnes or so and voyages may last up to 30 hours. Such ships are equipped with restaurant and bar facilities and usually have baths as well.

The cost for the cheapest class is usually lower than competing land transport and is often more enjoyable. The cheapest fare is for an open room with *tatami* floors that are shared by all passengers. During the busy summer season these may be crowded and smoky, while at other times they may be nearly empty. There are other classes including private cabins.

The only hazard of the *tatami* class is that there may very well be several parties of noisy *sake*-and *shochu*-tippling merry-makers nearby, particularly after harvest season when farmers who have brought in their crops set off for their annual vacation.

These groups of people are the real Japanese, rustic and simple, quite bawdy and an eye-opener for the person who knows only the prim and proper Japanese businessmen. The drunker they get, the happier they get and the louder they sing. They usually know many folk songs (which all tend to sound alike!), and when completely drunk, their dances become extremely earthy with blatant sexual themes.

Even though it may be at the cost of a few hours sleep, this is a good way to get to know another side of the complex personality of Japan and to meet the most genuine people in the country. Any gregarious traveller is sure to be invited to join in.

Many ferries leave at night so you can save the cost of accommodation but it can mean that you miss out on some excellent scenery. In summer, however, the sky becomes light as early as 4 am and much of the best part of the Inland Sea can be seen from one ferry (detailed later).

Many ferries carry cars and motorcycles. The charge for a motorcycle is about 1½ times the *tatami*-class passenger fare. Anyone travelling by bicycle would have no trouble taking the bike along on any boat, especially if it's a collapsible model in a carrying bag.

In addition to long-distance ferries, there are many boats operating in the Inland Sea between Shikoku and Honshu and between Kyushu and Shikoku. There are also many ships that operate between the main islands and small islands off-shore and sightseeing excursion boats that cruise for relatively short distances along the coast or loop back to the point of origin.

There are also several ships that operate among the chain of islands that extends south from Kagoshima to Okinawa. These services are described in the sections covering the port cities.

Following is a list of the main long-distance ferries, with the cheapest *tatami*-class fares.

Otaru (Hokkaido) to:

Niigata	5000

| Tsuruga | 6400 |
| Maizuru | 6400 |

Sendai (northern Honshu) to:
| Tomakomai (Hokkaido) | 8600 |

Oarai (northern Honshu) to:
| Muroran (Hokkaido) | 9300 |
| Tomakomai | 9300 |

Tokyo to:
Tomakomai	14,500
Kushiro (Hokkaido)	14,000
Nachi-Katsuura	8800
Kochi (Shikoku)	13,500
Tokushima (Shikoku)	8200
Kokura (northern Kyushu)	12,000
Naha (Okinawa)	19,100

Kawasaki to:
| Hyuga (eastern Kyushu) | 17,200 |

Nagoya to:
| Sendai | 9300 |
| Tomakomai | 15,000 |

Osaka to:
Takamatsu (Shikoku)	2300
Matsuyama (northwest Shikoku)	4300
Beppu (eastern Kyushu)	5700
Kochi (southern Shikoku)	4400
Shin-Moji (northern Kyushu)	4700
Hyuga	7400
Kagoshima (southern Kyushu)	10,000
Naha	15,000
Imabari (northern Shikoku)	3700
Sakate (Shodo Island)	1900

Kobe to:
Oita (eastern Kyushu)	4900
Kokura (northeast Kyushu)	4700
Hyuga	7400
Matsuyama	3400
Naha	15,000

Hiroshima to:
| Beppu | 3500 |

Hakata to:
| Naha | 12,600 |

Kagoshima to:
| Naha | 11,500 |

Kokura to:
| Matsuyama | 3400 |

For up-to-date information on scheduled passenger shipping, there are several useful sources. *Jikokuhyo*, the bible of all scheduled transport in Japan, shows ferry routes on maps at the front of the book. Ferries are shown as thin red lines, each with a number and a letter, which refer to the page and section in which the schedule and fare are printed.

The TICs have free info sheets listing a number of boat services, along with fares, schedules and dock locations. The lists are not complete however.

The sheet *Ferry Services in Northern Japan* covers the following services: Sendai-Tomakomai, Tomakomai-Hachinohe, Hakodate-Oma, Hakodate-Aomori and Hakodate-Noheji. This sheet does not list the Aomori-Hakodate and Aomori-Muroran services. The former are listed on the TIC sheet *Transportation for Northern Japan*; the latter are listed in the Hokkaido section of this book.

The TIC info sheet *Coastal Shipping Services* lists mostly ships from Tokyo and Kawasaki. They are Kawasaki-Hyuga, Tokyo-Kushiro and Tokyo-Tomakomai. It also details services from Osaka/Kobe to Matsuyama and Beppu.

CITY TRANSPORT
Train

In the Tokyo and Osaka area, JR trains operate as part of the city mass-transit system where they are called *kokuden* trains.

Loop lines circle the central district of both cities while other JR lines and private railway lines act as feeder systems from the outlying areas into the central districts. In Tokyo the loop line is called the Yamanote line; in Osaka it is the Kanjo line. Several other cities are also served by JR and private railways in a similar manner.

The private railway lines usually run for comparatively short distances (less than 100 km) and link the major cities with surrounding suburban areas or nearby resorts. In the Tokyo area, for example, 11 private railways connect directly to the Yamanote loop line. Some even act as continuations of subway lines.

In the early days of railway building, the founders discovered that it was good business to build department stores over the large stations, hence many lines bear the name of well-known stores such as Keio, Odakyu or Hankyu and many lines start from store basements.

In many cases, private railways run virtually parallel to JR lines and serve the same destinations. The private lines are usually less expensive (sometimes as low as half the JR fare) and also have a reputation for better service, cleaner equipment and more polite personnel, though this may not always be true.

Details of the rail services in each city or region are given in the appropriate sections.

Subway

There are subway systems in Sapporo, Sendai, Tokyo, Yokohama, Nagoya, Kyoto, Osaka, Kobe and Fukuoka. They offer a convenient means of getting around these cities because they run free of traffic congestion.

In each city the stations are well marked above ground and can usually be used by foreigners without difficulty because there is adequate information in English. City maps show the locations of stations.

In most of these cities the subways are augmented to a greater or lesser extent by private and JR railway lines. Subway maps, sometimes with romanised names, are usually available free at stations and tourist literature (particularly for Tokyo) often has maps.

Commuter Passes Passes valid for one, three or six months are available for all

forms of public transport in Tokyo and other major cities.

A single pass valid for travel on two separate systems (JR plus subway, for example) can be purchased at the office of either of the destination stations (except for small stations).

Day Passes The subways of Tokyo (and probably some other systems) offer a day pass valid for unlimited use on all subway lines for one day for Y600. It has the name 'One-day Open Ticket' and is available at any subway station.

Bus

Every Japanese city of any size has extensive bus services. Unfortunately it is difficult to use them because their destinations are written only in Japanese and the drivers don't usually speak English. One exception is the buses in Nikko which have signs in English because so many foreign tourists use them.

It is necessary to know bus routes in advance before they can be useful. Buses are also subject to traffic delays so they are usually much slower than trains and subways.

Two systems of fare collection are used. In Tokyo and some other cities, the fare is a flat sum paid on entering. The fare is normally clearly marked on the cash box beside the driver and there is usually a slot at the right side of the box that gives Y10 coins in change from a Y100 coin, from which the fare can be paid. There may be two slots on top of the cash box – the left one is for tickets, the right for coins.

In many other cities and on country runs the fare depends on the distance travelled. Passengers enter by the rear door and take a ticket from a dispenser beside the steps. On the ticket is a number indicating the fare zone at the place of boarding. At the front of the bus is an illuminated mechanical sign that shows the fare to be paid if you leave the bus at that point.

Most buses in Japan have recorded messages identifying the next stop, which is very helpful if you know the name of your stop. A separate fare must be paid for each bus boarded, except in Nagasaki, which is the only city that has adopted a system of transfers.

Taxi

Taxis used to be a bargain in Japan but now their prices match the high prices for everything else and are almost uniform throughout the country.

The flagfall is Y470 for the first two km, then Y80 for each additional 395 metres (in Tokyo; slightly further in other cities), plus a time charge when the taxi is moving at less than 10 km/h. The flagfall cost is displayed prominently in both windows on the left side of the vehicle and sometimes in the rear window.

A red-light sign in the left front window indicates an available taxi, green means that a night surcharge is in effect, and yellow indicates that it is answering a radio call.

Taxis can be flagged down on the street. In theory it is sufficient to stand at the edge of the road with an outstretched arm, fingers bent slightly downward; never whistle for a taxi.

Most taxi drivers are polite and patient (some are even very friendly) but some give the rest a bad name by passing by a foreigner and picking up nearby Japanese. The occasional one may be quite surly with foreigners he deigns to pick up but these drivers are probably just about as unpleasant to Japanese customers. Taxis can be summoned by phone in cities and there is a 20% surcharge for this service.

There are taxi stands near most stations and drivers are reluctant (or prohibited) to stop on the street near them. At night, in busy areas like Ginza, Roppongi, etc, a taxi stop is often the only place you can get a taxi.

From 11 pm to 5 am there is a surcharge of 20%. That, at least, is the official rate. Because the subways and trains stop running soon after midnight, drivers have a seller's market and it is often difficult to get a taxi after 10 pm, especially on rainy nights. One major cause of the problem is that companies give taxi coupons to employees and the employees don't mind giving two or more coupons to guarantee a ride. This they indicate by the number of fingers that they hold up.

Japanese taxi drivers are not linguists and most do not speak English, although I have been pleasantly surprised on occasion. Say your destination in Japanese, if possible, otherwise have it written in Japanese by someone so you can show it to the driver. Hotels have cards with their address in Japanese to help guests get back. Pick one up on the way out. Sometimes the hotel name is different in English and Japanese – for example, the Imperial (in Tokyo) is 'Teikoku hoteru' to the Japanese.

Addresses are notoriously difficult to find in Japan, so don't get upset and berate the driver if he takes a long time and has to stop at one or more police boxes to get you to your destination. This is simply standard operating procedure.

Tipping is not the practice in Japan unless the driver has performed some unusual service, like helping with heavy baggage, or has spent a long time finding a difficult address. A driver might even refuse to accept the money, although reports of this happening are not so frequent these days.

Do not try to open or close the passenger side (left) door. It is operated by the driver in almost all taxis. They get quite angry if customers close the door because it damages the mechanism, although you can turn this knowledge to your advantage and slam the door if the service has been particularly bad or surly.

Rickshaw

There are only a few rickshaws in use in Japan. They can be seen every day in the back streets around the Ginza, usually around dusk. When traffic is clear, the vehicle moves along surprisingly fast and smoothly.

These rickshaws are not for rent by the general public – they carry *geisha* to teahouses and restaurants where they will entertain in traditional style with songs, dances and stories.

At various places around Japan a few rickshaws have been dusted off and revived as tourist attractions but they are as much a novelty to the modern Japanese as they are to westerners. I have seen them at the charming old town of Kurashiki (near Okayama), at Furukawa (near Takayama) and at Nagasaki but reports are that tourists don't use them enough for the operators to make a living.

The rickshaw has its origin in Japan (not China) and the name is a corruption of the Japanese *jin riki sha* meaning 'man powered carriage'. However, Neil Pedlar wrote in an article in the *Japan Times* that the rickshaw was probably invented by an American, Jonathon Goble, who came to Yokohama as a missionary, wanted a carriage for his wife and commissioned one from a local craftsman (who then made many more). Further, the rickshaw is a copy of a vehicle called a 'brouette' first used in Paris in 1669! Goble copied the design from an encyclopaedia.

DRIVING
Driving Conditions
Ordinary Roads Roads in Japan are generally as good as they need be. This means that all are hard surfaced except for the rarely travelled ones high in the mountains.

With the exception of expressways, all roads are narrow relative to the heavy traffic that they carry, and minor country roads are so narrow that one car may have to pull off the road to let another pass.

The main roads are so built up that they seem at times to be one continuous town. Stop lights are very frequent along these highways and seem to be always red. Traffic-controlled lights for sideroads seem never to have been heard of and the

lights continue to operate through the night even when there is negligible traffic from such roads. The result is that it is impossible to make good time over long distances. In a typical good day's driving you can cover 200 to 250 km and this will require eight to 10 hours.

Passing slow vehicles is a near impossibility. Apart from the almost inevitable endless line of vehicles ahead and heavy oncoming traffic, there are few passing zones. Where there are straight and flat stretches (quite common in parts of Hokkaido and Tohoku) there will normally be a solid line on the road indicating no passing. Conversely and idiotically, when these roads get into the mountains and visibility is poor, dotted lines commonly extend around blind corners!

The single greatest frustration when driving – even a danger to one's mental health – is the speed limit. Incredible as it may sound, the maximum on highways in open areas is only 60 km/h. This limit, laughably low by international standards, is the maximum allowable, but it seems that the authorities feel that even this heady speed is rather risky so it is common to find limits as low as 50 or even 40 km/h in open areas in the countryside. Even more ridiculous, when going up mountain roads there are often signs calling for a reduction in speed!

The sad thing about these limits is that they are strictly, if unpredictably, enforced. A speed trap will always be located in the only straight and level section of an otherwise twisty and hilly road, where the temptation is greatest to ease the frustration of being held back by long hills and other lengthy and slow stretches of road.

Offenders are flagged down by a policeman with a red and white banded pole held touching the road. There is usually an 'office' complete with table and chairs set up in the wilderness to mass-process the victims, with 10 or more police sitting there writing out tickets. This waste of manpower explains why patrol cars are rarely seen on any but main highways and why driving habits on mountain and winding roads are so bad.

Expressways For drivers in a hurry to get from point A to point B, there is no substitute for the expressways. These now link Akita, at the far north of Honshu, to Yatsushiro, at the south of Kyushu, a distance of 2002 km. In addition, there are feeder expressways from country areas and in metropolitan areas there are several, often parallel to each other though separated by a few km. They are the only way to get through major cities quickly although they are expensive to use.

Tolls are incredibly high. For a car, from Tokyo to Nagoya (360 km) costs Y6100, which is substantially higher than the bus fare and a good portion of the cost by Shinkansen. It is less for a motor cycle, but not much. Speed limits on expressways are 100 km/h; they are the only roads in Japan with such 'high' limits.

Interchanges (*inta* in Japanese) are indicated in advance in both *romaji* and *kanji*, but at the exit it may be only in *kanji*, so memorise the characters of your exit when they first appear. It is also advisable to know the name of the desired exit in advance. For example, on the Meishin expressway (Nagoya-Kobe), the exit for Osaka is not named Osaka, but Toyonaka (which I found out by over-shooting and exiting at Amagasaki, a good distance further on). Road maps show the name of each interchange, but usually only in *kanji*.

Expressway signs in cities are largely only in *kanji*, so it is essential to know the *kanji* for your destination before starting out. For a year or so nationalism (or whatever) was leading the authorities to remove all *romaji* from signs but Japan has been overtaken by an 'internationalisation' (whatever it may be) wave, and the *kanji*-only policy conflicted with this new aim. As a result, more and more signs are

appearing with *romaji* on them, much to the great relief of foreign drivers.

Driving Habits The average Japanese driver is reasonably competent. There isn't the long history of mass motoring in Japan that there is in Europe and elsewhere – very few people owned cars prior to the mid-1960s, and the Japanese car industry was virtually non-existent – with the result that Japanese driving for a while was abysmal.

Fortunately, the gross stupidity that seemed prevalent in the early 1970s and earlier has been toned down in recent years, probably as a result of improved driver education and police law enforcement. Or perhaps most of the idiots just wiped themselves out. That is not to say that present driving habits are as good as they should be, it's just that they could be worse.

The main problem with drivers in Japan is a lack of foresight. Too many do not think ahead to predict what might happen and consequently have to slam on the brakes to avoid a collision. In this they are not always successful. Many drive so they are almost touching the vehicle ahead, relying solely on their reflexes to save them if a sudden stop is called for. This is probably a problem common to many countries but it seems to be a national characteristic in Japan, where every other aspect of life is overseen and controlled by parents, teachers or boss, and driving is one of the few activities where one has the freedom to do as one wishes.

The need for sudden braking could, of course, just be a consequence of the low speed limits that prevent drivers from gaining an appreciation of the increased distance required to stop from high speed.

When moving away from the curb, many drivers pull a metre into the road before looking behind them to see if anything is coming. Going around corners in the city at quite high speed, without thinking that there might be a pedestrian or car in the way, is all too common.

Too many drivers change lanes without looking, and, once a vehicle they are passing is out of peripheral vision, many drivers immediately begin to cut over, forcing the other driver to brake abruptly.

Beware of cars coming through the red lights. A large percentage of Japanese drivers seem to hold the belief that if a light they are approaching has been green at any time while in their view, they have the right to continue through it even if it has been red for several seconds. This makes things interesting when one road has the green light, yet cars from the cross-street continue to stream across in front.

Vestiges of the old days can be found on almost any mountain road, where every Japanese male driver seems to go silly, thinking himself highly skilled with the trained reflexes of a racing driver. The fact is that the low speed limits throughout Japan prevent them from gaining any experience at high speeds on any kind of road, let alone twisty mountain ones. Almost every driver cuts straight through curves, so it is advisable to sound your horn at every blind corner. Evidence of the bad driving is that there is scarcely a metre of guard rail in all Japan that isn't scraped or bent. Containers of flowers by the roadside, often with some personal possessions and a flat stick with a name written on it, are mute testimony to a fatal accident, and are a common sight.

Right-of-way at an intersection of equal-sized roads that have no markings goes to the vehicle on the left. Where a small road enters a larger road, all vehicles on the larger road have priority. That, at least, is the law, and it is useful to know in theory, but many Japanese appear to be unsure whether right of way is to the left or right and in practice there seems to be no clear rule. An objective evaluation is that the right of way lies with the bigger vehicle. Not for nothing has the *nihonglish* word *dumpu* evolved – it means a belligerent and reckless driver, and is a corruption of the English 'dump truck'.

Although most truck drivers are careful and sane, their numbers include some of the most dangerous drivers in the country. Too many drive irresponsibly, indulging in games of chase, driving almost touching the vehicle ahead and unmindful of the mass of their vehicle. I have seen a multi-tonne concrete mixer being put through manoeuvres in heavy traffic that I would hesitate to perform in a sports car on an open track. One of the worst smashups in Japanese road history is believed to have been caused by the driver of a large truck loaded with chemicals playing 'tag' with other drivers. The rear-end collision that he caused in a tunnel of the Tomei Expressway (Tokyo-Nagoya) killed seven people and destroyed 173 cars in the pile-up and ensuing fire. It is believed that many drivers take stimulant drugs to keep them awake for long hauls; one effect of these drugs can be hallucinations.

Again, most drivers in Japan are okay, but watch out for the crazies.

Actually, in fairness to Japanese drivers, one must remark that they are generally exceptionally well behaved in view of the small number of police patrolling the roads. For all the tight controls exerted by the police in many aspects of life in Japan, their road law enforcement is quite ineffective. Apart from the radar traps mentioned earlier, and some motorcycle cops monitoring speed, there seems to be negligible effort to stop drivers who are doing the silly things just described (or more dangerous ones) if this would involve more effort than setting up a radar trap and waiting for the flies to come into the web.

Every weekend in Tokyo (and probably in other large cities), numbers of motorcycle freaks called *bo-so-zoku* tear around the streets at night at high speed, making as much noise as possible. It is well known that they use the same streets week after week, yet the law enforcement seems to end at sundown.

The amazing thing is that there are relatively few accidents. As long as everyone has the same habits and expectations, a certain pattern of driving seems to develop and is expected. It would appear that other drivers just assume that it is up to them to allow for the problems caused by others.

Despite the problems and frustrations, the rewards can make driving worthwhile and independent driving through Japan can be recommended as the best way to see the country if time and costs permit.

For less exasperating driving conditions and the chance to see a more typical Japan, it is preferable to use the less-travelled highways, which are generally inland. Often they are little slower than the main roads and vastly more enjoyable, for the scenery is more traditional, with less of the ugliness that characterises the average Japanese city.

Fuel

Fuel is expensive but is readily available almost everywhere, the only exception being in remote areas with little traffic. The cost of regular has been in the range of Y140 per litre in recent years, while motor oil is incredibly expensive at up to Y1500 per litre.

There is no law prohibiting the import of gasoline and refined petroleum products, but when one entrepreneur brought in a tanker full of gasoline for sale at his gas stations at lower cost, he was prohibited from landing it by administrative decree and was forced to sell it to one of the major refining companies.

Drink Driving

The penalties for driving after drinking are very severe and can result in on-the-spot cancellation of licence for a year, with a good likelihood of jail or a stiff fine. Don't risk it.

Japan Automobile Federation

The Japan Automobile Federation (JAF) has a booklet which details the traffic laws. It is available by mail (within Japan) for Y1120 (including postage) from: JAF, 3-5-8 Shiba Koen. Minato-ku, Tokyo 105, or in person from JAF headquarters (opposite the entrance to Tokyo Tower) for Y1000.

Motorists may wish to consider membership in the JAF. It offers the same sort of road service as similar associations in other countries. Reciprocal benefits are given to members of the automobile associations of Australia, Canada, Germany, Great Britain, Holland, Hong Kong, New Zealand, Singapore and the USA. Membership also gives a discount when buying JAF publications and members can have strip maps made up for their journeys around Japan. Membership costs Y4000 per year plus a joining fee of Y2000.

Navigation

Finding your way around Japan, especially outside the cities, is not too difficult. International road signs are used for information, warning and prohibitions, so there is no need to be able to read Japanese. Where words are used on the sign there are often also numbers indicating times, dates or speeds so they can usually be understood.

As mentioned previously, many signs have both *kanji* and *romaji* and it is generally possible to find one's way using only the *romaji* signs, but the critical one that you need to know to make an exit or other sudden decision will invariably be only in *kanji*. When you see a sign in both scripts with your destination written on it, memorise the *kanji*!

When driving in large cities on ordinary streets, never try to take short cuts. Except in Kyoto and Sapporo, there are scarcely any two streets that run parallel for more than a few hundred metres and you can get so completely lost in such a short time that it is beyond belief. If you find you are lost, swallow your pride and go back the way you came, hoping not to encounter any one-way streets. On several occasions I have had to navigate in Tokyo with a compass!

Maps See the Facts for the Visitor section (and the Cycling section later in this chapter) for details of the maps available and the best ones to use.

Driving Licences

General Information A domestic licence of most countries or an International Driving Permit can be used for up to six months in Japan. If you are staying in the country longer, however, it will be necessary to obtain a Japanese driving licence. Arm yourself with a couple of 25 x 30 mm photos, your Alien Registration Card (or Certificate of Residence), a few thousand yen and your valid foreign licence and go to the *shikenjo* (licence office). In Tokyo this is near Samezu station of the Keihin Kyuko line (out of Shinagawa station).

A sign at the entrance of this office will direct you to the counter where an English-speaking person will explain the rest of the procedure, which is all routine and involves nothing more difficult than a simple eye test (glasses are allowed). An International Driving Permit can be obtained easily at the same office after you have been issued your Japanese licence. (Details for reaching the office are given in the Tokyo section.)

Long-term residents should note that the licence is valid for approximately two years, to your birthdate. No renewal notice is sent out, so you must keep track yourself.

Make sure you obtain your driving licence before coming to Japan as getting one in the country is a long, drawn-out and very expensive affair.

Travellers who are passing through Singapore and who will be away from their own countries for several years may find it useful to obtain a Singapore driving licence (very simple on presentation of your valid licence). The Singapore licence can be renewed easily by mail, something

that might be difficult in your own country if you have no permanent address. With the Singapore licence it is possible to obtain a Japanese or other licence as required. If the licence from home is valid for motorcycles it should be endorsed for the same in Singapore (as should an International Driving Permit from there or anywhere else).

Motorcycle Licences A visitor planning to tour Japan by motorcycle may ride any size of bike during the first six months while using an overseas licence. However, Japanese motorcycle licences are graded by the size of the bike for which they are valid and the maximum size for which a Japanese licence can be obtained by showing a foreign licence is 400 cc.

For larger bikes a test is required. This test is designed to be as difficult as possible, seemingly to minimise the number of riders who can have one. Among other things, it requires one to pick up a fallen 750 cc Honda, with the cute trick that it is an old police bike with a guard bar right where one would normally support the partially raised bike with a leg. (I have picked up a standard Honda 750 cc – with a full load of luggage – any number of times without difficulty, but had much trouble with their bike.)

Other tests are to ride their bike through a tight obstacle course, down a 300-mm-wide checkered steel plate, slowly, after passing first over a sharp bump while getting onto the plate, and several other difficult tricks, most of which are irrelevant to actual road riding. The test ground is right beside the harbour, so there is often a very stiff wind making precision riding that much more difficult.

CARS

Generally the only foreigners in Japan who buy new cars are those who will be staying for a year or more. A used car can save you money and can also be considered by short-term visitors who want closed-in private transportation.

New Cars

If you are staying in Japan for some time, ask friends if a car is really useful; they may advise, from experience, that a car is often more bother than it is worth in the city and getting out of the city into the countryside takes considerable time.

Within cities it is often more convenient to use public transport and taxis. Parking places are difficult to find, on-street parking is being actively discouraged by the authorities and commercial parking garages are expensive. It can be preferable and cheaper to use public transport to reach a vacation area and then use a rental car.

For those wishing to buy, there is (needless to say) an excellent choice of Japanese-made cars available, plus a number of imported models, though the latter are mostly sold for prestige and their price in Japan bears no relationship to that in their home countries.

Importing Cars It is possible to import motor vehicles (cars and motorcycles) into Japan for periods of one year on a carnet (explained later), or permanently if for more than a year. However, neither is recommended; shipping rates are high, customs clearance, port clearance and other charges will add substantially to the cost and if it is being imported for more than a year, tax (though not duty) will have to be paid, this being computed on the cost of the vehicle plus shipping costs.

In addition to these and other likely charges, many mechanical modifications will have to be made to bring the vehicle into conformity with Japanese safety and anti-pollution requirements; this is guaranteed to be expensive.

Unless there is a special reason for wanting a foreign car in Japan, it is simpler and cheaper to buy a Japanese model in Japan. Leave the overpriced and oversized foreign imports to the ostentatious local residents who have more money than sense. (Interestingly, large American cars are reputedly most popular with gangsters, politicians and doctors.)

Anyone still wishing to import a vehicle into Japan should contact a Japanese government representative overseas for up-to-date information on regulations.

Exporting Cars With the advent of design rules in various countries, cars built to Japanese specifications cannot generally be exported to them. As for exporting a car to a country without such design rules, the Japanese model might be more expensive than the car exported to that country because of anti-pollution equipment required in Japan. Because of agreements between overseas importers and Japanese producers, it is usually not possible to buy locally the export model of the type required. In addition, Japanese cars are (mysteriously) often less expensive overseas than in Japan.

Used Cars

Buying a second-hand car can be a money saver for the long-term resident and there are some good buys for someone who wants a car for only a few months of travel in Japan.

Buying second-hand involves the same worries as in any country – Japanese used car salesmen enjoy the same reputation for high business principles as do their brethren around the world. However a used car in Japan is likely to be safer than one bought in the USA or other countries where there is no system of compulsory vehicle inspection.

As a car gets older, the repairs required to meet the requirements of the bienniel *shaken* inspection (explained later) become progressively more expensive and a point is reached where the owner finds it cheaper to get rid of the car and buy another. (This enforced scrapping is probably a contributor to the good health of the Japanese auto industry: make 'em buy a new one!) Old cars with only a short time before the next inspection have little value and can be purchased cheaply, although finding them would require the assistance of a Japanese person.

Buying Buying a new vehicle is much less difficult than a second-hand purchase because the price and conditions are more or less fixed and finding a dealer is easy.

When buying a second-hand car or motorcycle, language may be the main problem because it is necessary to look around, use Japanese newspaper listings and negotiate with someone who probably doesn't speak English. A person belonging to one of the English conversation groups found in any large city might be willing to help with this in return for the language practice.

Used cars for sale by foreigners are advertised in *Tokyo Weekender* and other local papers aimed at the resident foreigner. Such advertisers would be easiest to deal with because they will more than likely speak English but it is still necessary to negotiate the hurdle of change of registration.

Shaken

One of the things to know about the regulations regarding cars and motorcycles is the *shaken* system. This is a combined road tax, registration fee, insurance premium and vehicle inspection. It is an expense every two years whether ownership changes or not. Any mention of the word usually makes car owners cringe, the reason being that the inspection usually requires money to bring the vehicle up to the standard.

The *shaken* system is disliked because it amounts to government-sanctioned extortion that benefits the great number of service centres that make the inspections. Even if no work is needed on the car and the check takes only a short time, the motorist is liable for the full charge just to have the papers filled out. Its purpose is supposedly a safety measure, but a study

showed that only about 0.0015% of motor vehicle accidents (apart from those due to tyre problems) were caused as a result of mechanical failure. This being Japan, however, it is unlikely that the system will change.

Motorcycles under 250cc are exempt from the inspection but insurance is still compulsory.

Rental Cars

For those not travelling on the tightest of budgets, a rental car can be a viable way of travelling in Japan, offering the opportunity to avoid the inevitable inconveniences of using public transportation, particularly in the back areas that often offer the most interesting sightseeing.

Rental costs are not cheap, but not unreasonable, especially if shared with two or three others. Rental cars are available near most major stations and elsewhere throughout the country.

Because it can take hours to get out of the big cities due to the absurdly low speed limits and the extremely crowded conditions on ordinary roads (and tolls are extortionate on the expressways), and because there are usually long dull stretches before reaching the good bits, it is not recommended to rent a car in a city like Tokyo. Rather, it is preferable to take public transport to the starting point and pick up a rental car there. Cars can be reserved in one city and picked up in another.

Two of the main companies are Nippon Rent-a-Car (associated with Hertz, which allows world-wide reservations) and Toyota. Both have brochures in English available at their desks at Narita Airport and at the TICs. Cars of several sizes and cost ranges are available.

The following rates for Nippon (Hertz) are for unlimited distance although the car must be returned with a full tank. Different companies have different policies regarding distance charges; unlimited travel is generally cheaper in practice. Vehicles can be rented for six-hour, 12-hour or multiples of 24-hour periods. The first price in the following list is for the first 24 hours, the second price is for each additional day.

1200cc	Y6800	Y4500
1300	Y7800	Y5000
1500	Y11,000	Y6500
1600	Y15,000	Y8600
1800	Y17,000	Y10,700
2000	Y21,500	Y12,800

A discount is often available. When I rented a Nippon (Hertz) vehicle for one day, I was signed up on the spot for their 'No. 1 Club', which entitled me immediately to a 20% discount. The other companies have similar schemes to reduce actual rental costs without actually cutting their listed rates.

It is generally possible to rent a car in one city and leave it in another but a rather stiff charge is added. Insurance is covered in the rental charge.

Cars can be reserved for pick-up almost anywhere in Japan through both companies by contacting the following offices:

		Nippon	Toyota
Tokyo	(03)	496-0919	264-2834
Osaka	(06)	344-0919	344-6831
Nagoya	(052)	203-0919	882-1310
Fukuoka	(092)	472-0919	441-1651
Sapporo	(011)	758-0919	
Sendai	(0222)	63-0919	
Yokohama	(045)	251-0919	
Kyoto	(075)	671-0919	
Hiroshima	(082)	245-0919	
Takamatsu	(0878)	61-0919	
Miyazaki	(0985)	51-0919	
Okinawa	(0988)	63-0919	

Other car rental companies are:

	Tokyo	Osaka
Japaren	352-7635	632-4881
Mitsubishi Rent-a-Car	294-4871	345-6188
Nissan Rent-a-Car	584-2341	458-7391
ACU Rent-a-Car	364-2211	

There are also car rental offices at some railway stations; these are indicated in *Jikokuhyo*.

Chauffeured Cars

Hire cars with drivers can be arranged through travel agencies or the larger hotels that cater to foreign tourists. They can also be contacted directly in the following cities:

Tokyo
Imperial Hire-Car Service (tel (03) 264-7441)
Kokusai Hire-Car Service (tel (03) 242-5931)
Nihon Hire-Car Service (tel (03) 213-6741)
Kyoto
Kyoto Hotel Hire-Car Service (tel (075) 211-1818)
Osaka
Nihon Kotsu Hire-Car Service (tel (06) 532-5671)

English-speaking drivers are available. The cost of a hire car is about double that of a taxi and is not really an option for budget travellers.

MOTORCYCLE

A person who likes motorcycles can have a very enjoyable time touring Japan by bike. The weather is favourable (or at least bearable) for at least eight months, there is the individual freedom afforded by any motor vehicle, plus the added advantage of being able to get through spaces that can stall a car for long periods when traffic gets snarled (which is quite often). I once got my bike across construction scaffolding where a road in the mountains had completely slipped away and down the side of a hill. Another advantage of bikes in Japan is that they can be parked almost anywhere – even on the footpath – as police never bother about them.

Most bikes in Japan are used for utilitarian purposes such as deliveries. Except in metropolitan areas (where wealth is concentrated), bikes larger than 250 cc are quite rare. Although many fire-breathing super bikes are built in Japan, most are exported. There are no new Japanese-made bikes for sale in Japan that are bigger than 750 cc. Any that you see have been exported, then re-imported, for there is no restriction on engine size for imported bikes.

The optimum size of a bike for touring Japan is 250 cc. This is the smallest size allowed on expressways and the largest allowed on the major streets of Tokyo between 11 pm and 6 am. An absurd law prohibits large bikes from using the major arteries between these hours. It penalises law-abiding riders and is scoffed at by the *bosozoku* who intentionally ride on these streets, making as much noise as they can, to taunt the police.

Best of all, a 250 cc bike is the largest size that is not subject to *shaken*. Because of the low speed limits there is little sense buying anything bigger anyway. A lady friend of mine rode from one end of the country to another on a 50 cc bike without problems. One thing you should be aware of, however, is that any bike of 125 cc or below is supposed to hug the side of the road and not ride in the lanes; a dangerous requirement in view of the way car drivers disregard space requirements of two wheelers.

My most earnest advice is to avoid even considering the purchase of one of the countless models of cute little mini-motorscooters that have multiplied like rabbits in the past few years. Though their prices are attractive, they are hazardous to drive because 60% of them (or more) are assembled with the rear wheel cocked out of line with the frame. The result is that the back end continually tries to go off to one side and riding one requires constant leaning to balance it. Looking at scooter riders in Japan might lead you to believe that every one of them suffers from curvature of the spine or a dislocated shoulder!

If you wish to buy a new bike bigger than 250 cc, the best dealers are in the large cities – Tokyo, Osaka, etc. Large dealers are better able to give discounts or may include accessories instead of a price reduction. The dealer can take care of the paperwork for registration, insurance, etc.

Honda has the largest dealer network in the country, followed by Yamaha then Suzuki. Kawasaki dealers seem comparatively rare. Remember that dealers in smaller centres don't normally work on large bikes so spare parts will not likely be sitting on the shelf in such places.

After considering the cost of a new bike you may decide to buy a second-hand one and sell it later. This is certainly less expensive than buying new, although even used bikes are rather expensive.

Conversely, it is difficult to get a good price when selling. This may seem surprising because Japan must be the ultimate throw-away society; things are usually discarded at the first sign of trouble.

Prices for used bikes have strange patterns. For example a used 400 cc bike won't be much cheaper than a used 750 cc (because the demand for the latter is less) and the price of bikes up to 250 cc is also high because they escape the very high recurring cost of *shaken*.

If buying a used bike in Tokyo, first check the *Tokyo Weekender*. Since advertisers are usually other foreigners there should be no language problem in negotiating. You could even run an advertisement yourself, saying what size bike you want (and the date of your arrival in Japan if you're doing it from another country). Write to: *Tokyo Weekender*, 55-11 Yayoi-cho 1-chome, Nakano-ku, Tokyo 164.

The Tokyo TIC sometimes has used motorcycles advertised on its bulletin board so you could check there or place your own ad (if they still permit this). Servicemen at US bases around Japan – there are several within an hour or so of Tokyo – sometimes have bikes for sale, but you would have to be sure that the registration could be transferred to a civilian.

The largest concentration of used bike shops is in the Ueno area of Tokyo, along the streets parallel to Showa-dori; this runs north-south past Ueno station (JR) and near Ueno subway station (Hibiya and Ginza lines). The dealers are to the north of the station.

Japanese newspapers also have bikes advertised and there are many motorcycle magazines with pages of bikes for sale. As with buying a car, you can get help over the language barrier with the aid of someone from an English-language study group.

Be sure to test ride any bike. There is a 50-50 chance it will pull to one side. Don't reject it immediately, as roughly half the bikes in Japan suffer from this malady. The most likely cause is simply that the rear wheel has been cocked sideways when adjusting the chain tension – one side has been tightened more than the other. This is easy to check by looking at the index marks on the arm, and is easy to correct.

If you're touring Japan by bike it is advisable to carry a tyre repair kit and pump. There is nothing worse than getting a flat high up on a mountain road.

When having a bike serviced in a small town, keep an eye on what's going on. I once had an oil change done in a town on Hokkaido. When I wasn't watching, the 'mechanic' tightened the drain plug with an immense wrench. At the next oil change, the plug didn't come out – the entire bottom of the oil tank broke free!

Elastic luggage straps are very useful and are available from motorcycle accessory shops. Worth looking for in small local bike shops are 'cottage industry' straps cut from old inner tubes, as they are long and very strong.

Another tip is to put your clothing in individual plastic bags and wrap them with elastic bands when you put them in your pack, to keep them dry if you get rained on (not uncommon!). Rain gear is useful to carry with you but it might be cheaper in other countries; a vinyl jacket and pants costs about Y1500.

Helmets are required by law for all riders. A name-brand helmet with chin guard costs about Y9000 after discount.

Road Dangers

Japan is no more dangerous than other countries for motorcyclists – possibly less so because the speed limits are so low – but you must be aware of a few local idiocies that persist.

Car and truck drivers have no appreciation of the space needs of bikes (or any other vehicles, for that matter) and drive close behind, unable to tolerate the sight of a clear space ahead of the vehicle in front. They will also go to ridiculous extremes to squeeze past a motorcycle, even if there is no space in front of it. It is not at all uncommon in city driving for a car to pass shortly before a corner, then abruptly cut across in front and make a left turn at the corner, instead of waiting a couple of seconds, pulling in behind, and making the turn leisurely.

Many car drivers simply don't know the law regarding motorcycles. Small bikes are required to hug the edge of the road and not exceed 50 km/h. Ignorant motorists – found in large numbers in small towns and remote areas – rarely see a bike bigger than 125 cc and just don't know that larger bikes have the same right to travel down the middle of the lane as a car does.

The necessity to stay by the edge of the road leaves you exposed to danger from another source – the road surface is often uneven due to deformation of the asphalt caused by heavy trucks and the heat. These ragged edges, along with uncertain shapes and slope of the gutter, can make riding hazardous.

Another road surface danger is the fact that many curves on mountain roads are cambered *toward* the edge, not (safely) toward the hillside.

Riders must always beware of taxis. Without warning they will cut across to the curb to pick up a fare, no matter how many lanes of traffic they have to cross. You must be on the watch for prospective passengers as much as the taxi drivers.

Another type of problem too-often encountered is the driver who pulls out from the curb or from a side road right in front of a motorcycle, even if the bike has the right of way and the road is completely clear once it has passed. It is also necessary to watch out for car doors opening in front of you, for few drivers look back to see if anything is coming.

The worst danger, however, is probably the riders of mini-motorscooters as they cut in with no regard for others. Among other things, they have no concept of the space needed for their own safety or that of other cyclists (both motor and pedal variety) nor of good road manners, stopping directly in front of other motorcycles at traffic lights.

The best safety measure is to be sensible and drive carefully. Just remember the old saying: There are old motorcyclists and there are bold motorcyclists, but there are no old, bold motorcyclists.

Rental

Motorcycles are not available for rental for long-distance touring, though in some popular tourist destinations they may be obtained for local sightseeing.

Transcyclist International

An organisation worth knowing about, Transcyclist International is the Japan chapter of an international association of touring motorcyclists and is active in 18 countries so far. The newsletter of Transcyclist International has news of enthusiasts who are touring the world, or their own countries. (Editor Volker Lenzner is obviously a workaholic, judging by the publications and correspondence that he puts out!) The club enables socialising with fellow motorcycle enthusiasts in Japan.

The feature of the club in Japan that would be of the greatest interest to overseas cyclists is the willingness of some Japanese riders to lend their personal machines on an exchange basis to overseas members of Transcyclist (in their own country or the Japan branch), meaning that they have the right to visit your country and borrow yours.

For details, send a self-addressed envelope and one international postal reply coupon (or a US$1 bill) to Transcyclist International, CPO Box 2064, Tokyo 100-91.

The H-D Phenomenon

An interesting sight in and around Tokyo and other large cities is the numerous Harley-Davidsons. These are the largest touring machines and are loaded down with every available accessory and their riders dressed to resemble American highway patrol police, right down to shoulder patches and badges on their tailor-made uniforms. (The badges are on sale in Ueno with a choice of cities and states.)

The H-D phenomenon is almost worth a trip to Japan just to observe, especially when you know how many thousands of dollars these get-ups represent. There are also numbers of other foreign exotica, but their prices keep them out of the reach of the hoi polloi.

Exporting a Motorcycle

Many years ago there was no problem with buying a bike in Japan, riding it while there, then taking it home. However, there are now so many different design regulations in various countries regarding lighting, switch operation patterns, reflectors and other things that a domestic model bike cannot be registered in the USA (for example), while the USA export model cannot be ridden on Japanese highways.

Export models that are manufactured in Japan can be bought in Japan and delivered to a shipping company. Some large-model bikes are being made in the USA and may not be available in Japan at all. The domestic models could, of course, be modified to meet foreign regulations, but the cost of this, together with all the shipping expenses, would very likely push the total price higher than what you would pay at home.

If you want a new bike duty free and are travelling through Singapore at a later date, it would almost certainly be cheaper to buy one there. There is no duty payable if the bike is exported within a certain period of time and it couldn't be as expensive to ship from there as it is from Japan. Even this way the shipping costs could still make the total price higher than buying new in most countries. Unless you plan to use a bike for touring in

the Singapore-Malaysia-Thailand area, check beforehand regarding the prices in the country to which you would take it.

Note also, if you do have thoughts of buying in Singapore, that shops there normally do not stock many bikes bigger than 400 cc, so it would probably be necessary to order well in advance to allow them enough time to get delivery from overseas.

CARNET

If you buy a car or motorcycle in Japan and wish to take it to another country for a period of less than a year, you can obtain a *carnet* (short for *carnet de passages en douane*) from the JAF that lets you do so without the problem of paying the duty in cash (almost always in US dollars) and trying to get it back (in dollars) when leaving.

The carnet is a book of several pages, each of which guarantees that the JAF will pay the duties owed if the vehicle is sold in the other country. The JAF does not do this out of the kindness of its heart of course – you must leave a cash deposit equal to the highest amount of duty that would be charged in any of the countries to which you tell them you plan to take the vehicle. For countries like Indonesia, the duty rate may be as high as 160% of the purchase price of the vehicle.

There is nothing in the carnet that identifies the countries for which it is valid nor the amount of deposit made to the JAF and there is no compulsion to state every country to which it will be taken. When you finish your travels in foreign countries, you send the carnet back to the JAF and obtain a refund on your deposit. It is not necessary to belong to the JAF to arrange a carnet.

Worth noting is that a carnet bought in Japan is extremely expensive – the administrative charges are possibly the highest in the world. For five pages (one page per entry into a country) the charge is Y9000; for 10 pages, Y15,000; for 25 pages, Y20,000. Also some countries near

Japan, like Taiwan, Hong Kong, Singapore and Malaysia have, in the past, allowed a Japan-registered motorcycle to enter without a carnet or other formalities. Check with the diplomatic missions of those countries if you plan to go there.

BICYCLE

Anyone in good health with the time and desire to see Japan in depth and at low cost should consider the bicycle. It offers the maximum interaction with nature and people in the countryside and the greatest convenience in seeing many cities.

A bicycle is a practical proposition because some models can be dismantled and packed into a special carrying bag that may be taken into the passenger compartment of a train or put in a car, enabling you to bypass boring stretches of countryside or to get out of the major cities more easily.

If you already own a good touring bike, you can transport it to Japan by air freight, by mail (if the frame isn't too big) or as part of your checked luggage either dismantled and packed or assembled. Policies vary with the airline, so speak to the agent of the one that you will be using.

Buying Bikes

Japan is one of the world's major bicycle producers and there are many high-quality machines available. The major problem is that they are generally rather expensive. Standard good-quality bikes are mostly Y40,000 plus and a custom-made one is difficult to find for less than Y80,000.

Another major problem is that stock bikes sold in Japan are sized for the Japanese. Not only are the Japanese shorter than tall westerners, but the *skelic ratio* of the Japanese is different from that of foreigners; a technical way of saying that the Japanese have legs that are short relative to body length.

Thus, even though catalogues may show some models as suitable for people up to 182 cm, keep in mind that this means 182 cm tall Japanese – westerners of the same height would find that they could never straighten their legs.

The good news is that anyone under about 175 cm tall will have a huge number to choose from. There will still be differences in the length of the top tube relative to that of the main down tube compared with bikes made to westerners' proportions, but this should not be a major problem.

For those people in this category, the bikes made by Bridgestone, Fuji, Maruishi, Miyata, Nishiki, Sekine, Silk, Tsunoda and National are all well regarded. Brochures of these and other manufacturers can be obtained by writing to: Japan Bicycle Promotion Institute (Att: Mr H Kono or Mr H Ise), Nihon Jitensha Kaikan Building, 9-3 Akasaka 1-chome, Minato-ku, Tokyo. The telephone number is 583-53444; both men speak good English.

Although many bikes are made for export, it is difficult to find these in Japan because they are too large for nearly all Japanese cyclists. Another problem when searching for a bike is that most dealers do not speak English.

I have found one shop in Tokyo where there are usually a few large-frame bikes in stock. (If business increases, this situation will probably become better.) The proprietor, Tsuneyuki Sumiyoshi, is a young man who speaks English quite well and can converse with no problems. He should be able to handle correspondence in English. He sells large bikes (frames in the 610-625 mm range), CrMo tubing frame, quick-release fittings and 700C rims/tyres in the Y56,000 range. The address is: Pro-T Dryad Cycle (tel (03) 714-1651) 1-6-28 Nakamichi, Meguro-ku, Tokyo. If you write, please enclose a US$1 note (or equivalent in a convertible currency), since postage costs out of Japan are high. He should be willing to credit this against a purchase.

To reach this shop, go to Meguro station (Yamanote line), then take any bus No 1 to 6, and get off at the third stop. This is past a major cross road and just past the crest of a longish hill. The next landmark is a small street on the right side (when going up the hill) between a Mitsubishi Bank and a small police station. About 120 metres up this street is a small street to the left, with a dry-cleaning shop on the far left corner. The bike shop is just around the corner on the left.

Another place where large-frame bikes are usually kept in stock is at bicycle shops near US military bases. There are two such shops along the main street in front of Fussa Gate of Yokota Air Force Base. The bikes are of good quality, sizes are like those that one would find in an overseas store and prices are reasonable, being in the Y30,000 to Y40,000 range.

Because the US servicemen are paid in dollars and the yen has gone up so much relative to the dollar, the shops must sell at very low prices if they are to maintain any sales at all to servicemen. An advantage of these shops is that the staff are accustomed to dealing with Americans and can communicate well in English.

To get to these shops, take a Chuo orange express train from Tokyo or Shinjuku station as far as Tachikawa. If your train has the terminus Oku-Tama or Ome, continue on the train. If it has any other destination (Takao, etc), exit at Tachikawa, go to platform 1 and take the local train. Go seven stations to Fussa. On the side of Fussa station with the large taxi stand, either take a taxi to Fussa gate (minimum fare) or walk about 10 minutes along the small street to the right of the taxi area. When you reach the large road running along the fence around the base, turn right and look for the shops.

Out of the hundreds of shops in Tokyo, two that I know and can suggest for buying an up-market bike are Spica in Shinjuku, and Narushima in Aoyama.

Types of Bike There are four main types of bike sold in Japan: Camping, Touring (or Randonneur), Sportif and Racing.

Camping bikes are very strong, but heavy and slow, and are built to carry large loads of camping gear over bad roads. They are a common sight in warm weather with loads of everything imaginable slung on everywhere, including bags hung

from the axles. It is not a recommended type for overseas visitors.

Racing bikes are also unsuitable for touring, being uncomfortable, twitchy in handling, lacking in comforts like mudguards, fragile (especially the tyres) and expensive. Road Racer bikes are between Sportif and Racing machines and can only be recommended for one-day runs.

The Touring and Sportif models are both quite light, typically 11 to 12 and 12 to 14 kg respectively. The major difference between them is the gearing. Touring bikes have a wider spread between the two front sprockets and may also have lower low ratios in the rear cluster. The end effect is that Touring bikes are a little stronger and are able to carry more on rougher roads, while the Sportif types are intended for higher speeds with less luggage.

Many bikes of all the main types are designed for quick disassembly, a definite plus feature. Such bikes are called *rinko* (short for *rinkosha*); in catalogues they are usually indicated by a wrench symbol. The main differences are that the balls of the steering column are captive, so they cannot fall out when the handle-bar stem is pulled out, the fenders remove more easily (some are in two parts, the outer section of which comes off) and the axles have quick-release handles instead of nuts. If you get a bike custom made, these extras cost little but add much to convenience.

A feature that improves the quality (at increased cost) is a frame made of chrome-molybdenum (Cr-Mo) alloy tubing instead of carbon steel, and 'double-butted' tubes (thinner metal in the middle of the length of a tube), both of which make the frame lighter. Aluminum rims are essential for light weight. The best tyres for touring are 'clincher' types, rather than 'tubular' (or 'sew-ups') that are delicate and a bother to repair.

Test Riding If you wish to try out a variety of bikes before buying one, there are two

complexes – near Tokyo (Izu-hanto peninsula) and Osaka – with a vast number of rental bikes of different types plus a variety of tracks on which to try them out. In Japanese it is called the Cycling Sports Center. There is also overnight accommodation (advance reservation recommended) and there are other sports and recreation facilities.

Custom-made Bikes Bikes can be custom-made to order. The problems are that it takes one to three months for delivery (slowest in the spring, before the summer riding season) and that there is still a limited number of sizes.

Frames are made up from tubing kits comprising tubes cut to length and the fittings for the joints. The latter determine the range of sizes and angles and thus the proportions, and the longest down-tube for which a kit is available is only 610 mm (24 inches). This is moderately large but still not enough for the tallest westerners.

It is realistic to order a custom frame only when in Japan, as it is necessary to determine if the proportions are suitable. With the value of the yen high, the price will not be attractive compared with an equivalent frame made in Europe.

Used Bikes Second-hand bikes are available in Japan but, as with buying anything else, the language problem has to be overcome.

Several bicycle magazines have ads. A Japanese friend or someone from an English school might be willing to assist. Other sources are police-recovered bicycle sales and suburban 'junk yards' that sell a great variety of second-hand merchandise.

Rental Bikes

At the time of writing, there are no rental bikes available for prolonged touring in Honshu. An Australian living in Hokkaido has been organising tours and has some bikes for rent for use in Hokaido. Write to *Oikaze* for details.

If it appears that sufficient numbers of

visitors would want to tour by rented bike, there is the possibility that someone could be encouraged to organise such a service. If you would be interested in touring Japan in this way, send a 'vote' by writing to *Oikaze* so that the editor can judge the amount of interest.

Bikes are available for rent by the day at a number of places in Japan. All the Cycling Inns (described in the section on Places to Stay) have bikes for rent at reasonable rates, so do several youth hostels. The *Youth Hostel Handbook* indicates these with a symbol but does not have a central listing of such hostels, although another of their publications *Hostelling Way in Japan* does. The booklet is free on request from the national headquarters in Tokyo.

Several shops in Kyoto have rental bikes but these (like most in Japan) are single-speed clunkers.

Cycling Information

A good introduction to cycling in Japan is the newsletter *Oikaze* (rough translation: 'Tailwind'), published six times a year by a bike addict of several years' residence, Bryan Harrell.

It has articles submitted by cyclists in various parts of Japan about travelling in the country. *Oikaze* is available overseas by air mail from: *Oikaze*, Futatsubashi 26, 2-24-3 Tomigaya-cho, Shibuya-ku, Tokyo 151. The cost is US$20 per year; send either cash (registered) or a cheque payable in the USA; this avoids sending remittances through the banks, which grab a large amount as a 'cashing charge'.

Back-issues are not available but the information of more than transient interest is being perpetuated in digests. For information on how to obtain these, for general information, and for the latest word on whether a booklet on the topic of bicycle touring in Japan has become a reality, send a letter to the same address, along with US$1 in cash or cheque to cover high mailing costs.

Another source of bicycling information in Tokyo is Marty Davidson (tel 705-5595). He used to be a manufacturer of bike bags but has now moved on to another line of work. However, he is still willing to act as a source of information on cycling.

Taking Bikes on Trains A bike that has been dismantled and put into a special carrying bag can be taken on any train. These bags are available from bike shops, including the two listed above. There is a possibility of a Y150 surcharge for each train ride unless one is a member of the Japan Cycling Association.

Membership in the Association may be bought by mail by writing to Japan Cycling Association, (Att: Mr Sakon), Tokyo Cycling Association, c/o Maeda Industry Co Ltd, 3-8-1 Ueno, Taito-ku, Tokyo, (tel 833-3967/8/9). If there are difficulties communicating with the JCA, call Mr Kono or Mr Ise at the Japan Bicycle Promotion Institute (tel 583-5444). The JCA has functions and activities like weekend rides.

Cycling Maps The general road maps suggested earlier for motor vehicles are equally useful for cyclists. In addition there are three maps that have been made up specifically with the cyclist in mind. They show the location of every youth hostel, places that rent bicycles (shown by a red bicycle symbol, with telephone number), special bicycle roads and touring routes, *Koku minshukusha* (accommodation), road gradients – even a rating system for the difficulty of the touring courses.

Of all the maps available for touring by road in Japan, these have by far the largest number of places identified in *romaji* as well as in *kanji*. The disappointing thing is that they only cover the central third of Honshu. Further maps in the series are intended to cover all Japan, eventually.

The maps are printed by the Bridgestone company and are called *saikuringu mapu* (cycling map); English is written on the back of the folder but the front is only in Japanese. They cost Y650 each and should be available at bookstores. If you have trouble obtaining copies, contact the Japan Bicycle Promotion Institute.

HITCHING

For saving money and getting to know some Japanese people, there is no better way of getting around than by hitching. The Japanese must be the kindest people in the world to thumbing foreigners and the main difficulty is to avoid taking unfair advantage of them. Tales abound of drivers going hours – even days – out of their way to take travellers to their destinations, all the while buying their meals and sometimes even taking them home overnight.

The official tourist authorities wish to discourage hitching but travellers have been doing it for years and gaining insights and experience in addition to simply a ride.

The Japanese themselves rarely hitch-hike and many drivers are not familiar with the meaning of an outstretched thumb. Many a foreigner has found himself taken to the next town and dropped off at the railway station.

It is useful to make up a large sign in *kanji* showing your destination, with the addition of the characters for *homen* which means 'area', otherwise a literal-minded driver may go past believing that only that destination will do, when he is going a slightly shorter distance. So carry stiff paper or cardboard and a felt tip pen. Another tip is to stand at traffic lights in towns (there are many) and ask drivers if they are going your way. Neighbourhood children may be willing to help.

In country areas hitching is no problem because it is easy to reach the highway and vehicles have space to stop. It is not permitted to hitch at the edge of the road on an expressway, so the best way to get started is to stand at the entrance toll gate. Attendants have been known to help

by asking drivers if they can give you a lift.

Once you have a ride, ask where the driver is going. If he plans to exit before your destination, ask him to let you off at the next rest stop by saying *tsugi no kyukeijo* (or 'rest area') *de orosh te kudasai*. You can then ask around truck drivers or other motorists. Failing that ploy, you can stand with your sign near the exit from the parking lot where it leads back to the road.

For straight-through long drives it is hard to beat trucks on the expressways, particularly at night when the long-distance truckers are in action. Drivers who have given a lift will frequently try to arrange a continuation with a truck going beyond their stopping point. Though they rarely speak more than a few words of English, they are invariably good natured and interested in their passenger. Often this is their first meeting with a foreigner. It gives them added prestige to be able to show off a *gaijin* in the cab of their truck.

They are usually quite earthy and the closest inheritors of the ancient Japanese spirit. They will most likely know and sing traditional folk songs and be familiar with other elements of the true folk culture, in contrast to the court culture that produced the refined tea ceremony, koto playing, etc.

Whoever your driver, you will probably be treated with such kindness that you are sure to want to return the favour in some way. This will be difficult, as they normally refuse to take money and will not let you pay for their meals; usually they will want to treat you! Before setting out, stock up on fruit, candy or *sembe* (rice crackers) and feed them to your driver as you go along; you can leave the rest of the box or package when you get out. Foreign cigarettes are also very popular (the Japanese smoke like chimneys) – bring them as your duty free allowance.

Be sure to try to talk to your driver; he will appreciate some attempt at communication even if he speaks no English. If two people are hitching together it is all too tempting to talk to each other all the time, and if the driver is alone he may get annoyed at being ignored after his kindness in stopping.

Any women hitching alone or in pairs who may have some doubts about the whole business would be well advised to stick to trucks with green number plates – they are company owned and the drivers are much more likely to behave themselves. Usually the drivers do not cause any problems, but some women have found themselves with a Romeo who has got the distorted idea from a film or magazine that all western women give their favours upon request. If you find yourself in this situation, you just have to persuade lover-boy that no means no.

Another potential risk for western women is the young Japanese male in his jazzed up car who wishes to impress her with his highly developed driving skills and finely honed reflexes. The fact is that, because of the low speed limits, he will have had very little experience with fast driving of any kind, especially on twisty roads. The presence of a western woman is likely to make him do something foolish, especially on mountain roads where young Japanese male drivers go silly anyway. One woman I heard of was given a ride and the driver did the predictable. When she protested, he reassured her that he had trained as a racing driver. Within five minutes they were in the ditch. Fortunately they were not injured.

Please don't ask the TIC for advice on hitching; it is not legal, they say, and they don't wish to get involved.

The following directions explain how to get to the entrances of the main expressways from the major cities of Japan.

Tokyo (Northbound) For many years, the Tohoku Expressway (*Tohoku Kosokudoro*) began at the city of Iwatsuki, more than 30 km north of Tokyo. Only in 1987 was the road complex completed through the city so that there was an expressway system from the north of Honshu to the south of Kyushu. The following instructions for hitching northward from Tokyo date from the earlier era but perusal of a map indicates that there are a few other places where there is an entrance near a train station, so if any traveller finds a nearer starting point, please write.

Take the JR Keihin-Tohoku line from any station between Shinagawa and Tabata to Omiya. Exit from the platform at the end closest to the front of the train; immediately to the left are stairs down to the Tobu-sen line. Take it to Iwatsuki, the fifth stop; the train fares total around Y500.

Exiting from the front of the station, walk down the main street until you reach the second large street on the right; ignore the side alleys. Walking for 10 to 15 minutes will take you under the overhead roadway, to the expressway entrance.

Tokyo (Southbound) Take the Shin-Tamagawa line to Yoga, the fifth station after Shibuya. Shin-Tamagawa line is a continuation of the Hanzomon subway line, so a train can be caught at any station along the line. At Shibuya station, the entrance is close to the statue of Hachiko, the famous dog. At Yoga, the overhead roadway of the Tomei Expressway (*Tomei Kosokudoro*) is about 500 metres to the south of the station; there is a police box near the station if directions are needed. Ask: *kosokudoro wa, dochira?*.

When you reach the roadway, pass under it and turn to the right. A few hundred metres alongside the roadway, a ramp rises to the right up to the entrance; a service road continues straight. You can stand in the vee between the roads (but be ready to run quickly if a car stops because the ramp is narrow and there is a risk of causing an accident); or you can take the safer course and stand further back on the service road before the ramp splits off. It might also be possible to enlist the help of toll gate operators.

Nagoya Take the subway bound for Hoshigaoka or Fujigaoka; the destination is Hongo station but many trains terminate before there at Hoshigaoka. In such a case, change to a following train that goes all the way. The entrance ramps for both northbound and southbound traffic are near Hongo station.

Kyoto From the front of Kyoto station take bus No 19 or 20 and watch for signs by the roadside for the Meishin Expressway. Get off and select the correct ramp for the desired destinations – Osaka, Kobe and points south, or Nagoya/Tokyo and points north.

Note that it is not worthwhile trying to hitch within the area bounded by Kyoto-Osaka-Kobe; they form one vast conurbation and trying to find your way by road

is more bother than it's worth. Trains are much quicker and more convenient, even if you have your own vehicle.

Because of the great build-up of towns around Kyoto, when heading toward the north coast, it is simplest to take the JNR train to Kamioka and start hitching from there.

WALKING

Few visitors to Japan are likely to have time to walk through the country but it can be done. As related in his interesting book *The Roads to Sata*, Japan resident Alan Booth covered the distance from the far north of Hokkaido to the far south of Kyushu in four months (in 1977). His experiences are actually typical of what any other traveller can expect to encounter while travelling in Japan, so his book can be recommended to any prospective traveller if for no other reason than to dispel some illusions.

Tokyo

Tokyo is one of the most populous cities on earth, the centre of government and commerce in Japan and a major industrial city.

It is difficult to put an exact number on the actual population because in the central part it varies by nearly two million between day and night. The actual Tokyo administrative area is 2031 square km and includes many sub-cities. Adjacent Kawasaki and Yokohama form one vast conurbation with Tokyo itself. Therefore, while the population of Tokyo is quoted at around 12 million, it totals 15 million or more when these areas are included.

Tokyo can be enjoyed for shopping and entertainment but it has relatively little of historic sightseeing interest; what did exist was largely destroyed by the 1923 Kanto earthquake or wartime bombing. It is better to go to Kyoto, Nara, Kamakura or Nikko for sightseeing. On the other hand. Tokyo is a very interesting place in which to live and explore slowly and in depth.

INFORMATION
Tourist Information Center (TIC)
The single best source of information for travel in Japan, and a surprisingly large range of other info of interest to overseas visitors, is any of the three information offices operated by the Japan National Tourist Organisation (JNTO). The offices are located at Narita Airport, in downtown Tokyo and in Kyoto.

The following are some of the publications available from the TIC.

Tourist Map of Tokyo is the best map of Tokyo available, showing parts of the city of most interest to visitors, plus detailed maps of some areas like Shinjuku. It has the best subway/railway map, colour coded to match the colours used to identify the actual cars (or the individual lines). Most importantly, station names are shown in both *kanji* and *romaji*, making it easy to figure destinations and fares.

A bonus is the map *Transportation Network – Tokyo & Vicinity* which shows all railway lines, both JR and private, for a considerable distance out of the city.

Map of Tokyo and Vicinity, also a JNTO publication, shows the area around Tokyo beyond the Fuji/Hakone/Izu area to the west, Nikko to the north and Chiba to the east. It is excellent for orientation.

Tokyo is the simple title of an information brochure on the city. It gives some history, general and sightseeing info, and has listings of some museums, galleries and the like.

Walking Tour Courses in Tokyo describes what you can see in walks around the Imperial Palace, Ueno-koen park, Asakusa, a bit of the Shitamachi area and other parts of the city.

A very useful publication is their listing of economical accommodation in the Tokyo area. (However, they do not arrange reservations.)

Also in their racks, behind the staff area, are other brochures for specialised aspects of Tokyo and Japan in general (summarised JR timetables, info on trains and buses to Narita airport) plus pamphlets on a large number of other cities and regions in the country. It is worthwhile looking at the titles of these publications. You can also talk to the staff and tell them exactly where you plan to go and request relevant information.

Staff at the TIC have filing cabinets bulging with miscellaneous information on every imaginable subject, so they can give information on everything from finding a dentist to where to find some unusual handicraft.

A telephone information service operated by the TIC (tel 502-1461) is available during working hours. There is also a recorded message giving info about current cultural events and festivals in the Tokyo area (tel 503-2911 for English or 503-2926 for French).

The office is open Monday to Friday from 9 am to 12 noon and 1 to 5 pm; on Saturdays from 9 am to 12 noon.

Tokyo TIC is near the Ginza area of Tokyo on Harumi-dori, about 200 metres from Mitsukoshi Department Store on the way to Hibiya-koen park. From Mitsukoshi you can see the railroad bridge (used by Shinkansen and local trains) down Harumi-dori; the TIC is just beyond the bridge, on the left. It is clearly marked with a large illuminated red sign with a question mark perpendicular to the front of the building; the name 'Tourist Information Center' is also written on the front of the building.

If travelling on the Yamanote or Keihin-Tohoku JR lines, get off at Yurakucho station. Walk to the end of the platform in the direction of Shimbashi station and look for the sign 'For Hibiya Area'. Note the Sogo Department Store on the right (it has a youth hostel booking office in the basement) and exit from the station on that side. Then turn left and walk along the street, keeping to the right of the elevated railway tracks. At the major road (Harumi-dori), the TIC office is clearly visible across the street.

If on the Hibiya line, get off at Hibiya station and leave the platform at the end closest to Ginza station (next stop). Walk up to the exit and double back between the exits (there is one on each side of the passageway). Bear to the left, watch for a sign for the Imperial Hotel, and follow it to the sign for Exit 4/5. Take Exit A4, walk up the steps, and the TIC sign is visible about 50 metres ahead.

From the Chiyoda and Mita lines, get off at Hibiya station on either line. Both stations are some distance from the Hibiya line's Hibiya station, but they are all connected by underground passages. After exiting from the platform, follow signs for the Hibiya line. This will lead to a long passage that has an entrance to the Hibiya line at the near end. Walk past this, along the passage as indicated by signs 'Passage for Ginza'. Exits 4 and 5 are to the right.

Immigration Office

The immigration office is in central Tokyo. It can be reached most easily by Chiyoda subway line to Otemachi station and exiting at the head of the train when going away from Hibiya. Leave by exit C2, walk to the corner, cross the street, and turn left. It is the official-looking place adjacent to the corner building.

Embassies

The following are the telephone numbers for some of the embassies in Tokyo .

Australia	453-0251
Austria	451-8281
Belgium	262-0191
Canada	408-2101
China	446-6781
Denmark	496-3001
Finland	583-7790
France	473-0171
West Germany	473-0151
Greece	403-0871
India	262-2391
Indonesia	441-4201
Ireland	263-0695
Italy	453-5291
*Korea	452-7611

Malaysia	463-0241
Netherlands	431-5126
New Zealand	460-8711
Norway	440-2611
Pakistan	454-4862
Philippines	496-2731
Singapore	586-9111
Soviet Union	583-4224
Spain	583-8531
Sri Lanka	585-7431
Sweden	582-6981
Switzerland	473-0121
*Taiwan	434-1181
Thailand	441-7352
UK	265-5511
USA	583-7141

*Korea Many travellers go to Korea from Japan, both for sightseeing and for obtaining Japanese visas. In addition to Tokyo, Korean diplomatic representatives are in the following cities:

Sapporo	(011) 621-0288
Sendai	(0222) 21-2751
Niigata	(0252) 43-4771
Yokohama	(045) 621-4531
Nagoya	(052) 935-9221
Osaka	(06) 213-1401
Kobe	(078) 221-4853
Fukuoka	(092) 771-0461
Shimonoseki	(0832) 66-5341
Naha	(0988) 55-3381

In Tokyo, visas are not issued at the embassy but at a separate building about 10 minutes away on foot. The easiest way to reach it is by bus. In all cases, get off at Ni-no-hashi bus stop; it has the same name on both sides of the road.

Of the buses listed, the first four let off passengers on the same side as the consulate building, the other three on the far side. The building is a tall white structure, about 100 metres along in the direction taken by the first four buses after leaving the stop.

The listing gives the bus number and the names of the starting and terminal JR railway stations.

85	Shimbashi	Shibuya
10	Tokyo (south exit)	Meguro
91	Tokyo (north exit)	Shinagawa
70	Shinjuku (west exit)	Tamachi
10	Meguro	Tokyo (south exit)
85	Shibuya	Shimbashi
99	Gotanda	Shimbashi

Visas are granted on the spot within an hour except to Japanese who have to wait several days. Cost is the yen equivalent of US$1.50 and one photo is required.

*Taiwan Since Japan recognised the People's Republic of China, Taiwan has been doing business in Tokyo under the name 'Association of East Asian Relations'. For visas, the office functions exactly as a consular office.

To reach it, take the Hibiya subway to Kamiyacho, then walk uphill along the major road (Sakurada-dori) in the direction of Tokyo Tower. Go straight across the large intersection at the top (keeping the Tower to your left) and continue downhill, on the left-hand side of the road. Look for the sign '39 Mori Building' on the front of a modern building with a glass-and-chrome theme and circular automatic door.

Office hours are 9 am to 12 noon and 1 to 4 pm Monday to Friday, and 9 am to 12 noon on Saturdays. The postal address is: 39 Mori Building, 2-4-5 Azabudai, Minato-ku, Tokyo (tel 434-1181).

Welcome Furoshiki
For newly arrived residents of Tokyo there is a very useful information service called Welcome Furoshiki. A *furoshiki* is a traditional Japanese square of cloth used to wrap and carry items; it is symbolic of a package of information that 'WF' offers free.

A WF member visits the homes of newcomers, gives the bundle (which contains a great deal of useful info) and answers questions about settling into this unfamiliar new land.

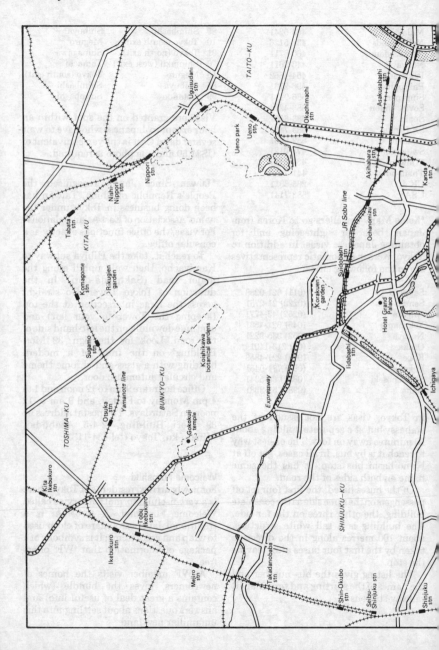

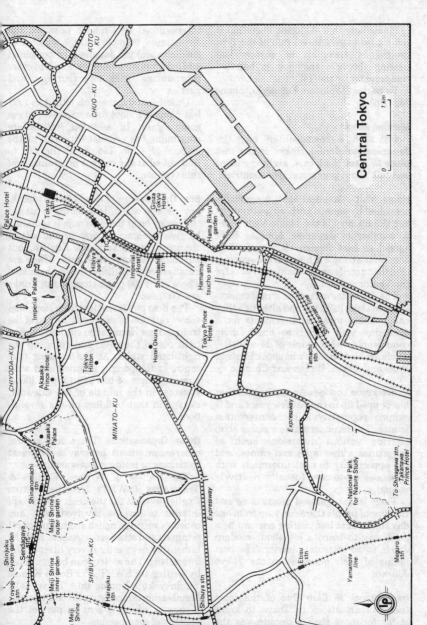

Central Tokyo

Please note that Welcome Furoshiki is not set up to give travel info of the type desired by travellers or anyone just passing through; that job is handled competently by the TIC.

To contact Welcome Furoshiki, phone 352-0765.

Meeting People

Being such a cosmopolitan city (by Japanese standards), Tokyo is the best place to meet the locals, exchange ideas and talk about your respective countries.

Home Visit An admirable programme organised by various authorities throughout the country is the Home Visit plan. A number of Japanese families have agreed to host foreign visitors in their homes for a couple of hours in the evening. (Further details are given in the Facts for the Visitor chapter.).

The TIC office makes the arrangements for such visits in Tokyo and although they can possibly make arrangements for a same-day visit they are much more comfortable with a couple of days notice. There are host families who speak English, French, German, Italian and Chinese.

Conversation Lounges An institution that has popped up in the last few years and is gaining popularity is the conversation lounge. The basic format is a coffee shop offering various diversions such as magazines, video tapes and games, and the opportunity to chat informally with Japanese customers (usually relatively young).

There is no organised programme and the type of people there can vary from one day to the next but visiting one can be a good way to learn a lot about modern Japan in an informal manner. The best listing of such places is in the *Tokyo Journal*.

International 3F Club One of the most useful organisations in Tokyo to know about for more than a decade was the International 3F Club. It provided the opportunity to meet a large number of English-speaking Japanese in congenial and informal surroundings, and had other programmes, such as excursions and parties.

Unfortunately, the club folded in 1987 but plans are afoot for a successor to get going again. In addition, others are continuing the original activities of the original 3F Club. Inquire at the TIC to find out what the current programmes of this type are.

Boss On the second Friday of each month, anyone who wishes is welcome to attend the goings-on at the Boss pub. It is mainly to give foreigners living in the city a chance to meet and talk English, but anyone is welcome to attend. There are usually several English-speaking Japanese. There is a Y300 cover charge, and drinks are Y600 each.

The Boss pub is reached from Roppongi subway station by exiting at the end of the train nearest Kamiyacho station, turning right out of the gate, and going up the right-hand stairs. At the crossing (the centre of Roppongi), turn left and walk along a couple of blocks to a pub like a streetcar in the middle of the sidewalk. Boss is in that building on the seventh floor.

Other Organisations There are several other organisations that may be of interest to visiting or resident foreigners.

The Society of Writers, Editors & Translators (SWET) has the written English word as the theme. It would be of interest to anyone involved with any aspect of writing English and has practical seminars and other get-togethers, and the bimonthly newsletter is very literate and interesting. The society can be contacted by writing to: SWET, PO Box 8 Komae Yubinkyoku, Komae-shi, Tokyo 201. Membership brings listing in the Directory, a copy of which is sent as part of the benefits of membership.

The Forum for Corporate Communications is an association of people involved in public relations and related activities. They have luncheons with guest speakers. Notices of forthcoming events are listed in the Announcements section on the back page of the *Japan Times*.

The Tokyo Gay Support Group (tel (03) 453-1618) can give information on what is happening in the gay scene in Tokyo and has a list and map of gay bars. The mailing address is: CPO, Box 1901, Tokyo 100-91.

Other groups include The International Feminists of Japan (tel (03) 783-9665, Anne Blassing). The IFJ can be contacted by mail at: IFJ, CPO Box 1780, Tokyo 100-91. The IFJ Newsletter is published monthly and is available overseas by subscription. There is also the Tokyo Women's Information Network – TWIN (tel (03) 354-8565). Notices of meetings appear in the English language dailies and in the *Tokyo Journal*.

Religious Groups There are numerous Christian churches in the greater Tokyo area, representing virtually all the major denominations. For listings, refer to a Saturday issue of the *Japan Times, Tokyo Weekender* or the *Tokyo Journal*.

The Jewish Community Center (tel 400-2559) near Hiroo subway station of the Hibiya line, has Friday, Saturday and holiday services, Talmud classes and provides other services and support to the Jewish community.

The Islamic Center (tel 460-6169) in Setagaya-ku provides a place for prayer and other activities.

For information regarding Hindu religious activities, contact the Indian Merchants Association (tel (045) 662-8685) in Yokohama.

Magazines & Newspapers
Tour Companion, a free weekly paper aimed at tourists, is available at hotels, airline offices, travel agents, the TIC and some supermarkets frequented by foreigners.

It is a superb source of information on events for the following week or two, with details of festivals, cultural and entertainment offerings in the Tokyo area.

It also lists phone numbers of embassies and airlines and has info on movies, gallery showings and concerts. There is also space devoted to shopping, restaurants and night spots and its maps show places of touristic interest, banks, shops and restaurants.

It is a commercial publication so its listings should be regarded in that light, with its advertisers expecting more favourable coverage.

Single copies (Y150 when ordered) and subscriptions are available in Japan and overseas from: Tokyo News Service Ltd, Tsukiji Hamarikyu Building 10Fl, 3-3 Tsukiji 5-chome, Chuo-ku, Tokyo 104.

Tokyo Journal is a monthly publication which covers a lot of ground. Its front pages have short articles on various subjects related to Japan, some of interest mainly to residents and others for anyone interested in the country.

Its format has varied through the years but it seems to have settled on presenting interesting articles on modern Japan, bringing an objective look to many facets (good and otherwise) of the country that is lacking from most sources.

The larger part is devoted to information about coming events such as concerts (classical and popular music), dance, *kabuki* and other traditional Japanese performing arts, films, and exhibitions at museums, galleries and department stores.

It also lists pubs and similar places which feature live music, a large number of restaurants and drinking places, conversation lounges, travel agencies and other services, Japanese language schools, miscellaneous classified ads, and a number of low cost accommodation places. It also has useful maps with banks and important buildings used as landmarks. Cover price is Y500.

It is available at most bookstores (especially in large hotels), the American Pharmacy, many travel agencies, supermarkets and restaurants popular with foreigners.

Single copies and subscriptions are available in Japan and overseas from: Cross Culture Jigyodan Cl Ltd, Magatani Building 3Fl, 5-10-13 Toranomon, Minato-ku, Tokyo 105; or in the USA from: Japan Cross Culture Centre, Japanese-American Community and Cultural Centre, Suite 305, 244 So San Pedro St, Los Angeles, CA 90012.

Tokyo Weekender is a weekly free newspaper aimed at foreign residents in Tokyo. The lead article may be on any topic under the sun but every issue has social, fashion, food and entertainment pages. There is a weekly film review and a listing of foreign-language films at Tokyo theatres.

Occasional articles deal with the Japanese and life in Japan (past and present) and give some insights rarely seen elsewhere, such as discussions of the plots and often anti-western slants of Japanese films and TV shows.

It provides good coverage of the six annual sumo wrestling tournaments and has a classified ad section for goods, services and accommodation of interest to foreigners. It is released on Fridays and can be picked up at the TIC, most large hotels, the American Pharmacy, many supermarkets and pubs or restaurants catering to foreign clientele (mostly in Roppongi and Akasaka).

Single copies and subscriptions are available in Japan and overseas from: Tokyo Weekender, Oriental Building, 55-11 Yayoi-cho 1-chome, Nakano-ku, Tokyo 164.

Books

There are numerous books available covering specific aspects of Tokyo and surrounds.

Footloose in Tokyo, by Jean Pearce (Weatherhill, Y1500), is a series of walking tours in the vicinity of the 29 stations of the Yamanote loop line. It gives background not only on the specific area but also on Tokyo and Japan in general.

Around Tokyo, Vol 1 & 11, by John Turrent & Jonathan Lloyd-Owen (Japan Times, Y1200), are compilations of columns from the *Japan Times* describing a large number of well-known and obscure attractions in Tokyo and vicinity.

Tokyo Now & Then, by Paul Waley (Weatherhill, Y5000), describes Tokyo in great detail as it is now and how it was then; with many interesting anecdotes to bring to life the things you can see.

More Footloose in Tokyo, by Jean Pearce (Weatherhill, Y1200), covers the Shitamachi area plus Narita in a manner similar to her earlier book – a walking tour with descriptions of what you're seeing and its significance/history.

Discover Shitamachi, by Enbutsu Sumiko (name written Japanese style, published by the Shitamachi Times, Y1500), deals with Shitamachi in greater detail than Jean Pearce's book, making it somewhat heavier reading but it contains more insights and information than the other book.

A Parent's Guide to Tokyo, by Hartzenbusch & Shabecoff (Shufunotomo, Y1500), is a collection of articles originally printed in the *Tokyo Weekender* with the theme of where to take children (and teens and tourists) for amusement in Tokyo. The articles were originally written in 1973 and generally updated in 1981.

Tokyo City Guide, by Connor & Yoshida, is (if not out of print) a well-regarded and lively aid for seeing and appreciating this giant city.

THINGS TO SEE

How do you begin to look around a city that is home to 12 to 14 million people? Is it even possible to explore Tokyo? Certainly not all of it but there are ways to nibble at parts to get some idea of the whole.

In the past, Tokyo was described as a collection of villages; except for the fact that many of these villages are now cities in their own right with city centres of large stores and commercial buildings, the description is still valid.

In Edo days (to about 1867) there were two major divisions of Tokyo – Shitamachi (pronounced 'Sh'ta-machi', meaning 'downtown') for the common folk, and Yamanote ('near the mountains') for the wealthy and powerful. (The Yamanote train line largely encircles the Yamanote area, hence its name.)

Although a centre of power since the early 1600s, there is little of historic interest in Tokyo. This is partly because Kyoto continued to be the imperial capital with the figurehead emperor, his court and the elaborate structures (such as temples and palaces) that went with it through this period, while Tokyo was more a military and administrative centre that did not attract such grandiose construction. It is also because the great Kanto earthquake and wartime bombing destroyed much of the city.

In the following pages are listed the major areas of interest, and it should be enough to keep most people busy for a couple of days. For more detailed explanation it is advisable to obtain one or more of the many guide books to Tokyo that have been published in recent years; they give vastly more detail on the attractions of this city than can possibly be crammed into a general book of this sort.

For a quick introduction to the city, ride the Yamanote loop for one circuit of the city, a trip of about an hour. This will show how so much of the city is made up of low (one or two-storey) houses interspersed with taller apartment and commercial buildings. Since the line passes through most of the major sub-city areas, it gives a view of the tremendous amount of development taking place in these clusters.

All of Tokyo, with the exception of some small pockets in the Shitamachi area, was quite literally flattened by bombing during the last stages of WW II. Photos from that time show vast expanses where not a building was left standing as far as the eye could see. The contrast with today, only 45 years on, is phenomenal.

The first post-war buildings were ticky-tacky, flimsy wooden structures, a few of which still stand here and there through the city. The next generation saw these replaced by generally drab and dreary, but functional, concrete structures. With the incredible increase in wealth in Japan in the past 10 years or so, these are progressively being replaced by archi-tectural showpieces, often of imaginative though sometimes non-functional (but eye-catching) shape.

These new buildings are giving an entirely new and stylish look to many parts of the city, initially in the fashionable areas, but also in local neighbourhoods. Walking through some of these nouveau riche areas (like Harajuku and Roppongi) makes one realise that Tokyo is developing into a city that ranks well in the world for physical attractiveness – something unimaginable 15 years ago.

Part of the enjoyment of Tokyo is just looking around at some of the more attractive, or outrageous, of its physical assets.

In the end, Tokyo is rather surprising. At first glance it appears to be a rather featureless jumble of uninspiring, often drab, buildings, but after a little looking around you come to appreciate it for what it is – a huge community with many interesting places to see and things to experience; a place that grows in appeal with each day or year.

There are many places in Japan with more readily identifiable attractions but none offers the combination of a giant metropolis with everything and the local village atmosphere that exists just under the surface.

For a better understanding of the character of the various elements that make up this enormous city, it is worth spending the money on Jean Pearce's book *Footloose in Tokyo*.

The best way to tackle Tokyo successfully is to read the following pages, pick up a map and literature from the TIC, obtain copies of *Tour Companion*, pick out the places of interest and go!

Ginza, Hibiya & the Imperial Palace

If any part of Tokyo were to be called its heart, it would be the Ginza district. In this one area are branches of nearly all the country's major department stores, many other high fashion shops and the most expensive restaurants and drinking establishments – for *very* big spenders only.

Close by is the Marunouchi financial district and just a short walk away is the reason why this area first came to prominence, the Imperial Palace.

Dating from Edo days, this was the area where the higher ranks of society obtained their necessities and fineries, and the tradition has continued.

Imperial Palace Grounds One might expect a magnificent castle to stand in Tokyo, as they once did in Osaka and Nagoya, but Tokyo never had such huge buildings despite the quite massive walls and embankments that can be seen. It is not possible to enter the actual palace grounds except on 2 January and 23 April – New Year and the Emperor's birthday. At other times visitors must be content with a stroll around the moats and a look at the fortifications and the scenic east garden.

If starting from the TIC, just turn left and go a couple of hundred metres to where a moat comes into view to the right, then continue along until the first road across the moat. This leads to a large open park area, Kokyo-mae Hiroba (Imperial Palace Plaza), and further on Kokyo Gaien (Imperial Palace Outer Garden).

The large, open, pedestrian-only area to the left leads to Nijubashi bridge which gives the only good view into the grounds. With the bridge in the foreground this is a typical Japanese castle view – a fortification wall with a white defensive building atop it. (A newspaper report said that Nijubashi was the most-photographed place in Japan – almost invariably as backdrop for a photo of visitors.)

A few minutes walk north (use the Tokyo map from the TIC for these explorations) brings you to the entrance of Higashi Gyoen (East Garden) which is open most days until 3 pm. Entry is through some of the massive stonework of the original defensive walls and the garden has many of the attractive features of Japanese gardens.

A small zig-zag bridge here is unusual, being of Chinese derivation and seldom seen in Japan. In Chinese mythology evil spirits can only move by hopping and can turn only with great difficulty. By walking in zig-zags, as here, the spirits hop into the water and drown. (The same story explains why there is a high sill to step over when entering the gate of a temple; the evil spirits cannot hop over it.)

The only other sightseeing relative to the palace is to stroll at leisure along the moats around the walls. Except during the cherry blossom season there is little incentive to go beyond the Sakuradamon gate. When the blossoms are out, however, the area at the top of the hill and beyond has some of the most magnificent displays of this short lived spectacle in the country.

The path around the palace is a well-known jogging route, with distance markers. The nearby Imperial Hotel (successor to the one designed by Frank Lloyd Wright) has a jogging map.

The moats, by the way, are home to a large number of graceful swans and in winter attract many migratory birds including some, like the mandarin duck, that are quite exotic for the centre of a huge city.

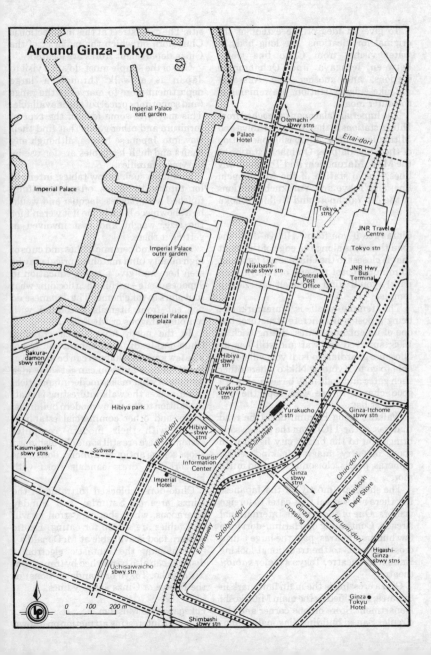

To give an idea of the extent of the original fortifications, the long body of water visible from Chuo line trains between Ichigaya and Ochanomizu stations, and another near Akasaka-mitsuke subway station, are remains of the outer moats.

The Imperial Palace can be reached from Hibiya stations of the Chiyoda, Hibiya and Mita subway lines; Nijubashi-mae station of the Chiyoda line; Otemachi station of the Mita, Marunouchi and Tozai subway lines; Tokyo station of the Marunouchi line; and Tokyo and Yurakucho stations of the JR Yamanote and Keihin-Tohoku lines.

Ginza Area If you follow Hibiya-dori (the road that runs along the edge of the moat that is closest to the Ginza area) for about 15 minutes (past the end of Hibiya-koen park) you'll find yourself at Zojo-ji temple.

The temple itself is unremarkable, being a post-war concrete structure, but one of its entrance gates, dating back to 1605, survived the war and still has its Niosama guardian gods. If you will not be able to go to Kyoto or Nikko where other such gates and gods may be seen, this is a good chance to see who kept the evil spirits at bay.

Walking along Harumi-dori (the road that passes the TIC) from the palace soon brings you to the bright city lights with shops of every imaginable kind selling cameras, pearls, cloisonne ware and much more.

The shops are mostly for the Japanese but there are several that cater to foreign visitors. One of these is the International Arcade. Continuing on Harumi-dori for a few hundred metres, past the large Ginza crossing, leads to the traditional-looking Kabuki-za theatre, Tokyo's major *kabuki* theatre.

Ginza crossing is the main landmark in this area, identified by the main Mitsukoshi Department Store on one corner and the circular San-ai building diagonally oppo-site. The cross street at this intersection is Chuo-dori, on which the majority of the Ginza department stores are located.

One of the simple must-do's of a visit to Japan is a walk through a large department store to marvel at the range (and sometimes price!) of goods available. This may give some idea of the type of furniture and other goods that find their way into Japanese homes, although any chairs and high-leg tables are for use by untypical families.

Furniture such as low tables, intended for *tatami* living, is often beautifully finished with flawless lacquer and would be a showpiece back home if it weren't for the size, weight and cost involved in getting it there.

Lacquer and ceramic dishes and cups of high quality (and matching price) may be seen here and give a quick education in Japanese taste – useful when deciding what souvenirs to take home. The Japanese do not eat from utensils decorated with temples, dragons or Mt Fuji.

To the north from Ginza crossing, Chuo-dori leads to Akihabara and Ueno. The few km to Akihabara can be walked in about an hour and you can get some idea en route of what makes modern Japan tick. What makes the walk interesting is that, in addition to the many modern buildings, banks and other commercial establishments with their modern computer systems, there are still some old-fashioned shops selling antiques, kimono, dolls, fans or zori (the dress sandals worn with kimono).

Chuo-dori is blocked to traffic in the Ginza area on Saturday and Sunday afternoons, when shoppers stroll at will and tables are set up for eating. Exotic western food is available at McDonald's.

Akihabara, the fantastic electronics district, can also be reached by train (from Yurakucho, Tokyo or Kanda stations) or the Hibiya or Ginza subway lines.

Fukagawa Edo Museum
This is an interesting attraction on its own

in an otherwise uninteresting area. It is worth seeking out as it has a masterfully produced representation of the appearance of the Fukugawa district of Tokyo (then Edo) around 1840.

In a large building specially constructed to house them are replicas of shops, houses, stalls and storehouses, exactly as they would have appeared at that time. There are eight complete buildings and three facades.

Although all new, the materials have been realistically weathered to look genuinely aged and every detail of construction is authentic. The lighting changes regularly to give a sense of changing time of day and sound effects reinforce the impression of being in a real community, from the crowing rooster to the sound of peddlers.

A sense of humour is evident, including a dog beside the fire watch-tower with raised hind leg. Admittance is Y300, and the English booklet (Y500) is a worthwhile investment. Professionally produced in perfect and enjoyable English, it describes the many features of the buildings that would not be self-evident. It tells the story of such a community from the point of view of the people who would have lived there and unobtrusively slips in the history of the area and the country.

The museum is reached by first going to Kiyosumi-koen garden (on the JNTO Tokyo map); across from it are two old-fashioned lanterns on each side of a narrow road. The museum is a couple of hundred metres down this road, on the left. The easiest way to get to Kiyosumi-koen is to go to Monzen-Nakacho station (Tozai subway line), take exit 3, and catch a No 33 bus from in front of the pachinko parlour. Get off at the fourth stop, Kiyosumi-koen park. You can also walk north along Kiyosumi-dori (near the station) for about 15 minutes, or south for the same amount of time along the same street from Morishita station of the Shinjuku subway line.

Akihabara

To gain a good appreciation of the state of technology in Japan it would be hard to beat a visit to Akihabara. This is the electrical wholesale and retail centre of Tokyo and has by far the largest concentration of electrical and electronics stores in the world.

There are literally hundreds of shops. Some are tiny hole-in-the-wall cubicles selling a single product line (transformers, electrical meters, etc), while others are huge multi-storey electrical department stores.

Even visitors from countries that are well served with a variety of electronic goodies will be amazed to see so many models and even some products that are never seen outside Japan. For details on buying electrical goods in Japan check the Things to Buy section in the Facts for the Visitor chapter.

Even if you are not buying, just wandering around the area and taking the escalators inside some of the buildings is an interesting way to spend some time.

The JR Akihabara station has an exit to the side of the tracks where most of the shops are located (to the left when arriving from Tokyo station, or toward Shinjuku if arriving from that station.)

It is a bit confusing getting out of the station; from the Shinjuku direction it is necessary to take the central stairs down to the next level of platforms, then find the correct exit. The Hibiya subway Akihabara station exits on the wrong side of the JR tracks, so it's necessary to find one of the cross streets to the main area. The simplest way to get to the main area is to exit from the rear of the train (when coming from the Ginza direction) and find the farthest exit in that direction. At ground level there is a service station on the corner. That road leads under the JR tracks to the main area.

Ueno

Attractions of the Ueno area are the zoo (not one of the world's greatest), the

National Science Museum (many working exhibits showing how some scientific and technological items function), Tokyo National Museum (primarily art and history), Toshogu shrine and a historic five-storey pagoda.

The zoo is very popular for its pandas, over which the Japanese went wild when they were first introduced. At the south of Shinobazu-ike pond is Shitamachi Fuzoka Shiryokan, which is a small museum of shops and houses of the type once common in Tokyo before WW II bombing and the 1923 Kanto earthquake destroyed them.

During the brief cherry blossom season, thousands of revellers set up parties on any patch of open ground in Ueno-koen park. The object is to appreciate the beauties of the blossoms, although after consuming copious quantities of sake, many have difficulty even distinguishing light from darkness, let alone appreciating the finer points of the blossoms. Still, it is an object lesson for many other cultures, how a huge number of people can get absolutely rotten drunk without becoming belligerent. Japanese usually just sing louder, if a bit more off key, the drunker they get.

An area that was the site of the post-war black market, and which has continued selling low-priced goods, is Ameyoko, across from the south exit of Ueno station. A sign over the entrance street identifies it in *romaji*.

Here you are likely to find 'Rolex' watches and 'Gucci' goods for a couple of thousand yen. Don't believe for an instant that they are the real thing. Counterfeiting famous-brand goods, while not as rampant as in Hong Kong, is still a big business in Japan and there doesn't seem to be a heavy emphasis on stamping it out. Even big-name department stores have been taken in by these goods. Have fun, but be careful.

The sub-map of the Ueno district in the JNTO map *Tourist Map of Tokyo* is sufficient for looking around this area.

From the station area, you can walk along the broad Asakusa-dori toward Senso-ji temple. It is a major thoroughfare, so local colour is lacking unless you wander around the back streets. There are many shops selling Buddhist funerary items, such as large and ornately carved *butsuden* (family altars where memorial tablets are kept) and large lotus leaves, all brilliantly decorated with gold leaf.

Along Kappabashi-dori (shown clearly on the JNTO Tokyo map), just north of the crossing with Asakusa-dori, are many stores selling equipment for restaurants. Several stores sell the incredibly realistic plastic replicas of food of the type seen in restaurant windows everywhere in Japan. Unfortunately, they are not cheap (a single piece of *sushi* costs about Y700) but they are all hand-made and the artisans making them take up to 10 years learning the craft. Anyone with the money could purchase an entire feast. Kappabashi-dori is between Inaricho and Tawaramachi subway stations, a little closer to the latter.

Shitamachi

In Edo days, Shitamachi was the area in which the common people lived and worked and where most of the ordinary trade was carried out. The people were unrefined, spontaneous and lacking in the reticence imposed on the general populace by the decrees of the Tokugawa rulers.

The people still living in this area regard themselves as a breed apart from the rest of Tokyo's residents and many of the old attitudes and ways of life survive, although it, like every other part of Japan, has changed much in the past decades.

There is no place marked 'Shitamachi' on a map; it is an ill-defined area generally to the east of the Yamanote line, from above Ueno to the Tsukiji area. It was an artificial creation of the shogun who wanted to keep all less-desirable elements in one area where they could be watched more easily.

The famous Yoshiwara pleasure district

was an important part of the scene, taking care of the sexual desires of all men of Edo. Although prostitution was made illegal in 1958, the same sort of activities go on under a different guise (*soaplands*), both in the old Yoshiwara district and everywhere else in Japan.

The heart of Shitamachi is Asakusa Kannon temple, properly known as Senso-ji. A visit can be combined with a walk through some of the back streets.

The temple is very active with worshippers praying for some sort of assistance, lighting bundles of incense and catching the smoke to rub on afflicted parts of their bodies to relieve an ache or pain, or just plain enjoying themselves. The approach is lined with shops selling all manner of tourist junk. The shopping street is often described in terms like 'street of gaily decorated souvenir shops'.

As a single place to visit, the temple is less than enthralling. Both Senso-ji and its five-storey pagoda are only post-war concrete reproductions, and thus lack any of the features of workmanship that make historic Japanese temples so remarkable. If you are going to Kyoto later, you will see much finer and older temples with extraordinary woodwork.

However, the temple can be interesting for just watching the people and it most definitely *is* worth visiting during its annual festivals in March and October. The festivities feature a Chinese-style dragon. Held up by numerous poles, it twists and writhes around the temple courtyard in a most remarkable way. Times are given in *Tour Companion* but they have sometimes been wrong in the past so get there an hour or so before the listed time to avoid disappointment.

Senso-ji temple can be reached by Ginza or Asakusa subway to Asakusa subway station, or by a special double-decker bus from Ueno station (as well as regular buses, but they have no markings in English). Upon arriving at the large Kaminarimon gate, look diagonally across the main road for the local

information office. It is set up to give assistance in English for sightseeing in the area. The books *More Footloose in Tokyo* and *Discover Shitamachi* are invaluable for exploring this area in depth.

After sightseeing near the temple, an alternative to the usual way back is to take the water taxi down the Sumida-gawa river. This trip takes about an hour and ends at Takeshiba pier, beside Shiba Rikyu and Hama Rikyu gardens, close to Hamamatsu-cho JR station at the edge of the harbour and near Tsukiji fish market. The starting point is just upstream (to the left) of the bridge across the Sumida-gawa river, a short distance beyond the subway station. The location is shown clearly on the JNTO Tokyo map.

Shinjuku

Shinjuku is the up-and-coming sub-city of Tokyo. Due to its geological stability (an important factor in earthquake-prone Japan) it has Tokyo's only collection of high-rise buildings. It is also the place to go for the best camera shopping and has a large percentage of the entertainment establishments of the city.

The high-rises are all located on the west

(or 'new city') side of Shinjuku station, which is reputed to be the busiest in the world, and a good contender for the title of 'most confusingly laid out'. On this side, down the small side streets, are the main stores of Yodobashi and Doi camera stores, as well as any number of other shops specialising in computers, watches and just about anything else you can think of.

The Highway Bus Terminal for buses to the Mt Fuji and Hakone areas is close to the main Yodobashi store and is clearly shown on the TIC map. This part of Shinjuku has also attracted a number of large hotels; in one small area there is the new Hilton, Century Hyatt, Keio Plaza, Shinjuku Washington and many others. Adjacent to Shinjuku station are two major department stores, Odakyu and Keio; trains of the same line leave from stations in their basements.

The east side of the station has most of the major department stores and many fashion-oriented shops. The two largest camera stores, Yodobashi and Sakuraya, have their 'showpiece' branches side by side facing the small square overlooked by a TV-type giant screen (which is made up of thousands of light bulbs). The Nakano building next door, by the way, is on the most valuable piece of real estate in Japan.

Nearby, the Kinokuniya bookstore has large numbers of foreign-language books (mostly English) and its ground level entrance is a popular meeting place because of the shelter it offers.

Nearby are hundreds, if not thousands, of restaurants and drinking places, many catering to the university graduates in their twenties through to unmarried office workers in their early-thirties, although sections of Shinjuku have attractions of interest only to males. Until a new law came into effect in February 1985, the sex scene was virtually uncontrolled, but police can now enter any establishment without a warrant and all such businesses must close by midnight and touts are prohibited.

One thing that hasn't changed is the large involvement of yakuza gangsters in the operation of many, if not all, of the sex-oriented (and even regular drinking) establishments and there is still the risk of being stuck with a horrendous bill for a single drink.

If you walk in or are enticed into a place with large numbers of hostesses sitting with customers, it is advisable not to sit down unless you have established in advance what it will cost you. The Y18,000 glass of beer was invented in places like these.

Meiji-jingu Shrine

Meiji-jingu shrine is probably the finest shrine in Japan and well worth a visit. It was built early this century to honour emperor Meiji who reigned during the eventful period from 1867 to 1912, which saw Japan change from a self-isolated feudal country to a world power, largely under the guidance of this emperor and his advisors. The shrine was destroyed during the war and rebuilt afterwards in the original style.

The shrine grounds are extensive and heavily wooded, offering a respite from the bustle of the city. Its broad paths lead to the main shrine building, a simple structure of traditional style and the finest of materials and craftmanship.

Because of its exalted status among the shrines of Japan, it is a popular place for blessings for various events and you can often see such ceremonies being performed by priests in traditional costumes.

Visiting the shrine is particularly worthwhile on 15 January, 'Coming of Age Day', when countless young women in beautiful kimono attend Meiji-jingu as part of the customary celebrations. It is very crowded but a wonderful opportunity to take many colourful photos.

Another good day to visit is Shi-go-san festival day on 15 November when young children dressed in very ornate kimono are taken there. New Year's Day, although a customary time to visit the shrine, is not recommended as the grounds are incredibly packed.

The entrance to the shrine is close to Harajuku station (Yamanote line) or Meiji-jingu-mae station of the Chiyoda line.

明治神宮御苑拝観券　　大人

Entry ticket to Meiji Jingu Garden

Yoyogi-koen Park & Harajuku District

Close to Meiji-jingu shrine are Yoyogi-koen park and Omote-Sando Boulevard, as well as the youth fashion shopping district of Harajuku.

Omote-Sando ('main approach to a shrine') is a high-fashion shopping district. Being one of Tokyo's few tree-lined streets (short though it may be), it has some of the flavour of a Paris boulevard. Any day of the week is a good day for fashion window shopping or buying and there are some tourist-oriented shops with reasonable prices.

On Sundays, Yoyogi park is the setting for the *take-noko-zoku* ('bamboo shoot tribe') – young people who meet here every weekend, share the same outlandish costumes that identify their group and dance to music from portable cassette players. Nearly all favour '50s rock 'n' roll classics, an era known to these people only as folklore, for the rebuilding Japanese nation did not participate in it. Greased-back hairstyles are the norm and the clothes date from the rock 'n' roll era back to the zoot suit. One of the sources of the wild clothes is the back streets of nearby Harajuku, the teen fashion centre.

Harajuku is more than just the crazy youth fashions though; it also has high-fashion and high-price clothing as well as some very high-style eating places. Anyone young at heart can enjoy a stroll and will see evidence that Japan has become one of the world's wealthiest nations.

Shibuya

Shibuya, one stop by the Yamanote line south of Harajuku, is another popular shopping and entertainment area. Like Harajuku and Shinjuku, the area appeals to a particular age group, in this case those of about senior high school age. For this reason there are plenty of fast-food and generally moderately priced restaurants. It is also a high fashion area with many modern and interesting buildings and imaginative window displays.

The most famous landmark in Tokyo is the statue of the dog Hachiko; just look for a few hundred people standing around in an open area on the northwest corner of the station and you'll find it. The real Hachiko was a dog that waited faithfully at a station for months for her master (who had died at work) to return home. It is not known if the story is completely true or if it was exaggerated by the pre-war military-run government to instill in the people such a sense of devotion to duty.

The area of greatest activity is diagonally across the large intersection from Hachiko. The mall continuing the diagonal leads past the most popular restaurants, with side streets holding many more, along with amusement arcades and other teen amusements.

There are shops of all kinds along both main roads of this intersection. To reach one that is out of the ordinary, follow the road running parallel to the tracks in the direction of Harajuku and take the left fork up the hill. This very fashionable street, with British-style phone booths, trees, buildings with imaginative fronts, and department stores, leads to the Olympic Stadium (dating from the 1964 Olympics). At one intersection part of the way up the hill is a Parco department store. Turning left at this corner leads to Tokyu Hands, a store that would be out of the ordinary in any country. It must surely be the ultimate leisure craft emporium in the world, with supplies for nearly every imaginable handicraft available on its many levels. Do you want a traditional Japanese saw or plane, an ultra-accurate micrometer or miniature lathe, a model boat kit, interior decoration supplies, art materials, the makings of metal or lapidary jewellery, electrical-electronic hobby equipment, a computer, or you-name-it? It's all here, and more!

Roppongi
Roppongi has become the main playground of the people of the modelling and TV world and has numerous discos and bars as well as many restaurants. Prices cover a wide range of budgets – from student to millionaire. There are several western franchise fast-food restaurants and countless other types. However, as is the case in most of Japan, few places fit into a traveller's budget.

Roppongi is most easily reached by Hibiya subway line. The exits at the front of the train when travelling toward Ginza lead to Roppongi crossing, the main intersection. On one corner is the best-known landmark and rendezvous point, the Almond coffee shop.

The majority of the favourite entertainment places are on this side of the expressway, on both sides of the major cross road and in the many side streets running off it. It could take a lifetime to explore this territory.

Gardens & Parks
Tokyo, like most Japanese cities, has only a small fraction of the park area per citizen considered usual in western countries. Cities in Japan are for commerce and housing, and little else.

Tokyo does have a few sizeable parks that make for pleasant strolls but they would be of more interest to foreign residents than those on a short visit looking for a garden with the traditional Japanese characteristics. (The best of these in the Tokyo vicinity is Sankei-en, in Yokohama.)

The best parks in Tokyo are Korakuen garden, Rikugien garden, the National Park for Nature Study, and Shinjuku Gyoen park. All are shown on the TIC map. Others are Hama Rikyu garden and Koishikawa Botanical Garden.

The parks are enjoyable in summer when the shrill sound of the *semi* (cicada) may be heard; indeed they are often loud enough to make conversation difficult. Their 'me-me-me-me' or chirring sound is one of the memories of Japan.

Museums & Galleries
Tokyo has a large number of interesting museums and galleries. Visitors to Ueno park can visit both the Tokyo Metropolitan Art Museum and the Tokyo National Museum.

The TIC pamphlet *Tokyo* lists the main

museums that would be of interest to visitors. The *Tokyo Journal* lists the major museums, galleries (art and photo) and department-store exhibits (a major type of gallery in Japan), and the displays/themes of each for the coming month, along with the prices and special features. *Tour Companion* has a similar listing, updated weekly.

The Saturday or Sunday issues of the English-language newspapers give details of the displays for the coming week; the page from the *Japan Times* is usually posted at the TIC.

Lookouts

Several tall structures around the city offer views of the huge expanse of Tokyo. In the clear weather of winter the view may extend to Mt Fuji.

Tokyo Tower, 333 metres tall, is a slightly enlarged copy of the Eiffel Tower and has an observation lounge at the top, along with a wax museum and restaurants. Access to the first level costs Y600 and it costs an extra Y400 to get to the 250 metre level. As Tokyo is a very flat city, built at the edge of the Kanto Plain, it lacks any notable features so one of the less expensive or free viewpoints may be preferable.

The World Trade Centre building has an observatory on its 40th floor; access costs Y400. The bargain, which gives as good a view as any, is the 52-storey Sumitomo Building in Shinjuku (west of the station). The observation level is on the 51st floor; several reasonably priced restaurants (by Tokyo standards) on the top floors offer a good view along with pleasant dining.

Tokyo Disneyland

In April 1983 Tokyo gained the first Disneyland outside the USA. Built at a cost of hundreds of millions of dollars, to strict Disney standards, it offers the same type of attractions as the US original, including 'theme lands' (Westernland, Adventureland, Fantasyland, Tomorrow-land and World Bazaar), plus a number of rides (such as a Mississippi paddlewheeler and the Western River Railroad) and a variety of other forms of entertainment. The 51-metre Cinderella Castle is the focal point and symbol of the park.

Tokyo Disneyland is open every day during summer (April to August); closed on Tuesdays from September to November; and closed Tuesdays and Wednesdays from December to February (except during holidays). In summer the hours are 9 am to 10 pm; and in winter, 10 am to 6 pm. Admittance-only tickets cost Y2700 for adults, Y2300 for high school students and Y600 for children but there is then a separate charge for each attraction. A 'passport', entitling you to enter all attractions as many times as you like, for one day, costs Y4200/3800/2900 (weekdays only); and a 'Big Ten' book of tickets gets you into 10 attractions.

There are two simple ways to get to Disneyland. The first is by Tozai subway to Urayasu station, from where a shuttle bus (from the nearby terminus) runs to the entrance about 20 minutes away. The bus costs Y200 for adults and Y100 for children. The second is by a 35-minute shuttle bus ride from Tokyo station, which costs Y600. The shuttle buses leave from the Yaesu (east) side of the station; on the Yaesu side, take the north exit (kita guchi) and follow the tracks to the left.

Festivals

There are festivals in Tokyo or nearby nearly every month. The TIC has free information sheets that list all festivals in Tokyo and all over Japan.

The weekly handout *Tour Companion* is also an excellent source of info. A major festival is often the front-page feature and others during the week are also described.

Festivals are least frequent in winter, begin in spring (rice planting time), are very numerous in late summer (*Obon* season) and climax in autumn with the harvest-related festivals.

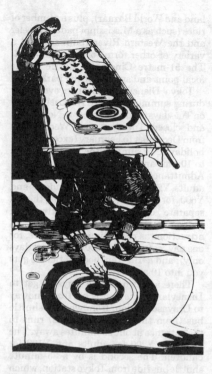

Tours

There is a variety of guided tours for seeing Tokyo. They cannot be recommended to the budget traveller as the same attractions can be seen by using public transport, this book and other tourist literature and maps, for a fraction of the cost.

However, for those who find climbing the seemingly endless stairs of the subway and train stations a bit tiring, or who only have a limited amount of time and no worries about watching their yen, a bus tour certainly offers convenience.

There are daily tours of the high spots of Tokyo for Y9000 to Y10,000, and a tour of the major industrial factories for Y10,000.

Night tours take in a glimpse (extremely brief and not really worth the high price) of a stage show, a *geisha* show, and the *kabuki* theatre, plus a *sukiyaki* dinner, for

Y12,000 to Y13,000. (Reports have stated that the stage show was abbreviated, the geisha show similarly short, and the dinner rather skimpy.) One can go to the Kabuki for as little as about Y1000 on one's own.

There are other tours to Kamakura, Hakone and Nikko but again they are very expensive compared with what it would cost using public transport.

Information about all available tours is given in *Tour Companion* and in pamphlets given out at all major hotels and the TIC.

Personally guided tours of central Tokyo and Shitamachi, using public transport for economy, are given by Mr Oka (tel (0422) 51-7673) for details.

Near Tokyo

There are many places of interest within easy travelling distance of Tokyo. They can generally be visited as day trips out of Tokyo, though an overnight stay away from the city will give a better appreciation of the more distant places.

Kamakura This is the home of the great Buddha statue, one of the most famous sights of Japan, and has several famous scenic temples.

Yokohama Yokohama has Sankei-en garden, one of the best in Japan, and also has the only Chinatown in the country.

Kawasaki The city of Kawasaki has an interesting park with numerous old thatched-roof farm houses that have been moved here from various parts of Japan. It offers the simplest way to glimpse what life was like a century or two ago.

Hakone This area takes in a scenic mountain and lake; in good weather you can get a magnificent view of Mt Fuji.

Mt Fuji The area around Fuji-san offers many scenic views of the mountain and surrounding lakes.

Kawagoe Kawagoe has a large number of well-preserved, century-old shops and houses and gives some idea of the appearance of a city of those days.

Matsumoto Matsumoto has the only

surviving authentic castle in the northern half of Japan.

Nikko Nikko city has the incomparable splendour of the Toshogu and Daiyuin mausoleums, plus lake and waterfall scenery.

Mashiko This place is the closest town to Tokyo where pottery is made in notable quantities.

PLACES TO STAY

There is a wide variety of accommodation available in the greater Tokyo area, ranging from hotels that match the world's best (with matching prices) to more modest and affordable places.

The good news for budget travellers is that the number of places catering to them has increased greatly in the last few years so the choice of places to stay is much more varied and the chances of finding a room much better. However, the number of people travelling in Japan has also gone up, so it may still be necessary to make quite a few phone calls to find a room, especially in popular seasons.

Listings of alternative sources of accommodation can be found in publications available at the TICs at Narita Airport and in the city (*Japanese Inn Group*, *Hotels in Japan*, *Japan Ryokan Guide*), in *Tour Companion*, and in *Tokyo Journal*. (The latter has the most advertisements of 'foreigner house' type accommodation, popular with travellers and those staying for longer periods.)

If you arrive in Tokyo and wish to stay at a top-end hotel, there is a desk at Narita Airport that can make on-the-spot bookings for more than 25 of Tokyo's top hotels.

Although there is private accommodation available with fewer restrictions and at similar cost, the youth hostels are quite central and they can be useful for obtaining info on the other hostels throughout the country.

If phoning for reservations, note that all seven-digit numbers listed can be dialled as local calls within Tokyo. If calling from Narita, the call is long distance and the Tokyo numbers must be prefixed by 03.

Youth Hostels

Tokyo Kok'sai (International) Youth Hostel (tel (03) 235-1107); the main youth hostel of Tokyo is a bit of a showpiece and one of the best in Japan, as befits the municipally operated hostel in the nation's capital. Located on the 18th and 19th floors of a new high-rise building, it has a good view over the north of the city and has enormous baths and comfortable rooms.

Hostel regulations are similar to those encountered throughout Japan, possibly a bit more relaxed; the doors close at 10.30 pm (and don't open until 6.30 am – which is a bit awkward if you need to catch an early flight) and visitors can normally stay for only three days.

The hostel is municipally owned so you don't need to be a YH member to stay; a passport for identification is sufficient.

Room charge is Y1650 per night plus about Y250 if heating or air conditioning is in use.

The hostel can be reached by JR and two subway lines as follows (all stations are named Iidabashi); the JR Chuo (yellow) line, running between Akihabara and Shinjuku, is the most convenient transport to the hostel. You can transfer to this line from the Yamanote and Keihin-Tohoku lines (through Ueno) at Akihabara, and at Ochanomizu from the Chuo (orange) line. Leave the station at the front of the train (if coming from Akihabara) then turn right at the street and walk downhill about 20 metres. Turn right into the open plaza area and walk into the arcade covered by the arched glass roof, to the elevators (on the left); the left hand bank of elevators goes to the top floors and the 18th floor reception desk.

The Yurakucho subway line, from Yurakucho (near Ginza) and Ikebukuro, brings you closest to the hostel at Iidabashi station, but it has the fewest transfers from other lines. These can be made only from the JR station at Yurakucho (walking distance from Ginza and Hibiya subway stations), at Nagatacho from the Hanzomon line (from Shibuya), and from the Shinjuku line. At Iidabashi station, exit from the station at the rear of the train (if coming from Ichigaya), follow signs for exit B2, and finally take exit B2a. At street level, walk uphill the short distance to the JR station, and turn left into the plaza described previously.

The Tozai subway line runs between Otemachi/Nihombashi and Takadanobaba. You can transfer at Otemachi (Marunouchi, Chiyoda and Mita lines), Nihombashi (Ginza line), Kayabacho (Hibiya line), Kudanshita (Shinjuku line) and Takadanobaba (Yamanote line); both the Ginza and Hibiya lines pass through Ueno.

The other hostel is *Yoyoji Youth Hostel* (tel (03) 467-9163) which is in one of the dorms constructed for the Tokyo Olympics. You can get there from the Shinjuku station of the Odakyu railway (on the west side of JR Shinjuku station) by local (non-express) train to Sangubashi, the second stop. Exit the station, take the small road to the left across the tracks, take the pedestrian bridge to the other side of the large road and continue to the right to the entrance gate of what looks like a university or school. The hostel is on the grounds.

The hostel can also be reached via Harajuku JR station or Meiji-jingu-mae or Yoyogi-koen stations of the Chiyoda subway lines, but these require a longer walk.

There are also youth hostels in Chiba city (tel (04757) 4-1850; in the region of Narita Airport), and in Yokohama (tel (045) 241-6503) and Kamakura (tel (0467) 25-1238), both within an hour of Tokyo on the west side.

Private Accommodation

Okubo House (tel 361-2348); this place is in a category all its own. Although it is privately owned, it requires guests to leave by 10 am and has a midnight curfew.

However, because of its singular nature and the fact that it has been a fixture for foreign travellers for years, it deserves some extra space.

Okubo House was originally a workman's dormitory until it was discovered by foreigners and it has been a mainstay since then. It has mostly dorm rooms (male only) for Y1500, but has some single/double rooms starting at Y2900/Y3900. (A good tip: take your bath early! The Japanese workmen living there have never heard of the Japanese etiquette that requires soaping before getting into the tub. They sluice one bucket of water over themselves, then hop into the tub and methodically start rubbing off all the dirt . . . into the water.)

Okubo House is near Shin-Okubo station (Yamanote line); turn left from the station exit, then left again at the first side street and walk almost to the T-junction about five minutes away.

Foreigner Houses

In recent years quite a few private homes have opened as communal-type accommodation with shared cooking facilities, one or more common-rooms with TV, and dormitory and individual bedrooms (singles, doubles).

There are no curfew regulations as there are with the youth hostels and Okubo House so guests can come and go at will. Most offer cheaper weekly and monthly rates and many guests stay on for months because of the community atmosphere that develops.

These 'foreigner houses' are the closest equivalent to the cheap hotels found on the travellers' route through South-East Asia and India.

Because of the number of places in the following list it is only possible to give their general location, so you need to phone ahead and ask directions. In many cases one of the guests will answer the phone so getting instructions in English should be no problem.

In some cases there is more than one

house; the phone number given is for the coordinating centre.

In the case of some of the popular places for which there is a waiting list (such as Yoshida House) the owner has alternative accommodation (sometimes dormitory style) where guests can stay while waiting for a private room.

The following list is alphabetical, with the lowest daily single room or dorm charge only. Most places have doubles at higher cost.

Ajima House (tel 366-0484) Y2000; Musashi-Sakai station of Chuo line, 20 minutes west of Shinjuku.

Apple House (tel 962-4979) Y1700; Oyama station near Ikebukuro station by Tobu Tojo line.

B I House (tel 200-7082) Y35,000 monthly; two locations; Oizumi-gakuen station and Chofu station.

Better Houses (tel 776-7023) Y12,500 weekly.

Bilingual House (tel 200-7082) weekly/monthly; three houses on Seibu-Shinjuku and Keio lines.

Cosmopolitan House (tel 825-0816) Y38,000 monthly; Shinjuku station.

Egerton House 'Masuoka' (tel 381-7026) Y2000; Nakano station.

English House (tel 988-1743) Y1700; near Mejiro station on Yamanote line.

Evergreen House (tel 713-4958) Yutenji station.

Fantasia Guest House (tel 372-5296) Y1600; Nakano-sakane station.

Foreigners' House Masuoka (tel 381-7026) weekly/monthly; Nakano (close to Shinjuku by Chuo line); several houses.

Friendship House (tel 314-7441) Y1300/1400; Hachimanyama (Keio line) or Higashi-koenji (Marunouchi line).

Fuji House (tel 967-4046) Y1200; Shimura-sanchome station (Mita line).

Fujikan (tel 813-4441) Hongo-Sanchome station.

Green Peace (tel 915-2572) weekly/monthly; Kami-Nakazato station (out of Ueno or Shinjuku).

Happy House; weekly/monthly; Ukimafunado station (JR Saikyo line; 16 minutes from Shinjuku).

House California (tel 209-9692) monthly;

Kami-Kitazawa station (Keio line) or Tanashi station (Seibu-Shinjuku line).

Ijinken (tel 235-1107) Y30,000 monthly; Edogawabashi station.

International House California (tel 209-9692, 376-7605) Y1600; Kami-Kitazawa station 12 minutes by Keio line ex Shinjuku.

Japan House (tel 962-2495) Y1300; Senkawa station (Yurakucho line from Ikebukuro) or Kamata station Keihin-Tohoku line from Shinagawa).

Kitty House (tel (0424) 84-6070) Y30,000 monthly; Keio-Tamagawa station.

Koma House (tel 915-4183) Y1000; very popular; Komagome station.

Kotani House (tel 962-4979) Ikebukuro station.

Let's Go World House (tel 479-1425/6) different locations out of Shibuya (one stop) and Shinjuku (15 minutes).

Magome House (tel 754-3112) Y1600; near Nishi-Magome station of Asakusa subway line.

Maharajah Palace (tel 748-0568/9) weekly/monthly; Ishikawadai station (Ikegami line from Gotanda, 12 minutes).

Mickey House (tel 936-8889, 371-2252) two houses; Y1300; near Kami-Itabashi station (Tobu Tojo line from Ikebukuro) Y1600; near Takadanobaba station (Yamanote line).

Midori House (tel 754-3112) monthly; Nishi-Magome station (Asakusa line).

Natural Stone House (tel (0473) 68-0802) Matsudo station.

Okubo House (tel 361– 2348) Y1400; Shin-Okubo station.

Rikko Kaikan (tel 972-1151) Y3500; Ekoda station.

Shinjuku Guest House (tel 353-5627) weekly/monthly; Shinjuku area.

Sun Academy (tel 904-0062) non-smoking; Shakuji-koen station (Seibu– Ikebukuro line; 10 minutes).

Taihei English House (tel 558-9351 (918-0709 after 7 pm] Y1300; Itabashi-Honcho station (Mita line).

Tokyo English Center) tel 360-4781 (360-1666 night); Y1600; Higashi-Nakano station (JR Sobu line).

Tokyo English House (tel 384-0918) Y1600; three locations: Honancho (Marunouchi subway, four stops past Shinjuku), Higashi-Ogikubo (10 minutes by Chuo line west from Shinjuku) and Toritsu Daigaku (just past Naka-Meguro by Toyoko line).

Tokyo House (tel 995-5306, 391-5577) Y1350; Shakuji-koen station (Seibu-Ikebukuro line) or Ogikubo station (JR Chuo or Marunouchi subway line).

Tokyo English Mansion (tel 384-0918) perhaps only monthly; two locations.

Tokyo International House (tel 945-1699) Y1000 to Y2000 (one week minimum); several locations in central Tokyo.

Tokyo Student Apartments (tel (0473) 96-9740).

Toyama Houses (tel (0422) 49-8938) several locations on the west side of Tokyo.

Yoshida House No 1 (tel 649-9544) Y900; popular place; Kiba station. *YTC House* (tel 946-5266, 576-5255) Y1600; Nishi-Sugamo (Mita line).

Ryokan & Minshuku

As mentioned previously, staying at a *ryokan* or *minshuku* is probably the best way to experience what life is like in a Japanese house. Most places have a range of prices (with and without private bath) and rates may be lower by the week. An asterisk (*) indicates a member of the Japanese Inn Group. The prices listed are for the cheapest category for single/double.

Only the closest stations are listed. If you have the JNTO Tokyo map, you can check if a listed subway station is close enough to a railway station (JR, Keisei, etc) to take a taxi instead of having to transfer to the subway. This could be more convenient for the *ryokan* near Ueno station.

Chujosu Minshuku (tel 378-3810) Y3300; near Shinjuku station of JR and Marunouchi subway.

Chome-ikan Ryokan (tel 811-7205) Y4500; Hongo-Sanchome station (Marunouchi subway).

Fuji Ryokan (tel 657-1062) Y5500; Koiwa station (JR Sobu line) or Keisrei-Koiwa station (Keisei line).

Fujikan Ryokan (tel 813-4441) Y3200; Hongo-Sanchome station (Marunouchi subway).

*Inabaso Ryokan (tel 341-9581) Y3900/7000; Shinjuku station (JR Yamanote and Sobu lines or Marunouchi subway).

*Katsutaro Ryokan (tel 821-9808) Y3600/6800; Nezu station (Chiyoda subway) or Ueno station (JR Yamanote or Keihin-Tohoku lines/Keisei line or Hibiya subway).

Kimi Ryokan (tel 971-3766) Y2000/4000; excellent information centrte; Ikebukuro station (JR Yamanote line or Marunouchi subway).

Kikaku Ryokan (tel 403-4501) Y12,000 (twin); Sendagaya station (JR Sobu line).

*Kikuya Ryokan (tel 841-6404) Y3500/5500; Tawaramachi station (Ginza subway).

Koshinkan Ryokan (tel 812-5291) Y4000; Nezu station (Chiyoda subway).

Miyako Hotel (tel 200-2180) Y3740/6820; Takadanobaba station (JR Yamanote line or Tozai subway).

*Mikawaya Bekkan Ryokan (tel 843-2345) Y4500/8600; Asakusa station (Ginza or Asakusa subway).

Nagaragawa Ryokan (tel 351-5892) Y5000/8000; Yotsuya-Sanchome station (Marunouchi subway).

Namiju Ryokan (tel 841-9126) Y4000/7000; Asakusa station (Ginza or Asakusa subway) or Tawaramachi station (Ginza line).

*Okayasu Ryokan (tel 452-5091) Y3600/6600; Tamachi and Hamamatsu-cho stations (JR Yamanote or Keihin-Tohoku lines).

*Sansuiso Ryokan (tel 441-7475) Y3800/6800; Gotanda station (JR Yamanote line or Asakusa subway).

*Sawanoya Ryokan (tel 822-2251) Y3600/6600; Nezu station (Chiyoda subway).

Seifuso Ryokan (tel 263-0681) Y6000; Iidabashi station (JR Sobu line or Tozai or Yurakucho subway).

Shimizu Bekkan Ryokan (tel 812-6285) Y6000; Hongo-Sanchome station (Marunouchi subway) and Suidobashi or Kasuga station (Mita subway).

Shinriki Business Hotel (tel 731-4706) Y4600/7600; Kamata station (east exit; JR Keihin-Tohoku line).

Shoheikan Ryokan (tel 357-0551) Y7000/12,000; Yotsuya station (JR Sobu line or Marunouchi subway).

*Suigetsu Hotel (Ohgaiso Building) (tel 822-4611, 828-3181) Y3500/6000; near Nezu station of Chiyoda subway, Ueno area.

Tokiwa Hotel (tel 202-4321) Y4400/9900; Shin-Okubo station (JR Yamanote line).

*Sukeroku-no-yado Sadachiyo Bekkan Ryokan (tel 842-64311) Y4000/7000; Tawaramachi station (Ginza subway).

Tsukuba Hotel (tel 834-2556) Y3700; Inaricho station (Ginza subway).

Yashima Ryokan (tel 364-2534) Y3000/4600; Okubo station (JR Chuo yellow line from Shinjuku station) or Shin-Okubo station (JR Yamanote line).

PLACES TO EAT

Tokyo has an incredible range of eating places, ranging from modest stand-up soba (noodle) shops to posh restaurants and nightclubs serving international cuisine at international prices. Although out of the price range of the average traveller, French cooking second only to the best offered in France is available in Tokyo, as is other top-rated international cooking.

A guide to the higher level places and a few moderately priced ones as well, is the book *Good Tokyo Restaurants* by Rick Kennedy.

There are extensive listings and advertisements for various kinds of restaurants in the *Tokyo Journal*, *Tour Companion* and *Tokyo Weekender*; the first two give some indication of the price range.

Japanese office workers and students depend on the countless restaurants in the vicinity of the major stations for the majority of their bought meals, so the prices there are about as reasonable as can be expected in Japan. All the popular entertainment areas, like Shinjuku, Harajuku, Shibuya and even Ginza, have many reasonably priced restaurants and beer halls. They usually have wax replicas of the food, with prices, in the window so it's easy to order and there are no surprises when the bill arrives.

There are many *Shakey's Pizza* and *Pizza Hut* shops throughout the city with a Monday to Saturday special from 11 am to 2 pm of all the pizza you can eat for about Y500. There are also other well-known American fast food outlets like *Kentucky Fried Chicken*, *McDonald's* and *Wendy's*. The young Japanese have taken to these with a passion so there will

only be more and more as time goes by. There is an outlet of at least one of them near every main train or subway station and they offer the greatest bargains in terms of value for money (with the bonus of being familiar).

There are also some branches of American restaurant chains like *Victoria Station* and *Red Lobster*, though these are not budget eateries. If you look around you'll find there is no problem finding virtually any kind of food in Tokyo.

ENTERTAINMENT

Visitors to Japan have the chance to see a variety of traditional Japanese performing arts, while foreign residents need not worry about being cut off from western varieties of entertainment.

Kabuki

There are several theatres in Tokyo where the colourful *kabuki* is performed. Kabukiza and Shimbashi Embujo are well set up for English-speaking audiences, having radio earphone commentaries on the play as it progresses. The earphone devices rent for Y600 plus a refundable deposit. (These may not be available for use in the cheapest seats.)

Programme notes in English may also be available at the theatre, giving a detailed description of the action, act by act.

Prices are lower for matinees and there is sometimes a reduction for foreign visitors with their passport. Prices start in the Y1500 range. There are performances much of the time but some weeks there will be none.

For listings of presentations playing, with a summary of the stories, look at *Tokyo Journal*, *Tour Companion* and the Saturday *Japan Times*. The TIC will also be able to give such information.

Noh

Noh drama performances are given at a variety of theatres. Up-to-date information is available from the same sources listed for *kabuki*.

Bunraku

Bunraku puppet plays are occasionally presented in theatres such as Kokuritsu Gekijo. Information is available from the same sources as for Noh and *kabuki*.

Music

In addition to the traditional Japanese performing arts, there is a surprising variety of western-type entertainment. Road shows of western pop and rock performers regularly appear in Tokyo (some famous western singers have actually springboarded to fame beginning in Tokyo).

Stage shows are popular. One of the best known is the Takarazuka Revue in which all parts are filled by women.

There are several symphony orchestras and smaller chamber groups of high quality. Concerts are given regularly. The best listing of these events is in the *Tokyo Journal* and *Tour Companion*. Prices are

high, typically Y3000 to Y5000 per ticket.

Cinema

Foreign movies are shown with their original soundtracks and Japanese subtitles. They are usually screened in Japan soon after their release overseas, with runs lasting between a few days and several weeks.

Typical admittance price for first-run films is Y1500. The best listing of films is *Tokyo Weekender*. There are also 'cheap movies', reruns at lower prices; check *Tokyo Journal* and *Tour Companion*.

THINGS TO BUY

Tokyo is probably the best place in Japan for shopping for Japanese antiques, handicrafts and modern optical and electronic goodies, but refer to the Things to Buy section in the Facts for the Visitor chapter before setting out.

The Akihabara area is the place for the greatest variety of electrical and electronic goods at their lowest prices. Several stores

have departments or floors to display models specially designed for use overseas (correct voltages and specifications). Another source of such models, though their prices may be higher and the variety more limited, is the shopping arcades in large hotels and the International Arcade, which is more-or-less under the railway tracks in the Yurakucho area, close to the TIC.

Japanese dolls are available in the department stores, as well as in other shops. There are several types (faces and hands, in addition to costumes and prices). The department stores are also a good source of items used by the Japanese in every day life such as lacquerware, pottery and other ceramic goods. Department stores are generally not the bargain centres they are in western countries but have a name for above-average goods, in both quality and price.

There are several flea markets held in Tokyo on an irregular and regular basis. Because of the changeable nature of the date, time and venue of these it is best to contact the TIC for details.

GETTING THERE & AWAY
Air

Nearly all international flights to Tokyo arrive at Narita Airport (Narita Kuko) located 66 km out in the countryside east of Tokyo. A minimum of 1½ hours (usually considerably more) is required to get from there to central Tokyo, making it one of the world's most inconveniently located major airports.

A high-speed rail service was included in the planning stage but less than 1% of the land required for the rails was ever purchased, and the present system for getting into Tokyo was cobbled up from existing rail lines plus a new bus service. (The authorities would prefer that the public not know but there is a blocked off station for the planned rail service beneath the terminal building.)

Narita 'errport' (as it has been called) is

Narita Airport

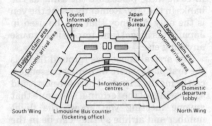

Japan's contribution to the world's collection of vast projects started on half-vast ideas. It would have been better to enlarge the existing and infinitely more convenient Haneda Airport, which would also have avoided the opposition to Narita (from farmers and student radicals) that still continues, with occasional sabotage and other disruptive tactics.

For this reason you will probably encounter a police check when entering the airport for outbound flights and will see scores of riot-control police around the airport. These security measures account for the high airport departure tax of Y2000.

There is one possible way to avoid all the problems of Narita Airport: fly China Airlines. Their flights land at Haneda Airport so you avoid the problem completely. Unfortunately this isn't possible for everyone as CAL is usually heavily booked.

Arrival at Narita

If you have to use Narita, you will find that the airport has well-signposted routes through quarantine/health, immigration and customs check points. If you are planning to obtain a Shore Pass, look for the mobile desk at the entrance to the immigration-check hall.

Before leaving the customs hall (after clearing customs) you can purchase Japanese currency at a window at the centre of the row of exit doorways. Other money changers are in the arrival lobby and on the departure (fourth) level. The rates at these places are the same as the banks in the city. Remember that the yen is the only currency that can be used in Japan; it is illegal (and impossible) to use anything else.

The arrival concourse (ground floor) is the first place where incoming passengers can be met by friends. There are north and south wings of the terminal so be sure that anyone meeting you knows the flight number and airline so they can be in the right place. It would be more courteous to arrange to meet them in Tokyo because of the inconvenience and cost involved in getting out to the airport.

Before heading into Tokyo, stop at the TIC office for any information and JNTO brochures and pamphlets. The small office is tucked away, almost out of sight, at the junction of the central block and the south wing, on the side nearest the runway; it is sometimes omitted from airport directories. Other 'information centers' in the centre of each wing are generally useless because most of the staff don't speak English.

The TIC information that will be of immediate use is *Tourist Map of Tokyo*

(405-E), *Map of Tokyo & Vicinity* and *Tokyo* (222-E); the last is available in several languages.

They also have listings of low-cost accommodation but these might be for reading on the premises only, not given out.

The *Tourist Map of Tokyo* has the best subway map available, with place names in both Japanese and Roman characters (*romaji*); it's very useful when faced with a fare chart written only in Japanese.

The TIC is open from 9 am to 12 noon and 1 to 8 pm on weekdays, and on Saturday mornings. Unfortunately the JNTO doesn't recognise that travellers arrive seven days a week at all times of the day and night.

Another counter in the concourse can arrange accommodation in one of more than 25 hotels in Tokyo. These hotels, however, begin in the moderate price range and work upward.

The Japanese Railways (JR) counter, at the centre of the central block, can give info on JR services, make bookings and sell tickets. There are usually English-speaking personnel on duty. They can exchange a Japanese Rail Pass voucher for

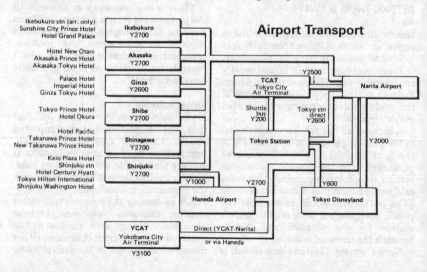

Airport Transport

Ikebukuro stn (arr. only) Sunshine City Prince Hotel Hotel Grand Palace	Ikebukuro Y2700	
Hotel New Otani Akasaka Prince Hotel Akasaka Tokyu Hotel	Akasaka Y2700	
Palace Hotel Imperial Hotel Ginza Tokyu Hotel	Ginza Y2600	
Tokyo Prince Hotel Hotel Okura	Shiba Y2700	
Hotel Pacific Takanawa Prince Hotel New Takanawa Prince Hotel	Shinagawa Y2700	
Keio Plaza Hotel Shinjuku stn Hotel Century Hyatt Tokyo Hilton International Shinjuku Washington Hotel	Shinjuku Y2700	

TCAT Tokyo City Air Terminal — Y2500 — Narita Airport

Shuttle bus Y200 / Tokyo stn direct Y2600

Tokyo Station — Y2000 — Narita Airport

Y1000 — Haneda Airport — Y2700 — Y600 — Tokyo Disneyland

YCAT Yokohama City Air Terminal Y3100 — Direct (YCAT-Narita) or via Haneda a pass. However this operation might be better done in Tokyo after you've had time to settle down and plan your travels; it does not have to be changed immediately. JR is not a recommended way of getting into Tokyo from the airport.

Next to the JR counter is an information and ticketing counter for the Keisei rail line, one of the two most convenient ways of getting into Tokyo. Reservations for their Skyliner train can be made here and they will probably have copies of their timetable in English.

On the other side of the JR counter are counters for Toyota and Nippon (Hertz) car rental agencies. No one in their right mind would try driving in Japan on first arrival but brochures could be useful for future reference.

Only two means of getting into Tokyo from Narita Airport are practical: Keisei railway and the airport bus; any others are too expensive or inconvenient. A taxi would cost a small fortune (about Y14,000 in fact) and a hire car about double that.

JR trains are costly, infrequent, slow and leave only from JR Narita station, a longish bus trip from the airport. Do not endorse your Japan Rail Pass just so you can use JR into Tokyo! JR can be recommended only if you're going immediately to the Chiba and Boso-hanto peninsula area. Buses for the JR Narita station leave from in front of the central block; more details are available at the JR info counter.

Narita to Tokyo

For many travellers, the most convenient transport (though not the cheapest) into the Tokyo area is by one of the many buses – misleadingly called 'limousines'. The bus service has the added advantage that you do not have to carry your baggage any further than the terminal exit.

Buses run from the airport terminal to a number of destinations in the city, some to hotels and railway stations and some to the Tokyo City Air Terminal (TCAT). The

hotel and station buses are the most convenient way into the city, then the Keisei railway and lastly the TCAT buses.

Hotel Buses Buses run to hotels and stations (between two and four hotels in any one area) in different parts of Tokyo as follows: Shinjuku (Keio Plaza, Century Hyatt, Shinjuku station); Shinjuku (Hilton, Shinjuku Washington, Shinjuku station); Akasaka (New Otani, Akasaka Prince, Akasaka Tokyu); Ginza (Palace, Imperial, Shinbashi Dai-Ichi, Ginza Tokyu); Shiba (Tokyo Prince, Okura); Shinagawa (Pacific, Takanawa Prince, New Takanawa Prince); Ikebukuro (Sunshine City Prince, Grand Palace); and to Tokyo station.

Only buses to Tokyo station and the Shinjuku area run throughout the day, leaving Narita as early as 6.50 am; services to the other area begin around 4pm and end around 9pm. The latest buses to Tokyo station are at 9.35 pm and to the two Shinjuku areas at about 10 pm.

The major shortcoming of the hotel buses is that they run no more frequently than once an hour, and may be much further apart. The trip takes from 80 to 120 minutes but can take up to an hour or more longer during the rush hour.

The fare to the hotels and stations is Y2700, half price for children and the handicapped. The buses leave from well-marked locations (just look for the incorrect word 'limousine') in front of both wings. Tickets may be purchased at counters inside both wings.

Keisei Trains The least expensive way into Tokyo is by one of the Keisei line trains which are more frequent and not much more complicated than the hotel buses. Trains leave from Narita-kuko station, six minutes from the air terminal by frequent shuttle bus (from position four in front of each of the wings of the airport terminal).

Tickets combining the bus and train

fares can be bought at the Keisei counter in the airport terminal, or separately on entering the bus and at the train station. The total price is the same.

There are two types of service on the Keisei line: 'Skyliner' trains which run non-stop to the terminus at Ueno on the northeast side of Tokyo; and two slightly slower (but cheaper) express runs – *tokkyu* (special express) and *kyuku* (express). The Skyliner takes one hour, and the *tokkyu* and *kyuku* take 73 and 90 minutes respectively. The cost of the latter two is about Y800, while the Skyliner has a Y700 surcharge.

Skyliner seats must be reserved; this can be done at the terminal counter or at Narita-kuko station. There is one non-smoking car (Kin-en-sha) that can be requested when reserving a seat. Skyliners leave from tracks 1 and 2; the others leave from tracks 3 and 4.

Ueno is the best station in the city for access to Tokyo International Youth Hostel and destinations in the northeast of Tokyo. From Keisei-Ueno station transfer is easy to JR Ueno station and the Ginza and Hibiya subway lines.

There are usually two Skyliner departures an hour, at about 20 and 50 minutes past the hour, although there is only one some hours. The last Skyliner leaves at 10 pm. Staff at the Keisei counter at the terminal or at the station can give information.

There is also a timetable available at the TIC office in the airport and another posted on a pillar facing the ticket machines at the station. On timetables lacking English, a Skyliner is usually identified by a blue dot, a *tokkyu* train by a red circle and a *kyuku* by a red triangle. The last train into Ueno leaves at 10.32 pm, reaching Ueno at 12.14 am.

Those travellers who do not wish to go to Ueno or that side of Tokyo may find the following useful. Some *tokkyu* and *kyuku* trains (about 15 per day) switch off the Keisei tracks at Aoto and run on the tracks of the Asakusa (pronounced 'Asak'sa') subway line as an Asakusa line train to its

normal destination. The terminus (marked on schedules) is Nishi-Magome, on the southwest side of Tokyo and the trains pass south of the centre of the city, skirting Ginza. You can transfer easily to JR lines at Asakusa-bashi, Shimbashi and Gotanda and to other subway lines as follows: Hibiya line at Ningyo-cho and Higashi Ginza; Ginza line at Asakusa; Mita line at Mita. Also, at Sengakuji, you can change to a Keihin-kyuku train for Kawasaki, Yokohama and through Yokosuka to the tip of the Miura-hanto peninsula.

The last of the direct Nishi-Magome trains leaves around 5.20 pm but don't despair if you arrive later. Take any regular (non-Skyliner) train bound for Ueno and get off at Aoto. Board the next train arriving at platform 1. This may go through to Sengakuji or Nishi-Magome, or may stop after six stations at Oshiage. If the latter, take a train from platform 1 for Nishi-Magome, or from platform 3 for one that switches off at Sengakuji for Kawasaki, Yokohama, etc. Staff at the Keisei counter or at the station can help with info.

Buying a ticket at Narita-kuko station is no problem despite the almost incomprehensible markings and fare chart. Just go and buy the lowest price ticket from machines three to eight and pay the difference at the destination; the cost is the same but make sure you hold on to your ticket. The mystifying sign over the machines 'Y1000 note available' is supposed to convey the message that the machine will accept a Y1000 note (and give change). This misleading use of English is typical of what you will find throughout the country. Welcome to Japan!

The first part of the trip in from Narita is through farming country with many rice paddies and even one thatched-roof house, visible to the right of the train.

TCAT Buses The other bus service into Tokyo (also misleadingly called a 'limousine') has as its destination the Tokyo City Air Terminal (TCAT) at Hakozaki, 2½ km from Tokyo station. Like the hotel buses, it is touted as offering the advantage that one has to carry bags only to the exit of the terminal and that the bus takes it directly to TCAT. What is not mentioned is that TCAT is off in a corner of Tokyo rather remote from subway or JR stations.

To proceed from TCAT, the choices are a taxi (rather expensive to almost anywhere in the city), the regular shuttle bus to Tokyo station (from where the JR tracks are about 10 minutes away and the subways even further) or a walk to Ningyo-cho or Kayaba-cho subway stations.

The closer of these is Ningyo-cho, on the Asakusa and Hibiya lines. To reach it, exit from the front entrance (to under the expressway), turn right, cross the street, and walk straight along the broad street; the station entrance is on the right hand side. After the trudge of about 15 minutes, with ever-heavier luggage, you find that this is one of the stations served by the train from the airport station to Nishi-Magome, and all the bother of the bus could have been bypassed completely.

Kayaba-cho station is reached by using the last directions to a few blocks along the broad street, then turning left at the first major cross-street and continuing over a bridge and on some distance more. This station is on the Hibiya and Tozai lines, the latter convenient for reaching Tokyo International Youth Hostel.

The cost of the bus is Y2500 (half price for children and the handicapped) and there are departures every five to 30 minutes. The nominal travel time into the city is one hour though this can be double or more during morning and evening peak traffic. Buses (identified by the word 'limousine') leave from in front of both wings of the airport terminal and tickets can be bought at well-marked counters inside the building.

Haneda Airport

Haneda is the airport that is used nearly all domestic flights; there are only about 10 from Narita. The most convenient way to transfer from Narita to Haneda is by bus (another 'limousine'). The fare is Y2700, departures are every 20 to 50 minutes and the trip is scheduled to take 80 minutes (except during traffic slow-downs). For safety, you should allow at least 4½ hours between scheduled arrival at Narita and scheduled take-off at Haneda.

An alternative to the bus (for the adventurous) is to take the Keisei/Asakusa line route to Shimbashi, transfer to the JR Yamanote or Keihin-Tohoku line as far as Hamamatsucho, then take the monorail from there. This might halve the fare but at the expense of much more time and effort.

If your first destination in Japan is a city other than Tokyo, it is best to try and get an international flight to a point closer to it. In most cases, however, Osaka and Nagoya are the only other major airports with large numbers of connections and there are no major international airports north of Tokyo.

Haneda to Narita Transfer between these airports can be made most easily by the 'limousine' bus (Y2700). Buses operate between 9.10 am and 8.50 pm. It's wise to allow about 4½ hours for connections between flights at the two airports.

Haneda to Yokohama The simplest way is by bus (from Haneda Tokyu Hotel) to Yokohama City Air Terminal (YCAT). The alternative is monorail to Hamamatsucho and JR from there.

Haneda to Kawasaki There is a bus service which runs between Haneda Airport and Kawasaki station every 20 to 30 minutes. The trip usually takes about 25 minutes and costs Y200.

Narita to Yokohama

Passengers destined for Yokohama will find that the bus service (another 'limousine') to Yokohama City Air Terminal (YCAT, not far from Yokohama station) is by far the quickest and most convenient way, taking a nominal two hours. Buses leave every 20 to 50 minutes, and the fare is Y3100. The 'adventurous' (and slower) way to Yokohama is via the Keisei/Asakusa line route. Transfer to either the JR Tokkaido or Yokosuka line at Shimbashi, or to the Keihin-kyuko line at Sengakuji. The JR route is much faster, though a little more expensive. Either way takes longer than the bus, but costs less than half the bus fare.

Because of the running contretemps between the governments of Taiwan and (mainland) China, Taiwan's national airline, China Airlines, was denied the dubious privilege of using Narita when Japan recognised the Peking government. China Airlines have been crying all the way to the bank ever since because they have the most convenient service into Japan of any airline. They have several flights a week from Taipei and the US west coast but advance bookings are required because of the airline's understandable popularity.

Nearly all Japan's domestic flights use Haneda Airport, which is connected to the JR rail system of Tokyo by the monorail. The way from the airport terminal to the monorail station is clearly marked and tickets are available from vending machines, which give change. The monorail terminus is at Hamamatsucho, on the south side of Tokyo, one of the stations on the JR Yamanote and Keihin-Tohoku lines.

Departure from Narita

Sage advice for anyone who is going from Tokyo to Narita Airport is to begin your trip four hours prior to your departure time. This allows for traffic delays and missed connections plus the security check (if using the Keisei route),check-in, immigration formalities and so on.

The most convenient ways to get out to the airport are (in order) hotel bus, Keisei train and TCAT bus.

Hotel Buses The earliest buses from the Shinjuku area, which stop at four hotels and Shinjuku station, leave at 6.24 and 7.04 am. Buses also leave the other hotels listed in the section on getting from the airport to the city. The Tokyo TIC has up-to-date information on the exact departure times throughout the day.

Keisei Trains Narita Airport can be reached using the Keisei railway starting from either Keisei-Ueno station (in Ueno) or from any station along the Asakusa subway line.

Keisei-Ueno station is close to Ueno stations of JR and of the Hibiya and Ginza subway lines. The easiest access from the JR station is to leave the train platform by the overhead passageway at the north end (away from Tokyo station), walk along the passage toward track No 1, exit, cross the road, turn left and walk down the hill; to the right, about 50 metres along is the entrance to the underground Keisei station. The transfer from the subway lines is well marked and should be no problem.

Skyliner tickets can be bought in advance at JTB offices and Keisei-Ueno station as well as the airport terminal and station buildings.

If you are travelling from the central or southwest parts of Tokyo, the service by the Asakusa subway line is the most convenient as it allows easy transfer from other lines, as described in the section covering the trip in from Narita. About 20 trains a day on this line continue past the usual terminus at Oshiage and go all the way to Narita-Kuko station. The trains are rather irregularly scheduled through the day so it is wise to plan in advance to be sure of getting the right train. The TIC usually has timetables of Keisei trains.

Top: View of Mt Fuji (IMcQ)
Left: Kaga Yuzen (silk printed by a resist process) is washed in the clear river water, Kanazawa, Central Honshu (AE)
Right: Daibutsu (the great Buddha) at Kamakura, near Tokyo (IMcQ)

Top: Nihon Matsuri festival, Tokyo (IMcQ)
Left: Dragon dance at Asakusa temple, very much of Chinese origin (IMcQ)
Right: Typical summer festival in Tokyo – carrying a mikoshi (portable shrine) (IMcQ)

The desired trains are listed as originating from Nishi-Magome.

If there is no Asakusa line train going directly to the airport at the time you want to go (or if you miss the right train), carry on to Aoto and catch one of the expresses coming from Keisei-Ueno bound for Narita (city) or Narita-kuko (airport) station. Some local trains also pass through Aoto, as do some that stop prior to Narita. Signs on the station (tracks 3 and 4) identify the terminus of every train, in *romaji*, so these local ones can be avoided.

Some trains of the Asakusa line terminate at Oshiage, six stations before Aoto. If you get one of these, simply take the next train on to Aoto and change as just described.

If your train goes only as far as Narita (city) station, walk to platform 5 and catch a train for the airport station, the next stop.

From Narita-kuko station (the terminus), take the shuttle bus for the short trip to the airport. There is a security check prior to boarding the bus so have your passport ready. They may inspect your baggage but the officials are usually more thorough with the luggage of Japanese passengers because of the continuing series of terrorist attacks on the airport by student radicals.

Bus from TCAT The third recommended way to get to the airport is the 'limousine' bus from TCAT which runs direct to the departures level at the terminal. Many (but not all) airlines permit complete check-in at TCAT, so you don't have to touch your bags again until your final destination. For these airlines, a bus is assigned to each flight and the flight is held if the bus is held up. To allow for potential traffic problems, check-in at TCAT is typically three to four hours ahead of departure.

At TCAT, everything is self-explanatory, buses operate throughout the day, departing at five to 30 minute intervals.

The fare is Y2500. The trip is scheduled to take one hour but this can double in heavy traffic.

Apart from taxi (not cheap) there are two ways to reach TCAT: subway and shuttle bus. From Ningyo-cho subway station (Hibiya and Asakusa lines), there is a sign, 'For Tokyo City Air Terminal' on each platform directing passengers. At the street-level exit, turn left and walk 10 to 15 minutes to the overhead expressway, under which TCAT is located.

If you're walking from Kayaba-cho subway station, the TIC Tokyo map gives clear enough directions. (Remember that the same Asakusa line that takes you to TCAT could also be used to go directly to the airport, as detailed above.)

The other way to TCAT is by shuttle bus from Tokyo station every 10 to 40 minutes, or from various hotels at irregular times. The bus from Tokyo station leaves from in front of the TDA office opposite the front entrance (Yaesu side, the side remote from the Tokyo Central Post Office). If you arrive there by Marunouchi subway line, you will have to walk 10 to 15 minutes under the station via an underground passageway (there are signs 'To Yaesu side'); from JR trains it is somewhat less. The shuttle bus costs Y200 and takes 10 minutes.

After check-in at Narita Airport, you can shop for duty free items in the terminal buildings; you can also buy after passing through immigration. Remember that airport departure tax is Y2000. Turn in any certificates for tax-free purchases just before the immigration check. The ground won't open up and swallow you if you fail to do this. It is largely an exercise to keep the bureaucrats employed.

YCAT to Narita As described in greater detail in the Yokohama section, the simplest way to Narita Airport is by bus from Yokohama City Air Terminal. Buses leave every 20 to 50 minutes, the trip takes about 90 minutes and the fare is Y3100.

Getting to Haneda
Tokyo to Haneda To go from Tokyo to Haneda Airport is a simple process; go to Hamamatsu-cho station (JR Yamanote or Keihin-Tohoku lines), follow the signs to the monorail, buy a ticket, ride the train, and you're there.

Yokohama to Haneda The most convenient way for one to reach Haneda from Yokohama is by bus from YCAT. They leave every 20 to 60 minutes and take about half an hour.

Domestic Flights
With the exception of a very few flights out of Narita, all domestic air transport to and from Tokyo goes through Haneda Airport. Haneda is easily reached by monorail from JR Hamamatsu-cho station.

There are direct flights from Tokyo to about 35 different cities, while even more are accessible with a transfer at the other major regional airports of Sapporo, Osaka, Nagoya, Fukuoka and Naha (Okinawa). Sample air fares are given in the Getting Around chapter.

TRAIN
Japan Railways (JR)
Shinkansen There are three super-express Shinkansen lines linking Tokyo with the most important regions of the country.

The Tokaido Shinkansen line runs through Nagoya and Kyoto to Osaka, at which point the name of the line changes to Sanyo Shinkansen (no change of train needed). The trains continue through Okayama and Hiroshima to the terminus at Hakata in northern Kyushu.

Tokaido Shinkansen trains leave from Tokyo station and do not stop in the metro Tokyo area.

The Tohoku Shinkansen runs northeast through Sendai to Morioka and the Joetsu Shinkansen runs north via Takasaki to Niigata on the north coast; both leave from Ueno station.

These are the most important trunk

lines in Japan, linking the majority of the biggest cities. They are explained in more detail in the Getting Around chapter.

Tokaido Line Trains of this line begin at Tokyo station, offer express service to Kawasaki and Yokohama (28 minutes) and continue some distance down the coast, generally as far as Atami, Odawara, Shizuoka or Toyohashi.

From these latter stations there are connections on to Nagoya and from there to Kyoto and Osaka. These trains stop at many stations and are considerably slower than Shinkansen service over the same route.

Within the Tokyo area, these trains stop only at Shimbashi and Shinagawa. This line, along with the Yokosuka line, is the quickest route to Yokohama.

The Tokaido line trains that stop at all stations are regarded as *kaisoku* express service and there is no surcharge for them.

Fast expresses (*kyuku* and *tokkyu* trains) that bypass nearly all stations are, of course, much faster but there is a surcharge.

Only trains leaving late in the day (after about 6 pm) run directly to Nagoya. About three trains leave late at night and reach Osaka early the next morning but these are uncomfortable as the seats are nearly bolt upright. One night train has sleepers and another has reclining seats available.

Yokosuka Line Trains begin at Tokyo station, provide express service to Yokohama (28 minutes) and continue on through Kamakura (about one hour) and Yokosuka (about 80 minutes) to Kurihama at the bottom of the Miura-hanto peninsula. All Yokosuka line trains are *kaisoku* expresses so there is no surcharge. Trains leave Tokyo station every five to 15 minutes.

Within metro Tokyo they stop only at Shimbashi and Shinagawa stations. Most begin as Sobu Hon-sen line trains from

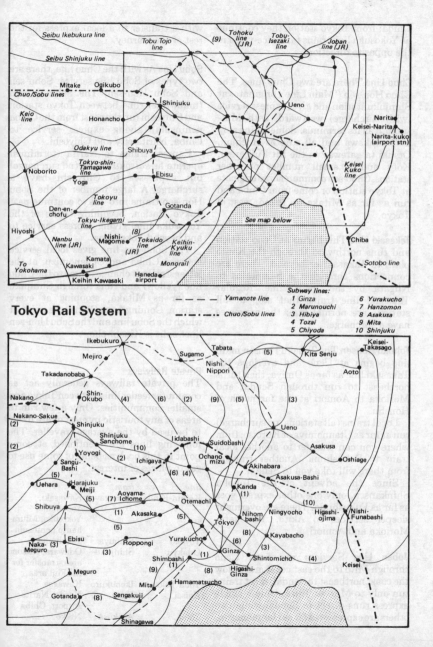

Tokyo Rail System

--- Yamanote line
-·-·- Chuo/Sobu lines

Subway lines:
1 Ginza
2 Marunouchi
3 Hibiya
4 Tozai
5 Chiyoda
6 Yurakucho
7 Hanzomon
8 Asakusa
9 Mita
10 Shinjuku

Chiba; from Tokyo station they continue as Yokosuka line trains (and vice-versa in the opposite direction).

Chuo Line There are two Chuo lines. The Chuo Hon-sen ('Main Line') originates at Shinjuku station and gives express service (with surcharge) westward, with Matsumoto as its terminus. Some trains stop at Tachikawa and all stop at Hachioji, Otsuki (a gateway to the Mt Fuji area), Kofu and a small number of other stations. Chuo-sen commuter lines originate at Tokyo station or come from Chiba and run as far as Mitaka or Takao, west of Tokyo.

Takasaki Line This begins at Ueno station and runs northward through the Kanto plain to Takasaki or beyond. There are connections through the mountains to Niigata by the Joetsu line. Regular Takasaki line trains that stop at all stations are normal fare; the expresses have a surcharge.

Tohoku Honsen The Tohoku Honsen main line begins at Ueno and overlaps the Takasaki line as far as Omiya, then turns northeast to run through Sendai and Morioka to Aomori at the far north of Honshu.

Local trains (all stations, no surcharge) run as far as Utsunomiya or Kuroiso, from where you can transfer to another local train to Fukushima. Another transfer from there will take you to Sendai.

Since the advent of the Tohoku Shinkansen, only one other express goes as far as Fukushima. There are overnight sleeper services to Akita, Yamagata, Morioka and Aomori.

Joban Line Services run from Ueno through Mito to the east coast and follow the coast northeast to Sendai; most trains run only to Mito or Taira. Only a single express runs direct to Sendai while two others are expresses as far as Haranomachi,

with a transfer to a local express for the rest of the journey.

Sobu Line As with the Chuo line, there are two types of Sobu line service: Sobu-sen and Sobu Hon-sen. The Sobu-Honsen (main line) runs between Tokyo station and Chiyoshi (up the coast from the Chiba peninsula) giving express service to Chiba, Narita city and Chiyoshi.

Express trains to Narita (terminus) operate as *kaisoku* trains (no surcharge) but expresses to Chiyoshi have a surcharge. A large number of the Sobu Hon-sen trains into Tokyo continue past Tokyo station, becoming trains of the Yokosuka line, giving express service to and beyond Yokohama.

The Sobu-sen line gives local service between Chiba and Ochanomizu; at the latter station it changes name to the Chuo line (yellow) and runs through Shinjuku as far as Mitaka, stopping at every station. Coming from Chiba, the point at which the Sobu line and the Sobu Hon-sen lines split is Kinshi-cho.

Private Railways

The private railways generally act as commuter feeder lines between Tokyo and smaller communities. Only a few run to areas of any touristic interest or are likely to be used by the average traveller. The following lines are mentioned at some point in this book as being of some use to get to places of interest.

line	from	to
Keihin-Kyuku	Shinagawa	Kawasaki, Yokohama, Yokosuka, Miura-hanto peninsula
Toyoko	Shibuya	Yokohama
Odakyu	Shinjuku	Odawara, Hakone area, transfer for Mt Fuji area
Tobu Tojo	Ikebukuro	Kawagoe
Keisei	Ueno	Narita, Narita Airport, Chiba
Tobu	Asakusa	Nikko

The JNTO's *Tourist Map of Tokyo* has one map showing the private lines and the subway lines that run to their starting stations. The subway lines are not identified by name but the accompanying subway map shows the private lines as black lines so the two maps can be used in conjunction to identify the starting points.

BUS

There is a growing number of expressway bus services out of Tokyo. These are described briefly in the Getting Around chapter.

Among these are buses to Nagoya, Kyoto and Osaka, Yamagata, Sendai, the Mt Fuji/Hakone areas and several other points toward the north.

Now that the expressway link northward has been completed from Tokyo, there will probably be in increase in services in that direction.

FERRY

Ferries from Tokyo and vicinity offer reasonably cheap transportation to a number of distant parts of Japan, with the bonus of a 'sea cruise' and the economy of saving accommodation costs for one or two nights.

From Tokyo, there are ferries to: Tomakomai and Kushiro (Hokkaido); Nachi-Katsuura (Kii-hanto peninsula); Kochi and Tokushima (Shikoku); Kokura (northern Honshu); and Naha (Okinawa).

There are also ferry services from nearby Kawasaki to Hyuga (western Honshu), from Oarai (near Mito) to Tomakomai and Muroran (Hokkaido) plus several boats to the nearby Izu islands.

GETTING AROUND

Tokyo has a comprehensive public transport system. Although large and complex, it is easy to use once you understand it and is the cheapest way to get around the city.

The system consists of suburban feeder buses, 11 private railways, 10 subway lines in two separate (though linked) systems, JR train lines, and city buses. The major shortcoming is that there is no system of free transfers between systems; a separate fare is required for each. You must keep your ticket and surrender it at the end of the journey (except on buses).

Try to avoid the peak periods of 7.30 to 9.30 am and 4 to 6.30 pm; there are millions of people on the move and it will seem they are all in your coach. It is also a time that will go a long way towards destroying any illusions about the 'exquisitely polite Japanese', as they have no compunction about squeezing past you to get ahead entering or leaving a train, or about putting a hand (or, more politely, the back of their wrist) in your back and pushing as soon as the doors open.

Using the System

On JR and private train lines and the subways, tickets are sold by vending machines. Fares are shown on a large map over the machines but they are almost invariably in *kanji* only. The JNTO *Tourist Map of Tokyo* is invaluable here for its two transportation maps. *Communications Network* shows the names of all private and JR railway lines in the greater Tokyo area in both *romaji* and *kanji*; *Subways in Tokyo* does the same for the subway lines within the city and the railway lines that continue from many of them. Each subway line has a colour code that is used to identify the line on maps and on signs in stations showing the route to follow for a transfer.

Most subway and JR stations have hand-out maps of the lines for the convenience of foreigners but they show the name only in *romaji*. To ask for a map, say: *Densha no chizu-o kudasai*.

One way around the fare problem is to buy the lowest fare ticket and pay the difference at the Fare Adjustment window at the destination (or to the ticket taker). A perplexed look when standing at the ticket machine will probably prompt some assistance.

Some ticket machines have a single large number, like '120'; they sell a single value ticket. Most machines have a row of buttons for selecting the fare (two rows actually; the bottom one is for children's tickets). The machines give change so it is safe to insert coins in excess of the fare. The most recent machines can be truly confusing, even for Japanese residents, as they have buttons for nominating the transfer station, the transfer line, the number of tickets, and other options. Fear not; you will be able to work it out!

If you put coins into the wrong machine and realise the mistake before pushing a fare button, you can get the coins back by pushing the button marked とりけし (torikeji). If you buy a ticket for a fare higher than required, take it immediately to the Fare Adjustment window (on the inside of the entrance wickets), or push the button marked よびだし (yobidashi) and ask for a refund. This is also the button to push if the machine jams and keeps your money. You cannot get a refund of excess payment at the end of your journey.

Commuter passes are available and permit an unlimited number of trips between any two stations in the Tokyo area (and all stations in between). A pass can cover travel on one other (connecting) transport system, so a JR pass could take in a transfer to a connecting subway line. Passes are for travel between two specified stations and are available for three or six months, so will be of more interest to residents.

Special day-excursion tickets are available. The JR pass is called a Free Kipu, and is valid for unlimited travel on JR trains for one day within the bounds of the Yamanote line. For the subways, posters advertise a 'Free Ticket'. It is tempting to write to the authority, thanking them for their generosity and requesting some free tickets, but I doubt that they would see the humour. This

misuse of English is all too common in Japan.

Note that it is often quicker to reach a destination by using a combination of JR and subway than to use one system exclusively but it will be more costly because separate tickets are required for each.

JR Trains

The government-operated JR (koku-tetsu in Japanese) runs several lines in the Tokyo area. Most important are the Yamanote loop line that circles the city in both directions, the Chuo line that crosses the city, and the Keihin-Tohoku line (which overlaps the Yamanote line between Shinagawa and Tabata). Other lines feed into these.

Fares are a minimum Y120 and are charged by distance. At any JR station in Tokyo it is possible to buy a ticket to any station in Japan, except for Shinkansen and reserved seat tickets which must be purchased at a station with a Green Window.

Every JR station in the Tokyo area (and generally throughout the country) is identified by signs over the platform in romaji as well as Japanese, but they are rather high and difficult to see when standing in a train. There aren't many signs so watch carefully when entering a station.

On either the overhead sign or on another sign at platform level there is normally the name of the station in large kanji and romaji, and in the lower left and right corners are the names of the next station in either direction.

On each platform, hanging overhead near the edge of the platform and at right angles to the tracks, is a small sign giving the names of major stations ahead along that line; there is usually one sign in romaji.

The number of signs in romaji indicating the route to follow to change trains, or for particular platform or station exit, varies widely. Tokyo station is well marked with illuminated and colour-coded signs in English, while Shinjuku, an extremely busy station, has the illuminated colour signs but nearly everything is in Japanese.

On JR lines, remember that *kaisoku* trains are semi-expresses, skipping several stations thereby giving faster service but without the surcharge usually applied to express services.

Yamanote (loop) Line Yamanote trains are green or have green stripes.

The Yamanote line circles the central part of Tokyo. Trains run in each direction at very frequent intervals through the day, tapering off later at night. Like all trains in the Tokyo area, service stops soon after midnight, although these trains are usually the last public transport to stop for the night.

There are 29 stations around the loop. Making a complete circuit takes about an hour and is a good introduction to the city. Three of the stations (Tokyo, Ueno and Shinjuku) are the starting points for JR intercity trains. All the 11 private suburban railways begin at their own stations adjacent to stations of the Yamanote line. (Many of these lines connect directly with subway lines.)

Keihin-Tohoku Line Keihin-Tohoku trains are blue.

Trains of this line run from south of Yokohama into Tokyo and north to Omiya, stopping at every station. From Shinagawa (southwest Tokyo) to Tabata (north Tokyo) they run parallel to the Yamanote line around the east side of the city, and either line may be used over this distance.

Chuo Line Chuo trains are yellow or orange.

There are three Chuo lines but as the Chuo Hon-sen line is an express line heading west from Shinjuku station it is not relevant here.

Chuo yellow trains stop at every station across the city from Shinjuku to Akihabara. Actually, they travel between Mitaka (some distance west of Tokyo) and Chiba (to the east), providing local service (every station). Between Akihabara and Chiba it is known as the Sobu line.

Chuo orange trains begin at Tokyo station and give *kaisoku* express service to Shinjuku (and vice versa). En route they stop only at Kanda, Ochanomizu, Yotsuya and Yoyogi. Passengers in a hurry to get to one of the intermediate stations across the city not served by the Chuo line take it to whichever of the latter three stations is closest to their destination, then take a Chuo yellow train the rest of the way. (Those going from Shinjuku to Akihabara can take the Chuo orange to Ochanomizu and change to the Sobu line just by walking across the platform.)

West of Shinjuku there are two types of Chuo orange service. 'Ordinary' *kaisoku* trains make the same stops as Chuo yellow trains as far as Mitaka, but continue west to Takao. (Some branch off at Tachikawa and run to Ome and Okutama.)

'Special' *tokubetsu kaisoku* make only one stop between Shinjuku and Mitaka and skip several stations between Mitaka and Takao. There are three *tokubetsu kaisoku* trains per hour, in addition to more frequent *kaisoku*. Both types of Chuo *kaisoku* train use the same platform so it is necessary to use a timetable to find out which is the fast service.

Yokosuka Line Yokosuka trains are cream and blue.

The Yokosuka (pronounced Yoh-kohs-kah) line starts at Tokyo station and provides express service southwest to Yokohama (28 minutes), stopping only at Shimbashi and Shinagawa in the metro Tokyo area. They continue beyond Yokohama through Kamakura (just under one hour) and Yokosuka (home of Yokosuka US Naval Base) to Kurihama on the Miura-hanto peninsula.

Tokaido Line Tokaido trains are orange and green.

The Tokaido line starts at Tokyo station and provides express service southwest to Kawasaki (not served by the Yokosuka line) and Yokohama. With the Yokosuka line it is the fastest way to Yokohama (28 minutes) and it also stops only at Shimbashi and Shinagawa in Tokyo.

Trains continue beyond Yokohama to various destinations and other trains of the Tokaido line run through to Osaka.

Main JR Stations

The multitude of platforms at some stations in the Tokyo area is confusing even to residents, and overwhelming to newcomers.

Tokyo Station Modelled closely on Amsterdam station, Tokyo is the main station of the city. Its services include the super-express Tokaido Shinkansen through Kyoto and Osaka to northern Kyushu, plus ordinary and express services southwest down the coast, and trains east and southeast. It is also the starting point for some commuter trains running west past Shinjuku.

The Tokyo Station table below is useful for general orientation but, because the Tokaido line trains (both locals and expresses) leave from the same platforms, it is necessary to check a timetable to be sure of getting the right type of train.

The last four lines (see table) offer plenty of scope for confusion as trains arrive from both directions at all platforms and depart in both directions from two of them. Consult a timetable to be sure of getting the right one. There is a large timetable (with English) at the foot of at least one of the escalators.

Tokyo station has two sides: Yaesu is the major side, Marunouchi the minor. An underground passage links them. It is one of the best stations in Japan in regard to English signs, colour coding and illuminated signs.

Tokyo Station		
track	*line*	*route*
1,2	Chuo orange	Express to Shinjuku and on to Takao.
3	Keihin-Tohoku	Local service north to Tabata, Omiya.
4	Yamanote	Loop line anti-clockwise to Ueno, Shinjuku, etc.
5	Yamanote	Loop line clockwise to Shinagawa, Gotanda, etc.
6	Keihin-Tohoku	Local service to Shinagawa, Yokohama, Ofuna.
7, 8, 9, 10, 12	Tokaido	Express to Yokohama; mixed local and express trains beyond to Odawara and Atami (with connections to Shizuoka, Kyoto, Nagoya and Osaka).
14 to 19	Tokaido Shinkansen	Super-express to Nagoya, Kyoto, Osaka and on to Hiroshima and Hakata.
underground (chika)		
1 to 4	a: Yokosuka and b: Sobu Hon-sen	a: Express *kaisoku* to Yokohama; local service on to Kamakura, Yokosuka and Kurihama. b: express *kaisoku* to Chiba and Narita; express (surcharge) and local service to both and beyond.

Tokyo station (Yaesu side) is the point of departure for highway buses to Nagoya and on to Kyoto/Osaka, as well as the night buses to Kyoto, Osaka and various points north such as Yamagata and Sendai. The shuttle bus to TCAT leaves from across the road from the Yaesu side exit. Information services are also on the Yaesu side.

The Marunouchi subway line is on the Marunouchi side; signs clearly indicate the way.

Ueno Station Ueno is the station for trains headed north and northeast. With the advent of the Tohoku and Joetsu Shinkansen lines it has become Japan's largest station.

It is not difficult to get confused but the station is fairly well signposted and with the Ueno Station platform table below it shouldn't be too hard to transfer trains.

For orientation, the important thing to remember is that the main concourse is above the tracks at the north end (the end away from Akihabara and Tokyo stations). The entrance to the Shinkansen lines is past line 12; escalators descend four levels to the tracks.

Platforms 1 to 4 serve trains that circle Tokyo or run to points nearby while others serve destinations farther away. As with Tokyo station, several lines depart at various times from any number of platforms, so check a timetable for the right one.

Transfers to tracks 13 to 18 require a little searching as they are not in line with tracks 1 to 12; they are to the east side of the station and downstairs from the overhead concourse. The way to the Ginza and Hibiya subway lines can be followed easily, as can the route to Keisei railway station.

Ueno Station

In the following table, abbreviations are used for the names of the lines:

To = Tohoku Hon-sen line;
Ta = Takasaki line;
Jo = Joshinetsu line;
Jb = Joban line;

track	line	route
1	Keihin-Tohoku	Local service to Tabata, Omiya (terminus).
2	Yamanote	Loop line anti-clockwise to Tabata, Ikebukuro, Shinjuku, etc.
3	Yamanote	Loop line clockwise to Tokyo, Shinagawa, Gotanda, etc.
4	Keihin-Tohoku	Local service to Shinagawa, Kawasaki, Yokohama, Ofuna (terminus).
5 to 8	To, Ta, Jo.	
9	To, Ta, Jo, Jb.	
10	Jb.	
11, 12	Jb (local).	
13, 14, 15	To, Ta, Jo.	
16	To, Jb.	
17	To, Ta, Jo, Jb.	
18	Jb.	
19, 20	Joetsu Shinkansen	Super express service through Takasaki to Niigata.
21, 22	Tohoku Shinkansen	Super express service through Fukushima and Sendai to Morioka.

Shinjuku Station Shinjuku is claimed to be the busiest station in the world, with several JR lines, two subway lines and three private railways delivering passengers to or near it. Only one long-distance JR line leaves from it, the Chuo Hon-sen. It has express trains west towards Kofu and Matsumoto as well as ordinary services terminating somewhat closer.

The main problem is that the station is very poorly marked in English and (on the east side) has ticket machines for two private railway lines side by side with those for JR trains. The information table below regarding trains and platforms will therefore be all the more valuable.

An underground passage on the north side of the station links east and west sides and has the entrance to Shinjuku station of the Marunouchi subway line. (Further east in the same passageway is Shinjuku-sanchome station.)

The tracks are accessible via two tunnels that are accessible from inside the JR wickets. The southernmost of these tunnels can be used to get to the Keio and Odakyu private railways (which have

their stations on the west side of the JR station) by purchasing a Keio or Odakyu ticket on the east side.

Shinjuku station is probably the most bewildering on earth; an architectural disaster with very poor planning of concourses, passages and stairs, and for visitors, the negligible signposting in English makes the whole thing even worse. Japan's great 'internationalisation' boom hasn't yet reached station labelling.

Subways & Private Railways

Tokyo has a good subway system. Trains are frequent and clean and the system covers the city intensively within the Yamanote loop line and beyond it some distance (especially to the east).

The system is made up of 10 lines: three municipally run *Toei* lines – Asakusa, Mita and Shinjuku (sometimes referred to on signs as Toei 1, 6 and 10 respectively, even though the lines were given names in the late '70s) and seven private *Eidan* lines – Ginza, Marunouchi, Chiyoda, Tozai, Hibiya, Yurakucho and Hanzomon.

Passengers can transfer among the

Shinjuku Station		
track	line	route
1, 2	Saikyo-sen Omiya,	Kawagoe
3, 4	Chuo Hon-sen	Expresses (surcharge) west to Kofu and Matsumoto.
5	Chuo orange	*Kaisoku* express to Tokyo station (morning rush hour only); local trains to Otsuki, Kofu, Matsumoto at other times.
6	Chuo orange	*Kaisoku* express to Tokyo station (all day).
7	Chuo Hon-sen	Local service to Otsuki, Kofu, Matsumoto
8	Chuo orange	*Kaisoku* express west to Mitaka, Tachikawa, Takao.
9	Chuo/Sobu (yellow)	Local service east through Akihabara to Chiba: after 10.10 pm, all but one go to Tokyo station.
10	Yamanote	Loop line anti-clockwise to Shibuya, Gotanda, Shinagawa, etc.
11	Yamanote	Loop line clockwise to Ikebukuro, Tabata, Ueno, etc.
12	Chuo yellow	Local service west to Mitaka for most of day; through to Tachikawa and Takao in late evening.

Eidan lines and among the *Toei* lines without extra charge but a transfer from one system to another requires a new fare to be paid.

The vending machines sell tickets that allow a transfer and cover both systems but the total cost is the same as two separate tickets. Similarly, a new fare must be paid when transferring to or from the JR system, private railways or buses.

There are times when it is advantageous to buy a through ticket (provided you can figure out the system in time). When changing from one subway line or system to another it is sometimes necessary to exit through the wicket and re-enter another station some distance away. In cases like this it is useful to have a ticket valid for the full fare through to the final destination lest the ticket taker at the first station want to take your ticket when you exit.

Every subway line connects with the JR Yamanote loop line somewhere, some also to the Sobu or Chuo line, and at least one subway line joins a JR line or one of the 11 private railway lines.

For changing to a private line, it is possible that no transfer will be required at all; some subway trains will continue along the tracks of the private line and operate some distance as one of its trains. (A new fare is charged as soon as the journey crosses the boundary of the second system.)

An example is the Hibiya line, many trains of which continue beyond the subway terminus of Naka-Meguro and continue along the tracks of the Toyoko line (which runs between Shibuya and Yokohama) as far as Hiyoshi. At the other end of the Hibiya line, some trains continue beyond the subway terminus, along the tracks of the Isezaki line through to Kita-Kasukabe. When a change of train *is* required, it usually requires nothing more than walking across the platform. At the most arduous, it might be necessary to walk a short distance to another platform.

At stations serving lines of both subway systems there are machines selling tickets for both, as well as ticket machines for transfer to any connecting private railway line. There may be up to a dozen machines, each one with different markings (only in *kanji*). It's complicated even for the Japanese, so don't be embarrassed to ask for help. Carry your copy of the JNTO *Tourist Map of Tokyo.*

The following is the colour scheme of the cars of the various lines; the colour is also used as a code to identify the various lines on maps.

Eidan
Ginza	orange
Marunouchi	red
Chiyoda	dark green
Tozai	light blue
Hibiya	grey
Hanzomon	purple
Yurakucho	yellow

Toei
Mita	dark blue
Asakusa	pink
Shinjuku	lime green

The name of every station in the subway system is clearly identified in *romaji* on walls and pillars in the station. Signs, also labelled in *romaji* and colour-coded the same as on fare maps, clearly indicate the direction to walk when transferring from one line to another.

The timetable for the line using each particular platform is posted over the platform. The symmetrical *kanji* identify services from Monday to Saturday (*heijitsu*); the other identify Sundays and holidays (*kyujitsu*). On private railway timetables the red, green or blue numbers represent express services; black numbers indicate local trains.

Commuter passes are available for travel between any two specified stations in the Tokyo area; periods are for one, three or six months. Commuter tickets (*kaisuken*) are also available for travel between two specific stations and give 11 rides for the price of 10.

Bus

There is a large network of bus routes throughout the greater Tokyo area. They act mostly as feeders to railway and subway lines, often through incredibly narrow streets. Most routes run between large JR stations. Buses generally stop running after 9 pm.

The drawback of buses is that the destination is written only in *kanji* and the drivers rarely speak English. However, since the destination is often a station, you can check if the *kanji* on a bus correspond to the characters for one of the JR stations. At every bus stop there is a sign with the names of the destination stations (in Japanese), a route map and the schedule.

Buses are, of course, subject to the delays of Tokyo's heavy traffic, so travel is slow in the morning and afternoon peak periods. In Tokyo the fare is paid when entering the bus and is marked on the cash box. Strips of tickets are also available.

Buses are most useful to residents who have the time to establish what lines go where they want to go. At least one map *Great Tokyo Detailed Map* (Nippon Kokuseisha, Y680 at bookshops), shows bus routes, but check the date of publication.

Streetcars

There is a single surviving tram line in Tokyo, running from Ikebukuro to Oji (on Keihin-Tohoku line), not a very useful route.

Near Tokyo

The region around Tokyo offers some of Japan's most interesting attractions including Kamakura, Mt Fuji and the Hakone area. Nearly all can be visited in day trips, though some might be more enjoyable if spread over two or more days.

West of Tokyo

There are several individual attractions and interesting areas to the west of Tokyo. Many can be visited as day trips or weekend outings or can be visited en route to Kyoto and other destinations in western Japan.

Although generally industrial/commercial in nature, Kawasaki and Yokohama have an attraction or two each and the many interesting sights of the historic city of Kamakura are only a short distance beyond Yokohama.

South of Kamakura is the Miura-hanto peninsula and west of the city lies Odawara, gateway to the Izu-hanto peninsula, the Hakone area and Mt Fuji.

Going west from the Hakone/Fuji area takes you along the south coast which is generally heavily urbanised and uninteresting. Going north leads inland via Matsumoto (site of the only historic castle

in the Tokyo region) through much more interesting and less-travelled regions.

KAWASAKI

Kawasaki is a typical Japanese industrial city with virtually nothing of interest to visitors, with one notable exception – a museum of traditional Japanese farmhouses.

Nihon Minka-en

The name means 'Japan Farmhouse Garden'. It is a collection of traditional thatched-roof buildings that have been moved to this peaceful forested site from many places around Japan.

The museum offers a very convenient way to get a glimpse of how Japan looked in centuries past. The oldest building dates from 1688.

A pamphlet in English, given at the entrance, explains the origin, use and unusual points of each building and there are many descriptive signs in English around the grounds.

Visitors are free to wander through the interiors of many buildings. On the second floor of one is a museum of traditional farming implements, utensils and tools plus some armour and weaponry.

The museum is is closed on Mondays and there is no entry after 4 pm.

Getting There & Away Access from Tokyo is by Odakyu line from Shinjuku station to Muko-ga-oka Yuen station; the express from track 5 takes about 30 minutes. From the south exit (*minami guchi*), look for the monorail and follow along to its right. Continue straight on at the main road where the monorail turns left. The museum is a 15-minute walk from the station.

With an early start it should be possible to take in Nihon Minka-en and Yokohama's Sankei-en garden in one day. To get to

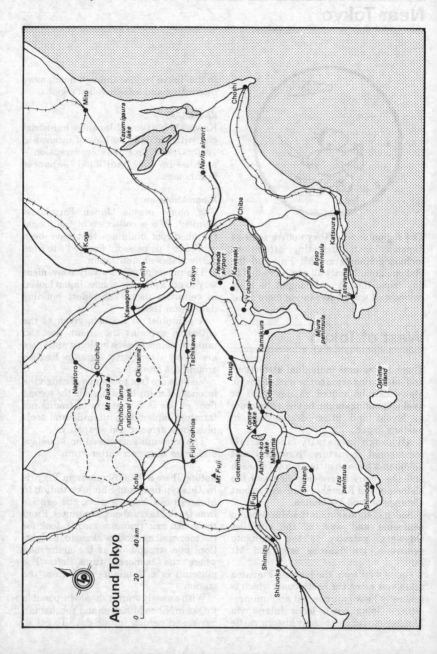

Around Tokyo

0   20   40 km

Mito
Kasumigaura lake
Koga
Omiya
Kawagoe
Kawagoe
Nagatoro
Chichibu
Mt Buko
Okutama
Chichibu-Tama
national park
Kofu
Fuji-Yoshida
Mt Fuji
Gotemba
Tachikawa
Atsugi
Tokyo
Haneda airport
Kawasaki
Yokohama
Kamakura
Odawara
Kome-ga-take
Ashi-no-ko lake
Mishima
Fuji
Shuzenji
Shimoda
Izu peninsula
Shimizu
Shizuoka
Narita airport
Chiba
Choshi
Katsuura
Boso peninsula
Tateyama
Miura peninsula
Oshima island

Yokohama from Muko-ga-oka Yuen station, backtrack one stop toward Tokyo to Noborito and change to the JR Nanbu line going south to Kawasaki, then change to a train to Yokohama. At Muko-ga-oka Yuen you can get a single ticket that permits the transfer to the JR line. Tickets are issued from the vending machine furthest to the left – buy a low-priced ticket and pay the difference later.

Other Attractions

Kawasaki is known for its red light district (named Horinouchi), and its many love hotels. It is one of the three or four most well known in Japan.

Kawasaki has one other attraction – the interesting annual festival, Jibeta-matsuri. This festival honours Kanamara-sama – deities of the metal phallus. It is based on a fable of a maiden (beautiful and rich, of course) who had an unusual and terrible affliction. She was 'inhabited' by a sharp-toothed demon that bit off the penis of two successive grooms who tried to perform their wedding-night duty.

A divinely inspired blacksmith took the girl with the aid of an iron phallus that de-toothed the demon and de-flowered the maiden. And everyone lived happily ever after, especially the Kawasaki businessmen who have revived the festival, which also honours the gods of businesses, growth, prosperity and reproduction, all of which are various forms of fertility.

Whatever the motives, everyone has a good time during the festival when phalluses are carried in procession, local smiths re-enact the forging operation and the whole thing is just a good-humoured celebration.

The festival is held on 15 April near Kawasaki Taishi station, beginning with music in the early afternoon, a parade of the sacred palanquin and masked people carrying phallic offerings (4 to 5 pm), followed by the forging (5 to 6 pm), then an outdoor banquet.

From Tokyo take the Keihin Kyuko line to Keihin Kawasaki station, then transfer to the Kawasaki Taishi line downstairs. Taishi station is about 10 minutes away. From the station (there is only one exit) cross the street outside, turn right and walk about 50 metres.

Getting There & Away

Train From Tokyo, Kawasaki can be reached by train by the Tokaido line (from Tokyo, Shimbashi or Shinagawa stations only). This runs non-stop from Shinagawa to Kawasaki.

The JR alternative is the Keihin-Tohoku line but the trains stop at every station. Both these lines continue to Yokohama (the next stop for a Tokaido train). You can also use the Keihin Kyuko line from Shinagawa station (or from Sengakuji station on the Asakusa subway line).

Boat There is a daily ferry service between Kawasaki and Hyuga in eastern Kyushu.

There is also a car-and-passenger service from Kawasaki across the bay (Tokyo-wan) to Kisarazu on the Boso-hanto peninsula.

Yokohama

Yokohama is a port and business city about 20 km from Tokyo. It has become the second largest city in Japan (nearly three million people) but both Tokyo and Yokohama have expanded toward each other (along with Kawasaki) and now form one vast conurbation.

Being a commercial city, it offers little for the sightseer; its large office buildings are much the same as those anywhere.

The city has a short history by Japanese standards. Before 1850 it was only a sleepy fishing village. With the signing of the treaty forcing Japan to open its doors after 250 years of seclusion, Yokohama became one of six ports open to the world and was the port for Tokyo. At the time it was an ugly expanse of mud and was chosen by the Japanese officials to keep unwanted and unclean foreigners as far from the capital as possible, in conditions less than pleasant. It has improved somewhat since then.

Information

Beside the Silk Center Building (facing the harbour) is the Kanagawa Prefectural Tourist Information Center (tel (045) 681-0506). It has a good selection of useful information on Yokohama and for travel elsewhere in Japan.

There is usually a free handout map but it may be one of the typical Japanese type with distorted scales, incorrect locations and north (unmarked) off in a strange direction.

Home Visit If you wish to visit a Japanese home in Yokohama for a couple of hours in the evening, arrangements can be made at the Tourist Information Centre (tel (045) 641-5824) in the Yokohama International Welcome Association on the ground floor of the Silk Center Building or at the Silk Center Hotel (tel (045) 641-0961).

Things to See

The attractions of Yokohama are limited and most are quite close to each other; Yamashita Park (along the harbour front), Marine Tower, Port Viewing Park, Chinatown and the Silk Center Building. The premier destination, Sankei-en Park, is a convenient bus ride away.

Silk Center Building This houses a permanent display of all aspects of the silk industry, from raw cocoon to beautiful fabric. The simplest way to get there from Yokohama station is by bus from the depot beside the Sky Building, opposite the East Exit. Bus 26 passes in front of the Silk Center; bus Nos 8 and 58 pass nearby (get off at the post office).

Marine Tower From the Silk Center it is a simple walk along Yamashita Park to the very visible Marine Tower. On a clear day it is possible to see distant Mt Fuji. This is more likely in the cooler months or following a day of strong winds.

From Yokohama station bus Nos 8, 26 and 58 pass nearby.

Port Viewing Park This park is an alternative to Marine Tower for viewing the harbour though not Mt Fuji. The road up to it can be found easily from the vicinity of the Tower. This area is known as the Bluffs and has been the prestige residential area, especially for foreigners, since Yokohama was opened to the outside world.

Chukagai Near the tower is Chinatown (*Chukagai* in Japanese), the only one in Japan. It is known for its restaurants and shops selling Chinese products and curios.

Sankei-en Park After the tower, catch a No 8 bus to Sankei-en Park. This is one of the most beautiful garden parks in Japan – in my opinion far more attractive than the 'Big Three' at Mito, Kanazawa and Okayama.

The garden dates only from the late 19th century and was built by Tomitaro Hara, a wealthy silk merchant. It is laid out around a large pond, with walking paths circling it and branching off to other places. Wooded hills totally obscure the ugly reality of the surrounding 20th century.

One of the side paths leads to the Inner Garden which is laid out in the traditional Japanese style and is an excellent example of the landscape gardener's work. Within the Inner Park are several historic buildings, including the traditional-style mansion Rinshun-Kaku. These have been moved here from other parts of Japan.

On the highest hill in the park is an old three-storey pagoda in excellent condition. It was built in the 15th century and moved to the park in 1914. A nearby lookout gives a good view of the harbour and on a clear

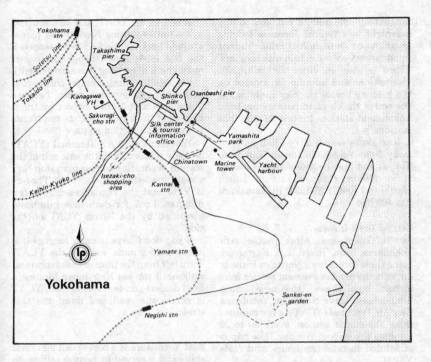

Yokohama

day you can see Mt Fuji, though the view is spoilt by a tall smokestack.

Yonohara Farmhouse This is near the pagoda in Sankei-en Park. It's a huge thatched-roof building which dates from 1750 and is held together only by straw ropes – there are no nails in it whatsoever. This one was moved here in 1960 when the opening of a new dam flooded the valley where it was located.

The only other similar buildings are in the Kiso area of Gifu-ken, so take this opportunity if you will not be able to see others.

To return to Yokohama station, or the vicinity of the tower or Chinatown, take a No 8 bus going in the same direction as the one that took you to the park. Get off anywhere near the Tower. The closest

railway station is Ishikawacho on the Negishi (Keihin-Tohoku) line.

Places to Stay

Kanagawa Youth Hostel (tel (045) 241-6503) is about 10 minutes from Sakuragi-cho station. From the station, in the direction of Yokohama station, you can see the 'Golden Center' Building (that's the name in Japanese if you have to ask someone); there is a wide street on the far side of it. Walk to the right along that street, keeping the elevated railway tracks to the right until you reach a short, steep incline leading up to a steep cobblestoned street to the left and a traffic bridge to the right. Turn left up the hill and the hostel is on the right about 100 metres along.

There are hotels of a variety of price

ranges to choose from. If you want to stay overnight in a typical Japanese lodging (*ryokan* or *minshuku*) the Tourist Information Centre can help with bookings. There is also an office for *minshuku* reservations and information located on the balcony beside the Sky Building, at the end of the elevated passageway from Yokohama station to one of the bus stations.

Kamakura is only about half an hour away from Yokohama (or an hour from Tokyo) and may be a preferable place to stay. *Nihon Gakusei-kaikan Youth Hostel* (tel (0467) 25-1234) in Kamakura has 400 beds.

Getting There & Away

Air To Yokohama: Most people visit Yokohama from Tokyo, but if you are going there direct from Narita or Haneda airports the most convenient service is by airport bus. Buses (the now-famous 'limousines') leave Narita for Yokohama City Air Terminal (YCAT), a few minutes from Yokohama station, every 20 to 30 minutes throughout the day. The trip is scheduled to take two hours, and costs Y3100.

From Haneda, buses run at five to 20 minute intervals throughout the day to the east exit of Yokohama station; the trip takes about 30 minutes, and costs Y400. (Some of these buses also stop at YCAT.)

From Yokohama: Buses to Haneda run very frequently (every six to 12 minutes) from Yokohama station (east exit). The fare is Y400, and the trip is scheduled to take 30 minutes. (Some of the buses to Narita from Yokohama City Air Terminal also stop at Haneda en route). To Narita, buses leave YCAT every 15-20 minutes through most of the day (Y3100). The trip is scheduled to take two hours for direct runs, although extra time should be allowed for traffic tie-ups. (Some of these buses stop at Haneda en route, and they should take 2½ hours.) For flights on participating airlines, luggage may be

checked in at YCAT and not touched again until reaching Narita, and planes are held back for checked-in passengers if the bus is delayed (though passengers must check in early for this arrangement).

For details of an alternative cheaper but more time-consuming route between Yokohama and Narita airport by trains instead of the airport bus, see the Narita to Yokohama section on page 192.

Yokohama City Air Terminal (YCAT) is easily reached from the east exit of the station. A shuttle bus runs from stop No 1 about three to five times an hour. The fare is Y110 and the trip takes only a few minutes. Look for dark blue minibuses identified by the letters YCAT on the side.

If you don't have to carry luggage it is about a 15-minute walk to the YCAT. Turn left from the front of the station and walk until you see New Japan Motors (a Ford dealer) across the wide road. YCAT is across the road and down the side street.

Boat Yokohama is a port of call for cruise ships and is served by regular sailings to and from Nakhodka (USSR) at the eastern extremity of the Trans-Siberian Railway. Passenger ships arrive at the modern International Port Terminal at Osambashi Pier.

To get to Yokohama station from Osambashi Pier you can walk, catch a bus or go by train from the nearer station.

After clearing immigration and customs, passengers walk to the mainland. At the entrance to the pier is a small square. On the right side is a map of Yokohama and the first of many indicators pointing the way to Sakuragicho Station (from where trains can be caught to Tokyo). On the left of the square is the nine-storey Silk Center Building. It is a simple 20 to 30 minute walk to Sakuragicho. If you follow the signs to a tree-lined avenue you can walk along that to Yokohama Park and through there to Kannai station. Both stations are on the Negishi (JR) line, a local line with trains to Yokohama station.

Buses No 8, 20, 58 and 81 go to Yokohama station via Sakuragi-cho station; buses No 11, 21 and 22 terminate at the latter. To get to the bus stop from the pier, walk straight ahead past the Silk Center Building (on the left) to the first major cross street (the post office is to the right). The bus stop is a little further along the street from the far right hand corner.

Train To reach Yokohama from Tokyo or Narita Airport there are five rail services – three JR and two private lines (Toyoko and Keihin-Kyuko).

From Tokyo station there are two express services, both taking 28 minutes to Yokohama. Both the Yokosuka and Tokaido lines stop only at Shimbashi and Shinagawa in the metro Tokyo area and each makes one more stop before Yokohama. The Yokosuka line stops at Shin-Kawasaki and the Tokaido line at Kawasaki. Trains of both lines depart at five to 15 minute intervals through the day. Trains on the Keihin-Tohoku line stop at all 12 stations from Tokyo to Yokohama.

From points near *Eidan* (private) subway lines, the most convenient and cheapest way to go is probably by the Toyoko line which starts from Shibuya. (You can transfer here from Ginza or Hanzomon subway or JR Yamanote lines but a separate ticket must be bought.) A direct transfer (without changing platforms) can be made from the Hibiya subway line at Naka-Meguro; a new fare zone begins here because it is the Toyoko line.

From stations on the *Toei* (Asakusa and Mita) subway lines, go to Sengakuji and transfer there to the Keihin-kyuko line to Yokohama. Many trains leaving Narita Airport station have the marked destination 'Nishi-Magome'. For Yokohama, take one of these trains to Sengakuji and transfer to the Keihin-kyuko line.

Getting Around

Train Yokohama station is a busy communications centre, being served by JR, three private railway lines, a subway and many buses. The station has undergone extensive remodelling in recent years and there are now relatively good markings in English, sufficient at least to find most connections.

The above-ground facilities over the station include a hotel and a department store and the actual station section is basically a broad underground passageway leading to most of the lines. The main entrance is the west exit (*nishi guchi*) and is the loading zone for most of the buses. The east exit (*higashi guchi*) is connected to another bus loading zone by a passage over a major expressway. The train platforms are numbered from the east exit end.

Tracks 1 and 2 are for Keihin-kyuko trains (private line). Track 1 trains go west to Yokosuka and the Miura-hanto peninsula. Trains from Track 2 run to Kawasaki and Shinagawa (Tokyo). Some of these continue past Shinagawa to Sengakuji. This station is on the Mita subway line and the train may terminate here or continue some distance along these tracks towards Oshiage. By changing trains when required (as described in the Tokyo section), this route can be used to get to Narita Airport. Expresses are marked with green or red *kanji* on the front and side of the trains while locals trains are marked in black.

Tracks 3 to 10 are JR services.

Track 3 is the Keihin-Tohoku line, providing local service as far as Ofuna (also a stop on the Yokosuka line). It becomes the Negishi line one stop out of Yokohama.

Track 4 is the Keihin-Tohoku line, providing local service to Tokyo and as far north as Omiya. It stops at all 12 stations along the way and costs the same as the much faster Yokosuka and Tokaido lines. In the Tokyo area it runs parallel to the Yamanote line for many stops. This is the line to take for connections with the Shinkansen at Shin-Yokohama station. Go one stop to Higashi-Kanagawa station and transfer to a Yokohama-sen line train bound for Hachioji; the third stop is Shin-Yokohama. Keihin-Tohoku trains are blue.

Tracks 5 and 6 are Tokaido line services west to Odawara, Atami and Nagoya. Many of these are expresses, for which there is a surcharge. It is necessary to consult a timetable to distinguish them in advance. The trains have red *kanji* destination signs for expresses, black for locals.

Tracks 7 and 8 are Tokaido line services to Tokyo, stopping en route only at Kawasaki, Shinagawa and Shimbashi, the latter two being stations in the metro Tokyo area. This is one of the two fastest services to Tokyo. Tokaido line trains are orange and green.

Track 9 is Yokosuka line (pronounced Yo-kos-ka) service west to Kamakura, Zushi, Yokosuka and Kurihama at the southeast side of the Miura-hanto peninsula. Some of these are expresses with a surcharge; refer to the notes for Tokaido line trains.

Track 10 is Yokosuka line express service to Tokyo, stopping only at Shin-Kawasaki, Shinagawa and Shimbashi en route. Beyond Tokyo, many of these trains continue to or toward Chiba as the Sobu line. Yokosuka line trains are cream and blue.

Tickets for all JR as well as Keihin-kyuko trains can be purchased from vending machines in the underground passageway.

The tracks of the second private line, the Toyoko (Tokyo-Yokohama) line are on the west side of the station. It runs from Sakuragicho (two stops beyond Yokohama) to Shibuya, on the west side of central Tokyo. It offers convenient transfer to the Hibiya subway line at Naka-Meguro, and to the JR Yamanote line and the Ginza and Hanzomon subway lines at Shibuya.

The entrance to the Toyoko line tracks is to the left when entering Yokohama station through the west exit. Ticket machines are nearby. The tracks can also be reached via an entrance directly from JR tracks.

Track 1 of the Toyoko line serves trains that go only two stops, to Sakuragicho.

Track 2 serves trains bound for Shibuya.

Trains with the destination marked in red are expresses (*kyuko*) and reach Shibuya 10 minutes faster than those marked in black.

Beyond Yokohama

KAMAKURA

Now a resort town for day-tripping Tokyo-ites and residence for many fortunate citizens, Kamakura was effectively the capital of Japan from 1192 to 1333 when the *baku* military government of the Minamoto family gained the upper hand in Japan. During that period it became very prosperous but it subsequently declined to a regional government centre. It finally lost all special status in 1603 and became a quiet backwater.

Kamakura, the most interesting single place in the Tokyo area to visit for historic remains, should be on everyone's 'must see' list. The best-known attraction is the famous Kamakura Daibutsu (Great Buddha) but there are other sights as well.

Information

Two useful leaflets, *Kamakura* and *Fuji-Hakone-Izu-Kamakura* are available from the Tokyo TIC.

There is a programme of volunteer student guides who show visitors around Kamakura at no charge in return for the opportunity to practice English. To fit in with the students' free time, the tours are given only on weekends. The Tokyo TIC has more information and can make arrangements.

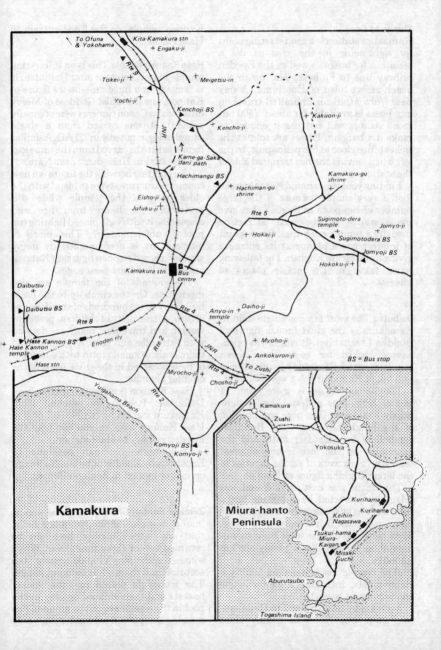

Kamakura

Miura-hanto Peninsula

To Ofuna & Yokohama
Kita-Kamakura stn
Engaku-ji
Rte 9
Tokei-ji
Meigetsu-in
Yochi-ji
Kenchoji BS
Kakuon-ji
Kencho-ji
JNR
Kame-ga-Saka dani path
Hachimangu BS
Kamakura-gu shrine
Hachiman-gu shrine
Eisho-ji
Jufuku-ji
Rte 5
Sugimoto-dera temple
Jomyo-ji
Hokai-ji
Sugimotodera BS
Jomyoji BS
Kamakura stn
Bus centre
Hokoku-ji
Daibutsu
Rte 4
Daibutsu BS
Daiho-ji
Anyo-in temple
Rte 8
Enoden rly
Myoho-ji
Rte 2
Hase Kannon BS
Hase Kannon temple
Hase stn
JNR
Ankokuron-ji
Rte 4
To Zushi
BS = Bus stop
Myocho-ji
Chosho-ji
Yuigahama Beach
Rte 2
Komyoji BS
Komyo-ji

Kamakura
Zushi
Yokosuka
Kurihama
Keihin-Nagasawa
Kurihama
Tsukui-hama
Miura-Kaigan
Misaki-Guchi
Aburutsubo
Togashima Island

Things to See

Kamakura station is a good starting point for sightseeing in the area as it's a terminus for buses as well as the Enoden railway line to Fujiwara and on to the beach resort town of Enoshima. A day pass (*furii kipu*) for unlimited travel on city buses is available for about Y500 but most visitors will not use it enough to make it a bargain. Passes are sold at the ticket office close to the police post, to the left when leaving the bus terminal side of the station.

Finding your way around Kamakura on foot is very simple because of the large number of signposts in English that give the distance to the next attraction (usually a temple or shrine). Every point of interest has a plaque at its entrance giving its history in English. The following route takes in the major places of interest.

Daibutsu The most famous single sight in Kamakura is the great bronze figure of Buddha (Amitabha). It sits in the open, having looked for more than seven centuries with half-closed eyes on the rise and fall of Kamakura as a seat of power.

The seated figure is more than 11 metres high, plus pedestal, and weighs nearly 100 tonnes. The pose and position of the hands represents the Buddhist symbolism for steadfast faith and the expression on the face is one of great serenity. It is a work of art far superior to the larger Buddha figure at Nara.

The statue was cast in 1252 and was originally protected by a temple but a tidal wave in 1495 swept this away and the figure has been in the open ever since. That tidal wave must have been monumental, as the Buddha is nearly one km inland!

(The temple has a welcome facility – clean toilets, including a western-style one *with* toilet paper!)

Access is by bus No 3 or 7 to Daibutsu-mae stop, bus No 8 to nearby Hase

Kannon temple, or the Enoden train to Hase station.

Hase Kannon Temple This is an interesting temple to visit before or after Daibutsu. It is famous for a huge nine-metre figure of Kannon, the Buddhist Goddess of Mercy (after whom Canon cameras were originally named). It was carved from a single camphor log, reputedly in 721 AD. A similar figure, said to be carved from the same log, may be seen in Hase-dera, near Nara.

The building housing the figure is a new concrete structure styled to blend with the older parts of the temple while still protecting the figure from fire and displaying it with well-placed lighting (no photos, unfortunately). This piece of religious art is accompanied by many smaller, carved wooden figures of Kannon and other Buddhist personages.

The grounds of the temple are also interesting. On the climb up to the main building you see hundreds of small figures of Jizo, patron deity of children, pregnant women and travellers; many are dressed with little bibs and hats. At ground level there is also a small grotto with a number of figures carved in the stone walls of the circular chamber.

Hase Kannon is about 200 metres from Daibutsu. It can be reached from Kamakura station by bus No 3, 7 or 8 to Hase Kannon stop, or you can take the Enoden railway to Hase station.

From here, you can continue to Enoshima by Enoden or by bus No 8 or go on foot or by taxi to Zeniarai Benten.

Zeniarai Benten Shrine The name means 'money-washing' shrine, from the belief that any money washed here will be returned two or three times over. While some search for Y10,000 notes, the sceptics limit themselves to loose change. The money is placed in little wicker baskets and then swished around in the pool in the small cave on the ground. The washing is supposed to be efficacious only on days related to the zodiacal sign of the snake.

Many wooden *torii* have been donated to the shrine and arranged in picturesque rows like short tunnels. The temple is finally reached through a tunnel cut through the rock after a steep uphill walk.

Zeniarai Benten can be reached by walking from Hase Kannon or from Hase station; the route is adequately signposted. There is no bus but you can catch a taxi.

Kenchoji Area From Zeniarai Benten you can either return to the station or follow the roads to the Kenchoji area. There are a few temples along the way and the final leg is along an unpaved road over a ridge and down the curiously named Kame-ga-saka dani – 'Turtle Slope Valley'.

From Zeniarai shrine it is about 1½ km as the crow flies but it is definitely a much longer hike. The slope is nicely wooded

though and you pass an interesting *ryokan* which, like Zeniarai shrine, is reached by a tunnel cut through solid rock.

From the station, the Kencho-ji area is quickly reached by bus No 9 or 10; get off at Kenchoji stop.

Kenchoji Temple The greatest and most picturesque of the temples of Kamakura, Kenchoji was founded in 1253. The main hall dates from 1646 and has the appearance of well-preserved age. The great *sanmon* gate and nearby belfry are equally picturesque.

Other buildings set in pretty gardens or other artistic settings can be glimpsed when wandering along the paths of the grounds.

Meigetsu-in Temple Close to Kencho-ji, this little temple is really worth visiting only in June when the huge number of hydrangeas are in bloom.

Engaku-ji Temple Close to Kita-Kamakura station, this temple dates from 1282 but virtually all the old buildings have been destroyed, many by the 1923 Kanto earthquake.

The great *sanmon* main gate is impressive and one of the buildings is reached through a wooden gate with intricate carvings of lions and dragons. There are glimpses of beauty here and there but the effect is not maintained and the main building is made of unromantic concrete. Superficially it resembles Kencho-ji temple in layout but has less to offer.

There are other temples nearby that may be explored if time allows but all are low-key. Downhill from Kencho-ji is a side entrance to Tsurugaoka Hachiman-gu shrine.

Hachiman-gu Shrine Occupying the place of honour in Kamakura, the shrine is built on a hillside overlooking the city and a long boulevard that leads to the sea. The boulevard is divided by twin rows of cherry trees that attract throngs of people in spring.

Hachiman is the god of war so it was natural for the military government (the *baku*) to dedicate the shrine to him. The present site was first used from 1191, the successor to an earlier one founded elsewhere in 1063. The present colourful orange buildings date from 1828. The small museum in the main building houses armour, swords, masks and other historic items.

At the foot of the staircase leading down from the shrine is a Noh stage from which a long stone-paved walkway leads to the front entrance; it is always crowded on weekends and holidays. To the left is the Kamakura Koku-hokan (municipal museum) which displays a number of treasures of the Kamakura and Muromachi periods (1192 to 1573) that belong to various shrines and temples in the area.

Near the main entrance to the grounds, to the right, is the Prefectural Modern Art Gallery. Also near the entrance is the steep Taiko Bashi (Drum Bridge) a sort of practical joke in stone as it is so steep that you cannot walk up and over. A running start is required to carry you over and crossing it is reputed to grant a wish. The shrine is unbelievably crowded on New Year's Day.

Hokoku-ji Temple Access is across Hana-no bashi bridge, an ordinary concrete structure, but look out for the colourful carp in the stream below. The temple is not noted for its buildings but for the beautiful bamboo grove behind which is interspersed with numerous historic gravestones. At the teahouse in one corner you can sit and contemplate the small but attractive garden behind the grove.

Hokoku-ji is a zen temple and zazen meditation is held in the garden before 8 am every Sunday. Anyone may participate.

Hokoku-ji can be reached from Hachiman shrine or the station by No 5 bus to Jomyoji stop.

There are several other temples and shrines along the same road, including thatched-roof Sugimoto-dera which is the oldest temple in Kamakura. Most of these temples however are of historical interest only and have little visual appeal unless you are familiar with Japanese history.

Komyo-ji Temple This temple is usually almost deserted, yet for visual appeal it is one of the most worthwhile destinations in Kamakura. It dates from 1243 although the main building is a modern concrete structure (but of traditional appearance).

What sets it apart from other temples in Kamakura is its *karesansui* garden of rock, gravel and greenery at one side of the temple, and another garden consisting of a lotus pond (best from late summer) and other picturesque elements arranged in front of an attractive building. Unlike most other temples, there is no charge to see either.

Other attractions of the temple include a large and old-looking *sanmon* gate, a bell tower with some of the finest wood carvings in Kamakura and a number of interesting tombs. Although many other temples in the city have extensive burial areas, this is the only one with a memorial for pet animals; look for a large monument on the right with food dishes left out.

To get there, take a No 2 bus from the station.

Getting There & Away

Kamakura is easily reached in just under an hour by Yokosuka line from Tokyo station (underground tracks 1 to 4), Shimbashi and Shinagawa stations in metro Tokyo, or from Kawasaki or Yokohama (track 9). From Yokosuka it is the fourth station.

ENOSHIMA

This is a popular beach resort town west of Kamakura. Because it is close to Tokyo it gets extremely crowded on summer weekends.

The main beach is Higashi-hama (higashi means east); on the Katase side of the Katase River is Nishi-hama beach (nishi is west), accessible by Katase-bashi bridge. Also on the Katase side is an aquarium and Enoshima Marineland.

In the harbour is Enoshima, the island that gives its name to the area. It offers the hillside Enoshima shrine (reached by steps or escalator), various recreation facilities and scenic views at Chigogafuchi, including two nearby caves.

Enoshima-jinja shrine has a nude statue of Benten, the Indian goddess of beauty and the only female among the seven Japanese deities of good luck. There is an observation tower that gives a good view of Mt Fuji in one direction and Oshima Island in the other. The latter can be reached by ferry from Shonan Harbour on the north side of the island. Enoshima island is easily reached by a footbridge.

Getting There & Away

To get to Enoshima from Kamakura you can go by Enoden train or bus No 8 from Kamakura station. There is also the monorail from Ofuna on the JR Yokosuka line.

To continue from Enoshima to the Hakone/Izu/Fuji area, take the Enoden line to Fujisawa and transfer to the JR to go to Odawara or Atami.

MIURA-HANTO PENINSULA

This peninsula projects into Sagami-wan Bay between Yokohama and Kamakura. The east side is mainly industrial and commercial and includes Yokosuka Naval Base, the largest US naval base in Japan. The west side and southeast coast is largely beach and resort territory.

A bus from Zushi station runs down the west coast to Misaki station. It passes beaches, the Emperor's walled-in villa at Hayama and several good views of the sea and pleasure craft. During clear weather (winter, late autumn) Mt Fuji is clearly visible.

Aburutsubo

Aburutsubo has a large aquarium – praised by some, a disappointment to others. It is named *Sakana-no-kuni* (Fish World). As well as displays of live fish, it has a dome onto which films are projected to give the impression of being underwater.

Buses run between Misaki-guchi station and the aquarium; the trip takes about 15 minutes. Loudspeakers, the bane of Japan, disturb the peace in all directions around the aquarium.

Jogashima Island

At the far southwest tip of the peninsula, Jogashima has preserved a picturesque cape as parkland, sparing it from development and the encroachment of urban sprawl. The shore is made of strangely twisted rocks, obviously of volcanic origin. There are several small pools, some with colourful little fish.

Anyone wanting a peaceful place for a picnic or just for relaxing by the sea will enjoy this place and it's a good destination for a day trip (or longer if you have the time) to escape Tokyo. It was almost deserted during my late-September visit but it might be more crowded in summer. There is a youth hostel nearby.

Buses run to Jogashima from Misaki-guchi station; the trip takes about 30 minutes.

Miura-kaigan Coast

North of the 'bulge' at the bottom of the peninsula is Miura-kaigan (coast), known for the very long Shonan-hama beach with good white sand and temperate water. Access is by Keihin-kyuko railway to any of the three stations: Miura-kaigan, Tsukuri-hama and Keihin-Nagasawa; local buses run along the coast. There are many *minshuku* and *ryokan* along the beach.

From Kurihama, a ferry crosses to Kanaya on the Boso-hanto peninsula (on the opposite side of Tokyo-wan bay); service is approximately every 35 minutes through the daylight hours.

KOZU

Kozu is the transfer point for JR train lines between the Tokaido Hon-sen line down the coast and the Gotemba-sen line to Gotemba, a major gateway for the Mt Fuji area. These services are described in detail in the section on Mt Fuji.

ODAWARA

Odawara's main attraction is a 1966 reconstruction of Odawara-jo castle. It preserves the outward appearance of the ancient castle but is not authentic. With a genuine 17th century castle at Matsumoto (just north of the Mt Fuji area) there is not much incentive to visit this one.

Odawara can be considered a gateway to the Izu-hanto peninsula to the southwest, and the Hakone area and Mt Fuji to the east and northeast.

Getting There & Away

Odawara can be reached by the JR Tokaido Hon-sen line (one hour from Tokyo by the fastest express; 1½ hours by local train, Y1240). You can also use the Kodama services of the Tokaido Shinkansen (40 minutes, Y3240) and the Odakyu (Odawara Kyuko) express line. Odakyu services are detailed in the section on Hakone because more travellers would use them for that purpose than for getting to Odawara.

Izu-hanto Peninsula

The Izu-hanto peninsula is probably the most popular seaside recreation area for Tokyo-ites. There are some interesting historical sites and some nice scenery but it is low key. The resorts are crowded during the summer season and it is really only an excursion destination for Tokyo residents and is of only secondary interest to short-term visitors.

For additional information the Tokyo TIC has a pamphlet *Fuji-Hakone-Izu-Kamakura* and an information sheet *The Izu Peninsula*.

A suggested way to see Izu-hanto peninsula is to take a bus down the east side from Atami to Shimoda and back up the west side to Numazu and Mishima. Trains of the Izukyu line run as far as Shimoda but about half that distance is through tunnels; buses pass closer to the water and give better views.

Atami can be reached from Tokyo by JR trains, either regular Tokaido-sen or Shinkansen (all Kodama, some Hiraki); the latter is faster but more than double the fare. Both lines also pass through Odawara. There is also a frequent bus service from Hakone along a scenic route over the mountains.

ATAMI

Atami is a favourite of weekend honeymooners and other hot-spring lovers but will be of limited interest to most western visitors as it is little more than countless hotels strung up the hillside. The Atami Bijutsu-kan (art museum) has a good

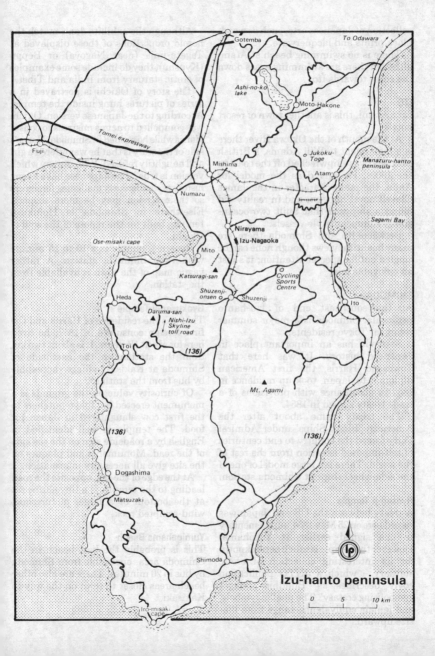

Izu-hanto peninsula

0   5   10 km

collection of Japanese arts, such as wood-block prints and lacquerware.

There is no swimming beach at Atami although there are swimming areas down the coast towards Ito.

ITO

Like Atami, this is another town of resort hotels.

At the mouth of the Okawa River there is a monument to Will Adams, a British pilot who was shipwrecked off the coast in the 1600s. He served as the model for Anjin, the main character in the James Clavell novel *Shogun*, and in reality did found a shipyard that built two ocean-going, European-style vessels.

Between Ito and Shimoda there are many beautiful views though none can be singled out for special attention; it's just an enjoyable trip.

SHIMODA

At the southeast end of Izu-hanto peninsula, Shimoda is a major summer resort for Tokyo residents.

Shimoda has an important place in Japanese history. It was here that Townsend Harris, the first American diplomat to Japan, took up residence in 1857 in accordance with provisions of a trade treaty signed in 1854.

The treaty came about after the American 'Black Ships' under Admiral Perry forced the country to end centuries of self-imposed isolation from the rest of the world. There is a large model of one of the side-wheel ships at Shimoda station.

Ryosen-ji Temple

A treaty between the US and Japan was signed here on 25 May 1854, supplementary to one signed earlier at Yokohama. However the temple is much better known for its interesting collection of erotic statuary – which a JNTO publication coyly describes as 'Buddhist images symbolising ecstasy'. The phallic symbols, and female equivalents, range from life-size upward.

Although the exhibits don't match the heroic proportions of those displayed at Tagata-jinja (near Nagoya) or Beppu (Kyushu), they do include some examples of erotic statuary from India and Tibet.

The story of Okichi is portrayed in a series of pictures hung inside the temple. According to the Japanese version, Okichi was compelled to act as mistress to consul Harris while he resided in Shimoda. Harris's side of the story is that he was offered a girl and haughtily refused. Who can say which version is true? The Japanese have a long history of slanderously maligning foreigners so their version may be more suspect. Elsewhere in Shimoda is Hofuku-ji temple, built for the repose of the soul of Okichi.

Ryosen-ji temple is a 10 to 15 minute walk from Shimoda station. A rather vague map of the town is available from the station.

Gyokusen-ji Temple

This was the residence of Harris and the first foreign consulate in 1857; he lived here for about 1½ years. It is about two km from the station on the east side of Shimoda at Kakisaki village (accessible by bus from the station).

Of curiosity value on the grounds is a monument erected by Tokyo butchers to the first cow slaughtered in Japan for food. The temple is well identified in English by a roadside sign on the sea side of the road. Monuments and plaques on the site give all necessary information.

At the edge of the sea, opposite the road leading to the temple, is a tiny shrine set at the bottom of a large, picturesque, wind-sculpted rock.

Yumigahama Beach

This is probably the best beach in the Shimoda area, accessible from Shimoda by bus in 20 minutes. There are also other beach areas closer to town on the way to Kakisaki.

Places to Stay

There are countless *minshuku, ryokan* and hotels around Shimoda but the town is very crowded during the summer and asking for a room at one place after another can be a waste of time. There is one accommodation centre at the station and another across the road from it. Both will phone and arrange a room.

Getting There & Away

As well as the train and bus services along the east coast, Shimoda can be reached by regular bus down the middle of the peninsula from Mishima and Shuzenji to Toi and Matsuzaki.

IRO-MISAKI CAPE

The southernmost tip of the peninsula is noted for its high vertical cliffs. You can get there from Shimoda by bus in 40 minutes but a boat ride from Shimoda, or an excursion out of Iro-Misaki port, gives a better view. Boat info is available from the station.

DOGASHIMA

The single most scenic place along the west coast is Dogashima. The geological structure of the area around this town is sedimentary rock that is banded in distinct layers.

Erosion or physical separation has resulted in a large number of huge rocks that jut out of the sea. It is scenic from the shore but can be seen much better from a cruise boat out of Dogashima.

WEST COAST

The west coast above Dogashima has fewer resort towns than the east coast. There are many lovely sea views along here and the travelling is more enjoyable than along the east coast.

Buses run north as far as Heda, then turn inland towards Shuzenji, so anyone wishing to continue around the coast to Mito would have to hitch across the gap between Heda and Ose-misaki cape.

NORTHWEST CORNER

The northwest corner of the Izu-hanto peninsula offers excellent views of Mt Fuji over Suruga-wan bay in clear weather (generally late autumn and winter). Suggested places are:

The top of Katsuragi-san, easily reached by cable car from Izu-Nagaoka town (accessible from Mishima via Nagaoka station).

The beach at Mitohama (near Mito).

Along the coast between Mitohama and Ose-Misaki cape.

The top of Daruma-yama, accessible by Nishi-Izu Skyline toll road.

By hiking from Shuzenji-onsen via Heda-toge pass, one of the best hiking trails on the peninsula.

An unusual sight along the coast between Mito and Ose is the old Swedish luxury passenger ship *Stella Polaris*, permanently berthed and serving as a floating hotel.

There is a boat service several times a day between Numazu and Matsu-zaki, stopping at Heda and Toi.

Mito

Of interest here is a natural aquarium formed by nets stretched between rocks. Dolphins and great turtles may be seen.

NORTH-CENTRAL AREA

Shuzenji-onsen

This town takes its name from Shuzen-ji temple which was founded in the 9th century. It is a typical hot-spring resort town with many hotels and *ryokan* using the hot water.

Unusual is a hot spring, Tokkonoyu, that bubbles forth at the edge of the small river that passes through the town. A roofed, slatted-wall bath house has been built around a pool of comfortably warm water. For those not too shy to disrobe and hop in (no one can see in from outside), there is no charge.

There is a youth hostel on the hill behind the town.

Shuzenji-onsen is reached by bus from

Shuzenji station, the terminus of Izu-Hakone Tetsudo railway from Mishima. Shuzenji is the transfer point for bus travel though the middle of the peninsula from Mishima to Shimoda. There is also service to Ito and other points on the peninsula from Shuzenji. Further information is available in *Jikokuhyo* or from tourist information sources.

Cycle Sports Center Less than half an hour from Shuzenji by bus is one of the two cycle centres in Japan. There are several courses and tracks of various types and lengths, and there are also hundreds of bicycles for rent. It is well suited for people who want to try a variety of bikes before purchasing and also offers a weekend recreation centre. It has reasonably priced accommodation.

Nirayama

Egawake, the oldest private house in Japan, is near this town. The 700-year-old building was the residence of the hereditary administrators of the Izu area, so it is large and has a pretty garden, canopied by a number of tall old trees.

Access is by bus from Nirayama station of the Izu-Hakone railway line between Mishima and Shuzenji.

Mishima

Rakuju-en landscape garden, which dates from late last century, is the main attraction of this town. Mishima is on the Tokaido Hon-sen line and is the starting point of the Izu railway line to Shuzenji which runs part of the way down the middle of the peninsula.

There are many buses through the day (more than 20 in summer) from Mishima to Kawaguchi-ko (north of Mt Fuji) via Gotemba and Fuji-Yoshida. The trip takes 2¼ hours and costs Y1700. There are also up to 10 buses a day to Shin-Gogome on the south flank of Mt Fuji – probably the most popular starting point for climbing the mountain.

WEST & SOUTH OF IZU/FUJI

West and south from the Izu-hanto/Fuji area, the road and train lines run very close to the coast; the inland area is inhospitable mountains with very few settlements. Apart from a couple of attractions around Shizuoka and Shimizu, there is little of interest to anyone except students of Japanese industrialisation.

Unless you want to go directly to Kyoto, there is little incentive to go this way by road, as Route 1 is incredibly busy and very slow to travel on – a continuous conurbation with countless stop lights. Only trains and vehicles on the Tomei expressway move quickly.

To see some of the 'real' Japan with rural areas and some historic remains, including one of the nation's finest castles, it is better to consider travelling through the Hakone and Fuji areas to Matsumoto (via Kofu).

However, for those who wish to take the coastal route, the following describes the few attractions along the way.

Okitsu

This was the 17th stage on the old Tokaido highway from Edo (Tokyo) to Kyoto. There is still a *honjin* (inn) that was designed to accommodate *daimyo* (feudal lords) during their periodic travels between Kyoto and Tokyo. The *honjin* still functions as a *ryokan*.

Seiken-ji temple has a very pretty landscape garden. It is about one km west of the station.

Fuji

The name of this city sounds inviting, but the place isn't. The only attractions are paper mills and other industries. On a clear day there is a good view of Mt Fuji from trains and motor vehicles passing the city.

Fuji is a junction of the Tokaido Hon-sen line and the Minobu line to Kofu and on to Matsumoto. For getting around to the scenic areas north of Mt Fuji, however, trains cannot be recommended as travel time can be as long as five hours.

The best way to reach the Kawaguchiko area is by bus from Fuji station or Fujinomiya and clockwise around the mountain. In summer, up to three buses a day run out of Fuji along this route. Out of season it may be necessary to take a train to Fujinomiya and go from there by bus.

Shizuoka & Shimizu
Tosho-gu Shrine On the south side of Kunozan hill (near the coast), and between Shimizu and Shizuoka (accessible from both cities by bus), is Tosho-gu shrine. Ieyasu Tokugawa was interred here before finally being laid to rest at the magnificent and famous Tosho-gu shrine at Nikko. The shrine, accessible after climbing more than 1100 steps, is very colourfully decorated and has much gold leaf.

Nihondaira This is a plateau atop Udo hill, one valley away from Kunozan hill. You can get to the top by a cable car that begins near Toshogu. Buses also run across it via Nihondaira Parkway between between Shizuoka and Shimizu stations. From the top there is an excellent view of Mt Fuji in one direction and the bay and Miho-no-matsubara (a narrow strip of pine forest along the water) in another.

Rinzai-ji Temple A couple of km to the north of Shimizu station is this temple best known for its beautiful garden. Nearby is Sengen-jinja shrine. Its festival is 1-5 April.

Toro In 1943 the remains of a settlement about 1800 years old were discovered in this area (in the vicinity of Rinzai-ji). Excavations have revealed a lot about life in those days, including the habitations of its people.

The term 'pit dwelling' given to the homes gives the impression of living in squalor but they were actually built on ground level and earth walls about a metre or so high were built around the base to keep out water. The dwellings were round with thatched walls built on a wooden framework.

Reproductions of such dwellings (and some elevated store houses) can be seen at the park in Toro; the houses were actually quite cosy. The museum has displays of implements excavated from the 16-hectare site.

Oikawa Valley
One of only two steam-powered train lines left in Japan, the Oigawa Hon-sen private line runs through this valley. (The other steam line, the JR Yamaguchi-sen in the far west of Honshu, reverted to special steam runs after being completely changed over to diesel power.)

In past summers there has been one run in each direction between Kanaya and Senzu, leaving Kanaya at 11.34 am, Senzu at 2.35 pm and taking about 1½ hours. Be sure to check the current schedule ahead of time.

The journey through the Oi-kawa river valley from Kanaya is pretty and at Senzu you can continue on a different line where the cars are pulled by a miniature diesel loco. This one really twists and turns, passing over deep chasms and climbing ever higher. Its terminus, Ikawa, is a popular starting place for climbing in the South Japan Alps.

There is a small youth hostel a short distance from Kanaya.

There is little of interest west of this area along the coast until Nagoya.

Hakone Area

Hakone (and its nearby attractions) is the closest resort to Tokyo and is therefore very popular with Japanese holiday makers. Because of its attractiveness to the local population, it is also heavily promoted for visiting foreigners – perhaps too much so in view of the differences in interests.

The major attractions of the Hakone area are good views of Mt Fuji, Ashi-no-ko lake, some interesting historic remains and other views of the volcanic terrain. Be warned, though, that much of the beauty and interest of the area comes from having Mt Fuji as a backdrop, and this mountain is notoriously bashful in spring, summer and early autumn, often being totally obscured by cloud even from close up. Because of this, the later in the season (late-autumn and winter) you visit, the better the chance of seeing the undeniably superb form of Mt Fuji.

Japanese visitors may not be too concerned with missing the view but foreigners who may only have a short time in Japan should plan their itinerary accordingly.

The following section describes a vaguely circular route through the Hakone area that minimises backtracking. The starting point is Odawara or Yumoto-onsen. Access is by JR and Odakyu train.

Getting There & Away

JR JR services to Odawara are described in the Odawara section. At Odawara station take the Tozan railway (platform 11 or 12) for the trip up the mountain. (It stops en route at Yumoto-onsen, the terminus for Odakyu Romance Car trains.)

Odakyu The Odakyu (Odawara-kyuku) line, running from Shinjuku (Tokyo) Odakyu station is the most convenient way to start a Hakone trip. Any of its trains can be taken as far as Odawara (70 minutes) for the *Romance Car* train (Y1050), while the local and express Odakyu trains (both Y550) take 112 and 92 minutes.

The Romance Car trains are the preferred way to go, however, for in addition to being substantially faster, they continue past Odawara to Hakone-Yumoto (Y1280), where the transfer to the Tozan line is more convenient.

The Romance Car train, though more expensive, is considerably more luxurious than the ordinary trains and this is one case when I can suggest that it is worth spending the extra money for first class. Passengers in the front car can look out through the panorama window at the front of the car.

A good buy for economy and convenience (no need to stand in line for tickets during busy times) is a 'Hakone Free Pass'. Sold by Odakyu railway, the pass covers the standard Odakyu rail fare (Romance Car or express is extra), plus cable cars, boats, etc, in the area for four days.

An alternative starting point for sightseeing in this region is Togendai, accessible by bus from Tokyo (Shinjuku Highway Bus Center), Gotemba and Odawara.

Tozan Railway This one or two car train, which resembles a municipal tram, starts from Odawara station. Once into the mountains, the 'little train that could' struggles valiantly against the steep gradient, groaning all the while. It makes a number of stops along the way to the terminus at Gora. There are three switchbacks along the way. Trains depart Odawara every 20 to 40 minutes.

Miyanoshita

The only attraction here is the Fujiya Hotel, a five-minute walk uphill from the station. It was the first western-style building to be constructed in the Hakone district (1878) and has since added wings that are more modern, giving an interesting blend of American colonial and Japanese architecture.

The main building has the mustiness of age, rather like a dowager who has known better days. It will appeal mostly to those of a nostalgic frame of mind who wish to see how expatriates once spent their summers. The library and its old books are still there, as is one billiard table.

Top: Children's kabuki on an ornate mobile stage, Nagahama (IMcQ)
Left: Costumed children at Asakusa Kannon temple festival (IMcQ)
Right: Typical aproned housewife and child dressed up for a festival (IMcQ)

Top: Cherry blossoms at Heian-jingu shrine, Kyoto (IMcQ)
Left: Autumn at a Kyoto temple (IMcQ)
Right: Pagoda of Sojiji temple near Monzen, Noto-hanto peninsula (IMcQ)

You can have coffee in the first floor lounge overlooking the pond and garden; prices are reasonable. In the lobby there is a display case with a large number of miniature figures playing 'native' instruments. (But they are native to Indonesia and Malaysia! They are leftovers from the days when officers from the British colonies vacationed in cooler Japan to escape the tropical heat.)

At basement level there are commercial exhibits of electronic and photographic equipment (and price tags) that have not been changed since about 1970, a sort of time capsule; one of the companies represented even went bankrupt several years ago.

There are several walking trails from Miyanoshita, such as the one to Sengen-san.

Chokoku-no-mori

This is the train stop and the Japanese name for 'Hakone Open-air Museum' where sculptures are arranged around a garden. Many western visitors have spoken highly of it though the garden and several other attractions are largely aimed at day-tripping Japanese who enjoy such 'exotic' western things. Parts of it can be seen from the right side of the train as it passes, so you can probably decide for yourself if it's worth a visit.

If you do get off the train here, you have the choice of walking the relatively short distance to the terminus at Gora or taking a later train.

Gora

Gora, the upper terminus of the Tozan line, is the base station for a funicular railway up to Sounzan. Cars depart every 15 minutes for the 1.2-km trip and cost Y280.

Sounzan

This is the base for a four-km cable car system of many gondolas, each holding 10 passengers. The line first rises to Owaku-dani station, passing over Souen-jigoku en route, where steam jets noisily into the air. It then continues almost level for a long span across a rolling highland plain, finally descending to Togendai beside Ashi-no-ko lake.

Cars depart as soon as they're full. If made non-stop, the trip to Togendai takes about half an hour. You can get off at Owaku-dani or Ubako-onsen for a walk around and catch a later car or a bus down to the lake. Although Owaku-dani is interesting, judge by the number of people waiting to continue from that station how long it will take to get another car if you get out for a look around.

Owaku-dani

The name means 'Valley of the Greater Boiling'. (There is also one of Lesser Boiling, the Kowaki-dani, but it is so much lesser that it is of negligible interest.) The 'Greater' is the crater of old Hakone-san volcano.

The road and walking route from Owaku-dani station leads upward; on one side is the bus stop (for the bus to and from Kojiri), and on the other is the entrance to a path that meanders among the traces of activity of the old volcano. Steam pours out of the ground in several places and grey mud boils endlessly at another. The hot water is used at one place to hard-boil eggs which are then sold; chemicals in the water turn the shells black. Each attraction is explained in English on an etched aluminium plaque.

Near the cable car station is the modern Shizen Kogaku-kan (Natural Science Museum) which explains the geology and wildlife of the area.

Togendai

The cable-car line terminates at Togendai on the shore of Ashi-no-ko lake. The station has restaurants, etc. The adjacent parking lot is also a bus terminal and behind it is a dock for cruise boats.

Transport services including Togendai are listed later in the section.

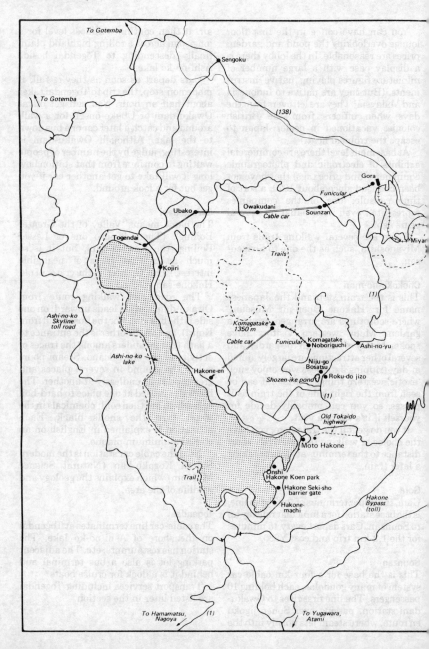

To Gotemba

To Gotemba

Sengoku

(138)

Gora

Funicular

Ubako   Owakudani   Sounzan
               Cable car

Togendai   Miyar

Kojiri   Trails

Ashi-no-ko
Skyline
toll road

                          Komagatake
                          1350 m
                                  Funicular   Komagatake
Ashi-no-ko   Cable car   Noboriguchi   Ashi-no-yu
lake
                                              Niju-go
                                              Bosatsu
               Hakone-en   Roku-do jizo
                          Shozen-ike pond

                                              (1)

                          Old Tokaido
                          highway

               Moto Hakone

Trail   Hakone
               Onshi   Bypass
               Hakone Koen park   (toll)
               Hakone Seki-sho
               barrier gate
               Hakone-
               machi

To Hamamatsu,   To Yugawara,
Nagoya   (1)   Atami

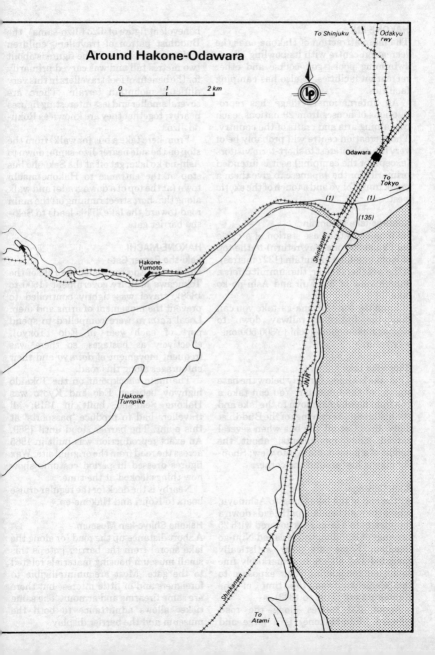

Around Hakone-Odawara

0   1   2 km

To Shinjuku

Odakyu rwy

Odawara

To Tokyo

(1)

(1)

(135)

Shinkansen

Hakone-Yumoto

Hakone Turnpike

JNR

To Atami

Shinkansen

HAKONE-EN

The main attraction of Hakone-en is the recreation centre with its bowling alleys, swimming pools, golf course and other recreation facilities. It also has camping facilities.

An 'International Village' has reproductions of houses from 29 nations, each containing arts and crafts of the country. The recreation centre will probably be of very limited interest to short-term visitors (except for the camping) as it is intended primarily for the Japanese to give them a break from Tokyo and a touch of the exotic west.

Koma-ga-take Mountain

Hakone-en is the base station of a cable car (Y550/900 one-way/return) to the top of Koma-ga-take mountain (1327 metres). If the weather is clear, the summit offers a superb view of Mt Fuji and Ashi-no-ko lake.

From the top of Koma-ga-take you can take the funicular railway down to Komagatake-nobori-guchi (Y300/500 one-way/return).

Shojin-ike Lake

This lake is almost directly below the base station of the funicular. You can take a bus from nearby Ashinoyu to the lake and the historic stone carvings of the Buddhist deity Jizo. Get off the bus when several carved stone monuments, about the height of a person, come into view; Shoji-ike lake is just around the corner.

Rock Carvings

At the end of the lake closer to Ashinoyu, where the road bends, a path leads down a few metres to a large rock covered with 25 carvings of Buddha; this is called Niju-go Bosatsu. Some are very artistically executed and all are in remarkably fine condition considering their exposure to the elements from the time of the Kamakura era (1192 to 1333).

About 100 metres along the road (toward Moto-Hakone) is a large and benevolent figure of Jizo (Jizo-sama), the Buddhist patron of travellers, children and pregnant women. The figure is about two metres tall and was carved primarily for the benefit of foot travellers in this very difficult mountain terrain. There are several smaller and less interesting figures nearby; together they are known as Roku-do Jizo.

From here take a bus (or walk) from the stop on the side nearer Jizo-sama, down to Ashi-no-ko lake; get off at the Seki-sho bus stop at the entrance to Hakone-machi town (at the top of a downgrade) and walk along the short street running off the main road toward the lake. This leads to Seki-sho barrier gate.

HAKONE-MACHI
Seki-sho Barrier Gate

During the Edo era under the rule of the Tokugawa military government (1600 to 1868), travel was tightly controlled to prevent the movement of arms and men. Local *daimyo* were compelled to spend part of each year in Edo (Tokyo), effectively as hostages, so there was frequent movement of *daimyo* and their entourages along this road.

The main checkpoint on the Tokaido highway between Edo and Kyoto was Hakone Seki-sho, built in 1619; all travellers had to produce 'passports' at this point. The barrier stood until 1869. An exact reproduction was built in 1965 across the road from the original site. Wax figures dressed in period costume show how things looked at the time.

Nearby is the dock for the regular cruise boats to Kojiri and Hakone-en.

Hakone Shiryo-kan Museum

A short distance up the road (or along the lake shore) from the barrier gate is this small museum housing materials related to the gate. Most are unintelligible to foreigners and of little interest but there are some firearms and armour. The same ticket allows admittance to both the museum and the barrier display.

Onshi-Hakone-koen Park
This is a park next to the museum, with peaceful walking paths through a small forest. During clear weather this area offers a good view of the upper part of Mt Fuji, complete with reflection in the lake.

On one of my visits there I was amused to see beautiful paintings of the lake, the opposite shore and Mt Fuji on the easels of a school class. The children had obviously been well prepared for their trip and were determined to portray the beauty of the area, despite the fact that they actually couldn't see more than 50 metres in front of them due to fog over the lake.

Suginami-ki
Just a short distance beyond the garden is the entrance to a section of the old Tokaido highway that runs parallel to the modern road for half a km between Hakone-machi and Moto-Hakone. It is lined with majestic cryptomeria (cedar) trees that were planted in 1618 to provide shade for travellers. The trees make the walk to Moto-Hakone town most enjoyable. From the shore at Moto-Hakone, near the bus station, you get the best shoreside view of Mt Fuji in the area.

MOTO-HAKONE
Hakone-jinja Shrine
A short walk from Moto-Hakone (and about two km from Hakone-en and the Komaga-take base station) is Hakone-jinja shrine. The present main building dates from 1667 although the shrine is believed to date from the 8th century. The buildings are not particularly noteworthy as shrines go but the mysterious atmosphere of the place is. The path is lined with venerable cedars and the shrine is set among equally huge trees dating from the 17th century.

There is a picturesque *torii* gate in the lake just offshore. Be satisfied looking at it from a distance as it is made of practical but unromantic concrete.

The shrine festival takes place on 31 August when lanterns are set adrift on the lake as part of the Obon ceremonies.

Old Tokaido Highway
A short distance up the hillside road from the lakeside bus terminal of Moto-Hakone (by the large *torii*) is the beginning of a stretch of the original Tokaido road. A pedestrian overpass leads up to it. Because of the hill, the road was paved with stones for a considerable distance to make walking easier and to prevent rain from destroying the path.

Most people will be content with a look and a photo at the beginning but a walk of about 20 minutes takes you to a coffee shop and restaurant in a traditional-style building that also houses Edo-era exhibits. Buses return to Moto-Hakone and also go to Odawara (opposite direction) but service is not frequent (about two per hour until mid-afternoon).

PLACES TO STAY
There are many hotels, *ryokan* and *minshuku* of all price ranges in the many hot-spring resort towns and other centres in the Hakone area. The most famous is the *Fujiya* at Miyanoshita, the oldest hotel in the area, while the most luxurious might be the *Prince* beside the lake. As for all accommodation in Japan, reservations may be made in advance through any travel agent in the country.

There is a *Youth Hostel* (tel (0460) 2-3827) at Sounzan, very close to the base station of the cable car to Owaku-dani.

From the Hakone-machi/Moto-Hakone area there is a variety of ways to continue.

GETTING AROUND
Bus
Buses run between Togendai and Odawara (Y970; 60 minutes) at 10 to 20 minute intervals through the day (until about 8.45 pm in summer from Togendai) following a route over the mountain via

Sengoku and Miyanoshita (roughly parallel to the Tozan railway).

About nine buses per day run between Togendai and Gotemba station (Y780; 45 minutes) via Sengoku, but the last one from Togendai is not much after 4 pm.

In past years there were buses between Togendai and Shinjuku (via Gotemba and the Chuo expressway) but these are no longer listed in *Jikokuhyo*. There are no other bus services listed from Togendai but several run to/from nearby Kojiri, which is not a long walk away.

Check for local buses running along the shore to connect to the other towns along the shore (Moto-Hakone, etc).

About 23 buses per day run between Kojiri and Odawara over the mountain via Owaku-dani, Miyanoshita and Hakone-Yumoto. About 10 of these buses start/finish at Hakone-en (toward Moto-Hakone from Kojiri). The fare from Odawara to Kojiri (55 minutes) is Y900 and from Odawara to Hakone-en (65 minutes) is Y1000. To/from Hakone-Yumoto is somewhat less.

There are two bus services between Hakone-Machi/Moto-Hakone and Odawara (via Hakone-Yumoto), both going over the mountain but following slightly different routes. The station for Komagatake is listed for one (but only a single bus per day is shown as stopping there) and some of the buses start from the barrier gate Seki-sho. Service is every 15 to 30 minutes until after 8 pm. The fare to Odawara is Y920 (60 minutes; 40 minutes to Hakone-Yumoto).

Buses also go from the Ashi-no-ko area south to Atami via two routes. From Moto-Hakone/Seki-sho there are regular buses south (about 12 per day) via a route over the mountains, passing through Jukoku-toge pass with its good views of Mt Fuji. One of the stops is Jukoku-toge nobori guchi, the base station for a funicular railway up to a scenic viewpoint. The bus trip takes an hour and costs Y900.

The alternative route is the bus from Moto-Hakone/Hakone-machi via Yugawara (one hour, Y1000) to Atami (85 minutes, Y1150).

About 8 buses a day run from Moto-Hakone/Hakone-machi to Mishima (50 minutes) and Numazu (75 minutes); the highest fare is Moto-Hakone to Numazu (Y1050), and is less to/from Hakone-machi and/or Mishima.

Boat

Boats run at about 40-minute intervals through the day (final sailing at 5.30 pm from Togendai) along the lake going from Togendai to Hakone-machi (50 minutes), then on to Moto-Hakone (10 minutes). The fare to either from Togendai is Y850; between Hakone-machi and Moto-Hakone it is Y250.

Another boat service runs from Kojiri to Hakone-en, Moto-Hakone and Hakone-sekisho-ato (Y600 and Y800).

Mt Fuji Area

Every visitor to Japan wants to see Mt Fuji, or Fuji-san as the Japanese call it (*never* Fuji-yama!). It is the symbol of Japan recognised universally and is truly one of the world's most beautiful mountains. It was revered, understandably, for centuries as a sacred peak and is a spectacular sight no matter how many times you see it.

Almost the ideal of what a volcano should look like, the now-dormant Fuji-san last erupted in 1707 covering the streets of Tokyo 100 km away with a thick layer of black volcanic soot. Its symmetrical, snow-capped cone rises 3776 metres from an almost perfectly round base. Around its north side are five lakes, Fuji go-ko, that add their own beauty.

Several places offer superb views of the mountain: from the Shinkansen train as it passes near Fuji city; from the Tomei expressway; from Nihondaira, near Shizuoka; from several places in the northwest corner of the Izu-hanto peninsula; from several places in the Hakone area; from Nanao-toge pass, between Hakone and Gotemba.

There are also clear views from many points along the roads that nearly encircle the mountain, chiefly beside Yamanaka-ko lake and between Yamanaka-ko and Sai-ko lakes. West of Sai-ko lake the view is not as good because of a shoulder at the base of the cone which diminishes the symmetry of the mountain as seen from other directions.

Visitors should be forewarned, however, that the famous volcano is very bashful for most of the year. In spring, summer and early autumn, Fuji-san is usually partly or totally obscured by clouds, even from close up.

From the Tokyo area, the two major access routes to the Mt Fuji area are Fuji-Yoshida/Kawaguchi-ko and Gotemba. The former can be considered the main one of the two for sightseeing if you don't plan to climb Mt Fuji. Refer to the end of the section for information on transportation to the places mentioned.

GOTEMBA

Gotemba is a typical, rather nondescript, Japanese city with no particular attraction apart from providing a bus connection to Shin Go-gome ('New Fifth Station'), which has become the favourite starting point for the ascent of Fuji-san. (Bus services to Shin Go-gome and the older Go-gome are detailed in the section on climbing Mt Fuji.)

Going by road, views of Mt Fuji are negligible or unexciting almost anywhere in the Gotemba area. From the city, the road climbs for several km to the tableland (Gotemba kogen) that surrounds much of the mountain, which finally comes into clear view near Yamanaka-ko lake.

Travellers with a limited amount of time to see Mt Fuji and the lake area would probably be best advised to go directly to Fuji-Yoshida from Tokyo, but if time permits a route from Gotemba past Yamanaka-ko lake will give a more complete view. There are about 24 buses a day between Gotemba and Fuji-Yoshida; most of these go further in each direction – to/from Mishima (1½ hours south of

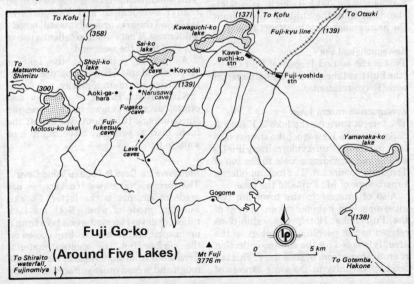

Fuji Go-ko
(Around Five Lakes)

Gotemba) and to/from Kawaguchi-ko lake (10 minutes west of Fuji-Yoshida).

Yamanaka-ko Lake

This lake, and the resort town on its shore, is a popular recreation area offering swimming, boating, coffee shops, other sports (such as tennis) and other entertainment that appeals to young Japanese. There are many *minshuku*, pension, etc, in the area. Rental boats and water-skiing are available by the hour.

Fuji Yoshida

Other than its annual festival on August 31, the only interest in this city is as a transportation centre. The many bus services for travel around the north side of Mt Fuji are described later in this section.

Fujikyu Highland Amusement Park

This park is more of interest to residents than to visitors (except perhaps those with children). It is close to both the bus station and Fujikyu Highland station of the train line between Otsuki and Kawaguchi-ko lake (which is understandable since the Fujikyu railway built the amusement park to attract money).

Kawaguchi-ko Lake

This is the second largest of Fuji Go-ko (the Fuji five lakes) and is a popular resort with Tokyo residents.

Kawaguchiko-machi Town

The largest town on the lake is Kawagu-chiko. Close to Kawaguchiko station (the terminus of the Fuji-kyuko railway line) is a cable car providing access to the top of Tenjo-san mountain. The lookout offers a superb view of Mt Fuji and the lake.

Also of interest in the town are two museums. Fuji-hakubutsukan, in front of the Fuji Lake Hotel, has exhibitions related to the people and geology of the area. It is noted for the Amano collection of erotic items from bygone days. This is a good opportunity to see some aspects of

the large role that fertility symbols played in the lives of the Japanese not so long ago. This very earthy element within Japanese society is not as apparent these days as it once was. The museum is a 10-minute walk from the station.

Yamanashi-ken Visitors' Centre is a museum of material relating to the natural history of Mt Fuji. It is about 15 minutes walk from Kawaguchiko station.

NORTH OF MT FUJI

The next attractions lie west of Kawaguchi-ko lake along the road around the north of the mountain. Scheduled buses running between Fuji-Yoshida station and Fuji-nomiya pass within walking distance of the places of interest mentioned.

There are up to 13 buses a day as far as Motosu-ko lake; most go considerably farther, to Shiraito falls and Fujinomiya on the west side. There are many sightseers in their own cars so hitching should be no problem.

Sai-ko Lake

This picturesque lake is less developed than Kawaguchi-ko and Yamanaka-ko lakes and the area around it is still largely wilderness. There is an excellent view of Mt Fuji from the west end.

A vantage point near the lake is Koyodai (Maple Hill), along one of the roads from the main highway.

Saiko Youth Hostel is close by and offers a good view in picturesque surroundings. It is about two km off the main road so you may have to hitch or walk to it.

Narusawa Ice Cave & Fugaku Wind Cave

The former, Narusawa Huoketsu is not made of ice, nor is the latter, Fugaku Fuketsu, made of wind. Both are lava tubes (or caves) formed when lava from a prehistoric eruption of Mt Fuji cooled on the surface but the molten material flowed out from underneath, leaving the rough and jagged inner surfaces. Both are cold, even in mid-summer, so a sweater is recommended.

The entrances to the caves are quite close to the main road (Route 139) and each has a bus stop. They are about 20 minutes apart on foot.

There are several other similar caves in the area, including Fuji Fuketsu on the Shoji trail which has a floor of solid ice much of the time.

Shoji-ko Lake
The smallest of the five lakes of Fuji Go-ko is regarded as the prettiest.

Eboshi-san
If you have the time you could climb Eboshi-san to take in the view from Shoji Panorama, the scenic lookout at the summit. There is a superb view over the Aoki-ga-hara Jukai ('Sea of Trees') to Mt Fuji. It is a climb of 60 to 90 minutes from the road. Inquire locally about bus services.

Aoki-ga-hara
The 'Sea of Trees' is an area of wild forest. The Shoji trail to Mt Fuji passes through it but general exploration is not encouraged because it is very easy to get lost and mineral deposits in the area prevent a compass from functioning. It is well known among Japanese as a place where people intentionally get lost and die.

Motosu-ko Lake
This is the westernmost and the deepest of the five lakes that stretch around the north side of the mountain and is of little interest to visitors.

Shiraito-no-taki Waterfall
This is a very pretty and unusual waterfall. The drop is not great (only a few metres) but the falls make a semicircle of considerable length. The name translates as 'White Threads', which is an apt description of the countless rivulets of water. It is accessible by bus from Motosu-

ko lake. Nearby is another waterfall, Otodome-no-take.

Fujinomiya
This city is of no inherent interest other than as a transportation centre for buses to Shin Go-gome.

NORTHWEST OF MT FUJI
From the Mt Fuji area there are many further destinations. Those to the east, south and southwest have been described. It is easy to continue northwest through Kofu to Matsumoto and the many other interesting places described later in the Central Honshu chapter.

Kofu
Near Kofu is a scenic gorge, Shosen-kyo. The most scenic part begins at Sen-ga-taki waterfall and continues for four km through the rocky gorge. Access to the entrance is by bus from Kofu station.

Getting There & Away Kofu can be reached from the Mt Fuji area by bus (up to 17 a day; Y1350) from Fuji-Yoshida/Fuji Highland/Kawaguchi-ko. It is also served by many daily buses from Shinjuku Bus Terminal and by JR trains.

GETTING THERE & AROUND
Gotemba and Fuji-Yoshida/Kawaguchi-ko can be reached by both train and bus from Tokyo.

Gotemba
Odakyu trains Though few in number, the most convenient services to Gotemba are the four daily expresses from Shinjuku (Tokyo) which instead of veering south to Odawara at Shin-Matsuda, switch to the JR tracks at Matsuda and run directly to Gotemba. These take about 1½ hours and cost Y1770.

Other Odakyu trains can be taken as far as Shin-Matsuda, from where you need to change to the JR Gotemba-sen line at adjacent Matsuda station.

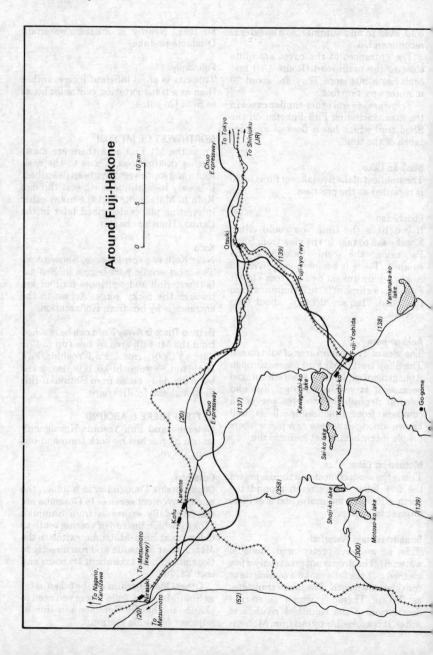

Around Fuji-Hakone

0   5   10 km

To Tokyo

To Shinjuku (JR)

Chuo Expressway

Otsuki

(139)

Fuji-kyo rwy

Yamanaka-ko lake

(138)

Fuji-Yoshida

Kawaguchi-ko lake

Kawaguchi-ko

Sai-ko lake

(137)

Chuo Expressway

(20)

Kanente

Sho-ko lake

(358)

Kofu

Shoji-ko lake

Motoso-ko lake

(300)

(139)

Go-gome

To Matsumoto (expwy)

To Nirasaki

To Matsumoto

(20)

(52)

To Nagano, Karuizawa

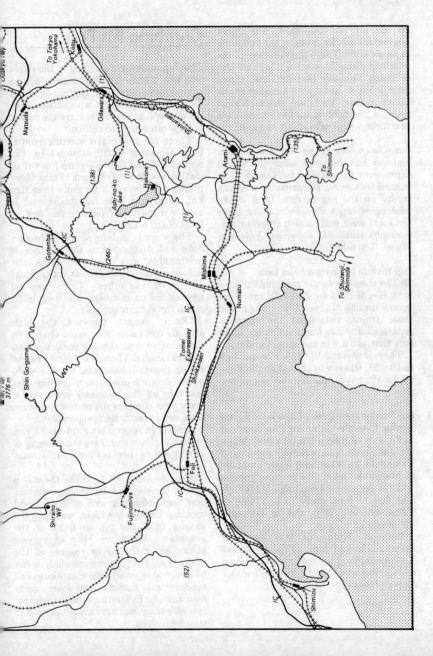

JR By JR to Gotemba, the most convenient service is one of the two daily expresses from Tokyo station or one of the four from Shinjuku station. There are also ordinary Tokaido Hon-sen line trains from Tokyo to Kozu, with a change to the Gotemba line. There are about 15 local trains a day from Kozu to Gotemba via Matsuda, which take about one hour.

Bus Gotemba can be reached by the highway bus that runs along the Tomei expressway from Tokyo to Nagoya. The buses do not go into Gotemba but stop at a lay-by on the expressway, from where passengers can walk a short distance to the local road and local transportation. Gotemba station is about one km from Tomei-Gotemba bus stop.

Fuji-Yoshida & Kawaguchi-ko Lake
JR The simplest way of reaching the area is by one of the four direct JR expresses from Shinjuku (Tokyo). If you take one of these trains, note that the train is separated into two parts at Otsuki, so be sure that you are in the correct end.

There is also the JR Chuo Hon-sen line to Otsuki, where you change to the Fuji-kyuko (Fujikyu) line for the rest of the trip.

Bus During the summer there is very good service from the Shinjuku Bus Terminal to Fujikyu Highland bus terminal. Many of these continue on to Kawaguchi-ko and Yamanaka-ko lakes, and lesser numbers to Motoso-ko lake. One or more goes to 'old' Go-gome on the north side of Mt Fuji. The fare to Kawaguchi-ko is Y1450, to Yamanaka-ko Y1700 and to Go-gome Y2100.

Between Kofu (to the north of Kawaguchi-ko) and Fuji-Yoshida/Kawaguchi-ko there are about 17 buses a day (90 minutes, Y1200). Kofu is a major stop on the way to Matsumoto.

Climbing Mt Fuji

The Japanese have a saying to the effect 'He who climbs Mt Fuji once is a wise man; he who climbs it more than once is a fool'. Those foreigners who believe they are wise will be pleased to know the ascent of Fuji-san is not too difficult.

There are two major starting points, (old) Go-gome ('fifth station') on the north flank, and Shin Go-gome ('new fifth station') on the south flank. From these places the climb is little more than five km, takes just over five hours and is mostly a matter of putting one foot in front of the other.

The official climbing season is through July and August when the weather is predictable and the conditions not hazardous to climbers wearing normal cool-weather clothes. There are no restrictions on climbers, and people do climb throughout the year.

Out of season, however, the high altitude can cause very rapid change in the weather and the temperatures can plunge rapidly. There is a definite risk of strong snowfall, blizzards, etc. If you do decide to climb in winter, make sure that you take all the necessary precautions; every year climbers die on the mountain because of insufficient preparation.

Anyone in reasonably good health can make the climb and there is no danger of getting lost as there is a continual stream of climbers.

Most people used to make the climb during the day but increasing numbers now begin climbing well after dark and continue through the night, watching the sunrise from the top or flank of the mountain. There are huts at various places along the upper reaches of the major trails but they are crowded, do not have a good reputation for cleanliness and everyone gets turfed out at a very early hour anyway. By starting around midnight or a bit earlier, you may avoid the need to stop for a sleep.

The major aim of climbing Fuji-san is to witness the amazing experience of *goraiko*, the sunrise. Although the sunrise is so often spoken of, the fact is that in early morning the top is often shrouded in mist and visibility is not good until later in the morning. One guide who has made the climb several times (from the north side) recommends watching the sunrise from Hachigome, the eighth station.

The descent can be made more quickly on the north side than the south because a large patch of the mountain side is covered with volcanic sand and you can slide down it very quickly. This is called *sunabashiri* ('sliding on sand').

In olden times before buses went to points high up on the sides, it was customary to walk the distance from the railway stations and then climb to the top. Several trails still exist but these days they would be better regarded as hiking paths for a day's outing without climbing.

The most well known trails are the Yoshida trail from Fuji-Yoshida station, the Kawaguchi trail from the town of that name (it joins the Yoshida trail at the sixth station), the Shoji trail from the Shoji-ko lake area (which passes Fuji-fuketsu cave along the way) and Gotemba trail from Gotemba. There is also a circular trail around the mountain about half way up.

The following description of climbing Mt Fuji is reprinted with kind permission of Jean Pearce who writes a regular column in the *Japan Times* and well-regarded guides for exploring Tokyo on foot.

I know what I should have been doing a year ago. I should have been jogging every morning, doing deep knee bends and running up the subway steps in preparation for what everyone should do once but never twice – climb Mt Fuji. But I know now how to answer this question: What should I take along on the climb?

You don't need much of anything, but you must be a stoic if that is your choice. We climbed in the heat of late July but it was

freezing after the sun went down. You can have a year's variety of weather – it rains, the sun beats down, you'll be groping in the mists. Be sure to have a cover-all plastic raincoat. After the storm, you can put it between the layers of your clothing when you get cold to seal in your body warmth, if you have any. And beware of the sun. Have a hat to shade your face and wear long sleeves. Even on a hazy day, Fuji-san's sun can inflict a painful burn.

You can buy lemons, hard boiled eggs, soft drinks, beer and sake, and such standard foods as soba and oden. Prices are high but remember, you didn't have to carry them. Take along foods that don't spoil easily such as cheese, cucumbers, nuts, chocolate and sliced meat, and a bottle of water. Toilet facilities are adequate but don't expect them to be clean or to flush.

Take gloves. Climbing Fuji is not a stroll; you'll be pulling yourself along with a chain over some rocky areas. You'll want them if you come down by way of the lava slide in case you fall. Cinders can leave scars with the persistence of a tattoo. Have a backpack so your hands will be free and outer clothing with plenty of pockets for immediate necessities like tissue and money. For your feet, sturdy hiking boots and two or three pairs of wool sox.

Accommodation is cozy; your own futon on your own tatami mat in friendly proximity with a hundred or so other hikers. If you don't have reservations at the top, stop early to be sure of space and don't necessarily believe the resthouse keeper who tells you there is room at the next station. He does not know. Some like to sleep a few hours along the way and finish the climb the next morning before dawn. Since dawn usually arrives about 4.30 am, it seems easier to me to do it all in one piece.

Be prepared for an early morning at the summit as well. Someone will likely be pulling off your covers at, say, 3 am (that's morning?) and if you don't get up then, attendants will be back for your futon some 10 minutes later. The room must be readied for breakfast service for the morning climbers who are just arriving.

There are 10 stations but don't be lulled by that statistic as you look up and count. You can't see the top from the bottom, and there are a number of resthouses between each official station that can delude the unwary.

Climbing the mountain on the same day I did – I climbed with a group from the Press Club and recommend that you find companions – were four blind men, two boys with their bicycles (later I saw them riding around the summit), a one-legged man, an 88-year-old lady and a gentleman of 93. Not everyone gets to the top but it is worth all the exertion you can expend to make it.

I don't believe there is a mirror on all of Fuji-san, except perhaps a sacred one in the shrine at the top, but it doesn't matter. You won't care after a while. At one stop I saw a woman powdering her nose. It looked pretty silly.

The best season to climb Mt Fuji? There isn't one. Climb it early in the official season (it begins on 1 July and ends on 31 August) and it's bitterly cold; later you'll likely have rain, perhaps a typhoon and pathways lined with discards of earlier climbers, though it wasn't the huge garbage heap that I expected, thanks in part to the tractors that, unseen, ply the back slopes carrying up supplies and returning at least some of the empty bottles. You will still marvel at the old men who jog up the mountains with three cases of beer and a dozen litre-bottles of sake on their backs for their resthouse concession; their sons, if they stay on the mountain, hire the tractor.

Oh yes, on the way back, it took us 4½ hours by bus from the fifth station to the highway at the foot of the mountain, normally a 20-minute drive. Sturdy climbers make the summit in less. When you climb Mt Fuji be prepared for anything. Ganbatte!

Getting There & Away

There is direct access to Mt Fuji's base stations from Tokyo and regular bus services from the nearby towns.

To Go-gome (north side) From Kawaguchiko station there are 10 or more (depending on the day) buses a day (Y1450). The latest of these during the peak climbing season arrives shortly after midnight, obviating the need to sleep at any of the huts.

From Shinjuku Bus Terminal (Tokyo), one bus (April to July, September to November) or two (main climbing season, from around 11 July to 31 August buses go directly to Go-gome (2100) in just under three hours. The second one (in season) arrives just before 10 pm. It stops at Fujikyu Highland en route.

To Shin Go-gome From Gotemba station

there are up to six buses a day to Shin Go-gome (eastern entrance), the last one arriving in the late afternoon (45 minutes, Y900).

From Mishima station there are several buses a day (numbers depending on the week and day) to Shin Go-gome, the last one arriving as late as 8.35 pm (two hours, Y2150).

From Fujinomiya station there are also several buses a day (again, numbers depending on the day) to Shin Go-gome (western entrance) the last arriving as late as 10.15 pm (about 95 minutes, Y1850).

These bus frequencies are representative of mid-summer schedules and buses are likely to be much less frequent at other times of the year. Be sure to check with *Jikokuhyo* or a source of travel information.

Saitama-ken

This section covers the Chichibu-tama National Park, Kawagoe and Sakitama kofun-koen. Other attractions of Saitama-ken are included in descriptions of the Nagano-ken and Tochigi-ken (Nikko) areas.

CHICHIBU-TAMA NATIONAL PARK

This large national park is northeast of Kofu and Yamanashi. It is divided into two areas: Chichibu and Okutama, in parallel valleys.

Both areas offer enjoyable nature walks and are especially popular with day-tripping Tokyo residents. A hiking trail extends between the two sections of the park.

Okutama Area

This section of the park is easily reached by JR Ome line which begins at Tachikawa (on the Chuo line).

Ome The attraction here is the JR Railway Museum, Ome Tetsu-do koen. Around

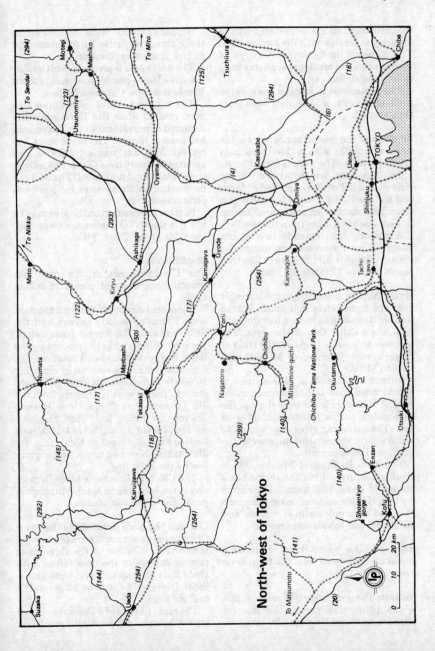

North-west of Tokyo

0 10 20 km

the main building are several steam locos formerly in service with the former JNR. The museum has moving displays of model trains and meals are available in an elegant old dining car.

The museum is in Hikawa-koen to the north of the city, a 15-minute walk from Ome station.

Hinatawada The general appearance of the town is scenic, with a low mountain looming over it. The town is famed for its plum blossoms which attract many visitors in late February and early March and an interesting festival is held at this time. The best-known groves are Yoshino Bai-en, less than a km from the station.

A walking trail extends beyond the Yoshino area via several low mountains (Sampo, Hinode and Mitake). The trail passes close to Mitake-jinja shrine.

Mitake Mitake *keikoku* (gorge) is visible from the train before you reach Mitake station; it can also be seen on foot from the path along either side of the river. The best way to see it is to get off the train at Sawai station (one before Mitake) and walk to Mitake.

Mitake-san mountain (930 metres) is well forested with tall cedars and other trees. A cable car runs close to the top; the base station can be reached by bus or on foot. The cable car gives easy access to Mitake-jinja shrine; this intersects the Yoshino-Hatonosu trail.

The main building of Mitake-jinja is about a century old but the shrine has a history of about 1200 years. The shrine festival, Hinode-matsuri, takes place on 8 May and has a procession of *mikoshi* and people dressed in samurai armour.

Hatonosu The gorge here, Hatonosu-keikoku, can be seen from the train or on foot.

Okutama The terminus of the railway, this is the point of departure by bus for Nippara cave and Okutama-ko lake.

Nippara shoyudo is the largest cave in the Kanto area; it is lit for about 280 metres to allow exploration.

The whole area is pretty in late October when the leaves change colour. It is about 40 minutes from Okutama by bus.

The southern shore of Okutama-ko lake, created when the Tama river was dammed to provide water for Tokyo, still has natural terrain. The north shore has typical Japanese tourist facilities and about 6000 cherry trees that are usually at their best around mid-April. The lake can be reached in 20 minutes by bus from Okutama station.

Further information on the area may be found in the JNTO publication *Okutama*, available at the Tokyo TIC.

Chichibu Area

The Chichibu part of the park has beautiful scenery and plenty of hiking trails.

There are two approaches into the park area: Chichibu-tetsudo railway and the Seibu railway. The former passes along the river valley and is intersected by the Seibu line near Ohanabatake station. The Chichibu line can be reached by changing at Yorii from the Tobu line (from Ikebukuro station, Tokyo) or at Kumagaya from the JR Takasaki line (from Ueno station, Tokyo). By Seibu line from Shinjuku station (Tokyo) the trip takes 1½ hours by limited express, longer by local train. By JR it takes about two hours, and slightly less by the Tobu line.

The Chichibu line route takes in more and is the only way to reach Mitsumine-guchi, the innermost station.

Chichibu The main attraction of the city is Chichibu-jinja shrine, 200 metres west of the station. It is one of the three most famous shrines of the area (along with Hodo-jinja at Nagatoro and Mitsumine-jinja). It is noted for large buildings and its tall, old trees.

The night festival of 3 December is well known throughout Japan for the procession

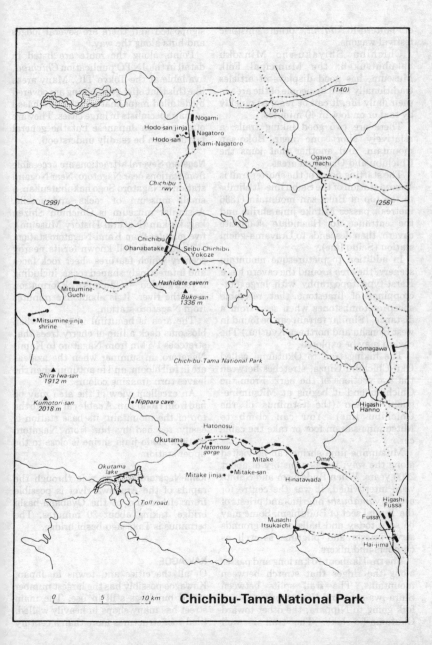

Chichibu-Tama National Park

(140)

Yorii

(299)

Nogami

Hodo-san jinja

Nagatoro

Hodo-san

Kami-Nagatoro

Chichibu rwy

Ogawa-machi

(256)

Chichibu

Ohanabatake

Seibu-Chichibu

Yokoze

● Hashidate cavern

Buko-san

1336 m

Mitsumine-Guchi

● Mitsumine-jinja

shrine

▲ Shira Iwa-san

1912 m

● Nippara cave

▲ Kumotori san

2018 m

Chichibu-Tama National Park

Komagawa

Higashi

Hanno

Hatonosu

Okutama

● Hatonosu

gorge

● Mitake

Mitake jinja ● Mitake-san

Okutama

lake

Hinatawada

Ome

Musashi

Itsukaichi

Higashi

Fussa

Fussa

Toll road

Hai-jima

0   5   10 km

of lantern-lit *dashii*, ornate historic festival wagons.

Chichibu Shiyaku-sho Minzoku hakubutsukan, the Municipal Folk Museum, has good displays of articles traditionally used by people of the area in their daily life. It can be reached quickly by taxi or on foot in 40 minutes.

There are two good hiking trails: a relatively short one near Buko-san mountain, and another that joins the Chichibu and Okutama areas.

The starting point of the shorter trail is Yokoze station of the Seibu line. It climbs to the top of Buko-san mountain (1336 metres), passes Mitake-jinja shrine and the entrance to Hashidate stalactite cavern, then descends to Urayama-guchi station (Seibu line).

In addition to picturesque mountain scenery, the area around the cavern has a Karst-type topography with large outcroppings of limestone that resemble sheep or tombstones when seen from a distance. (Similar terrain can be found in west Honshu and northern Kyushu.) The cavern may be explored.

The hiking trail to Okutama, called Oku-Chichibu Ginza, stretches between the two sections of the park. From the Chichibu end it begins at Mitsumine-guchi station (the terminus of the Chichibu line). You can climb to Mitsumine-san on foot or take the cable car.

Mitsumine-jinja shrine can be visited along the way; it has a history of about 2000 years. When Buddhism and Shinto were intertwined, it was the centre for ascetic *yamabushi* pilgrims and priests of the Tendai sect of Buddhism. Some may be seen today and halls on the grounds serve priests and pilgrims as well as climbers and hikers.

The trail is about 10 km long and passes along the ridges that stretch between mountains. The trail splits between Shira-iwa-san and Kumotori-san, one fork going to Nippara, the other toward Okutama-ko lake. The trail is well

signposted and there are several lodges and huts along the way.

Points along the route are listed in detail in the JNTO publication *Chichibu*, available at the Tokyo TIC. Many areas like this that offer good hiking are covered by detailed maps that may be purchased at map specialists in large cities. They are often only in Japanese but the general features can be readily understood.

Nagatoro Several attractions are accessible from stations near Nagatoro. Near Nogami station is Nagatoro Sogo hakubutsukan, a small museum of rocks and fossils. A similar museum is Chichibu Shizen kagaku-kan (Natural History Museum), five minutes from Kami-Nagatoro station.

Nagatoro is well known for its nearby scenery which features sheer rock faces and interestingly shaped rocks, including a 'rock garden' – a famous rock formation near the river. It is about five minutes from Nagatoro station.

The area is beautiful in spring when blossoms deck a line of cherry trees that stretches 1½ km from Nagatoro to Kami-Nagatoro, in summer when the azaleas are in full bloom, and in autumn when the leaves turn amazing colours.

An excellent view of the area may be had from Hodo-san. A cable car goes to the top of the mountain; its base station is easily reached by bus from Nagatoro station. Hodo-jinja shrine is close to the upper station.

Kami-Nagatoro A boat ride through the rapids of the Arakawa river is possible from either end of the Oyabana-bashi bridge, taking about 30 minutes. The terminus is Takasago-bashi bridge.

KAWAGOE

Of all the cities and towns in Japan, Kawagoe possibly has the largest number of old buildings still in use. The main street has many shops in heavily walled, tiled-roof structures more than a century old. For a glimpse of 'old Japan', a visit to Kawagoe is recommended.

In addition to walking around the town looking at the charming old buildings, it is worth a visit to Kita-in temple to see its attractive main building and garden, visible from an elevated corridor. Nearby is the garden of Go-hyaku rakan with 500, 40-cm-tall statues of Buddhist characters in a variety of poses. They are a little unusual and of moderate interest.

Kawagoe has an interesting annual festival on 15-16 November. On display around the city on those days are 23 or so *dashii* – incredibly ornate festival wagons, some of which are prefectural treasures about 200 years old.

On the second night of the festival the wagons are pulled through the streets, some in each direction of the route so that they pass each other. At every encounter, the costumed dancer on each wagon tries to out-perform the other. Each wagon carries its own musicians and supply of *sake*, so these performances become increasingly enthusiastic as the night wears on.

The festival dates back to 1648 and is typical of several that used to be held in the area, including in Tokyo. The *dashii* in Tokyo were destroyed during the war, however, so the Kawagoe festival is the only survivor.

Getting There & Away

Train From Tokyo, the most convenient way to get to Kawagoe is by the Seibu line from Shinjuku, as its terminus (Hon-Kawagoe) is closest to the centre of the city. Alternatives are the Tobu railway (Tojo line) from Ikebukuro (Tokyo) to Kawagoe station, or by JR from Ueno station (Tokyo) to Omiya, where you change trains to the Kawagoe line and go on to Kawagoe or Kawagoe-machi stations.

SAKITAMA KOFUN-KOEN

The Kanto plain has been settled for more than 2000 years, as shown by excavations of ancient relics throughout the region. One of the three largest clusters of ancient tomb mounds in Japan can be found near Gyoda. It consists of eight burial mounds and there's a museum containing artefacts dug up in the area.

Getting There & Away

Sakitama kofun-koen (Sakitama Tomb Park) is reached by taking a JR train (Takasaki-sen line) from Ueno station to Fukiage station, then changing to a bus bound for Gyoda via Sama. The stop is Sangyo-doro; from there the park is a 15-minute walk.

Chiba-ken

To the east and curving around the south of Tokyo is Chiba-ken. The areas adjacent to Tokyo (Chiba-shi city and beyond) are largely residential suburbs. Much of the rest of the peninsula is used for market gardening of vegetables and flowers.

Apart from beaches of the southeast and east coasts, attractions for tourists are quite thin on the ground and the area is of interest mainly to Tokyo residents looking for a weekend excursion.

CHIBA

Chiba city is noted for the enormous Port Tower which is open June to September from 9 am to 9 pm and October to May from 9 am to 7 pm; entry is Y400. It is about 10 minutes walk from Chiba Minato Station of the Keiyo line.

The city is also well known for the large number of soaplands.

NARITA

The city of Narita, after which the nearby airport is named, is famous among the Japanese for Narita-san temple (properly Shinsho-ji). It has stood on the present site since 1705 but succeeded another elsewhere dating from 940. Its pagoda dates from 1711 and Niomon gate from

1838, but the large main building is a recent (1968) concrete structure fashioned to resemble the traditional wood. It is a temple of the unusual Shingon sect of esoteric Buddhism which is known for ascetic practices.

It is possible that you may see pilgrims bathing in icy water in winter or walking endlessly around the temple chanting sutras.

Visitors have a good chance of seeing the interesting ceremony of blessing a car for safety. Results are not guaranteed but any help is useful for driving in Japan.

Behind the temple, occupying much of the 20 hectares of the grounds, is the very attractive Narita-san-koen, a landscape garden of traditional design with ponds and artfully formed and arranged 'hills'. Also nearby is Narita-san historical museum.

Narita-san is easily reached by taxi or bus from the stations of both JR and the Keisei line.

Only a couple of km away is Boso Fudoki-no-oka (Ancient Cultural Park) which comprises ancient tomb mounds approximately 1500 years old, and a modern museum housing relics excavated in the area.

BOSO-HANTO PENINSULA

The main attraction of the Boso-hanto peninsula is the seaside. Popular resorts are Shirahama, Tateyama, Hoto and Katsuyama. In the area of the latter two is Pearl Island where pearls are cultured. Demonstrations by women divers may be put on. Contrary to common belief, these women do not dive for pearls but for edible seaweed and shellfish. Indeed, anyone staying at one of the many *minshuku* along the coast may have the freshest possible seafood, caught in the afternoon by the lady of the house.

Further north is a very long beach named Kujukurihama – which means 99 Ri Beach, a *ri* being a measure of length.

Note that some of the beaches are

hazardous due to strong undertows. Further information about this area, including a good map and booklet, can be obtained from the Tokyo TIC.

Izu Seven Islands

Within the bounds of Tokyo are, among other things, two active volcanoes. They present no danger because they are located on two of several small islands south of Tokyo that are included in the Tokyo-to administrative area. The islands, part of the Fuji volcanic chain, are called Izu Shichi-to, meaning Izu Seven Islands. There are in fact more than seven but some are very small.

Until recently the islands were relatively isolated and some were used during the Edo period as a place of exile. They have now become popular as a holiday resort, especially among young Japanese.

Getting There & Away

The islands can be reached by boat and by air but schedules change by season so it is best to get up-to-date information on reaching any of the islands from the TIC in Tokyo.

OSHIMA

This is the largest of the islands (91 square km) and the name means 'Big Island'. Its high point, literally and figuratively, is Mihara-yama (758 metres) which last erupted in 1986 and forced evacuation of the island for several days. At the time of this writing it is rumbling again.

Activities on the island include swimming at several beautiful beaches, climbing the volcano (on foot or by bus from Okada or Motomachi), and visiting the 'Hawaiian' Botanical Garden of tropical and subtropical plants that can be grown in the mild climate.

The town of Saki-ichi and the nearby area are known for old houses and customs which differ from those on the mainland.

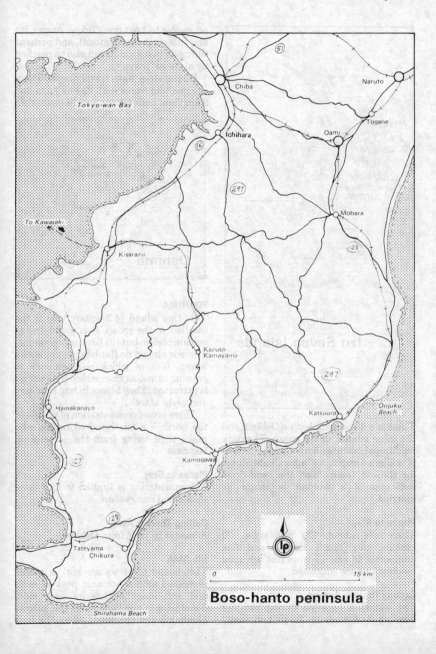

Boso-hanto peninsula

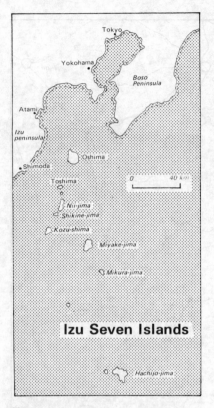

Izu Seven Islands

There is a distinct dialect on Oshima and the other islands in the group. The dark traditional costume with a white pattern is unlike a kimono; an 'apron' substitutes for the *obi* (sash), and the head-dress indicates if a woman is single or married.

Places to Stay
There are about 120 *minshuku*, 70 *ryokan*, two *Youth Hostels* and five campsites to choose from but advance reservations are suggested.

Getting There & Around
The island is crowded during summer because it is close to Tokyo and easily accessible by boat from Tokyo, Atami, Ito and Inatori (near Shimoda), and perhaps Shimoda in season. It can also be reached by air from Tokyo.

Bus services make travel simple. There are two tour buses each day at 7 am and 9 am from both Okada and Motomachi.

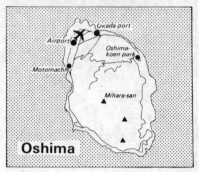

Oshima

TOSHIMA
This tiny island (4.2 square km) is the smallest of the group. It is round and of volcanic origin but the fires have gone out. There is almost no flat land on the entire island, 60% of which is given over to growing camelias from which fragrant oil is extracted. They bloom in late February and early March.

There is one concentration of people in the north – a few hundred people who make their living from the camelia oil business.

Places to Stay
Accommodation is limited to four *minshuku* and one *ryokan*.

Getting There & Away
Access is by boat from Oshima.

NII-JIMA
This island (23.4 square km) is rather elongated with a volcanic peak at each end and long beaches on each side. Swimming is excellent at several places. Maehama (on the west) offers the best

swimming and white sand but is very crowded in season. There is a campsite to the north. In the area is a museum, hot spring, temple and a cemetery from the days of the exiles. Habushi-ura beach has very high cliffs (up to 250 metres) but it is better for surfing than swimming.

The houses on the south of the island are interesting because they are constructed of lightweight volcanic rock that is mined in the area; they are known for their unusual architecture. Objects carved of the rock are on sale as is locally distilled *shochu*.

Places to Stay
There are plenty of places with about 235 *minshuku* and seven *ryokan* but reservations are recommended in the summer because the island has become very popular in recent years among young Japanese.

Getting There & Away
The main town, Honmura, is reached by boat from Oshima and Tokyo.

SHIKINE-JIMA
Despite its diminutive size (3.8 square km), this island has more than its share of interesting attractions. The scenery along the rugged shore is spectacular, with 10 to 30-metre high cliffs encircling the island; inland it is mostly flat. Most of the population is found in fishing communities to the northeast such as Nobushi and Kohama.

Shikine-jima and Nii-jima were once the same landmass but tidal waves in 1688 and 1704 separated them.

There are several beaches around the island, with surfaces ranging from rock to sand. There are two beaches where hot-spring water gushes out to form a natural (and free) *onsen*. The water of both is too hot to enter directly but at Ahizaki you can bathe at the seashore where the 60°C water mixes with the sea. At Jinata the sea mixes with the hot water only at high tide and cools the 80°C water enough to be enjoyable. Play it by ear as to whether a swimsuit is needed.

This was one of the penal/exile colonies and some traces of those days still remain.

A festival is held around 24 January for the return of the souls of sailors lost at sea. In mid-June there is a sea festival.

Places to Stay
On the island there are about 100 *minshuku* and five *ryokan*, so there are plenty of places to stay but reservations are suggested in summer because it is also popular with young people.

Getting There & Away
Shikine-jima can be reached by boat from Nii-jima.

Getting Around
Bicycles can be rented at shops but the island is small enough to walk around easily.

KOZU-SHIMA
This gourd-shaped island (18.5 square km) has a dead volcano in the centre. Most of the population lives on the west side; fishing, farming and catering to tourists are the main activities. The island is an excellent place for fishing from the rocks, swimming is good at Tako-wan (a white sand beach) and you can also climb the central peak.

There is a boat festival on 5 January, Juria matsuri festival on the third Sunday in May, Bon odori festival from 13-16 July and a shrine festival on 1-2 August.

Places to Stay
There are about 200 *minshuku* and five *ryokan*.

Getting There & Away
Access to Kozu-shima is by boat from Oshima and other islands and in summer from Tokyo as well.

Getting Around

Bus transport is good in summer and bicycles can be rented.

MIYAKE-JIMA

A round island with a live volcano, this is the third largest (55.1 square km) of the group. The most prominent feature is Oyama volcano (815 metres) which last erupted in 1962, leaving a stark black area resembling a collapsed sand castle. Much of the island is surrounded by cliffs 20 to 30 metres high. Activities include swimming and hikes inland through the forests.

The main beach is Miike-hama. It is unusual for its black sand and is the centre of seaweed harvesting. There is camping nearby but it tends to be crowded and littered in season. Less crowded is Okubo-hama where swimming is good and there is a nearby camping ground.

There are two small lakes – an unusual feature on such an island. Shin-Myo-ike dates only from 1763 following an eruption. It is less than one square km in area (the Japanese name means 'pond'), and is largely surrounded by cliffs 70 to 80 metres high. The water is salty and

Miyake-jima

Okuba hama

Oyama

Miike-hama beach
Miike-Mura village

Airport

Shin-myo-ike   Tairo-ike

0   10 km

mysteriously takes on seven different colours through the day. You can climb to the rim and look down on the water.

The other lake, Tairo-ike, is only a little bit bigger (1.2 square km) but much older (2000 years or so). It contains fresh water and is used as a water supply reservoir so swimming and camping are banned.

Although the island has an almost tropical climate the lake has many qualities of a mountain lake, an interesting contrast on such a small island.

There is a boat festival on 2 January, a shrine festival on 8 January and the *ajiisai* (a type of blue flower) festival in mid-June.

Places to Stay

As on the other islands, there are plenty of places – 130 *minshuku*, 12 *ryokan* and a *Youth Hostel*.

Getting There & Away

Access is by boat from Oshima or Hachijo-jima or by air from Tokyo.

MIKURA-JIMA

Although this smallish (20 square km) circular island is only 20 km from Miyake-jima (an hour by boat) there is only infrequent service, six or seven times a month. It is rugged, with cliffs 100 to 300 metres high round the periphery, a 100-metre waterfall on the west side and a dead volcano in the middle. There is not a single stretch of level road on the island, there is no public transport and the entire population lives on the north side.

Places to Stay

There are 12 *ryokan*, adequate for the few who can wait out the period between boats. Camping is not allowed.

HACHIJO-JIMA

The most southerly of the Izu group, this is the second largest (71 square km). It is characterised by two volcanic peaks, Higashi-yama (Mihara-san) in the south-east and Nishi-yama in the northwest, and there are cliffs along most of the rugged coast. It has a mild and wet climate all year round.

Hachijo-jima was the outermost of the islands used for exile and some relics, such as the ruins of large houses, may be seen.

Tourism is a relative newcomer to the

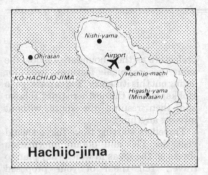

The scenery can be seen by bus tour beginning at Hachijo shi-yaku-sho (city hall) daily at 9.30 am, or by rented bicycle. Another attraction is Jiyugaoka-yuen park, where bullfights are held. Like those on Shikoku, Okinawa and some other islands of Japan (and as far away as Indonesia) the fights are not between man and beast, but are a test of strength between two bulls; the winner pushes the other out of the ring.

The exiles festival is held on 28 August.

Places to Stay

There are nearly 100 *minshuku* and 22 hotels or *ryokan* on the island.

Getting There & Away

There are boats from Tokyo and flights from Tokyo and Nagoya.

island and some old customs may still be found. A local type of cloth, *ki-hachijo*, is still woven and coloured with vegetable dyes from local sources. It is one of the souvenirs of the island; others are sake, and shell and coral products.

Northern Honshu

North of Tokyo are some of Japan's best attractions. A few are man-made relics but most are natural scenic beauties or curiosities. Perhaps most interesting, especially for the traveller with time to spare and a real interest in Japan, is the well-preserved local culture.

The northern part of Honshu, called Tohoku ('east-north'), was late in being developed and in this respect it still lags behind other parts of the country. This is to the disadvantage of the people who live there (though conditions are improving) but to the distinct advantage of foreign visitors who want to see at least some aspects of Japan as it used to be. (There are modern amenities, of course, so there is no hardship involved when travelling in the area.)

I would rank the Tohoku area with the Noto-hanto peninsula (Ishikawa-ken), northern Gifu-ken and Nagano-ken areas as the best in Japan for independent exploration. More folklore, dances and traditions survive in these areas than in most other parts of the country.

This chapter describes a route northward along the east coast and through some of the centre, and a southbound route along the west coast and other parts of the centre. This covers the maximum of territory with a minimum of backtracking and also allows description prefecture by

prefecture as their boundaries follow the same geographical features used for laying out this itinerary. You can also go to Hokkaido from the northern tip of Tohoku and then resume the route without missing anything.

Travellers starting from Tokyo should visit the TIC and obtain information sheets on the areas in which they plan to travel. Tell them of your proposed itinerary and ask for their suggestions for places to stay.

Several information sheets are now available, and others are added yearly. Sample titles are: *Towada-Hachimantai National Park* (MG-31), *Morioka & Rikuchu Kaigan (coast) National Park* (MG-38), and *Sendai, Matsushima & Hiraizumi* (MG-023). These sheets have up-to-date transportation schedules and fares and list several hotels, as well as giving sketchy sightseeing information.

A very detailed guide book covering only Tohoku appeared in 1982 and has become very popular with travellers. *Exploring Tohoku* by Jan Brown (Weatherhill) is almost of the 'telling too much' type but its plenitude of information has something for everyone and will certainly be invaluable for foreign residents in the area. Time has caught up to a few entries but it is still very usable in almost every way, especially if its information is combined with that of this book.

For details on getting around Northern Honshu, refer to the section at the end of this chapter.

Ibaraki-ken

Tokyo is on the edge of the Kanto plain, one of the largest areas of flat terrain in Japan, which is why it was one of the most prized fiefs in feudal times. The plain is

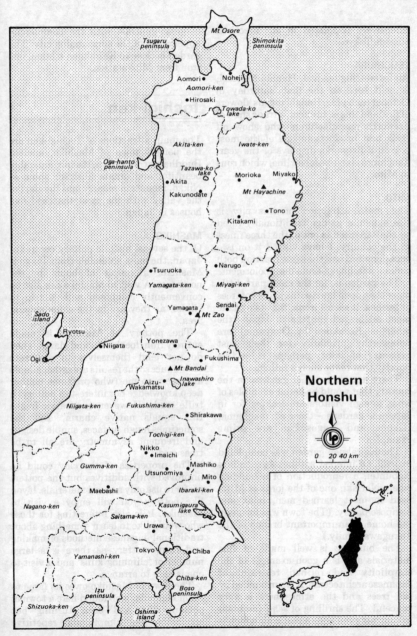

Northern Honshu

0   20   40 km

intensively populated in all directions outside Tokyo.

TSUCHIURA

An interesting festival, Hanabi Matsuri, is held here on the first Saturday in October each year. Hanabi means 'flowers of fire' and this is, in effect, a trade show of fireworks manufacturers who show off their best products in one of the most colourful fireworks displays of the year. Tsuchiura is on the Joban line, which runs to Mito.

MITO

The main attraction of this city is Kairakuen, a garden traditionally rated by the Japanese as one of the three finest in the country. I have visited it on two occasions and had the same reaction both times – a feeling of acute disappointment.

The garden is, for the most part, little more than open lawn with clusters of trees or bushes. It seems ironic that two of the most celebrated gardens in Japan (the other is Korakuen in Okayama) are noteworthy primarily for their vast expanses of lawn; perhaps it is this novelty that reaps such a rating.

There are many other gardens in the country that would be better examples of what foreign visitors are looking for in Japanese gardens – those at Yokohama, Hikone and Kagoshima are prime examples.

The Kairakuen garden was completed in 1843. Of interest within its grounds is Kobuntei, a reproduction of a building where Nariaki, one of the lords of Mito, used to meet learned men, relax and compose poetry. (The town was formerly the home of an important branch of the Tokugawa family.)

The building is well made of fine materials and is a good example of the simplicity and refined restraint of Japanese architecture. It is surrounded by tall trees and the atmosphere is very peaceful. The shrilling of *semi* (cicadas) in summer even adds a rustic air which is in great contrast with the commercial appearance of the surrounding city. The garden is close to Kairakuen station, one stop from Mito station.

Tochigi-ken

The main attractions of Tochigi-ken are the pottery town of Mashiko, ancient Buddha statues at Oya, the incomparably beautiful and ornate Toshogu shine at Nikko, mountain scenery and the start of the valley with the most thatched-roof houses in Japan.

MASHIKO

Of the several historic pottery centres of Japan, the most accessible from Tokyo is Mashiko, a couple of hours to the northeast. A visit to Mashiko can also be conveniently combined with a trip to Nikko, as they are in the same general area.

The pottery of Mashiko is made entirely from local clays and glazes. They do not lend themselves to elaborate techniques so the results are rather simple and seem to me (who professes neither deep knowledge nor interest in pottery) a trifle crude. However, to ceramic freaks this equals native charm, and the sometimes rough surfaces, simple designs and frequent asymmetry are all to be treasured.

The properties of the clay could be improved with additives but the potters prefer to use only natural materials. If you like pottery you will enjoy a visit to Mashiko. It is also interesting for those who would like to learn something about traditional Japanese methods of making and firing pottery as there is a large number of 'climbing kilns' and a visit to one is easy to arrange.

The town of Mashiko owes its fame to Shoji Hamada, who found here a town of potters who had been turning out serviceable but simple and repetitive

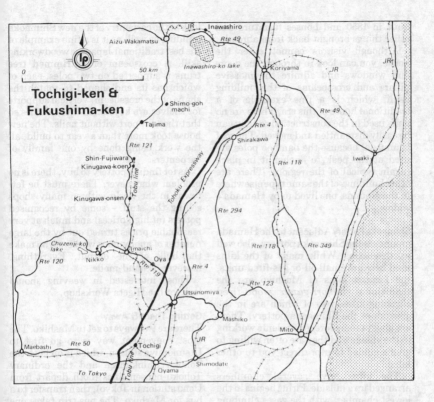

**Tochigi-ken &
Fukushima-ken**

designs since 1852. He settled in the town, absorbed their traditions and then built on them, establishing his own kiln in 1930. As his fame spread, it reflected back to the town that had nurtured him.

Adding to the fame of the town and the name of Shoji Hamada was the English potter, Bernard Leach, who lived and studied here for several years before returning to his homeland to spread the Mashiko influence.

Things to See

The town is filled with shops selling the local wares, so it could take a week to explore it thoroughly. There is a free handout map available at most shops in town. A good starting place is the Hamada

Home which houses a small museum and other attractions.

The Hamada Home This is made up of thatched-roof houses moved from elsewhere in the area, plus two stone *gura* (storehouses) of the type found throughout the region.

The *gura* houses the Mashiko Sankokan (Reference Collection Museum), a collection of odds and ends that Shoji Hamada gathered during his travels outside Japan. There are few treasures and little of his own work. I found the place more interesting for the old farmhouses that Hamada had brought to this place in 1943. The largest one was built in 1850 and houses furniture and other things brought back from abroad.

Although visitors cannot enter the house, you can look in through the doors and windows and admire the massive pillars and crossbeams of the building itself, which is a fine example of a traditional house of this era. There are no nails used in the construction so they can be easily dismantled and moved. The roof is unusual because the bamboo poles are used at the peak to anchor it in place (again typical of the region). There are other buildings of the same type elsewhere in the grounds, one lived in by Hamada's widow.

Shimaoka Pottery Adjacent to the Hamada grounds is the Shimaoka pottery, also well worth visiting. While many of the kilns used here are small oil-or gas-fired units, the famous kilns of Mashiko are the traditional *nobori-gama* wood-fired climbing kilns, two of which are in the grounds of the Shimaoka pottery. There are always some foreign students working in the village and they are often willing to give a guided tour or direct you to other kilns.

The kilns have several chambers arranged up a hillside. Firing begins in the lowest chamber, with the gases climbing and pre-heating the other chambers. When the first chamber has been thoroughly fired, fuel is then added to the second chamber and the first allowed to burn out. This sequence is repeated until all chambers have been fired. Because of the size of the kilns and the fuel consumption, many of the large kilns are fired only three or four times a year. It is an awesome sight as the flames and sparks shoot high over the stacks at the top of the hill.

There are many of these kilns scattered around the hillsides and they can be found easily enough, but the distances become appreciable. A look at the Shimaoka kilns will probably be adequate.

If you are able to arrange a visit, try to look at the carpentry of the new Shimaoka building as well, as it is a fine example of the best traditional Japanese woodworking skill. A crossbeam of untrimmed tree trunk is supported on two poles, each of which has its end shaped to match the shape of the crossbeam. Vertical supports for shelves are keystoned into notches so that they support without nails. The new house took more than a year to build, all the work being done by one family of carpenters.

As for finding pottery to buy, there is no problem whatsoever. There must be few towns in the world with so many shops selling the stuff – some by recognised potters (at high prices) and much at very reasonable prices turned out by the large number of anonymous workers who make the bulk of the output. Everything, however, is hand-made.

Those interested in weaving should look for the Higeta Workshop.

Getting There & Away

There are two ways to get to Mashiko. The most convenient way is to go first to Utsunomiya station, which is on both the Tohoku Shinkansen and the ordinary Tohoku-honsen lines (both depart from Ueno station in Tokyo), then transfer to a bus for Mashiko. The bus trip takes one hour and costs Y1000 each way. There are more than 20 buses a day in each direction.

Those who wish to go entirely by JR train should go from Ueno to Oyama (same JR lines), transfer to the Mito-sen line (32 a day) and go as far as Shimodate (the fifth station, or fourth by express), then change to the Moka-sen line (eight per day), which goes through Mashiko (seventh station). The train travel alone by this route totals nearly an hour and there will be waits between trains.

OYA

At Oya, near the city of Utsunomiya, there are 10 Buddha images carved in relief in the rock wall of the protective overhang. The temple building of Oya-ji extends back into the shallow cavern, protecting the images. It is believed that they date from the early Heian period (794 to 897 AD) and are the oldest stone statues of Buddha in Japan.

Near the temple is a 27-metre concrete statue of Kannon, the goddess of mercy, finished in 1954 – you can't miss it.

Visible in the surrounding countryside are the quarries and nibbled-away hills that are the source of the soft stone (tuff) used in structures such as the granaries (gura) throughout the region and beyond Nikko. Many small workshops can be seen where the stone is cut into building blocks.

Getting There & Away

The easiest way to reach Oya is by bus from Utsunomiya station; the trip takes about 25 minutes.

NIKKO

Nikko is one of the 'must-sees' of Japan, to be included in even the shortest visit. Adjacent to the town are some of the most beautiful buildings in the world, ornately coloured and covered with gold leaf.

The surrounding area is also famed for its natural scenery – waterfalls, a lake resort, forests and volcanic mountain peaks.

Information

The trip to Nikko is so popular that the Tokyo TIC has prepared free notes that give useful and up-to-date information on trains, accommodation and sightseeing. Be sure to get them before leaving Tokyo.

Things to See

The term 'sensory overload' was invented just for Nikko, particularly the Toshogu and Taiyuin shrines, as well as for lesser shrines in the area.

Superlatives become exhausted before the sightseeing does; you should allow a full day to absorb it all. The best way, if

time permits, is to spend a night in Nikko and stretch your sightseeing over two days.

Keep in mind that during the summer it may rain heavily for an hour or two from about midday, so try to get an early start.

Rinno-ji Temple At the top of the hilly main street stands Shin-kyo, the Sacred Bridge, an orange structure closed to traffic. Follow the road around to the left of the hill, to the footpath up the hill. This leads to one corner of the compound of Rinno-ji temple.

The major point of interest of this temple is Sambutsudo, Temple of the Three Buddhas, the largest in the Nikko mountains. It houses three gilded wooden statues (five metres tall) of Kannon (a Buddhist saint with 11 faces and 1000 arms), Amida-Nyorai and the Bato-Kannon (believed to be the incarnation of animal spirits).

The large avenue at the left side of Rinno-ji is named Omote-sando ('main approach') and it leads to Toshogu shrine, the most important single attraction in Nikko. To the left of the path is a five-storey pagoda, 32 metres tall, built in 1818 and redecorated in recent years. At the entrance to the shrine is a tall granite torii gate.

There is a basic fee of Y230 for admittance to the Toshogu shrine, Rinno-ji temple and Futaara-san shrine.

Toshogu Shrine Entry to this shrine is through Otemon, also called Nio-mon gate, with its statues of the guardian Nio-sama (Deva kings). The decorations are but a hint of what is to come.

From the gate, the path bends to the left. The decorated buildings encountered on the right are the lower, middle and upper storehouses. On the upper storehouse are noted relief carvings of elephants, created by a sculptor who had only ever seen drawings of elephants.

To the left of the path, opposite the

middle storehouse, is the sacred stable, the only unlacquered building in the compound. Overhead are various carvings of monkeys; second from the left is a famous panel featuring the three monkeys in the 'see, speak, hear no evil' poses. Carvings of monkeys were reputed to fend off diseases in horses. Visitors can feed the sacred horse (which obviously relishes the tid-bits) by purchasing a small dish of carrot slices.

Facing the upper storehouse, and to the left of the bronze *torii*, is the Kyozo (Sutra Library), which houses nearly 7000 volumes of Buddhist sutras (sacred writings). Beside it is the sacred fountain where Japanese visitors rinse out their mouths to purify themselves before proceeding farther. The water is safe to drink.

Yakushido Temple The next flight of stairs leads to the middle court. The similar

buildings on each side are the belfry and the drum tower.

Beyond the drum tower is Yakushido, the only Buddhist-style structure in the shrine. Yakushido is famous for its Crying Dragon (Naki-ryu), a ceiling painting in an inner chamber.

Admittance to this inner shrine requires a separate ticket, which may be paid for when first entering Toshogu. Visitors stand on a marked spot, clap their hands together, and the echo sounds like the reverberating roar of the dragon. The painting is quite recent as the roof was destroyed in a fire in 1961, as was a very famous painting by Yasunobu Kano (1607 to 1685).

Gate of Sunlight (Yomeimon) Returning to the courtyard and climbing the next set of

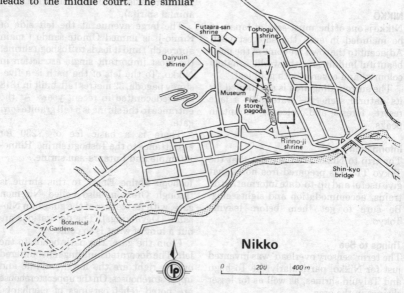

Nikko

steps, you come to the most beautiful gate in Japan and one of the most elaborately decorated structures on earth.

Yomeimon contains a wealth of intricate carvings, gilt and lacquer work, any detail of which would be worthy of display on its own.

The Japanese nickname is Higurashi-mon (Twilight Gate), the implication being that you could admire it until overtaken by night. You'll understand the sentiment when you have seen the gate.

Among the 12 supporting columns are two seated figures, and on the beams atop the columns are the white figures of stylised lions. From these beams, a complex and attractive branching of brackets spreads out to support the balcony that surrounds the second storey. On the ends of the beams are carved *kirin* (mythical Chinese animals), and between the black and gilded brackets are carvings of a Chinese prince, sages and immortals of Chinese mythology.

The balcony surrounding the second storey incorporates panels depicting Chinese children. The beam ends are decorated with white dragon heads, and a

dragon cavorts on the central beam. Above that, the rafter ends are detailed with lacquered and gilded dragon heads.

A low fence, also decorated, runs from either side of the gate and surrounds the courtyard. On the inside of the gate, back to back with the seated figures, are colourful *koma-inu* (guardian lions or dogs).

Through the gate and to the left is the *mikoshi-gura*, where the *mikoshi* (portable shrines) are stored. These shrines are carried in the two annual festivals (17-18 May and 17 October). Kaguraden, in the courtyard, is the stage used for performances of *kagura* (sacred shrine dances).

The closed gate facing the courtyard is Karamon (Chinese gate). It is predominantly white, in contrast with the fantastically brilliant colours and gold leaf of the other buildings and structures. The door panels are decorated with carvings of various flowers and bamboo, and the pillars with dragons. The figures around the support beams depict Chinese celebrities.

Karamon gate and the Sacred Fence (Tamagaki) surround the Haiden (oratory) and Honden (main hall), the central buildings of the shrine. The innermost chamber of the Honden (the Gokuden), with its splendid interior (the supply of

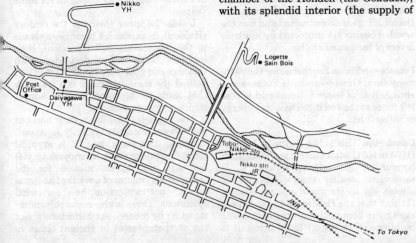

superlatives is becoming exhausted!) is where the spirit of Ieyasu Tokugawa is enshrined. His body is buried in a simple tomb on the hill behind the shrine. It is a Shinto custom for illustrious historical figures to be considered *kami* (gods or spirits) so it is natural for the shrine of his spirit to be the more magnificent.

The spirits of Hideyoshi Toyotomi and Yoritomo Minamoto are enshrined in the same hall. You can visit the innermost chamber but it is forbidden to take photos, which is unfortunate because the interiors are brilliant.

The last area of interest at this shrine is the tomb of Ieyasu Tokugawa, reached through the doorway to the right of the Sacred Fence. Over the doorway is the famous carving Nemuri-neko – the sleeping cat. There are said to be no mice or rats in the building because of its presence. The tomb is reached by climbing about 200 steps set among immense cedar trees. The tomb itself is severely simple and resembles a small bronze pagoda.

Back on Omote-sando, around the corner from the pagoda, there is an avenue through the trees. On the left, close to the pagoda, is the shrine museum which houses a good collection of armour and other relics. It has exhibits showing how the buildings are constructed and how the wooden beams are protected by multiple layers of lacquered cloth.

Futaara-san Shrine Further along the path, away from Omote-sando, is Futaara-san shrine. It is of lesser interest and is best left to see at the end if you have any energy or interest left.

Daiyuin-byo This is the shrine to Iemitsu (1604 to 1651) who constructed Toshogu in honour of his father, Ieyasu. It is somewhat smaller than Toshogu but almost up to its standards in beauty. (I think that the Haiden and Honden are even more beautiful than the equivalent buildings of Toshogu.) In addition, it is

possible to stand back some distance to take in their beauty and gain some perspective, as well as to photograph them. (The buildings of Toshogu are closely surrounded by a wall and photography is prohibited.)

Approaching Daiyuin-byo, you first walk through Nio-mon (Deva king gate) with its guardian statues. You then pass a small garden and can see the sacred fountain ahead and to the right. Turning left, you climb the stairs to Niten-mon (Two Heavens Gate), named for the two Buddhist deities Komokuten and Jikokuten. On the other side of the gate are the Gods of Wind and Thunder; the former is holding shut the opening of the bag of winds.

After climbing more stairs, you pass through Yashamon (named for its four figures of Yasha, a Buddhist deity) and arrive at the middle court with its belfry and drum tower. Between the middle court and the inner shrine is a Chinese gate, beautifully decorated and flanked by the sacred fence. Time and weather (it snows profusely in Nikko) take their toll of the decorations and they must be continually repaired or repainted. The intricate carvings of birds were retouched in 1978 so should stay colourful for some years.

Inside the inner shrine is the oratory (Haiden), from which a passageway leads to the inner main hall (Honden), both interiors being richly decorated with carvings and gold leaf. To the right of and behind the main buildings is a walkway that leads to the tomb itself, a simple structure by comparison.

The aesthetes look down their noses at Nikko because it is not 'typically Japanese', claiming it is too gaudy. It is atypical (though representative Momoyama style) but still not to be missed for the tremendous amount of work that has gone into it – not to mention the sheer visual splendour. There is also some misunderstanding by modern art historians about the aesthetic tastes in ancient times in

Japan. Many statues as we see them now are plain and undecorated but when they were new they were often decorated with gold leaf and were spectacular to behold.

Nikko Museum & Botanical Garden Beside Hanaishi bus stop (en route from Nikko station to Chuzenji), is Nikko Botanical Garden. A short distance back toward town is Tamozawa villa, a former imperial residence, now a museum. Set in a quiet garden, the building is constructed of the finest materials and is a good example of good Japanese architecture, though it is larger than most wooden buildings in Japan.

Festivals Nikko is noted for several annual festivals. On 17 October and 18 May there is a great procession of hundreds of people dressed in samurai armour and other costumes of the Tokugawa era. *Mikoshi* (portable shrines) carry the enshrined spirits of Ieyasu, Hideyoshi and Yoritomo.

This is a big event and always crowded but worth seeing for both the glimpse of pageantry and the feel of bygone days. On 17 May, the Ennen-no-mai (Longevity Dance) is also held in front of Sambutsudo, with two priests in elaborate costume performing ancient dances.

On 5-6 August there are very popular folk dances (Waruku-Odori) during the *Obon* season, which honours the souls of ancestors. Similar dances are held in communities throughout Japan at this time, but the Nikko dance is particularly famous.

Other days with festivals are 17 May (at Sambutsudo), and 14 and 17 April at Futaara-san jinja shrine.

Places to Stay
As befits one of the most popular tourist destinations in Japan, there is no shortage of places to stay in Nikko but it is wise to book ahead through a travel agent (JTB or the *minshuku* association) to be sure of a room.

Much of the available accommodation is of the high-quality, high-cost type. However, there are two youth hostels. *Nikko Youth Hostel* (tel (0288) 54-1013, 70 beds), once infamous for its surly, officious staff, has been transformed by new management into one of the best in Japan, with a relaxed, open-house atmosphere. *Nikko Daiyagawa Youth Hostel* (tel (0288) 54-1974, 26 beds), is an alternative.

Not far away by train is *Shinko-en Youth Hostel* (tel (0288) 26-0951, 26-0817; 33 beds) at Imaichi. It is near Shimozuke-osawa station, two stops out of Nikko on the JR line.

Getting There & Away
From Tokyo there are two train lines, JR and Tobu. The latter is the more convenient as there are many more trains each day, they are quicker and the fare is lower.

Tobu trains leave from Tobu station in Matsuya department store in Asakusa, not far from Asakusa station of the Ginza subway line. There are about 21 *tokkyu* expresses (Y2000), a couple of *kyuko* expresses (Y1500) and about 11 *kaisoku* expresses (Y1000).

The first seven *tokkyu* trains of the day (the last leaving at 10 am) take just over 100 minutes to get to Nikko and no change of train is required. The other *tokkyu* take between 107 and 118 minutes and require a change at Imaichi (one station before Nikko). The *kaisoku* take between 119 and 130 minutes and no change of train is required (except for two in the afternoon). There are local trains but they take an eternity and cost the same as the *kaisoku*.

NIKKO TO CHUZENJI
Regular buses from Nikko run several km up the twisting Iroha highway to Chuzenji-ko lake, a popular summer resort. One of the bus stops along the way is Akechi-daira, a lookout and the base station for a cable car that leads up 300

metres to a higher lookout (*tempodai*; three minutes, Y600 round trip).

This lookout has a much better view, taking in Kegon-no-taki waterfall. The source of the water is Chuzenji-ko lake which can be seen clearly, backdropped by the conical peak of Nantai-san (2844 metres).

From the *tempodai* there is a trail (for those who wish to take the cable car only one way) that leads to a ridge surrounding the lake (possibly the rim of an old volcano). A 30-minute walk leads to Chanoki-daira, the top station for a one-km cable car that leads down to a point close to Kegon falls (Y320/600 one-way/return).

A handout map/brochure of the area is available from the Nikko Youth Hostel (and possibly elsewhere in town). On the many walks in this area you will find enough points of interest to last for several days.

In uncrowded times the bus trip takes about 50 minutes but on weekends, in the summer when the cooler weather is an attraction, and in the autumn when the coloured leaves are beautiful, the road is clogged and the trip can easily be doubled or trebled and it would not be worth the bother.

Chuzenji-onsen

This is an extremely popular and very crowded resort town. The lake can be toured by regular excursion boat from various points, either by circling the lake (55 minutes, Y700) or crossing it from the town to Shobugahama (20 minutes, Y400).

South from the town, on the shore of the lake, is Chuzen-ji temple, which is worth a visit. The principal attraction is a tall, 1000-year-old wooden statue of Kannon-bosatsu. The carving, made from a single tree, has far fewer than 1000 arms, and the 11 faces are worked into a crown on a single benevolent visage.

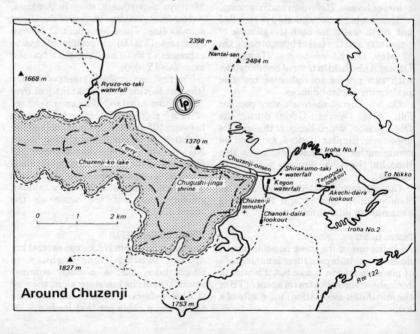

Around Chuzenji

The present temple dates only from 1902 when it was moved from a point west of Chugu-shi shrine when the buildings were washed away. A booklet in good English explains other details of the temple.

Chugushi-jinja Shrine This is the middle shrine of the three that make up Futaarasan. (The first is at Toshogu.) A museum here has a reasonably good collection of armour and swords, as well as portable shrines. The collection is similar to those of many Japanese museums.

A trail begins in the shrine grounds and leads to the peak of Nantai-san, a four-hour climb.

Kegon-no-taki Waterfall Kegon waterfall drops 100 metres from an escarpment into a wide basin below. The falls are not visible from the surrounding cliffs; the best view is from the tempodai lookout (as described earlier).

A lift takes you to the foot of the falls where the full power of the plummeting torrent can best be appreciated.

Shirakumo-taki ('White Cloud') Falls This waterfall, one of the many in the area, is a short distance from Kegon falls. The best vantage point is Kasasagi-bashi bridge which crosses the ravine near the midpoint of the plunge.

IMAICHI

Travellers going to Nikko from the Utsunomiya or Tokyo direction by train might wish to consider getting off at Imaichi first, then taking a bus to Nikko (13 km) instead of going all the way by train.

The reason is that the road is lined for much of the distance with thousands of tall, straight cedar trees. They were planted by a feudal lord over a period of years. He lacked the money to contribute a sumptuous structure when the shrine was being built, so he had the trees planted instead.

About 13,000 trees still stand and although the narrow avenue is crowded with traffic during the summer season (especially on weekends) it still retains its stately dignity.

Check with the TIC in Tokyo about schedules and bus connections to ensure there won't be a long wait in Imaichi. Remember that noon rain!

Thatched-roof Houses

Route 121 runs north from Imaichi to Aizu-Wakamatsu (in Fukushima-ken). Along this road is the largest concentration of thatched-roof houses that I encountered during 50,000 km of road travel around Japan.

The road follows a river valley for much of the journey; the scenery is nearly always beautiful and often rustic, with many old houses. Many changes have taken place in the last 10 years though and it is now much a part of modern Japan.

There is a bus service the full length of the valley from Imaichi through Kinugawa-koen and Tajima to Aizu-Wakamatsu. There are enough buses to guarantee connections but there may be waits of an hour or more.

It is also possible to make the first leg to Kinugawa-onsen or Kinugawa-koen by Tobu line train and the last leg from Tajima to Aizu-Wakamatsu by JR, but because the houses of interest are along the road, the bus will be more interesting (at least until it reaches the start of the flat and open country around Kami-Miyori, and that place is so close to Aizu-Wakamatsu that there is no reason to change to a train).

OZENUMA

A little farther into the hinterland beyond Nikko (westward) is the very popular swamp of Ozenuma. Swamps don't usually sound exciting but this one is a bit special and is very popular with the Japanese.

It is set on a plateau 1400 metres high, with a generous amount of pretty scenery including a lake that reflects nearby low mountains that have patches of snow on them, right into late spring.

Trails of logs are laid out as hiking tracks through the swamp but they're usually wet and slippery so take appropriate footwear.

The entry road branches from Route 120 at Kamata, about 50 km from Nikko, and from there it is another 25 km or so. The Ozenuma area can be reached by public transportation. There are up to nine buses a day from Tobu-Nikko station to Yumoto-onsen (about 1½ hours) where you change to one of the three daily buses as far as Kamata (about 1½ hours). From Kamata, nine buses a day go to Oshimizu (40 minutes) and another 10 run between Numata and Kamata.

Ozenuma can also be approached from the north. Up to three buses a day (2½ hours) run from Aizu-Tajima station in the thatched-roof valley.

There is a *Youth Hostel* at Tokura and *ryokan* and *minshuku*.

Gumma-ken

From Nikko you can travel on through Gumma-ken to Numata. (Gumma-ken is described in the chapter on Central Honshu.)

NUMATA

One route through this part of Japan is between Nikko and Nagano via Numata and Kusatsu. In addition to being the gateway for visits to Ozenuma, Numata also has one historic relic that might be worth a look. It is the house of a wealthy merchant, built two and a half centuries ago and believed to be the oldest in eastern Japan. It is in Numata-koen park.

Fukushima-ken

TAJIMA

A little more than halfway up the valley from Imaichi lies Tajima. It has a museum of folk craft housing items that were used in daily life. One traveller rated it better than the similar but more famous museum at Kurashiki in Okayama-ken. Ask for the Mingei Hakubutsukan.

Shimo-goh machi

In this region of thatched-roof houses, this small town is noteworthy for a street with

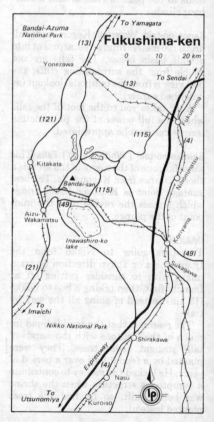

more than a dozen such houses side by side. The appearance of this area must be almost as it was one or two centuries ago.

AIZU-WAKAMATSU

This city was the site of the strongest castle in Tohoku (northeast Japan) at the end of the feudal era. At the time of the Meiji restoration, the local lord resisted in favour of the Tokugawa who had ruled Japan for about three centuries. Imperial troops battled the garrison for a month and the castle was destroyed.

There is a realistic replica of the castle in the city today but there are still authentic castles extant elsewhere so this is not of great interest. There are, however, several attractions nearby.

Aizu buke-yashiki

This is a reconstruction of samurai housing as it looked at the time of the civil war. (Most of the city was destroyed by fire in 1868.) Museums on the grounds show various aspects of Aizu-region culture and history.

Iimori-yama

During the civil war fighting of 1868 between the forces of the Tokugawa shogunate and those seeking to restore the emperor Meiji, a detachment of teenage army cadets was facing defeat on this hill. Rather than surrender, they ritually killed themselves. The hill, with its graves and monuments, can be climbed on foot or by long mobile sidewalks. A museum, Byakkotai kinnenkan, has exhibits from this time.

The most interesting and unusual structure is the strange Sazaedo, a sort of Buddhist shrine that is probably unique in Japan. Although the roof over the entrance is of the traditional shape found at many temples and shrines, the main building is a tall, octagonal wooden structure. Inside, ramps spiral upward both clockwise and anti-clockwise, meeting at the top after two complete revolutions.

The 'bridge' at the top, joining the two ramps, passes over 33 figures of Kannon.

INAWASHIRO-KO LAKE

The lake area is a popular resort destination in summer and winter (for swimming and skiing) so there are many in the vicinity. The land around the lake is flat and there are few vantage points for a good view. Probably the best point is at Okinashima (take a bus from Inawashiro station).

The popular Okinashima-so kokumin-shukusha is located on a hill above the road; it's a good place to stay, almost as large as a hotel, but an advance booking is usually necessary. There is an excellent view over the lake from the grounds and, when the atmospheric conditions are right, a superb view of of the volcanic peaks of Bandai-san.

The house next door to Okinashima-so is a bit of a curiosity. It is a very large house of turn-of-the-century western style, named Tenkyokaku. The characters translate as 'heavenly mirror house' and refer to the fine view of both the lake and Bandai-san (although trees obscure much of the Bandai view now). The villa was built early in the century by Prince Takamatsu and Emperor Hirohito spent his honeymoon here in 1924. It is open to the public and is still richly furnished and decorated with its original fittings.

Kitakata

Kitakata is a short distance north of Aizu-Wakamatsu and is noted for the very large number of old *gura* (rice storehouses) scattered around the town. Walking or cycling (bicycles are available for rent) around the streets is an enjoyable way to spend a few hours. There are also horse-drawn carriages, structured like miniature gura, that carry passengers throughout the town.

Making *geta* is one of the cottage industries of the townspeople. Pieces of wood in various stages of being made into these characteristic Japanese clogs can be

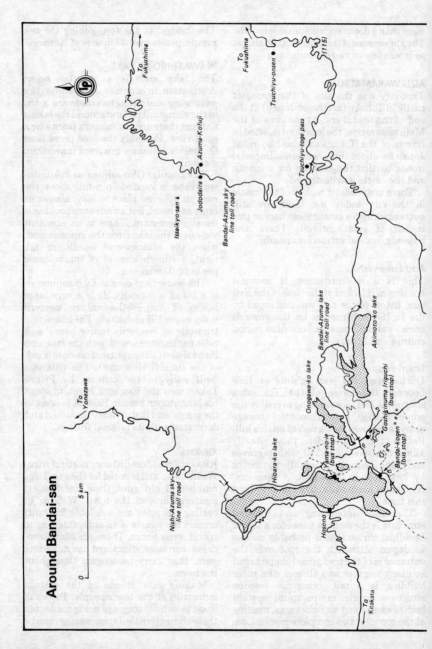

Around Bandai-san

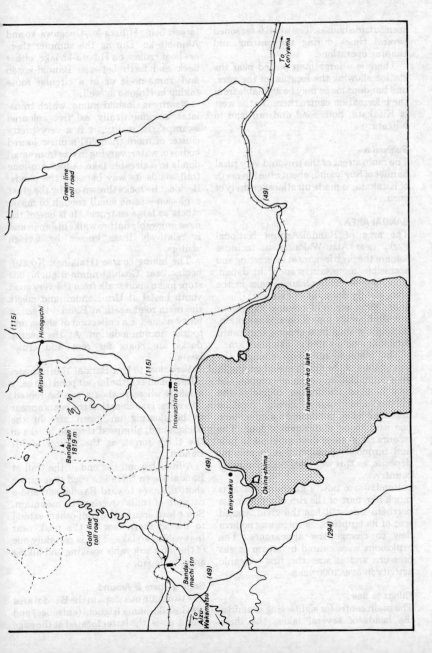

seen outside houses. The wood is seasoned several times during the cutting and shaping operations.

There is a large map posted near the station showing the location of the gura, and handout maps may be available from the information centre there. To the west of Kitakata, both road and rail lead to Niigata.

Sugiyama

The main street of the tiny and very rural hamlet of Sugiyama, about nine km north of Kitakata, is made up almost entirely of *gura*.

BANDAI AREA

The area of Bandai-Azuma National Park, near Aizu-Wakamatsu, includes some of the prettiest, most interesting and accessible mountain scenery in Japan. There are several volcanic peaks in the area, mostly dormant or extinct.

In 1888 a series of colossal explosions literally blew the top off Bandai mountain, hurling the rock in a general northward direction over an area of 70 square km.

The 'instant excavation' changed the topography of the entire area, burying 11 villages and killing nearly 500 people. The rock blocked the former course of the Hibara and Nagase rivers, creating dozens of lakes, ponds and swamps, each one said to be a different colour. The colours range from deep emerald to jade and turquoise, possibly due to mineral deposits, as this was once copper-mining country.

Bandai-san, now a group of peaks, is much like part of the rim of a crater. Its northern side still has the vivid, jagged scar of its eruption, as there was no lava flow to change the appearance. The explosions were caused by steam or gas pressure and it was the first volcanic activity in over 1000 years.

Things to See

The main centre for sightseeing is amidst the heads of several lakes, the three largest being Hibara-ko, Onogawa-ko and Akimoto-ko. During the summer there are boat cruises on Hibara-ko lake, either back and forth between Bandai-kogen and Yama-no-ie or in a circular route taking in Hosono as well.

Nearby is Goshiki-numa, which translates unromantically as 'five coloured swamps'. In reality, it is a very pretty cluster of more than 200 multi-coloured bodies of water, varying in size from small ponds to a sizeable lake. A four-km-long trail wends its way between the ponds. Beside it lie rocks thrown out by the great explosion – some small enough to move, others as large as trucks. It is one of the most enjoyable nature walks in Japan and is relatively little known by foreign visitors.

The hiking course (Haikingu Koosu), begins near Goshiki-numa-iriguchi bus stop, just a short walk from the very good youth hostel at Ura-Bandai, and meets the main road again at Bandai-kogen, a fancy name for a collection of shops and tourist accommodation. At the nearby docks are boats for rent and cruise boats.

Very close to Ura-Bandai Youth Hostel is Bishamon-ike, the largest pond (actually a lake), where rowboats can be rented. The water is so clear that the boats appear to be floating on green air. In the background, glimpsed through breaks in the thick forest, is the stump of Mt Bandai.

A little beyond the end of the trail at Bandai-kogen there is a road that runs a short distance toward Bandai-san and a network of trails covering the mountain. Some lead around the rim; others extend to the southern foot of the peak near Inawashiro-ko lake. This is certainly one of the most enjoyable walking and hiking areas in Japan.

Getting There & Around

The two main bus stops in the Bandai area are Goshiki-numa Iriguchi (entrance) and Yama-no-ie, the latter located at the edge of Hibara-ko lake. Buses connect these places (and other bus stops in the area, of course) with Aizu-Wakamatsu, Inawashiro and Fukushima.

Towards Yonezawa, the route includes the Nishi-Azuma 'Sky Valley' toll road; towards Fukushima, there are two toll roads, the 13-km-long Bandai-Azuma ('lake') Rine ('line'), and Bandai-Azuma Skyline – definitely worth travelling on.

The Bandai-Azuma Rine begins near Ura-Bandai Youth Hostel and passes between the lakes Onogawa-ko and Akimoto-ko, providing views of Bandai-san and Hibara-ko lake. It intersects route 115 which goes from Ura-Bandai to Fukushima, either directly or via the Bandai-Azuma Skyline.

Nearly 30 km long, the skyline road runs mostly along ridges and the crests of the mountain range, passing through the collection of peaks known as Azuma. The most interesting of these are Azuma-Kofuji (Azuma-Little Fuji) and Issaikyo-san, its neighbour. Both are moderately high (1705 and 1949 metres) but the space between them has filled in considerably so that the road passes very close to the northern rim of Azuma-Kofuji. You can climb up in less than 10 minutes and look or climb down into its crater – probably the most accessible one in Japan.

On the other side of the road is Isaikyo-san, an active volcano that jets steam with a continuous roar. Anyone who is the least bit energetic can scramble to the top in 30 minutes or so and be rewarded by a superb view over the conical-cratered top of Azuma-Kofuji and the rapid drop to the valley floor and Fukushima city.

Jododaira bus stop is between the two mountains, and buses between the Bandai area and Fukushima can be used to get there. A stop-over is possible, continuing on or returning by a later bus. There is also a daily round trip out of Fukushima to Jododaira, with a 50-minute stop. The bus circles back via Tsuchiyu-toge pass and Tsuchiyu-onsen. The trip takes 3¼ hours and leaves at 1 pm.

The area is very popular with sightseers so hitching should be good.

Miyagi-ken

SENDAI

The largest city in northern Honshu, Sendai was flattened during WW II and has been rebuilt like any typical Japanese commercial city, with many large buildings and straight streets in the central area.

One of the main streets, Aoba-dori (Green Leaf Avenue), is very attractive in the stretch where the trees are growing. It is rather up-market with many shops and good hotels and the feeling is of a European city street.

The rest of Sendai is unexceptional however, though foreigners there say it's a good place to live as the mountains are an hour in one direction and the sea an hour in the other.

Short-term visitors will find only a small number of attractions, namely Osaki-Hachiman shrine, Rinno-ji garden, Zuihoden mausoleum and possibly the grounds of the former castle, Aoba-jo.

Information

Useful maps and information in English for sightseeing in the city are available from the information centre in the station.

A guide book prepared by foreign residents gives good sightseeing and other info on Sendai and vicinity. Simply titled *Sendai*, it should be available at Maruzen bookstore, Sendai station and downtown hotels for about Y1300.

Aoba-jo Castle & Grounds

Aoba-jo (Green-leaf Castle) stood on this hill until 1872. Now only the fortification walls remain and the grounds have been made into a municipal park. A museum in the grounds has art and objects related to the history of the city and castle.

Sendai was founded and Aoba-jo was

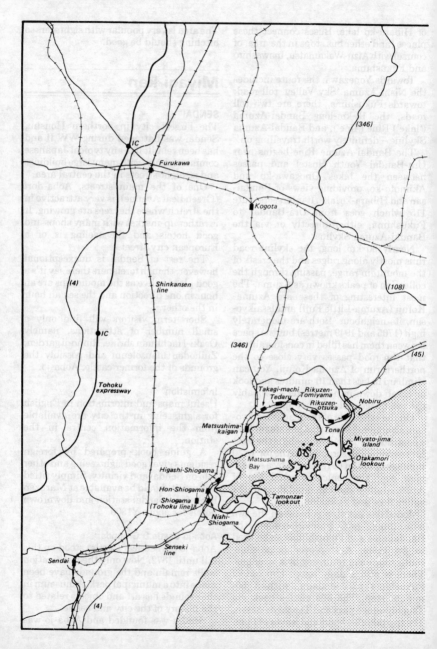

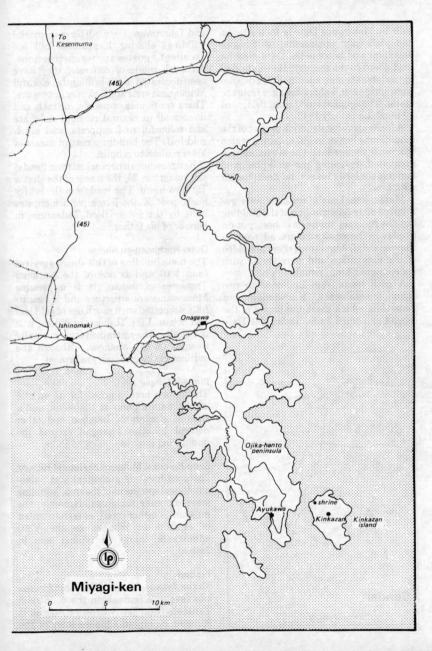

To Kesennuma

(45)

(45)

Ishinomaki

Onagawa

Ojika-hanto peninsula

Ayukawa

shrine

Kinkazan

Kinkazan island

Miyagi-ken

0   5   10 km

built by Masamune Date in 1600 after he had defeated opponents of Shogun Toyotomi and become the third greatest feudal lord in the country. He was buried in an elaborate mausoleum (Zuihoden) on Kengamine hill, a short distance from the castle. The original stood until destroyed by bombing in July 1945.

A five-year reconstruction project of the mausoleum began in 1974, during which the vault underneath the structure was excavated, revealing the well-preserved bones of the lord plus several items buried with him.

Masamune Date's remains were re-interred after construction of the building but the funerary items have been put on display in the small museum adjacent to the memorial. Also shown there is a video of the excavation and re-interring with appropriate Shinto ritual.

A path leads from Zuihoden to two other mausoleums, Kansenden and Zennoden, which mark the tombs of the second and third lords, Tadamune Date

and Tsunamune Date. All three memorial buildings sharing Kengamine hill are excellent post-war reconstructions. Although made of concrete, they have been decorated in the brilliantly colourful Momoyama style and look very impressive. There are figures of people, animals and flowers all in natural colours, elaborate and colourful roof supports, and much gold leaf. The buildings cost in excess of Y800 million to rebuild.

Kengamine can be reached from Sendai station on bus 25; the name of the stop is Tamaya-bashi. The road from the bridge leads past Zuiho-ji temple which was built by the second lord Tadamune in honour of his father.

Osaki-Hachiman-gu Shrine
The main building of this shrine survives from 1607 and is one of the National Treasures of Japan. It is a genuine Momoyama-era structure and is beautifully decorated with much use of gold leaf and colour. Like Toshogu in Nikko, it is not at all in the restrained style normally thought of as Japanese, although the outlines of the building are typical.

Rinno-ji Temple
The garden here is noted for its artistic layout, with a pond as the focus, and a stream, clusters of bamboo and other natural beauties arranged around the undulating grounds.

Saito Ho-onkai Museum of Natural History
Featured here are geological and palae-ontological specimens of the area, including some dinosaur skeletons. However, the museum is rather small, as is the number of exhibits in relation to the Y300 admittance charge (a typical sum in Japan).

Festival
To the Japanese, one of the most famous and favourite festivals in the country is Tanabata (Star Festival) on 6-8 August. It is based on an old Chinese story of the

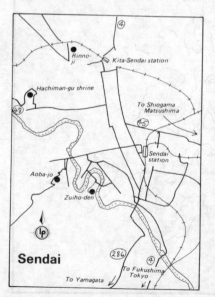

Sendai

princess and the peasant shepherd who could only meet once a year.

During the festival the city is adorned with elaborate paper decorations but there is almost no action worthy of note and the average westerner would find it about as exciting as a submarine race.

Places to Stay

There are many hotels and ryokan in Sendai as well as four *Youth Hostels*.

Getting There & Away

Ferry From Sendai, long-distance ferries ply daily to and from Tomakomai (Hokkaido) and Nagoya. The terminal is on the coast at Tagajo which can be reached by JR train or bus from Sendai station.

SAKUNAMI-ONSEN

This resort town, 28 km from Sendai, grew up around a hot spring occurring at the edge of a small river. The spring, at the bottom of the gorge that runs parallel to the road, can be reached via the lobby of the Iwamatsu Hotel. The baths, or *rotemburo*, are five small pools sheltered from rain and snow by a simple wooden roof. The only wall is the gorge face; the other three sides are open to nature, and a favourite winter pastime is to sit in the hot water and drink sake while admiring the snow.

Getting There & Away

Access is by JR Senzan line to Sakunami station; the line runs between Sendai and Yamagata. There is also a regular bus service from Sendai that runs directly to Sakunami-onsen.

SHIOGAMA

This is the port for Sendai and is of limited interest. The main feature is Shiogama-jinja shrine, a large structure mostly painted orange and white, although inner buildings are built in a traditional manner with very simple lines and natural wood. In the grounds is a museum of historic

relics and exhibits related to whaling, which used to be carried out here. The shrine is on a wooded hill near Shiogama station.

Getting There & Away

Boat Boats run regularly between Shiogama and both Matsushima-kaigan and Otakamori, passing by many of the little islands for which Matsushima Bay is famous.

Details on boat services is given in the following section on Matsushima.

TAMONZAN

One of the best places to view Matsushima Bay is Tamonzan hill. To get there, take a bus from Shiogama station to Tamonzan stop (the road continues on to a couple of inviting ocean beaches) and walk along the little road to the left of the electric power station (you can't miss it).

After a couple of hundred metres there is a concrete staircase which leads up Tamonzan to a little shrine and a good view over the water to the white-shored, tree-covered islands and the small boats passing through the narrow channels between them.

Around the shrine, which is likely to be totally deserted, are many figurines of foxes (the messenger of Inari shrines) plus small, 40-cm-high shrine-shaped houses to shelter them.

MATSUSHIMA

About 40 minutes by train (JR Senseki line) from Sendai lies famed Matsushima Bay, which is dotted with more than 250 small islands of strange shapes all covered with twisted pine trees. Some of the islands are inhabited, while others are little more than dots in the water. (Matsushima means 'pine islands'.)

The area is regarded as one of the traditional 'big three' of Japanese natural scenery (along with Amanohashidate, north of Kyoto, and Itsukushima, near Hiroshima). It is certainly pretty and worth seeing both by regular cruise boat from Matsushima or Shiogama and on foot around Matsushima.

Oshima Island

The red-lacquered Togetsukyo bridge connects the mainland (just near Matsushima-kaigan station) with this small scenic island. In former times Oshima was the site of ascetic practices by the Buddhist faithful. The only evidence of those days are the many interesting niches and small caves cut in the rocks, and many carved stone memorials and Buddhist figures. The island offers good views over Matsushima Bay.

Kanrantei

The 'Wave Viewing Pavilion', or Kanrantei, is one of the best places for viewing the bay and is just a short walk from the station past the large park. Kanrantei is a teahouse dating from the early 1600s and was originally part of Momoyama-jo castle in Kyoto. It was given to Masamune Date and moved here when the castle was demolished and its major buildings scattered around Japan.

Matsushima Hakubutsukan Museum

Next to Kanrantei, this museum has an excellent collection of Japanese suits of armour, swords, pikes (used by foot soldiers to fight cavalrymen) and a number of pieces of high quality lacquerware, all of the Date clan.

Zuigan-ji Temple

This Zen temple was established more than 700 years ago although the present buildings date only from 1609. They were built under the direction of Masamune Date and are of Momoyama style. The paintwork is faded and peeled but you can still admire the numerous ornately carved wooden panels and the decorated sliding doors. The temple is a National Treasure, which is surprising since this area was a backwater until quite recently.

The grounds are very restful; tall trees shade the large area and you can see the rooms carved out of solid rock that were once the quarters of monks. The temple is located across the road from the dock area, down a sidestreet signposted in English.

Godaido

At the left extremity of the dock area are two short red bridges that lead to Godaido on the tiny island of Godaido-jima. Godaido, which could be described as a worship hall, is part of Zuigan-ji temple and houses five statues of Buddhist figures.

The colour that might once have existed on the building has weathered away but the wood has survived the centuries well and the carved animals under the eaves, the complex supports of the roof, and other details are worthy of note. The interior is said to be beautifully decorated but the building is opened only once every 33 years.

Fukura-jima Island

The entrance to Fukura-jima is easily identified because the long red bridge out to the island is visible from anywhere near the harbour. There is no historic significance to the island but it is a sort of natural botanical garden.

Saigyo Modoshi no Matsu-koen Park

The best, all-encompassing view of Matsushima Bay is from this park on the hill behind the town. The view is good at any time of the day but the best way to enjoy it is to spend the late afternoon on the verandah of the Panorama restaurant with a coffee or a beer and watch the last rays of the sun on the bay. There are also two lookouts that afford views of other parts of the bay. The simplest way to get to the park is by taxi; you can go on foot if you feel like a two-km climb.

Festivals

On 15 August the Matsushima-Toro-Nagashi festival is held at Matsushima-kaigan. Thousands of tiny lanterns are set adrift from the beach (at about 7 pm) after which there is a fireworks display. The festival is part of the Buddhist observances of *Obon*, the Festival of the Dead, which is held throughout Japan. There is also a lesser festival the following day.

Places to Stay

There are more than 40 *ryokan* around Matsushima-kaigan. The *Matsushima Youth Hostel* is on Miyato Island and can be reached from Nobiru station or by boat to Otakamori and then bus (or on foot) the three km to the hostel. From the dock at Otakamori, go left past Otakamori-kanko Hotel and take the left fork in the road further along.

Getting There & Around

Boat cruises There are both scheduled public boats and charter cruises available around the islands that dot Matsushima Bay. These offer one of the most pleasant ways to see the sights of the area.

Scheduled one-hour cruises leave hourly between 10 am and 4 pm and take in a major part of the bay's scenic areas. Seats cost Y1800; standing is Y1200 for adults, Y600 for children, with a discount for groups of 15 or more.

Charter boats also cruise the bay at a fixed price (regardless of the number of passengers) determined by the route taken. This can be Y3000, Y4000, Y6000 or Y15,000.

In addition to round-trip cruises, there are up to 16 boats per day in each direction between Matsushima-kaigan and Shiogama (Y1400; 60 minutes).

Between Shiogama and Otakamori (Miyato-jima island) there are three boats daily in each direction; between Matsushima-kaigan and Otakamori there are two boats daily in each direction (Y1200 minimum; 60 minutes).

At Matsushima-kaigan the boats dock at the central pier which is easily reached from Matsushima-kaigan station. At Shiogama, boats leave from Shiogama-ko port, a five-minute walk from Hon-Shiogama station (Senseki line).

OJIKA-HANTO PENINSULA

A trip down the beautiful south coast of this peninsula can be recommended, especially if you have your own transport and can stop at the many lookouts. The coastal views include a succession of bays, interesting rock formations, little fishing villages, many fishing boats and of course the ocean itself. This is not good territory for cyclists as there are many steep hills.

There are seven buses a day (Y1400, 1¾ hours) from Ishinomaki to Ayukawa near the southern tip, and a daily boat in each direction that leaves Ishinomaki at 9.40 am and Ayukawa at 7.30 am.

Beyond Ayukawa (no public transport listed) the road leads around the top of the peninsula to a fine view of Kinkazan Island, just a short distance off the coast. You can sit and admire the view from the restaurant close to the entrance to the toll road.

Ayukawa is a whaling port and the museum (near the dock for the Kinkazan boat) has an exhibit about whales and the industry.

KINKAZAN ISLAND

A mysterious atmosphere seems to surround this island which is just off the coast of Ojika-hanto peninsula. Various visitors have mentioned the peace at night, especially when staying at the youth hostel at Koganeyama-jinja shrine. The name Kinkazan means 'Gold Flower Mountain', which seems to be a reference to the sparkle of mica in rocks on the island.

The island is covered with dense bamboo groves and forests, and monkeys and deer roam free.

Koganeyama-jinja Shrine

This is one of the main attractions of the island and is surprisingly large for such a remote place. There may be an early-morning service (about 6.30) featuring sacred dances by shrine maidens, with traditional music and chanting by priests.

Behind the shrine a two-km path leads to the top of the mountain where there is another shrine. The walk to the top takes an hour or so.

Getting There & Away

Boat Up to 10 ferries a day run between Ayukawa-ko port and Kinkazan (Y750); the single boat between Ishinomaki and Ayukawa is one of these. In addition there are up to five ferries a day between Kinkazan and Onagawa, which is the terminus of a JR line (Y1600 minimum; 85 minutes).

Road & Rail Above the Matsushima/Ojika-hanto peninsula area you can go inland along Route 4 to the attractions in Miyagi-ken and beyond in Iwate-ken, or along the east coast. There are several roads and railway lines linking Route 4 with the coast, so it is possible to criss-cross to take in nearly all the attractions without backtracking.

Heading inland, Route 4 is slow, crowded and not very interesting but *shi kata ga nai* – it can't be helped. To get to Narugo and its nearby geyser turn off on to Route 47 at Furukawa, or take the train.

NARUGO

This town, actually the collective name for a series of hot-spring resorts, has numerous *ryokan* and hotels catering to the hot-spring crowd, as well as an unmemorable (but adequate) youth hostel.

The town is not particularly noteworthy – basically a string of buildings up the sides of a hill – but some very attractive lacquerware is produced here, and the town is famous for its Narugo-kokeshi dolls.

Kokeshi are very simple, with a cylindrical (lathe-turned) body, round head and simple, painted features. The Narugo dolls 'cry' when the head is

turned, one explanation (veracity not guaranteed) being that families made them years ago to honour the souls of girl babies that had been abandoned in the open to die because there was not enough food to support them (being less-useful females). Many dolls are made in shops along the main street and you can watch the process.

Onikobe-onsen

One of Japan's few geysers, and probably the highest spurting, is at Onikobe-onsen (a collective name for several onsen, this one meaning 'ogre's head').

About 14 km north of Narugo, the geyser can be reached by bus from Narugo station; just ask to be let off at Onikobe kanketsu-sen-onsen. From the stop, the small park surrounding the geyser is down a side road.

The geyser is artificial to the extent that a hole was bored to tap the underground pool, but the eruption, every 30 minutes or so, is entirely natural. Water shoots at least 15 metres into the air for several minutes. Close by is a warm water swimming pool that can be used by those who have already paid to see the geyser.

Narugo-kyo Gorge

About three km outside Narugo, near

Nakayama-daira-guchi, this gorge is an enjoyable place to walk. It follows a small river for about four km. To get there take a bus from Narugo station.

The Tsuruoka area of the west coast is easily reached from this point.

Iwate-ken

HIRAIZUMI

Taking the inland route you come to this ordinary looking town, once the cultural centre of the area, which contains the most historic temple in northern Japan. Nearby are two interesting gorges and beautiful views of typical farmland with some of the largest and finest farmhouses in the country.

Chuson-ji Temple

This temple was founded in 1105 to accompany a fortress in Hiraizumi built by the Fujiwara family. Of the more than 40 buildings then standing, only two have survived. One, Kyozo, is not particularly noteworthy, but the other, Kon-jiki-do, is a marvel of finely executed, ornate decoration.

Kon-jiki-do ('golden hall') was originally protected by an outer structure but recently a new concrete building was put up around it to provide a climate-controlled environment. At the same time, it was restored to its original splendour, using authentic materials from the same sources as the ones used initially.

The exterior is lacquered black and there are large panels of mother-of-pearl and gold leaf. Inside are three altars, each with 11 Buddhist deities (three Amida, six of Jizo and two of Ten). The building is small (only 5½ metres square) but you can stand for a long time admiring it through the protective plate glass. The remains of three of the Fujiwara rulers lie under the central altar.

The grounds of the temple are very restful, set at the top of a large hill that overlooks fertile farming country. An avenue of tall trees lines the stone-paved road up from the entrance. The entry fee also covers the nearby Sankozo museum.

There are many buses to the temple from the station throughout the day and the entrance is a drop-off point for the bus that runs between Hiraizumi station and Ichinoseki station (the next large town).

Motsu-ji Temple

During the era of the Fujiwara this was the largest and greatest temple in northern Honshu. All the buildings from that time have been destroyed over the years and nothing but foundation stones and Oizumi-ga-ike pond and garden remain, although there are some picturesque buildings of more recent vintage around the grounds.

The temple grounds would be very peaceful if it wasn't for several PA systems with different recorded messages, two of which can usually be heard at any one time.

The youth hostel is in the temple grounds and guests are allowed to walk around without paying the admittance charge.

The temple is about half a km from Hiraizumi station. You can get there by

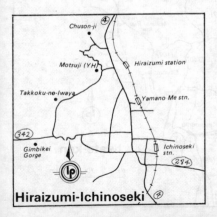

Hiraizumi-Ichinoseki

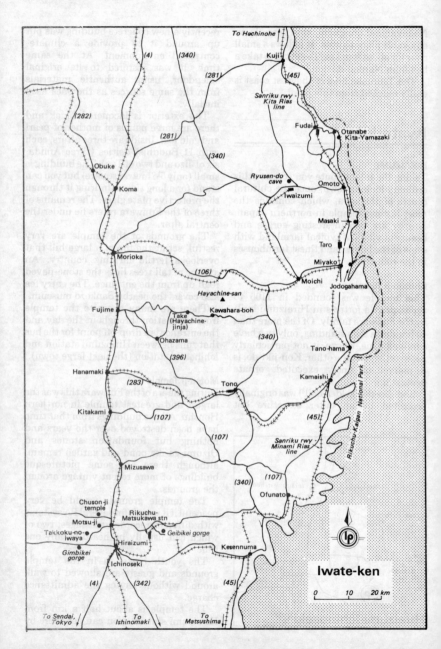

To Hachinohe

Kuji (45)

Sanriku rwy -
Kita Rias line

(4) (340)

(281)

(282)

(281)

(340)

Fudai

Otanabe
Kita-Yamazaki

Obuke

Koma

Ryusen-do cave

Omoto

Iwaizumi

Masaki

Taro

Morioka

Miyako

(106)

Moichi

Jodogahama

Hayachine-san

Kawahara-boh

Fujime

Take
(Hayachine-jinja)

Ohazama

(340)

Tano-hama

(396)

Hanamaki

(283)

Kamaishi

Kitakami

(107)

Tono

(45)

(107)

Sanriku rwy -
Minami Rias
line

Mizusawa

(107)

(340)

Chuson-ji
temple

Ofunato

Motsu-ji

Rikuchu-
Matsukawa stn

Takkoku-no-
iwaya

Geibikei gorge

Gimbikei
gorge

Hiraizumi

Ichinoseki

Kesennuma

Rikuchu-Kaigan National Park

(4) (342) (45)

To Sendai,
Tokyo

To Ishinomaki

To Matsushima

Iwate-ken

0   10   20 km

bus or by walking out of the station and across the main road (Route 4), then continuing along the road on the other side of it.

Takkoku-no-Iwayu Temple

A few km further along the road that curves past Motsu-ji is a small interesting temple in the mouth of a cave. It is built on pillars, like a small scale Kiyomizu-dera (Kyoto). The temple is a 1946 reproduction of a much more ancient structure.

Faintly visible in the large rock near the temple is an image of Dainichi-Nyorai, believed to date from the late 11th century.

Gimbikei Gorge

This gorge is only about one km long and never more than a few metres deep but the river has carved the solid rock into a most picturesque and intricate natural sculpture. You can walk its full length along the banks where there are many Jacob's wells (circular holes bored into the rock by the action of rock-bearing water). It is a very pretty place and well worth a visit.

The gorge, which is past Motsu-ji and Takkoku-no-Iwayu, is easily accessible by bus from Hiraizumi station. The trip there passes through pretty countryside and by large prosperous-looking farmhouses.

Geibikei Gorge

Near Hiraizumi is another gorge but this one is of heroic proportions and is one of the great bargains of Japan. For about Y1000 you can take a truly memorable 90-minute boat trip up the river and back. The flat-bottomed boat is poled by two boatmen up the slow-moving Satetsu-gawa river between grey and blue streaked cliffs and large rocks.

On the way upstream the only sounds are the splash of the boatmen's poles, the ever-present cicadas (in summer), plus wheeling, raucous crows (which by the way, have a Japanese accent, and say 'haw' instead of 'caw'!). The ride ends at Daigeibiga, a cliff that rises straight and flat for about 100 metres. It is a fitting climax to the ascent.

On the way down, the boatmen serenade their 50 or so passengers with plaintive, traditional songs that echo off the rock walls. This was one of the most beautiful, peaceful and relaxing moments of my travels in Japan.

MIZUSAWA

Anyone interested in an unusual souvenir of Japan should look for a little shop in the main street of this town that sells fish traps. These are the simple type, centuries old in design, that funnel water through the trap so the fish is caught in an inner chamber.

KITAKAMI

Though it is not one of the famous Tohoku festivals, Kitakami's annual extravaganza is quite interesting. Its history goes back only 30-odd years but the format varies from year to year as dancers, floats, etc, from other festivals in Japan are invited to participate.

There are usually lion dances, kagura dance displays, sword dances, drumming and fireworks. The festival is held from 7 to 9 August. It is best to inquire locally to determine the best day to visit.

TONO

Tono is a large town in a long agricultural valley east of Kitakami on the road toward Kamaishi and the coast. Its relative isolation until the turn of the century has meant that many of the old legends and folk tales have remained more a part of people's lives here than in most other parts of Japan. And that's the way the people of Tono want to keep it. They have rejected industrialisation and are endeavoring to retain as much of the atmosphere of the past as is practicable.

The town itself is unremarkable, like almost any other in the country, but there are still several *magariya* (thatched-roof houses) in the valley, either lived in or

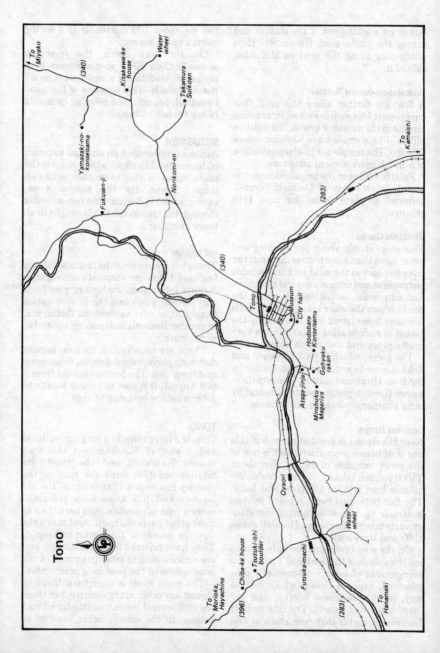

used for storage or animals, and some of the old waterwheels are still in use.

Information

To the right when leaving Tono station is the combined information and accommodation booking office. They have two maps of Tono; one is an all-too-typical Japanese colour pamphlet with cute little pictorial representations of the local sights which give absolutely no indication of where they really are; the other is a proper map. When the two are used together, the first is handy for finding the kanji name for the attraction, while the second can be used for actually getting there.

The various attractions around Tono and the roads to them are conveniently signposted.

Chiba-ke

This imposing structure, sited on a hill about nine km from Tono (along Route 396), was the home of the Chiba family, who were very wealthy farmers. It dates back about two centuries and was restored recently because it is regarded as one of the ten most important historic farmhouses in Japan.

Waterwheel

One of the few functioning (rather than decorative) waterwheels in the area can be found along the road that runs south from Iwate-Futsukamachi station (the second east of Tono station). The word for waterwheel is *suisha*.

Gohyaku-rakan

Carved in relief on boulders in a shallow ravine and on the hillside are several hundred images of faces, the 500 *rakan* (disciples) of Buddha. They were carved in the mid 1700s by a priest to console the spirits of the hundreds who died of starvation following two years of crop failures. A few of the images can be found easily; the rest of the nearly 400 known to

survive could take quite a while to locate.

The gohyaku-rakan can be found by first locating Atago-jinja shrine, which is near Route 283, across from a major bridge west of the bus terminal. The stone carvings are about 300 metres up the hill in a peaceful wooded area behind the shrine.

Fukusen-ji Temple

There are several shrines and temples in Tono itself but perhaps the most interesting to visit is Fukusen-ji, about six km from the station. There is a large Ming-style gate at the entrance but the feature is a very tall statue of Kannon, the goddess of mercy. It is, it must be said, more impressive for its 17 metre height than for the artistry of the woodcarving, even though it was carved from a single piece of 1200-year-old wood.

Norikomi-en

The main attraction here is an old *magariya* house with authentic furnishings to give an idea of what life was like in days gone by. Both in the house and in an adjacent building there are demonstrations of old crafts such as weaving and straw sandal making.

Another building houses hundreds of Oshira-sama dolls – simple figures that are little more than a 30-cm stick with a crude face, dressed in a square of brightly coloured cloth. There are also other displays and an old steam locomotive in the grounds of Norikomi-en, which is just past the turn-off for Fukusen-ji temple.

Places to Stay

Near Gohyaku-rakan is *Minshuku Magariya*, a typical L-shaped thatched-roof house about 80 years old that offers accommodation. The owner is friendly and very hospitable. To make a reservation (tel (01986) 2-4564).

There are numerous other *minshuku* and *ryokan* in Tono and bookings can be made at the office near the station.

Getting There & Away

The train line serving Tono (JR) runs between Kitakami (on the Tohoku Shinkansen) and Kamaishi, a nondescript industrial city on the east coast, from where a JR line runs north to Miyako and beyond.

The Sanriku railway Minami Rias sen line runs south from Kamaishi to Ofunato, where JR services resume.

HAYACHINE-SAN

The mountain of Hayachine-san has been regarded as a sacred place for centuries. These days it has become a popular destination for walkers and on 31 July and 1 August every year a very interesting festival is held in the little village of Take on the flank of the mountain.

TAKE

The festival of Hayachine-jinja shrine in Take (pronounced 'Tah-kay') begins on the night of 31 July with performances of a very rare type of theatre unique to this part of Japan.

Yamabushi-kagura is a collection of stories acted out in dance. Prior to WW II, farmers in Tohoku used to regularly act out these very energetic masked dance-dramas in their farmhouses during the winter nights, a tradition hundreds of years old. Since the arrival of television, however, the performances are limited to this annual festival and others on 3 January, 17 December and the second Sunday of June.

Performances are given on the stage in the courtyard of Hayachine-jinja shrine on the night of the 31st. (Take is tiny, so it's not hard to locate the shrine). The music, drumming and cymbals are quite simple, somewhat reminiscent of Balinese music.

The next morning (try to get there by 9 am), there is a procession from the main shrine to a smaller shrine nearby. The preliminaries include the blessing of *mikoshi* (portable shrines), a time-honoured Shinto ritual. Then out comes

the most fascinating attraction of the festival, the *shishi*.

Twenty or more *shishi* – townspeople dressed in lion costumes that are topped with very large and magnificent wooden masks of lion heads – parade along the road, the heads held high overhead so that the 'animals' are much taller than a man. The masks have glossy black lacquered faces, fiery eyes and gold teeth outlined in red. The mane is made of white tassles of paper and the lower jaw is hinged so it can open and shut to make a resounding clack.

The procession, which includes many children dressed in white, is led by long-nosed, red-faced Tengu. The *shishi* stop periodically to give dance demonstrations, accompanied by musicians on drums, flutes and gongs. The jaws of the lions clack resonantly in unison with the music, producing an effect that can only be described as truly eerie. But for the onlookers, you feel as if you've been dropped into a surreal world.

There are further performances of *yamabushi-kagura* at the shrine following the procession. At the same time, Sumo wrestlers perform in a ring in a nearby field.

Places to Stay

Because Take is a base camp for walking in the mountains, there are several places in the town that offer accommodation, nearly all in the form of very large open rooms with one or more *tatami* mat per person. The rooms are big enough to hold 60 or more people. There is an information service for the festival (tel (0198) 48-5864); they may also be able to help with reservations for accommodation.

Getting There & Away

Take is part of the town of Osama, from which there are up to eight buses a day; three of these originate at Hanimake station and a fourth at Kitakami station. Two buses continue on through Take to Kawahara-no-boh, a high point along the road used as a starting point for walking on Hayachine-san.

MORIOKA

The centrepiece of Morioka is Iwate-koen park, formerly the site of Morioka-jo castle but now just a respite from the crowds. It can be reached from Morioka station via Saien-dori, one of the two main shopping streets (the other is Odori). Across the river and to the left is the Gozaku area, a series of old shops looking much as they did one hundred years ago.

The attractions of the Tazawa-ko lake area are a relatively short distance to the west of Morioka, easily accessible by train and bus, as are Akita and the Oga-hanto peninsula also to the west, and Miyako, Kuji, Hachinohe and Towada-ko lake to the east and north.

COASTAL ROUTE

Northward from the Matsushima area you can continue along Route 45. The road runs close to the sea for much of the way but except for near Ofunato there is little in the way of coastal sights until Miyako. At Kesennuma you reach the beginning of Rikuchu-Kaigan National Park.

OFUNATO AREA

Scarcely worth being called a peninsula, the little extension of land below Hosoura has enough natural attractions to interest the traveller who is not in a hurry.

The first place of interest, almost at the tip, is Goishi-hama, which means 'Go stone beach'. Go is a popular board game played with black and white stones; the stones found on the beach here are round and black, and in the past provided many pieces of the right size for the game.

The beach is less than a km before the Goishi-kaigan bus terminus where there is a booking office for the many minshuku in the area, a restaurant and a delightful wooded park.

Back toward town is another attraction definitely worth seeing if you're into

seascapes. Anadoshi is a triple arch of rock formed from centuries of erosion.

Getting There & Away

There are regular buses from Ofunato bus terminal or station, via Hosoura to Goishi-kaigan, some of which go on to Anadoshi.

From Kamaishi, Route 283 leads inland to Tono, Hayachine and the attractions along Route 4.

MIYAKO

The city of Miyako is a major gateway for travel up the Sanriku-kaigan coast, and with the opening of the Sanriku railway Kita Rias line, travel in the region is now faster and more reliable than on the local buses. The main problem with the line, however, is that more than half its length is though tunnels, which limits the sightseeing en route.

There are two Youth Hostels in Miyako, both near the station, and there is an accommodation office at the station that can help you find a ryokan, though you might have to persist a little if they say they have no rooms.

The coastal attraction nearest to Miyako is Jodogahama – 'Paradise Beach'. A finger of the cliff reaches out and descends into the water, forming a sheltered cove for swimmers. Walking trails stretch along the coast north of Jodogahama and are marked on the handout map given out at Miyako station.

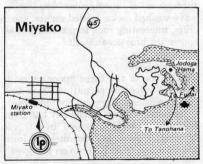

SANRIKU-KAIGAN

In summer there is a daily cruise boat that goes from Jodogahama to Otanabe, leaving at 8.30 am and arriving at 11.15 am (Y2200; return departure is at 2.10 pm). This boat passes the most spectacular sight, the cliffs of Kitayamazaki, which are well over 100 metres high.

From Otanabe it is possible to go back by bus to Kitayamazaki-tempodai, an excellent viewpoint built specifically to overlook the cliffs, then continue on by another bus to the next train station and use it either to return to Miyako or continue on to Kuji.

There are also five other boats in each direction from Jodogahama to Taro (Y900; 40 minutes) and Masaki (Y1000; 60 minutes), both much closer to Miyako. From any of these boats you can see at least some of the cliffs for which this coast is famous and the boat goes close enough to shore to see the specific points of interest clearly.

TARO

The first sight north of the Miyako area is the picturesque stone column Sanno-iwa at Taro. The finger of the cliff that formerly stretched into the ocean has been eroded away from both sides, leaving this solitary tower about 50 metres tall and 10 metres across the base.

There are three buses a day from Miyako and the cruise boats from Jodogahama stop at Taro harbour.

The rest of the coast north to Fudai is a succession of spectacular headlands, wave-washed rocks, eroded arches, sheer cliffs, interesting rock formations and of course the blue ocean itself.

Ryusendo Cave

This is one of the three major caves in Japan. Visitors are permitted 300 metres into it, passing stalagmites and stalactites.

Ryusendo can be reached by bus from Iwaizumi (which is served by JR via Moichi). Buses also run directly from Morioka and from Komoto on the coast.

There are *ryokan* and *minshuku* at Iwaizumi and at other tourist spots in the area.

Aomori-ken

This is the northernmost part of Honshu and is of interest mainly for access to Hokkaido. If you are travelling up the east coast, Hachinohe is the first ferry port; others are Aomori, Noheji and Oma.

HACHINOHE

This coastal city is most noteworthy as the port for regular daily boats to Tomakomai on Hokkaido. By using this route to Hokkaido it allows you to bypass the relatively uninteresting northern tip of Honshu.

Those interested in archaeology can visit Kokokan, a small museum in Hachinohe which houses several thousand Jomon-era relics dug up in the area.

Another attraction of Hachinohe is the city's annual festival (one of many in the region during the first week of August). The festival is a lengthy procession of floats depicting a theme from Japanese or Chinese history or mythology – castles, lucky gods, demons, warriors, dragons and, of course, beautiful maidens – and each float is accompanied by a large *taiko* (drum) beaten tirelessly by a relay of young men. Each float is a group effort of a neighbourhood of the city.

MISAWA

Travellers through Misawa with time to kill while waiting for a train could venture into the amazingly kitsch Komaki-onsen.

This large Japanese-style resort complex includes a large bath of several pools, a park area with reconstructions of famous historic structures, and a lake for boating. Komaki-onsen is about five minutes walk from Misawa station. Admittance is Y800.

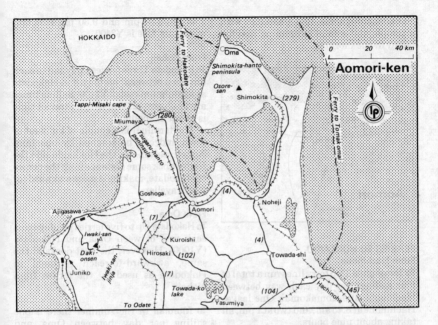

SHIMOKITA-HANTO PENINSULA

The eastern horn of northern Honshu is quite flat and rather bland. There are beaches all along the inner coast but they collect all the floating debris of the area so are not good for swimming.

With the exception of festival time at Osore-san, most visitors only come here to take the ferry from Oma to Hokkaido.

Osore-san

This mountain has been regarded as sacred since at least the 9th century. Entsu-ji temple was built on its flank on the north shore of the small lake Osoresan. The landscape around the lake is desolate, stark and white, the result of underground minerals deposited on the surface by hot springs.

The temple is associated with *itako*, or mediums. This is the main purpose of the annual festival (20-24 July) when blind women (the mediums) go into trances and

attempt to contact the souls of departed members of the worshipping families.

These activities take place in tents set up on the temple grounds and are the only remnant in Japan of minkan shinko shamanist rites, once practiced all over the country until they were absorbed and changed by Shinto.

AOMORI

Aomori is famous for its Nebuta festival (3-7 August), when very large floats move through the streets at night. The floats are unusual, huge three-dimensional representations of men and animals that are illuminated from the inside. The sight is memorable. An explanation of the origin of the festival is given in the section on Hirosaki, which has a similar festival called Neputa.

Places to Stay

The *Youth Hostel* can be reached from Aomori station by bus No 1; get off at

Sakaimachi-ichome. It is associated with a temple and a faint drumming may be heard in the morning.

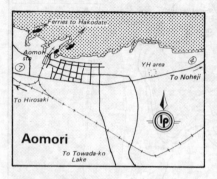

FERRIES TO HOKKAIDO
From Hachinohe
To Tomakomai Two ferry lines run a total of four sailings per day each way between Hachinohe and Tomakomai. One leaves Hachinohe at 8.45 am, and two at 1 pm, all taking about nine hours.

Another boat, which leaves at 10 pm, reaches Hachinohe the next morning at 6.30 am, saving on a night's accommodation.

The boat dock can be reached by city bus from Hachinohe station; get off at Shin-sankaikan-mae stop. Minimum fare is Y3900.

From Aomori
To Hakodate Until 1988 this was the port used by most travellers for getting to and from Hakodate by ferry. With the opening of the Seikan tunnel, however, the JR train service under the sea to Hokkaido now does the job and this ferry route no longer operates.

To Muroran There is a ferry service from Aomori to Muroran on Hokkaido. Muroran is very convenient for reaching the popular Shikotsu-Toya area of Hokkaido but the arrival times in Muroran are very awkward. Departure/arrival times are

2.45 pm/9.30 pm and 9.30 pm/4.30 am; minimum fare is Y3400.

From Noheji
To Hakodate Three ferries a day sail in each direction between this town and Hakodate at a minimum cost of Y1400. Sailing times are 12.35 am, 12.30 and 5 pm; transit time is about 4½ hours.

The terminal is a couple of km west of town and can be reached by bus from Noheji station. On the Hokkaido side the ferries dock some distance from the centre of Hakodate, making it more awkward for foot travellers.

From Oma
To Hakodate Up to five ferries per day cross each way between Oma and Hakodate (Y1000). However, the boat docks at the same, awkward-to-reach terminal in Hakodate as used by the ferries from Noheji.

To Muroran In the summer there is one sailing per day between Oma and Muroran, leaving Oma at 9 am, and Muroran at 3.15 pm (Y1400).

TSUGARU-HANTO PENINSULA
The western pincer of Mutsu Bay, at the top of Honshu, is the Tsugaru-hanto peninsula. A spine of low mountains up the middle and a west coast of small lakes and marshes limits the habitability.

Only the east coast is very populated and is, in fact, one endless fishing village squeezed between the water and the hills almost immediately behind. Nets can be seen drying everywhere. By road it is slow going; the JR line runs along this coast and would probably be faster and more relaxing.

The most notable scenic view is from the northern tip, Tappi-misaki cape, with its semi-circular bay, rocky shoreline and green-covered cliffs that slope into the sea.

Few visitors come here, as the previous major attraction of a ferry connection between Miumaya and Hokkaido has been suspended. To reach the cape, take one of the six daily trains from Aomori to Miumaya (95 minutes), then a bus from the station to the Tappi-misaki lookout (*tempodai*).

The Seikan tunnel under the strait to Hokkaido plunges underground near here.

NORTHWEST COAST

A train trip down the west coast from the base of the Tsugaru-hanto peninsula is an enjoyable way to see this section of Honshu. The JR line (five per day) between Hirosaki and Higashi-Noshiro (between Akita and Odate) runs as close to the water as practicable and offers excellent vistas over the ocean and rocky coastline for nearly its full length.

JUNIKO

Those who like walking, or nature, or both, should consider a stop at Juniko. Juniko means 'Twelve Lakes' and takes its name from the many bodies of water dammed by a landslide caused by an earthquake. All are quite small, some big enough for an enjoyable row around, others almost small enough to jump over.

There are walking trails through the forest and around the larger ponds; a circuit takes a couple of hours. An engraved wooden sign at the bus terminal shows the routes.

Juniko can be reached from Mutsu-Iwasaki station by bus. Buses are scheduled to meet all five trains from

Noshiro (to the south) and three of the five from the Hirosaki direction. They remain at Juniko for 50 to 100 minutes before returning to the station. Four of the five make good connections with trains bound for Hirosaki and three connect well with trains for Noshiro.

AOMORI TO TOWADA-KO LAKE

The shortest route to the area around Towada-ko lake (and recommended if you're in a hurry) is the direct road south through scenic woodland areas. An enjoyable stop en route is Suiren-numa, a small pond backdropped by four mountain peaks, still snow patched in late July. The area is at its best in autumn. There are at least 11 buses a day.

For those in less of a hurry, the route south via Hirosaki is more interesting.

HIROSAKI
Information

The information office at Hirosaki station may have a copy of the city-produced brochure *Hirosaki* showing a couple of temples that might be of interest – Chosho-ji and Seigan-ji.

Hirosaki-jo Castle

This lovely original castle dates from 1610. The moat and walls are also intact, the gates are original (or authentically restored) and the grounds are covered with cherry trees.

In any season it is pretty; during the cherry blossom season (late April-early May) and from mid-October when the maples are at their autumn best, it is a truly beautiful place to visit.

Saishoin Temple

Standing in the temple grounds is a five-storey pagoda dating from 1672. Although many people believe that Japan is full of such pagodas, they are in fact relatively rare and therefore worth a visit.

Festivals

Hirosaki is famous throughout Japan for

its Neputa festival (1-7 August) which is very similar to the Nebuta festival of Aomori.

The floats of the festival are smaller than those of Aomori and of a different format – rather like a three-dimensional fan, with scenes from Japanese or Chinese mythology painted on the two faces and the edges. Lights inside them, either candles or electric, illuminate the scenes beautifully.

The numerous *dashi* (carts carrying the floats) parade through the streets on a different route each night accompanied by drummers and other musicians. A map showing the route for that day is available from the information office at the station.

The origin of the Neputa (and Nebuta) festival is unknown. One version is that a Japanese military commander used giant figures similar to those carved in the floats to terrify the Ainu (whom he was fighting at Hirosaki) and that he celebrated his victory on reaching Aomori. The *Official Guide* indicates that a military commander, Sakanoue, used such figures in the late 9th century to subjugate rebels (who might well have been Ainu or other tribesmen fighting against the southern

Japanese who were advancing into their territory).

These two festivals, along with ones at Hayachine-san (31 July – 1 August), Yamagata (6-8 August) and Akita (5-7 August), make early August an excellent time to visit this part of Japan, especially as its climate is cooler and less humid than that of the southern regions.

Buses are available from Hirosaki or Kuroishi to Nenokuchi and Yasumiya on Towada-ko lake (described later).

IWAKI-SAN

The cone of this 1625-metre dormant volcano dominates the flat countryside west of Hirosaki. It can be climbed in about four hours (7.3 km) from Hyakuzawa-onsen or can be approached the easy way by bus and chairlift. Five buses a day go from Hirosaki station to the top of the mountain (*sancho*) from where the chairlift begins.

On the mountain you may see white-garbed pilgrims wending their way up the paths. They are members of the *yamabushi* sect, an offshoot of Buddhism that includes many elements of Shinto.

If you are considering a trip to the top, observe the weather carefully; if clouds can be seen near the summit the view from there may be totally obscured by fog.

Iwaki-san-jinja Shrine

On the southeast flank of Iwaki-san, this shrine is surrounded by a large grove of tall, ancient trees. The buildings are painted a reddish-brown and some doorways and other details have elaborate carvings overhead.

According to the *Official Guide*, the shrine is often called 'Nikko shrine of northwest Honshu'. Well, the shrine is pleasing in appearance but bears no resemblance to Toshogu (Nikko) and is not worth a special trip for its beauties. It is popular with pilgrims and bus loads of them may be seen being guided through the rites of the shrine by the priests, to the sound of drumming.

Similarly, Iwaki-san's description in the *Official Guide* is: 'The mountain is often called Tsugaru-Fuji because of its remarkable resemblance to Mt Fuji'. Most mountains will resemble Fuji if they are volcanic cones and Iwaki-san is one of at least 12 in Japan described in this way!

Akita-ken

TOWADA-KO LAKE

One of the most popular destinations in northern Honshu is the Towada-ko lake area. The main attraction is natural scenery and an escape from the built-up city areas.

The lake is the third deepest in Japan (334 metres) and is in an old volcanic crater. The sides of the crater rise sharply, as you'll see if you arrive by bus from Tawada-minami; the road snakes down around countless twists and switchbacks on its way to water level.

The area invites exploration on foot but there is a road around the entire circumference of the lake and buses pass along all parts of it at some time during the day.

The main centres of population around the lake (all small) are Yasumiya, Uta-

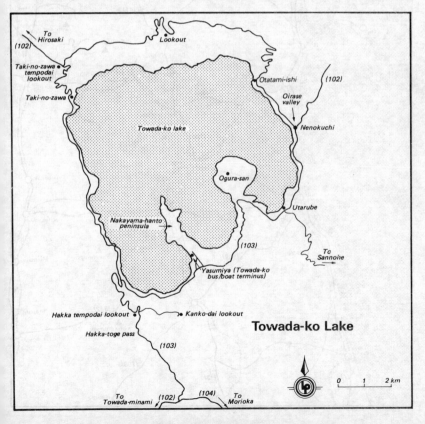

Towada-ko Lake

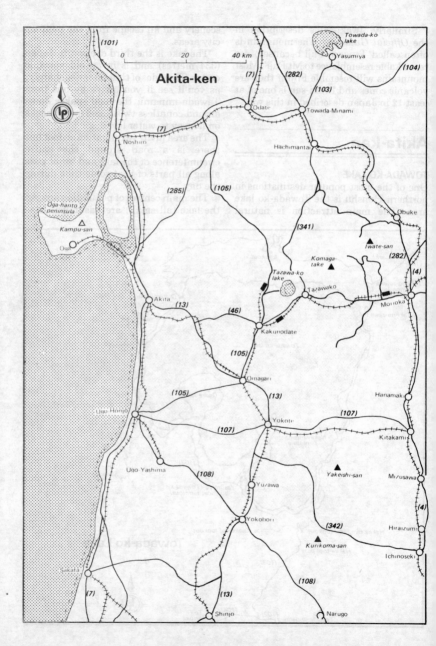

rube and Nenokuchi. Most of the shore has been left in its natural state, without the rows of souvenir shops that characterise too many resorts in Japan.

Oirase Valley

The most popular walk in the area is through the Oirase valley which stretches 14 km northeast from Nenokuchi. The Oirase-kawa river originates at the lake and flows through the only break in the crater wall. Along the way its character varies between shallow and placid to a narrow torrent rushing around rocks and plunging over falls. A tree-canopied path follows the river and in October the leaves are amazingly colourful.

From Nenokuchi you have the option of returning to Yasumiya by bus or boat. Boats run every 30 minutes between Nenokuchi and Towada-ko. The trip takes one hour, costs Y1100 and passes by the most scenic parts of the lake. These include the volcanic cone of Ogura-san, which bulges into the lake, and Nakayama-hanto, the peninsula on which Yasumiya is located.

Oyu-onsen

Between Towada-ko and Towada-minami (20 minutes from the latter) is Oyu-onsen. Anyone interested in archaeology should stop here to see the mysterious stone circle, Oyu-iseki, which is about 20 minutes by local bus into the countryside.

The attraction is not so spectacular in itself but for what it represents. It is an arrangement of stones in a circle about 46 metres across, with a central group of stones and an upright rock; the origin is unknown but it is believed to be about 4000 years old. It was discovered in the early 1930s and excavated 20 years later.

Of the 30 or so stone circles known to exist in Hokkaido and Tohoku, this is the largest and finest.

There are plenty of buses every day that pass through Oyu between Towada-minami and Towada-ko, or run direct to

Oyu-onsen so it is quite easy to make this a day trip. There is also a youth hostel in Oyu about 100 metres from the bus station.

Places to Stay

There are many hotels, *ryokan* and *minshuku* in addition to the youth hostels. It is possible to inquire about accommodation in Yasumiya but because of the popularity of the area it is risky to turn up without a reservation (particularly during the October school excursion season).

Yasumiya, on the south shore, is the transportation centre of the lake area; the name of the bus stop is Towada-ko. *Hakubutsukan Youth Hostel* (Museum YH) is quite close; *Towada Youth Hostel* is between Yasumiya and Wainai, on the lake near Hotel Hakka. The other nearby hostels are at Towada-ko machi, Nishi-Towada and Oyu.

Getting Around

Starting from Yasumiya, any of the 17 daily buses to Odate or Morioka can be taken a few km along the mountain road up the south rim to Hakka-toge *tempodai* (Hakka pass lookout), which gives an excellent view of the lake. Another lookout nearby is Kogakudai.

From Wanai, on the lake, there are four daily buses running clockwise around the lake (toward Hirosaki) to Takizawa-tempodai, for probably the best view of the lake. After that it is possible to get a bus coming from Hirosaki and take it as far as Nenokuchi to have a look round the Oirase-dani valley.

There are also round-the-lake cruises out of Towada-ko (up to seven per day) that last one hour and cost Y1100.

NOSHIRO

This small city has an interesting festival during the same period as the other main Tohoku festivals. On the night of 6 August there is a parade of lantern-lit festival wagons similar to those featured in the

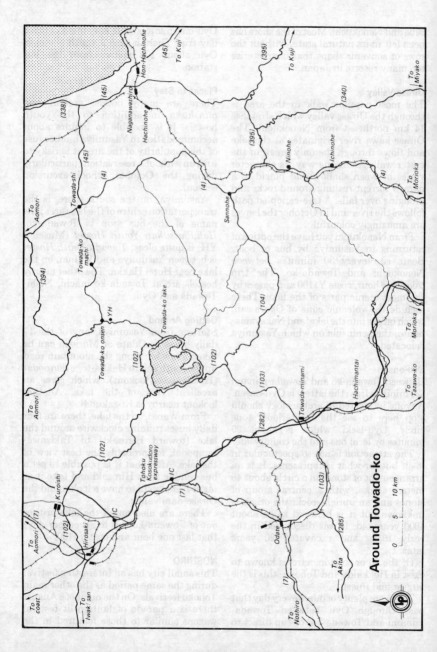

Around Towado-ko

festivals of Takayama, Furukawa and Kyoto. For up-to-date info (in Japanese only) you can ring 0185 52-2111.

OGA-HANTO PENINSULA

This promontory, formed by submarine volcanic activity long ago, has an indented coastline with many unusual and scenic rock formations and reefs.

A good starting point for seeing the peninsula is Monzen (reached by bus from JR Oga station; up to 14 through the day). Between late April and the end of October boats cruise along the coast from Monzen to Oga-Suizokukan aquarium. About six buses per day make the trip between the aquarium and Oga station. (It should be easy to hitch back if desired.) The boat schedule is posted at the Monzen bus terminal, and both it and the bus schedule are also printed in *Jikokuhyo*.

Oga-suizokukan Aquarium

This aquarium is definitely worth visiting. In addition to commonplace ocean fish, it has some truly weird and wonderful creations of nature that outdo anything that a Walt Disney cartoonist could dream up – some incredibly beautiful, others equally ugly. There are also several alligators, crocodiles and large turtles.

A very unusual sight here (and at Monzen) are dugout boats still in everyday use (with outboard motors!). The availability of large trees in the area makes them very practical.

Nyudo-saki Cape

From Oga-suizokukan, you can continue by bus to Nyudo-saki cape via Oga-onsen. From the cape, a toll road runs along another stretch of cliff and between two small green lakes, ending at Nomura.

At the cape (and elsewhere) you are likely to see masks and costumes of *namahage* (ogres). In a traditional festival at New Year, groups of young men in similar ogre costumes visit homes of the town, where they are formally received by the master of the house. They pause to

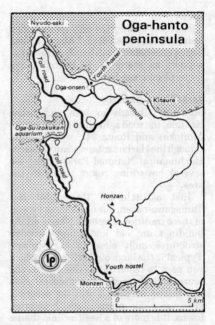

honour the family shrine, then walk around the house shouting 'Any good-for-nothing loafers here?'

Because this festival has become so well known throughout Japan, many outsiders want to see it, so there is a special performance on New Year's Eve for their benefit. The real festival is held later among only the residents.

Places to Stay

There is accommodation available at several centres on the coast, including Oga city and Monzen. *Oga Choraku-ji Youth Hostel* at Monzen is better than usual. It is part of a 1200-year-old temple; an alarm clock is unnecessary because drumming, which is part of the religious ceremony, begins at 6.30 am.

At Oga-onsen there are several *ryokan* and *minshuku*, plus another youth hostel.

AKITA

This city is noteworthy only for its famed annual Kanto festival (5-7 August) when young men balance tall bamboo poles that support as many as 50 lighted paper lanterns on cross-bars.

TAMAGAWA-ONSEN

South of Towada-ko lake and below Kazuno, the road splits into Route 282 (to Morioka) and Route 341, which passes through the Hachimantai plateau (Towada-Hachimantai National Park). There are several hot-spring resort towns in the area.

Just a little off Route 341 lies Tamagawa-onsen, one of the most typical of these traditional resorts. Nearly all the buildings are old and simple wooden structures built close to the springs. Typical is the large old bath-house which you pass to reach the ravine that is the source of the hot water. It has several pools and mixed bathing is still the practice. However, like many such hot-spring towns, it is more of a health clinic than a resort and the bathers are mostly geriatrics.

In the ravine, there is one stream that has some of the most unusual water you're likely to see – it is brilliant orange. Further upstream, a violent bubbling and boiling marks the emergence of many gushers of hot water, one of which boils two metres high in winter.

Water from the different streams is sluiced separately to various pools, each of which is believed to provide a cure for, or effective relief from, specific ailments. Some streams are laden with yellow minerals and this water is led into settling chambers, cooled and the minerals are collected for sale.

A common sight up in the ravine is one or more people lying on straw mats. The earth is hot (potatoes cook if buried a short distance underground) and people believe the heat is healthy. Nearby is a small concrete pool in the open air filled with hot water and free to the public.

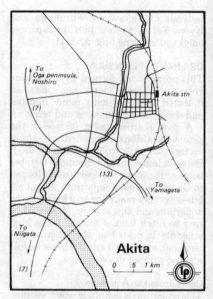

Akita

0   .5   1 km

Getting There & Away

Tamagawa-onsen is linked by eight buses a day to and from Hachimantai station and seven a day to Tazawa-ko station. There is a reasonable amount of traffic for hitching.

A toll road, the Aspite Line (Japanese name), leads across the mountain range from Route 341 toward Routes 282 and 284, past several peaks. It's enjoyable if you happen to be going that way but not worth a special trip.

TAZAWA-KO LAKE AREA

In the area around this lake are several interesting individual attractions, such as the lake itself, nearby mountains and plateaus, Kakunodate town, Dakikaeri gorge, and the general countryside. It sticks in my mind as one of the most enjoyable areas I visited while researching this book.

Tazawa-ko Lake

This is a classic caldera lake and the

round shape of the old crater is apparent. The swimming is good and the water shallow for some distance off shore before it plunges to 425 metres, the deepest in Japan.

Tazawako-kogen Plateau

A few km from the lake, the plateau offers some of the most interesting and scenic nature walks in Japan. The scenery ranges from highland scrub (low trees and bushes) to a dormant volcano.

There are several trails, the most interesting of which takes in Koma-ga-take mountain and vicinity. The scenery is quite outstanding (if the highland area is not fog-bound) and the walking and climbing are within the range of anyone except cardiac patients.

Koma-ga-take erupted in October 1970 – a fascinating event I was lucky enough to see. Following an explosion, gases shrieked from the earth like the exhaust of a hundred jet engines, then molten rock from underground slowly clogged the entrance, finally sealing the tube. For many minutes the air was silent until, as amazed onlookers watched, a dome began to form and smoke rose over it. Finally, when it had reached a height of about four metres and a diameter of perhaps 10, the pressure became too much and the dome shattered, hurling fragments high into the air. Toward dusk, the red glow of rock chunks could be seen as they traced arcs in the air. The cycle repeated itself again and again.

The tens of thousands of tons of rock hurled out then now lie in a 'river' of rough-textured boulders that stretches down one side of the hill. It is quite fascinating to explore this area to see the amazing forms and shapes of the lava. Some of the boulders have a rippled surface caused by the hot gases that blasted past them. Others rocks were torn asunder while hot and toffee-like and the strings of then-sticky rock can still be seen, looking like stretched bread dough.

The easiest way to reach the top is by bus from Tazawa-ko station (three per day) to Komagatake-Hachigome ('Eighth Station') and then a 40 minute walk up a clearly marked trail. Two other trails start lower down, one beginning at the road near the Seishonen Sports Centre, the other at the top of a string of three ski lifts. The base of the bottom lift is called Mizusawa Daburu Rifuto (double lift). There is some road traffic and hitching is possible but you might have to wait a while.

The first route takes you to the rim of a bowl that looks down on a couple of mini-cones and the high 'bump' of Me-dake (the peak that erupted in 1970). Its black top, and to the right, the river of boulders ejected at that time, shouldn't be missed. On the rim of the bowl is a small hill, on the left side of which is a path that leads down to the foot of Me-dake and the floor of the small, green valley, as well as the mini-peaks.

On the other side of the hill is a long trail down to the lava river and Me-dake. ('Me-dake' means 'female peak'; there is also an Odake – 'male peak'. By pre-Shinto custom, all natural features came in matched pairs, or a male and female aspect was found when there was only a single feature.)

The last bus leaves Hachigome at 3.45 pm, which restricts extended walks in the area if you intend to take the bus back down. There are two other trails down but to find them it is better to have used them to climb up as well, as there are unmarked forks that can lead you astray (as I can certify). It is advisable to carry food and a lot of water as there are no sources on the mountain and the climbing generates a healthy thirst.

The region around Tazawa-ko is ideal for exploration by those with their own transport, although buses do cover several routes. The farmland is good and the people prosperous so the houses (some with thatched roofs) are large and handsome.

Residents take pride in their homes and

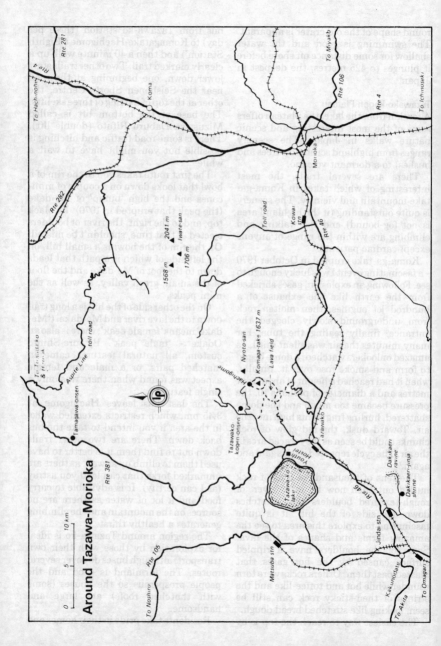

Around Tazawa-Morioka

To Miyako

To Ichinoseki

To Ichinuseki

Rte 106

Rte 4

Rte 281

To Hachinohe

Koma

To Hachinohe

Morioka

Rte 282

Kowai stn

Rte 46

Toll road

2041 m ▲ (Iwate-san)

1568 m ▲   1706 m ▲

1637 m ▲ Nyoto-san

Komaga-take

Lava field

Aspite Line toll road

To Tsukidoto & B--h

Tamagawa onsen

Hachimantai

Tazawako-kogen onsen

Youpi Hostel

Tazawako onsen

Tazawa-ko Lake

Dakikaeri ravine

Dakikaeri-yinja shrine

Tazawako stn

Jindai stn

Rte 46

Matsuba stn

Kakunodate

Rte 105

To Noshiro

To Akita

To Omagari

0   5   10 km

To Omagari

the surroundings and one of the delights is the sight of long stretches of flowerbeds along the roadside.

There is a youth hostel at Matsuba that looks nicer than usual (it is a private home).

Places to Stay

There are several *ryokan*, hotels and *minshuku* around the lake so accommodation is plentiful although reservations would be advisable in summer.

There is a good *Youth Hostel* near the lake. The evening meal is *sukiyaki* and the large dining room usually becomes the scene of a big party. Definitely light years ahead of most hostels and worth a trip to enjoy.

KAKUNODATE

This town is very unusual and offers a good chance to see daily life in picturesque surroundings. Although located in the far north (almost a cultural backwater), it preserves a number of 350-year-old samurai houses in surroundings of tall, old trees, quite unlike almost any other place in Japan.

The old houses stand mostly on a single street, not far from the station, where a large map is posted as a guide. The houses are open to the public for a reasonable fee and provide an interesting glimpse into the past. Most have simple but elegant tree-shaded gardens and are built with the best materials.

A guide for sightseeing in the samurai area can be obtained (for a reasonable fee) by calling the Yakuba Shoko-kanko kan (tel (0187) 54-1111). The Densho-kan hall, in the samurai area, serves as a museum and training centre for making articles of cherry bark and has a tour information centre as well.

Many cherry trees have been planted along the Hinokinai-gawa river which flows through the town so the area is especially beautiful in spring.

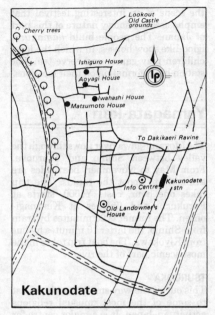

Kakunodate

Dakikaeri-keikoku Ravine

A few km outside Kakunodate is this small gorge, near Jindai station, accessible by train or bus. While offering no spectacular vistas, it provides an enjoyable hour's walk through relaxing surrounds to the upper reaches. The most memorable impression is the intense turquoise colour of the water. The swimming is good in several places.

IWATE-SAN

This mountain (1706 metres), which dominates the area northwest of Morioka, is conical when viewed from the east but in fact has two peaks. (Naturally it is called Iwate-Fuji.) It is quite easily climbed; two popular starting points are Yanagisawa and Amihari-onsen, both accessible by bus from Morioka.

YOKOTE

On 15-16 February each year, this town is

the scene of an interesting festival that emphasises the snowy nature of this part of Japan. The people build *kamakura*, igloo-like snow houses, in which the local children play games and serve tea. The station has information on their locations.

Yamagata-ken

The Mogami-gawa river flows through the valley between Shinjo and Tsuruoka. From May to November, boat rides are available to shoot the rapids. The trip takes one hour, costs Y1500, starts at Furukuchi and finishes at Kusanagi-onsen. The former is 20 minutes by train from Shinjo, the latter 10 minutes by bus from Kiyokawa. The boat trip takes in the most scenic part of the river.

TSURUOKA

This out-of-the-way small city plays host to some of the most unusual religious activity in Japan. It is a major centre for Shugendo which combines Buddhist and Shinto beliefs.

In the city itself is the famous Zenpo-ji temple which has a picturesque pagoda and a building with hundreds of images in every imaginable pose lining its walls. It can be reached by bus from the station.

The friendly people at the station information centre can put you on the right bus and are well prepared with any other info or assistance you might need.

HAGURO-SAN

Of the three mountains of Dewa (Dewa-sanzan), Haguro-san is the closest to Tsuruoka, the most accessible and the most interesting to most people.

There two ways to reach the top. The most prosaic (but quickest and easiest) is by bus from Tsuruoka station via a toll road. The scenic route is the traditional way, starting from the village of Haguro (accessible from Tsuruoka by bus). Near the bus station is a gateway that leads to

steps down to a wooded gorge, one of the most beautiful forest glades in Japan.

Tall trees line the walking paths and along the way there are several small shrines, a waterfall and a picturesque bridge. The only sound in the summer is the breeze and the ever-present *semi* (cicadas). The path leads to a five-storey pagoda, then to the base of the very long staircase that leads to the top. There are more than 1000 steps (believe me, I counted them!).

At the top is Haguro-san-jinja, a large thatched-roof structure looking like a combination of a shrine and temple. Near it you can still see the tiny huts used by pilgrims when they visited for prayer, fasting and other forms of religious penance.

Anywhere on the mountain there is a good chance of seeing *yamabushi* pilgrims, dressed in white and carrying rosaries and bells. During the day you can sometimes hear the sound of a conch shell being blown by priests as part of their religious observances.

Places to Stay

Many temples and homes at Haguro offer accommodation. Help can be obtained at the Haguro (bus) or Tsuruoka (train) stations if you wish to stay pilgrim-style.

The *Youth Hostel* is several km down the coast from Tsuruoka and can be reached by train. The information centre at the station can help with other *minshuku, ryokan* or hotel accommodation.

GASSAN & YUDONO-SAN

Together with Haguro-san, these form the three sacred mountains of the Shugendo sect. Gassan is the main peak and Yudono is an outcropping on one flank.

At the top of Gassan is Gassan-jinja shrine, to which pilgrims and others climb in summer. Climbers are advised to take warm clothing as it gets cold even in mid-summer. A toll road runs to the top of Yudono-san.

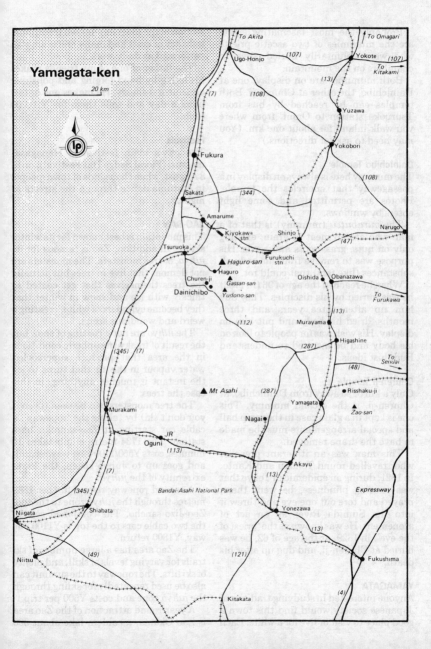

Yamagata-ken

0   20 km

Probably the most fascinating sights are the mummies of two ascetic priests who were voluntarily buried alive in chambers on the mountain.

Both mummies are on display, one at Dainichibo, the other at Churen-ji. Both temples can be reached by bus from Tsuruoka station to Oami, from where you walk inland for about one km. (You may need to ask for directions.)

Dainichibo Temple

The mummy here is always on display in a passageway that encircles the temple. Photos are permitted and some light enters by windows.

The *mirabutsu* (mummy) is that of a man who ate no meat or grain, existing only on nuts, grass-roots and seeds. His purpose was to remove from his body all substances (like fats) that could rot.

When he reached the age of 96 (in 1783) he was buried by his disciples. They dug him up after three years and three months, dried his body and put him on display. His wish was for people to look on his body and be inspired to understand Buddhist ideas.

Churen-ji Temple

Only a km or so away from Dainichibo, at Churen-ji, is the second mummy. This one is kept in a glass case in the main hall and special arrangements must be made to have the drape removed.

This man was an itinerant preacher who travelled round Tohoku and Kanto. In 1821, during an epidemic in Tokyo that was causing blindness, he went there, prayed and tore out one eye and threw it into the Sumida River as an act of atonement. He was known as the 'priest of the eye'. In 1829, at the age of 62, he was buried at Churen-ji, and dug up after his death.

YAMAGATA

Anyone interested in studying traditional Japanese society would find this town a good place to visit or live for a while. Each section of the town has its own traditional industry or craft and many crafts are still performed as daily work.

The father of one of my friends makes his living by hand-forging and polishing agricultural shears. He makes one or two pairs a day and sells them for Y20,000 each.

Festivals

The city's main festival is Hanagasa-matsuri (Floral Sedge Hat Festival), on 6-8 August, when thousands of townspeople in costume dance through the streets at night.

ZAO-SAN

This mountain is best known for its winter skiing. In addition, Zao is famous for its *juhyo*, or tree monsters. The monsters are not demons that live in trees but actually the trees themselves that get coated so thickly with ice and snow in winter that they become cylinders of white, creating a weird and wondrous scene.

The *juhyo* are not a coating of snow but the result of freak atmospheric conditions in the area that produce supercooled water vapour in the air that turns to ice the instant it touches anything, in this case the trees.

The tree monsters can be seen (even if you don't ski) by taking the 'ropeway', a cable car starting at Zao-sanroku base station. The 1734-metre climb takes 15 minutes, costs Y550/1100 (one-way/return), and goes up to Juhyo-kogen, the lower extremity of the *juhyo*.

A second ropeway rises a further 1839 metres through the *juhyo* zone to the top, Zao-Jizo-sancho. The combined cost of the two cable cars to the top is Y1100 one way, Y1800 return.

The Zao area has a large number of ski trails for varying levels of skill, and plenty of ski lifts. The ropeway to the summit can also be used repeatedly for skiing through the *juhyo* zone and costs Y500 per trip.

A year-round attraction of the Zao area is Zao Okama, a caldera lake about 300 metres across. The scenery here is desolate and interesting for the shapes and colours of the rocks.

Places to Stay

There are many hotels, *ryokan* and *minshuku* scattered around the mountain, many at onsen (hot spring sites). The largest concentration is along the Zao Echo Line toll road that passes along the southern flank.

There are also some lodges on the upper levels, including *Juhyogen Lodge* at the peak. Almost any travel agent can provide information and make reservations.

Getting There & Away

The simplest access to the Zao area is from Yamagata station by the hourly bus to Zao-onsen (45 minutes). An alternative is to take the less frequent bus from Kaminoyama station to Zao-bo-daira and Karita-chushajo, or from Yamagata station to the same two places via Zao-onsen.

As with other popular ski areas, there are direct bus services in winter from locations in Tokyo; buses for Zao leave from Ueno station.

YAMADERA

The main attraction of the Yamagata area lies several km out of town. Yamadera ('mountain temple') is properly known as Risshaku-ji. The buildings are scattered around the heavily wooded mountainside. Some are perched at the edge of precipices and look as if they will topple at any time. It takes two to three hours of climbing on foot to visit the various temples. Access is from Yamadera station, which is reached by bus or train from Yamagata or Sendai.

YONEZAWA

Formerly a castle town of the Uesugi family, the small town is now noted for the tombs of 12 generations of the family. They resemble 12 small wooden shrines laid out in a row beneath tall trees. A bus runs from Yonezawa station.

From Yonezawa, a local road connects with Nishi-Azuma Skyline toll road, which leads to the Bandai-san area (described later).

Route 121, which goes over a mountain range from Yonezawa to Kitakata and Aizu-Wakamatsu, is a twisty gravel road in parts, with no buses listed and little traffic.

The west coast is also easily accessible from the Yonezawa area, and from Kitakata and Aizu-Wakamatsu Route 49 takes you the 120 km westward to Niigata, a gateway to Sado Island.

Niigata-ken

NIIGATA

Situated on the Japan Sea almost due north of Tokyo, Niigata is an international port of entry and one of the ports for sailing to nearby Sado Island.

Tsuruoka (Yamagata-ken) is straight up the coast but the terrain is not terribly interesting along the way as Niigata lies on a large flat plain in an area that produces more rice than any other prefecture in Japan.

The trip southwest is also unexciting. Travellers planning a journey in that direction can make a trip to Sado Island, then return to Honshu at Naoetsu, from where road and rail lead south to Nagano

Niigata

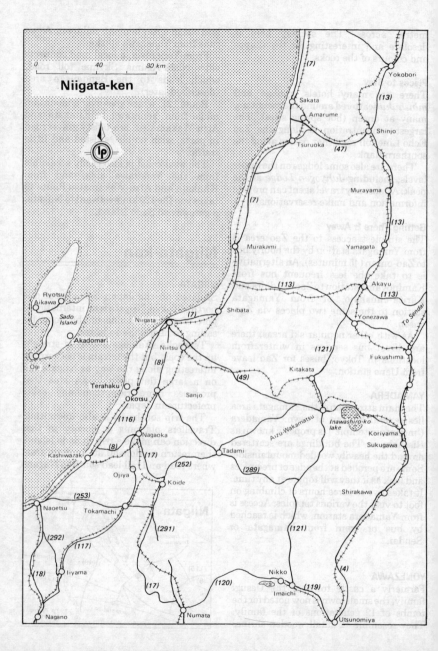

and Matsumoto (Nagano-ken); or west to the Northern Japan Alps/Noto Peninsula areas and inland to Gifu-ken.

Information

There is little to see in Niigata. If you have a few hours to kill, pick up a copy of the glossy brochure *Sight Seeing Niigata* (trilingual – in Russian even!) and see if there's anything that interests you. Copies are available at the information office at the station.

Festivals

One feature of the Hakusan-jinja matsuri festival from 12-18 April is the masked dances by shrine maidens.

The Niigata-matsuri festival is on 20-23 August and on the last day there is a spectacular display of fireworks near Bandai-bashi bridge.

Places to Stay

There are hotels and other accommodation in Niigata. Assistance may be obtained at the information office in the station.

There is a *Youth Hostel* (tel (0252) 290-0935) on the outskirts of town.

Getting There & Away

Air Niigata airport receives international flights from Khabarovsk (USSR). Many passengers on the Trans-Siberian Railway use this service as there are not enough ferries to Yokohama.

The airport is a few km northeast of the city centre; buses connect with Niigata station.

Train Niigata is the northern terminus of the Joetsu shinkansen super express train.

By the fastest service (the Asahi), Tokyo (Ueno station) is less than two hours away. By regular (and cheaper) expresses the trip takes about four hours.

Boat Niigata is the main port for ferry and hydrofoil services to Sado Island (there is

also an air service). Further details are given in the section on Sado Island. The dock can be reached from the station in about 20 minutes on foot, or by bus 14.

The ferry from Niigata to Otaru (Hokkaido) is the most economical way to reach Hokkaido from the north coast. Ferries leave from Yamanoshita-futo pier, which can be reached by bus 7 from the station.

NAOETSU

Situated on the coast southwest of Niigata, Naoetu's main attraction is the ferry service from Naoetsu-wan bay to Ogi on Sado Island.

If you're travelling south by road (along Route 18) through Naoetsu toward Nagano, keep your eyes open for the many old-fashioned, pre-war wooden buildings.

These old wooden houses and shops have sliding wood and glass front doors, and canopies that extend over the sidewalk from the buildings. They aren't worth a special trip but do provide a glimpse of something that has vanished almost everywhere else in the country in the rush to plate glass and brick.

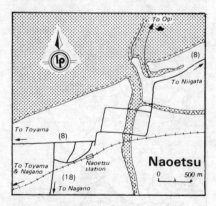

SADO-GA-SHIMA ISLAND

Sado-ga-shima Island is the fifth largest of the islands of Japan. The main attraction is its remoteness. Despite the large number of sightseers annually (about one million), the people of Sado continue much as they have done for decades or even centuries. It is like most island communities – the people are more friendly and the pace of life is slower. These, of course, are not things a visitor can actually see but if you have a feeling for atmosphere you should enjoy a visit.

The island is made up of two long, oval-shaped mountain ranges with a fertile valley sandwiched between them.

Ryotsu

The main town on Sado is Ryotsu, a small port city at the northeastern end of the valley. Starting from here, one route (along the south side of the valley) first passes Honma-ke Noh theatre, where performances of local dances and folk theatre are given during the summer. Check locally about these performances.

Konpo-ji Temple

This is in a forest setting, 30 minutes from Ryotsu by bus.

Myosen-ji Temple

Set in a forest, this temple has a 21-metre-high pagoda.

Ogi

This city lies near the southwest corner of the island. It is the other major port for boats to Honshu.

In Ogi harbour there is a chance of seeing 'washtub' boats – perfectly circular, flat-bottomed boats made in the manner of staved barrels. They were once a common sight around the island, and were originally used for harvesting seaweed and shellfish. Their main use these days is as a tourist attraction. If you see one, you can pay for a ride.

Other routes to Ogi are by circling southwest along the coast from Ryotsu, or by crossing the hilly spine of the southern range by one of three small roads. One source indicates a bus service on all, while another shows buses only on the western route across to Akadomari and around the eastern tip; inquire locally. There is definitely a section of the south coast without buses.

Past Ogi, toward Nansenkyo, there are many old houses built over 200 years ago. Along the way is the Ogi mingei hakubutsukan (folkcraft museum). The coast becomes rugged around the Nansenkyo-Sawazaki area then becomes quite gentle until the far side of Mano-wan bay, past Sawada.

Sado is of volcanic origin and the rock outcroppings have the weird shapes typical of once-molten lava, aided by the erosion of the sea. There are many beautiful views.

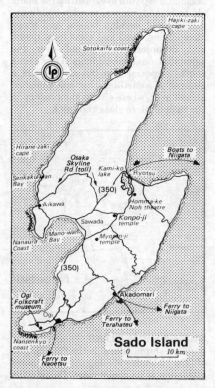

Sado Island
0   10 km

Aikawa

This was formerly the major gold mining centre of Japan, once the largest producer in the Orient. Its miners were often prisoners, many of whom died here.

The gold is nearly gone now but visitors can tour one of the mines, Sodayu-ko, which started about 360 years ago. Most of its passages are low and narrow. Mechanised displays (robots) show how the mining was done by hand.

Continuing up the coast, you pass more pretty coastal scenery and indented bays, with the Sotokaifu-kaigan coast the most attractive.

Getting There & Around

The main port for boats to the mainland is Ryotsu. During the peak season there are up to 10 hydrofoils a day to and from Niigata. The trip takes one hour and costs Y5300. There are also up to nine ordinary boats per day from the same port; they take about 2½ hours and cost a minimum of Y1730.

There is one boat a day between Niigata and Akadomari; it costs Y1550 and takes three hours, leaving Niigata in the afternoon and Akadomari in the early morning.

There are up to three boats a day each way between Akadomari and Terahaku (near Okotsu JR station); the fare is Y1190 and the trip takes two hours. Between Ogi and Naoetsu there are up to five boats a day that take 2½ hours and cost Y1910. There is also an airport near Ryotsu.

Buses run between the major centres on the island, so there is no problem getting around. There are also tour buses offering tours lasting four to eight hours. They leave from Ryotsu and Ogi.

Getting Around Northern Honshu

The following times and frequency of trains and buses are provided as samples of services available at the time of writing. Although there is a large degree of repetitiveness of schedules from year to year, there is no guarantee that any particular service will be as listed.

Be sure always to check travel plans with an up-to-date *Jikokuhyo* (book of timetables). Because of lack of traffic or roads impassible due to snow, many of the services described are suspended from early November to late April.

TRAIN

There is a good network of JR lines in northern Japan: a line along both east and west coasts, two roughly parallel lines up through most of the middle, and several crosswise linking lines.

In addition there are two Shinkansen super express lines (up to 240 km per hour) linking cities in this region with Tokyo.

Tohoku Shinkansen

This line was originally intended to go through Aomori on its way, via a tunnel under the Tsugaru strait to Hokkaido. However, economic reality struck hard and the line was terminated at Morioka, about 80% of the way to Aomori.

On the quickest express, the time from Tokyo to Sendai, the largest city in the region, is one hour 53 minutes; to Morioka, 2¾ hours.

Joetsu Shinkansen

This line links Niigata (almost directly north of Tokyo) with Tokyo. On the fastest train, the distance can be covered in 108 minutes.

BUS

There are long-distance overnight bus services from Tokyo to Sendai, Yamagata, Hirosaki, Aomori, Morioka and several other places in the Tohoku region. These are detailed in the general Getting Around chapter.

In addition to these long-distance

buses, there are many other bus routes within the region to places not served by railways, or between large centres via mountainous routes where railways would be difficult to build. These are

shown in *Jikokuhyo* as thin double-blue and double-red lines (JR services on which a Japanrail pass may be used), and a single thin blue line (others).

Hokkaido

Hokkaido is the northernmost major island of Japan. Although it was settled quite late in Japanese history and, visibly at least, has little of historic interest, it is the home of an aboriginal people who are not related to the Yamato Japanese (who comprise almost the entire population of Japan). There is evidence that the island has been occupied for about 23,000 years.

Hokkaido's strong suit is natural beauty and outdoor activities, with a definite flavour of eastern North America. In the river valleys, where most of the population has settled, the terrain features broad, rolling valleys flanked by low wooded hills.

Because the climate of Hokkaido is colder than that of the south islands, traditional farming methods and crops did not succeed, so foreign experts (mostly American) were brought in as advisors in the late 19th century. With them came large farms, dry-land crops, barns, silos and cows (a rarity elsewhere). These are very exotic to the Japanese but of limited interest to foreign visitors.

Most travellers will prefer the coastal, mountain and lake regions where the characteristic Hokkaido scenery, mostly of volcanic origin, can be enjoyed.

HISTORY & PEOPLE

Hokkaido was long a frontier region of little interest to the central governments in the south of Japan. The major groups of inhabitants were native peoples of various origins (mostly unknown), including the Ainu, Gilyak and Oroke.

Not much is known about the Ainu, who also live on Sakhalin Island. It is generally believed that they are a Caucasian race but next to nothing is known about their origins. It seems their languages have no known relatives elsewhere in the world, although there are tribes in Siberia with similar shamanist forms of worship based on a cult of the bear, and it has been observed that Ainu and Navajo music is similar.

It has also become known that they are recent arrivals on Hokkaido, having settled only about 800 years ago, displacing an even more mysterious people who seem to have occupied the island for much longer. Ainu used to live on Honshu as well and possibly as far south as Kyushu. They were a peaceful people and no match for the more aggressive Yamato Japanese so they were slowly pushed back into the remoteness of Hokkaido.

Ainu men are very hirsute and the large number of Japanese men (compared to Chinese and Korean) with a heavy beard is probably a legacy of intermarriage early in Japanese history.

Up to the end of the last century, the Ainu lived a life of hunting and fishing and engaged in small-scale agriculture of dry-field crops (no rice). By the last decade of the century the encroaching settlements of the southern Japanese had almost destroyed the Ainus' way of life and they were a dispirited people seemingly on the way to extinction.

The central government adopted a policy to forcibly assimilate the Ainu into the mainstream of Japanese life. They

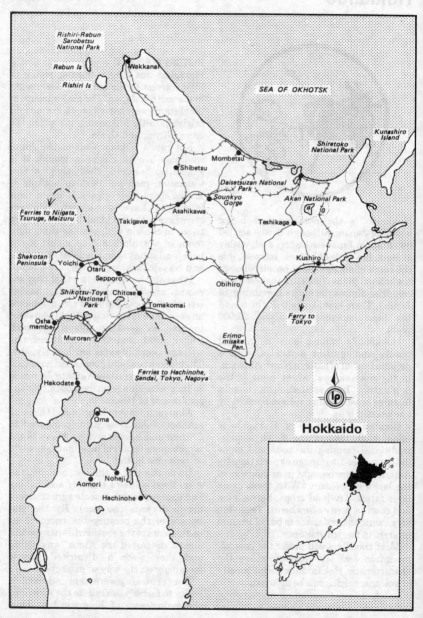

Hokkaido

were forced to take Japanese names and forbidden to use their own languages. As a result they have adopted Japanese names, language and customs and would be difficult to identify by sight.

In Japan there is discrimination against those who are different, so most Ainu do not advertise their racial heritage. There are perhaps only 15,000 full-blooded Ainu left in Hokkaido.

The only Ainu wearing traditional garments do so for the benefit of visiting tourists. They may be seen at Shiraoi, Noboribetsu-onsen, Asahikawa, in the area around Akan-ko, Kutcharo-ko and wherever tourists gather.

No one speaks any of the Ainu languages fluently but many place names are of Ainu origin. This can cause problems because nearly all are written in kanji, and southern Japanese are unable to read many place names correctly because of their unique pronunciation. Many of the pronunciatons do not even appear in kanji dictionaries.

The Gilyak were a hunting and fishing people like the Ainu and were largely found in Sakhalin. They also lived along the lower Amur River on the mainland and are a Mongolian race.

The Oroke lived on Sakhalin and were nomads who lived off their reindeer herds. They are a Tungas people and are related to the Orochi of the Amur River delta region. They were not originally inhabitants of Hokkaido but the takeover of Sakhalin by the USSR after World War II caused several Oroke to move to Hokkaido. There are about 30 Oroke scattered around the island, one of whom has opened a small museum at Abashiri.

INFORMATION

If you are in Tokyo prior to going to Hokkaido, visit the TIC and request any literature they would suggest for the area which you plan to travel to. Also pick up a copy of their listing of festivals of the month and check it for Hokkaido events.

A useful book describing 23 festivals unique to the island (some Ainu), with articles from a local English-language newspaper, may be available from some news-stands. It can also be obtained by mail (price Y980) from: Tast Corporation, Tokan Building, Kita 7, Nishi 4 Kita-ku, Sapporo.

GETTING THERE & AWAY

Hokkaido can be reached from Honshu by sea, air, and, with the opening in 1988 of the Seikan tunnel, land.

Air

The main airport is at Chitose, serving Sapporo. There are also local airports around the island fed via Chitose.

Train

At the time of writing the first edition of this book, announcements promised Shinkansen train service in 5½ hours from Tokyo to Sapporo by 1982. The fast connection from Tokyo is still a long way off because the Shinkansen goes only as far as Morioka in northern Honshu.

However, after 20 years of construction and the expenditure of countless billions of yen, the tunnel under the Tsugara Strait between Honshu and Hokkaido has been finished and trains are now making the 54-km trip on a regular basis. The railway-operated ferries that ran between Aomori (Honshu) and Hakodate (Hokkaido) for a century or so have been stopped, but other ferries continue to run.

Most trains to and from Hokkaido run just between Aomori and Hakodate, requiring a change of train at each end. There are 13 daily trains each way. Nine of these are *kaisoku* expresses starting from one of these two stations and requiring no surcharge; the other four are 'L' *tokkyu* expresses originating elsewhere and incurring an express surcharge. The trip takes about 2½ hours and the *kaisoku* trains will cost the better part of Y3000.

Few travellers going directly from a southern area (like Tokyo) to, say,

Sapporo, would choose to go by train unless they had a Japan Rail Pass that would otherwise be going to waste.

A train trip from Tokyo involves a Shinkansen trip to Morioka (the terminus for Shinkansen trains for the foreseeable future; typically 3 hours 20 minutes), an express from there to Aomori (about 2 hours 20 minutes), then a change to the train under the strait, and another train onward from Hakodate. It is rather long, and the overnight trains are popular among those who don't mind the surcharges for the sleeper (not covered by a Rail Pass). The exceptions here are three overnight express trains from Tokyo (Ueno) that run through to Sapporo nonstop, a small number of overnighters from Ueno to Aomori, and one from Osaka that ends at Hakodate.

By comparison, the base express fare from Ueno to Sapporo is Y15,800, and the cheapest berth is Y5000 extra. The airfare is Y25,500 and obviously the trip is much faster. (The tunnel was started before air travel become common. After the tunnel was finished there was serious discussion of just abandoning it, or even using it for growing mushrooms.)

Ferry

There are several ferry lines servicing Hokkaido. Listed here are the main ferry ports in Hokkaido and the cities in Honshu with which they connect. The schedules change from year to year, so these are only a guide. Up-to-date information for all sailings is printed in *Jikokuhyo*.

Hakodate to Aomori Although the JR train ferries were stopped when the Seikan tunnel was opened, the Highashi Nihon Ferry company (HNF) continues to operate up to 11 daily sailings for vehicles and passengers between Aomori and Hakodate, though the majority are in the evening and early morning. Crossing time is about 3¾ hours and the fare Y1200.

At both Hakodate and Aomori, the HNF terminal is some distance to the west of the city. Ask at the station for directions to the dock.

If you arrive at Hakodate by HNF, you can reach the JR station by taking the road from the terminal, turning right at the first T-junction, left at the next corner and continuing until you come to the intersection of a major road. The bus stop is across the road and to the right. The name of the stop (written only in Japanese) is Hokudai (Hokkaido University). Take bus No 1 to the station.

Hakodate to Noheji HNF has at least three sailings a day in each direction between Hakodate and this small city about 45 km east of Aomori. Sailing time is about 4¾ hours and the cheapest fare is Y1400. The terminus is a few km to the west of the JR station; a bus from the station makes the connection.

Hakodate to Oma HNF has up to three sailings daily in each direction between Hakodate and this small town at the north of the Shimokita Peninsula. The sea distance is shorter (sailing time of two hours) and the fare is slightly less than from Aomori (Y1000), but this is balanced out by the longer land distance to reach Oma (road only; no train service).

Muroran to Aomori There are two ferries a day (sailing time about 7½ hours) in each direction and the minimum fare is Y3400. They leave from Muroran at 8.20 am and 11.30 pm, and from Aomori at 2.45 and 9.30 pm. The ferry terminus ('Ferry Noriba') at Muroran is easy to find and is one km from the JR Muroran station. It can be reached by bus from the station.

Muroran to Oma In the summer there is a service between Muroran and Oma; the fare is Y1400. Check the schedule in *Jikokuhyo*.

Muroran to Hachinohe There are one or two daily sailings between Muroran and

Hachinohe, a port on the east coast approximately halfway between Aomori and Morioka (the Shinkansen terminus). Using this port can save travel time in Honshu. Minimum fare is Y3900.

Muroran to Oarai There is service three times a week in each direction between Muroran and this small city north of Tokyo and the Chiba Peninsula. Sailing time is 19 hours and the minimum fare is Y9300.

Visitors with only a few days for Hokkaido should note that Muroran is very close to the Toya-ko Shikotsu-ko area, one of the two most popular and interesting regions for travellers in Hokkaido.

Tomakomai to Hachinohe Boats of two lines sail three times a day; the trip takes nine hours and costs Y3900.

Tomakomai to Sendai There are daily services (by different lines; sailing time 14½ to 17 hours) to and from Sendai. One of these runs between Nagoya and Tomakomai, stopping at Sendai in each direction. The minimum Sendai-Tomakomai fare is Y8600.

Tomakomai to Oarai There is one daily sailing at midnight in each direction between Tomakomai and this small city north of Tokyo and the Chiba Peninsula area. The trip takes 19 to 20 hours and costs a minimum of Y9300.

Tomakomai to Tokyo There are two sailings a week in each direction. The trip takes 31 hours and costs a minimum of Y11,500.

Tomakomai to Nagoya The trip between Tomakomai and Nagoya takes about 39 hours (with a three-hour stop at Sendai) and costs a minimum of Y15,000. Departures are in the early evening.

Kushiro to Tokyo Kushiro gives easy access to Akan National Park. There is a ferry

every one to two days in each direction, operated by Kinkai Yusen Ferry. The trip takes 33 hours; cheapest fare is Y14,000.

Otaru to Niigata, Tsuruga & Maizuru These services are run by Shin Nihonkai Ferry. Tsuruga and Maizuru are on the north coast of Honshu, conveniently close to Kyoto. From both places there are three or four sailings a week in each direction (32 hours from both ports).

From Niigata there are five sailings a week in each direction; duration is about 20½ hours. The cheapest fare from Niigata is Y5000, and from the other two ports is Y6400.

Getting Around
There are JR lines around nearly all parts of the island, and a good system of long-distance buses has developed in recent years. In addition to these, other bus routes serve the more mountainous or unpopulated regions.

A peculiarity of the bus services here (and in other similarly isolated parts of the country) is that the summer is considered to end on 15 August – after which services may be reduced or even cease altogether.

HAKODATE
Hakodate was the primary port of entry to Hokkaido from Honshu, being the terminus of train ferries from Honshu. The Seikan tunnel under the strait has changed all this and the ferries no longer operate from here.

Information
There is an information office at the JR railway station. It should have maps of the city detailing the old section of the city and be able to help in finding accommodation.

Hakodate-san
The city of Hakodate is dominated by Hakodate-san (335 metres), a large hill of volcanic origin at the end of a small

peninsula that forms a natural shelter for ships. The view of Hakodate at night from this hill is considered the finest night view in Japan; a carpet of coloured lights stretches into the distance.

It is possible to walk up but it is easier to take the cable-car ('ropeway') that runs to the top from a base station part of the way up the hill (Y600 one way; Y1100 return). The base station is easily reached from tram stops Horaicho on line No 2, or Jujigai on lines 3 or 5. From the latter, go one street west, then uphill.

Motomachi (Old Section)

The first impression of Hakodate is that it is an unattractive city, but its appeal grows. It has character – something that most Japanese cities lack.

In the port area and on the hill side at the base of Hakodate-san, the Motomachi district has many old and decrepit buildings, distinguishable because they are American or European in style. They

date from the Meiji and Taisho eras (late 1800s and early 1900s) and have been recognised by the authorities as comprising an area of historic architecture. The area is charmingly seedy for the most part but it seems the buildings will be preserved and maintained, and probably restored in part.

There is no particular street to see these buildings; it is interesting just to wander around. Tram No 3 passes by a number of such buildings near the harbour terminus and the streets of nearby hill sides are a good area to explore. One place to look for is an old public hall, Kokaido, a large, ageing and sagging wooden building that resembles a Civil-War-era mansion from the American south.

In the same area is the Japan Orthodox Hakodate Resurrection Church, a Byzantine-style building dating from 1916 and starting to show its age. It's especially pretty at night when lit up. Nearby is the Hakodate branch of the

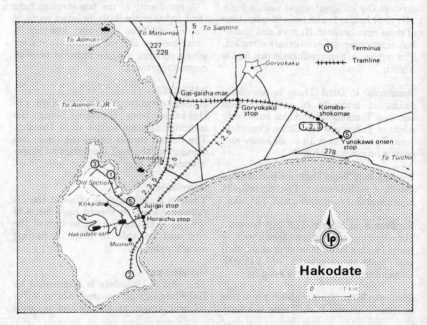

Higashi Honganji temple. An amusing sign post, one of many directing the pedestrian explorer to places of interest in the area, shows a sweating priest frantically beating a *mokugyo* (wooden gong), a feature of prayers of that sect.

Like some of the old buildings, the trams in Hakodate are also a trifle decrepit and add an air of nostalgia to the place. Only wooden cars (dating from 1949) are in use – the modern metal ones rusted away in the salt air.

Hakodate Museum
On the other side of the hill is Hakodate-koen park, an attractive wooded area noted for its cherry blossoms in late April.

In the park is Hakodate Hakubutsukan museum which has a good collection and modern display of artefacts of the aboriginal races that inhabited Hokkaido. If you have time to see only one museum in Hokkaido, this would be the best choice. It is close to the last two stops on tram line No 2 and is not too far from the Horaicho stop.

Goryokaku Fort
This is an interesting fort, being the only one in Japan built in a European style (finished in 1864). It is shaped like a five-pointed star, a design which allows defenders to rake all approaches with gunfire.

The fort was the scene of a siege in 1868 when supporters of the Tokugawa *shogunate* resisted the Meiji restoration for more than a month. A small museum inside the walls has relics of the battle and a small tower allows a view over the area. The walls themselves are low (perhaps five metres high) and there is no superstructure, only the walls and moats. It is now a park, and cherry trees in the grounds make it pretty in late April and early May.

The fort is close to Goryokaku-gyoen-mae tram stop which is the common point for all tram lines in the city.

Trappist Convent & Monastery
The convent is five minutes from Yunokawa station by bus. It is famous in Japan for its butter and candy and is the only Trappist convent in Japan.

The Trappist monastery is at Oshima-Tobetsu, 26 km from Hakodate.

Places to Stay
There is one youth hostel in Hakodate, *Hokusei-so Youth Hostel* (tel (0138) 57-3212); it is several km from the station in the hot-spring town of Yunokawa ('hot water river'), a suburb of Hakodate. From the station take a tram No 5 and get off at Yunokawa-onsen (the second-last stop on the line). Be sure to get a No 5 going the right way. (Trams No 1, 2 and 3 go only as far as the car barn, one stop before Yunokawa-onsen, which would add over half a km to the distance to the hostel.)

The hostel is located amidst resort hotels and its bath is fed with the same naturally hot (and *very* hard) water, so you can enjoy the privilege without the cost of a resort hotel. The hostel tends to be quite full on weekends. If you arrive early in the day, consider staying in the scenic Onuma area, about 25 km away.

Getting Around
There is an all-day tram-and-bus ticket for about Y600 and a 10-tickets special (Y1000) at both the train station and the bus station.

Hitching If you wish to hitch to Sapporo and elsewhere immediately, it is necessary to get to Route 5. If arriving by ferry from Honshu, get off the bus at Gas-gaisha-mae, which is near a large gas holder. Just before reaching it the road from the ferry terminal follows an overpass that curves to the left and intersects a major road at right angles; that is Route 5. Gas-gaisha-mae can also be reached by bus from Hakodate station.

AROUND HAKODATE
West of Hakodate

Matsumae This was the capital of Hokkaido from the 16th century when the island was known as Ezo. It was the site of the last feudal castle to be built in Japan (and the only one in Hokkaido) but a fire destroyed the original buildings. A concrete reproduction shows the former appearance and about 5000 cherry trees make the place one of beauty from late April.

East of Hakodate

Mt Esan This is an active volcano (618 metres) with steaming vents at the summit and an oval crater. It can be climbed in about an hour. Access to the base takes about 2¼ hours by bus from Hakodate.

North of Hakodate

The view from either the train or the road (Route 5) leaving Hakodate is typical of the valley scenery anywhere in Hokkaido – rolling farm land interspersed with numerous towns. After 25 km or so, road and rail pass through a tunnel and the scenery changes abruptly.

You are suddenly confronted with the very scenic Lake Konuma, which reflects the squat volcano Komagatake. This is the entrance to Onuma Kokuritsu-koen National Park, a very enjoyable place to spend a day or two. Travellers arriving at Hakodate might consider making their way here for the first night in Hokkaido instead of staying in Hakodate.

Koma Visible for the next 20 km or so, Koma consists of three peaks – Sawara, Kengamine and Sumidamori. It is an ugly brown ulcer on the green countryside but is nevertheless very scenic. Originally conical, explosions have blasted the top off, leaving an elongated flat and sloping top.

Mt Higure As well as the view over Lake Konuma, the best outlook is considered to be Konuma Hill; another is the top of Mt Higure (313 metres). It is an easy walk to the top where there are three smaller craters within the large horseshoe-shaped outer rim; the rim is two km from east to west and 1½ km north to south, sloping towards the sea. Any of the three youth hostels in the area will have information on the best routes.

It is also possible to circle the mountain by train. From the sea side on a clear day you can see distant Mt Yotei across the bay.

HAKODATE TO OSHAMAMBE

As Komagatake falls behind, the road and railway run parallel to the shore of Uchiura Bay for the next 70 km or so to a point slightly beyond Oshamambe. They are seldom far from the water and travellers with the time to stop will find beachcombing in this area probably the best in Japan because the bay seems to act

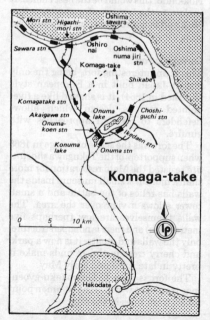

Komaga-take

as a collection point for anything floating in the area.

Stop anywhere distant from habitation and the beach is almost sure to be littered with hand-blown glass fishing floats that have been washed ashore. I stopped at random three times and each time found more than 20 floats within half a km of where I started; carrying them all became a problem! It appears they are replenished regularly because one beach I picked over on the way north had another 25 or so by the time I returned just a month later.

The road passes through many fishing villages; draped everywhere are fishing nets, with fishermen making repairs. On flat areas you can often see large pieces of *kombu*, an edible seaweed, laid out to dry.

OSHAMAMBE TO SAPPORO

There are two suggested routes between these cities. One follows the railway and Route 5 inland in a northward loop, while the other continues around the bay, then cuts inland and touches on the Toya-ko lake area before continuing through mountainous terrain to Sapporo.

The first route passes mostly through river valleys and, near Sapporo, a dismal succession of unappealing towns, but it offers the option of a looping side trip through Shakotan Hanto peninsula. The second route passes through much more attractive scenery for most of its length.

The traveller who has adequate time and who plans to circle back to the Toya-ko area can combine the best of both these routes by taking the first to Yoichi, circling the Shakotan Peninsula to Iwanai, then cutting over to Kutchan and Kimobetsu and carrying on from there by the second route to Sapporo.

Oshamambe to Kutchan

Both road and rail run parallel through this region of river valley farmland. Between Niseko and Kutchan it skirts Mt Yotei (1893 metres), which is now extinct.

The top is mostly lava-covered but the lower sections are wooded.

Climbing Mt Yotei is popular with the Japanese and is not particularly difficult. (Most 'mountain climbing' in Japan is simply a matter of putting one foot in front of the other for a long enough period.) One popular route is via Hirafu station by bus to Nangetsu-ko lake from where you begin the climb. The walk up takes about four hours, plus an hour at the top to walk around the three cauldrons. For up-to-date information try the Niseko Youth Hostel in Kutchan.

Mt Nisekoan-Nupuri (1309 metres), also near Kutchan, is rated as one of the four best ski areas in Hokkaido. There are nearby *onsen* for relaxing in afterward. Kombu-onsen is noted for its autumn leaves.

Kutchan to Yoichi

Yoichi is best regarded as the gateway to the Shakotan Peninsula. The town has an aquarium and offers tours of the Nikka Distillery, near Yoichi station (Monday to Saturday).

Shakotan Peninsula

The Shakotan Peninsula is noted for its rugged scenery – cliffs rising out of the sea as high as 250 metres, and the peaks of two mountains, Yobetsu (1298 metres) and Shakotan (1255 metres).

Two capes mark the tip of the peninsula, Kamui and Shakotan; the former has a huge rock rising abruptly about 40 metres from the sea.

Buses run from Yoichi as far as Yobetsu. In past years there was a boat around to Kamoenai and Iwanai that connected with a bus, but the boat was not shown in *Jikokuhyo* in 1987.

Yoichi to Sapporo

The short distance between these two cities includes the best sand beach on Hokkaido (at Ranshima), as well as shorter stretches of beach at irregular intervals.

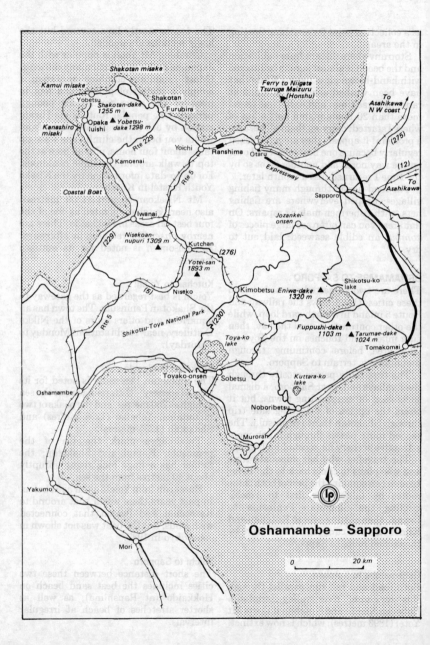

Oshamambe – Sapporo

0   20 km

There are several prehistoric relics in the area. Oshoro Stone Circle is a rough circle of large stones about one metre tall, located on Ranshima-kawa river, southeast of Ranshima station.

Other indications of early settlement have been found in the area, such as traces of a dwelling, pottery, tools, Oyachi Shell Mound, a fort and a cave with more than 200 pictographs on the walls (both in the Fugoppe area, estimated to be about 1500 years old).

Mt Tengu, three km southwest of Otaru station offers good skiing.

Otaru is a ferry port with services to and from Niigata, Tsuruga and Maizuru. There is also an overnight boat from Otaru to Rishiri Island off the far north coast of Hokkaido. More details on that are given later.

To Sapporo via Toya-ko Lake

This route continues around the shores of Uchiura Bay, then turns inland to Toya-ko lake and continues through highland scenery to Sapporo. It is by far the more scenic route and is recommended for travellers in a hurry or for those who will be going in this direction only once.

From Toya station (on the bay) there is a regular bus service to Toya-ko *onsen* on Toya-ko lake. (The many attractions of the Toya-ko area are described in detail in the section on Shikotsu-Toya National Park).

From Toya-ko, Route 230 climbs to a plateau, passing areas of forest land with broken-top trees smashed by rock ejected in the 1977 eruption of Usu-san. As the road climbs beside the lake, you get a superb view of Nakajima, a cluster of small volcanic islands poking up in the middle of Shikotsuko (Nakajima means 'middle island').

Other points of interest are Usu-san (probably steaming profusely) and Showa Shinzan. Once on the plateau, the road leaves the lake and the view of Yotei-san begins to dominate the landscape. From there to Sapporo the road passes through a very pretty mountain and farming region with few built-up areas.

The road passes through Jozankei-onsen, one of the best known spas in Japan. (Mixed bathing, formerly the custom here, has gone the way of the auk.) Autumn is the best time for a look around as the leaves are beautiful at that time.

SAPPORO

A rarity among Japanese cities, Sapporo is laid out with streets at right angles and has an address system that makes sense to foreigners. (This is true for many other

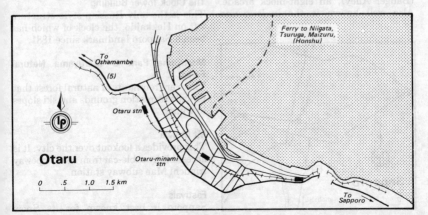

Otaru

cities on Hokkaido). The reason for this is that Sapporo was founded only in 1869 when the Kaitakushi (Commissioner of Colonisation) was stationed here to establish the city as the capital of Hokkaido. Like other 'instant cities' it lacks the soul and the element of disorder that gives older cities their character.

The somewhat sterile atmosphere is, however, offset partly by many parks and gardens. Foreigners find it a pleasant place to live, but as a tourist goal it is rather low-ranking. It is at its best when the bright lights of the Susukino district give it a magical touch.

Those with a larger budget will find it has the best night life north of Tokyo with more than 3500 bars and cabarets.

The main street, O-dori, is famed for its great width (105 metres) but this is a deceptive statistic because most of the space is occupied by a park-like boulevard. This is a popular place in summer when visitors sit around, usually huddled under the inadequate number of trees. (Why do city planners always go for huge open spaces which become intolerably hot under the summer sun?) At the east end of the boulevard is the TV tower (147 metres) which gives a good view over the entire city.

The main shopping area is Tanuki-koji (Badger Alley), an eight-block arcade. Also well known is the underground

shopping arcade that stretches from the TV tower under the boulevard and then turns to run to Susukino. It reflects the cold winter climate.

Information
The first move is to pick up a map and pamphlet from the tourist information centre in the station. The map shows the points of interest and subway and other transportation lines. The JNTO map of Japan also has an adequate Sapporo map on the back.

The Botanical Garden
The Botanical Garden has about 5000 species of plants from Hokkaido and the rest of the world. It is an attractive setting for a stroll or picnic.

The Clock Tower Building
This is the only Russian-style structure left on Hokkaido, the clock of which has been a Sapporo landmark since 1881.

Maruyama Park & Maruyama Natural Forest
There are remnants of natural forest that provide recreation grounds and ski slopes in winter.

Mt Moiwa
This provides a lookout over the city. It is accessible by cable-car from near Ropeway Iriguchi Mae subway station.

Festivals
Sapporo is best known for its Snow

Festival in the first weekend of February when O-dori boulevard (and other open areas) are built up with huge snow-and-ice sculptures of people, famous buildings and mythological figures. These sculptures are probably the most impressive of any winter carnival in the world.

Places to Stay

There are three *Youth Hostels* in the Sapporo area. By far the most convenient to reach is the one near the station.

Getting There & Away

In addition to the JR and road connections, Sapporo is easily reached by air from other parts of Japan. The actual airport is at Chitose, about an hour away by bus. (The JR bus terminal is beside the station.)

The city of Tomakomai is only a short distance beyond Chitose and it is the port of entry for ferries connecting with Tokyo, Sendai and Hachinohe in Honshu.

Getting Around

Sapporo has the nicest subway in Japan. Like those in Montreal and Paris, it runs on rubber tyres and is therefore very quiet. Stations are marked in *romaji* at the station, but next and previous stations are labelled only only in Japanese, as are trains, maps, etc.

ASAHIKAWA

In the Chikabumi district of Asahikawa, the Ainu Kinenkan (memorial hall) combines a reasonably good museum with a large number of souvenir stands that sell Ainu handcrafts – mostly identical wooden bears and statuettes of Ainu people.

Many Ainu live in the area. One or two (usually elderly) people may be dressed in traditional costume and delegated to satisfy tourists' cameras. Dances are performed – when a tour bus turns up. If you are going to Noboribetsu, Akan or Shiraoi, it is not worth bothering with Chikabumi.

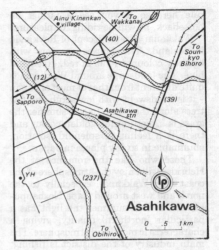

From Asahikawa you can make a side trip north to Wakkanai or proceed east to the major attractions of that area.

Places to Stay

The *Youth Hostel* is quite good, has a ski tow in the back yard and you can get information on buses to Wakkanai or elsewhere.

If you arrive early in the day and are not going to Wakkanai, consider pressing on to Sounkyo, where there are two *youth hostels* in the midst of beautiful gorge scenery near good hiking territory.

RISHIRI-REBUN-SAROBETSU NATIONAL PARK

The islands of Rebun and Rishiri are combined with a part of the mainland to form the Rishiri-Rebun-Sarobetsu National Park.

Wakkanai

Wakkanai is as far north in Japan as it is possible to go. It is 250 km from Asahikawa and the road passes mostly through flat land where the scenery consists of spreading farms, barns and silos. Modern farming machinery is the rule here so if you see a farmer on horseback, he will be riding for pleasure.

Wakkanai is reminiscent of Reykjavik in Iceland. The houses are low with brightly coloured roofs in red, green and blue. The landscape around Wakkanai is quite different from that of most of Japan – it is windswept with low scrub and few trees along the coast. In late summer the grass is a picturesque golden colour and there is a feeling of splendid isolation, obtainable in so few places in Japan.

Those who like the romance of the Hebrides will enjoy the atmosphere of the coast near Wakkanai, especially to the north and west around Cape Noshappu-misaki. In late summer the light has a particular 'northern' quality, giving a characteristic mood and atmosphere. The main industry of the district is fishing, which also adds to the local atmosphere.

Rishiri & Rebun Islands

A very popular excursion with the Japanese is the boat trip from Wakkanai to the islands of Rishiri and Rebun. Although close together, the two islands have totally different histories.

Rebun has been there for millions of years and was formed by an upward thrust of the earth's crust. Rishiri, on the other hand, is a comparative youngster (only a few hundred thousand years old) formed when a submarine volcano built itself above the ocean surface. The picturesque cone of Rishiri-san (1719 metres), now gullied by eons of rain, remains as a reminder of the eruption.

The magnificent isolation, unspoiled environment, beautiful scenery, sea birds, wildflowers in profusion, and little fishing villages, are the main attractions of these islands.

An almost circular road runs around Rishiri and bus transport is available (six per day, each way). Hiking courses are set out and connect the major points of interest around the island. Scenic spots include the view of Rishiri-san over the small lakes Hime-numa and Otadomari-numa, and many seascapes and capes that jut into the sea.

Rebun is very low but nonetheless offers scenic views near Nishi-Uedomani, the view of Tadoshima Island from Cape Sukoton-misaki, and the towering rock Jizo-iwa.

Places to Stay There are three *Youth Hostels* on Rebun and one on Rishiri.

Getting There & Away Access from Wakkanai is by Higashi Nihonkai ferry; two boats a day go to Oshidomari (Rishiri) and to Kafuka (Rebun), and there is one a day to Funadomari (Rebun) and to Kutsugata (Rishiri).

Other ferries of the same line run from Katsugata to Kafuka (one per day) and from Oshidomari to Kafuka (two per day).

There is a similar number of sailings in the opposite direction. There is also an overnight boat from Otaru (near Sapporo) to Kutsugata and Kafuka (Y7500), returning to Otaru in the evening. It could be of interest to those who wish to see the northern islands and the tip of Hokkaido but don't relish the idea of the return trip by land from Wakkanai as it doesn't have the most exciting scenery.

More information on the boat connections is available at the TIC in Tokyo, the information centre at Sapporo station and in Wakkanai.

Getting Around Roads and transport facilities are not overly developed on either island, but are adequate. Hiking is enjoyable and, since the islands are small, it is a good way to look around.

On Rebun you can take the bus one way and hike back in one day. There are sure to be young Japanese people doing this and they're usually happy to have an extra person tag along. Many will be camping.

Sarobetsu

Sarobetsu is an area of swampy coastline and sand dunes known for the beauty of its

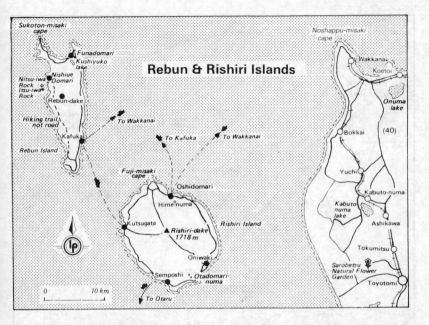

wildflowers. It can be reached by bus from Wakkanai to Bokkai, by train to Bokkai (the northernmost point of entry), or by going to Toyotomi, from where a bus is available (through the middle of the park) to Wakasakanai.

The most important part is Sarobetsu Gensai-kaen (Natural Flower Garden); it is about 15 minutes from Toyotomi station. Forget it in the spring as the area floods annually.

DAISETSUZAN NATIONAL PARK

Daisetsuzan Kokuritsu-koen is one of the most well-known scenic areas in Hokkaido and would rank just behind Akan and Shikotsu-Toya parks as an attraction. For those who enjoy hiking it is superb, and is very popular among the Japanese. The entrance to the park is 16 km east of Kamikawa on Route 39. (Kamikawa is about 45 km east of Asahikawa.)

From Kamikawa ('upper river') onward you get occasional glimpses (to the right)

of a group of volcanic peaks known collectively as Daisetsuzan.

The most pronounced peak is the sloping cone of Asahi-dake ('Sunrise Mountain', 2290 metres), the highest mountain on Hokkaido. Climbing and hiking in summer and skiing in winter are popular activities in this area.

Soun-kyo Gorge

The single most scenic attraction of the park is Soun-kyo gorge, a canyon on the Ishikari river extending 24 km from the entrance to the park. Rock walls rise sharply on both sides of the road and outcroppings of jagged rock jut from cliff faces.

In the middle of the gorge is the hot-spring resort town of Soun-kyo-onsen with a number of resort hotels and two youth hostels. It is a base for climbing and hiking through the Daisetsuzan area.

About three km further along the gorge are two picturesque waterfalls, Ryusei-

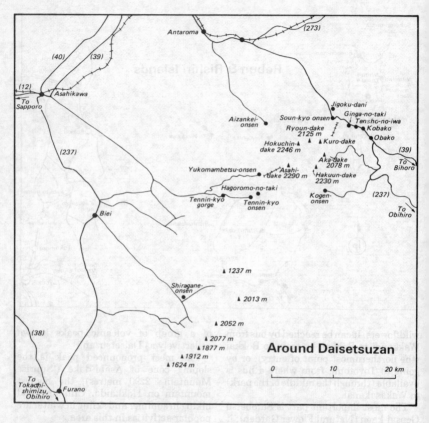

Around Daisetsuzan

no-taki and Ginga-no-taki, which are close to each other but separated by huge Tensho-iwa ('Heavenly Castle Rock').

Near the end of the gorge are Kobako and Obako ('small box' and 'large box'), closely enclosed sections of the gorge where you feel as if you're at the bottom of a box. The walls of the 'boxes' and much of the gorge are columnar basalt, lava that cooled into large crystals. Australians from Victoria will find the gorge like a hundred Hanging Rocks laid side be side. The way in which both were formed is similar.

Exploring Daisetsuzan

The area known as Daisetsuzan (Great Snow Mountain) consists of a number of volcanic peaks, all about 2000 metres high. They do not require climbing gear or great skill but do invite exploration as the terrain is easy to walk through.

It is basically an undulating plateau that fills in the area between the various peaks that make up the mountain. The view is one of small craters (some steaming), wildflowers, the crater of Daisetsuzan and open spaces with no signs of civilisation. A network of trails makes walking easy.

The best-known trail runs from Soun-

Top: Interior of an old farmhouse at Nihon-Minka-en, Kawasaki (IMcQ)
Bottom: Old lady and one of the characteristic walls of Kurashiki (IMcQ)

Top: Interior of Tagata-jinja shrine, typical of any large Shinto shrine (IMcQ)
Left: An Ainu elder, Noboribetsu (IMcQ)
Right: Shinto priest at Meiji-jingu shrine (IMcQ)

kyo-onsen to Yukomambetsu-onsen; it can be walked in a day with little effort. From Soun-kyo-onsen, a cable-car runs a good part of the way up the side of Kuro-dake ('Black Mountain', 1984 metres). From there the path is easy to follow past Ryoun-dake (2125 metres), Hokuchin-dake (2246 metres) and Asahi-dake (2290 metres) to the upper station of the 'Daisetsuzan Asahi-dake ropeway' that leads down to Yukomambetsu-onsen. This resort has a good youth hostel, with a view of Asahi-dake, as well as other accommodation.

Continuing along the path you come to Hagoromo waterfall, Tennin-kyo-onsen and Tennin-kyo gorge. Tennin-kyo ('Heavenly Maiden') gorge is similar to Soun-kyo but its sides are less steep and the cliff faces have crumbled more.

Hagoromo-no-taki, a beautiful waterfall, is a few hundred metres from Tennin-kyo-onsen; it is a cascade of seven falls set in a high ravine. Tennin-kyo-onsen and Yukomambetsu-onsen are about four km apart. The road joining them passes through Tennin-kyo and both *onsen* are linked to Asahikawa by bus.

There are many other trails across the plateau of Daisetsuzan – nicknamed 'the roof of Hokkaido'. A short one runs from Soun-kyo-onsen to Aizankei-onsen, while a slightly longer one goes to Kogen-onsen; both are shorter than the hike to Yukomambetsu/Tennin-kyo-onsen. A bus service is indicated to Kogen-onsen.

More information is available locally, especially at youth hostels.

SOUN-KYO TO SHIRETOKO PENINSULA

Route 273 runs south to Obihiro and is mentioned only as a short cut for those pressed for time who wish to circle back to Shikotsu-Toya National Park. Part of the road is rough gravel. The preferred alternative is to continue on toward Bihoro and the attractions of the Akan-ko/Kutcharo-ko/Mashu-ko area.

After leaving Soun-kyo, Route 39 continues eastward through Onneyu-

onsen, Rubeshibe, Kitami and Bihoro. The fields around Kitami are planted with peppermint (claimed to be the world's best) and at Rubeshibe Youth Hostel there is a well-preserved steam engine of the type used in Hokkaido up until the early 1970s. Otherwise there is little of interest along the way.

Bihoro to Akan National Park

Those with a limited amount of time will head for Akan at once; it ranks with Shikotsu-Toya National Park (detailed later) as one of the two most scenic and interesting travel destinations on Hokkaido.

The most direct route is Route 243 which goes to Teshikaga, more or less in the middle of the park. You could turn off it at Kutcharo-ko lake; this gives an excellent view over the lake from Bihoro-toge (mountain pass). Another way is via Route 240 to the west entrance of the National Park but it would probably cause a considerable amount of backtracking.

Bihoro to Abashiri

Abashiri is a fishing port with some remains from prehistoric times as well as the recent past. The slightly musty but enjoyable Municipal Museum in Katsuraoka-koen park has a good display of Ainu artefacts from the area, plus pottery and stone tools (relics of aboriginal dwellers who predated the Ainu) excavated at nearby Moyoro Shell Mound. The museum is one km southeast of the station and the shell mound is northeast of the station on the left bank of the Abashiri river.

Late in the summer of 1978, Daahennieni Gendaanu, one of the few Oroke people who moved to Hokkaido from Sakhalin Island, opened a museum to keep alive the memory of his people, nomads who lived by herding reindeer. (There are still Oroke living on Sakhalin Island.) The Oroke word for the museum is Jakkadohuni; it may be known in Japanese as Oroke Kinenkan. It is worth visiting and the curator is very friendly.

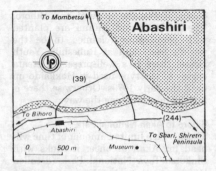

North of Abashiri are two lagoons, Notoro and Saroma. In this area, and noted on the map in the TIC brochure on Northern Japan, is the intriguing 'Coral Grass Gregarious Spot' but, alas!, there is no further explanation. (It might refer to an unusual red plant that grows on swampy ground; in September the fields are quite bright red.)

The nearest youth hostel is at Gensai-kaen (next section) or you can go slightly farther north or south to one of the others.

Abashiri to Akan National Park

There are two suggested routes to follow: one is direct, while the other circles around the Shiretoko Peninsula. Both offer better scenery than the route back through Bihoro.

East of Abashiri along Route 244, the first attraction is Gensai-kaen (Natural Flower Garden). This is a strip of coastal sand dune that is heavily overgrown by wild-flowers (the result of a dune stabilisation programme) which bloom in late June and early July. It begins at Kitahama and continues along the road for about 30 km to Shari. It is always the target for swarms of Japanese photographers.

At Hokuto, before Shari and about 25 km out of Abashiri, the road turns off to Koshimizu and then goes on to Kawayu and Teshikaga. Kawayu is the centre of many of the attractions of Akan National Park.

Instead of turning off for Koshimizu, you can continue along Route 244 to Shari and beyond (on Route 334) to Utoro on the untamed Shiretoko Peninsula.

Beyond Shari, you can look inland and see the jagged cone of Shari-dake (1545 metres), and later, the rounded outline of Kaibetsu-dake (1419 metres). Shari-dake is also visible along much of the length of the direct route.

SHIRETOKO PENINSULA

Shiretoko is an Ainu word meaning 'end of the Earth', and it lives up to its name. The end of the peninsula is a national park, the least developed in Japan. There is a small number of hiking trails and roads go along both the northwest and southeast coasts but not to the tip. A single road crosses it from Utoro to Rausu.

From the middle to the tip there are three major mountains, Rausu-dake (1661 metres), Io-san (1563 metres) and Shiretoko-dake (1254 metres). At the base of the peninsula is Kaibetsu-dake and between it and Rausu-dake is a smaller peak.

Io-san is one of the most unusual volcanoes on earth – when it erupts, it emits pure sulphur. During its most recent eruption (in 1936) more than 15,000 tons of sulphur poured out.

The volcanoes (all but Io-san are extinct) are a continuation of the chain that extends through the Kuril chain to Alaska; on Hokkaido, this is the Chishima volcanic zone.

It is almost impossible, however, to see the mountains while travelling along the road as it passes close to the base of the hills and in many places has been hacked out of the rock. The best way to see the beauty and splendour of the peninsula is by boat (detailed later).

The cape is famous for its rugged cliffs that rise as much as 200 metres from the sea and stretch up to 10 km without a break. The cliffs are noted for their black and white stripes, layers of volcanic rock alternating with sedimentary rock. Time,

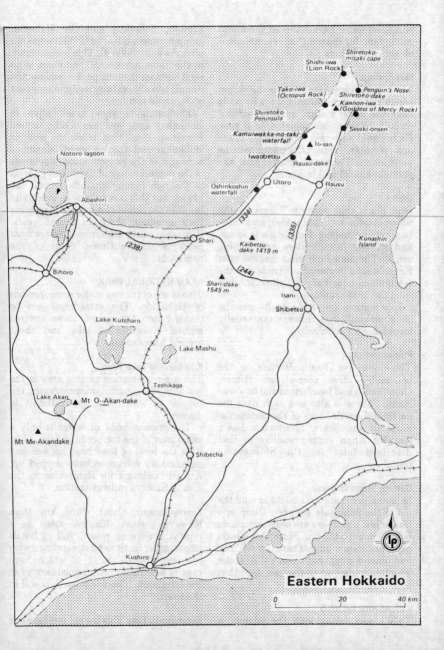

Shiretoko-misaki cape

Shishi-iwa (Lion Rock)

Tako-iwa (Octopus Rock)

Penguin's Nose

Shiretoko-dake

Kannon-iwa (Goddess of Mercy Rock)

Shiretoko Peninsula

Seseki-onsen

Kamuiwakka-no-taki waterfall

Io-san

Iwaobetsu

Rausu-dake

Notoro lagoon

Oshinkoshin waterfall

Utoro

Rausu

Abashiri

Kunashiri Island

(334)

(238)

Shari

(335)

Bihoro

Kaibetsu-dake 1419 m

(244)

Shari-dake 1545 m

Isani

Shibetsu

Lake Kutcharo

Lake Mashu

Lake Akan

Teshikaga

Mt O-Akan-dake

Mt Me-Akandake

Shibecha

Kushiro

Eastern Hokkaido

0   20   40 km

wind and water have sculpted them into many fanciful shapes that resemble real objects and beings.

Hot Springs
There are several places along the shores where hot-spring waters collect in pools near the water's edge, making natural *rotemburo* (open-air pools). One is near Kamuiwakka-no-taki waterfall. These are popular, especially with young vacationers. There's no charge; just take your clothes off and hop in.

Walks
One place that rewards hikers is the Shiretoko-Go-ko (five lakes) area near Iwaobetsu. Another destination is Io-san and its two large craters and fuming vents. The four-hour hike begins near Kamuiwakka waterfall. Visible on the sea-bottom near here is yellow sulphur from the 1936 eruption.

Information on other trails can be obtained locally; youth hostels are usually invaluable for such help.

Places to Stay
There are five *Youth Hostels* on the peninsula, three near Utoro (Utoro, Utoro-onsen and Iwaobetsu) and two near Rausu. There is also one each near the north and south bases of the peninsula, Shibetsu and Shari. The former has a Genghis Khan supper similar to that described later for the Shikotsu-ko hostel.

Getting There & Away
In past years there were boats around the tip of the peninsula between Utoro and Rausu but now there are only excursions out of Utoro to the tip, Shiretoko-misaki cape, in summer only. There is a 3¾-hour trip (once a day) that costs Y4770 and a 90-minute trip (up to five per day) that costs Y1850.

KUNASHIRI ISLAND
This island, along with the islands of Etorofu, Shikotan and the Habomai group, was seized by the USSR two weeks after the end of WW II. This was contrary to the Yalta Agreement and there is no legal basis for the occupation because the islands had always been indisputably part of Japanese territory.

The issue is very much alive in Hokkaido and you are likely to see numerous signs that show the map of Hokkaido and the occupied islands, a reminder of the Soviet action. Residents of the peninsula would like to have access to the rich fishing grounds around the islands but this is not likely to eventuate because the Soviets have been increasing their presence there in recent years. Kunashiri can be seen from a boat or from parts of the southeast coast of the peninsula.

AKAN NATIONAL PARK
This is one of the two major scenic regions of Hokkaido. The attractions can be divided into two areas, those centred around Kutcharo-ko lake and those around Akan-kohan.

Kutcharo-ko Lake Area
The main attraction of this area is the remnant of a gigantic volcanic crater, the bounds of which are now difficult to discern.

The present body of water is only a small part of the former huge lake. Over time the level of land has changed and new smaller volcanoes have popped up. A good landmark for sightseeing in the area is Kawayu railway station.

Kawayu-onsen About three km from Kawayu station, Kawayu-onsen is a typical hot-spring resort, full of hotels (most rather costly) and streets lined with souvenir shops – most of which have captive bear cubs or Ainu wood carvers as the attraction. There is a youth hostel in the town.

Kutcharo-ko Lake This is a caldera lake but

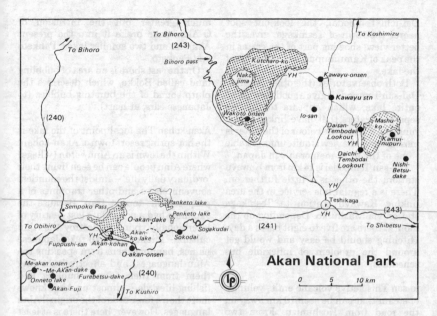

its circular shape has been changed beyond recognition by the intrusion of later volcanoes. Due to the high mineral content the water is a very unusual green but the nearby terrain is the same level so there are few vantage points high enough to see the colour of the lake. The best view can be obtained from high ground like Bihoro-toge pass on the road from Bihoro. The lake is an enjoyable place to relax.

Because the youth hostel on the lake shore uses the baths of the neighbouring hotel, you have the advantage of a visit to a resort without the painful cost. The bath is quite memorable, with continually overflowing hot water in a pool four metres square and about knee-deep; smooth flat pebbles on the bottom give an unusual feeling underfoot. Large windows give a view out over the lake toward Mokoto-san (1000 metres).

Wakoto-hanto A small bump on the map at the south end of the lake indicates this mini-peninsula, little higher than water level. Hot-spring water rises from below and feeds two open-air baths at Wakoto-onsen, (both are free and mixed); at Sunayu it warms the sand of the beach (Sunayu means 'hot sand').

There is a camping ground on the peninsula as well as others along the shore. There may be performances of Ainu dances at Sunayu during the summer.

Mashu-ko Lake Nearby is the remarkable and beautiful Mashu-ko lake. Situated part of the way up the side of a sprawling mountain, its water is claimed to be the clearest in the world. In 1978 it was clear to a depth of 34.8 metres (41.6 metres in 1911). However, it would be extremely difficult and dangerous to try to reach the water's edge to try to see for yourself. Like many other calderas, the walls of the old volcano that encloses it rise very steeply, giving negligible foothold.

It is better to be content admiring the incredible blue of the water from the two observatories, or walk around the rim.

Dai-ichi-Tempodai, the look-out spot nearer the town of Teshikaga, gives the better view, showing part of the crater in the peak of Kamuinupuri on the far side of the lake.

Both observatories (the other is called Dai-san Tempodai) give a good view of the entire lake, which appears to fill two separate craters that have linked. On a sunny day, when the colour of the water is most intense, the view is quite unforgettable – one of the most memorable in Japan.

Dai-san Tempodai is 14 km from Kawayu station; the other is a little further on. There is a regular bus service in the area linking Kawayu station to Teshikaga station via Mashu-ko. Depending on the month, there are five to eight buses a day. Hitching should be easy and would get around the problem of inflexible bus schedules.

Io-san This active volcano emits volumes of steam that can be seen 10 km away on the road from Koshimizu. From two ravines in the side of the earth-brown mountain, sulphurous (smelly!) steam issues forth, gently wafting from some vents, violently jetting with a great roar from others. Around these holes, vivid yellow needles of sulphur have crystallised out of the steam. Io-san means 'sulphur mountain'.

For the ultimate in natural foods, you can buy eggs cooked by the heat of the earth in one of the little saucepan-size pools that boil endlessly. Look for the old women near the base of the ravines.

Akan-ko Lake Area

The area around Akan-ko lake is noted for scenic beauties, mountains, Ainu people, and a weed that behaves like a submarine. Like Kutcharo, Akan-ko is in the remnants of a huge volcanic crater, the shape of which has also been changed beyond recognition by subsidence and the incursion of the smaller volcanic peaks, O-Akan-dake and Me-Akan-dake.

The size of Akan-ko lake was originally much greater but the intrusion of O-Akan-dake broke it into the present Akan-ko and two smaller lakes, Panketo and Penketo.

On the east shore is an area of bubbling mud called Bokke, which describes the plurp sound of the bursting bubbles (to Japanese ears, at least).

Akan-kohan The focal point of the lake is the hot-spring resort town of Akan-kohan. Within the town is an Ainu *kotan* (village) where Ainu people can be seen living their 'ordinary daily life' – amidst the countless souvenir shops and other trappings of a purpose-built tourist trap. Because the Japanese had a policy late last century of intentionally trying to destroy the Ainu culture – forcing them to take Japanese names, banning them from speaking the Ainu languages, and effectively barring them from their former hunting and fishing lifestyle – almost no Ainu knows more than a few words of the original Ainu languages. However, here there is at least a chance to obtain a small idea of the old ways. Ainu people may also be seen at shops in town, carving an endless succession of wooden bears.

Marimo Weed Another attraction of the Akan-ko lake area is this curious weed. It's not just any old garden-variety weed, mind you, but one that acts like a submarine, with the ability to rise and sink in the water. Marimo is actually an intertwined mass of hair-like green algae that forms into spongy spheres up to 15 cm in diameter. Other species live in Lake Sakyo (in Aomori-ken), Yamanaka-ko lake near Mt Fuji and in some lakes in Siberia, Switzerland and North America, but it is quite rare elsewhere.

The Akan variety is the largest and is considered the most attractive. In the past so many people were taking marimo home as a souvenir that there was a danger they would be wiped out, but they are now under government protection.

All excursion boats on the lake stop at a

small island on which a marimo 'sanctuary' has been built, and visitors can see them lying on the bottom of concrete tanks, doing their thing. There is also a glass tank containing many marimo at the Akan-kohan town information office beside the police station on the short street across the road from the Akan Kanko Hotel.

On 10 October each year there is a 'traditional' Ainu festival in honour of the marimo, supposedly celebrating Ainu legends about the marimo. In reality it is of quite recent origins, conceived more for touristic value than for preserving Ainu culture. (Part of the ceremony involves Ainu elders carrying a type of tray used only in Shinto observations, and Shinto is part of the Yamato Japanese tradition, totally foreign to the original Ainu culture and worship.) However, Ainu from all over the country do congregate here at this time and have their own celebrations apart from the official ones.

O-Akan & Me-Akan The most prominent peaks in the vicinity of the lake are easily climbed and offer beautiful views as a reward. Closer to the town is O-Akandake, the trail to which begins at O-Akanonsen; ask for the 'O-Akan Hiking Course'. The summit is 10.7 km from the *onsen*.

Me-Akan-dake probably offers the more beautiful and unusual scenery from its summit – a weird view of extinct and active volcanic cones, steam jets, and the overall impression of being on the moon. It can be climbed from either Akan-kohanonsen or from Me-Akan-onsen, which is 20 km west of Akan-kohan. From the former the summit is 10.7 km, but from the latter it is only 2.2 km.

Lookouts There are two well-known scenic lookouts on the road (Route 241) between Teshikaga and Akan-kohan. Sogakudai ('Two Mountains Lookout') gives a good view of Me-Akan-dake and O-Akan-dake; while Sokadai ('Two Lakes Outlook')

overlooks (need it be said?) two pretty lakes, Penketo and Panketo. The whole area is at its finest in autumn when the leaves turn into masses of reds, oranges and yellows.

Places to Stay There are three *Youth Hostels* near the lake, as well others in the general area, plus many hotels of varying prices (tending toward the high, this being a hot-spring resort town).

Getting There & Around
Akan National Park is readily accessible by JR via Teshikaga and Kawayu-onsen stations (Kutcharo-ko lake area) from Kushiro (due south on the coast) and from Abashiri and the Shiretoko Peninsula areas (on the coast to the north).

There are also several bus services. The most picturesque run goes from Bihoro (inland to the north) via Bihoro pass, the lower shore of Kutcharo-ko lake, Kawayu-onsen, Mashu-ko lake, and thence to Akan-kohan. This is a sightseeing excursion bus and can be used to get up to Mashu-ko lake. Another bus service goes to Kawayu-onsen from Abashiri, but this is less frequent at best and does not run through to Kawayu-onsen at all out of season. There is also service from Kushiro to Kawayu-onsen.

Direct to the Akan-ko lake area (Akankohan) there is bus service from Bihoro and Kitami (to the north), Kushiro (to the south), and Ashoro and Obihiro (to the southwest), all of which are on JR lines.

The area is very popular with Japanese tourists so there will be no trouble arranging transport to the various attractions, either by tagging along with other travellers or by hitching with one of the many passing motorists.

KUSHIRO
Kushiro, on the south coast, and the coast itself, are of no particular interest, but Kushiro is connected with Tokyo by regular ferry service.

The main attraction of this largely

industrial city is the sanctuary for rare red-crested white cranes at Tsuruoka (20 km west of Kushiro station). The number of resident cranes is small, but several hundred come to feed in the winter.

The other attraction that the local authorities promote is Harutori-koen park with its lake and an Ainu 'village'. These would be best regarded as something to see while waiting for a train or boat connection.

AKAN TO TOMAKOMAI

This route includes some of the prettiest countryside in Hokkaido and leads to Tomakomai, a port for ferries to Honshu and gateway to Shikotsu-ko lake and Shikotsu-Toya National Park.

The first destination along Route 241 is Obihiro, an unexceptional town with a nice youth hostel very close to the station; the staff rush out with banners to greet and send off hostellers.

Beyond Obihiro, Route 38 leads to Tokachi-Shimizu; from there you branch onto Route 274 as far as Hidaka and then to Route 237 to Tomikawa on the coast. From Hidaka you have the option of the JR line to Tomakomai.

The road from Tokachi-Shimizu to Hidaka (Nissho Highway) passes through almost total wilderness and offers many lovely views of the Hidaka mountains as the road snakes up and down over crests.

There are also glimpses of the green Saru river as it nears the coast. It is a contrast with most roads on Hokkaido, which follow valley floors.

About 15 km before Tomikawa is the town of Biratori, known for its large Ainu population, but similar in appearance to any other Hokkaido town. From Tomikawa it is another 45 km to Tomakomai.

Cape Erimo

At the bottom of the peninsula is Cape Erimo and Erimo Prefectural Park. The tip of the cape is noted for 60-metre cliffs that become a line of rocks and reefs protruding several km out into the ocean like a line of sentinels. The cape is desolate, swept clear of vegetation by winds, and is usually blanketed by thick fog in summer.

TOMAKOMAI

This port and industrial city is the gateway to the attractions of nearby Shikotsu-Toya National Park. It is close to Chitose Airport (which also serves Sapporo, 65 km away), and is connected to Hachinohe, Sendai, Tokyo and Nagoya by regular ferry service. From Tomakomai ferry terminal, bus No 41 runs to the station, from where you can make bus and train connections to other parts of Hokkaido. The bus of the same number goes to the ferry terminal but service is infrequent, so a taxi may be necessary if you are rushing to catch a boat.

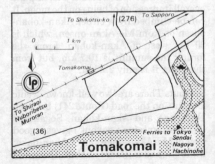

SHOKOTSU-TOYA NATIONAL PARK

If a visitor to Hokkaido could go to only one part of the island, the area of Shikotsu-Toya should be it. The major attractions are around the lakes Shikotsu and Toya, plus the town of Noboribetsu. Some might want to add the town of Shiraoi. Attractions are both natural and human.

Shikotsu-ko Lake

Shikotsu-ko is the deepest lake on Hokkaido (363 metres) and the second-deepest in Japan, after Tazawa-ko on Honshu. The classic round shape of a caldera lake has been intruded on by the cones of Eniwa-dake (1320 metres) on one side and Fuppushi-dake (1103 metres) on the opposite shore. The altitude of the lake itself is 248 metres.

Boat cruises are available on the lake from a point near the bus terminal at Shikotsu-kohan. Swimmers should take note that the bottom slopes gently for the first 10 or so metres from the shore, then plummets sharply.

Eniwa-dake The low cone of this volcano is the most prominent feature of the lake shore. It is steep but can be climbed easily, and makes a good day's excursion. The starting point is Poropinai, accessible by a toll road along the lake (beginning near the bus terminal), or by boat, also from near the terminal.

The climb to the crater top takes about three hours and on a clear day the view extends as far as Sapporo, as well as to Okotampeko lake on the far side and the other mountains around the lake.

Fuppushi-dake The outline of this low mountain is visible across the lake from Shikotsu-kohan.

Tarumae-dake Behind Fuppushi is this unusual volcano. During its 1909 eruption, a dome of lava 450 metres across and 100

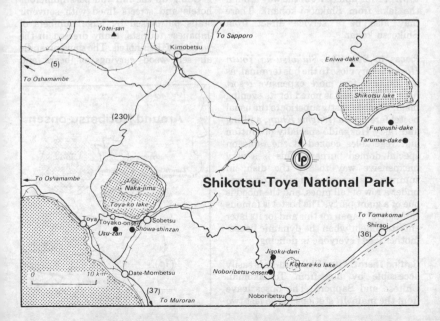

Shikotsu-ko lake

metres high formed in the central crater. It varies in its activities these days; sometimes it shows few signs of life, but most of the time it sends plumes of steam into the sky. It erupted in May 1978 and February 1979.

The rim of the crater can be reached by a 40-minute walk after a bus ride from the town of Morrapu (part of the way around the lake from Shikotsu-kohan). There may also be a service direct from Shikotsu-kohan.

Places to Stay The *Shikotsu-ko Youth Hostel* is very close to the bus terminal, as are quite a few more expensive resort hotels. The hostel is noted for its evening meal, which is vastly superior to the usual hostel fare. It is a *Genghis Khan*, a filling and tasty Hokkaido specialty of mutton and vegetables cooked at the table on special domed burners. This is a very inexpensive way to try the dish; in summer it is prepared on tables outdoors under a row of tall pines, and the mood is one of a giant party. The hostel is famous throughout Japan for this and for its later entertainment when the dynamic house-mother leads everyone in dancing.

Getting There & Away Shikotsu-ko is easily accessible by bus from Tomakomai, Chitose and Sapporo. The buses leave from the main JR stations in the last two (plus from Chitose Airport), and from the bus terminal in Tomakomai. The trip takes less than an hour from the first two, about 80 minutes from Sapporo.

Noboribetsu-onsen

If a foreign visitor was to sample only one hot-spring resort in Japan, this would be a good choice. It is one of the few that a foreigner can enjoy fully, as *onsen* can usually be sampled only by staying at an expensive resort hotel. In Noboribetsu, however, the famous baths are open to the public and are among the largest and most magnificent in Japan. There are also other attractions in and around the town to add to its interest.

The town is a few km inland from the coastal town (and railway station) of Noboribetsu-shi. It is built on the slope of a hill, with the bus stations part of the way up. Akashiya-so Youth Hostel is a short distance down the hill from them and the other youth hostels are in the town.

Going up the hill you pass numerous hotels and streets lined with souvenir stalls patronised by large numbers of Japanese tourists, many dressed in the *yukata* of their hotels. The souvenir stalls all sell wood carvings of bears and

Around Noribetsu-onsen

representations of Ainu people (some of fancifully beautiful maidens). The only glimpses of originality are a few anomalies like a Vishnu-on-Garuda, as seen everywhere in Bali, or a large and incongruous Polynesian-like figure – both carved by a Japanese who read many books on folkart. Some of the carvings are well done and would be classed as sculpture if they were not all so nearly identical.

The Baths Continuing up the hill, the road levels off, and where it branches to the left there is a large brown hotel. This is the Dai-ichi Takimoto Hotel, famous for its enormous bath room – and one experience a visitor should not miss.

The entrance for non-guests of the hotel is to the left of the building. After undressing (take your own towel), you enter the cavernous bath room, at least 100 metres long and half that in width. There are nearly 20 large pools, plus a small number in the women-only section, all of differing size and shape, with water of varying mineral content and temperature. At the far end is a shallow wading pool that has the only cool water in the place – which is worth remembering!

There are numerous fonts where you can sit and wash before taking the waters. The little squirrels gush drinking water; drink frequently to avoid exhaustion from dehydration.

This was, until recently, one of the few major hotels where mixed bathing remained, but prudery (and resultant peeping at the women who did continue to go into the mixed section) led the hotel to change its policy to one of separating the sexes.

The bath closes to non-guests at 5 pm, although it may be possible to stay on after that time, and it seems possible to go in the evening if you get permission from the front desk.

Jigokudani A further 150 metres or so up the hill beyond the baths is the unusual and beautiful Jigokudani (Valley of Hell),

so named for the evil smell and noise of steam and boiling water that pours forth from the earth. The colourful valley is a ravine with small hills and gullies where the yellow earth has been stained in bands and patches by the minerals deposited over the centuries by the water. The valley is the source of the hot water used in the baths of the town, and different pools have different kinds of water. At maximum flow, it can exceed 75,000 litres per minute – a householder's dream.

The path through the valley (the dangerous areas are roped off) begins above the car park at the end of the main street through the town. There is no admittance charge. The sense of 'hell' is very appropriate – if you broke through the crust, you could be scalded to death before being rescued. Pleasant thought! Down in the valley is a Buddhist shrine to ward off evil.

Oyunuma The path through Jigokudani hooks sharply to the left; at that point a small gravel path (labelled in Japanese only as leading to Oyunuma) leads up to a gravel road, across which is the observation point which overlooks the boiling pond. Oyunuma ('hot water pond') is an intriguing large pool of muddy water that boils continuously. It sits in what is believed to be the crater of an extinct volcano. It is simultaneously scenic and ugly.

Beside the path are some small stone statues with cloth bibs and a sad story. These are figures of Jizo, the protector of children (as well as travellers and pregnant women). One of his responsibilities is the souls of dead children, and sewn to each bib is the name of the dead child whose soul is to be helped into the underworld. Areas of subterranean activity like Jigokudani are obviously entrances to hell.

The road crossed while walking to the lookout leads to Kuttara-ko lake (to the right) to the left it leads back down to the car park at Jigokudani.

Kuttara-ko Lake This is a classic caldera lake – almost perfectly round, with the surrounding shore rising steeply to an almost level rim. On a crystal-clear sunny day, the water is an intense sapphire-blue, said to be even deeper in colour than that of famed Mashu-ko lake. On a hazy day (judge from conditions over Noboribetsu) only the outline of the lake will be visible and the water will be a characterless grey, making the trip to the lake a disappointment.

From the lookout over Oyunuma it is about three km to a lookout over Kuttara-ko. It is a further 2½ km down to the bus terminus/rowboat rental/restaurant at the edge of the lake. Buses leave Noboribetsu-onsen at 10 and 11.40 am and 1.20 pm (check locally) stopping at the lake for five minutes. Taxi, hitching and walking are alternative ways of getting there.

Kumayama Overlooking Noboribetsu-onsen is the high hill Kumayama ('Bear Mountain'). A trip here could be recommended if it weren't for the extortionate Y1800 return charge for the cable-car (10% discount with a youth hostel voucher). The main attraction (to foreigners) is a reproduction of an Ainu settlement, with five or six buildings built in the traditional Ainu style – grass thatch over a wooden framework. The bottom building houses a small museum.

Four times a day a number of elderly Ainu re-enact several of their traditional dances, chants and ceremonies – centred on the bear. According to tradition a bear was raised from a cub, then ceremoniously killed, thus releasing the soul of the dead Ainu believed to be trapped within. Nowadays a bewildered bear cub is 'shot' with a blunt arrow that does it no harm. Yes, the whole thing is for the tourists, but it is the only way to get a first-hand idea of their former customs. The participants in the ceremonies are mostly in their 70s, so even this remnant of Ainu culture may not be around for much longer.

The performances (at 10.30 am and 3.30, 7.30 and 8.10 pm) are held in the second building from the bottom of the slope. No photos may be taken during the ceremonies and it is unlikely that anyone will pose afterward. To guarantee a good seat, be at the base station of the cable-car more than half an hour before a performance (especially in the busy summer season) to be sure of getting a car up the mountain in time.

Another attraction of the mountain is a large enclosure full of very large and dangerous Hokkaido bears. They are obviously bored by a life of sitting around on unyielding concrete, and have devised many tricks to cadge biscuits from visitors. Although these bears lead a much better life than those in cages at Shiraoi, both places exemplify a definite shortcoming of the Japanese – a total disregard for animals and their basic welfare. Another building houses a Bear Museum that shows and tells you everything you ever wanted to know about bears – but the text is in Japanese.

Minor entertainment at the top of the mountain includes goose races. The view from the top over the sea, neighbouring mountains and Kuttaro-ko lake is very good on a clear day.

The base station of the cable-car is reached by walking up a short side street off the main street of Noboribetsu and either walking up a flight of steep steps (past a number of souvenir shops) and following the path, or by taking a chair-lift that runs parallel to it. (The distance is so short that the latter is only for the very tired.) The base station is just a short distance away in the large building.

Getting There & Away During the summer months there are six buses a day over the mountains from Noboribetsu-onsen to Toya-ko-onsen. The trip takes 1¾ hours (Y1300) and is much quicker and more scenic than by train around the south of the peninsula.

Toya-ko Lake Area

The remaining area of interest in the Shikotsu-Toya National Park is around Toya-ko lake. In addition to the beauty of the lake and its central islands, there is much evidence of past and ongoing volcanic activity. The lake is another circular caldera, much larger than Kuttaro-ko. In its centre are the islets that collectively comprise Nakajima ('middle island'); they are the remains of the volcano whose crater forms the basin of the lake.

Lookouts An excellent view of the lake, Toya-ko-onsen and Usu-san is offered by the lookout near Abuta beside the road to the coast. From the T-junction near the bus station and police station, it is 1.6 km up the hill.

Other good views can be found by following the road clockwise around the lake (Route 230 to Kimobetsu). From the same T-junction, the road goes at lake-level for a short distance before beginning to climb to a broad plateau. Just over six km up the hill (one km above the entrance to the Toya Country Club) there is an excellent view over the lake. On the plateau there are other good views of the lake and its islands, and visible inland is the tall cone of Mt Yotei. Beyond the red barn-like restaurant/bus-stop, the road goes inland and the lake is lost to sight.

At the other side of the lake there is a road down to Toya-machi (the town of Toya) at lake level, and from there a road circles the lake, back to the youth hostels and hotels. However, the road down is loose gravel and risky on a bike, and the view from the lower road is only so-so.

Showa Shinzan 'New Mountain of the Showa Era' is one of the most remarkable pieces of rock on Earth. On 28 December 1943, earthquakes hit the area around Toya-ko. Near Sobetsu, southeast of the lake, the flat farmland began to rise and,

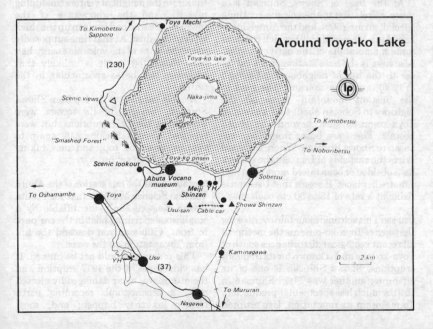

during the next two months, formed a hill nearly 25 metres high. Between late June and late October, many volcanic eruptions took place and the hill continued to grow. By November it had reached a diameter of 800 metres. The climax came when a tower of hardened lava started to rise through the crust of the earth. By September 1945 it had reached an altitude of 408 metres above sea level, a respectable 150 to 200 metres above the surrounding terrain. There it sits today, a chunk of colourful yellows and browns, bare of vegetation and issuing steam from many crevices.

A friend once said that he feels a sort of affection for sharks, tidal waves and volcanoes, for they remind man just how powerless he is against nature. A realisation of the immense forces at work lifting this huge chunk of rock should push any ego back into place. The rock showing above the surface weighs at least 100 million tons!

At the base of Showa Shinzan is a museum relating to the volcano (nothing special; about Y500), and the Ainu Kinen-kan (Ainu Memorial Hall), which contains some memorabilia of the native peoples. Also here is the base station of the cable-car to the top of neighbouring Usu-san (Y1200), an active volcano. The road to the 'instant mountain' turns off the highway to Sobetsu about four km out of Toya-ko-onsen, just beyond the youth hostels. There are buses from Toya-ko-onsen to Showa Shinzan. Where this road skirts the east side of Usu-san the surface has subsided or been raised more than half a metre in places. It seems that Usu-san is rising at a rate of 15 to 30 cm each year.

Usu-san This volcanic mountain overlooking the town of Toya-ko-onsen is the mother of all recent geological disturbances south of Toya-ko lake and is known for its frequent eruptions. Showa Shinzan is one of its offspring; another was Meiji Shinzan in 1910, a much less spectacular production. To maintain its reputation, Usu erupted in August 1977, and for more than a year afterward there were a dozen or so earthquakes a day that could be felt, plus about 200 measurable by seismograph.

The 1977 event was its most spectacular eruption, as photos on sale around Toya-ko-onsen clearly show. An immense cloud of black ash and soot was blown about 10,000 metres skyward and 30 cm of fine ash fell on Toya-ko-onsen, causing some buildings to collapse, burying crops, forcing the evacuation of the populace, and causing a giant headache for those who had to clean up the mess. Chunks of rock hurled out during the eruption damaged much of the forest land near the town, and broken tree tops and stripped branches along the roadside remain as silent witnesses to the event.

Usu-san's activity since then has been confined mainly to blowing out great volumes of steam and gas, although it erupted again in July 1978, sending another cloud of ash and dust high into the air, to the delight of visitors (including myself), and the annoyance of the townspeople who had to clean up the thick layer of fine dust. At that time supposedly more than 80% of the volcanic energy had been dissipated, so it is unlikely that activities will be as spectacular in the future.

A cable-car runs to the top from Showa Shinzan. Several of its towers were wrecked by the 1977 eruptions, but were repaired when it became safe again to venture near the top, and new hiking trails have been set out.

Museum Near the bus station is the Abuta Volcano Science Museum (ask for 'Abuta Kazan Kagaku-kan'), identifiable by a small wooden fishing boat in the car park in front, visible as you descend the hill from Toya station on the coast.

This museum should not be missed. It has videotapes of the 1977 eruption and the aftermath; a car damaged by ejected rock; a seismograph recording earth tremors as they happen; and, most interesting of all, a projection room with a model of the volcano complete with 'pillar of smoke'. To the accompaniment of actual recordings of the eruption, 'lightning' flashes through the plume and the floor shakes with terrifying realism, simulating the earth tremors and explosions that actually took place. The museum also has an excellent display of relics from the area and an exhibit of items used until recent times by people in their daily work. The museum is open from late April to mid November.

Places to Stay The shore of the lake has been heavily built up with tourist hotels and is a popular summer retreat from the heat of Honshu. Swimming and boating (commercial cruises available) are popular activities. The town of Toya-ko-onsen is the largest centre on the lake, and has several deluxe resort hotels.

The two *Youth Hostels* are about four km out of town on the road to Sobetsu. Some of these places may still bear witness to the changes in terrain resulting from the eruptions. At *Toya-Kanko-kan Youth Hostel*, all the window frames and doorways were pushed out of square, and the bath pool had a distinct tilt.

Getting There & Away Toya-ko-onsen is linked eight times a day by bus with Muroran and Noboribetsu-onsen, the latter by a scenic mountain pass. The JR station on the coast is called Toya, but the actual town of Toya (Toya-machi) is on the lake, several km inland, and it is necessary to take a bus to the lake area from the station. The main touristic centre is Toya-ko-onsen. (Toya-machi is on the opposite side of the lake.)

Refer to the Noboribetsu-onsen section for information on the bus service between there and Toya-ko lake.

Getting Around There is a regular bus service around the lake and surrounding area. Bicycles can be rented near the bus station and are a very convenient means of getting around.

SHIRAOI

About 3000 Ainu have settled in this town which is about 20 km from Noboribetsu on the way to Tomakomai. It was originally known for its reproduction of a small Ainu *kotan* (village) but is now more famous for its commercialism. To get in to see five or so Ainu-style buildings, the bored, frustrated and pitiable bears in tiny cages, and a five-minute performance of chants and dances by a few Ainu women who look as if they'd rather be elsewhere, you first have to pass through a very large and modern building full of stall after stall of Ainu souvenirs – all staffed by ethnic Japanese.

The redeeming features of the place are a well-presented modern museum of Ainu artefacts and life-size reproductions of daily activities in traditional times, plus an excellent booklet, *Shiraoi & Ainu*. This gives a great deal of information about the traditional way of life, far more than is available from sources other than scholarly journals, and is presented from the Ainu point of view – which is generally quite different from that appearing in official Japanese publications.

Compared with this village, however, the 'settlement' on Kumayama is *much* less commercialised, gives a better view of Ainu customs and, comparing costs, is not that much more expensive to visit. Kumayama would normally get the nod as the better place to visit except for the attractions of Shiraoi's good, modern museum and the excellent publication already mentioned.

Shiraoi can be reached easily from Tomakomai or Noboribetsu by train or bus. The bus stop (Shiraoi-kotan) is right in front of the village; from the train station, you walk along the road toward Tomakomai for about 20 minutes until you see a large archway over a side road.

MURORAN

At the tip of the peninsula is the city of
Muroran. Apart from the annual festival
(28-30 July), and the cliffs of Chikyu-
misaki cape, the sole attraction of this
dark steel-producing city is that it is the
terminus for ferries to Aomori and
Hachinohe (northern Honshu). These
give the option of skipping Hakodate and
the not-so-interesting 150 km to Shikotsu-
Toya National Park. From Muroran to
Toya-ko-onsen (Toya station) it is no more
than 50 km by bus (eight per day) or train,
and Noboribetsu-onsen (Noboribetsu
station) is only about 25 km away by bus
(eight per day) or train. The train goes to
Noboribetsu town on the coast (from where
buses go the short distance to Noboribetsu-
onsen), and on to Tomakomai and
Sapporo. All trains for Toya, and about

half of those for Noboribetsu/Tomakomai/
Sapporo, leave from Higashi-Muroran
station, three stops from Muroran
station.

Central Honshu

This section covers much of what is traditionally regarded as Chubu, or central Japan. For the traveller who wants a feel for the 'real' Japan, this is one of the best regions of the country to visit.

Until only a few years ago much of the area was quite isolated and, except for boats on narrow rivers, some places were completely cut off during winter. As a result, many folk traditions that have disappeared elsewhere still survive quite strongly here. The region also offers natural beauty, historic remains (including a fine authentic castle) and some of the most interesting festivals in Japan.

The areas covered here are parts of Gumma-ken, Nagano-ken, northern Gifu-ken, Fukui-ken, Ishikawa-ken, Toyama-ken and northern Aichi-ken.

KUSATSU (GUMMA-KEN)

This is one of the most well-known hot-spring towns in Japan and has more than 130 *ryokan* in the central part of town. Yuba (Hot Water Field) is the origin of the hot water, which gushes, boiling, from the ground. Sulphur residue is left behind as the water cools, is collected and sold as *yunohana* (hot-spring flowers), a home remedy.

Netsunoyu (Heat Bath) is the main public bath and is famous for its exceedingly high temperature. It is so hot that (reputedly) a 'drill master' has to enforce discipline to ensure that bathers stay in for the prescribed time. Anyone who stays in accommodation with Japanese people knows that they can withstand water that would boil a lobster, so this must really be hot!

Kusatsu is also a ski resort and has several pleasant walking paths nearby.

Nagano-ken

KARUIZAWA

Much touted in tourist literature as the ideal resort, Karuizawa is in fact a place of high-fashion for the summer; it's more of interest to residents of Japan who are seeking an escape from the heat of Tokyo.

It is largely for the rich, as indicated by the fact that more than 250 shops based in Tokyo and Yokohama have branches here. As a result, it has aspects of a shrunken, transposed Tokyo and in summer it is extremely crowded.

The city is divided into several parts, the main area being Kyu-Karuizawa. The station is two km away. Most places likely to interest the budget traveller lie outside the town.

Information

More information on Karuizawa is available in the JNTO pamphlet *Karuizawa-kogen*, available at the Tokyo TIC (and possibly at Kyoto).

Asama-yama

The backdrop of Karuizawa is Asama-yama, a conical volcano that is still active. Its last major eruption was in 1783 when awesome amounts of lava poured forth. This lava field, Onioshi-dashi, can be seen easily by taking a bus (55 minutes) from

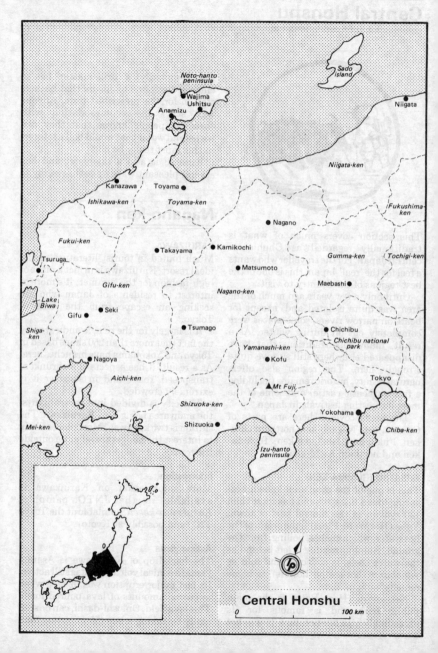

Central Honshu

0   100 km

either Karuizawa or Naka-Karuizawa stations.

Asama-yama can be climbed quite easily from several starting points, the favourite ones being the two stations just mentioned. It is advisable to check before climbing because the volcano still erupts from time to time and climbing is banned when it is active.

There is a good view of Asama-yama, as well as the surrounding countryside, from Usui-toge pass which can be reached on foot in 30 minutes. Kumano-jinja shrine is nearby.

The pass itself was part of the old Nakasendo Highway between Kyoto and Tokyo. Some old towns along this route that still retain much of their original appearance are described in the section covering the Kiso Region (southern Nagano-ken).

A 30-minute walk from Karuizawa station leads to Shiraito falls, three metres high and 70 metres wide.

About 300 species of wild birds inhabit the sanctuary near Hoshino-onsen. They can be watched from two observation huts or from along the 2.4-km walking path.

Places to Stay

There are many hotels, *ryokan*, *minshuku*, villas, camping grounds and two *Youth Hostels* around Karuizawa.

NAGANO

The city of Nagano lies in a valley hemmed in by mountain ridges on two sides. Nearby are the best skiing areas (such as Shiga Heights) in the Tokyo region. Snowfalls in the mountains can reach as much as 15 metres over a winter. It was an area near here, in neighbouring Niigata-ken, that Nobel Prize winner Kawabata wrote about in *Snow Country*.

Zenko-ji Temple

The main attraction of Nagano is Zenko-ji temple which draws several million visitors a year. It houses historic statues that are shown only every seven years (the

Around Karuizawa

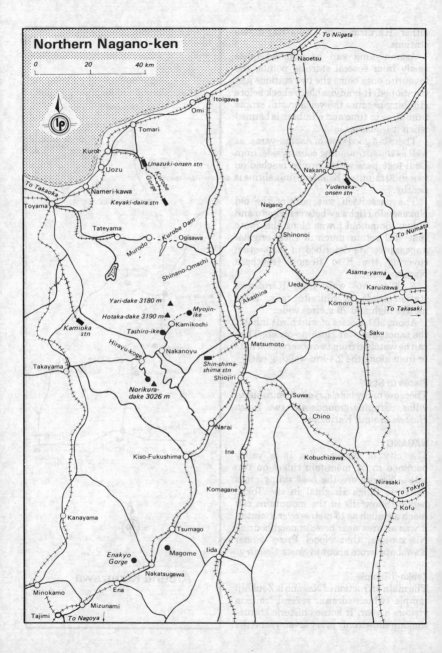

Northern Nagano-ken

0   20   40 km

To Niigata

Naoetsu

Itoigawa

Omi

Tomari

Kuroh

Uozu

Nameri-kawa

To Takaoka

Toyama

Tateyama

Murodo

Unazuki-onsen stn

Kurobe Gorge

Keyaki-daira stn

Kurobe Dam

Ogisawa

Shinano-Omachi

Nakano

Yudanaka-onsen stn

Nagano

Shinonoi

To Numata

Yari-dake 3180 m

Hotaka-dake 3190 m

Myojin-ike

Tashiro-ike

Kamikochi

Kamioka stn

Hirayu-koge

Nakanoyu

Norikura-dake 3026 m

Takayama

Shin-shimashima stn

Shiojiri

Akashina

Ueda

Asama-yama

Karuizawa

Komoro

To Takasaki

Saku

Matsumoto

Suwa

Chino

Narai

Kiso-Fukushima

Ina

Kobuchizawa

Komagane

Nirasaki

To Tokyo

Kofu

Kanayama

Tsumago

Magome

Iida

Enakyo Gorge

Nakatsugawa

Minokamo

Ena

Mizunami

Tajimi

To Nagoya

next showing is 1994); the rest of the time they are concealed.

A totally dark tunnel passes beneath the altar, along which people grope their way hoping to touch the 'key of Paradise' that is supposed to guarantee easy entry to Heaven.

There is nearly always a service in progress for the benefit of visiting pilgrims and the interior is richly decorated with Buddhist motifs. It is one of the better temples in Japan to visit for a glimpse of the ceremonies of one branch of Japanese Buddhism.

Yudanaka-onsen

Into the mountains from Nagano (about 25 km northeast) is the hot-spring resort town of Yudanaka. It has open-air pools which are famous from the photographs of snow-covered monkeys sitting in them keeping warm in winter.

Beyond Yudanaka you can continue by the Shiga-Kusatsu Kogen toll road to Kusatsu, then cross to Nikko and Ozenuma via Numata.

MATSUMOTO

The city of Matsumoto is in the basin of mountain ranges. It possesses one of the finest castles in Japan and this alone makes it worth visiting.

Matsumoto-jo Castle

Matsumoto-jo castle is the most easily reached feudal castle in the region around Tokyo. The trip can be made in four hours from Shinjuku station (Tokyo).

The castle stands an imposing six storeys above its surrounding moat and is unusual among Japanese castles because it is black, rather than the usual white.

The original castle on this site was built in 1504 but the present structure is from a somewhat later date. However, it is important enough to rate as a national treasure. Swans swimming in the moat add a note of grace to its beauty.

In the compound of the castle is the Minzoku-kan (folklore museum) which

houses an exhibit of 60,000 items of history, archaeology, folklore and geography.

The castle is a little over one km northeast of Matsumoto station and even closer to Kita-Matsumoto station. Streets near the castle are narrow and winding, typical of castle towns.

The TIC in Tokyo has an information sheet that gives more details on transport, sightseeing and accommodation in Matsumoto.

Getting There & Away

Train From Tokyo the easiest and quickest way to get to Matsumoto is by JR train from Shinjuku station (tracks 3, 4 and sometimes 7; consult a timetable).

Nearly all trains are 'L' *tokkyu* expresses (about three hours; Y5900). There is one *kyuko* limited express very early in the morning (3 hours fifty minutes) and a few that leave Shinjuku in the late evening. The ones closest to midnight reach Matsumoto between 4.50 and 5.20 am. These would save on a night's accommodation at the cost of a probable stiff neck. *Kyuko* trains cost Y4900.

The only local trains from the Tokyo area leave from Takao, some distance out along the Chuo line from Shinjuku, and would take about five hours.

Other train lines run to Matsuyama from Nagano/Naoetsu and from the north coast (Itoigawa).

KISO REGION

As well as the very enjoyable scenery, the Kiso River valley (southwest of Matsumoto) is also worth visiting to see three villages that have remained relatively unchanged for nearly two centuries. Narai, Tsumago and Magome were on the old Nakasendo ('Middle Way') highway between Kyoto and Edo (Tokyo).

Every year there were grand processions of *daimyo* along this road between the two cities. Their retinue often numbered in the thousands (at least one of 30,000 was recorded), a measure of the power and wealth of the baron. Because the distance between the cities was great, there were post stations where travellers could rest overnight. To meet the exalted demands of their guests, the *ryokan* had to be of high standard; some of these fine buildings are still standing.

A visit to one or all of these towns is highly recommended. Apart from a few collections of old buildings that have been gathered from other parts of the country, there are relatively few places in Japan where you can see more than one or two old buildings in any one place. In these three towns, however, you can see a large number side by side, with only a few newer buildings interspersed.

The towns retain their old appearance mainly because they were bypassed when the railways were built late in the last century. Their future is assured because of the interest (rather belated) by the Japanese in their past, and they are popular destinations for Japanese sightseers.

Kiso-Hirasawa

South of Shiojiri, this is the first town of interest along the valley. It is noted for the production of lacquerware and there is a lacquer museum near the station.

Narai

One station (JR) away from Kiso-Hirasawa is one of the 62 post towns used by travellers along the Nakasendo Highway. The old buildings are easy to find as they line the main street and are only a few minutes on foot from Narai station (turn left when leaving the station).

The majority of the buildings fronting the street are old although there is a larger proportion of newer structures than in the other two towns. However, Narai is less accessible so there are fewer fellow sightseers to contend with and you can enjoy the atmosphere a little better.

There are several buildings open to the public and money would be well spent visiting a few.

Kiso Fukushima

During the Tokugawa era this was the most important barrier gate of the Nakasendo road. Traveller's documents were inspected here to verify that they had permission to travel. Life was very strictly regulated in those days (down to such details as to what kind of clothes one might wear and even the position in which one had to sleep!) and most people were not allowed to leave their appointed work or home village. Some mementos of those days survive in the form of old buildings and exhibits in museums.

Yamamura Daikan Yashiki This was formerly the residence of the Yamamura family, high officials in the Kiso region. It is 15 minutes on foot from Kiso-Fukushima station.

Kiso-Fukushima Kyodo-kan This is a museum of historic artefacts and materials related to the Nakasendo road and the barrier gates. It is five minutes by bus or 25 minutes on foot from Kiso-Fukushima station.

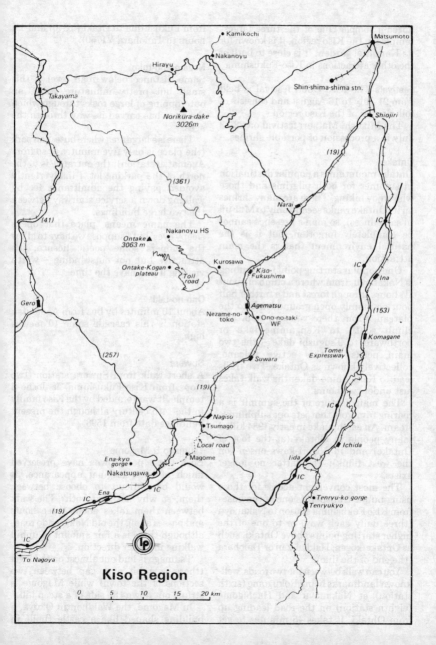

Kiso Region

Matsumoto

Shin-shima-shima stn.

Kamikochi

Nakanoyu

Hirayu

Takayama

Norikura-dake
3026m

(361)

Shiojiri

(19)

Narai

IC

(41)

Nakanoyu HS

IC

Ontake
3063 m

Ina

Ontake-Kogan
plateau

Kurosawa

Kiso-
Fukushima

Toll
road

(153)

Gero

Agematsu

Nezame-no-
toko

Ono-no-taki
WF

(19)

Komagane

Suwara

Tomei
Expressway

Ojika

IC

Nagiso

Ichida

Tsumago

Local road

Magome

Iida

Ena-kyo
gorge

IC

Nakatsugawa

Ena

IC

Tenryu-ko gorge

(19)

Tenryukyo

IC

To Nagoya

0   5   10   15   20 km

Kiso Region

Kozen-ji Temple One of the three largest temples in the Kiso region, it is known for its Kanuntei garden. It is close to both of the other attractions in Kiso-Fukushima.

Festivals The Kiso Odori festival is held from 21 July to 16 August and consists of folk dances of the Kiso region.

The Mikoshi Matsuri festival on 22-23 July is a procession of portable shrines.

Ontake

Ontake mountain is a popular destination in summer for both pilgrims and those who enjoy hiking. There are many shrines on it (Ontake ranks second only to Mt Fuji in sacredness), so man's presence cannot be completely forgotten, but it is the natural environment that is the main attraction.

One popular starting point for climbing is Nakanoyu, from where a climb of about 1½ hours through forest and a further half hour on mainly open ground leads to the plateau. From there you can walk and climb south to Kengamine-dake or northward to Tsugushi-dake – the two main peaks of this active volcano, collectively known as Ontake. Two trails lead to Kengamine-dake; the walk takes just under two hours.

The main feature of the summit is a roaring fumerole that jets out sulphurous steam. An earthquake in early 1984 killed many people in Ohtaki (at the foot of Ontake) and in Nigori-kawa-onsen (on the west flank); the latter no longer exists.

The most convenient access for those using public transport is one of the buses from Kiso Fukushima station to Nakanoyu (three daily each way) or to one of the higher starting points above Ohtaki, such as Ontake-kogen, Hakkai-zan or Tanohara (the end of the line).

You can walk between the two roads, well-known landmarks being Rokugome (sixth station) at Nakanoyu and Hachigome (eighth station) on the road leading up from Ohtaki. It takes 45 minutes to get from Fukushima to Otaki (Y840) and 1¾ hours to Tanohara Y1750).

Nezame-no-toko

Some distance below road level is this small but pretty miniature gorge, an outcropping of large rocks through which the river has carved its way through the ages.

There is a large area where buses can park (the place is only five minutes or so from Agematsu station); the entrance is to the north of the parking lot. I inadvertently avoided paying the admittance fee by walking down a service stairway between the two large buildings.

The name means 'place that opens sleepy eyes' but I suppose we have to allow the namers some poetic licence; it's attractive but not outstanding – worth visiting if you have the time.

Ono-no-taki

About 10 minutes by bus from Agematsu station is this cascade some 10 metres high.

Suwara

A short walk from Suwara station (two stops from Kiso-Fukushima) is Josho-ji temple. It was founded by the Kiso family in the 14th century although the present buildings date from 1598.

Tsumago & Magome

Both these post towns have preserved much of their original appearance. It would be difficult to choose between them, so why not visit both? The walk between them takes about three hours and passes along the old Nakasendo road, although there is a fair amount of uphill walking in either direction.

Tsumago is laid out almost on the level (there is a bit of a gap between two sections of the town) while Magome is strung out down the side of a steep hill.

In Magome, the Wakihontin Okuya, a building shaped like a castle (built in

1877), has an exhibition of material regarding the old post towns.

Festival The Tsumago-matsuri festival on 23 November takes the form of a procession of townspeople dressed in the style of ancient times re-enacting one of the processions of the *daimyo* who travelled along the Nakasendo road in feudal times.

Places to Stay There are buildings open to the public in both towns and many have been converted to *minshuku* so travellers can stay overnight.

The towns are very popular with tourists and the accommodation is usually fully booked in season so it would be advisable to make reservations if possible.

Getting There & Away Both Tsumago and Magome are linked with the city of Nakatsugawa by regular bus service (Meitetsu line). From Nakatsugawa station it takes about 30 minutes to Magome and a bit over an hour to Tsumago.

There is also a direct bus connection to Magome from Nagoya; the trip takes about two hours. If you are coming from Matsumoto or Shiojiri, Nagiso is the closest station to Tsumago.

More information can be obtained from the TIC in Tokyo which has a handout on the Kiso region.

Nakatsugawa

Nakatsugawa is the JR station closest to Tsumago and Magome on the line between Nagoya and Matsumoto, and also affords access to nearby Ena-kyo gorge. It is on the bus route from Nagoya to Iida (in the next valley), the gateway to Tenryu-kyo gorge.

Ena-kyo Gorge This scenic gorge near Ena city is about 12 km long. In past years, jet boats carried passengers along half its length but recent *Jikokuhyo* have no

listing. If you are really keen to make such a trip, enquire about boats at Nakatsugawa or Ena station, from where the connecting buses used to leave.

Tenryu River Valley

Another route from Matsumoto southward (branching off at Shiojiri) is through the Tenryu (Heavenly Dragon) River valley to Iida along Route 153, or by the parallel JR line.

The scenery is pleasant enough to make the trip enjoyable and there are a few points of special note. At Ina, the grounds of the former Takata-jo castle are very pretty in the cherry blossom season (probably a couple of weeks later than in Kyoto and Tokyo).

Tenryu-kyo Gorge The major attraction of the river valley is the scenic Tenryu-kyo gorge, accessible from Iida. Tenryu-kyo station (JR) is near the gorge but the most enjoyable way to see this and other parts of the Ina valley is by boat through the Tenryu rapids. There are at least two points of departure.

The longest trip (20 km) begins near Ichida (JR) station, from which three of the eight boats of the day depart (Y2700; 1½ hours); all eight boats can be taken from Benten, 10 minutes by bus from Iida station (Y2500; one hour). Both terminate near Tenryukyo JR station.

Another boat trip leaves from Tenryukyo station and goes to Karakasa (one hour, up to seven per day, Y2400) also on the JR line.

In addition to JR trains, Iida can be reached from Tokyo (Shinjuku Bus Terminal) by buses (11 daily, 4 hours 15 minutes Y4000). It can also be reached by one of the 15 daily buses (2½ hours, Y2250) from Nagoya (Meitetsu Bus Center). These buses pass via Nakatsugawa (gateway to Tsumago) in the next valley, and can be taken between that city and Iida. This permits a trip down one valley from the Matsumoto area, crossing to the other valley via Route 256 and returning along that valley to the Matsumoto area.

MATSUMOTO TO TAKAYAMA

The trip from Matsumoto to Takayama via Kamikochi can be recommended as a chance to see an area of relatively unspoiled rural Japan. The route is definitely off the beaten track for most foreign tourists (although I suspect that you may encounter some others holding this book!) but the route uses well-established scheduled transport and takes you through a scenic region of mountains, beautiful valleys and picturesque little farms.

The first leg of the trip is by Matsumoto Denki Tetsudo private railway from Matsumoto to Shin Shima-Shima (22 minutes, Y590, about 25 trains per day with the first at 3.52 am). Do not mistake this stop with Shimojima, which is three stops before Shin Shima-Shima.

The next leg is by bus from the terminus across the road from the railway station. You can go either as far as Nakanoyu and transfer directly for Takayama (55 minutes, Y1400, up to 14 per day), or to the end of the run to the scenic delights of Kamikochi (another 20 minutes, Y1750 total), and return to Nakanoyu after looking around for a few hours. In the opposite direction, some buses go beyond Shin Shima-Shima to Matsumoto Bus Terminal.

From Kamikochi and Nakanoyu there are up to 10 buses a day to Hirayu-onsen (55 minutes from Nakanoyu, 70 from Kamikochi; Y1250 from either). Six of these continue to Norikura (1¾ hours from Nakanoyu).

To Takayama there are up to four buses a day from Norikura (1½ hours, Y2250) and up to three a day from Hirayu-onsen (one hour, Y1200) and vice versa.

Schedules are such that you can begin at Kamikochi/Nakanoyu, go to Norikura and spend a couple of hours walking around, then continue on to Takayama the same day. (The same type of connections are, of course, possible in the opposite direction.)

On the other hand, if the first look at Norikura does not appeal to you, a Takayama-bound bus leaves Norikura within 10 minutes of the arrival of a bus there from Nakanoyu. The climb to Norikura and approach to it across the highland plateau in the bus is probably the most scenic part of the trip.

If you don't want to go all the way to Takayama, an alternative is to travel to Norikura from Matsumoto then return to Shin Shima-Shima directly by bus (Y2550, up to four a day).

The schedules for all these trains and buses are given in *Jikokuhyo* so it is possible to schedule your travels through the region with military precision.

Kamikochi

Some people believe that this highland basin west of Matsumoto is the most beautiful area in the northern alps. The most impressive single view is the one seen during the last few minutes of the trip in from Nakanoyu, just before reaching the cluster of lodges and inns and the parking area.

The valley opens up on to a broad flood plain with the wall of mountains behind forming an impressive backdrop. This view alone justifies the trip, though there are some very pleasant walks through wooded paths beside the river.

There is no lack of company on these walks and it is interesting to observe how the normally reserved Japanese greet each other while enjoying the natural surroundings. The number of previous hikers can be judged by the height of the cairns – piles of stones built up one at a time by people leaving a marker of their passing.

Several trails begin at Kamikochi. The main trail from the car park leads to Kappabashi, a famous suspension bridge across the Azusa-gawa River.

From the bridge there is a beautiful view of Mt Hotaka and nearby is a rock

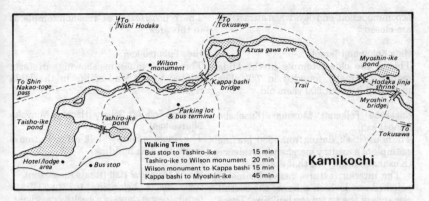

Walking Times

Bus stop to Tashiro-ike	15 min
Tashiro-ike to Wilson monument	20 min
Wilson monument to Kappa bashi	15 min
Kappa bashi to Myoshin-ike	45 min

Kamikochi

sculpture of Walter Weston, a Briton who was the first alpinist to explore the Japan alps in the last century. Prior to this the alps were regarded as sacred or inhabited by evil spirits and were avoided.

Apart from the general ambiance, fresh air and scenic views, other attractions are Tashiro-ike and Taisho-ike ponds and Myojin lake.

A three-hour walk from Kamikochi takes you past Myojin lake, Tokusawa and Yokowao. Trails continue beyond here to nearby high peaks such as Yari-dake (Spear Mountain – the 'Matterhorn' of Japan) but scaling them is for the experienced only. Every year dozens of Japanese are killed in falls from slopes.

Mt Norikura Despite its 3026-metre height, this is the most accessible peak in these alps as a toll road runs most of the way to the top, crossing an alpine plateau en route.

Buses via the Norikura Skyline go as far as Tatami-daira (2½ hours from Kamikochi; less from Nakanoyu or Hirayu-koge) from where a three-km hike (90 minutes) leads to the top. It is high enough that a few patches of snow can be found as late as August.

As mentioned previously, there are regular bus services from the Norikura area to Takayama.

Information The TIC in Tokyo has an information sheet on this area.

Northern Gifu-ken

TAKAYAMA

The city of Takayama ('High Mountain'), often called Hida-Takayama, has been a prosperous area for several centuries and there is a tradition of cultured living that you would not expect to find in an isolated river valley.

Several fine old houses and other buildings survive in the city. These and other attractions make wandering around the city interesting and pleasurable and make Takayama one of the most worthwhile places in Japan to visit.

Information

Your first stop should be at the information booth in front of Takayama station to pick up a copy of their English-language booklet *Hida-Takayama*. It lists all the places of interest to visitors, with a brief description of each, and they are marked on a map.

If you are starting from Tokyo you should also obtain from the TIC a copy of the information sheet on Takayama; it has up-to-date details on train connections, accommodation, and days when attractions are closed.

Hida Kokubunji Temple
This is the oldest temple in the Hida region, originally founded in 746. The main hall is about 500 years old.

Kusakabe Folkcraft Museum (Kusakabe Mingei-kan)
The house itself, dating from 1880, is a fine example of a wealthy merchant's residence (Kusakabe family) of that era.

The interior features heavy beams of polished wood which enhance the overall elegance of the rest of the building. There is also a collection of regional folkcraft items. It is closed Wednesdays from December to February.

Yoshijima House
Next door to the Kusakabe house, this building was the residence of the Yoshijima ('Old Island') family, also wealthy merchants. The two are among the finest houses in Takayama. Yoshijima House is closed on Tuesdays from November to February.

Shishi Kaikan
This is an exhibition of the elaborately carved and ornately lacquered wooden lion-heads used for dances during processions.

Hachiman Shrine
The shrine is the site of the autumn festival. In the grounds is Takayama Yatai Kaikan, an exhibition hall containing four of the 23 elaborately decorated festival wagons (*yatai*) arranged as you would see them in an autumn or spring procession. This gives at least an idea of the magnificence of the festival for those who are unable to see the real thing.

Higashiyama Teramachi
Teramachi means 'temple town'; the name comes from the row of 10 temples at the foot of Higashiyama (East Mountain).

The *Youth Hostel*, at Tenshoji temple, is in this area.

Hida Fubutsu-kan
This is a museum showing artefacts related to the way of life in the Hida region.

Hachiga Folk Art Gallery (Hachiga Minyoku Bijutsu-kan)
The Hachiga family's folk-art collection is housed in this building.

Hirata Memorial Hall (Hirata Kinen-kan)
Art objects belonging to the Hirata family, descendants of a wealthy merchant, are displayed in this museum.

Kyodo Gangu-kan
This museum houses about 2000 traditional toys from different regions of Japan.

Municipal History Museum (Takayama Kyodo-kan)
Built in 1876 and formerly a storehouse, this building belonged to the Nagata family and now houses many items of local history as well as a famous Enku statue. The latter is one of many well-known statues roughly sculpted with a hatchet by the itinerant priest Enku.

Shorenji Temple
Shorenji temple (main building dating from 1504) is built in a unique ancient style and is famous for the elegant curve of its roof. It was moved here from Shirakawa-go when the Miboro dam was built in 1961.

Furui-Machinami
Step back in time with a stroll down Furui-Machinami where old houses and shops line both sides of the street. Many buildings are restaurants, coffee shops or souvenir shops (the owners have to make a living too) but the overall impression is that of a century ago.

The buildings with the large spongy-looking 'ball' hanging from the eaves are old sake warehouses, where various kinds of sake are still on sale. For more than a millennium, Takayama has been known for its carpenters and woodworkers, so have a look at the small chests, trays, bowls and chopping blocks on sale in the shops.

Some of Japan's most tasteful souvenirs (such as woodblock prints, papier-mache figures and special sake flasks) are made and sold in Takayama.

Takayama Jinya

This imposing building was the residence of the local governor in the Tokugawa era and was originally the heart of a large complex of buildings. Most are now gone except for eight *samurai* barracks and a garden behind the main building; closed Wednesdays.

Hida Folklore Village (Hida Minzoku Mura)

With the mountains that surround Takayama as a backdrop and the interesting setting of the park itself, the first impression here is that of a functioning ancient village.

It is probably the best park of its kind in Japan, with many traditional farmhouses (mostly thatched) and other buildings (up to 500 years old) set up around a pond. The reservation includes houses from a number of districts in the mountains around Takayama, including the Shirakawa-go area. Because the buildings were held together with ropes and not nails, they could be dismantled and reassembled without damage. A pamphlet in English describes the salient points of the various buildings.

The park is a couple of km from the station and can be reached by bus (half hourly; Y200), taxi or on foot. It is especially beautiful in autumn. (Parks on a similar theme can be found in Kawasaki, Kanazawa and on Shikoku.)

Other Attractions

There is also a number of museums and exhibitions worth visiting. They include

the following: the Shunkei Lacquerware Hall (Shunkei Kaikan), Fujii Folkcraft Museum (Fujii Bijutsu Mingei-kan) and the Hida Archaeology Museum (Hida Minzoku Koko-kan).

There is also a pair of delightfully grotesque statues of pot-bellied goblins with long arms in the middle of the main river bridge.

Festivals

Takayama is justly famous throughout Japan for its spring and autumn festivals, two of the most magnificent and interesting in the country. Huge, incredibly ornate festive wagons are put on display for most of the day and later pulled through the streets.

The tradition of building *yatai* began a couple of centuries ago as a supplication to the gods to protect the inhabitants of the city from a plague that was ravaging the country. Their prayers seemed to be successful so the custom continued (a sort of preventive medicine) and the carts became more magnificent each time as a spirit of competition developed among wealthy merchants.

As Takayama was a wealthy town, the best materials and construction could be afforded. To duplicate a wagon today would cost about half a million dollars! A booklet is available giving the history of each *yatai*; some are nearly 300 years old.

During the rest of the year the wagons are stored in *yatai-gura*, tall concrete (fireproof) storehouses with no windows and *very* tall doors. As mentioned earlier, there is a permanent display of four *yatai* during the rest of the year at Yatai-kaikan, in the grounds of Hachiman shrine.

The wagons (which are hard to describe as they resemble nothing known in western countries) include intricate wood carvings that form panels and pillars of the structure, antique tapestries of European origin, and other embellishments.

In addition, a few of the *yatai* have

mechanical 'dolls' that perform amazing movements and tricks, all controlled by wires and push-rods; the ingenuity of their designers deserves greater recognition. A typical doll walks out along a beam, rotates and bows to the audience, pivots around completely a couple of times, then releases a shower of flower petals. One *yatai* even has a couple of acrobats that swing from perch to perch.

The performance times of the dolls during the display of the *yatai* is indicated on a board near the wagons. It pays to arrive early for a performance to get a good place as the crowds are very heavy.

The spring Sanno-matsuri festival is held on 14-15 April near Hie-jinja shrine; the autumn Yahata-matsuri festival on 9-10 October in the grounds of Hachiman-jingu. There is a total of 23 *yatai*; 12 are shown at the spring festival and the other 11 in the autumn.

There are also parades of people in various feudal costumes. An interesting feature is one of the musical instruments, a circular metal pan that is struck with a wooden mallet to produce a peculiar 'ging' sound; it seems to be found only in this district.

Places to Stay

There is a *Youth Hostel* (tel (0577) 32-6345) in Takayama at Tenshoji temple.

As might be expected in a town that is very popular with Japanese sightseers, Takayama has plenty of *minshuku* and *ryokan*. Reservations may be made at offices near the station set up for the purpose. One is at the information booth in front of the station, another is down the street to the left and a third is at the far side of the department store opposite and to the right. They are signposted only in Japanese but the *kanji* for '*minshuku*' are prominent and can be recognised easily.

To contact the Takayama Minshuku Association (tel (0577) 33-8501/2; for the Takayama Ryokan Association (tel (0577) 33-11810). Try to have someone call in

Japanese as it is unlikely that anyone will understand English.

There is also a *Kokumin-shukusha (Peoples' Lodge)* (tel (0577) 32-2400). The cheapest hotel is the *Meiboku* (tel (0577) 33-5510) which has double rooms for Y8000. The *Hida Hotel* (tel (0577) 33-4600) and *Green Hotel* (tel (0577) 33-5500) are more expensive.

Getting There & Away

From the south, Takayama is easily reached by JR train from Nagoya via Gifu. There is also a year-round bus service to and from Gifu.

From mid-May to mid-October there is the combination of two buses and a train via Shin Shima-Shima from Matsumoto. From the north, there is JR service to and from Toyama and possibly a bus service.

Highway 41 is a major road linking Nagoya with Toyama and there is quite heavy traffic so hitching should be no problem.

Getting Around

Since the city is laid out with streets at right-angles (a rarity in Japan) it is easy to find your way around Takayama and it is small enough that the energetic can see it on foot or by bicycle. The latter can be rented from at least two shops on the main street (to the left when leaving the station, on the opposite side of the street) for Y1500 per day.

There is a regular bus service that goes to or near most of the attractions of the city and circles back to the station. A 'free pass' costing Y770 is available; it gives unlimited travel for two days and can be bought at the station. Buses run every 20 minutes between 9 am and 4.40 pm.

SOUTH OF TAKAYAMA
Gero

Gero is a typical hot-spring resort, basically a collection of concrete hotels that feature the mineral-laden water, mostly for therapeutic benefits.

The only attraction of Gero is the Chubu

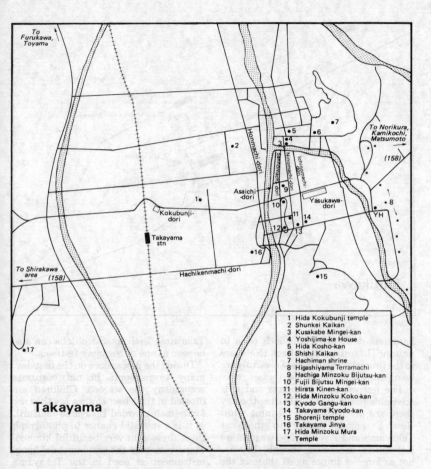

1 Hida Kokubunji temple
2 Shunkei Kaikan
3 Kusakabe Mingei-kan
4 Yoshijima-ke House
5 Hida Kosho-kan
6 Shishi Kaikan
7 Hachiman shrine
8 Higashiyama Terramachi
9 Hachiga Minzoku Bijutsu-kan
10 Fujii Bijutsu Mingei-kan
11 Hirata Kinen-kan
12 Hida Minzoku Koko-kan
13 Kyodo Gangu-kan
14 Takayama Kyodo-kan
15 Shorenji temple
16 Takayama Jinya
17 Hida Minzoku Mura
* Temple

Takayama

Sangaku Kohkogaku Hakubutsukan (Archaeological Museum).

Zenshoji

One stop north of Gero is Zenshoji station. Nearby is Zenshoji temple, the largest in the Hida region. Hida is the name given to the region roughly from Gero to beyond Takayama.

Furukawa

About 15 km north of Takayama is the small city of Furukawa ('Old River'). It has a number of old houses and the appearance of some of its streets is, overall, perhaps more traditional than that of Takayama. It is a pleasant place to walk around and there is a chance that a rickshaw will be available for short rides.

Festival Furukawa is probably best known for its annual festival which is well worth trying to see. Furukawa-matsuri festival is held on 19-20 April. The feature is a night procession of a huge drum on which two men sit back to back and swing their

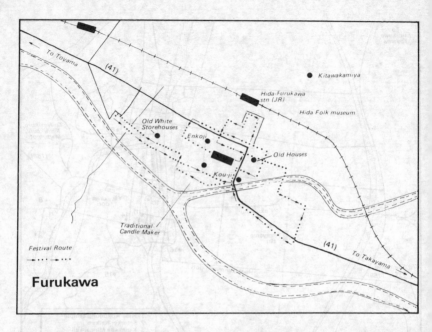

Furukawa

hammers down to strike both ends in unison. The festival dates back 1500 years to the time when drums were used to scare boars away from the crops.

The festival lasts two days and it is advisable to see all of it. During the day there are processions of the nine *yatai* (festive wagons similar to those at Takayama and Kyoto). The wagons are elaborately decorated, though they are not as large or imposing as those in the other two cities. Two of them also have ingenious mechanical dolls which are on display on the second day of the festival. Times for their performances are posted beside the *yatai-gura* (the concrete buildings where they are stored for the rest of the year).

The times for the *kirintai yatai* (a *kirin* is a mythical dragon) are 1.30 and 3.30 pm, while the *seyutai yatai* can be seen at 10 am and 3 pm. The dolls are at least 165 years old (*circa* 1820) and are marvels of design skill, similar to those described for the

Takayama festivals. Such dolls can also be seen at one of Nagoya's festivals.

During the processions on the first day, many townspeople in old costumes accompany the wagons. Children are dressed in their best clothes (as they are for the more crowded Takayama-matsuri), so it is a splendid chance to photograph them dressed in very beautiful kimono. Many boys play the same unusual 'ging' instrument as used in the Takayama festival.

Throughout the festival young men go from door to door performing a *shishi-mai* (lion dance). The *shishi* has a magnificently carved wooden head with jaws that clack shut in a most amusing way. If there are children nearby, the dancer operating the head may get right down to the ground to try to scare the child – usually he or she laughs with delight. Two assistants manipulate the lion's body and the dancers are accompanied by a small troupe of flute players and a drummer

Top: Rickshaws can still be found, especially at tourist destinations (IMcQ)
Bottom: Young women in their best kimono at the Furukawa Matsuri festival (IMcQ)

Top: After the ceremony, Hachiman shrine, Autumn festival, Takayama (AE)
Left: Tagata-jinja fertility festival (IMcQ)
Right: Shishi Mae (Lion dance) performer, near Wajima, Noto-hanto peninsula (AE)

who keeps rhythm with healthy wallops on a wheeled drum.

After dark on the first night bonfires are lit at several intersections of the town, and at about 10 pm the lids of the *sake* casks are broken open and the contents liberally distributed to the young men carrying the drum, as well as to any passers-by who wish to indulge. Any foreigners present (usually few) receive special attention and it becomes a problem keeping sober enough to see the rest of the festivities, let alone take pictures.

The fires and sake help to keep the young men warm as the nights are cold (nearby ski-grounds still have large patches of snow on them) and they wear nothing but *haramaki* around their waists, and a loincloth. After they have become sufficiently soused, one after another demonstrates his balancing skills by scaling a bamboo pole and lying on it, all his weight held by his belly pressing on the small circle of the pole.

Soon after, the procession with the large drum begins. The drum (at least 1½ metres in diameter), the two drummers and at least 10 other people carrying lanterns are supported on a large structure of bamboo poles and beams that is carried through the streets on the strong shoulders of many (usually inebriated) young men. The drum is preceded by a large number of people in costume who carry lighted paper lanterns; the effect is beautiful.

Most houses, *ryokan* and *minshuku* along the parade route (it circles through the town several times through the night) have upper-storey windows that can be removed completely to give a good view of the parade – by far the best vantage point. The celebration and inebriation are, by the way, historically part of Japanese festivals and have been for the last 2000 years.

During the festival there is a special table set up at the station to help people find rooms. However, many of the rooms are at ski lodges many km out of town,

accessible only by taxi, so it would be worth trying to arrange accommodation in advance. There is a youth hostel at Takayama but the drum procession takes place too late at night to allow time to see it and get back in time for lights-out.

48 Waterfalls

Between Takayama and Furukawa there is a turn-off (signposted in Japanese) pointing the way to 48 Waterfalls (Yonju-hachi taki), about eight km off the main road.

They are a pleasant low-key bit of scenery (the water flow and the drops are moderate) but they provide a peaceful walk relatively remote from the rest of humanity (most of it, anyway).

SHOKAWA VALLEY AREA

Not far west of Takayama is a very interesting region, the Shokawa River valley. (It is also accessible from the south from the Gifu area, and from the north from Takaoka.)

The area was settled in the 12th century by survivors of the Heike (Taira) clan who were defeated by the Genji (Minamoto) clan in the great battle of Dan-no-Ura (near Shimonoseki) for control of Japan. The Taira fled to this and other remote areas to escape slaughter by their foes.

The area was still considered remote as late as 1961 when construction of the Miboro dam brought it to greater attention. Even until 1978, the only communication during winter was by boat along the river. Nowadays there is a year-round bus service.

Gassho-zukuri (Thatched-roof Houses)

The outstanding feature of the region is its characteristic large three or four-storey thatched-roof *gassho-zukuri* houses. These are the largest traditional farmhouses in Japan and many are 200 to 300 years old.

Surrounded as they are by hills and mountains, and remote from most influences of the late 20th century, they

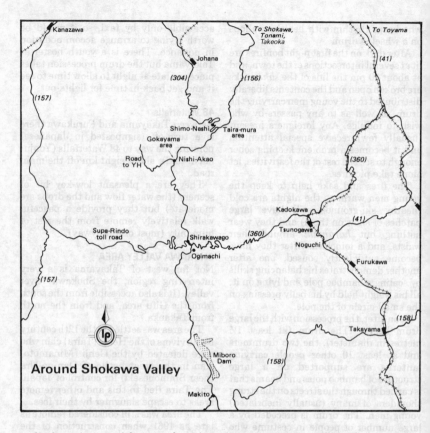

Around Shokawa Valley

make the region one of the most charming and traditional in Japan. A visit to such an area (there are relatively few left) should be on the itinerary of any visitor who wishes to get a feel for 'old' Japan.

'Gassho-zukuri' means 'hands held in prayer' (ie, Buddhist-style, with palms together and fingers stretched straight up). In former times, a single house accommodated 30 to 100 people on the ground floor; upper storeys were used for the production of handicrafts (utilitarian in those days, not for sale to tourists) or for raising silkworms, and the attic was used as a storehouse.

The area is increasingly popular with Japanese tourists seeking what remains of the traditional Japan. As a result, a large number of the houses function as minshuku and take in guests, thus producing an income and ensuring their survival.

Shirakawa-go
This village is made of several buraku (hamlets), each containing some of the thatched houses. Ogimachi is by far the most interesting as it has the lion's share of gassho-zukuri clustered together (11 of which are now minshuku). Other nearby buraku are Hatogoya and Iijima, both of which have only a few thatch houses.

The original village of Shirakawa was

inundated when the Miboro dam filled in 1961, so its buildings were moved elsewhere. Some can be seen at Takayama's Hida Folklore Village, Yokohama's Sankei-en garden and at Kawasaki's Nihon Minka-en.

The present village of Shirakawa is small and the main activity for visitors is just to look around and savour the atmosphere. All the houses are within walking distance of each other and there are rice paddies in the immediate vicinity, so the mood is certainly rural. Many of the houses have old farm implements hung outside as an open-air museum display.

A good vantage point can be reached by walking (or taxiing) a couple of km up the Supa Rindo highway, which links the village with Kanazawa. Another is from the foundations of a former castle.

Information All the *minshuku* give out copies of a sketch map which is quite adequate for sightseeing. The largest house in Ogimachi, formerly the chief's residence, is a museum.

Places to Stay One of the most memorable experiences of a visit to Japan is a night spent in one of the many *gassho-zukuri minshuku*. Although modern amenities have been added, the traditional appearance of the exterior has been retained in all cases and the common rooms often have the original hearth over which is suspended a pot hook. All guests eat together and, if my experience at the *Juemon* was typical, the lady of the house keeps everyone company, pours beers and *sake* for them (paid for separately) and even sings folk songs of the region and performs local folk dances.

Listed here are the names and phone numbers of almost all the *minshuku* in Ogimachi. In the July-August season this area is very popular and it is advisable to phone ahead to be sure of having a place to stay.

None of the proprietors speak English so you will need a Japanese person to

phone for you. It might be possible to book through an agency in Tokyo or other large city, or at the station in Toyama or Gifu. The number in brackets is the approximate age of the house (in years). The charge per night is uniform for all *minshuku*. The area code for Ogimachi in Shirakawa-go is 05769.

Juemon	6-1053	(300)
Yosobe	6-1172	(230)
Nodaniya	6-1011	
Kidoya	6-1077	(200)
Gensaku	6-1176	(170)
Magoemon	6-1167	(280)
Iicha	6-1422	(200)
Koemon	6-1446	(200)
Furusato	6-1033	(150)
Yoshiro	6-1175	

The hostess at Yosobe seems very pleasant and friendly but the people in charge of the last two *minshuku* were not very interested or helpful to me, although a Japanese friend recommended the *Yoshiro* highly.

While it is not a *gassho* house (only a country farmhouse), some travellers have had only the highest praise for a *minshuku* they stayed in near Shirakawa-go; it is *Minshuku Osugi* (tel (05769) 6-1345) at Okubo Shirakawa-mura.

A few km north of the *buraku* of Shirakawa-go is another small cluster of gassho houses to the west of the road and down near the valley floor. There is a *minshuku* (tel (07637) 3632) advertised on a sign at road level *Toichin-so*, but the surroundings are not as picturesque as they are at Shirakawa-go.

Getting There & Away The Shirakawa-go area can be reached by public transport from Gifu and Nagoya to the south, from Takaoka to the north, and from Takayama to the east.

From Nagoya, a simple way is by JR train to Mino-Ota (nine per day; one hour), and from there by JR to Mino-Shirotori (also nine per day but generally not connecting; two hours). From Shirotori there are five buses a day (two hours) to Onimachi (via Makito), which terminate at Hatogaya, a short distance beyond Onimachi.

There is also a single bus from Nagoya station to Onimachi (5¼ hours) and Hatogaya. From Gifu, not far from Nagoya, there are many JR trains to Mino-Ota (40 minutes), plus many buses through the day from Shin-Gifu station through to Shirotori (just over two hours).

From Takaoka, JR trains run as far south as Johana (20 per day) from where two buses a day run south to Hatogaya (one hour). Two buses a day also go from Takaoka station to Shimonashi (bypassing Johana; 1½ hours) where you can transfer to a Johana-Hatogaya bus. From Takayama, you can go by bus to Makito (six per day; 1½ hours) and then change to a Shirotori-Onimachi bus.

There are two routes to and from Kanazawa. The old one is via Route 304 to Taira-mura, where it meets Route 156; buses run on this route. The new Supa Rindo ('Hakusan Super Forest Pathway') toll road runs much more directly through the mountains and links Shirakawa-go with Route 157 straight to Kanazawa, but there is no bus service. Unfortunately, two-wheeled vehicles are not allowed on this road.

Gokayama

A little further north, across the boundary into Toyama-ken, are the *gassho* houses of Gokayama (which is technically part of Kami-Taira, or 'upper Taira village'), beginning at Nishi-Akao. There are so few that they can be identified by name.

First comes the Iwase family; a little farther on, at Suganuma (Kami-Taira), you find the houses that make up the Gokayama Seishonen Ryoko Mura (Youth Tourist Village) which offers accommodation.

Near the Tourist Village is a road that turns off and runs inland to the west. This leads to *Etchu Gokayama Youth Hostel*

(tel (07636) 7-3331), itself a *gassho* house.

Another house (Murakami family) can be found at Kami-Nashi (Upper Nashi), a hot-spring town. At Shimo-Nashi (Lower Nashi) you can see traditional Japanese paper (*washi*) being made at Goka-shi Kyodo Kumiai (Goka-city Paper Producers' Cooperative).

Toga

You can also find *gassho-zukuri* in the Kami-Momose section of Toga village where there are five thatched houses close to each other. Being not at all well known and very more remote, it is guaranteed not to be touristy. There should be at least one *minshuku* in the area.

You need your own vehicle to get to Toga. One map shows a good road direct to the village from just north of Furukawa/Takayama, with a minor road linking that road to Inokuchi, a little north of Taira. Another major map gives no hint of such a road.

Going north from this area along Route 156 leads to Takaoka. JR trains can be taken from Tonami. Branching off Route 156 onto Route 304 first leads onto a twisty gravel road but passes through some pretty scenery. This route leads to Johana (soon after the road reaches flat land), where a JR line begins; the road goes on to Kanazawa.

SOUTH TO SEKI

The scenery along Route 156 to Seki is pleasant for most of the journey, with typical small farms and farmhouses, few towns and few signs of rampant modernisation. The only town of note is Gujo-Hachiman.

Gujo-Hachiman

There isn't much to see here but the town is renowned for its celebrations of the *Obon* festival when large numbers of townspeople dance in the streets every night throughout August. This 'madness' is known as Gujo Odori and is famous throughout Japan. The peak nights are around 13-16 August but any night from late July to early September would be equally good for a visit.

Toyama-ken

TAKAOKA

Near the eastern base of the Noto-hanto peninsula is Takaoka. The city is noted for its lacquerware as well as copper and iron products, and is the main source in Japan of large cast bells. If you are interested in artistic foundry work you might be able to arrange a visit to a workshop; try the town hall (*shi-yaku-sho*) for contacts.

Sightseeing potential in the city is limited but it does have the third largest Daibutsu (statue of Buddha) in Japan. However, although it is described as being made of bronze, it looks more like green-painted concrete and cannot be compared with the serene beauty of the famous Daibutsu at Kamakura near Tokyo.

Zuiryuji Temple

The best place in Takaoka to visit is, in fact, the *Youth Hostel* (tel (0766) 22-0179), No 3207, because it is a large and venerable temple about 350 years old.

Zuiryuji is a Zen temple of the Soto sect. The main building and the ceremonial entry gate are large and the spacious grounds are surrounded by a traditional wall. It is unusual to find such a splendid structure in such a remote area as this. There is a peaceful feeling because there are no hordes of tourists.

It is not worth a special trip but for anyone who plans to stay overnight in the area it can be highly recommended. As a bonus, the wife of the priest speaks good English and can tell you a bit about the place.

Other Temples

Other temples in Takaoka are Kokutaiji and Shokoji. Shrines include Imisu and

Keta. The foundations of the old castle and its moats still stand and are rather pretty during the cherry-blossom season. The castle grounds house the buildings of the civic centre and are not otherwise interesting.

Festivals

There are festivals on 14 January and 2-3 June as well as the following:

1 May: Procession of *dashi* (large carved and decorated wagons). The *dashi* used in this procession are old but not as fantastically elaborate as those of Takayama or Kyoto.

15 May: Night processions of at least seven large floats lit by lanterns.

3-7 August: Tanabata, with pretty paper decorations on the streets – but not much action.

23 September: Daibutsu festival.

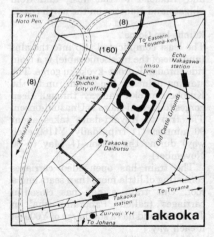

Around Takaoka

As well as using Takaoka as the starting point for trips around the Noto-hanto peninsula, you can take Route 156 south to the very interesting Shokawa River valley and the old houses of Shirakawa-go area described earlier. There are buses from Takaoka station through the valley.

There is also a JR line as far as Johana, from which another road links up with Route 156 at Taira-mura, the northern extremity of the area of old houses mentioned previously.

TOYAMA

Toyama has little in the way of attractions but is the starting point for two good excursions into the northern Japan alps.

Two of the routes into the mountains that can be followed by anyone (no need for climbing) have Toyama as the most convenient starting point. One is an excursion to nearby Kurobe-kyo gorge, the other a route from Toyama to Shinano-Omachi in Nagano-ken. (A third is the route between Matsumoto and Takayama.)

Toyama can be reached from the Shokawa River valley area, from Kanazawa and Takaoka to the west, and from Niigata and Naoetsu on the north coast.

Kurobe-kyo Gorge

The least complicated trip into the alps (and one of the most enjoyable) is a train ride through Kurobe-kyokoku gorge. The starting point for the 20-km run by the Kurobe-kyokoku railway through deep gorges to Keyaki-daira is Unazuki-onsen. The trip to Keyaki-daira takes about 90 minutes (11 trips daily; Y1160 each way) during the season (1 May to 30 November).

The train has open-sided carriages consisting of little more than seats and a roof. One train a day has closed-in carriages (called 'Panorama sha' in Japanese) and has a surcharge of Y600 on it each way.

It is not possible to go on past the end of the gorge; you must return to the coast or Toyama. There are several stations along the way through the gorge so it is possible to walk part of the way. It would be best to ride all the way in, then decide which sectors would the be most enjoyable on foot.

Unazuki-onsen is easily reached by the Toyama-chiho Tetsudo railway from Toyama (Den-tetsu Toyama station; separate from JR station) by transfer from the JR stations at Namerikawa, Higashi Namerikawa or Uozu, or at Kurobe (separate station); there are up to 26 trains a day (Y1400 from Toyama ordinary, Y1550 express). It can also be reached by road.

Tateyama-Kurobe Alpine Route

Although the excursion from Toyama to Keyaki-daira is easily made, probably the most popular journey in the alps passes through territory that was the province only of alpinists until recent times. The Tateyama-Kurobe Alpine Route takes in the peaks of the Tateyama group, centred around Tateyama itself (3015 metres).

The route runs between a point near Toyama (Toyama-ken) and Shinano-Omachi (Nagano-ken) and is enjoyed by many Japanese, partly for its variety of transport (including train, bus, cable car, funicular and trolley bus). The drawback is cost; transport alone comes to more than Y8000 and you may have to rush through to avoid an overnight stay at Y4000 and up prices. The fares are expensive but prior to 1971 no such route existed except for those willing to walk the distance.

TOYAMA TO OMACHI

From Dentetsu Toyama station, the Toyama-chiho Dentetsu line runs frequently to Tateyama town (about one hour and Y940 ordinary; about 50 minutes and Y1090 by express).

At Tateyama, the route continues by a funicular up to Bijo-daira (Y600). From there a bus ride leads to Murodo (55 minutes; Y1600). En route it passes scenic but rather distant Shomyo-taki waterfall (Japan's longest, including a drop down a sheer, 126-metre cliff face) and there's the vista offered at Midagahara over the surrounding area. The route is open from 15 May to 5 November; if you travel soon after it opens, you may find yourself in a

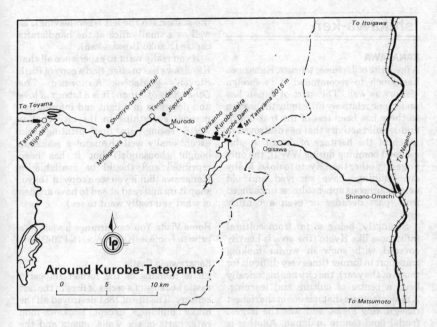

Around Kurobe-Tateyama

To Toyama / To Itoigawa / To Nagano / To Matsumoto

Tateyama / Bijo-daira / Shomyo-taki waterfall / Midagahara / Tengu-daira / Jigoku-dani / Murodo / Daikanho / Kurobe-daira / Kurobe Dam / Mt Tateyama 3015 m / Ogisawa / Shinano-Omachi

0   5   10 km

canyon cut through snow up to 10 metres deep. (Murodo can be reached by private vehicle; beyond here it is necessary to use public transport or go on foot.)

Murodo is a base for walking to Mikura-ga-ike lake or Jigoku-dani ('Hell Valley'), an area of steaming solfataras (volcanic vents), or for climbing Tateyama (Oyama) or Tsurigi-dake. The climb from Murodo to Oyama is steep and is nearly five km long. The view from the top takes in a number of surrounding peaks and valleys.

The route continues from Murodo by a 10-minute bus ride (18 per day) through a tunnel to Daikanho (Y2000; oh, to have that franchise!). From here the route takes a cable car (seven minutes, Y1200) across a wide valley, and a funicular train (five minutes, Y800) down to Kurobe-ko lake, behind Kurobe dam (the largest arch dam in the orient).

From the end of the dam there is the option of going up to Kurobe-daira, a lookout over the dam, before going to the

station for the trolley bus. The only such line left in Japan, it takes travellers to Ogisawa (16 minutes; Y1200) for an almost immediate connection with a regular bus that runs to Shinano-Omachi (35 minutes; Y1150). There are 11 trips a day in each direction by the trolley bus and the connecting bus. The cable car and funiculars run more frequently and generally dovetail for minimum delay, so you can take some time to look around and continue by a later departure without a long wait, or continue almost at once.

An economical alternative that takes in most of the best scenery of the northern alps region but which saves money is to make a day trip out of Toyama, going only as far as Murodo before returning. As one traveller expressed it, 'A dam is a dam anywhere' and the scenery eastward from the dam to Omachi is not particularly noteworthy.

The Tokyo TIC has an information sheet with up-to-date prices and times.

Ishikawa-ken

KANAZAWA

A favourite of Japanese tourists, Kanazawa has much to recommend it to foreign visitors as well. This part of Japan has undergone relatively little industrialisation so there has been less of the tear-down-and-rebuild activity that has destroyed so much of the heritage of Japan. It also escaped bombing during WW II, the only large city other than Kyoto to do so. Many old buildings have survived and old neighbourhoods appear almost unchanged from past decades or even a century ago.

Strangely, being so far from cultural influences like Kyoto (the area is heavily covered with snow in winter making transport in former times very difficult for much of the year), the city has historically been a centre of culture and learning. A major factor is that it is one of the richest rice-growing areas, and was the largest feudal land tenure in Japan. Another is that the Maeda clan who controlled the city and region (beginning with Toshiie Maeda, who captured the city in 1583) valued education and a cultured life. They spent the wealth wisely and promoted such crafts as lacquerware and weaving, encouraged artisans to settle, and established fine buildings and traditions that survive to this day.

A large proportion of the attractions of Kanazawa are near Kanazawa-jo castle (mostly around an irregular loop encircling Kenrokuen garden) and can be seen on foot. The castle can be reached by bus in 15 minutes from Kanazawa JR station (about 2½ km away); the stop is pronounced 'Kenrokuen-sh'ta'.

Information

The photocopied information sheets provided by the Tokyo TIC give useful additional details on accommodation, etc. In Kanazawa there is a large guide map and an information office in front of the station (to the left when leaving), as well as a small office at the handicrafts centre (Kanko Bussan-kan).

If you really want to experience all that Kanazawa has to offer, find a copy of Ruth Steven's guidebook *Kanazawa: The Other Side of Japan*. It is a labour of love and describes in a light and informative manner everything in the city that is worth seeing. Its first printing sold exceptionally well (Kanazawa residents bought thousands!) but it has been reprinted and should be available in Kanazawa (but if you see a copy in Tokyo, snap it up and read ahead to have an idea of what you really want to see).

Home Visits You can arrange a visit to a private home in Kanazawa, (tel 20-2075).

Kanazawa-jo Castle

Little remains of the former imposing castle because of a series of fires in the last century. The fire of 1881 destroyed all the major buildings except Ishikawa-mon gate, parts of the walls, moats and the armoury. The site of the castle has been used as the campus of Kanazawa National University but this should have moved out by now. In one corner of the grounds is Oyama-jinja shrine.

Oyama-jinja Shrine The gate of this shrine is very unusual in design and history, and is unlike that of almost any other in Japan. It was designed in 1870 by a Dutchman, a scientist who was teaching in the city during the westernisation period. The top two storeys of the gate strongly suggest two squared arches, one atop the other, of traditional Chinese design.

Filling the top arch is a stained-glass window that was originally used as a lighthouse for ships on the Sea of Japan. The shrine itself dates from 1599 and was built to honour Toshiie Maeda, the founder of the Maeda clan. It was moved to its present site in 1873.

Other arches similar to those of this

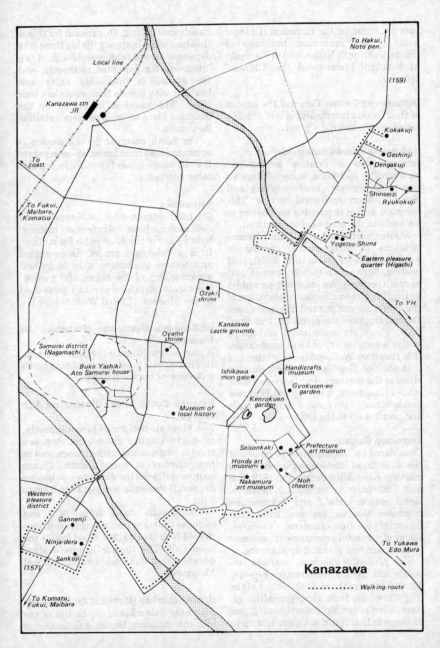

To Hakui,
Noto pen.

(159)

Local line

Kanazawa stn
JR

To
coast

To Fukui,
Maibara,
Komatsu

Kokakuji

Geshinji
Dengakuji

Shinseizi
Ryukokuji

Yogetsu Shima

Eastern pleasure
quarter (Higashi)

To YH

Ozaki
shrine

Oyama
shrine

Kanazawa
castle grounds

Samurai district
(Nagamachi)

Buke Yashiki
Ato Samurai house

Ishikawa
mon gate

Handicrafts
museum

Gyokusen-en
garden

Kenrokuen
garden

Museum of
local history

Western
pleasure
district

Seisonkaki

Prefecture
art museum

Gannenji

Honda art
museum

Ninja-dera

Sankoji

Nakamura
art museum

Noh
theatre

To Yukawa
Edo Mura

(157)

To Komatu,
Fukui, Maibara

Kanazawa

·········· Walking route

gate are found on the Karamon (Chinese gate) of the innermost buildings of Toshogu shrine in Nikko, and in Nagasaki at Kofukuji (nicknamed the 'Chinese' temple).

Gyokusen-en Garden

This was the garden of the Nishida family and is laid out in a circular style around a pond.

Ishikawa-ken Kanko Bussan-kan

Ishikawa-ken is famous for several handicrafts, including some of Japan's finest lacquerware, cloth weaving and dyeing, pottery and wood carving. This museum makes it possible for visitors to see some of the crafts being practiced.

Master craftsmen give daily demonstrations in lacquerware, carving of wooden heads for *shishi* (lion dolls), gold beating, *kaga yuzen* (fabric dyeing), and *kutani* (pottery). An excellent pamphlet in English gives sufficient explanation of the crafts to understand the processes. Demonstrations are given on the third floor. There are restaurants and shops selling a wide variety of local handicrafts. It is closed on Wednesdays in winter.

In addition, there is a tourist information office at the entrance, but beware of their map of Kanazawa; it is a typical Japanese handout map – very stylised, not to scale and north is off to the left.

Kenrokuen Garden

Considered by the Japanese to be one of the three finest landscape gardens in the country, Kenrokuen dates from 1819. It is quite extensive, covering 10 hectares. Roku means 'six', and Kenrokuen combines the six features considered essential to fine gardens: vastness, solemnity, careful arrangement, coolness (water), age and pleasing appearance.

The garden is spacious, encloses two ponds and has many attractive aspects. To me it is by far the most attractive of the 'Big Three' gardens. However, although Kenrokuen is certainly worth seeing, my feeling was that it did not quite live up to

its advance billing. One reason for this is that because it is among the big three (the Japanese *love* to rank everything), it is a 'must-see' for Japanese sightseers, and the garden is invariably noisy and bustling with people from countless tour buses. The mood is not aided by the constant blare of loudspeakers extolling its virtues.

The north entrance to the garden is across the road from Ishikawa-mon gate of the old castle grounds but there are also other entrances.

Seisonkaku

On the southern edge of Kenrokuen is Seisonkaku, a beautiful two-storey mansion built by one of the *daimyo* for his mother. It is a fine example of Shoin-zukuri architecture. In addition to the design and workmanship of the house and garden, there is also an exhibit of many items used by the Maedas. (Closed Wednesdays.)

Ishikawa-ken Bijutsu-kan (Prefecture Art Museum)

A very short distance from Seisonkaku, this museum is most worthy of note for its collection of *kutani* pottery.

Nohgaku Bunka Kaikan (Prefectural Noh Theatre)

Noh plays are performed here frequently, mostly by amateur groups, but there is a regular professional performance on the first Sunday of every month. (Some sources claim the third Sunday, so be sure to check!) Performances last from 9 am to 5 pm.

The theatre dates from 1972 and includes the stage that was salvaged from the old Noh theatre that stood beside the town hall. The theatre is just a short distance south of Seisonkaku. (Closed Mondays.)

Honda Zohin-kan (Memorial Art Museum)

Also near Seisonkaku, at the top of the hill, this museum houses a collection of items used by the Honda family, the chief retainers under the Maeda.

Nakamura Kinen Bijutsu-kan (Memorial Art Museum)

Close to the Honda Museum, this is a large Japanese-style house that belonged to a wealthy *sake* dealer named Nakamura. He donated the house and his collection of oriental art (including fine lacquerware and utensils for the tea ceremony) to the city. It is closed on Tuesdays and the day after national holidays.

Kyodo Shiryo-kan (Museum of Local History)

This museum has a variety of exhibits of local archaeology, folklore and history, including one relating to the processions required of local *daimyo* to Edo (Tokyo) in feudal times (which often involved thousands of people).

The building looks incongruous as it is a western-style red-brick structure built as a high school in 1891 at the time when westernisation was in full swing. On the map included with the information sheets available at the Tokyo TIC, this is labelled 'History Museum'. (Closed Mondays.)

Samurai District

Walking through the little lanes of the old *samurai* town of Nagamachi gives at least an impression of olden times. There are several typical narrow crooked streets lined with packed-earth, tile-topped walls that keep out curious eyes. Most of the houses, however, are actually from the Meiji era (1868 to 1910), rather than genuine *samurai*-built houses.

One authentic *samurai* house which has been restored and is open to the public as a museum is Buke Yashiki Ato (closed Wednesdays). Another old house, Saihit-suan, is used for demonstrating *yuzen*, the traditional method of hand-painting patterns on silk for kimono. (Closed Thursdays in winter). For a look over two former *samurai* gardens, have a coffee at

either Kaga-no-niwa or Nokore (both closed Thursdays).

After visiting the *samurai* area and shopping in the many stores along the nearby main street, you can return to Oyama shrine or leave it until last along with a more leisurely look at the handicraft-making displays at the handicrafts centre.

Higashi (Geisha) District

Higashi is one of Kanazawa's two old districts, most popular with visitors because they preserve much of the atmosphere of former times. According to one story, the Maedas decreed that *geisha* areas and temples be placed on the banks of both the Agano and Sai (west) rivers, so that invaders would be distracted by one or the other. More likely it was a way to minimise their effect on daily life, just as Tokyo had the Yoshiwara area set aside for its *geisha* houses.

The main attraction is just wandering along the back streets among the old houses and temples. Visitors are allowed into one of the still-functioning *geisha* houses, the Shima (usually open from 9 am to 5 pm, closed Mondays). Another, the Yogetsu, has been turned into a *minshuku*.

Teramachi

This is the second of the old districts. The *geisha* houses are no longer here but the temples still remain, including Myoryuji, one of the most unusual in Japan.

Myoryuji Temple

Dubbed Ninja-dera (Ninja temple), this is not merely a temple but a type of fortress with labyrinthine secret passages, hidden traps and exits that would serve to hold off invaders while the *daimyo* escaped.

Myoryuji was the Maeda family temple. There are tours lasting 20 minutes but the temple is so popular that it is generally necessary to make reservations (tel 41-2877, in Japanese); on Sundays and holidays it may be impossible. The best time to go is mid-afternoon. If there are not many people scheduled for a tour, it may be possible to squeeze in without a reservation. Some of the guides may speak English. (Closed on the 1st and 13th of each month, and New Year.)

Edo-mura

Of interest to many is Edo-Mura, a 'village' of Edo-era (17th to 19th century) buildings that were moved here from different parts of Japan. Some of the buildings are luxurious mansions and houses while others give an idea of the less exalted conditions of the ordinary people. The village is well done but the number of buildings (about 20) is rather small in view of the rather high admittance charge (Y650).

Included in the price, however, is entry to nearby Danpuen, a small village concentrating on crafts; a minibus goes every 20 minutes between the two villages. The village rather suffers in comparison with the similar park in Takayama but it is worth seeing if you don't have to pinch pennies. Access is by Hokuriku Railway bus No 12 from Kanazawa station to Yukawa Onsen; Edo-mura is a short walk uphill.

Festivals

There are many festivals through the year. Most are small neighbourhood affairs but there are some very large and well known ones as well.

10-16 February: Performances of *dekuma-washi* (a kind of puppet theatre unique to the area) at the community centre of Oguchi. Performances are at night so it is advisable to make prior arrangements for accommodation in the village.

19-20 April: Gokoku-jinja Spring Festival featuring dances by shrine maidens.

15 May: Shinji Noh performance given outdoors at Ono Minato Jinja (in Kanaiwa); a 370-year-old ritual.

13-15 June: Hyaku-man goku matsuri festival celebrates the entry into Kanazawa, in 1583, of Toshiie Maeda,

first lord of the Maeda clan. (Other sources say 12-14 June, so check in advance.) Features include a procession of people in colourful feudal costumes (on the last day), folk dancing in the evening, geisha show at Kanko Kaikan, tea ceremony at Kenrokuen and Seisonkaku, and martial arts displays.

24-25 July: At Ono, three mountain demons (villagers in bright costume) spend two days going from house to house exorcising demons with flutes and drums. Ono can be reached by bus from Musashi.

1-3 August: Ono-minato-jinja matsuri festival, held in Kanaiwa town, is famous for its carved wooden floats.

15 August: Obon dances at Hatta village (night); its Sakata Odori is one of the few in Japan in which old costumes are worn and music is live, not recorded.

October: Through the month there are local shrine festivals.

19-20 October: Dances by shrine maidens at Gokoku shrine.

15 November: Shichi-go-san festival, celebrated everywhere in Japan. Go to Ishiura-jinja shrine to see children dressed in beautiful kimono.

Places to Stay

There are two *Youth Hostels* in Kanazawa, one of which is the cheapest in Japan (Y750), but it is so far out in the country that it is not worth trying to find. It also has a very early (and noisy) reveille.

There are many hotels, *ryokan* and *minshuku* (especially in Higashi); bookings can be made at the station. There is a very interesting inn/restaurant in a 150-year-old farmhouse, *Zenigame* (tel 35-1426), a few km out of town toward Edo-mura.

Getting There & Away

Kanazawa is easily reached by train from Tokyo, Nagoya, Kyoto, or Osaka via Maibara (on the Shinkansen), or by plane to nearby Komatsu Airport.

KANAZAWA TO THE NOTO-HANTO PENINSULA

Between Kanazawa and Hakui are two large and venerable houses, Okabe-ke and Kita-ke, the homes of local governors in the Tokugawa era. In addition to administering the law, these officials collected taxes in the form of rice.

Okabe-ke is somewhat larger but both houses (which are about 10 km apart) have collections of relics from that age. Okabe-ke is accessible by bus from Kanazawa station and is close to Menden station (JR); Kita-ke is near Minami-Hakui station and there may be a bus service as well.

Keta-jinja Shrine

There is nothing of interest at Hakui itself but just a few km north is Keta-jinja shrine, which faces the sea and is set in a picturesque grove of trees.

Myojiji Temple

Only a short distance north and a little inland of Keta shrine is Myojiji, one of the great temples of the region. Its five-storey pagoda looks out over the surrounding flat countryside, and the view of the temple at the top of a long flight of stone steps is quite beautiful and memorable (except for the inevitable wires draped right across the middle of the scene, which will spoil any photo).

The temple was established in the 13th century, although most of the present buildings date from the 17th century. There is a handout pamphlet in perfect English that explains the history of the temple and each of the main buildings.

NOTO-HANTO PENINSULA

The Noto-hanto peninsula contains some of the most picturesque scenery in Japan. There are still large rice paddies, farmers working diligently and typical rural scenes that have remained almost unchanged for decades.

Cyclists will particularly enjoy this area as there are relatively few hills, a continuation of the pleasant cycling of the Echizen coast from Fukui northward.

The outer (*soto*) coast of the peninsula is much more rugged and scenic than the calm inner (*uchi*) shore. The finest scenery begins just north of Kanazawa and continues around to the eastern tip at Cape Rokugo, while there are beautiful (though less dramatic) views past the cape down to Nanao on the east coast.

Information

The information sheets from the TIC in Tokyo are very useful for train, bus and boat schedules and should be picked up for up-to-date information.

Places to Stay

There are 12 youth hostels around the peninsula, nine peoples' lodges and probably hundreds of *minshuku*, as well as hotels and *ryokan*.

The hostels are listed in the *Youth Hostel Handbook* and on the information sheet *Noto Peninsula* given out by the Tokyo TIC. One hostel I found very pleasant was the *Noto-Katsurazaki Youth Hostel*, right beside the water near Kafuto station.

Getting Around

There is a frequent and convenient bus service to all places of interest around the Noto-hanto peninsula, making it the recommended means of transport.

Briefly, there are special sightseeing buses around the northeast end of the peninsula between Wajima and Anamizu/Ushitsu, and regular buses that cover the following steps: Kanazawa-Togi, Togi-Monzen, Monzen-Wajima, Wajima-Ushitsu, and Monzen-Anamizu.

Trains run Hakui-Nanao-Wajima, and Nanao-Takojima. There is a JR service to Wajima and Takoshima (a little east of Suzu) but for the loop around the peninsula there are only buses. Since Wajima is more or less in the middle, it is not a useful starting point.

As there are many places to see and

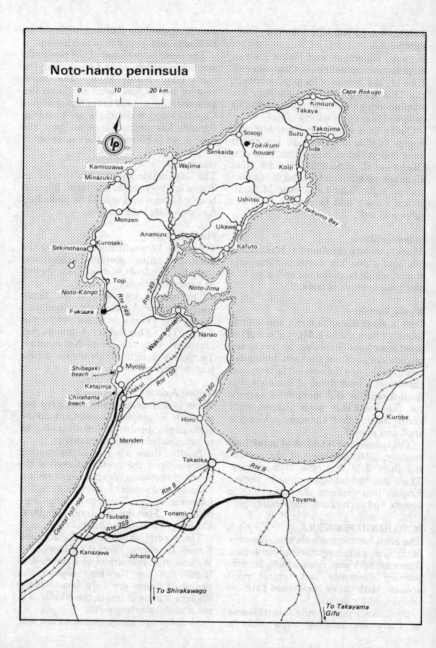

Noto-hanto peninsula

0   10   20 km

Cape Rokugo

Kinoura
Takaya
Takojima
Sosogi   Suzu
Senkaida   Tokikuni   Iida
              houses
Kamiozawa   Koiji
Minazuki   Wajima

Monzen   Ushitsu   Ogi
                                          Tsukumo Bay
Kurosaki   Anamizu   Ukawa
Sekinohana   Kafuto

Togi
              Noto-Jima
Noto-Kongo
Fukuura
                          Nanao
              Wakura-onsen
Shibagaki
beach   Myojiji
Ketajinja   Himi
Chirahama
beach   Hakui   Kurobe

         Menden   Takaoka
                              Rte 8
                                        Toyama
Coastal toll road   Rte 8

              Rte 359
Tsubata   Tonami
Kanazawa   Johana

              To Shirakawago

                   To Takayama
                   Gifu

visit, and because the land is relatively level all around the peninsula, it is one of the best areas of Japan to explore by bicycle. Cyclists and other independent travellers should have detailed maps to enable them to follow little roads closer to the coast. The preferred direction of travel is clockwise, the Kanazawa area being a good starting point, so the sun will be to your left or behind you through the most scenic parts.

Noto Kongo

About 15 minutes north of Myojiji, a small roads turns off Route 249 to Fukuura and the shore. Between Fukuura and Togi is a 14-km stretch of coast known as Noto-Kongo, noted for its scenic formations of eroded rock. Most memorable are Gammon, a grotto 54 metres deep and 15 metres wide, and Taka-no-su (Hawk's Nest), a rock that rises 27 metres and projects far over the sea.

Buses run along this coast, leaving from Hakui (50 minutes away), or Sammyo (30 minutes). Boat cruises lasting about 20 minutes leave from Fukuura.

Seki-no-hana

North of Togi, a small road turns off Route 249 and runs to and along the coast, rejoining the main road farther along. The scenery is attractive most of the way, especially around Seki-no-hana. This road is part of the regular tourist route between Togi and Monzen.

Monzen Near Monzen is Sojiji temple. Strangely located in this remote area, it was the national headquarters of the Soto sect of Zen Buddhism (founded in 1321) until 1818 when most of the buildings were destroyed in a fire. After that, the headquarters were moved to Sojiji in Yokohama. The present buildings are attractive, especially in summer when the cicadas are chirring loudly.

Sojiji and Monzen are accessible by bus from Anamizu (on the *uchi* coast) as well as being on the regular bus run around the

soto coast. The temple is a five-minute walk from Monzen bus station.

Sojiji is a functioning Zen temple and visitors may obtain accommodation and participate in meditation. It is best to make reservations in advance (tel (07684) 2-0005) or by writing to: Sojiji, Monzen-machi, Fugeshi-gun, Ishikawa-ken. It is not possible to obtain accommodation on the spot. Costs range from Y3500 to Y5000.

Monzen to Wajima

Inveterate sea-coast buffs armed with a sufficiently detailed map can find roads along parts of the coast between Monzen and Wajima, but the area isn't generally famous for scenery. Your own transport would be useful, though there are buses along the main roads. There is a 5½-km hiking trail along the coast (no road, so it is still quite remote) between Minazuki and Kami-Ozawa. The former can be reached by bus from Monzen; the latter from Wajima.

Wajima

This small city on the northern coast is noted for its large-scale production of good quality lacquerware (on sale everywhere in town). About 25% of Wajima's population is engaged in some aspect of the craft.

There are several places were you can see the process of lacquerware making. In the area near the harbour, countless little shops turn out chopsticks with interesting patterns, the result of repeated dipping.

The best single demonstration of the whole process can be seen at the main store of Inuchu (daily except Sunday). It can involve 18 or more steps, from forming the wood to the addition of layer after layer of lacquer, interspersed with careful polishing to make the finished product perfectly smooth. Good lacquerware is a true work of art and requires more demanding detail than the better-known craft of pottery. Somewhat directed to the tour-bus trade, but also good, is Wajima

Shikki Kaikan (which also has a small museum of lacquerware on the second floor). Wajimaya store also has demonstrations.

Omatsuri-kan In the grounds of Sumiyoshi-jinja shrine is this interesting museum containing local folk art and objects related to the major Wajima festivals.

Kiriko-kaikan This is an exhibition of floats used in festivals around the peninsula.

Sodegahama Sodegahama is a pleasant beach near Wajima.

Markets Every day (except the 10th and 25th of the month) there is both a morning market (*asa-ichi*) and an evening market (*yu-ichi*). The former is from 8 am to midday at Honcho-dori of Kawai-cho, the latter on the grounds of Sumiyoshi-jinja shrine from 4 to 7 pm. Goods sold include handicrafts and other tourist items as well as food.

Divers In the winter months, women divers operate off the coast looking for shellfish and edible seaweed. (In the warmer weather they migrate to nearby Hegura Island.) The days are long gone when the women dived wearing only a loincloth, so the photos of lovely, shapely, topless, smiling divers are fakes. The true *ama* (divers) are older, stocky and bashful.

Festivals There are annual festivals on 4-5 April and 23-25 August.

Places to Stay Wajima is an extremely popular destination but there is generally no shortage of accommodation, except in July-August. In addition to youth hostels, there is a large number of *minshuku*. Near Sodegahama beach there is a Kokumin-shukusha.

Getting There & Away Wajima is the terminus for the JR line from Kanazawa and further south (Maibara). It is also

served by the bus service that circles the peninsula.

Wajima to Sosogi
About 10 km inland on the road to Anamizu is a very picturesque village of farmhouses built on the hills surrounding the rice fields. From all reports it is worth going out of the way to see.

Continuing along the coast east toward Sosogi, the coastline is very pretty. There are two places you should especially look out for. One is Senkaida ('1000 terraces'), a suitably poetic description for a broad ravine in which paddies have been built in terraces from sea level high up the side of the tall hill. Just before harvest time (late August – early September) is the most colourful of all times to see this as the rice then takes on a rich green-gold hue. (The same is true of all rice fields of course but few are as beautifully situated as Senkaida.)

A little farther on is a fine view of the kind that is comparatively rare in Japan these days as modernisation continues to take over. Terraced rice fields drop down to the sea, surrounding a small Shinto shrine. Its *torii* gate stands before the tiny building, and behind the shrine is a small, thick grove of trees.

Sosogi
At this town, a road branches inland from Route 249 toward Ushitsu. About 400 metres from the junction stand two of the largest traditional farmhouses in Japan. They are worth a visit both for their historic value and their design. Both are thatched-roof buildings of the highest quality materials and traditional Japanese carpentry.

One of the highest ranking court families (the Tokikuni) has lived in this area since the forces of the Taira clan (also called Heike) were defeated by the Genji (Minamoto) in the battle for control of Japan at Dan-no-ura in 1185.

The Taira fled to this area and the nearby inland mountain regions of the

Sho-kawa river to escape extermination. Their descendants live in the Shirakawa-go/Gokayama area.

Tokikuni Houses The house closer to Sosogi (they are a five-minute walk apart) is Shimo-Tokikuni-ke (lower Tokikuni house); it is at least 300 years old. Inside its spacious interior are many relics of the past. Foreign visitors are given a recorder with a taped explanation of the house, room by room.

The nearby Kami-Tokikuni-ke (upper Tokikuni house) is newer, having been built in the last century to replace the first house which had become unusable. It shows few signs of age; the finest materials and workmanship were employed in its construction over a period of 28 years. It is intriguing to find such a fine building and garden in such an out-of-the-way place but it was built to suit a person of very high rank, a descendant of the Kyoto nobility.

Visitors are given a notebook with a handwritten explanation of the house's history and a description of the high points and exhibits, room by room. A story in the notes tells how one of the rooms was reserved for receiving guests only of Daina-gon rank or higher, which was above that of the local governor and many court officials, so these people were not allowed to enter.

On one occasion it was necessary to receive a person of lesser rank but before he was allowed in, the golden carving of a swallow-tailed butterfly (symbol of the Heike, and indicating the resident's rank) had to be covered.

Buses of Hokuriku Railway run from Wajima station to Kami-Tokikuni-ke bus stop in 45 minutes, and from Suzu station (further east) in one hour.

Museums There are two other museums in Sosogi. Wajima Minzoku Shiryokan, which houses local folk art and items of daily use, is between the Tokikuni houses. The other is Noto Shuko-kan and is a more general art museum with no particular relation to the Noto area. It is southeast of Sosogi and separate from the other attractions.

Places to Stay There are several *minshuku* and some hotels near the two old houses. There are, in fact, *minshuku* in virtually every town and hamlet along the coast.

Around the Coast to Takaoka

The coast east of Sosogi is pleasantly scenic with outcroppings of eroded rock at intervals. Route 249 doesn't go out to the tip of the peninsula but a good road does lead out to Cape Rokugo (Rokugo Misaki) near the town of Noroshi.

An 11-km hiking trail (Misaki Nature Trail) begins at Takaya and continues through Kinoura to Noroshi. At Noroshi, Cape Rokugo and its lighthouse can be reached in 10 minutes on foot.

South of Noroshi, the *uchi* or inner coast becomes much more placid and peaceful. While there are many pretty views, there are not the outstanding scenic areas found along the outer coast.

Suzu The main attraction of this hot-spring and port town is a large house (Kiheidon) which serves as a museum for local artefacts.

Koiji There is a nice white beach here, 10 minutes walk from Koiji station or six minutes by bus from Iwatsunami station.

Tsukumo The name means '99 indentations' and indicates the scenic attraction of this bay. It can be seen from any of the sightseeing boats that leave from Ogi (Noto Ogi station).

Ushitsu Ushitsu's Toshimayama Park affords an excellent view of the bay. The park, which incorporates two old houses that act as local museums, is 10 minutes by bus from Ushitsu station. The town's annual festival is on 7-8 July.

Noto-shima Island Little fishing villages

and outdoor activities (swimming, hiking and camping) are the main attractions of this island. Inquire locally if boat service is still available. There is a festival on the island on 31 July.

Wakura-onsen This is a typical, rather expensive, hot-spring resort of hotels and *ryokan*.

Anamizu This town is also of little interest but it has a festival on 22-23 July.

Nanao to Hakui Along Route 159 between Nanao and Hakui there are many beautiful old wooden houses, particularly between Nanao and Kue.

Fukui-ken

FUKUI

The city of Fukui, while of little intrinsic interest, can be used as a base for visiting several nearby attractions.

Eiheiji Temple

Beautifully located at the foot of a mountain amongst ancient trees, Eiheiji is one of the most famous temples of Japan. As well as being a large, functioning Zen temple with shaven-headed monks silently meditating, the natural beauty of the setting makes it well worth a visit.

Founded in 1244, it is one of two head temples of the Soto sect of Zen Buddhism (the other is Sojiji in Yokohama, near Tokyo).

Set on 33 square km, the 70 or so temple buildings spread up the hillside and are surrounded by trees up to 600 years old. A pamphlet in English is given at the entrance and gives a good description of the main buildings.

The temple authorities allow foreign visitors to stay at the temple and participate in Zen meditation. (Refer to the section on Zen meditation in the Facts

for the Visitor chapter.) At Eiheiji, visitors are expected to follow the same discipline as Japanese participants, starting with meditation at 3.30 am. Arrangements should be made in advance by writing to: Sanzenkei, Eiheiji, Eiheiji-cho, Yoshida-gun, Fukui-ken.

The temple (less than 20 km southeast of Fukui) is easily reached by Keifuku Dentetsu railway or by bus. The train is most easily caught from the east side of Fukui station (behind the building). A bike path between Fukui and Eiheiji runs mostly along scenic river banks.

Kuzuryu & Managawa Gorges

Both of these gorges, noted for their scenery, are in the vicinity of Ono. The former is close to Echizen-Shimoyama station (JR) and it is likely that buses run to the latter from Ono station (JR). Ono is on the road to Shirotori, the junction for going north to Shirakawa-go.

IMADATE

Imadate is a town noted for paper-making – not machine-made but the traditional *washi* hand-made paper. There are about 120 establishments making paper in the district (which is not far from Fukui) and about half of these are in the village of Otaki.

The process of paper making is illustrated at Washi-no-Sato-Kaikan (open daily). Paper and paper products are on display and for sale.

Paper making by traditional methods is a cottage industry carried out by many families. To see one of these workshops (*kojo*), contact the Washi Kumiai (Papermakers' Cooperative) which will then arrange a visit. The Kumiai also sells paper of the area. These hand-made papers are not cheap but, as they require a large amount of hand labour, the asking price is justified.

Getting There & Away

Access is from Takefu (18 km south of Fukui by JR) by a local line, the Nan-etsu-

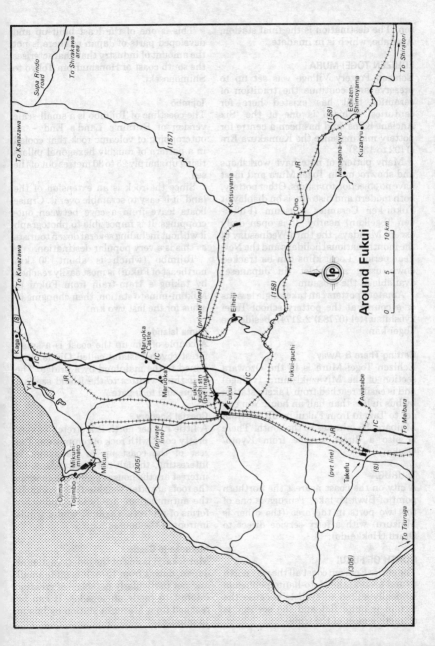

Around Fukui

sen. The destination is the final station, Awatabe, which is in Imadate.

ECHIZEN TOGEI MURA

Echizen Pottery Village was set up to preserve and continue the tradition of ceramics that has existed here for centuries. Echizen is one of the 'Six Ancient Kilns' and has been a centre for pottery making since the Kamakura Era (1192 to 1333).

Many potters of note have workshops and showrooms in Togei Mura and most have no objection to visitors. Other pottery, both modern and historic, is on display at Fukui-ken Ceramics Museum (Fukui-ken Togeikan) nearby. It is open daily except Mondays, the third Wednesday of the month, national holidays and the New Year period. Local kilns can be tracked down using a booklet (in Japanese) available at the museum.

Amateur potters can take single lessons or a course at the pottery school Togei kyoshitsu (tel (07783) 2-2174), beside the Togei-kan.

Getting There & Away

Echizen Togei Mura is in the Ozowara section of the Miyazaki-mura (village) and is easily reached from Takefu station by bus in less than half an hour. You can get to Takefu from Fukui by JR, or from Maibara, 55 minutes to the south. There is also a direct service from Kyoto/Osaka.

TSURUGA

A city on the coast nearest the northern point of Biwa-ko lake, Tsuruga is one of the two ports in the area (the other is Maizuru) with a ferry service direct to Otaru (Hokkaido).

NORTH OF FUKUI

The entire Echizen coast all the way north to and around the Noto-hanto peninsula is ideally suited to cyclists because the terrain is quite flat and the scenery is attractive most of the time.

This is one of the least built-up and developed parts of Japan so there is not the amount of industry that characterises the south coast of Honshu from Tokyo to Shimonoseki.

Tojimbo

The coastline of Tojimbo is a small-scale version of Britain's Land's End – an outcropping of volcanic rock that cooled in a pattern of roughly hexagonal pillars rising up sharply 25 to 30 metres out of the sea.

Since the rock is an extension of the land, it is easy to scramble over it. Cruise boats leave from a cove between outcroppings. It is impossible to photograph it without including several dozen tourists as this is a very popular destination.

Tojimbo (which is about 30 km northeast of Fukui) is most easily reached by taking a tram-train from Fukui to Mikuni-minato station, then changing to a bus for the last two km.

Ojima Island

A couple of km up the coast is a small forest-covered island called Ojima. It is joined to the mainland by a bridge. The first thing visitors to the island see is a shrine and *torii* gate.

Coastal Scenery

A little further north is a stretch of very pretty coast with rock outcroppings. The rest of the coast up to Kanazawa is interesting, though not outstanding. Of interest are the houses facing the coast as the roofs are often weighted with rocks. In the autumn there are boards and other forms of protection against winter winds in front of the houses.

Maruoka-jo Castle

Maruoka-jo is one of the oldest castles in Japan, dating from 1575. It is quite small and not particularly notable – of greatest interest to castle aficionados. It can be reached from Maruoka station by bus in 15 minutes.

Places to Stay

Of the hostels in the Fukui area, I found *Youth Hostel No 3404* (in Fukui) to be rather institutional. More pleasant, though some distance out of town, is *Gankeiji Youth Hostel*, which is a large functioning neighbourhood temple near Kaga. The temple's history goes back several hundred years (though the present buildings are comparatively recent), and the house-mother is exceptionally kind and pleasant.

There are some *minshuku* right on the northern coast overlooking the water which would probably be a good place to spend the night.

Kinki District

The Kinki district, one of the traditional divisions of Japan, traditionally comprises the region from around Biwa-ko lake west through Hyogo-ken (Himeji), and from the north of Biwa-ko lake to the bottom of the Kii-hanto peninsula. However, this chapter stretches the definition somewhat in order to describe as a lump all the places of interest that can be reached easily while in the area. For that reason it also includes the region around Nagoya, including the nearby areas to the north (Gifu and Inuyama).

This region, together with eastern Kyushu, is the part of Japan longest settled by the present-day Japanese. The original inhabitants of Japan, about whom little is known, were swamped by later arrivals who settled first in Kyushu, then established a series of military outposts along the south coast up to the Tokyo area.

The origin of the name Kinki is lost but the characters of the name mean 'near the moat', possibly related to the mysterious remains in mountains in the Nara region of a defensive wall more than 60 km in circumference.

Within the Kinki region are many of the prime attractions of Japan: Kyoto, the imperial capital for nearly 1000 years and a repository of temples, palaces and gardens as well as historic arts and crafts;

Nara, the capital before Kyoto, with even more ancient temples and other remains from the past; Toba, with its cultured-pearl industry and nearby coastal scenery; Himeji and Hikone with historic and picturesque castles; and many other historic and natural attractions.

For detailed information on travelling in the Kinki district, see the Getting Around section at the end of this chapter.

Southern Gifu-ken

The attractions of Gifu-ken can be divided into two general groups. The first are found in several cities in the south that have always been in the mainstream of Japanese life. Some attractions of bordering prefectures are also included here, either because access is easier from Gifu-ken, or because there are no neighbouring attractions that would otherwise draw you to that area.

The other attractions are found in a number of locations in the northern mountain highlands where isolation has preserved many traces of 'old' Japan, and these are covered in the Central Honshu chapter.

GIFU
The city of Gifu is most famous among foreign travellers for *ukai* (catching fish by the use of trained cormorants), paper lanterns and paper umbrellas.

Gifu is beside the large Nagara River, at the northern edge of a large rice-growing plain. It is a typical commercial city with few places of historic interest as the city was flattened by an earthquake in 1891 and by bombs during WW II. The one exception is Shohoji temple.

Kinki District

0   20   40 km

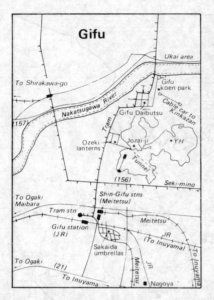

Gifu

Ukai area

To Shirakawa-go

Gifu koen park

Nakatsugawa River

Gifu Daibutsu

Cable car to Kinkazan

(157)

Tram

Ozeki lanterns

Jozai-ji

•YH

Tunnel

(156)

Seki-mino

To Ogaki Maibara

Shin-Gifu stns (Meitetsu)

Tram stn

Meitetsu

Gifu station (JR)

JR (To Inuyama)

To Inuyama

Sakaida umbrellas

To Ogaki (21)

Meitetsu

JR

To Inuyama

Nagoya

Shohoji Temple

A very unusual Daibutsu (statue of Buddha) is housed in the large orange-and-white building visible from the road. The statue is made of 1000 kg of paper *sutras* (prayers) pasted to a bamboo frame, which was then covered with clay and stucco, lacquered and gilded.

The hall is very dim and the artistry not the ultimate but it is interesting and worth a look. The statue is 13.7 metres tall and one ear (elongated very much as a symbol of wisdom) is over two metres long. It was finished in 1747 after 38 years of work and was constructed to console people who had lost relatives in earthquakes and famines.

Jozai-ji Temple

The original temple dates from 1450 but the present one (not far from Gifu Youth Hostel) is quite recent. Visitors should regard the large structure simply as a neighbourhood temple and can watch daily life go on around it. It is popular as a playground for toddlers and their ever-watchful mothers.

Kinkazan

The backdrop to Gifu is Kinkazan (Silver Mountain). On it are the Gifu Youth Hostel and a concrete reproduction of the castle that stood at the peak until the earthquake of 1891. The new castle (1956) houses a small prefectural museum. Exercise freaks can walk up from the city or from the hostel; the lazy can take the cable-car ('ropeway') from Gifu-koen park.

The castle and mountain, however, are not attractions of great merit. The castle looks very pretty (and *very* high up) at night when it is floodlit. It can be seen clearly from the *ukai* fishing area.

Ukai

From 11 May to 15 October there are nightly displays on the Nagara River (just above Nagara-bashi bridge) of the ancient practice of using trained cormorants to catch fish. The birds are kept on a leash and a ring around their neck prevents them from swallowing any but the smallest fish. The action takes place at night when the *ayu* (river smelt or sweetfish) can be attracted to the surface by torches blazing over the bow of each boat.

One *usho*, (fisherman) in each boat, dressed in mediaeval grass-skirted costume, controls several birds, pulling in each one as it makes a catch, then taking the fish and putting the bird back in the water for another dive.

A large number of people can see the spectacle at one time as there are more than 130 covered boats of different sizes (capacity of 10 to 30 people). Tourists usually go out an hour or two before the fishing starts and dine (meals by prior arrangement), drink, sing and set off fireworks. It becomes a grand party and probably more than a few revellers are unable to focus by the time the boats and birds appear. The sightseeing boats are

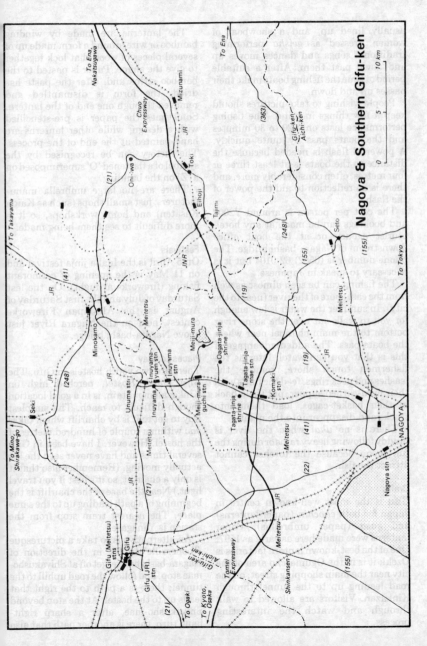

Nagoya & Southern Gifu-ken

usually lined up, and a showboat of women dressed as *geisha* performing traditional songs and dances moves up and down past them. After a suitable period of time the fishing boats make their passes up and down.

People wishing to take pictures should keep a few things in mind. The fishing performance lasts only 20 to 30 minutes and the boats pass by quite quickly. A powerful flash is needed because the distance to the boats is at least three or four metres, often considerably more, and there is no reflection to aid the power of the flash.

The cost per person is around Y2000 and bookings can be made at any hotel, tourist agency or at the boat office downstream of Nagara-bashi bridge. The phone number is (0582) 62-0104 but it is necessary to speak in Japanese.

The fishing can be seen almost as well from the east shore of the river (near to the city). In summer the water is low enough for you to walk out over the stone river bottom to the main channel near where the boats pass. The added advantage of this is that you can watch later as the fishermen touch shore, remove the leashes and neck rings, feed the birds with their hard-earned supper, put them back in their basket-cages, load them into trucks and disappear into the night.

There is no *ukai* when the river is muddy following heavy rains or during the full moon because the torches cannot attract the fish.

Crafts

Gifu is the most well-known centre in Japan for both *chochin* (paper lanterns) and *kasa* (paper umbrellas). Paper lanterns were made here as early as 1597. One of the best-known lantern factories is Ozeki; it is in the Oguma-cho area of the city near the main shopping street, on the road leading up to the tunnel through Kinkazan. Visitors are allowed to walk through and watch the interesting process.

The lanterns are made by winding bamboo or wire around a form made up of several pieces of wood that lock together to give the shape. Paper is pasted to the bamboo strips and, after the paste has dried, the form is dismantled and removed through one end of the lantern. Sometimes the paper is pre-stencilled with a design, while other lanterns are hand-painted at the end of the process. The factory can be recognised by the symbol of a flattened 'O' superimposed on a 'Z' on the building.

There are no large umbrella manufacturers, just small shops (such as Kaida Kasaten) and home workshops, so it is more difficult to see them being made.

Festivals

On 5 April is the Inaba jinja festival and on 11 May is the opening of cormorant fishing (fireworks at night). On the last Saturday of July and the first Saturday of August is the All-Japan Fireworks contest, held on the Nagara River just above Nagara-bashi bridge.

Places to Stay

There are two youth hostels in Gifu. The *Gifu Youth Hostel*, perched high on Kinkazan mountain, is in a good location though difficult to reach. The simplest way to get to it is by chairlift which takes you within a couple of hundred metres of the hostel. However, I have been in Gifu several times and have never seen the lift actually moving. (Remember also that it is only a chairlift, so it's best if you travel light.) Near the base of the chairlift is the beginning of a path leading up to the same place. The nearest tram stop from the station is Yanagase.

An alternative is to take a picturesque 'Toonerville' trolley in the direction of Nagara-bashi bridge, get off at Shiyakusho-mae stop, and follow the road uphill to the tunnel; there is a path to the right that leads up to the hostel. At the stop beyond Shiyakusho-mae, after a sharp right-hand turn, there is another path that also

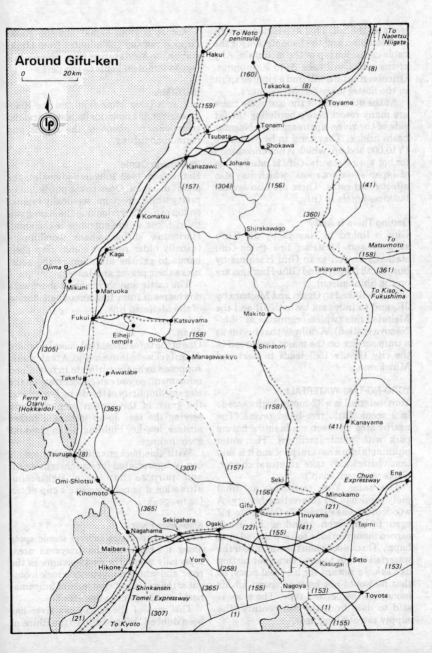

Around Gifu-ken

0   20km

To Noto
peninsula

To Naoetsu
Niigata

Hakui
(160)

Takaoka   (8)

Toyama

(159)   Tonami

Tsubata

Shokawa

Kanazawa   Johana   (156)

(157)   (304)   (360)

Komatsu

Shirakawago

To Matsumoto

Kaga   (158)

Ojima   Takayama   (361)

Mikuni   Maruoka   To Kiso,
Fukushima

Fukui   Katsuyama   Makito

Eiheji
temple   Ono   (158)   Shiratori

Managawa-kyo   (158)

Takefu   Awatabe   Kanayama

(305)   (8)

(365)   (41)

Ferry to
Otaru
(Hokkaido)

Seki   Chuo
Expressway   Ena

Tsuruga   (8)   (303)   (157)

Omi-Shiotsu   (156)   Minokamo

Kinomoto   Gifu   Inuyama   (21)   Tajimi

(365)   Sekigahara   Ogaki   (22)   (41)

Nagahama   (155)   Kasugai   Seto   (153)

Maibara   Yoro   (258)   Nagoya

Hikone   (365)   (155)   Toyota

Shinkansen
Tomei Expressway   (153)

(21)   (307)   (1)   (155)

To Kyoto

leads up the hill. This stop is close to both the Daibutsu and the base station for the cable car to the top of the mountain. Any of the walks will take 20 to 30 minutes. Orienteering fans will find a kindred spirit in the hostel manager, Mr Nomura.

At the other end of the cost scale there are many resort hotels bordering the far side of the river, upstream from Nagara-bashi bridge. They tend to be expensive (Y10,000 and up) which is not uncommon for hot-spring resorts. Gifu is rated as one of Japan's 'sex hot spots', which may also affect room rates. There are also several business hotels in Gifu.

Getting There & Away
Gifu is linked to Nagoya by JR (Gifu station) and Meitetsu line (Shin-Gifu station), as well as to Gifu-Hashima by bus. (Both Nagoya and Gifu-Hashima are on the Shinkansen).

Gifu is linked to Ogaki and Maibara by JR, and to Inuyama by both JR and the Meitetsu line (which originates at Shin-Nagoya station). A railway that begins as a tram service on the major cross-road in the city (Route 156) leads to Seki and Minokamo.

YORO-NO-TAKI WATERFALL
Yoro waterfall is a 32-metre-high cascade in a scenic little tree-lined ravine. The nearby area has been made into a nature park with picnic facilities. The water plummets into a natural pool and it is said that visitors may take a natural shower. (Take your own soap.)

The name Yoro translates as 'filial piety' and has an interesting history. A woodcutter was extremely faithful to his aged father, even spending his hard-earned money on *sake* to keep the old man happy. On one occasion the water near the waterfall is said to have come out tasting like *sake*, a reward for his filial piety, so that he would not have to spend all his money on the bottled type. The story is said to date from the 8th century (the supply ran out long ago).

Access is from Ogaki via the Kinki Nippon railway (25 minutes from Ogaki station) to Yoro station from where a bus (seven minutes) leads to the park.

INUYAMA
Inuyama (Dog Mountain), on the Kiso-gawa river, is known for its historic castle, river scenery, shooting the rapids and cormorant fishing.

Inuyama-jo Castle
Dating from 1440, Inuyama-jo castle is the oldest in Japan. Open to the public, it is a pretty white structure, scenically located on top of a cliff overlooking the Kiso-gawa river. Close to the entrance is the small Haritsuna shrine where worshippers (usually older people) come, clap their hands to get the attention of the gods, make their prayer and leave.

The castle and shrine are a short walk downstream from Inuyama-yuen station of the Meitetsu line.

Jo-an
One of the three finest teahouses in Japan, Jo-an is close to Inuyama-jo. A teahouse is supposed to be the ultimate in restrained refinement, so you can concentrate on the elegant simplicity of the utensils used and the grace of the person preparing and serving the tea. Jo-an is thus a rather austere, low-key building, set in pleasant surroundings.

With this background information, it can be appreciated for its inherent worth and purpose but as a sightseeing attraction it is not everyone's cup of tea (so to speak).

Kiso-gawa River
Kiso-gawa river has several scenic spots along its banks in the Inuyama area, especially where the castle overlooks the river and where a mysterious rock looms out of the water just upstream of Inuyama-bashi and Inuyama-yuen station.

This area of the Kiso-gawa river has been dubbed 'Nihon Rhine' (the Rhine of

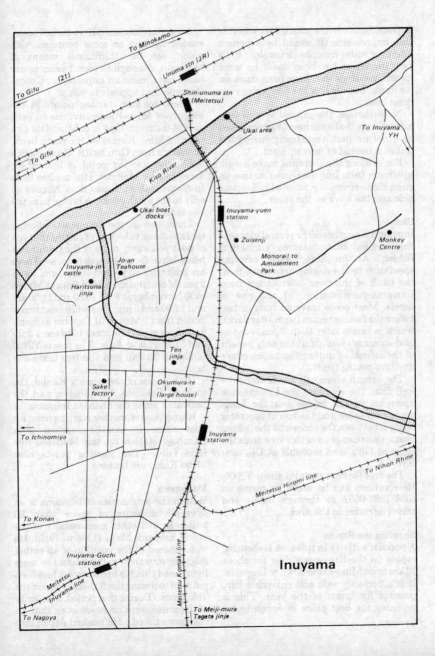

Inuyama

Japan), but only the strange rock fulfills this impression. (It would be a perfect home for water nymphs or Lorelei.) It's a pity the effect has been spoilt by some garish buildings that have been stuck on its flank, but such is the way things are done here.

Nevertheless, the general area is very attractive as the banks have been preserved as a nature park thus being spared the dubious benefit of development.

Rocks along the shoreline make a walk upstream from Inuyama-yuen station an enjoyable excursion – forested hill on one side and the river on the other.

Ukai

Inuyama is another of the several places in this region that features cormorant fishing. At Inuyama, boats carrying spectators to the fishing area leave from the bank of the river downstream from Inuyama-yuen station, at the row of hotels. Most boats leave an hour or two before the fishing begins (soon after dark), which is rarely later than 7 pm, even in mid-summer (just about the only benefit of the refusal of authorities to introduce daylight saving time).

The overall scene can be viewed quite well from the shore on the Unuma side upstream of the bridge but the boats anchor off shore and the row of spectator boats is between the shore and the fishing boats. (You can get a better view from the shore at Gifu, and probably at Uji, near Kyoto.)

The cost for boat rental is about Y2000. Reservations can be made by phone on (0568) 61-0057 or through hotels and travel agencies in the area.

Shooting the Rapids

A popular activity in this area is shooting rapids on the Kiso-gawa river for about 13 km from Mino-kamo down to Inuyama. It is a perfectly safe and enjoyable trip, possible for much of the year. This is probably the best place in Japan to try it.

Long, flat-bottomed Kiso-kudari boats, guided by two or more boatmen with poles, are the traditional means of transport although in recent years power boats have made an appearance. Choose the type that appeals to you.

There are two starting points in the vicinity of Mino-Kamo city, one on each side of the river. One is at Mino-Ota city (part of Mino-Kamo) on the north bank, accessible from Gifu by JR. On the south bank, the starting point is Imawatari, accessible by Meitetsu Hirome line from Inuyama station. Buses from Nagoya go only to the south docks. A bridge joins the two sides.

There are several companies offering tours so check to be sure of getting the type of boat you want; more of the traditional boats leave from the south docks. There are boat trips all year at 10 am, and 1 and 2 pm. More trips are added from 15 March to 30 November at 9.30, 10.30 and 11.30 am and 12.30 and 3 pm. One additional trip is added from 1 May to 31 October at 9 am, and there is yet one more between 1 July and 31 August at 4 pm. The fare is Y2750 (children Y1350) and the trip takes one hour.

High points of the trip are Kaniai, the rocks at Sekiheki, Rhine-yuen, and the park area along the shore at Inuyama.

Rhine-yuen is another starting point for boat rides. It can be reached from Sakahogi station on the Meitetsu line from Gifu. (The starting points near Mino-Kamo are better.)

Meiji-mura

Within the boundaries of Inuyama is an open-air museum of more than 50 buildings and other memorabilia of the era of Emperor Meiji (1868 to 1910). He was restored to the position of an actual reigning monarch, rather than the mere figurehead that his predecessors had been reduced to during the 300-odd years of the Tokugawa. (During that period, a majority of Japanese were unaware even that an emperor existed.) He pushed Japan into the modern age after three centuries of almost total isolation from the rest of the world.

The innovations of Emperor Meiji's rule ran the gamut of every aspect of Japanese life and, within 10 years of his taking power, there was a railroad operating in Japan – quite an advance on horses and hand-carried palanquins.

This period is called the 'Meiji Restoration', though 'Meiji Revolution' would be more accurate, both for the many changes in Japanese life during that time, and the many military battles required to secure his rule.

To most westerners, the items in the museum have symbolic rather than inherent interest. Most of the buildings, for example, are 19th-century western style and rather commonplace in appearance, though to the Japanese they are somewhat exotic.

Depending on the starting point, Meiji-mura can easily be reached from Inuyama or Nagoya. From Inuyama, the bus takes 20 minutes and costs Y300. There are four per hour from 9.40 am until late in the afternoon. From Nagoya, the bus from Meitetsu bus centre (near Nagoya station) takes one hour and costs Y1030. There are several in the morning but the last one leaves at 1 pm.

Places to Stay

There are many hotels and *ryokan* in Inuyama, including a number just downstream of Inuyama-yuen station.

The *Youth Hostel* is about 800 metres upstream of this station and a further 400 metres uphill. It is quite pleasant (bar the noisy PA system) and a bargain – at Y600 it's one of the cheapest youth hostels in Japan.

Getting There & Away

Meitetsu line trains run to Inuyama from both Gifu and Nagoya. From the Nagoya area, the Inuyama line runs from Meitetsu station (adjacent to the JR station) and the Komaki line runs from

Kami-Ida station in the northeast of the city.

Inuyama station is near the edge of the city; the next stop, Inuyama-yuen, is the station closest to Inuyama-jo castle. The Inuyama and Kami-Iida lines join at Inuyama. Shin-Unuma is the terminus for trains from Nagoya and from Gifu.

The name of the JR station for Inuyama is Unuma; it is on the line from Gifu to Takayama and Toyama. Inuyama-bashi, the bridge between the main part of the city and the Unuma railway stations, is the only place where I have seen a train caught in a traffic jam; both cars and trains use the same bridge.

FERTILITY SHRINES

The second and third stations out of Inuyama along the Komaki line toward Nagoya (don't take an express!) are near two shrines devoted to fertility, both for crops in this rich rice-growing valley, and for humans. There are shrines of this sort scattered around Japan but these are among the best known and the most accessible in the country.

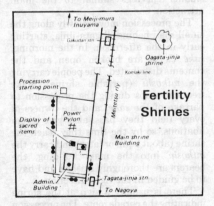

Oagata-jinja Shrine

This is the female shrine and it houses several natural phenomena, such as a cleft rock that resembles the female genitalia. It is a popular place of veneration for women about to marry and those who want children.

The shrine is reached from Oagata station by turning right when leaving the station and walking across the tracks and up the road for about 15 minutes toward the forested hills.

Tagata-jinja Shrine

This is the male shrine. In the small building to the left of the main building is a quite amazing collection of phallus carvings ranging in size from a few cm to about two metres – all donated by grateful parents. The shrine is close to Tagata-jinja-mae station, the next after Oagata. Souvenirs are on sale at both shrines.

Shrine Festivals

Tagata-jinja has a very interesting festival each year on 15 March. A carved wooden phallus, about three metres long, is carried in happy procession from another shrine about one km away, accompanied by Tengu (a Shinto deity with a very long nose, also of phallic significance) and several women carrying smaller carvings similar to the main attraction.

The procession moves slowly along the small road behind Tagata-jinja, starting early in the afternoon. In the morning, *sake* casks are broken open and the contents distributed. The people carrying the *mikoshi* (portable shrine) make frequent stops during the procession to partake of the *sake*, and the owners of every field they pass also give them libations, so by the time they reach the shrine (about 3 pm or later) and carry the *mikoshi* into the main building, the bearers are thoroughly sloshed and have to be guided in the right direction.

There is usually a sign at the shrine indicating the parade route. The procession used to pass along the main road but has now been relegated to the back road for safety and better control, so its format will likely remain unchanged unless the puritanism of the police increases.

Oagata-jinja has a festival on the first weekend after 15 March. The procession features a number of pretty young women (brides-to-be?) on decorated floats, as well as the shrine's *mikoshi*, a discreetly covered tree-root that serves as a female symbol. If you are interested in this festival it might be possible to get more information from the TIC in Tokyo or Kyoto.

MIZUNAMI

Palaeontologists passing through this town might find the Fossils Museum of interest.

TAJIMI

About 80% of the porcelain for the Japanese market, and more than half of the porcelain for export, is produced in Tajimi's pottery plants. Those interested in pottery could probably arrange to visit one of the 1300 or so plants.

ONI-IWA (OGRE ROCK)

Travellers between Toki and Mino-Kamo might wish to stop to look at this interesting gigantic granite formation rising from the edge of the river near Oni-iwa onsen (hot-spring resort).

SEKI

The small city of Seki has been known for centuries as the centre of production for many of the finest swords in Japan. To this day there are still many people in the city who make their living solely from this craft; this includes 12 swordsmiths plus polishers and other assistants.

Seki Swordsmiths

The Japanese sword is the finest weapon of its kind ever created anywhere in the world; it is the ultimate expression of the swordsmith's art. It is unfortunate that their *raison d'être* is killing, as they could truly be described as 'jewels in steel'.

When making a sword, a balance must be struck between hardness (for cutting) and resilience (so that it doesn't snap in service). To accomplish these conflicting goals, Japanese swordsmiths use two processes together; they combine high carbon steel (hard) and low carbon steel (soft) in the same blade, and the tempering (heating and cooling the steel quickly to bring it to the correct degree of hardness) is varied over the width of the blade so that the back remains soft while the cutting edge is hard. This process takes a long time.

A swordsmith is permitted by law to make only two swords per month, though it is not likely he could make more swords of quality in much less time than this anyway.

It is generally very difficult to see the process of making swords, for the smiths are busy and do not relish a continual stream of sightseers. Fortunately, however, demonstrations (open to the public) are given six times a year at Seki city, on the first Saturday of each of the odd-numbered months.

The demonstrations are given in a corner of the grounds of Kasuga-jinja shrine, where a workshop has been set up duplicating the equipment found in a traditional smithy. Kasuga shrine is straight down the street leading from the town hall.

If you are seriously interested in sword making and are not in Seki at demonstration time, there is a city official (Mr Shigeru Matsui) who speaks a little English and *might* be able to arrange an introduction to a practising swordsmith. (Modern smithies, however, are equipped with power-operated machinery, unlike the demonstration smithy.) Mr Matsui's phone number is (05752) 2-3131; it might be advisable to have a Japanese-speaking friend make the call.

At the Kasuga-jinja demonstration, a master dressed in traditional costume is accompanied by several apprentices (also in costume). The first striking is the most spectacular. The spongy mass of steel, after being heated in the fire by the master smith, is mashed into a cohesive blob by the hammer blows of the apprentices, a process which sends out a spray of sparks in all directions.

The process of heating and beating is repeated a couple of times until the metal has become a small bar about 60 x 200 mm and 20 mm thick. Water is poured onto the anvil and the red-hot bar is placed on it when struck; the water prevents the metal from oxidising. This slab is scored with a chisel and then folded back on itself.

Now follows the most important stage. The smith rolls the glowing metal block in a small pile of black, carbonised rice husks. When the metal is completely smothered in black, he pours a brown liquid over both sides and returns the metal to the fire. The liquid is a type of clay and the coating protects the carbon from burning in the fire. When the metal reaches red-hot temperatures again inside its 'blanket', the carbon is actually absorbed into the surface of the metal.

The rest of the process is a repetition of the same procedure. The number of times it is repeated determines the carbon content of the finished steel, and thus its potential hardness. For the hardest steel, to be used for the edge of the blade, the metal is folded 20 to 25 times. The result of this folding is an incredible number of layers of alternating carbonised (hard) and pure (soft) steel. After 20 folds there will be more than a million layers; after 25, more than 33 million! Softer steel for the inner structure of the blade will be doubled only 10 to 12 times and steel for the side plates (and back, if one is used) might be folded 12 to 15 times. The layered structure imparts a measure of resilience and flexibility that a solid blade would not have.

During the demonstration (from 10 am to 4 pm) there is time to make only a couple of the required pieces of steel. When all the pieces are available, they are forged together into a single mass, which is then beaten out into the rough shape of a sword. The individual pieces made for the edge, core and sides keep their relative positions through the beating stage and the boundaries can be seen when the sword is polished. The final stages (shaping and straightening a previously made sword) are usually shown during the demonstration.

After the sword has the proper shape, two stages remain – tempering and polishing. To enable the edge to be tempered to a high degree of hardness while keeping the back relatively soft, the blade is covered with clay so that only one edge is exposed. The clay is often made wavy so that varying widths of the edge are exposed. After heating, plunging the blade into water, and polishing, this pattern can be seen, and is one of the signs of beauty looked for in a sword. (The parts of the sword protected by the clay do not cool so abruptly, so they remain softer and more flexible.)

An interesting finale to the demonstration is a display of the use of some of the finished swords. Bamboo poles are set up, and swordsmen, dressed in traditional costume, show how effortlessly the swords can cut through pieces of bamboo. In olden times it was customary to demonstrate the sharpness of a new sword by testing how many condemned criminals it could cut through, one lying atop another.

Other craftsmen in Seki make the elaborately decorated handles, hand guards, etc, while most factories in the city make everyday knives and other cutting utensils.

If you're thinking of picking up a sword while in town, you may want to know the price so you can save up – a sword of the type being made and demonstrated would sell for about Y6,000,000.

Ukai

During the season mid-May to mid-October there is cormorant fishing at Seki, as well as the better-known centres of Gifu and Inuyama.

Places to Stay

There are several *ryokan* and *minshuku*

around the city, including at least two that are operated by cormorant fishermen. It is therefore possible to stay at one of the houses and have dinner on a boat for an all-inclusive price of Y7000 to Y8000 (which is rather high by *minshuku* standards, even including Y1800 or so for the performance). Two such fishermen are Mr Adachi (tel (05752) 2-0799) and Mr Iwasa (tel (05752) 2-1862).

Getting There & Away

Seki is easily reached from Gifu by the train that begins service in Gifu as a tram but continues far into the country parallel to the road to Seki and Mino. By JR, you could go from Nagoya, Inuyama, Mino-Kamo or Takayama.

Nagoya

Nagoya, Japan's fifth largest city, is best regarded as just a transportation centre; a place to go through. It has some direct international flights and could be a convenient place to first set foot in Japan as there are several attractions in the general region.

The city itself is of very limited interest because, due to its concentration of industries, it was a prime target during WW II and was flattened. As a result virtually all historic relics, such as the castle and Atsuta shrine, were destroyed.

After the war, Nagoya was rebuilt as a city planner's dream. Streets run broad and straight and everything is neat and tidy – and totally lacks any soul. It is as exciting as any commercial and industrial city.

Nagoya is close to Gifu and Inuyama and could be used as a base of operations to those places. It could also be used as a base for places as far away as Tsumago/Magome because of convenient transport. By Shinkansen train it is only 46 minutes from Kyoto.

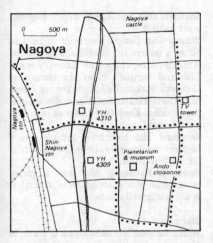

Information

Before setting off on the limited sightseeing of the city, stop at Nagoya City Tourist Information Office (tel (052) 541-4301) at the JR station and pick up a copy of the city map and other brochures. These give more information on the city. A full-colour 32-page booklet *Nagoya* gives greater information than space allowes in these pages.

The information centre is inside the station, to the left of the building when walking out. It is open daily from 8.30 am to 7 pm. The JNTO map of Japan has a usable Nagoya map on the back.

Home Visits A visit to a Japanese home in Nagoya can be arranged through the Home Visit Program. You can apply at the city information office (tel 961-1111, extension 2245), Nagoya Tourist Information Office (tel 541-4301), JTB offices and major hotels. There is no charge for the service but a day is usually required to make arrangements.

Nagoya-jo Castle

Formerly one of the greatest castles of Japan in both size and importance, Nagoya-jo castle was destroyed during WW II. The present building retains the original stone foundations and moats but the building is a concrete reproduction completed in 1959. It preserves the grand external appearance of the original structure but its interior is laid out as a museum instead of the original residential arrangement.

From late September to late November there is an interesting display of 'dolls' made of chrysanthemum bushes that have been shaped so that the flowers form faces and hands. They are dressed in costumes and set out in tableaux of famous historic events. The building in which they are displayed is in the central castle grounds.

On entering the castle, visitors are given a brochure describing its history and structural details extremely well. It is also available from the information centre at the station.

The castle is most easily reached in seven minutes by city bus No 5 or 17 from the station. The stop is Nagoya-jo-minami.

Tokugawa Art Museum (Tokugawa Bijutsukan)

This is a highly rated museum containing historical treasures that formerly belonged to the Tokugawa family.

Literature about the museum usually has wording like 'it contains nearly 10,000 items' like armour, swords and scrolls. But, while the museum may *house* so many treasures, only a disappointingly small portion is on display at any one time. The Y500 admittance charge could be better spent at several other museums.

The museum is accessible from the castle by bus No 16 from bus stop 6 at Shiyakusho subway station. The stop is Shindeki-machi. The same bus can be caught for the return trip from across the street going the opposite way. The museum is on a back street and a little tricky to find. It is closed on Mondays.

Atsuta Shrine

This 2000-year-old shrine site ranks with the greatest shrines in the country, second only to those at Ise. It is dedicated to the sacred sword, one of the three imperial regalia. The original buildings were destroyed in WW II and the present structures, which are made of concrete, are not as attractive.

However, the shrine is still revered and worshippers come in large numbers. The day that I visited, mothers in beautiful kimono were taking their newly born babies to the shrine for blessing.

The shrine is easily reached by subway; the stop is Jingu-nishi ('Shrine west').

Nagoya-shi Hakubutsukan (Nagoya City Museum)

Opened in 1977, this large building houses items related to the history and folklore of the Nagoya area. (Closed Mondays.)

Municipal Science Museum

Along with general scientific exhibits, this museum has a planetarium.

Nagoya TV Tower

This tower, not far from the station, is promoted as a tourist attraction. Considering that the city is laid out at the edge of a vast plain, it is industrial by nature, and the street plan is regular, I never felt it necessary to look over the city from the tower's 180-metre height. (Sorry, city fathers.)

Higashi-yama-koen (East Mountain Park)

The 84-hectare park is one of the few areas of greenery in the city. It houses one of the largest zoos in the orient, along with a botanical garden and a conservatory with many species of flowers.

Temples

There are four temples in the Nagoya area that might be worth visiting, but only if you have no chance to go to Kyoto.

Kosho-ji This has a five-storey pagoda, built in 1808.

Nittai-ji This temple was built in 1904 to house a relic of the Buddha, a gift of the King of Siam; the name means 'Japan-Thailand temple'. Near the temple is Gohyaku Rakan hall. It takes its name from the 500 statues of Rakan, disciples of the Buddha. Each face and pose is said to be different.

Kenchu-ji The Kenchu-ji temple has a historic two-storey gate at the entrance, dating from 1651.

Ryusen-ji Ryusen-ji also has a large, picturesque gate at its entrance, though it is not historically noted.

Crafts

World-famous Noritake china is made in Nagoya and visitors may tour the factory at 10 am and 2 pm daily (except Sundays and holidays). English-speaking guides are provided.

Visitors can watch the process of hand-painting cloisonne ware daily from 10 am to 12 noon and 1 to 5 pm (except Sundays and holidays) at Ando Cloisonne. The workshop can be reached by subway to Sakae station. Ando is 10 minutes walk along Otaumachi-dori Avenue.

Festivals

There are several festivals in the Nagoya area that are worth seeing.

1 January: New Year's rites at Atsuta shrine.

13 January: (lunar) Naked Men's festival at Konomiya. (They wear loincloths.)

Early April: Cherry Blossom Festival at Nagoya castle.

16-17 April: Toshogu jinja matsuri festival is a small local shrine festival, but interesting nevertheless. On the 16th there are performances of Kagura, ancient sacred masked dances with equally ancient and strange gagaku court music.

18 May: Toyokuni-jinja-matsuri yagumo koto and dances.

1 June: (lunar) Tenno-matsuri festival of

Tsutsui-cho area (but celebrated throughout the city).

5 June: Atsuta shrine festival.

20-21 July: Port festival (fireworks, etc.).

26 July: Shimono-ishiki-kawa (river) festival of Sengen- jinja.

Late September to late November: Chrysanthemum Doll show (Nagoya castle).

Mid-October: Nagoya-matsuri festival has music, dancing, tea ceremony, folk songs & dances, *kagura* (sacred dances & music) scheduled for the second Saturday and Sunday of the month. The high points are the procession of the Three Feudal Lords (both days) and the parade of eight *dashi*, elaborate wooden festival wagons of the type seen at the famous festivals at Kyoto, Takayama and Furukawa.

A very interesting feature of these *dashi* is the display of mechanical dolls that are associated with some of the carts. These ingenious dolls, well over a century old, perform an amazing number of tricks and movements, all controlled by wires. Similar ones can be seen at Takayama and Furukawa (Nagano-ken).

Places to Stay

There are three *Youth Hostels* and many hotels and business hotels in Nagoya. One of the hostels is *Miyoshi Ryokan* (tel (052) 583-0758), a small *ryokan* about 10 minutes from Nagoya station. It is shown on the map.

Two other hostels in the city area are *Aichi-ken Seinen-Kaikan* (tel 221-6001) and *Nagoya Youth Hostel* (tel 781-9845).

The information office at the station can help find accommodation. It is also possible to stay at nearby places like Inuyama and Gifu.

Getting There & Away

Air Travellers from Hong Kong, Seoul, Guam and Manila can fly direct to Nagoya. As the airport is only 30 minutes away from Nagoya station by bus (every 15 minutes), it is very convenient, especially when compared with the mess at Tokyo. Processing is quick as there are few international flights.

The airport is not far from Kasugai station of the Meitetsu Komaki line that goes to Inuyama/Gifu, passing the shrines of Tagata and Oagata on the way.

Train Nagoya is a stop for all Shinkansen trains and is also served by regular JR trains and several private lines. All connections to other points in the Kinki district are detailed in the Getting Around section at the end of this chapter. Shinkansen services are given in the Getting Around chapter earlier in the book. Private lines to other nearby destinations are outlined here.

All JR lines use Nagoya station. Kintetsu trains leave from Kintetsu-Nagoya station which is attached to Nagoya station. Trains of the Meitetsu line (north to Inuyama and Gifu, and south to the Chita Peninsula) leave from Shin-Nagoya station in the basement of the Meitetsu department store, to the right when leaving Nagoya station.

There is a second Meitetsu station at Kami-Ida, within the city limits but some distance from Nagoya station. It can be reached by bus No 1 from the latter, but it is simpler, for passengers who wish to use it (to Meiji-mura or Tagata/Oagata shrines), to go to Inuyama from Shin-Nagoya station, change trains at Inuyama and backtrack slightly along the other line.

Bus There are regular bus services west to Kyoto/Osaka and east to Tokyo; these are also detailed at the end of this chapter.

Ferry There is a daily ferry in each direction linking Nagoya with Sendai (northern Honshu) and Tomakomai (Hokkaido). The boat leaves Nagoya in the early evening, reaches Sendai the next morning, and Tomakomai the morning of the third day. More details are given in the Getting Around chapter.

Ferries leave from Nagoya Ferry Terminal which can be reached by city bus from the station. It is not too far from Nagoya-ko subway station.

Hitching To hitch out of Nagoya along the Tomei expressway (to Tokyo or Kyoto/Osaka), take the subway from Nagoya station (platform 1) to Hongo. About half the trains terminate before Hongo at Hoshigaoka; if yours does, wait for the next one, which will terminate at Fujigaoka. Trains bound for Fujigaoka are shown in red on the timetable in stations. On ticket machines, the line is shown in yellow.

The entrance to the expressway is close to Hongo station.

Getting Around

Airport Transport Buses to the airport leave from Nagoya Bus Terminal, which is in the Meitetsu department store, to the right when leaving the JR Nagoya station.

Subway Nagoya has a subway system of three lines. It is easy to use and has stations marked in *romaji* (although the station names on maps are not). The free handout map from the information centre shows the stations.

SOUTHEAST OF NAGOYA

To the southeast of Nagoya are the peninsulas of Chita and Atsumi, looking like pincers poised to close on Mikawa Bay. Their attraction for Nagoya residents is a glimpse of nature, especially wildflowers in season, but they are of limited interest to foreigners.

The Chita Peninsula can be reached by Meitetsu train from Shin-Nagoya station. From the terminal stations (it branches near the end) buses run from both places to Morozaki at the tip. The most exciting attraction here is the sight of buildings and other park facilities covered with sea

shells. (One train terminus is Kowa, a beach resort.)

From Morozaki, ferries cross eight times daily in both directions to Irako (Y500). Ferries also cross Ise Bay to Toba (five times daily, Y750) and there is a service to Toba from Irako (14 daily, Y750). There is a service to Toba from Gamagori as well but at Y3000 it is much more expensive.

There are also island-hopping services in the Mikawa Bay area, along the route Kowa (noted for beaches), Himaka-jima, Shino-jima (considered the most attractive) to Gamagori. Morozaki is another starting point to Himaka-jima to pick up the route.

At Irako, bicycles can be rented at the service centre of the Toyotetsu railway (near the port) and at Irako Koku-min Kyuku-mura (vacation village). The Toyotetsu line itself does not begin until half way along the peninsula, so it is just as easy to go by bus from Irago all the way to Toyohashi station.

Those wishing to hitch on the Tomei expressway to Tokyo or Kyoto/Osaka would find it easiest to take JR from Toyohashi to Mikawa-Ichinomiya and backtrack a couple of km to the Toyohashi interchange (*inta* in Japanese). Route 1 passes through Toyohashi but this road is very congested, slow to travel on and the scenery is depressing nearly all the way to the Mt Fuji area.

SOUTHWEST OF NAGOYA

To the southwest are the attractions of the Toba area and the Kii-hanto peninsula.

The following are the major places between Nagoya and Toba, and are to the east of the mountain range dividing them from the Nara area.

Yokkaichi

There is nothing of interest in this industrial city except for its annual festival on 26-27 September – a procession of a feudal lord and townspeople in costumes of that era. Inland about 20 km

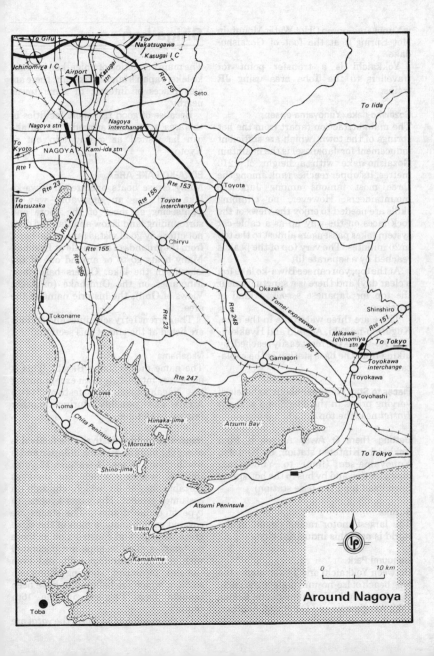

Around Nagoya

0   10 km

is Yunoyama-onsen ('Hot Water Mountain Hot Spring'), at the foot of Gozaisho-dake.

Yokkaichi is a transfer point for travellers to the Toba area using JR trains.

Gozaisho-dake/Yunoyama-onsen

The main attraction (apart from the hot springs of the town, which are sufficient inducement for Japanese) is the mountain Gozaisho-dake with a height of 1210 metres. Its upper reaches rank among the three most famous among Japanese mountaineers. However, no climbing skills are needed to enjoy the views of the rock faces on the way up as a cable-car system takes passengers almost to the top in 20 minutes. The very top of the peak is reached by a separate lift.

At the top, you can see Biwa-ko lake (on a clear day) and there is a sanctuary near the top for Japanese *serow*, a kind of antelope.

There are three waterfalls in the area, Kugurido-no-taki, Ao-taki and Hyakken-taki. Ao-taki is the most easily reached, by hiking from the base station of the cable-car.

Places to Stay There are about 30 hotels of varying prices in the *onsen* and a *Youth Hostel* near the top.

Getting There & Away Access is from Yokkaichi Kintetsu station, by Kintetsu Yunoyama-sen (line) to Yunoyama-onsen station and by bus to the hot-spring town itself (and the base station).

Suzuka

The largest motor racing circuit in the world is near this industrial city.

Isenoumi Park

Between Yokkaichi and Tsu stretches the long beach of Ise-no-umi prefectural park. Beaches include Tsutsumi-gaura, Chiyo-zaki, Akogigaura and Gotemba. Another, nearer Tsu, is Niezaki.

Shiga-ken

The main attraction of Shiga-ken is Biwa-ko lake, Japan's largest lake, but there are also places of interest in some towns nearby.

Because of good transport facilities in this area, attractions around Biwa-ko lake can be visited as a day trip out of Kyoto.

BIWA-KO LAKE AREA

Many cruise boats operate on Biwa-ko lake and are an enjoyable way of sightseeing as most of the shore and surrounding land is low and flat and does not offer any good vistas (apart, perhaps, from the grounds of the castle at Hikone). Many boats go to or around one of the islands in the lake. Others base their itineraries on the Omi-hake (or Eight Views of Omi), the historic name of the area.

The current ferry schedules and options are listed at the end of this section.

Nagahama

The name means 'Long Beach'. This is not a very interesting town except during the Nagahama-matsuri festival (14-15 April) and possibly during another festival in October.

Nagahama-matsuri Festival This festival is one of the more interesting in Japan and is worth trying to see. It features 12 *yatai* (festival wagons) which are used as portable stages on which children in costume present Hikiyama-kyogen (a type of comic drama). The stages are covered with miniature roofs of the same graceful shape and construction as those on temples. The wagons are decorated with elaborate carvings, gilt and even Gobelin tapestries showing European soldiers, which are believed to have been brought from Belgium in the 16th century.

On the evening of 14 April, the *yatai* are

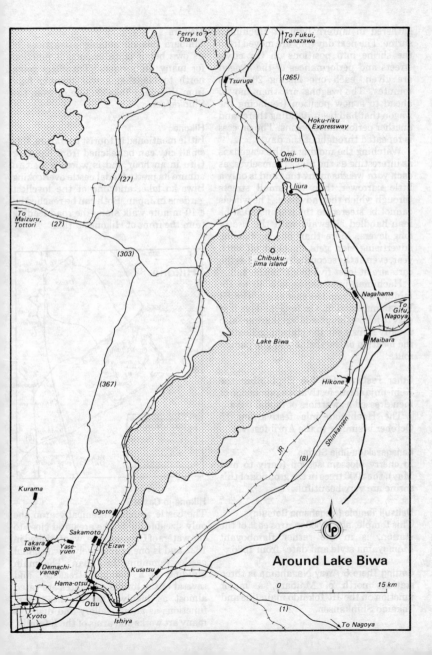

Around Lake Biwa

0   15 km

Ferry to Otaru

Tsuruga

To Fukui, Kanazawa

(365)

Hoku-riku Expressway

Omi-shiotsu

Iiura

(27)

To Maizuru, Tottori

(27)

(303)

Chibuku-jima island

(367)

Lake Biwa

Nagahama

To Gifu, Nagoya

Maibara

Hikone

Shinkansen

JR

(8)

Kurama

Ogoto

Sakamoto

Takara-gaike

Yase-yuen

Eizan

Demachi-yanagi

Kusatsu

Hama-otsu

Otsu

Ishiya

Kyoto

Ishiya

(1)

To Nagoya

gathered in lantern light at Hachiman shrine. The next day they are moved from the shrine into positions on the city's streets and performances of the *kyogen* are given, each one lasting 20 to 30 minutes. The wagons are then moved ahead to a new position (replacing the wagon that had been standing there) and another performance begins. The process is repeated throughout the day.

Watching the moving of the wagons is as interesting as the plays themselves, as each *yata* weighs many tons and is only a little narrower than the small streets through which they advance. The wheels cannot be steered so the wagons must be man-handled sideways with the use of long levers. More than one protruding advertising sign gets knocked off each year, even at the second-storey level as the carts are at least five to six metres tall.

Hachiman-jinja shrine is a 10 to 15-minute walk from the east exit of the JR Nagahama station. On festival days it is easy to follow the crowds but there are also usually signs near the station indicating the location of the shrine and the parade route.

Other Festivals On 2-5 September the Kehi-jinja shrine festival is a procession of men dressed as warriors of feudal days.

The Hachiman-jinja festival on 15 October is similar to the April festival.

Kanagasakigu-jinja Shrine
In cherry blossom season (early to mid May), the 2000 trees in the grounds of this shrine are very beautiful.

Daitsuji Temple (Nagahama Betsuin)
This temple, about 500 metres east of the station, is in the rather flamboyant Momoyama style and dates from 1586.

Getting There & Away Nagahama is three stations north of Maibara, a major junction on the JR Tokaido main line and Tokaido Shinkansen.

Maibara
Maibara has no notable attractions of its own but it is an important junction for many JR services. Travellers going north to Nagahama will transfer here from the main Tokaido line or from the Shinkansen.

Hikone
Little mentioned in tourist literature, this small city can be reached from Kyoto or Gifu in an hour and is worth a visit to admire its pretty feudal castle overlooking Biwa-ko lake, and one of the loveliest gardens in Japan. Both can be reached by a 10-minute walk along the road leading from the front of Hikone station.

Hikone-jo Castle
The castle, perched scenically atop the only sizeable hill in the area and close to the waters of Biwa-ko lake, was finished in 1622 and is one of relatively few original castles remaining in Japan. The main building is a national treasure, and several of the towers and gates are rated almost as highly. One of the towers functions as an art gallery and displays many art works and arms of the Ii family,

the owners. (Tall people, watch your head on the beams!)

Two of the original three moats remain and their banks give good views of the walls and the castle itself. Cherry trees line the banks and during the cherry blossom season (usually early to mid April) the castle and grounds are one of the most beautiful places in Japan. Graceful swans swimming in the moat add a note of serene beauty.

A booklet in English is usually available (free) when entering the castle; it gives a good description of the various features of the castle and other attractions of Hikone. If the booklet *How to See Hikone in Japan* is not available at the castle or Genkyuen garden, ask at the *shi-yaku-sho* (city office).

Genkyuen Garden Just north of the castle moats is Genkyuen, a landscape garden dating from 1678, patterned on the garden of the same name in China. Although it is not as famous as the 'Big Three' gardens, I consider it far more attractive than any of them and one of the loveliest in Japan. This view was shared by a Japanese garden lover I met while strolling around the central pond; according to her it is beautiful in all four seasons. If you take bread you can feed the colourful carp in the pond. The admittance ticket for the castle also includes the garden.

Other Attractions Other attractions in the Hikone area include Taga-jinja shrine and its garden, nearby Konomiya shrine and garden, Ryotanji temple and its highly regarded Zen-type rock garden, Seiryoji temple, Daido Benzaiten temple, and Tenneiji temple.

Festivals

Early April: Sakura-matsuri festival (Cherry Blossom Festival).

22 April: Taga-jinja matsuri festival.

1 August: Fireworks display.

8 August: Hikone Bayashi dance in the centre of the city.

Autumn: Shiro-matsuri castle festival, a procession of children in costumes of feudal days.

Getting There & Away Hikone is on the JR Tokaido (main) line between Kyoto and Maibara, one stop before the latter. It can be reached from Kyoto in less than an hour and can be seen easily as a day trip. There are many trains through the day from Kyoto (and Osaka).

The fastest access using only the Tokaido line (except for one early express) are the four Shin-Kaisoku trains (near-express service but with no surcharge) that reach Hikone with enough time for adequate sightseeing; from Kyoto these take 56 minutes, and from Osaka 82 minutes. Regular trains (about 12 during this same period) take 69 minutes from Kyoto and about 108 minutes from Osaka.

Those travellers with a Japan Rail Pass (or who are not counting pennies) could take the Shinkansen to Maibara (only Kodama trains; 28 minutes from Kyoto, 45 from Osaka) and backtrack one stop by the Tokaido line (six minutes travel time plus waiting time).

Getting Around Biwa-ko Lake

Up-to-date schedules are published in *Jikokuhyo* and are also available at the TICs in Tokyo and Kyoto or from any travel agent, so check one of these as schedules change from year to year.

(With the towns of Takeijima and Iiura, *Jikokuhyo* gives no guide to pronunciation so the closest approximation is given here. Locals should recognise the sound of the names, even if they are not totally correct.)

Excursion to Islands (With Stopover)

From Hikone to Takeijima there are up to four sailings between 10 am and 3.10 pm. The trip takes 30 minutes, there's a stopover of 30 minutes and the fare is Y1660 for the round trip.

From Imazu to Chikubu-jima island there are several sailings (Y2300) between 10.10 am and some time after 2 pm. The actual sailing time is 40 minutes going and 35 minutes returning from early March to 30 June , and 20 minutes each way from 1 July to the end of November. The stopover is about 90 minutes early in the year, 65 minutes for the second half.

Other Excursions to Islands

There are two choices to Chikubu-jima island, but with only a brief stop. One makes a round trip out of Hikone, leaving at 10.10 and 11 am, and at 1.10 pm, taking 35 minutes in each direction (Y3100). The other makes a round trip out of Iiura at 1 pm. From April to the end of June the trip each way takes 40 minutes. From 1 July to extended to 85 minutes, with a 25 minute return (Y1430).

There are also cruises to Chikubu-jima island with only a brief stop. Three leave from Nagahama (10.45 am, 1.15 and 3.45 pm; 65 minutes total; Y3100), ending at Hikone, and one leaves from Imazu (11.40 am, 40 minutes, Y2840), also ending at Hikone.

Omi-hake Cruises There are cruises around the lake to take in the Omi-hake. The most convenient of these are those starting from Hama-Otsu lasting 2¾ hours (up to four per day; Y2790).

The Michigan Totally non-Japanese but worth considering as an attraction nonetheless, the *Michigan* is a 900-ton, stern- wheeler (paddle-wheel ship). With its one-metre draft, it is ideal for the shallow lake. The ship is 59 metres long and 11.7 metres wide and was outfitted virtually on a money-no-object basis. (Its Y1.7 billion cost could have purchased a 20,000 ton cargo ship.)

There are four decks, the first three with dining facilities of increasingly higher

quality (all with a foreign theme). On the third level is a stage where Dixieland music is played during the 'Showboat' evening cruise.

The 'Showboat' cruise is a round trip from Hama-Otsu departing at 6.30 pm. It takes 2¾ hours and costs Y4100 and up. Reservations are essential for the Michigan; (tel (0775) 24-5000 in Japanese).

The Hama-Otsu Cruise This is a round trip which departs twice in the morning at 10 and 11.50 am and twice in the afternoon at 1.40 and 3.30 pm. It takes 90 minutes and the cost is Y2000 to Y4500.

Kyoto

If there is one city in Japan that every foreign visitor should visit, it is Kyoto. As it was the imperial capital for nearly 1000 years it has the finest temples, palaces, villas and gardens in Japan, as well as the most refined culture and lifestyle.

Some over-enthusiastic writers have described Kyoto as one of the most beautiful cities in the world. It isn't. Kyoto is a modern Japanese metropolis with its full share of Japanese urban ugliness. However, dotted through the city and clustered around the edges are oases of tranquillity and beauty, exemplifying the best of Japan.

By the way, the name is pronounced so that the 'y' is hard as in 'yet'. The first syllable is 'Kyo', not 'Kie-o'. The last syllable is the same as the English word 'toe'. Some foreigners in Japan have been heard to garble the name into 'Kyota' (or worse). The name Kyoto simply means 'capital city'; Tokyo, the successor capital, means 'east capital'.

Orientation

There is no problem whatever in finding your way around Kyoto, even if you do not speak a word of Japanese. Kyoto is one of the few cities in Japan which is laid out on

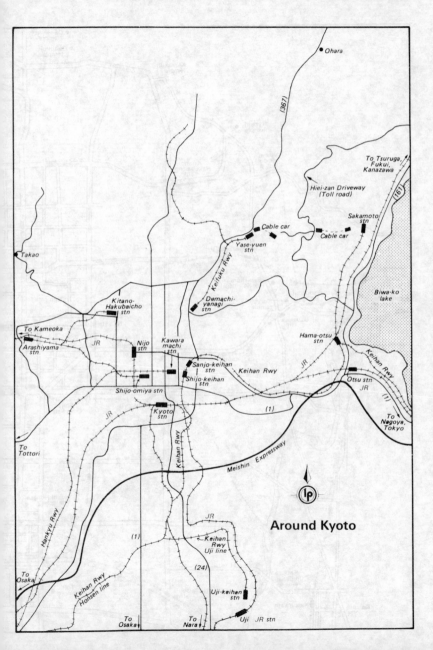

Around Kyoto

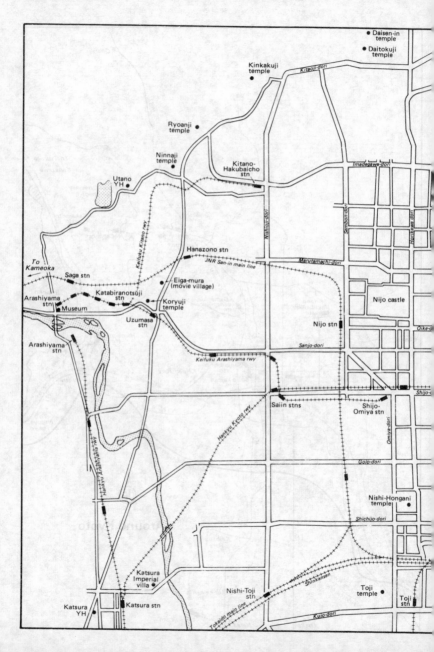

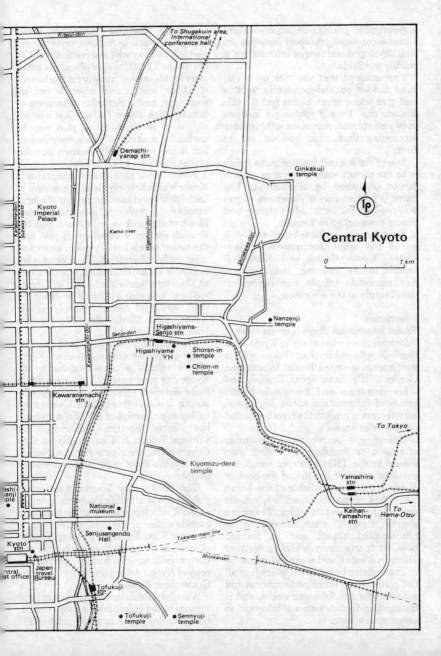

Central Kyoto

0   1 km

a rectangular grid (modelled on ancient Chinese capitals), transport facilities are well developed and tourist information is readily available.

I recommend that you pick up a TIC map and set out independently, as this will give you a much better feel for this historic city. Even if you do get lost you may well stumble across something more interesting than what you set out to find.

One of the few commercial maps which is to the correct scale is the area map of Kyoto published by Shobunsha. The name is printed only in Japanese, so you will need to ask for it. Most streets and places are marked in English.

Bus tours are available but virtually all go to the same destinations: Nijo-jo castle, Kyoto Gosho and Kinkakuji temple in the morning; Heian shrine, Sanjusangendo temple and Kiyomizu-dera temple in the afternoon.

Information

Tourist Information There is no shortage of information on what to see in Kyoto. It is the only city other than Tokyo with a government-operated Tourist Information Center (TIC). Staff speak English and other languages and are absolute gold mines of information about any place, activity, art or craft in the Kyoto area and elsewhere in Japan.

Unless you arrive on a Saturday afternoon or Sunday, your first stop should be the TIC to pick up one of the excellent maps of Kyoto and the booklet *Kyoto Nara* (also available at the Tokyo TIC), and to ask any specific questions you may have about travelling. They have a great deal of other information on photocopied sheets and in printed booklets (particularly useful is *Walking Tours in Kyoto*), and some rail maps.

The bulletin board in the office lists all the cultural and other performances and activities for the following weeks, and is the most up-to-date source of information about such events.

The TIC also has information about accommodation in various price ranges and will call to make reservations (unlike the Tokyo TIC). Cheaper places are listed later in this section, mostly for the benefit of those who arrive after 5 pm on weekdays, or on Saturday afternoon or Sunday. The Tokyo TIC also has a handout list of accommodation that may be useful for making advance reservations but it has occasionally omitted popular places (like Mrs Uno's house).

A very handy booklet is *Monthly Guide Kyoto* which lists events of the month in useful detail and has descriptions of a large number of temples, shrines and palaces. Much of the book is in Japanese but the English section is excellent. It also lists the better hotels (with prices), tours and other useful information. The booklet is not available at the TIC but may be obtained at the large hotels that cater to foreign visitors. It is also available in Japan by mail for Y600 from: Monthly Guide Kyoto, 30-5 Chajiri-cho, Arashiyama, Nishikyo, Kyoto-shi.

The Monthly Guide should not be confused with another publication, *Kyoto Monthly Guide*, which is produced by the Kyoto city government. This one is much more detailed regarding events for the month. It is available at the TIC or by mail in Japan on receipt of a Y70 stamp from the Tourist Section, Department of Cultural Affairs & Tourism, Kyoto City Government, c/o Kyoto Kaikan, Sakyo-ku, Kyoto. Both publications are very useful.

The Kyoto City Tourist Association publishes a worthwhile guide book simply called *Kyoto*. It contains useful information such as airline phone numbers, etc, and is a steal at Y300. For a very good explanation of many of the attractions of the city and their significance in history, purchase a copy of *Kyoto, A Contemplative Guide* by Gouverneur Mosher.

A useful publication for residents of and visitors to the Hanshinkei region (Osaka-Kobe-Kyoto) is the monthly publication

Kansai Time Out which has evolved from a newspaper format of several pages into a well-produced glossy magazine covering social, cultural and other events of interest to foreigners, including festivals and films. It should be on sale at bookstores selling English-language publications. It can be ordered by subscription (Y3000 per year) in Japan or surface mail anywhere from: *Kansai Time Out*,(tel (078) 232- 4516/7) 1-13 Ikuta-cho 1-chome, Chuo-ku, Kobe 651. It might be possible to arrange for single copies.

Another publication, more of interest to residents, is *A Resident's Guide to Kyoto*, a compilation of nearly every bit of information that one needs when arriving to stay in Kyoto for a while. It can be purchased at the YWCA for Y500, by domestic mail for Y1000, or by foreign mail for Y1500, from: YWCA Thrift Shop, Muro machi-dori, Demizu-agaru, Kamikyo-ku, Kyoto-shi 602.

There is a thrift sale at the YWCA on the third Saturday of every month. It's a good place for bargains, exchanging information with other foreign residents, and even home-made western-style munchies and crunchies.

Tickets and any other travel bookings are available from the JTB offices near the north entrance of Kyoto station, and on Sanjo, east of Kawaramachi. There is generally English-speaking staff on duty to help with inquiries.

Post Office The post office offers basic services 24 hours a day, including mail pick up from poste restante. A passport or other identification is required. Postal rates are conveniently noted in English in the main section.

Home Visit It is possible to visit a private home in Kyoto for a couple of hours in the evening to see what Japanese home life is like. Members of the participating families speak English or other foreign languages.

Arrangements should be made as far in advance as possible. Usually this can be done in a day, but more time should be allowed. Travel agencies and large hotels can make arrangements or you can contact the Kyoto City Information Office (tel 371-2108) at Kyoto station.

Markets
There are two monthly flea markets; one at Kitano-jinja on the 5th of every month, the other at Toji on the 21st. Be sure to check with the TIC if these dates are still valid.

For the best selection, arrive early in the morning. Don't expect to find any valuable antiques as these people know the worth of their goods.

Don't pick up any antiques; some unscrupulous dealers carefully assemble already broken items so they 'break' when touched, and the hapless victim is charged for the breakage.

Zen
If you wish to practise zazen meditation while in Kyoto, you will be disappointed to learn that this is not possible on a casual basis without an introduction. The reason is that many other foreigners joined in, didn't know what to do, would not conform to the customs, and distracted those who wanted to participate properly.

Anyone who is seriously interested should contact the TIC or arrange an introduction through a previous teacher elsewhere. Those just becoming interested would be better advised to go to Tokyo where there are facilities for teaching Zen in English.

Museums
There are many museums other than the few detailed here. If the following sound interesting, inquire at the TIC for more information. Japan Historical Museum (Nippon Rekishi-kan), Kiyotaki Folkcraft Museum (Kiyotaki Mingei-kan), Kyoto Ceramic Hall (Kyoto Tojiki-kaikan), Kyoto Folkcraft Museum (Kyoto Minzoku-kan), Kyoto Municipal Museum of Art,

Kyoto National Museum of Modern Art, Kodai Yuzen (has old yuzen-dyed items), and the Steam Locomotive Museum (Umekoji Joki Kikansha-kan).

Arts & Crafts

Kyoto is famous for a number of handicrafts of the highest quality. These are a legacy of its past as the capital for nearly 1000 years, a period when there was a continual demand for fine fabrics and lacquerware, etc.

Many of these goods are still produced by the traditional methods evolved centuries ago, and you can see several types of craftsmen at work. As well as the crafts mentioned here, it is possible to arrange an introduction to other specialists through the TIC or City Information Office.

Kyoto Handicraft Centre This is well worth a visit to watch a variety of crafts in action. Goods may be purchased on the spot.

Tatsumara Silk Fine silks are on display here and demonstrations are given on fingernail weaving. Inquire at the TIC for more details.

Inaba Cloisonne Demonstrations are given of making cloisonne ware. Inquire at the TIC.

Municipal Museum of Traditional Industry This has displays of many handicrafts of the very highest quality, along with live demonstrations of some crafts.

Yuzen An interesting and quite extensive live display here shows the historic process for producing the incredibly beautiful material used for one kind of very expensive kimono. Yuzen Bunka Kaikan (Yuzen culture centre) is on the west side of the city near Nishi-Kyogoku station (Hankyu railway Kyoto-sen line). A leaflet and more information are available at the TIC.

Pottery There are several potteries in the area but they do not encourage visitors because of the interruption to their work. An exception is Kotobuki Toshun, which has set up special facilities in the Kiyomizu-Yaki Danchi building so that visitors can see how pottery is made, and even make some for themselves. This is usually only for group tours so inquire at the TIC if you are interested.

Cherry Blossoms

The exact time of the blossoms varies over a range of several weeks from year to year but is generally around early to mid April. The best places to see blossoms are Kiyomizu-dera, Heian-jingu, Daigo-ji, Maruyama-koen park, Arashiyama-koen park and Nanzen-ji. Yoshino (Nara-ken) is a mountain side planted with thousands of trees and can be seen as a day trip from Kyoto. Also highly recommended is Hikone; its castle grounds are covered with cherry trees and the moats are lined with them.

Maple Leaves

The temples of Kyoto in autumn are among the most beautiful places in the world. The founders planted maples in the grounds of the temples, which are generally in the hills around the city.

The leaves of the trees change colour in a fiery display of reds and oranges rarely matched anywhere else in the world (a difficult admission for someone who comes from eastern Canada!) and their beauty underscores the fine lines of the walls and roofs of the buildings. The peak period is usually early to mid November.

Temples noted for their foliage are Eikan-do, Nanzen-ji, Kiyomizu-dera, Tofuku-ji, Sekiya-Zen-in, Kinkaku-ji and Ryoan-ji. Areas close to the city include Arashiyama, Sugino, Kiyotani valley, Yase, Ohara (Sanzen-in and Jakko-in), Mt Kurama and Kibune, and Takao (Jingo-ji and Kozan-ji).

Kyoto Gosho Palace

This is the Imperial Palace in Kyoto and is considered to be the centre of the city, from where you go 'up' or 'down'. The palace itself is of only moderate interest but the office of the Imperial Household Agency is at the entrance. You apply here for permission to visit some other places associated with the Imperial family.

Kyoto Gosho was the residence of the emperor in the days when he lived in Kyoto. The present building dates from 1855, replacing one destroyed in a fire. Although the capital was Kyoto from 794, this site was not used until 1788 when a palace was built to replace an older one that was also destroyed by fire. The main buildings are replicas of the former structures and are quite simple in design, though made with the finest materials and construction methods. A guide accompanies all visitors, so the details are explained.

To enter you must fill in an application and show your passport, so arrive about 20 minutes before the tours, which start at 10 am or 2 pm. There are none on Saturday afternoon or Sunday.

The palace is one of the most peaceful places in Kyoto because Japanese must wait for months to get permission to enter, and few do. Any Japanese accompanying you will have to wait at the entrance. It is a privilege for foreigners to be able to enter so easily.

Before or after the tour, file your application to visit Katsura Imperial Villa, Sento Imperial Palace, and Shugaku-in if you plan to see any of them. Permission will be given for a specific date and hour, usually within a day if requested, but you should apply soon after arriving in Kyoto to allow for delays.

Go-jinja Shrine

This little shrine, across from the west side of the Gosho, is unremarkable except that instead of the usual *koma-inu* guardian dogs/lions at the entrance, it has two pigs.

Sento Imperial Palace

There is another palace on the southeast side of the same grounds. In addition to the buildings, which have been rebuilt many times, there is a garden completed in 1630 and designed by Kobori Enshu, possibly the most famous of all landscape-garden designers. As mentioned earlier, advance permission is required to enter.

Nijo-jo Castle

Although called a castle, the main building here (Ninomaru) was used as a luxurious residential palace, with extensive grounds and minimal defences (primarily the moat, walls and watch towers). A more defensive building once existed but was destroyed by fire.

The castle was built in 1603 by Tokugawa Ieyasu, the founder of the Tokugawa shogunate. Features to watch for are the architectural details of the huge Ninomaru palace, including the famous nightingale floor that 'chirps' when a person's weight activates mechanisms under the floorboards (installed to warn of potential assassins). To hear the chirp clearly, fall to the rear of the group so the stomping herd passes ahead.

The garden is one of the finer landscape gardens in Japan and makes for a pleasant stroll. The grounds hold no other great surprises but you are free to wander around the moat and walls as you wish, or leave to go on to other places.

The castle is extremely popular with visitors and is over-run with literally dozens of bus loads during the peak morning and afternoon periods. The best visiting times are early in the morning, during lunch time, and later in the afternoon; the first and last are better for taking photos.

The beautiful Karamon gate, passed through on the way to Ninomaru palace, was originally part of Fushimi castle. When the castle was dismantled, parts were distributed to a number of temples and shrines around Kyoto and many other parts of Japan.

Separate tickets are available for the garden alone or for the palace and garden; the latter is recommended. Like many of the major attractions of Kyoto, a large plaque at the entrance gives detailed information about the castle in English.

Shinsen-en Garden

To the south of Nijo-jo castle lies this small and unpretentious garden, all that remains of the 700-year-old pleasure gardens of the palace. It can be seen while walking through to Nijo-jinya. There is at least one traditional-style restaurant overlooking the garden, with sliding doors opening onto the view; the reflection in the pond and the Japanese food make eating at one of these places a memorable experience (but be prepared for a little language difficulty).

Nijo-jinya

This building looks like any ordinary house but was actually a fortress-residence for a person of rank approximately equal to baron. The interior has an ingenious collection of concealed traps, escapes and places for ambush that would allow the resident to escape any attempt at capture.

The drawback is that there is no explanation in English and foreigners are not admitted without a Japanese-speaking escort. Gouverneur Mosher's guide book on Kyoto gives a detailed explanation of the purpose of the house and the action of the defences. An advance appointment is necessary. Obtain further details from the TIC.

Kyoto Station Area

From the Gosho/Nijo-jo castle area you can proceed to the Kyoto station area along Horikawa-dori, or by bus or train from JR Nijo station. The main attractions northwest of the station are Nishi-Honganji and Higashi-Honganji temples, while to the east is Sanjusangendo and the National Museum.

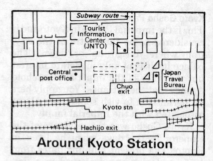

Around Kyoto Station

Nishi-Honganji Temple This is regarded by many as the finest example of Japanese Buddhist architecture. The temple dates from 1592 but the original buildings were destroyed in 1617. The present Boei-do was rebuilt in 1636, and the Amida-do in 1760; the former is the northernmost of the large main buildings.

The Shoin building was originally part of the old Fushimi castle and was moved here when the castle was dismantled. Not to be missed is the very colourful Karamon gate in the south wall (viewed from inside the grounds). Of typically flamboyant Momoyama style, it has much gold inlay on the metal fittings and brightly coloured carved figures of animals and humans, many obviously of Chinese derivation.

There are four tours a day, at 10 and 11 am, and 1.30 and 2.30 pm. Though lengthy (if the explanation is being given only to Japanese visitors), this is the only way to see the interior buildings, the two Noh stages, Komei-no-en (a pretty garden of rocks, gravel and greenery), and other glimpses of beauty such as wide verandahs made of a single plank of wood. Not open to the public, unfortunately, is the more beautiful Hyakka-en garden.

Costume Museum Close to Nishi-Honganji temple is an interesting museum with costumes (both original and replicas) worn in Japan over the past 2000 years. It is on the 5th floor of the Izutsu Building.

There is an English-language pamphlet, and the costumes are also labelled in English.

Higashi-Honganji Temple This temple has the largest wooden structure in Kyoto. It was founded in 1602 but the present buildings date from 1895. It is worth a look around.

Kikokutei Garden This large garden was a villa of the abbot of Higashi-Honganji temple. Unfortunately it has been neglected and allowed to run down but it is little visited and provides a haven of relative peace. An interesting scandal has been hovering around it, as the abbot transferred ownership to a private individual without consulting the 10,000 or so temples affiliated with Higashi-Honganji.

Toji Temple To the southwest of the station and therefore a little off the track, this temple on extensive park-like grounds has the tallest pagoda in Japan (55 metres). The *kodo* (lecture hall) is a simple building containing only a few large gilded statues. This was the first temple I visited in Kyoto, and in the late afternoon, with the sun shining in the doorway and reflecting off the floor, the effect was quite mystical.

The first Europeans here must have been similarly impressed by the unfamiliar symbolism. The pagoda dates from 1644, the lecture hall from 1598, and the main hall from more recent times.

East of Kyoto Station

Sanjusangendo The name means '33 bays' and refers to spaces between the pillars of this long, narrow structure which dates from 1266. The spaces are filled with a huge and intriguing collection of 1001 life-sized statues of Kannon, Goddess of Mercy. If they look small, remember that the Japanese were once very short; many old people in the countryside are no taller than these figures.

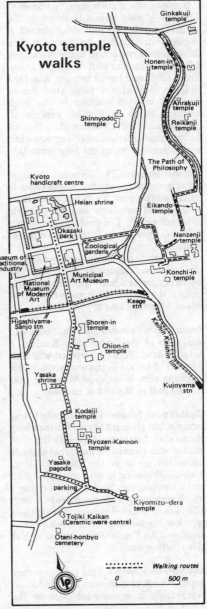

Kyoto temple walks

- Ginkakuji temple
- Honen-in temple
- Anrakuji temple
- Shinnyodo temple
- Reikanji temple
- The Path of Philosophy
- Kyoto handicraft centre
- Heian shrine
- Eikando temple
- Okazaki park
- Nanzenji temple
- Zoological gardens
- Museum of Traditional Industry
- Municipal Art Museum
- Konchi-in temple
- National Museum of Modern Art
- Keage stn
- Higashiyama-Sanjo stn
- Shoren-in temple
- Chion-in temple
- Keihin Keishin line
- Yasaka shrine
- Kujoyama stn
- Kodaiji temple
- Ryozen-Kannon temple
- Yasaka pagoda
- parking
- Kiyomizu-dera temple
- Tojiki Kaikan (Ceramic ware centre)
- Otani-honbyo cemetery

·········· Walking routes

0   500 m

Some of the statues wear 'necklaces'. The face of each statue is different; if a visitor sees one that resembles himself, it is customary for him to donate such a decoration. The central figure is a seated 3.3-metre statue of 1001-handed Kannon (from 1254) and her 28 helpers. Also take time to look at the large (but dusty) sculpted wooden statues in the back corridor. Signs in English explain all attractions briefly. The temple is famous for its archery festival on 15 January when arrows are shot along the long verandah.

National Museum The National Museum is just across the road from Sanjusangendo and is worth a visit for its large collection of Japanese artefacts from prehistoric to recent times. The pottery from about 2000 BC shows how little this craft has changed.

Although the museum is conveniently reached from Sanjusangendo, it might be worth saving for a rainy day. Admission is free on the 15th of each month but it is closed Mondays and at year-end.

Kawai Kanjiro Pottery This is the house and workshop of the late Kawai Kanjiro, a noted potter. Those interested will find displays of his work, the workshop, and a climbing kiln. It is closed Mondays, mid August and at the end of the year.

Chishaku-in Temple Of somewhat less interest, but pleasant to visit during a long Kyoto stay, this temple has an attractive garden with an unusual pond that extends under the porch of the main building. A special building is used to exhibit wall and door paintings from the 16th century which survived fires in the main building. They are considered masterpieces of their type but are not of great interest to non-Japanese. An English-language pamphlet gives further details.

Kiyomizu-dera Temple This temple is very popular with visitors and is included on every tour. It is unusual because the

honden (main hall) is built out on pillars over a hill side. The grounds are especially lovely during the cherry blossom season and autumn. The present buildings date from 1633 and include a picturesque Sanmon gate at the entrance and a three-storey pagoda, as well as the famous verandah.

Access from the south is gained by walking up the long hill from Gojozaka bus stop, either through the cemetery (southernmost road) or up the shop-lined road. These shops, and those along the other approaches, have a large variety of pottery and other crafts, as well as countless souvenirs and Kyoto-type nibbles.

Exploring the Back Streets Several little streets near Kiyomizu-dera temple make this possibly the most enjoyable area of Kyoto for strolling. When leaving Kiyomizu-dera, take the right hand of the two downhill roads and note the first street that branches off to the right, down a set of stone steps; this is Sannen-zaka. Explore the main road as desired (also the road off to the left when leaving the temple) but return to Sannen-zaka.

Like the main road, Sannen-zaka has numerous little shops selling a variety of knick-knacks. If you see something of interest in any of the shops in the area, I suggest you buy it there, as some shops have goods that can't be found anywhere else.

A short distance along Sannen-zaka, to the right, you will see the entrance to Sakaguchi, a lovely little garden tea house with a pond. For a few hundred yen you can order *soba* (noodles) or tea and have them while enjoying the view. Pleasant, tinkly koto music provides the background and guarantees one of the most 'Japanese' experiences available.

A little farther along is a coffee shop that I enjoyed, the Boga *tei*. The front and interior are modern and European in appearance but there is a pleasant courtyard at the rear with the incongruous combination of traditional Japanese garden with stone lanterns and trees, and a Mediterranean-style patio; for contrast, the adjoining gift shop is in a traditional house. The coffee shop is easily identified by the decorative little Japanese shelter (to the right) over the pay phone.

A little beyond here, Sannen-zaka curves off to the left and Ninen-zaka branches to the right, down another set of steps. There are more knick-knack shops, teahouses and coffee shops along the way, some in garden settings.

Sannen-zaka, by the way, continues on to a pagoda, the five-storey Yasaka Gojonoto, all that remains of a once grand temple. The grounds are closed, however, so it is not worth a walk to see. Photographers will find that the view along the road is ruined by numerous power lines but the little uphill road to the east shortly before the T-junction gives a good silhouette of the top four storeys. A telephoto lens is needed to cut out foreground clutter.

The road forming the T-junction at the end of Ninen-zaka leads up to Ryosen Kannon, a large concrete seated figure of Kannon. The figure is of no historic importance but the appearance of the statue is peaceful and reassuring. It is surrounded by a wall but you can see through the gate without paying the entry fee if you don't want to go in.

Continuing on the road that runs along the foot of the grounds of Ryozen Kannon (reached by zig-zagging left from the end of Ninen-zaka) you pass another couple of tea gardens, and temples which can be looked into. The road ends in a T-junction at Kodai-ji temple, which can be identified easily by the strange looking spire coming out of the roof.

Just before the end of the road, on the right hand side, is Rakusho coffee shop. At first it appears to be like any of the other countless coffee shops in Japan, but this one has an interesting attraction of its own – a charming little garden with a long narrow pond. The garden is actually a

century old and earlier was the centrepiece of a more classical tea garden, but it has moved with the times.

Around the pond are typical Japanese decorative motifs, like a stone slab across the water to serve as a bridge, many colourful flowers and tastefully positioned moss. The most interesting sight is the large number of huge decorative carp in the pond. They have won the Kinki district championship for several years and are the pride and joy of the distinguished-looking owner who potters around carrying out maintenance. It is not necessary to buy anything as visitors are allowed to enter just to look, but it is a good place to take a break. Prices are typical for Japanese coffee shops and the owner's daughter-in-law speaks English.

This area around Kiyomizu-dera temple (also described in the pamphlet on walks in Kyoto) is, more than any other area in Kyoto, conducive to a relaxing stroll rather than a rushed attempt to see everything in a day. Not all visitors will have the luxury of time but those who do are sure to enjoy it as the area has a mood difficult to find elsewhere in Japan.

Yasaka-jinja Shrine Not far away from the Rakusho is Yasaka-jinja shrine. It has several photogenic brilliant-orange buildings as well as one of the largest granite *torii* gates (on the south side) in Japan, dating from 1646. It is one of the best places in Japan to see people 'waking the gods' – shaking and whipping a thick rope attached to a rattly gong at the eaves, then putting their hands together in prayer. It is said to be a favourite of *geisha* from the nearby Gion entertainment area.

Adjacent Karuyama-koen park has a pleasant little pond and Japanese-style garden arranged around it. It is as much of interest to see how Japanese enjoy their leisure as for its own attractions. In cherry blossom time there are parties everywhere, with much happy imbibing and singing. It provides a path to nearby Chion-in temple.

Chion-in Temple The huge Sanmon gate at the south (main) entrance to this hillside temple is the largest in Japan and dates from 1619. It also has the largest bell in the country. The main building is impressively large and is best viewed in its entirety from the large open area in front.

The interior is equally impressive and is an excellent place to examine the great range of Buddhist symbols and other ornate gilded decorations; it is a feast for the eyes.

The temple is active (not just a type of museum as is the case with many temples) and there is a good chance of observing priests chanting prayers for deceased members of visiting families.

The garden and large building behind the main temple are also worth visiting. Although there are always other visitors around, the temple is rarely overcrowded. An English-language pamphlet gives the history of the temple and serves as a primer on the Jodo sect, of which it is the head temple.

Shoren-in Temple This is one of my favourite temples. It is off the beaten path enough for it not to be over-run with hordes of sightseers, so you can enjoy its lovely little garden, the peace, and the blending of the buildings (and their architectural details) with the setting at the foot of a hill. Birds can be heard in nearby trees. It is delightful in the late afternoon, especially in autumn when the trees are beautiful; 2 to 3.30 pm is good in November, later in summer when the sun is higher.

After exploring the buildings and the views from there, return to the entrance, don shoes, and walk around the garden, which is entered by a tunnel under one of the corridors (to the right when leaving the building). An English-language handout gives the history of the temple.

Northeast of Kyoto Station

Nanzen-ji Temple Another highly recommended temple to visit, especially when the autumn leaves are at their colourful best, is Nanzen-ji. This temple began as a villa for a retired emperor and was made into a temple in 1291. The present buildings date from after 1600. The grounds have many tall, venerable cedar trees so the approach to the entrance is canopied by nature.

The buildings of the temple feature the finest construction techniques, rooms with exquisite details (some opening onto lovely little gardens), sliding doors with fine, treasured paintings, and several rock-and-sand Zen gardens. Nanzen-ji means 'south Zen temple'. A leisurely walk is rewarding.

To the right inside the main entrance is a simple room where you can sip tea for Y200 extra. It is a good chance to appreciate the beauty of the tea ceremony (the spirit of it, anyway), sitting in the simple room on *tatami* mats and looking out at the little waterfall. An English-language pamphlet gives the history of the temple.

Toriyasu Another peaceful and beautiful place for rest and refreshments is Toriyasu, a teahouse-restaurant-garden just across from the right-hand corner of the grounds of Nanzen-ji temple. *Koto* music provides the background and the area is shaded by tall trees.

Eikando Temple The grounds of this temple are gorgeous during autumn, and enjoyable at other times. A graceful stone bridge arches over the pond and the temple buildings enclose small gardens, including one of rocks and sand raked into elaborate patterns. Unfortunately, loudspeakers babble incessantly and destroy any potential for peaceful exploration.

Kyoto Dento Sanyo Kaikan (Centre of Traditional Industry) This museum is worth visiting for its beautiful lacquerware, masks, and robes for *bugaku* dances. (Interestingly, one mask with a small dragon atop the head of the mask is very similar to masks used in festivals in Bolivia.)

The museum also has a reproduction of a typical, traditional Kyoto house with its long corridors (nicknamed *unagi-no-nedoko*, 'bedrooms for eels') as well as exhibitions of hand-forging knives and other traditional crafts.

The museum is to the right of the National Museum of Modern Art and can be recognised by its unusual architecture, with a curved wall up to the second floor and a traditional square form for the upper storey. The TIC map has only the English name, which no Japanese would understand to give help with directions. The Kyoto Municipal Art Museum and the zoo are nearby.

National Museum of Modern Art This has many large and attractive works. 'Modern' refers to the past century or so.

Heian-jingu Shrine A Johnny-come-lately among Kyoto's shrines and temples, Heian-jingu shrine was built in 1895 to mark the 1100th anniversary of the founding of Kyoto as the capital of Japan. It is a 60%-scale reproduction of the palace built in 794; the present buildings are large so the imagination runs overtime picturing the originals. Actually, the present buildings do not even date to the last century; a mysterious fire in 1976 caused extensive damage, resulting in the reconstruction of the main hall and several other buildings.

The shrine has an extensive and pretty garden, known especially for cherry blossoms in the spring. It is a popular place for wedding parties so keep your eyes open for brides in beautiful wedding kimono. Also, take bread crusts to feed the carp in the pond. At 23 metres, the huge *torii* at the front entrance is the largest in Japan.

Kyoto Handicraft Centre Although a commercial establishment, this is a good attraction. On its several floors craftsmen

may be seen using their traditional skills in damascene, wood-block print making (carving the plates and actually making the prints), pottery (making and painting), doll making, and several other crafts. Work is in progress every day of the week but some of the people take Sunday off. For a convenient one-stop look at a number of traditional crafts, it can't be beaten.

Like Heian-jingu shrine, it is on the route of almost every tour, although a visit on your own would be more enjoyable, allowing you to move at your own pace. The products being made are sold on the premises, along with a large variety of other good-quality souvenirs (plus some tourist rubbish).

Ginkaku-ji Temple This temple was originally built in 1489 as a hillside retreat of a *shogun* and was converted into a temple after his death. The intention was to cover the walls of the main building with silver foil; although this was never done, the name Ginkaku (Silver Pavilion) was given to it anyway. In Japan, intention can count as much as performance, a tradition carried on into many aspects of modern life, for better or worse.

The effect of the buildings, the rock-and-sand garden (including some unusually shaped piles of gravel) and careful use of greenery, is one of restrained elegance. It should perhaps be visited before the more flamboyant and spectacular Kinkaku-ji temple (Gold Pavilion Temple) for it may seem to suffer by comparison, although it is probably a better expression of Japanese taste.

It is about two km from Heian-jingu and the others, so a bus or taxi will save time. A plaque at the entrance gives the history in English.

Northwest of the City Centre

Daitoku-ji Temple Daitoku-ji is a functioning Zen temple made up of 22 separate temples, eight of which are open to visitors. Each one is explained on the ticket and payment is separate for each. Three of the best known are Daisen-in, Zuiho-in and Koto-in. The whole place has been criticised for the commercialisation of the temples.

Kinkaku-ji Temple This is probably the best known temple in Kyoto (if not Japan) because its pavilion is covered with gold leaf. Set beside a large pond in which it is reflected, the pavilion is very beautiful and worth a visit. It is on the itinerary of virtually every full tour of Kyoto.

The present building dates only from 1955, replacing the previous structure (1397) that was destroyed in 1950 when it was set on fire by a student-monk with deranged metaphysical notions. (Mishima based his well-known Kinkaku-ji on this story.)

The building was completely re-covered in gold foil in 1987 so it should retain its beauty for many years. The foil is much thicker than that applied originally, which was during times before Japan had become the wealthy country that it is today.

Even though it is popular with every visitor to Kyoto and is therefore crowded, a visit is recommended for the lovely views around the pond and the wooded grounds. It is especially beautiful when the leaves change colour in November. An English-language pamphlet tells the history of the temple and its high points. Access from other parts of Kyoto is convenient by bus or taxi.

Ryoan-ji Temple This temple houses the most famous rock-and-sand *seki-tei* garden in Japan. It is an enigmatic arrangement of 15 rocks in groups of various sizes in a sea of grey-white gravel that is re-raked daily into set patterns. A tile-topped earthen wall surrounds it on three sides; the fourth side is a verandah of the temple where viewers may sit and admire it. The unknown designer in the 1470s left no explanation of the meaning of the garden (if any), so numerous interpretations have been concocted, any one of which is as valid as the next.

There's more to the temple than just the garden – small groves of trees, a pond, a giant *moku-gyo* (wooden gong that makes a 'tonk' sound when struck), a carved stone well in the shape of a coin (the water is safe to drink), the paintings on the interior sliding doors, and many details of the buildings. Ryoan-ji is in walking distance from Kinkaku-ji. (Pronounce the 'Ryo' of Ryoan-ji as one syllable if you want Japanese to understand you.)

Ninna-ji Temple The great gate of this temple fronts onto the street and on either side of the entrance is a huge, fearsome Nio-sama guardian god. One has an open mouth, the other closed, like Koma-inu. These are some of the finer Nio-sama in Japan and they are better lit than most (good for photos). The grounds are large and at their best when the cherry blossoms are out; at other times the temple is only of moderate interest.

The area between Kinkaku-ji and Ninna-ji is covered by the TIC publication *Walking Courses in Kyoto*.

Kitano-tenmangu Shrine Quite the opposite of the flamboyant Heian shrine, Kitano is old (1607) and of a restrained Japanese style in natural wood. Its size and the beautifully coloured details and carvings set this apart from most shrines.

Day Trips

Kyoto is close to a good deal of the really interesting sightseeing territory in Japan. A number of places can be visited in a day using Kyoto as a base, or you can go out on circling routes and return after a few days. Day trips include Nara, Hikone, Himeji, Osaka, Ise, and Yoshino (in cherry blossom time).

Extended trips would be the area around Nara and around the Kii-hanto peninsula. Information on train services in the region is given at the end of this chapter.

Festivals

There are many festivals in Kyoto but because information is so easy to obtain there is no need to list them all here. The JNTO pamphlet on Kyoto/Nara has a good listing, as do the monthly booklets listed earlier.

The most famous festivals, worth making a point to see, include the following:

15 May: Aoi Matsuri festival is a procession where people in costumes of centuries ago pass through the streets from Kyoto Gosho Palace to Shimogamo and Kamigamo shrines.

16-17 July: Gion Matsuri festival is probably the supreme Japanese festival. Huge festival carts (yatai) are pulled through streets on the 17th of month. There are 29 in all, of various sizes, all several tonnes in weight and built like miniature temples, small boats, etc, with the finest lacquer covering, gilded ornamentation, and some with European tapestries – they are a fantastic sight. The night before, they are on display in little side streets; many may be entered on the payment of a fee. Also open are some of the old nearby houses where families display their treasures, such as suits of armour. The TIC can give information on the route and display sites. Accommodation is hard to find at this time so it is necessary to book ahead or to commute from a nearby city or town.

16 August: For the Daimonji festival five huge bonfires on separate mountains surrounding Kyoto each traces out a Chinese character. City lights are doused to add to the effect. It is the culmination of the Bon season when the spirits of the dead are believed to return to earth. During this season you may find neighbourhood dances with hundreds of people in kimono moving in great

circles and performing the slow and graceful movements of the dance. The best vantage points are Shogun-zuka hill (Hagashi-yama) and Yoshida-yama hill, near Kyoto University.

22 October: Jidai Matsuri festival; the name means Festival of the Ages, and it is a procession of people in historical costumes of the 13 main periods of Kyoto's history.

Places to Stay

A large number of places offer reasonably priced accommodation in Kyoto but there are hotels of the international luxury class and some ryokan that are even more costly.

For the full listing of cheap places to stay it is best to obtain the photocopied sheets Moderately Priced Accommodation in Kyoto from the TIC in either Kyoto or Tokyo.

There are six Youth Hostels in and around Kyoto. Those nearest the station are Higashiyama (tel 761-8135) and Matsusan (tel 221-5160). Because of their proximity to the station they are more likely to be booked.

Both Utano Youth Hostel (tel 462-2288/9) and Kitayama (tel 492-5345) are about 50 minutes by bus to the north of the city (a little less if you take the north-south subway line and go by bus from there); the latter is more out of the way.

Some distance into the country (more than an hour by bus) are Ohara Youth Hostel (tel 744-2721) and Oharago Youth Hostel (tel 744-2721).

Favourites with travellers who don't care for the restrictions of youth hostels are two private homes, Tani House and Uno House.

Tani House (tel 492-5489) is a spacious, traditional-style house with several rooms, one each set aside for males and females, plus several smaller rooms suitable for couples or whoever happens to get there first. The only disadvantage is that it is a considerable distance from Kyoto station. Access is by subway to the north terminus, then a west-bound bus No 214, 204 or 222 to Funaokakoen stop, where a small road can be seen across the main road from a tailor shop. Follow this and turn right at the third little side street. (It faces an earthen wall inset with tiles.)

Uno House is conveniently located not far from the southeast corner of the Kyoto Gosho. Access from Kyoto station is by bus No 4, 14, 54, 200 or 215 to Kawaramachi-Marutomachi stop. From the large intersection, walk west to the second small street on the south side and turn left (there's a bank on the corner). The house is on the east side; a very small sign says 'Uno'. Travellers arriving in Kyoto by bus from Osaka Airport should get off at Kyoto Hotel (on Kawaramachi-dori), a 20-minute walk to the south of Uno House. The house is something of a wonder and quite untypically Japanese, with so many added-on rooms and wings that it is a bit of a rabbit warren. Be sure a record is made that your payment has been received. Uno house has the convenience of offering simple cooking facilities for economical eating, and closeness to the city. Occasionally a room is available for long-term occupancy.

One of the benefits of staying at these two places is that the other travellers you meet there often have useful information and interesting stories.

There is another private home (tel 681-7437) run by a family named Tani. It is to the south of the city.

One more place that welcomes foreigners is called the English Guest House (tel (075) 223-1059 mornings, (075) 722-0495 evening and weekends), northeast of the city. Shared accommodation is Y1300 per night, with slight reductions by the week or month. It is accessible by subway to Kitaoji station (terminus), then by east-bound bus Kita 6, Kitaoji to Takanoshako-mae stop. Phoning ahead is advisable.

The least expensive ryokan are Ichiume (tel 351-9385, Y1500), Sanyu (tel 371-1968, Y1500) and Yuhara (tel 371-9583).

Other ryokan include: Rakutuso Bekkan (tel 761-633, Y3900) and Rakutuso Honkan (tel 761-6336, Y8000 for two), both near Heian-jingu.

The Kyoto YWCA (tel 431-0351) costs Y3500 and takes women only.

Some western-style hotels include:

Pension Utano, (tel 463-1118), Y3200
Traveller's Inn Honkan, (tel 771-0225), Y3800, near Heian-jingu shrine Traveller's Inn Hotel
Sun Shine,(tel 771-0225), Y3800
Hokke Club, (tel 361-1251), Y4000
Kyoto Business Hotel, (tel 222-1220), Y4000
Kyoto Central Inn, (tel 211-1666), Y5080
New Ginkaku Inn, (tel 341-2884), Y5500
Tokyu Inn, (tel 593-0109), Y5900
Pension Shimogamo, (tel 711-0180), Y8200

Those on large budgets who wish to sample a really fine ryokan in beautiful surroundings should enjoy Rankyokan, which is on a hill side overlooking the Hozu River, just above Arashiyama and set among tall trees. The price is over Y10,000 per person.

Temple Accommodation Many people wish to stay in a temple in Kyoto. Unfortunately, as with Zen meditation, previous foreign guests have not conformed with customs and rules of the temples and soured any desire of temple staff to have foreign visitors.

Anyone seriously interested in staying at a temple and able to demonstrate both some genuine interest in the religious aspects and a willingness to conform to custom should contact the TIC for further information.

Places to Eat
To help with the search for a good restaurant, the Kyoto Restaurant Association has printed a pamphlet, Kyoto Gourmet Guide, available at the TIC. Staff at the TIC would also probably be willing to suggest a good restaurant and

perhaps even a sample menu if your visit was not at one of their busy times.

For budget diners there are many little restaurants with realistic wax displays that show you the available dishes. A former student of Kyoto University recommended *Nakagima* for economical food (open Monday to Saturday).

For years the bargain of the city was the all-the-pizza-you-can-eat deal at *Trecca Pizza*, but this near-institution on one of the main streets has closed. The restaurants of the *Shakey's Pizza* chain in Tokyo and elsewhere have the same deal (for Y550) and there is probably a Shakey's in Kyoto by now. The hours at Shakey's for this deal are between 11 am and 2 pm, Monday to Saturday.

As in other Japanese cities, there are *McDonald's, Kentucky Fried Chicken* and other familiar American fast-food shops; they provide more food for the yen than just about any restaurant serving Japanese food.

Entertainment

If you aren't worn out after a day's sightseeing, or if you want a break during the day from a seemingly endless round of temples and shrines, what else is there to do in Kyoto?

There are many events that would fit into the cultural category – performing arts that have been passed down through the centuries and which represent some of the highest levels of achievement in these fields in the world. Naturally these are not going to be everyone's cup of *o-cha*, but it would be a pity to ignore this side of Japanese life.

Dance & Theatre Through the year, at various times and theatres, there are performances of the traditional arts Noh, *kabuki, bunraku, kyogen* and others. As Osaka is less than an hour away by train, performances of *kabuki* and *bunraku* (puppet theatre which originated in Osaka) given there are also in easy reach.

A highly recommended condensed version of all the major Japanese arts – dances by *geisha*, traditional *bugaku* dances, *koto* music, *bunraku*, flower arrangement – can be seen between 1 March and 29 November twice daily at Gion Kaburenjo Theatre. The show is called Gion Corner and lasts an hour; performances begin at 8 and 9 pm. Each act is long enough to give a feel for the skill, but short enough not to be dull (most seem too short). Tickets can be bought at the door but bookings or advance purchase may be advisable during busy seasons.

There are many performances of traditional dances at certain times of the year. Examples are Miyako-odori (Cherry Blossom Dance) throughout April, when numbers of beautifully dressed *maiko* (apprentice *geisha*) perform traditional dances, and Kamogawa-odori in May, when *geisha* of the Ponto-sho area perform.

To check on what is happening, obtain the booklets mentioned earlier, and be sure to stop in at the TIC where the bulletin board lists all the events of that month and the staff can give further details.

Coffee Shops Other entertainment includes the many coffee shops. Some are only places to sit and chat; a coffee-shop date is a common activity among young couples, which helps explain the high prices – you're not paying for the coffee, but for the space.

Many shops offer music, either recorded or live; the latter is usually jazz, while recorded music may be jazz, classical or in between. The TIC people can suggest which are the current popular places. It is possible to meet people at such places, but it's all the luck of the draw.

Bars & Clubs There is a huge number of places for drinking, as is true of any large city in Japan. Some are reasonable in cost and quite enjoyable to visit, but beware of what would be called 'clip joints' in any other country – these are accepted in Japan because of generous expense accounts. It is not unknown to be billed well over Y10,000 for a beer!

There are many small pubs and 'stand-bars' (Japanese term), many of which are run by companies that make or distribute whisky. These reasonably priced places can be identified after a little practice. Don't be embarrassed to ask prices – remember the possible consequences!

Avoid any place that has touts in front enticing customers in, and places with hostesses, unless you are able to check prices for all services. Hostess charges can skyrocket. The TIC may be able to give suggestions.

There are many lower-class clubs where strippers and similar entertainment may be found. Finding them on your own may be difficult, if not impossible, so a Japanese friend would be invaluable in locating one.

Things to Buy

Kyoto probably offers the largest variety of traditional Japanese handicrafts of any city in the country. There are many shops near the station and near many of the major temples and other tourist attractions. There are also several department stores and the Kyoto Handicraft centre. A commercial map, *Shopping Guide Map of Kyoto*, is useful for locating specialty shops. It is available at the TIC and hotels. The TIC staff can also help you find anything out of the ordinary.

I found that the tax-free shops along Kawaramachi-dori gave somewhat less discount on photographic equipment than the cheapest shops in Tokyo, but the difference wasn't enough to worry about. If Kyoto is your first stop in Japan, it is better to spend the extra yen and have a camera available to photograph the beauties of Kyoto rather than saving a small sum and having no photo souvenirs.

Getting There & Away

Air You can reach Kyoto easily from many points in Japan as well as from overseas because Osaka International Airport serves Kyoto as well as Osaka.

Hitching To hitch out of Kyoto east to Nagoya or Tokyo, or west to Hiroshima and Shimonoseki, take bus No 19 or 20 from the station until signs for the entrance of the Meishin expressway (marked in English) come into view. Find the entrance for the direction you want and hold up a sign (in Japanese) showing your destination.

If going to a point beyond Osaka, such as Hiroshima, it is vastly preferable to pick up a car going directly that way (at least beyond Osaka) because there are several expressways in the Osaka area and, if your drive turns onto one, you could have a great deal of difficulty getting back in motion. It is illegal to hitch beside the expressways; the only way to change vehicles is to get off at a rest stop and try other drivers.

Osaka is so close that it is not worth hitching to; take the train.

To hitch toward Tottori (north coast) it is simplest to take the train to Kameoka and start there, but you could also take one of several buses (or Hankyu train) to the Katsura area and hitch on Route 9.

However, it seems the authorities are beginning to discourage hitch-hikers out of Kyoto (possibly because there are too many people doing it), so ask among other travellers for an up-date.

Getting Around

Airport Transport Buses run every 20 minutes throughout the day in each direction, making the rounds of several of the better-known hotels (the Miyako, Kyoto, JAL, International and Grand) as well as Kyoto station.

Bus Kyoto is covered by an extensive network of bus routes. The major ones are shown on a sub-map on the TIC Kyoto map. A much more detailed map (in Japanese only) is available at the bus centre in front of Kyoto station. If possible, however, it is advisable to chat to the TIC staff because some of the buses are infrequent.

Briefly, there are two loop bus lines, No 206 and 214. The former goes along Higashi-oji, Kita-oji and Karasuma streets on the way to and from the station, while the latter uses Kawaramachi, Kita-oji and Nishi-oji streets. The character following the number tells the direction.

A one-day pass for unlimited travel on city buses is available but you might not use it enough to justify the cost. There is also an '11 tickets for the price of 10' deal. Both are available at the bus centre, and further information can be obtained at the TIC.

Subway Kyoto has a modern subway line running from Kyoto station north along Karasuma-dori to Kita-oji-dori on the northernmost major east-west road. The Hankyu private railway line (Kyoto-Osaka) intersects it at Shijo-Karasuma and provides east-west service via four stations along Shijo-dori. Several JR and private rail lines can be used for transport within Kyoto. These are shown on the TIC map.

Taxi Taxis are plentiful. Don't worry about telling the driver your destination; if he doesn't understand your pronunciation he can read it in Japanese on the TIC map.

Bicycle Bicycles may be rented at the Bridgestone bike shop on the corner of Muromachi and Shimocho-jamachi streets, and from a couple of shops near Sanjo station. The TIC will know if any other shops now offer them.

The bikes are single-speed clunkers but most of Kyoto is flat so this is no great problem. A bike is probably best regarded as convenient, rather than economical, for the savings in bus fares might be negligible.

Kyoto Area

WEST KYOTO
Arashiyama
This area is on the western edge of the city, where the Hozu River emerges from a gorge, and tree-covered hills appear. Though it is often promoted as a tourist attraction, most of it is of limited interest to visitors unless nature walks are of particular appeal. It *is* of great appeal to the Japanese, who are confined to cities much of the time.

Arashiyama-koen park is a pleasant area at the end of a picturesque foot-bridge across the river from Arashiyama station (Keifuku railway); it is at its prettiest in spring because of the many cherry trees on the grounds.

The area north and west of Arashiyama is shown on the TIC's *Walking Tour Courses in Kyoto*, but it does not detail east of the museum, so you will need to rely on the TIC Kyoto-Nara map or the one in this book.

Arashiyama Museum One of the better museums in Japan, this is at the north end of the bridge near the station. Kyoto-Arashiyama Hakubutsukan, to give it its proper name, will be of greatest interest to war buffs, but also has general appeal. It has one of the best collections in Japan of ancient armour, helmets, swords, halberds and other weapons, as well as incredibly ornate and fine lacquerware.

What sets the museum apart from others, however, is its display of WW II weapons, including the only Zero fighter left in Japan (all were destroyed by American authorities, but this one was fished out of Biwa-ko lake in 1978), a midget suicide submarine (raised from off Izu-hanto peninsula), and an enormous gun barrel from the sunken battleship *Mutsu*. This immense piece of steel is 19.3 metres long and about two metres wide at the breech end; it projected a 1000-kg shell anything up to 40 km.

Tenryo-ji Temple

The landscape garden behind the abbot's quarters is well known, although the buildings are of recent vintage (about 1900).

Nison-in Temple

The grounds of this temple, northwest of Tenryo-ji, are planted with maples that are famous for their autumn colour.

Ukai

Every night between 1 July and 31 August (except on nights of full moon or after heavy rains when the river is muddy), there is a performance near Arashiyama bridge of fishing using cormorants as the divers. (Details of this activity are given in the Gifu section in the chapter on Central Honshu.) The best view and the most fun is on a boat, but the river is not too wide so the action can also be seen from shore or the bridge.

Koryu-ji Temple

One of Kyoto's oldest buildings, and a very large number of exceptionally old Buddhist images, are found in this out-of-the-way temple. The original temple was said to have been constructed in 603 AD by Prince Shotoku. The Lecture Hall (*kodo*) was built in 1165, while the Hakkakudo building dates from 1251.

The new fireproof Reihohan (treasure museum) has on display a large number of historic carved wooden statues including the famous Miroku-Bosatsu, which was crafted in the Asuka period (552 to 645) and which is still in remarkably good condition. There are many other figures nearly as old. Even if you don't understand any of the significance of the figures, you can still appreciate their workmanship and marvel at how well these wooden figures have survived the years.

Although the temple is close to Usumasu station of the JR San-in line, trains are rather infrequent compared with buses. You can take a bus No 71, 72 or 73 from in front of Wimpy's, to the left when leaving Kyoto station.

Eiga-mura

The name means 'Movie Village', and the place is a studio used for making films that require a traditional Japanese setting. There are streets of buildings of the style of the *samurai* era, and others of later eras.

Visitors are welcome to watch filming, when a camera, dolly and crew show up at some spot on the set, actors go through their lines with action, and the camera rolls. One suspects there is no film in the camera because only a single take is made of each scene, but movies are an illusion anyway, aren't they? It's all good entertainment.

There are also exhibitions explaining some of the special effects used in films. The studio is within walking distance of Koryuji temple, so refer to that section for access information. Many people can usually be seen walking to it, so there's a good chance you can follow the crowd. If not, ask 'Eiga-mura dochira?' Everyone seems to enjoy it.

Saiho-ji Temple

Saiho-ji was very popular with visitors because of the unusual beauty of the 200 or so varieties of moss that have been planted in the garden. However, the hordes of sightseers caused neighbours of the temple to protest, with the result that the garden has been closed. Entry is still possible, but only to those who write for an appointment and are willing to pay Y3000 as well as fulfill some other obligations.

I visited the garden several times before the closure and found it nice but not special, and consider the fee exorbitant. If you really wish to see it, send a reply-paid postcard, giving your name, address, age, occupation and desired date of visit to: Saihoji, 56 Kamigatani, Matsuo, Nishikyo-ku, Kyoto-shi.

SOUTHWEST KYOTO
Katsura Rikyu Imperial Villa
This villa was built for the brother of an emperor and was finished in 1624. It was painstakingly repaired and restored over several years up to 1982. The buildings are of very simple design but are made of the finest materials by the best craftsmen available. It is considered the zenith of restrained elegance; the highest point in purely Japanese architecture.

The villa is under the control of the Imperial Household Agency and it is necessary to make an appointment in advance. (Details are given under Kyoto Gosho at the beginning of this section.) Although there may be a wait of two to three days, it is sometimes possible to go the same day. The villa is closed Saturday afternoons, Sundays, national holidays and from 25 December to 5 January.

It can be reached from Arashiyama/Saihoji, or from central Kyoto (Shijo-dori area) by different branches of the Hankyu railway.

SOUTH & SOUTHEAST KYOTO
The TIC has a small photocopied map that is useful for general orientation in this area (as far south as Nara).

Tofuku-ji Temple
This temple is at its best in November when the maples in the ravine (crossed by picturesque Tsuten-kyo bridge) are at their best. Some of the architectural details of the buildings are noticeably different from those of most temples, and the *karesansui* garden of mixed greenery and raked sand has a beauty of its own.

Access is from Tofukuji stations of both JR Nara line and Keihan hon-sen (main line).

Fushimi-Inari Taisha Shrine
This is the largest of the 32,000 Inari shrines found throughout Japan. They honour the patron deities of agriculture and business, two of the most important activities in the country, which ensures their continued popularity. For this reason you are likely to come across a family or members of a small business praying for success in a new venture. The fox is the messenger of the shrine deities, which explains the large number of fox statues on the grounds.

The shrine is famous for the huge number of orange-painted *torii* erected over some of the paths that wind up the mountain side. There are more than 1000 of them and they are so close together that they form a tunnel. They have been donated by worshippers whose supplications were answered. (You may read reports that there are 10,000 or more, but I counted them.)

At various shrines along the route you may see hundreds of miniature *torii* (sold at the entrance) that have been left by worshippers – they can be seen stacked like firewood at the end of the season.

Those energetic enough to climb to the top – there are many paths branching off, many leading considerable distances away – may find a stone monument engraved with the profile of Charles Bronson! He is used as the symbol of virility by a line of male cosmetics called Mandom.

There is a good chance of seeing some sort of ceremony at the main building; there may also be performances of the slow and graceful sacred *kagura* dances by shrine maidens.

The shrine is reached easily from Inari station of the JR Nara line, or Fushimi-Inari station of Keihan hon-sen line. It is one of very few in Kyoto with no admittance charge.

Daigo-ji Temple
The oldest structure in Kyoto is the five-storey pagoda of this temple in the far southeast corner of the city; it dates from 951. Nearby Sambon-in has one of the finest landscape gardens in Japan. There is no nearby train station; ask the TIC for access information.

Fushimi-Momoyama Castle
This is marked on the TIC map and you may be tempted to see it. The original castle that once stood here was torn down centuries ago and many of its parts given to other temples, palaces, etc. Some are at Nijo-jo, Nishi-Hongan-ji and other Kyoto temples, and can be found as far away as Matsushima, in the northern part of Honshu.

However, the present structure is only a modern concrete reproduction and offers nothing that can't be seen better elsewhere such as Himeji or Hikone, both easily reached from Kyoto, which have genuine historic castles.

Manpuku-ji Temple
This is the head temple of the Obaku sect of Zen, probably the least known of the three Zen 'schools' in Japan. It was introduced from China in the mid-17th century and, until the mid-1700s, was headed by a Chinese monk. Every attempt is still made to preserve Chinese traditions. The buildings are of Chinese architectural style, which makes them unique in Kyoto.

Access is from Obaku stations JR Nara line or Keihan main line. The former is closer.

Uji
For centuries this has been a resort for the wealthy and powerful of Kyoto. It is best known for Byodo-in temple and *ukai*.

Byodo-in Temple This temple is unusual for its elongated structure dating from 1053. It is meant to portray a phoenix-like bird of Chinese mythology, and is the building seen on the Y10 coin; it is considered to be the finest structure of the Fujiwara era. However, most of the painted details inside the main building have disappeared with time and you may be somewhat let down by the temple and grounds.

Ukai A suggestion is to go and see Byodo-in temple late in the afternoon, have an evening meal or a snack, and then watch the cormorant fishing on the river at Tonoshima island (very close to the temple).

Ukai is held every night from 11 June to 31 August, except during full moon or after heavy rains. You can rent a boat only, or arrange for a party/supper with food and drink. (A person who speaks Japanese would be helpful for this; the TIC might be able to offer suggestions.)

The actual fishing lasts only 20 to 30 minutes, so the Japanese watchers make a party lasting the evening out of it. The fishing takes place close to shore and can be seen quite well without taking a boat, but the boat is more fun if the moderate cost is not a problem.

Access to Uji is by the JR Nara line, or the Keihan line, for which Uji is the terminus. Byodo-in temple is on the same side of the river as the JR station; from the Keihan station you cross the bridge and turn left.

NORTHEAST KYOTO
Shugaku-in Rikyu Imperial Villa
This villa dates from 1629. The upper garden is built around a pond and is considered the most scenic part of the grounds. The landscape is mostly lawn and rolling hills and I regard it as not worth a special trip to see, at least not until after you have seen a good number of the other places first. It is at its best in autumn. Advance permission must be obtained from the Imperial Household Agency. (Refer to the Kyoto Gosho details at the beginning of this section.)

Kyoto International Conference Hall (Kokusai Kaigi-jo)
A source of civic pride, the Conference Hall is a six-storey building constructed in 1966 beside the Takara-ga-ike pond and used for many international gatherings. It can be reached from Kyoto station by bus No 5, 36 or 65; it is about one km from Takaragaike station of the Keifuku line out of Demachi-Yanagi station (to the

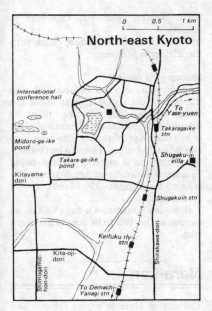

North-east Kyoto

0   0.5   1 km

International conference hall

To Yase-yuen

Midoro-ga-ike pond

Takaragaike stn

Takara-ga-ike pond

Shugaku-in villa

Kitayama-dori

Shugakuin stn

Keifuku rly stn

Kita-oji-dori

Shirakawa-dori

Shimogamo-hon-dori

To Demachi-Yanagi stn

northeast of the city). The fastest access is by subway north to Karasuma-Shakomae, which is linked to the hall by bus No 36.

The Ohara area is easily reached as the Conference Hall is close to the bus and rail connections to Yase-yuen and Ohara.

Enryaku-ji Temple

This is a very large temple complex on Mt Hiei, the highest point in the ridge that separates Kyoto from Biwa-ko lake. Temples have stood here since 788 when Emperor Kammi (who founded Kyoto as the capital) ordered its construction to guard against 'evil spirits' from the northeast. One theory suggests that the spirits were actually Ainu or another race who predated the ethnic Japanese (Yamato).

Enryaku-ji grew to an astounding 3000 temples and its private army of several thousand armed monks was more powerful than any government force. They terrorised other Buddhist sects and often attacked

Kyoto itself if their wishes were not met. In 1571 Nobunaga Oda, who began the unification of Japan after the civil war, killed or dispersed the monks and destroyed every temple. After this, Enryaku-ji was limited to 5% of its former size. Today there are still 130 temples on the mountain. The main building is the huge Kompon-cho-do.

There are four possible routes to Enryaku-ji temple. The first two are either by Keifuku private railway from Demachi-Yanagi station, or by bus from Kyoto station to Yase-yuen and then cable railway to the top.

The third route is by train to the west shore of Biwa-ko lake, then a cable railway to the top of Mt Hiei. There are two stations near the base station: Sakamoto station of the Keihan line (from Sanjo-Keihan station in Kyoto, with a change of trains at Hama-Otsu), and Eizan station (JR), which is on the Osaka/Kyoto – Nagahara/Omi-Shiotsu line. Fourth, there are also at least 10 buses a day from Kyoto station to the temple. The third is the most scenic route.

Ohara

This small village is well known for the Jakko-in and Sanzen-in temples. The women of Ohara have long been famous for their characteristic costume and customs. Unusual in Japan, they carry loads on their heads. They may be seen on occasion in Kyoto selling produce from Ohara; in Ohara itself they may be working at souvenir stalls.

Access to Ohara is by bus that originates at Kyoto station and passes by Sanjo-Keihan and Yase-Yuen stations on the way, or by Keifuku railway Eizan-sen line to Yase-Yuen (the base station for the cable railway to Mt Hiei) and then by bus to Ohara. During the leaf-viewing season the buses are packed, so a start from Kyoto station is advisable to guarantee a seat (or even somewhere to stand!).

Sanzen-in Temple Like most other temples,

this temple has images of historical interest which become rather repetitive to westerners who know little of Buddhism and its art. However, the main temple has a setting of lush green and the grounds are extremely beautiful in late October and early November when the leaves change colour. It is, naturally, very crowded at that time but still well worth going to see. An English-language pamphlet gives historical information.

Kurama-dera Temple

Accessible by Keifuku railway from Demachi-Yanagi station (continuing from Takaraga-ike station on the Kurama-sen line) is Kurama-dera temple. Although the temple dates from 770, the present main hall was only built in 1971 so it is of little architectural interest. However, the grounds are very pretty in late October and early November, so this is the best time for a visit. There is also an interesting festival on 20 June.

There is a good hiking trail between Kurama-dera and Kibune-jinja shrine; it also is most recommended during autumn.

NORTHWEST KYOTO

Takao

This is possibly the supreme area for maple viewing, several km into the mountains northwest of the city. There are three temples to visit while admiring the foliage. These temples are: Jingo-ji (at Takao), Saimyo-ji (at Makino-o), and Kozan-ji (at Togano-o); all are within walking distance of each other.

On the approach up to Jingo-ji temple, tables and mat-covered areas are set up on level patches of ground and on platforms so visitors may lunch beneath the canopy of brilliant colours. The view of a Japanese family, with one or two of the women dressed in kimono, eating amidst such beauty is a memorable picture of Japan at its best.

Visitors may find a specialty of the season on sale – maple-leaf tempura. The

batter tastes good but the leaf is terrible.

Buses run as far as Takao; check with the TIC for schedules.

Shooting the Rapids

An enjoyable excursion, especially during the heat of the summer, is to shoot the Hozu rapids. The starting point is Kameoka, accessible by JR Sanin-sen line or bus from Kyoto station. The dock is at Hozu-ohashi bridge. The trip lasts about two hours and is exciting without being dangerous. It finishes at Arashiyama. The season lasts from 11 March to 30 November.

Boats leave six times a day (Y3000), so inquire at the TIC to be sure of getting a seat.

Nara-ken

The city of Nara is a very famous and popular destination for visitors to Japan. It predates Kyoto as the imperial capital and some temples from that period actually still survive.

The Nara plain was one of the most important areas in the early history of Japan and historic remnants abound. There are also other attractions in the southern parts of the prefecture and the adjoining Kii-hanto peninsula.

NARA

Usually mentioned in the same breath as Kyoto, Nara is another ancient Japanese capital. It is only 42 km from Kyoto and is usually included in any tour. It was the first permanent capital of Japan, from 710 to 784, prior to which the capital was moved after the death of each emperor.

Nara witnessed the introduction of Buddhism into Japan, with the resulting far reaching effects on culture and the arts. Amazingly, some of the temples and other structures from that period still stand. Although they were then in the city

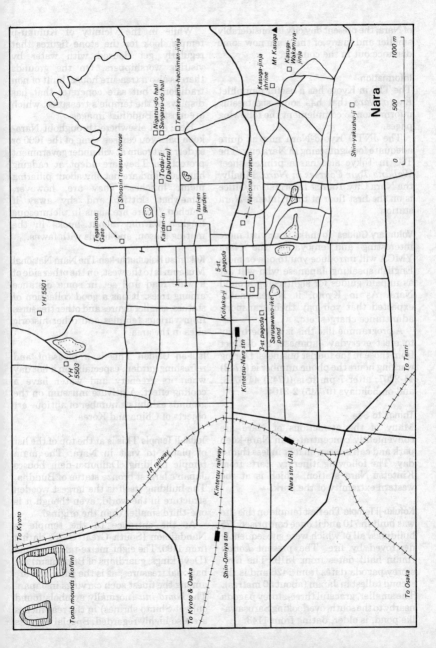

Nara

1000 m

500

0

To Kyoto

To Kyoto & Osaka

Tomb mounds (kofun)

Y H 5503

Y H 5501

Tegaimon Gate

Shosoin treasure house

Nigatsu-do hall
Sangatsu-do hall

Todai-ji (Daibutsu)

Kaidan-in

Isu-en garden

Tamukeyama-hachiman-jinja

Kasuga-jinja shrine

Mt Kasuga

Kasuga Wakamiya-jinja

Shin-yakushu-ji

National museum

5-st pagoda

Kofuku-ji

3-st pagoda

Sarusawano-ike pond

Kintetsu-Nara stn

Kintetsu railway

JR railway

To Tenri

Shin-Omiya stn

Nara stn (JR)

To Osaka

of Nara, the present day city is considerably smaller and many of them are now some distance out in the country.

Information

The TIC in Kyoto has a useful pamphlet *Kyoto Nara* that has some sightseeing information to complement the following pages.

The JNTO Kyoto-Nara map is quite adequate for sightseeing in Nara city. The TIC in Tokyo also has a printed sheet *Walking Tour Courses in Nara*. Finally, the Nara City Tourist Information Office is on the first floor of the Kintetsu-Nara station.

Voluntary Guides To make your visit more interesting and enjoyable, the Nara YMCA will introduce you to one or more English-speaking Japanese who will act as unpaid guides for sightseeing around Nara. As in Kyoto, it is reasonably expected that you pay their transport, admittance charges, etc.

A programme like this is a superb way to meet everyday Japanese, as distinct from those in the tourist business. During working hours the phone number is (0742) 44-2207; after 7 pm it is (0742) 44-6718, and on holidays (07745) 2-3104.

Things to See

Many of the attractions of Nara are conveniently concentrated in Nara-koen park and can be seen on foot in less than a day. The following itinerary starts from Kintetsu-Nara station, which is at the western extremity of the park.

Kofuku-ji Temple The first temple on this site was built in 710 and it once comprised 175 buildings, all of which were subsequently destroyed by fire. The present *kondo* (main hall) dates from 1819. The five-storey pagoda dates from 1426 and is the second tallest in Japan (about 50 metres). The smaller, graceful three-storey pagoda nearby to the south, overlooking Sarusawa-ike pond, is older, dating from 1143.

While in the vicinity of Kufuku-ji temple, look for the stone figures that regularly get doused with water by visiting worshippers. On the grounds there is also a treasure house, built of non traditional but safe concrete, that has displays of the temple's treasures, which are mostly Buddhist images.

Here and elsewhere throughout Nara-koen park you can see some of the 1000 or so deer that roam at will under government protection. They are adept at cadging handouts and are not shy about pilfering picnic lunches. They are, however, somewhat skittish and shy away if touched. There are signs in picturesque English warning about bucks in the mating season, and hinds with fawns.

Kokuritsu Hakubutsu-ken The Nara National Museum is to the west, on the other side of a wide road and set in some distance among trees. It has a good collection of statues, smaller figures and other treasures from various temples and other historic sites in the area.

Isui-en Garden This is a pleasant and refreshing garden, especially on a hot day when its greenery and water have a cooling effect. A private museum on the grounds exhibits a number of antique art objects of China and Korea.

Todai-ji Temple This is at the top of the list of places to visit in Nara. The main temple building, Daibutsu-den, houses Japan's largest bronze statue of Buddha. The building itself is the largest wooden structure in the world, even though it is one-third smaller than the original.

At the entrance to the temple is Nandaimon (South Great Gate) dating from 1199. The eight-metre-tall Nio-sama (Deva kings, guardians of Buddhism) are national treasures, as is the gate, and are among the finest such carvings in Japan. The *koma-inu* (normally symbols found only at Shinto shrines) in the rear niches are also highly regarded. Special biscuits for the deer are on sale in this area, and not surprisingly, the deer are also found here in the greatest numbers.

Daibutsu-den was built in 1709, the latest in a series from 752; it has recently had extensive renovations. The Daibutsu (Great Buddha) statue in the incense-filled interior was first cast in 749 but subsequent damage in fires has required replacing the head (at least twice), the right hand and other parts. Possibly as a result of this later work, the statue lacks the artistry and serenity of the Daibutsu at Kamakura (near Tokyo). The statue is 16 metres tall and weighs 437 tonnes.

The two large statues in front of the Daibutsu are Nyoirin-Kannon, who grants prayers and wishes, and Kokuzo-Bosatsu, who possesses wisdom and happiness. The figure in the left-hand corner behind the statue is Komokuten, one of the four heavenly guardians who destroy all obstacles in the path of Buddhism. Another of the guardians, Tamonten, is found in the right-hand corner; he is trampling a demon.

Kaidan-in is a separate temple west of the Daibutsu-den; it contains clay images of the four heavenly guardians; all are national treasures.

Sangatsu-do is the oldest structure of Todai-ji, dating from 733. Many statues of national treasure merit are displayed.

Kasuga-taisha Shrine One of the best known places in Nara, Kasuga-taisha is famous for its forested setting and lanterns. There are approximately 3000 lanterns, some of stone and standing as tall as a man, others of bronze and hung from the eaves of the various buildings that make up the shrine. Seen against the bright orange and white of the buildings, the effect is striking.

Lanterns line nearly all the paths of the shrine grounds, and this is within the area roamed by deer, so one of them is quite likely to poke its head out between two of the lanterns for a very cute picture.

The lanterns are all lit twice a year, on the day of the Setsubun festival (2 or 3 February) and on 15 August. The annual festival of the shrine, Kasuga-matsuri, is held on 13 March and features a colourful procession.

In addition to the four shrines (surrounded by a gallery) that make up the main shrine, there is also Kasuga-Wakamiya-jinja to the south. Here it may be possible to see Kagura (sacred dances) in the Kagura-den, the southernmost of the three buildings. The annual festival of this shrine is the greatest in Nara and is a procession of large numbers of people in costumes and armour of ancient times. It is held on 16-17 December.

Shin-Yakushi-ji Temple This temple is of modest interest and is known primarily for its central seated image and 12 clay figures of 12 divine generals.

Places to Stay

Most foreign visitors to Nara probably make it a day trip out of Kyoto. However, anyone wishing to explore the area in greater detail will find a good range of accommodation available. Accommodation can be booked in advance through any travel agent in the country (though JTB is the biggest) and help is available at the railway stations in Nara.

There are two youth hostels in Nara. *Nara Youth Hostel* (tel (0742) 22-1334) should be avoided if there is any choice in the matter. The staff, even temporary help, act as if they are doing the hostellers a great favour by letting them stay, insist that both meals be taken there without option (many people, including myself, do not care for a Japanese breakfast, and a hostel supper is rarely a gourmet feast), and are generally officious.

The alternative is *Nara-ken Seishonen-Kaikan Youth Hostel* (tel (0742) 22-5540, 26-4305), which is much better. It can be reached by following the main road that passes the Kintetsu station downhill to the north-south road that begins north of where the overpass road ends. Follow it

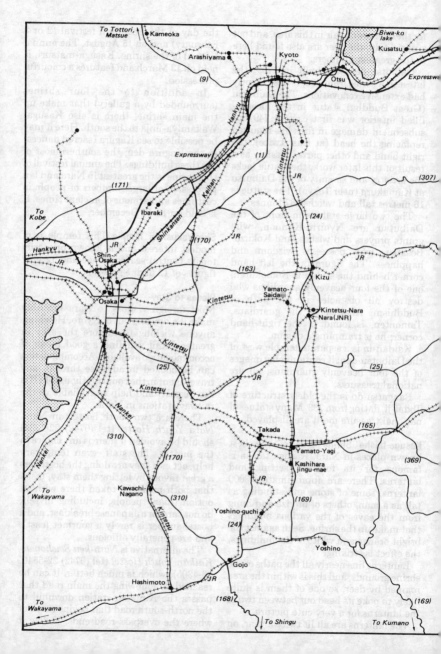

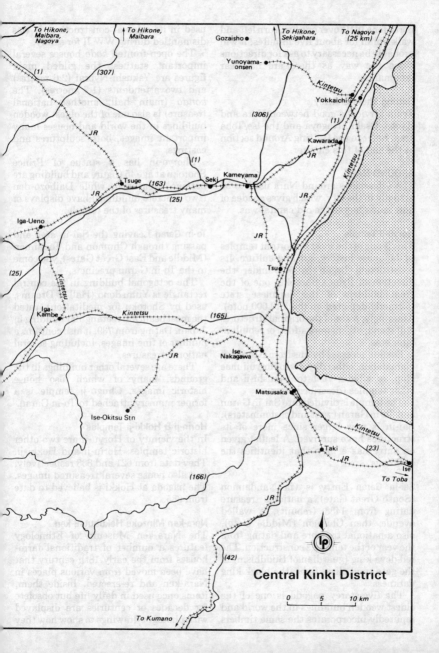

To Hikone,
Maibara, Nagoya

To Hikone,
Maibara

Gozaisho

To Hikone,
Sekigahara

To Nagoya
(25 km)

(1)

Yunoyama-
onsen

(307)

Kintetsu

Yokkaichi

(306)

(1)

Kawarada

(1)

JR

Kameyama

Tsuge   (163)   Seki

(25)

JR

Iga-Ueno

(25)

Kintetsu

Kintetsu

Iga-
Kambe

(165)

JR

Ise-
Nakagawa

JR

Matsusaka

Kintetsu

Ise-Okitsu Stn

Taki

(23)

JR

Ise

To Toba

(166)

(42)

To Kumano

Central Kinki District

0   5   10 km

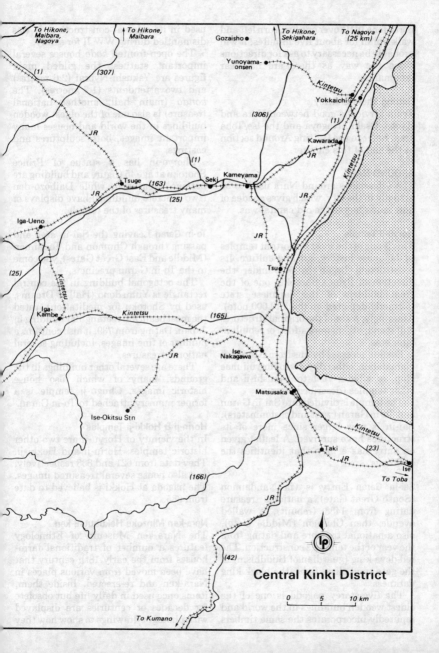

north for a little over one km, turn left and walk uphill for about five minutes; it will probably be necessary to ask for directions along the way as there are no clear landmarks.

Getting There & Away

Train service is good between Nara and Kyoto, Osaka, Nagoya and the Ise/Toba area. Refer to the Getting Around section at the end of this chapter.

AROUND NARA

The attractions around Nara used to be actually in the city, which gives an idea of how much bigger the old capital was.

Horyu-ji Temple

This is one of the most important temples in Japanese history, art and culture. Its construction began in 607 under the direction of Prince Shotoku, one of the great builders of the Japanese state (formerly depicted on the Y10,000 note). Amazingly, some of the original structures still stand; others were added or rebuilt in later eras.

Easiest access is by bus from Kintetsu-Nara station, either directly to Horyuji-mae stop, or after a visit to Yakushi-ji and other temples (described later).

The temple is divided into Sai-in Garan and To-in Garan (west and east minsters). Sai-in is now larger since more of its structures have survived. A leaflet given on entry has a map that identifies the buildings.

Sai-in Garan Entry is via Nandaimon (South Great Gate), a national treasure dating from 1438 (rebuilt), a walled avenue, then Chumon (Middle Gate), also a national treasure and dating from the year of the temple's construction. The red deva king (guardian of Buddhism) in the gate symbolises light; the black king darkness.

The five-storey pagoda is one of the oldest wooden buildings in the world and reputedly incorporates the same timbers used in its original construction. It was dismantled during WW II for safety.

The open-fronted *kodo* houses several important statues: the gilded main figures are Yakushi-Nyorai (2.6 metres) and two attendants (1.7 metres). The *kondo* (main hall, another national treasure) is also one of the oldest wooden buildings in the world and houses many important images, both sculptures and castings.

Shoryo-in has a statue of Prince Shotoku at age 45 (figure and building are national treasures), while Daihozo-den (two concrete buildings) have displays of many treasures of the temple.

To-in Garan Leaving the Sai-in area and passing through Chumon and Todaimon (Middle and East Great Gates), you come to the To-in Garan precincts.

The octagonal building in the central rectangle is Yumedono (Hall of Dreams, used by Shotoku for meditation), rated the most beautiful rectangular building in Japan. Dating from 739, it also contains a number of fine images, including several national treasures.

There are several other buildings in the grounds, many of which also house historic images. Chugu-ji temple is a former nunnery attached to To-in Garan.

Horin-ji & Hokki-ji Temples

In the vicinity of Horyu-ji are two other historic temples, Horin-ji and Hokki-ji. They date from 621 and 638 respectively, and also house several treasured images. The pagoda at Hokki is believed to date from 685.

Nara-ken Minzoku Hakubutsu-kan

The Nara-ken Museum of Ethnology features a number of traditional farmhouses from the early 18th century that have been moved from various places in Nara-ken and re-erected. Inside them, items once used in daily life but obsolete for decades or centuries are displayed with photos or drawings to show how they

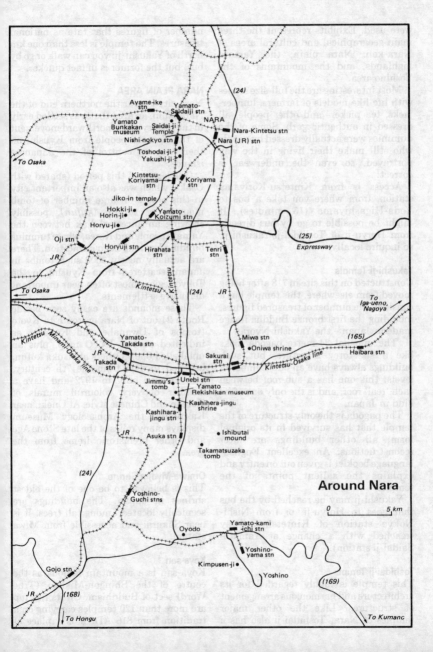

To Osaka

(24)

Ayame-ike
stn

Yamato-
Saidaiji stn

NARA

Yamato
Bunkakan
museum

Saidai-ji
Temple

Nara-Kintetsu stn

Nishi-nokyo stn

Nara (JR) stn

Toshodai-ji
Yakushi-ji stn

Kintetsu-
Koriyama
stn

Koriyama
stn

Jiko-in temple

Hokki-ji
Horin-ji

Yamato-
Koizumi stn

Horyu-ji

Oji stn

Horyuji stn

Hirahata
stn

Tenri
stn

(25)
Expressway

To Osaka

Kintetsu

Kintetsu

(24)

JR

Kintetsu Minami-Osaka line

To
Iga-ueno,
Nagoya

Yamato-
Takada stn

Miwa stn

Oniwa shrine

(165)

JR

Takada
stn

Sakurai
stn

Kintetsu-Osaka line

Haibara stn

Jimmu's
tomb

Unebi stn

Yamato
Rekishikan museum

Kashihara-jingu stn

Kashihara-
jingu shrine

Ishibutai
mound

Asuka stn

Takamatsuzaka
tomb

Around Nara

0   5 km

(24)

Yoshino-
Guchi stns

Oyodo

Yamato-kami-
ichi stn

Kimpusen-ji

Yoshinoyama stn

Yoshino

(169)

Gojo stn

JR

(168)

To Hongu

To Kumano

were used. Exhibits represent the three main geographical and cultural areas of Nara-ken: Nara plain, the Yamato highlands, and the mountains of the Yoshino area.

Most interesting are the full-size scenes with life-like models of farmers, lumberjacks, tea pickers and other people, all dressed in authentic garb. Some of the dummies were actually dressed by people who still make their living in the way portrayed, so even the underwear is correct!

Access is from Kintetsu-Koriyama station, from where you take a bus to Yoda-Higashiyama (15 minutes). It might be possible to go by bus directly from Horyu-ji or Toshidai-ji/Yakushi-ji, so inquire locally.

Yakushi-ji Temple

Constructed on this site in 718 after being moved from elsewhere, this temple has a considerable number of treasured figures, including the first bronze Buddha image made in Japan – the Yakushi-Nyorai.

The unusual 34-metre pagoda looks like a six-storey structure, but such buildings always have an odd number of levels; this one has a sub-roof between each 'real' roof, and is the only one of its kind in Japan.

The pagoda is the only structure of the temple that has survived in its original form; all other buildings are later reconstructions. An excellent English-language booklet is given out on entry and explains the salient points of the temple.

Yakushi-ji may be reached by the bus that goes to Horyu-ji, or from Nishi-Nokyo station of Kintetsu railway (reached with a change at Yamato-Saidai-ji station).

Toshidai-ji Temple

This temple is highly regarded for its architecture and harmonious arrangement of structures. Like the other major temples of Nara, Toshidai-ji also has a number of figures that rate as national treasures. The temple is less than one km north of Yakushi-ji; you can walk or go by bus, but the former is in fact quicker.

NARA PLAIN AREA

Nara city is near the northern end of the Nara plain, an area that was settled early in the history of the northward movement of the Yamato people from Kyushu on their way to control of the Japanese islands.

One legacy of this period (shared with Osaka, which was also an important city in this era) is a large number of tomb mounds, or tumuli (*kufun*), possibly showing an ancestral link between the Yamato people and Korea, where tumulus building has long been a tradition. There are actually nearly 3000 such tombs in Japan, scattered from Kyushu to the Tokyo region, most often near important defensive settlements.

These mounds are easily seen beside Route 24 out of Nara en route to Kyoto (tombs of Uwanabe and Konabe, as indicated on the JNTO map, plus an unlabelled one). Others at Asuka kufun, believed to date from the 7th century, were opened only in 1972 and have a number of very colourful murals of Korean and Chinese style. At Uneki, near Kashihara, the Archaeology Museum displays many relics of the late Stone Age and other prehistoric items from the area.

Omiwa-Myojin Shrine

This is believed to be one of the oldest shrines in Japan. The buildings are scenically located among tall trees. It is near Sakurai and accessible from Miwa station.

Koya-san

Koya-san is a mountain famous as the centre of the Shingon-Mikkyo (True Word) sect of Buddhism. On its flat top are more than 120 temples carrying on a tradition from 816 AD. It is a place of pilgrimage for the faithful, especially for those with family members buried in the extensive cemetery, which is actually one of the most interesting things to see.

Koya-san has also become a mountain resort providing an escape from the heat and humidity of the lower areas.

Information Koya-san is best visited for its symbolic value, being a community of temples. As an object of architectural study, it is not worth a special trip, especially when compared with the beautiful buildings of Kyoto.

The Tokyo TIC distributes an information sheet that gives some more details on Koya-san, although its map is typically not to scale.

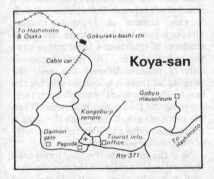

Things to See Buses run from the upper cable-car station into the centre of the small community, or you can take a taxi or walk the three km or so into town. The road is lined with tall cedars and leads to the main temple on the west side of the community.

Gobyo If a bus is available, it is better to go directly to Gobyo. This is the mausoleum of Kobodaishi, the founder of the temples and a great teacher of Shingon, who also devised the *hiragana* syllabary for writing Japanese in a simpler form than using *kanji*.

From Gobyo there is a very pleasant

and peaceful walk through the great cemetery, where tombs and memorials are set in a forest of very tall cedar trees. The path leads to Ichinohashi (First Bridge), from where you can walk through the town and visit any of the large number of temples on the way. There is only one main street so it is impossible to get lost. At the intersection with the main road is an information office that can supply a map, some literature and give assistance in finding a room.

Kongobu-ji Temple Just a short distance beyond the town is Kongobu-ji (Temple of the Diamond Mountain, rebuilt in 1861), the chief temple of the sect and the best one to visit if time is limited.

Other Attractions Nearby (downhill and across the road) is the Daito pagoda in a large courtyard, built in a style uncommon in Japan (rebuilt 1937). The interior features brilliantly coloured beams and it houses five sacred images of Buddha in different incarnations. Other buildings are the Golden Hall (for ceremonies) and Miedo.

Further along the road below the latter cluster of buildings is Daimon (Great Gate), a large wooden structure from 1705; it is similar to such gates at other old temples. The youth hostel (at Henjosan-ji) is near here.

Places To Stay There are 53 temples on the mountain that provide accommodation. Most, if not all, have been developed into attractive places to stay, with lovely little gardens.

Each of these temples is virtually owned by its abbot, and then inherited by his son (natural or adopted). By charging about double the tariff of most temples elsewhere in Japan (about Y5000 a night), the abbots have turned them into a very lucrative business, and many are reputedly quite weak in the theology of their sect.

Since wealth is required to advance in the religious hierarchy of the sect, this operation of the temples as money making ventures is encouraged. Remember that this applies to the Shingon-Mikkyo sect only; other sects are still close to the original tenets of their faith.

Getting There & Away The direct route is by Nankai private railway from Namba station (Osaka). From other centres (such as Kyoto and Nara) you can go via JR to Hashimoto station and change there for the final 21 km by the Nankai line to the terminus at Gokuraku-bashi station. From there a cable car runs to the top of Koya-san.

Getting Around From Koya-san you can go west to Wakayama and continue around the Kii-hanto peninsula. From Gojo, Route 168 runs south to Hongu, Shingu and other attractions of the peninsula.

Three buses daily make the scenic run between Gojo and Shingu, and another two go from Gojo to Hongu.

Yoshino

The view of the cherry blossoms on the side of Yoshino-yama (northeast of Koya-san) is famous throughout Japan. There are about 100,000 cherry trees and in season the blossoms form a massive blanket of pink stretching a long distance up the slope. Because of the differences in temperature from the top of the mountain to the bottom, the trees mature at different times, so the *sakura* season on Yoshino can last for a couple of weeks.

From Yoshino station of the Kintetsu railway, a nearby cable car rises to the main road that passes through the settled areas of the mountain side. You can then walk or take a taxi to the main temple area.

The mountain has been regarded as sacred for centuries and is a centre of Yamabushi religious activities. The main temple, Kimpusen-ji, belongs to this sect; the old wooden gate (Kuramon) encountered during the climb up the road from the cable car belongs to the temple. Kimpusen-ji is a national treasure and its age shows in the weathered timbers and inside pillars. It is reputed to be the second largest wooden building in Japan.

Typical of almost any tourist destination in Japan, the main street is lined with souvenir shops and eating and drinking places. Several of the latter have balconies overlooking the trees on the hillside. The little shop with the giant toad sells Chinese-type traditional medicines.

Part of the way along this level stretch, just past the small temple with an unusual low pagoda, stands a stone *torii* gate. Pass through it, on the road downhill, and you come to the most historic place on Yoshino. Sho-in dates from 1336 and was a resort villa used by a number of emperors through the years. It is very famous in Japanese history, although it would be of more interest to students of traditional architecture than the casual visitor. The small garden is only of passing interest but near the parking lot there is a lookout offering the best single view over the sea of cherry trees covering the facing mountainside. When the blossoms are at their peak the sight is magnificent and explains the popularity of Yoshino for successive emperors.

Near the *torii* gate the road forks; take the road uphill to Kizo-ji temple, which is now a combination youth hostel and commercial *ryokan* providing accommodation for travellers and pilgrims.

Nearby is Chikurin-in, a villa built by the famous tea master Sen-no-rikyu, who was forced to commit *seppuku* (ritual suicide) for preventing *shogun* Hideyoshi from taking his daughter as a concubine. The present main building is a highly regarded (and expensive) *ryokan* open to the public when not being used by visiting members of the royal family. The beautiful garden behind the *ryokan* should not be missed.

Numerous roads wind their way up and across the Yoshino mountain side and can be followed into the mass of cherry trees.

There are several large maps posted in prominent places in the village.

To the east and south of Yoshino is a heavily wooded wilderness area that would appeal to hikers. Accessible from the Nara plain side of the mountains is a point on the flank of Mt Odaigahara (1695 metres) that is the starting point for hikes to Owase (on the east coast of Kii-hanto peninsula) and Doro-kyo gorge to the south. These are both described in the section on southern Kii-hanto peninsula, along with the rest of the coastal region. The Odaigahara area is the wettest region of Japan and the mountain top is often shrouded in fog.

Getting There & Away Yoshino station is the terminus of the Kintetsu line from Abeno-bashi station (Osaka); travellers from Kyoto transfer at Kashiwara-jingu-mae. You can also go most of the way by JR, changing to the Kintetsu line at Yoshino-guchi.

During many months of the year there are three buses a day to Odaigahara from Nara-Kintetsu station. The bus passes through Yamato-Kami-Ichi (two stops before Yoshinoyama station).

There are also two buses a day between Nara and Kumano (on the southeast coast) which pass Wasabi-dani, the point where the toll road to Odaigahara branches off Route 169; it should be possible to get off there and transfer to the other bus (if schedules match) or hitch the rest of the way.

Mie-ken

East of Nara-ken, Mie-ken is divided by a coastal ridge of mountains. On the Nara side of this ridge is the area around Iga-Ueno. Most of the other attractions of Mie-ken are on the coastal side of the mountains. From there you can conveniently travel clockwise around the Kii-hanto peninsula and up the west coast to Wakayama and Osaka.

IGA-UENO

This small city east of Nara has some unusual history and an attraction almost unique in Japan. The name simply means 'Ueno of the Iga region' to distinguish it from other places called Ueno, which is a common name in Japan.

Information

A pamphlet on Ueno in quite good English is given out at Ueno castle and may also be available at the TICs in Kyoto and Tokyo. It also contains information on some other places of lesser interest.

Ueno Castle

Ueno has a small but picturesque castle. Although the present building dates from only 1953, it is a reminder of when the rulers of Iga had to defend their fertile lands against neighbouring, powerful Kyoto and Yamato.

As part of their defences (beginning around the 1200s) they developed the Ninjutsu art of stealthy combat to defeat foreign armies in the mountains. *Ninja*, the practitioners, were trained in invisibility, poisons, sabotage, espionage, assassination and other genteel arts. *Ninja* are featured in the James Clavell novel *Shogun*, and have become well known in the west through films that are often quite inaccurate.

In the grounds of the castle is Ninja-Yashiki (Ninja House), an ordinary looking building that actually has a number of hidden passages, hiding places and weapons caches. These are demonstrated frequently during the day for visitors by a lithe young woman dressed in black.

Elsewhere in the grounds is Ninjutsu Shiryo-kan, a museum of weapons, clothing, climbing devices and other ingenious items used by *ninja* in their work. Things such as an iron claw that would tear a victim as if by the claw of a bear, armour, and several kinds of throwing weapons. This is one of very few places in Japan with such a large display of items of this black 'art'. (Another is nearby at Akame 48 Falls).

Ninjutsu is explained well in Stephen Hayes' book *The Ninja & Their Fighting Art* (Tuttle).

Festival

23-25 October: Tenjin-matsuri festival is a 400-year-old Demon Procession. It features a procession of more than 100 'demons' in masks and costumes, as well as nine ornate festival wagons, similar to but smaller than those of Kyoto's Gion-matsuri. Masks and other items from the procession are displayed at the museum beside the Ninja-Yashiki.

Getting There & Away

The castle is reached by walking up the hill from Ueno-shi station of the Kintetsu line; this can be reached by transferring from the JR Kansai hon-sen line at Iga-Ueno station, or by branching off the Kintetsu Osaka line at Iga-Kambe.

The Kansai line runs between Osaka and Nagoya via Nara, the latter between Osaka and Matsuzaka. Both are easily reached from Kyoto and Nara.

AKAME 48 FALLS

Due south of Iga-Ueno is a very pleasant gorge known for its 48 waterfalls. Many are rather small, especially those higher up near the source, but the large ones are quite impressive. The riverside walk is a rare way to enjoy nature with no sound but the shrilling cicadas, some birds and the rushing water. There is a good chance you will see some of the large and very colourful butterflies for which Japan is noted. Higher up the gorge there is an inviting pool.

Just inside the entrance to the park is a very nondescript concrete cage containing some equally nondescript animals; they are giant salamanders, found only in this area.

Before the entrance to the park (on the left going in) is a small building that houses a good (if modest) museum of historic articles used in daily life. Possibly of greater interest is a sizeable collection of *ninja* weapons and devices. If you can't find the building, ask for 'Ninja hakubutsu-kan'.

Getting There & Away

The entrance to the falls (Akame Taki) is reached easily by bus (12 per day) from Akame-guchi station of the Kintetsu-Osaka line, three stations west of Iga-Kambe station.

SHIMA-HANTO PENINSULA & ISE

The Shima-hanto peninsula and the vicinity of the city of Ise is one of the longest-settled parts of Japan. Passing through the area, it is easy to understand its attraction to early settlers. The land is flat and ideal for rice farming, and the climate is the mildest in north-central Japan due to the warm Black Current that passes nearby. It was settled first by the Yamato tribe, which ultimately became the dominant power in Japan.

Many legends come from this part of the country regarding the origin of Japan and its people. It is not surprising, therefore, that the most important Shinto shrine of the 80,000 or so around Japan is here, in the city of Ise.

The grand shrines of Ise represent much that is characteristic of Japan and the Japanese. There are two shrines, Geku (Outer Shrine), and Naiku (Inner Shrine). The latter is somewhat more important as it honours and is considered the abode of Amaterasu, the sun goddess.

Prior to WW II, when the emperor was still considered to be divine, it was claimed (and taught in schools) that the Japanese royal family was directly descended from this goddess. By extension, since all Japanese were descended from that family, they therefore had a special place in the world. The claims of divinity have been given up and Shinto has been disestablished as the state religion,

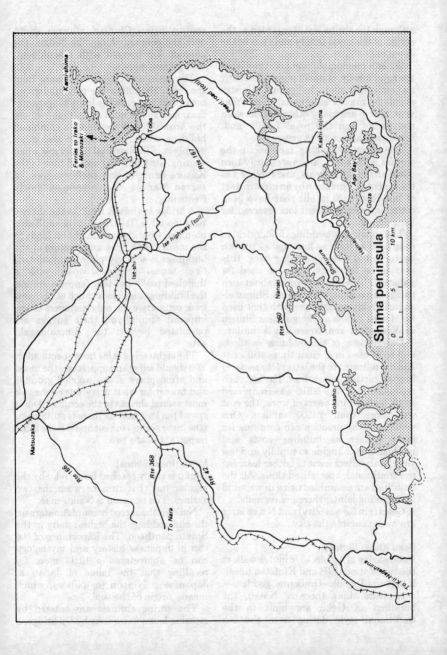

Shima peninsula

Kami-shima

Toba

Ferries to Irako & Morozaki

Pearl road (toll)

Rte 167

Ise highway (toll)

Ise-shi

Kashi-kojima

Ago Bay

Goza

Tsukumo

Shinmei

Nansei

Rte 260

Gokasho

Matsuzaka

Rte 368

Rte 42

To Nara

To Kii-Nagashima

Rte 166

0 5 10 km

although the shrine is still regarded as the shrine of the royal family and thus of the Japanese.

When a memorable event occurs within the royal family, it is still reported here by an emissary, and the prime minister normally makes an annual New Year visit. There are many other ties between the shrine and the royal family and, therefore, the people in general.

The most interesting fact about the shrines is that they are customarily torn down after only 20 years, and replaced as the centre of veneration by an identical set of buildings (220 in all) that have been constructed on adjacent lots reserved for the purpose.

The style of the buildings is identical to that used at least as long ago as the 8th century, and possibly further back. It is said to be the style that was used for palaces. Those who are curious about such things can compare the Yuitsu-Shimmei-zukuri architectural style with that used for Hongu Taisha at Hongu (near Shingu in Wakayama-ken) to see if it is similar.

Descriptions of the building methods and tools used in ancient times still exist and are followed to the letter (character?) in constructing new shrines. The last such reconstruction, the 60th, was completed in 1973 after nine years of work; the cost was more than Y4500 million. One wonders if the practice can continue for much longer as building costs and methods are changing so rapidly and few young carpenters want to bother learning the traditional, specialised skills. All the buildings are assembled using dowels and interlocking joints; there are no nails.

Geku is in Ise-shi (city) and Naiku is six km away, outside the city.

Geku (Outer Shrine)

Geku shrine is within 15 minutes walk of the two stations (JR and Kintetsu lines). It honours Toyouke-Omikame, goddess of agriculture. Like those of Naiku, the buildings of Geku are built in the traditional style dating from the 5th

century before Chinese influence swept over the country. Also, like Naiku, the grounds are covered with magnificent, tall, ancient cedars.

The main entrance is easily seen from the road. You follow the path under two *torii* gates and past the large Magatama-ike pond. To the right of the first *torii* are the Anzaisho and Sanshido, a combined building where the emperor and other members of the imperial family rest when visiting. Just past the second *torii* is the Kagura-den, where performances of sacred dances are presented fairly frequently.

A bridge to the left leads to the shrines Kaze-no-miya, Tsuchi-no-miya and Takano-miya. Continuing straight on leads to the main shrine. The architecture of the buildings is severely plain – unpainted, fine, *hinoki* (cypress) wood, with a thatched roof – but four fences surround the buildings and block much of the view from ordinary eyes; only members of the imperial family and their envoys are permitted beyond the Tonotamagaki gate.

The sightseeing is far from spectacular. You should enjoy and appreciate the mood and atmosphere of the wooded grounds and take it for what it is – one of the two most sacred shrines in the country. Don't spend too long here as there is still Naiku (the inner shrine) to visit and it is the more important of the two.

Naiku (Inner Shrine)

Naiku is easily reached from Geku by the regular bus that runs between the two shrines. The bus stop is Naiku-mae.

Naiku is the sacred home of Amaterasu, the sun goddess, the highest deity in the Shinto pantheon. The importance of the sun in Japanese history and mythology can be appreciated a little more by recalling that the name of Japan in Japanese is Nippon (or Nihon), which means 'origin of the sun'.

The shrine grounds are entered by crossing Isuzu-kawa river by Uji bridge, a

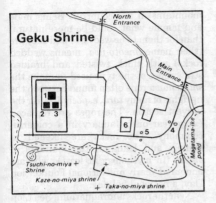

Legend for both maps

1 Shoden (main hall)
2 Saihoden (west treasure hall)
3 Tohoden (east treasure hall)
4 First torii
5 Second torii
6 Kagura-den (sacred dance hall)

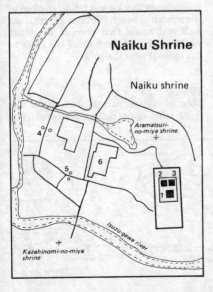

picturesque structure. From here the faithful follow one of several paths to the

riverside where they wash their hands and rinse their mouths as purification. The many tall cedars on the grounds give a peaceful mood, and the 66 hectares of grounds swallows up the large number of people who visit.

The usual route takes visitors through the first and second *torii*, past the Kagura-den (hall of sacred dances) and on to the main shrine Shoden. As with Geku, the four rows of fences block a large part of the view of the buildings – after all, a lady (especially a goddess) needs her privacy. Photos toward the shrine building are prohibited and it is customary for men to remove hats and overcoats.

Again the style of architecture is ancient and severely simple, with thatched roofs. Beside the shrine is the open space where the previous shrine stood until 1973, when the present buildings were finished and consecrated, and the goddess (along with her belongings) moved into her new quarters with very solemn ceremony.

On the same compound with the Shoden (main hall) are two treasure houses, Tohoden and Saihoden (East and West treasuries), in which are housed about 2500 treasures of the shrine – fine clothing, lacquerware, swords, etc. These are made anew each time along with the buildings and represent the finest of craftmanship in the best Japanese tradition. In previous times these were destroyed when the new shrines were opened. But today, because of these objects' great value as the work of perhaps the last of the old generations, they are preserved and displayed at Chokokan, the shrine's history museum.

Included among the treasures in the two treasure buildings (not on display) is the sacred mirror, one of the three sacred imperial throne treasures. The others are the sword and jewel. The sword was lost in the battle of Dan-no-ura in Kanmon Strait, Shimonoseki, and the jewel is kept in Tokyo.

A news item stated that some antique

rickshaws (*jin-riki-sha*) were being operated at the shrines (entrances). If you wish to try one, keep your eyes open. Proceeds are for charity.

ISE TO TOBA

There are two main routes to Toba, Ise-Shima Skyline and Route 167/Railway.

Ise-Shima Skyline

From a point near Naiku, a toll road runs along and over a ridge of the Asama mountains to Toba-shi (city). The scenery is pretty, with distant water views and the indented coast (though it is not worth a special trip from elsewhere just to see). At the ridge top is Kongoshoji temple. Two buses an hour make the trip from Naiku to Toba station; the last is in the mid afternoon.

Route 167/Railway

Travellers by Route 167 or JR from Ise to Toba might want to stop for a look at a sight dear to the hearts of the Japanese – Futami-ga-ura. This is a pair of rocks that jut out of the sea close to each other, not far from shore.

In keeping with the traditional Japanese view of nature as representations of *kami* (spirits/gods), or other 'semi-animate' objects, the rocks have been regarded as male and female (in exactly the same manner as gender is assigned to nearly all

mountains in the country). Being male and female what could be more natural than for them to be wed? So, wed they are (their name, *meoto-iwa*, means wedded rocks) with thick twisted and braided straw ropes of the type used to make the *shimenawa* rope often found between the uprights of many *torii*, especially after the harvest season. The ropes are replaced every year on 5 January in a colourful ceremony. The rocks are likened to Izanagi and Izanami, the founders of Japan (in mythology at least), who are honoured yearly on National Foundation Day, a national holiday.

Near the rocks is an aquarium, Sea Lion House, and Marine House where women divers give demonstrations. The *Taiko Youth Hostel* (tel (05964) 3-2283, No 4404) which is also a temple, is not far from the rocks.

The rocks are about one km from Futami-no-ura station (JR). Buses from the station, as well as from Toba, Ise-shi, Uji-yamada, Naiku and Geku, go close to the stretch of beach (Futami-ga-ura), sea wall and hotels that precede the short walkway around the base of the cliffs to the lookout near the rocks.

TOBA

Toba is famous as the place where the cultivation of pearls was perfected. The

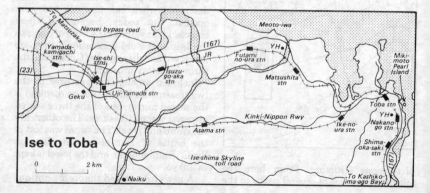

Toba area is still one of the most important pearl farming areas in Japan.

Until Kokichi Mikimoto began his research in the late 1800s, the only pearls were accidents of nature. If a grain of sand or other foreign material happened to find its way into the shell and irritate the oyster, the irritant would be covered with layers of nacre, forming a pearl. Mikimoto reasoned that it should be possible to introduce such an irritant artificially, so he began experimenting in 1888. By 1893 he had succeeded in producing a pearl, though it was not spherical, and by 1905 had succeeded completely.

Since then his company has continued to grow and his name is now well known around the world. He died in 1954. Always dedicated to top quality, and also a bit of a showman, Mikimoto once burned hundreds of kg of inferior quality pearls that he had rejected, but which his competitors would have sold. Such pearls are now used to decorate cheaper items.

Tatoku-shima island, where he performed his experiments, is now the site of a very interesting museum where all stages of producing cultured pearls are shown, both as a static display of photos and materials (with English text), and exhibitions by young women of how they insert the irritant, remove a pearl from an oyster, match pearls by colour and size, then drill and string them. Also on display are some fabulously valuable displays utilising pearls, such as a small scale model of the Liberty Bell in solid silver (16.9 kg), with 336 diamonds and 12,250 pearls.

The complete pearl-making process begins with a pearl oyster usually about two years old. Its shell is prised open, an incision is made in its body, and two spheres about six mm in diameter (the irritant) are introduced into the wound. For trivia buffs, the irritant is made from the Pig Toe shell, a variety found along the Mississippi River. After trying thousands of materials, Mikimoto found this to be the best.

Along with the two spheres, a small piece of tissue about a mm square, from the body of another oyster, is introduced. This piece is cut from the tissue band at the junction between the oyster's body and its shell; it is the tissue that excretes the nacre that deposits as mother-of-pearl. The oyster 'adopts' this and uses it to coat the irritant with layer after layer of nacre. By this method, one oyster can be used to produce two pearls.

The oysters are suspended in special racks hung below rafts in the sea. These rafts can be seen in Ago Bay and other sheltered bodies of water in the region, where the temperature and other conditions are ideal. The nearby Black Current guarantees a plentiful supply of plankton, the food on which oysters thrive.

The racks are pulled up four to six times a year and the shells are cleaned of marine growths, then they are lowered again. After about three years they are lifted out for the last time and the pearls are taken out, sorted to remove imperfections and odd shapes, classified by colour, then drilled and strung. The colour range is quite amazing, going from pink and gold through silver to a distinct blue tint.

Only about 50% of oysters produce pearls after all that effort, and only about 5% of these are suitable as gems. In past years, the lifespan of oysters was six to seven years, with the seeds being implanted at age two, but pollution is raising its ugly head these days and the pearls must now be harvested after only two to three years in the water instead of four to five years as before. The pearl quality is also said to be slipping.

There is, if it needs to be said, absolutely no difference in composition between cultured and naturally occurring pearls; the former just increase the harvest and guarantee consistent quality.

Where do the oysters come from? They grow on trees. When females are spawning, they release thousands of larvae into the water, to come to rest where they may. Trees are lowered into the water and, with luck, larvae will cling to the branches. After two to three months they are raised and transferred to a better place where they can grow to sufficient maturity to allow the irritant implantation.

Every 40 minutes there is a display of women divers. Similar divers may be seen in action near Toba and in nearby sheltered bays and coves, like Ago Bay. There are still about 3500 of them actively diving, but this is only half the number of a few years ago.

There is so much nonsense written about these white-clothed divers that it is time to put the record straight. They do not dive for pearls. Before Mikimoto's successful experimentation, their ancestors did dive for the gems of the sea, but they could not make a living at it today. The whole idea of cultivating pearls is to sidestep the hit-or-miss (mostly miss) business of looking for natural pearls. Also, natural pearls are often mis-shapen and/or discoloured, while cultivating them gives a good yield of nearly perfect spherical ones.

What the women do dive for is seafood, both shellfish (such as abalone) and octopus, as well as edible seaweed. Any pearl oysters that they find can be used to grow pearls by implantation of a nucleus. But they do not dive for pearls, and publications and tour pamphlets that repeatedly refer to them as 'women pearl-divers' are verging on dishonesty. Their activities are interesting enough, with their peculiar whistling breathing sound, that such hype is uncalled for.

Other Attractions
The aquarium at Toba is considered one of the best in Japan. Other related attractions are Dolphin Island (Iruka-jima) and the marine museum (Burajiru-maru).

Getting There & Away
There are regular boat excursions out of Toba to nearby islands, including Kamishima, scene of Mishima's story *Sound of Waves*.

There is a ferry service across the bay to Irako at the tip of Atsuma-hanto peninsula (at least 13 times daily), as well as to Gamagori on the mainland between the peninsulas (at least six a day); these places are all on the east side of the bay, south of Nagoya, and offer a convenient way to bypass that city if you're planning to travel to Tokyo via the south coast. It should be said that this is the least desirable and interesting way to get to Tokyo; routes via the Kiso region and the Noto-hanto peninsula are much more interesting.

AGO BAY
This bay, sheltered from the ocean tumult and incredibly indented, offers the beauties of nature and the finest scenery of the Shima-hanto peninsula. A common sight is the number of rafts from which pearl oysters are suspended in the water. They should not be mistaken for even rows of poles protruding from the water near the shore; these have nets strung horizontally among them, and edible seaweed grows on them. Ago Bay is ideal for pearl oysters because the water temperature is always between 17 and 22°C and there is plenty of food.

Getting There & Away
Most travellers who plan to continue from the Ago Bay area to southern Kii-hanto peninsula destinations (like Shingu) by road will find it better to backtrack to Ise and beyond to connect with Route 42 (or railway) rather than following Route 260 along the coast.

Few roads require more time to travel a given distance than Route 42. It winds in, out, up, down, over and around every combination of cape, ridge, hill, valley and promontory imaginable. The scenery is pleasant as it passes through fishing villages and coves of pearl rafts or seaweed frames, but it tends to quickly become variations on a theme rather than new melodies.

From the youth hostel at Isobe I followed

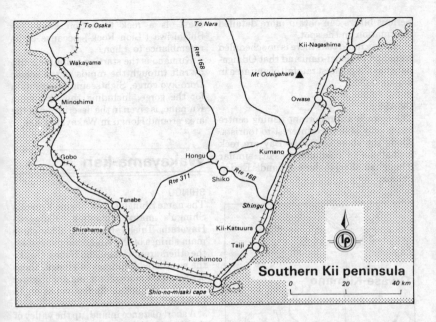

Southern Kii peninsula

0   20   40 km

the road by motorcycle for what seemed like hours and only reached Shukuura, a relatively short distance down the coast, at which point I turned back to Ise and went around it.

KASHIKOJIMA

This is the main town on Ago Bay. From it, sightseeing boats leave regularly on excursions that circle the bay. It would be a good way for a closer look at the rafts, and there is a good chance of seeing *ama* (women divers) at work. Near Kashikojima station is Shima Marineland which houses an aquarium.

Places to Stay

There is a *Youth Hostel* (No 4406) not far from Kashikojima, at Isobe. It is on a hill, giving a good view over a smaller bay. However, it is a JYH hostel, and has some of the less-than-favourable characteristics of one as the house-father is a regional JYH executive.

The biggest drawback of the place is that the rooms are almost hermetically sealed and are very stuffy; a shame because it is so close to all that fine sea air.

GOZA

From Kompira-san hill, this town affords a good view of both the Pacific Ocean and Ago Bay. It can be reached from Kashikojima by boat or bus.

USUGI-DANI

Inland from a point 10 km or so north of Owase (just a short distance south of Funa station), a road leads inland to Usugidani, considered one of the grandest valleys in Japan. A publicity photo shows a very pretty series of cascades and pools and a rustic suspension bridge.

The valley leads close to Mt Odaigahara, a mountain much more easily reached from Yoshino. There are trails in the area between Odaigahara and Owase (32 km), and to Doro-kyo gorge (described later).

Serious hikers can obtain more detailed information on the spot.

Keep in mind that there is no scheduled transport to Usugi-dani and that Odaiga-hara has the greatest rainfall of any area in Japan.

OWASE

The town is an important fishing centre but is only of limited interest to tourists. Along the shore of Owase Bay are rock formations of columnar basalt, similar (though smaller) to those of Land's End in Britain.

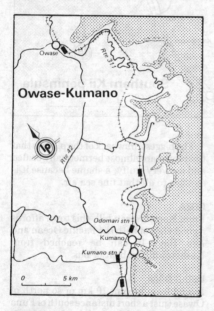

KUMANO

The attractions of Kumano ('Bear Field') are the sea and cliffs. A popular sight is Onigajo ('Ogre's Castle'), a large chamber in the cliffs. Near it the rock has been weathered to an unusual texture, slightly resembling the exterior of the brain. It is about a km east of the station, along the coast.

In the opposite direction, also along the

coast, is a rock formation known as Shishi-iwa ('Lion Rock') because of its resemblance to a lion.

Kumano is the starting point for a trip by raft through the rapids of the scenic Doro-kyo gorge. Sightseeing information for the gorge, including this trip from Kumano, is given in the description of the area around Hongu in Wakayama-ken.

Wakayama-ken

SHINGU

The name Shingu ('New Shrine') reveals Shingu's main attraction, Kumano-Hayatama Taisha shrine, one of the three main shrines of the Kii-hanto peninsula; the others are at Hongu and Nachi. Unlike the weathered buildings of Hongu, those of Shingu are more recent and are brighter and more colourful. Its festival is on 15 October.

A short distance inland, up the valley of the Kumano-kawa river, are Hongu and Doro-kyo gorge. Between Shingu and Hongu the road passes through the Kumano-kawa valley. The pretty, relatively unspoiled scenery makes the trip enjoyable. Hills rise on both sides of the valley and the water is a beautiful emerald or jade-green. In seasons of heavy rainfall, like the September-October typhoon season, several waterfalls thunder close to the road or can be seen clearly nearby.

Buses run from Shingu station to Hongu (70 minutes) and on to Gojo (4¾ hours).

HONGU

Hongu, which means 'Main Shrine', is the most important of the three great shrines of Kii. Nearby are a couple of typical mountain hot-spring resorts with *rotemburo* (open-air, hot-spring baths).

The area near the Kii-hanto peninsula was settled early in Japanese history and the mountains of the peninsula appealed to the religious feelings of the people. The early folk religion, the predecessor of

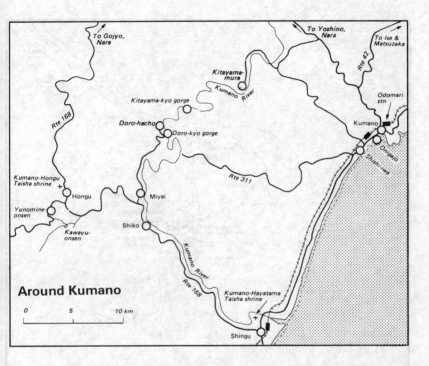

Around Kumano

```
0        5        10 km
```

Shinto ('Way of the Gods'), was animistic in nature, closely related to similar beliefs still found in Korea and in many other regions of Asia. The mountains, valleys, forests, rocks – in fact all of nature – appeared to be a special habitat of the gods and were areas of special veneration 15 to 20 centuries ago.

With the advent of Buddhism in Japan, the beliefs and form of worship changed somewhat as the people accepted the idea (promoted by Buddhist teachers in the manner used also by Christianity and other religions to make their new message acceptable) that their old religion was an earlier manifestation of the new one, and that the gods were manifestations of the Buddha.

This culminated in the development of Shugendo. *Yamabushi* (pilgrims) of this belief may be seen here (as well as at areas

like Haguro-san near Tsuruo-ka and elsewhere in Tohoku), dressed in white with unusual 'ornaments', perhaps ringing bells as they proceed. Such *yamabushi* indulge in ascetic practices, like bathing under icy mountain waterfalls and other forms of corporal mortification. More information is included in the section on Tohoku.

The main shrine is at Hongu and is set in wooded land near the town of the same name. The present buildings are quite large and have a natural weathered colour. Their architectural style is an uncommon form used in the early 10th century for palaces. Its festival is 15 April.

Access is via a long path attractively lined with tall cedars. This is not too far from the wettest place in Japan, so lush greenery can be expected. In other areas of

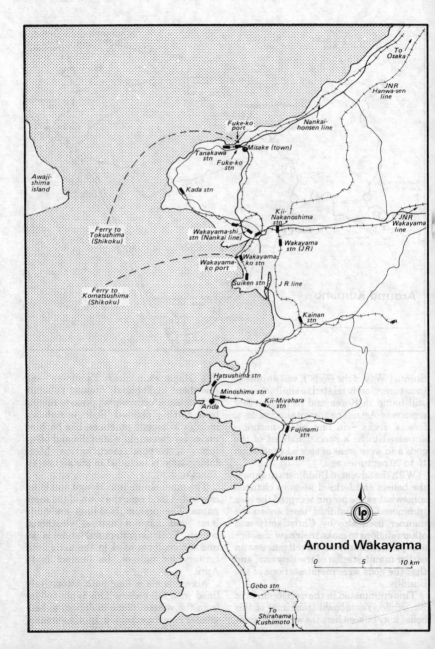

Around Wakayama

0   5   10 km

the Kii-hanto peninsula there are still virgin forests with some trees 600 to 1000 years old. The name 'Kii' is a contraction of Ki-no-kuni, or 'country of trees'.

YUNOMINE

In past days *yamabushi* pilgrims included bathing in the hot springs of Yunomine as part of their devotions. These days it is more like a typical *onsen*, with visitors who indulge in the hot water for the same reasons as elsewhere – for health and pleasure.

Along with hotels (large and small), and their private baths, there is also a *rotemburo*, a natural hot-spring pool in the middle of the stream, surrounded by a simple wooden fence and an equally simple and quite traditional bath-house.

KAWAYU

This is another hot-spring resort town. It also has a *rotemburo* open to all comers. There is a *Youth Hostel* (No 5612) here.

DORO-KYO GORGE

This gorge on the Kitayama-kawa river is considered the finest in Japan. Cliffs rise 50 metres vertically from the green water, naturally sculpted rocks decorate the way, and in June azaleas and rhododendrons bloom on the cliff faces. The gorge stretches several km, and the river has rapids alternating with wide, calm areas. The three major sections are Oku ('inner') doro, Kami ('upper') doro, and Doro-hatcho. Shimo-Doro ('lower Doro') is the entrance and is not so noteworthy. Doro-hatcho means 'eight cho', signifying eight cho of tranquil water, a *cho* being an old measurement of 109 metres.

There are three ways to see the gorge. First, from Shiko (on the road through the valley), long glass-roofed boats leave from docks behind a a restaurant and go as far upstream as Kami-Doro.

The day I went to the area (in mid September), the river was swollen from heavy rains and boat trips were suspended. There are usually eight trips a day, the first at 8 am, the last at 3.15 pm. The trip up takes 50 minutes, there is a 20-minute rest, and the return takes 45 minutes. Check with the TIC in Kyoto or Tokyo to ensure that these boats are in operation before making a trip there.

Shiko boat terminal can be reached by bus from Shingu station in 30 minutes, or from Kawayu-onsen in 20. The four buses a day from the latter are timed to connect with a boat departure. Further information is available at the youth hostel.

The second way to see the gorge (if you have your own transport) is to take the road to Doro-hatcho. Maps indicate future road construction to link this point with Kitayama-mura. An offshoot to join Route 311 to Kumano is also likely but the completion date is uncertain.

The third way has been in operation for several years, so is likely to continue. It is a ride through all the rapids on a long, narrow, 20-man raft. Rides are exciting and you need waterproof clothing because of frequent spray.

Rides begin at Kitayama-mura, a village accessible from Kumano station by a once-a-day bus to Shima-oi, plus a minibus ride from there to the starting point. The ride lasts three hours, ending at Miyai (not far from Shiko) and costs about Y5000. The contact telephone number is (073549) 2331 but you have to speak in Japanese. The TIC in Kyoto should know if this is still running.

NACHI-KATSUURA

This is the collective name for the district between Nachi and Kii-Katsuura, south along the coast from Shungu; both are station names. The several attractions of the area give it the most concentrated sightseeing possibilities of the southern Kii-hanto peninsula.

Nachi-taki

The high point of the Nachi area is the 130-metre-high Nachi-taki waterfall – one of the deepest plunges in Japan. The falls are reached by taking a short bus ride

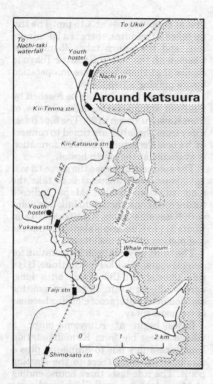

Around Katsuura

from Nachi station. From the stop, they are reached after a brief and enjoyable walk down steps between rows of tall and very old cedars.

Nachi-Taisha Shrine

Beside the falls (and located there from ancient times because of its obvious strong connection with the Shinto spirit world) is Nachi-Taisha shrine, one of the three great shrines of the Kii area. It was founded in the 4th century. Its festivals are 1-7 January and 14 July.

Seiganto-ji Temple

Immediately beside Nachi-Taisha is the temple Seiganto-ji.

Myoho-ji Temple

At the top of the twisty toll road is the Myoho-ji temple.

Kii-Katsuura

From a place near Kii-Katsuura station you can take a boat ride around a group of pine covered islands called Kii-no-Matsushima. The name implies a comparison with the 'real' Matsushima near Sendai, one of the scenic 'big three' that are supposed to send the Japanese into fits of ecstasy. The ones at Kii are scenic, one islet being perforated, another (visible from shore) resembling a camel in silhouette, while others come in a variety of other shapes. A good lookout point is from the narrow peninsula on which Katsuura-onsen is located.

Places to Stay

There are *Youth Hostels* at Nachi, Katsuura, and Taiji.

Getting There & Away

Between Shingu and Nachi-Katsuura is the Nachi-Katsuura terminal for regular long-distance ferry services to Tokyo and Kochi (on the island of Shikoku).

The terminal ('ferry noriba') is close to Usui station, north of Nachi. There are 12 trains a day between the two places, but note that the ferry leaves for Tokyo hours after the last train.

TAIJI

Taiji has been the centre of the whaling industry in the Kumano district. On a small peninsula a little more than one km from Taiji station, five minutes by bus, is Kujira-hama-koen (Whale Beach Park). Its main attraction is Geirui-hakubutsukan (Whale Museum) which has displays of articles associated with this unpopular industry.

There are also some full-size reproductions of whales to show their immense size. Unfortunately, Japan is one of the few countries still hunting these behemoths of the deep.

KUSHIMOTO

This city is at the base of the Kii-hanto peninsula and is the entrance to the Shio-no-misaki cape. A short distance northeast of the city, and a little closer to Kii-Hime station, is the unusual rock formation Hashi-kui-iwa, a row of about 30 large rocks, spaced quite regularly in a line and stretching into the sea. They do resemble what their name means, 'bridge pillars'. Other writers likened them to a procession of hooded medieval monks.

KOZAKAWA-KYO GORGE

Inland a short distance from Kushimoto is a pretty gorge, Kozakawa-kyo. The Kozakawa river has eroded the rocks of its bed and flanks into interesting shapes and textures. Much of the rock was apparently formed with trapped bubbles; the water has removed the solid surface, leaving a strange perforated appearance.

The road through the gorge turns off Route 42 at Koza, and the gorge begins shortly after at Taka-ike ('High Pond'). It continues for 15 km to Mito-gawa, from where a local road returns to the coast while the main road continues some distance inland before rejoining Route 42.

Northwest from Kushimoto along the coast there are pleasant views from both the road and train, although there are not as many identifiable attractions as there are on the southeast coast.

SHIRAHAMA

Along with Atami and Beppu, this is regarded by the Japanese as one of the three best hot-spring resorts in Japan. This information, however, is not likely to excite foreigners who do not have such a history of enjoying 'the waters'.

As consolation, in addition to the delights of the flesh (or at least partial amelioration of the aches, pains and troubles of corporal existence), there are also scenic pleasures at the water's edge and the enjoyment of a very good white sand beach; 'Shirahama' means 'White Beach'.

A short distance to the north of the beach is the islet of Engetsu-to ('Round Moon Island'), known for the hole in its middle. South of the beach are the layers of rock 'plates' of the Senjojiki formation, and just around the promontory are the cliffs of Sandankei. The seascapes are considered among the best on the Kii-hanto peninsula and there is a good view from Heisogen hill, behind the town. A cable car runs to the 130-metre summit from Shirahama. During the summer festival, large sand sculptures are built on the beach.

Places to Stay

In addition to over 100 hotels of all types, some with floor shows at night, there is also a *Youth Hostel* at nearby Tanabe, very close to Kii-Tanabe station (third stop from Shirahama station).

TANABE

There are several good swimming beaches near this port city. The best known is

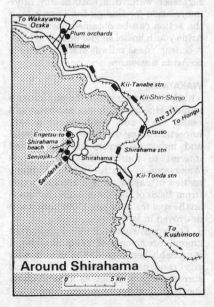

Around Shirahama

Ogigahama. The name of the station is Kii-Tanabe.

MINABE

In late January to mid February, Minabe-gawa-mura is a popular destination for tourists who flock to see the huge plum groves, which have about 300,000 trees, on the surrounding hills and valleys. They are a couple of km inland from the station; buses are available.

GOBO

Near this small city there is a good white sand beach, Enju-ga-hama, which is about 500 metres long.

ARIDA (ARITA)

On the Arita-kawa river there is nightly *ukai* (cormorant fishing). In other places the fishermen ride in boats that have a blazing fire in an iron grate at the bow, but here the fisherman wade in knee-deep water, holding a torch in one hand and the leashes of the cormorants in the other. Sightseers watch from boats nearby. More information for finding the exact site of the action can be obtained on the spot. Arida youth hostel should be able to help; it is near Yuasa railway station. There is no Arida station.

WAKAYAMA

This is the city for which the prefecture is named. Historically it was important as a castle town and residence of a very important *daimyo*. It is now a commercial and industrial centre of very limited interest to tourists. Its trademark is Wakayama-jo castle but, like many castles in Japan, it is a reconstruction (from 1958) of the historic one that stood on the spot from the late 1500s until it was destroyed in WW II.

The reconstruction is well done and the grounds are an oasis of tranquillity, but it is probably best regarded as an escape for city residents from their rather drab surroundings and not as a particularly special attraction for foreign visitors.

There is a regular ferry service between Wakayama-ko port and Komatsushima on Shikoku. Details are given in the Komatsushima section.

FUKE

From Fuke-ko, not far from Wakayama, there is a ferry service to Toku-shima on Shikoku island. See the Tokushima section for details.

Osaka

Osaka is one of the most important cities in Japanese history and was a thriving trading centre almost 2000 years ago. It is now a commercial and industrial city, second in importance only to Tokyo, though as far as population goes it has slipped behind Yokohama to third position.

Despite its history as a power centre (as narrated in *Shogun*), there is very little of historic interest within the city due to the passage of time and heavy bombing during WW II. There are a few attractions north of the city, across the Shin-Yodo River.

Osaka can be recommended as a port of entry as it is in the centre of the main island of Honshu and it is close to Kyoto, the single most important tourist destination in Japan. The airport serves Kyoto as well and is actually closer to both cities than Narita is to Tokyo.

Osaka is also a hub for train services so it is easy to get to other parts of the country. There are also some bus services and long-distance ferries to several cities.

Information

At Osaka station there are two information offices, one at the front of the station and one at the rear; the front one is more likely to have pamphlets. If out of stock, they should be able to refer you to the Osaka city information office. One of the offices

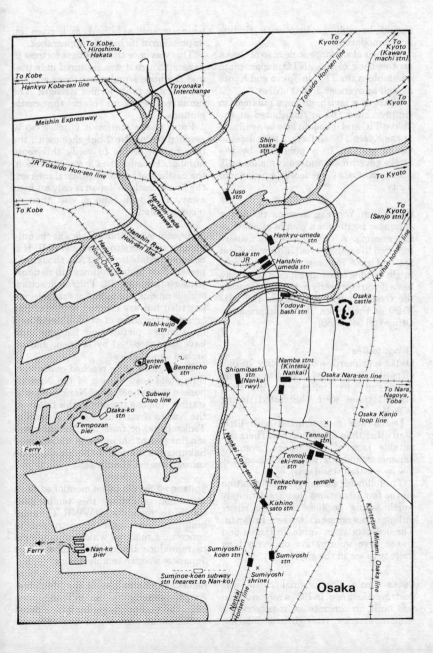

To Kobe, Hiroshima, Hakata

To Kobe

Hankyu Kobe-sen line

To Kyoto

To Kyoto (Kawara machi stn)

Toyonaka Interchange

Meishin Expressway

JR Tokaido Hon-sen line

To Kyoto

Shin-osaka stn

JR Tokaido Hon-sen line

To Kobe

Juso stn

Hanshin Ikeda Expressway

To Kyoto

To Kobe

Hanshin Rwy Hon-sen line

Nishi-Osaka line

Hankyu-umeda stn

To Kyoto (Sanjo stn)

Osaka stn JR

Hanshin-umeda stn

Keihan-hon-sen line

Yodoyabashi stn

Osaka castle

Nishi-kujo stn

Benten pier

Bentencho stn

Shiomibashi stn (Nankai rwy)

Namba stns (Kintesu Nankai)

Osaka Nara-sen line

To Nara, Nagoya, Toba

Subway Chuo line

Osaka-ko stn

Tempozan pier

Ferry

Osaka Kanjo loop line

Nankai Koya-sen line

Tennoji stn

Tennoji eki-mae stn

Tenkachaya stn

temple

Kintetsu Minami Osaka line

Ferry

Nan-ko pier

Kishino sato stn

Sumiyoshi-koen stn

Sumiyoshi stn

Suminoe-koen subway stn (nearest to Nan-ko)

Sumiyoshi shrine

Nankai Hon-sen line

Osaka

should be able to help with finding accommodation.

There is also a large-scale map of Osaka on the back of the JNTO Japan map, available at the TICs in Tokyo and Kyoto as well as overseas JNTO offices.

There is a lavish, 48-page publication simply called *Osaka* distributed at the Tokyo TIC and it should also be available at the Kyoto TIC and one of the offices in Osaka station. It is published by the Osaka government and really makes a silk purse out of what is generally a pig's ear of a city.

Home Visit You can arrange to visit a Japanese family for a couple of hours in the evening. A day or more is usually required to arrange a visit, although if you are in Osaka for only a short time you might be able to arrange it on a same-day basis if you start early in the day. Contact the Osaka Tourist Association (tel 261-3948) or the Osaka Tourist Information Office (tel 345-2189).

Things to See
Osaka is primarily a business city. Its day of political greatness and power is long past, and what relics were left from ancient times were obliterated during WW II.

Osaka was reconstructed with little plan other than for commerce. There is a notable lack of park space, even by Japanese standards (which are lamentably low by western standards).

The following section gives information on the few attractions that are definitely worth seeing because they are either unique or uncommon elsewhere in Japan. The booklets *Your Guide To Osaka* and *Osaka* give information on everything there is to see in the city.

Osaka Castle The original castle was destroyed long ago. In 1931 a reproduction was built, in concrete, so it preserves a similar exterior (though not interior,

which even has lifts!) and gives an impression of its historic appearance.

This was once the mightiest fortress in Japan (though it was captured in battle) and the huge foundation stones and the gates testify to its former strength. The municipal museum is in the castle grounds.

From Osaka station it is most easily reached by bus No 2 but check with the information centre to verify this route number. Because it is a reconstruction, the castle is of limited historical interest; the finest castle in Japan is only an hour away, at Himeji, and a visit there is recommended.

Sumiyoshi-taisha Shrine This was the only historic structure to survive WW II. It is believed to date from 202 AD, though the present four main buildings (all national treasures) are from 1810. Their architectural style is unique; the roofs, for example, are not tiled but are covered with multiple layers of thin strips of wood. The grounds have many picturesque lanterns that have been donated by seamen, and an arched stone bridge.

The shrine can be reached easily from Sumiyoshi-koen station of the Nankai-honsen (main line) out of Nankai-Namba station. You can transfer to this line from the Nanka shuttle line out of Tennoji at Tenkachaya, or from the Nankai-koya-sen line (out of Shiomibashi station, near Sakuragawa station of the Sennichimae subway line) at Kishinosato.

Shitenno-ji Temple Often mentioned as an attraction of Osaka, this temple was totally destroyed during WW II. The main buildings were later reconstructed in concrete, a material which cannot begin to reproduce the qualities inherent in Japanese wooden temple design.

Keitaku-en Garden Beside the Municipal Art Museum (Bijutsu-kan) in Tennoji-koen park, this very pretty garden is considered an excellent example of the Japanese

Top: Old man with bicycle, Nagasaki, Kyushu (AE)
Bottom: Young shrine attendants, Autumn festival, Takayama (AE)

Top: Kintai-kyo (Bridge of the Brocade Sash), Iwakuni, Hiroshima-ken (IMcQ)
Bottom: Hakuro-jo (White Egret) Castle, Himeji, Japan's finest (IMcQ)

circular garden. It is open without reservation on Tuesdays, Thursdays and Sundays, and with reservation on Wednesday, Fridays and Saturdays. It is easily reached from Tenno-ji JR or subway stations.

The Mint There is a museum of coins from around the world, but the main attraction is during the cherry blossom season when the grounds are open so that the public can see the many beautiful trees planted there.

Other Attractions For combined shopping and sightseeing, the underground shopping centres are worth a look, as they are usually very attractive. They are usually at the terminuses of the various private railway lines. The arcade at Hankyu Umeda station is a good starting point; it has one section that resembles the arched roof of a cathedral, with stained-glass windows.

Although Osaka is unlovely by day, with lots of large buildings, parts of it are quite pretty at night, particularly the Dotombori area where the lights of large multi-coloured advertising signs are reflected in the water of a canal. Fountain sprays in the canal serve the double duty of adding a note of beauty while helping to purify the water. Many shops and restaurants line the nearby streets.

Places to Stay

Because it is such an important business centre, Osaka has a large number of hotels of various prices, from luxury class to business hotels and *ryokan*. Help in finding a room is available at Osaka station.

There are several youth hostels in and near Osaka. *Nagai Youth Hostel* (tel (06) 699-5631/2) is in the municipal sports ground. It has 102 beds, is quite pleasant and is one of the cheapest hostels in Japan. It is reached from Nagai station of either the JR Hanwa line (south from

Tennoji station) or Midosuji subway line. No card is required, only a passport.

Hattori Ryoku-chi Youth Hostel (tel (06) 862-0600) is north of the city in the same park as the Farmhouse Museum. It has 108 beds and is reached via Ryokuchi-koen station of Midosuji subway line.

The 24-bed *Sayama-Yuen Youth Hostel* (tel (0723) 65-3091) is to the south of the city. It is reached by Nankai railway Koya-sen line via Sayama-yuen-mae station.

Other hostels in the area can be found with the help of the information service at the station. Failing that, a Japanese person could ask for additional phone numbers by telephoning any of the hostels listed. The hostels of Kyoto and Nara are also within range of Osaka, but if Osaka hostels are full the others probably will be too.

Entertainment

Bunraku Osaka's contribution to the world's performing arts is *bunraku* puppet theatre. The puppets are more than a metre tall, have realistic faces, and are beautifully costumed.

Each doll is manipulated by one to three people standing behind it, moving the head, arms and legs in such a realistic manner that it seems to take on a life of its own. The master puppeteer is visible and dressed in traditional costume, while his masked assistants are dressed in black. There is a narrator and musical accompaniment by *shamisen*.

In early 1984, *bunraku* acquired a permanent home in Osaka, the Kokuritsu Bunraku Gekijo (National Bunraku Theatre), a five-storey, Y65-billion building in Minami-ku (ward). Inquire locally about performances of this interesting art. The TIC in Kyoto should be able to help.

Kabuki Performances of *kabuki* are given at various times throughout the year; the theatre is Shin-Kabuki-za, near Namba station of the subway or Nankai line. Information is available from the TIC in Kyoto.

Takarazuka Girls' Opera This is an institution in the Kansai area, a music hall in which all performers are young women. Programmes include revues, musicals and adaptations of light operas.

The 4000-seat theatre, the largest in the orient, is part of Takarazuka Family Land, a large recreation centre with cinemas, gardens, etc.

Access is by Hankyu-Takarazuka line from Hankyu Umeda station. It was originally built to attract users to the Hankyu railroad, which had been built through new housing developments but was losing money.

Clubs & Bars Being a large business centre, Osaka has all the nightclubs, cabarets, hostess bars, etc, found in any large Japanese city. The same warnings also bear repeating – that many (if not most) are aimed at expense account spenders and can be *very* expensive. If prices aren't posted, ask before ordering anything. A safe and relatively inexpensive way around the problem is to take an evening tour that includes a nightclub and cabaret.

Festivals

9-11 January: Imamiya Ebisu-jinja (Niniwa-ku).

22 April: Shitennoji temple.

14 June: Sumiyoshi-taisha.

24-5 June: Tenmangu shrine (Tenjin matsuri).

30 July – 1 August: Sumiyoshi-taisha.

11-12 August: Ikutama-jinja shrine (Osaka Takigi Noh performances at night).

Things to Buy

Because of the relatively small number of foreign visitors to Osaka, there is a correspondingly small number of tax-free shops.

Based on a very small sample, I found that discounts were smaller than those available in Tokyo and about the same as (or a little less than) those in Kyoto, but it might be possible to shop around and do better than this.

One place to look for would be Doi Camera, one of a chain of shops across the country; their Tokyo branch in Shinjuku has very favourable prices. Kimura Camera is another well-known chain store but their prices in Tokyo vary from branch to branch, so there is no assurance of matching Tokyo prices.

Getting There & Away

Air Osaka has air connections with approximately 30 cities in Asia, Europe and the USA. Cities include Bangkok, Beijing, Bombay, Calcutta, Cheju (Korea), Guam, Hong Kong, Honolulu, Kaohsiung (Taiwan), Manila, Pusan, San Francisco, Seattle, Seoul, Shanghai, Singapore and Taipei.

Osaka Airport is close to the city and convenient to reach. Travellers who plan to visit Kyoto should consider landing at Osaka instead of Tokyo.

Clearing immigration and customs is straightforward; the immigration officials here have a reputation for being among the most reasonable in Japan and they seem more willing than those at some other international ports of entry to give a 90-day entry period if you are entitled to it by bilateral agreement.

Train Kyoto, Nara and Kobe can be reached in less than an hour by train from Osaka. To Nagoya and a large number of other places in the Kinki district it takes somewhat longer. For details of services in the Kinki district, refer to the transport section at the end of this chapter.

For longer distances, the Shinkansen offers very fast service to Tokyo (about three hours), and Hakata (Fukuoka, in northern Kyushu) is 3½ hours in the opposite direction. Shinkansen services are detailed in the Getting Around chapter.

The stations for inter-city train services are Shin-Osaka (New Osaka) station for the Shinkansen (one stop from Osaka station), and Osaka station (the main JR station), used by Shin-Kaisoku and other trains of the Tokaido and Sanjo lines.

Shin-Osaka station is on the Midosuji subway line, while Osaka station and the Umeda stations of the Hankyu and Hanshin lines are all served by the Midosuji, Yotsuhashi and Tanimachi lines. The Keihan line intersects the Tanimachi, Sakaisuji and Midosuji lines at the three stations following Kyobashi station (JR Sanjo line) and Kyobashi is also the transfer point from the Katamachi line (to/from Nara) before it terminates at Katamachi.

Tennoji, on the Kanjo, Tanimachi and Midosuji lines, is the starting point for the JR line to Wakayama, the Kintetsu line to Koyasan, and the Nankai Koya-sen (to Koyasan) and Nankai Hon-sen to Wakayama.

Namba stations of the Kintetsu/Nara line (to Nara) and Nansai Koya line (to Koyasan) are close to stations of the Yotsuhashi, Midosuji and Sennichimae subway lines. Transfer to the Kintetsu Nara line is also possible where it intersects the Sakaisuji and Tanimachi lines. The JR Minato-machi station (for trains to Nara) is close to the Namba stations.

Ferry There are both international and domestic boat services from Osaka. There is a regular service to both Pusan (Korea) and Shanghai (China), and ferry services to Shikoku (Takamatsu, Matsuyama and Kochi) and Kyushu (Beppu, Moji, Hyuga and Kagoshima). The domestic ferries generally run daily and sail overnight, saving on accommodation costs.

Ferries from Osaka to points on Shikoku and Kyushu leave from three different piers – Benten-futo pier, Tempozan pier and Osaka Nanko pier.

To get to Benten-futo pier, take the JR Kanjo-sen (loop line) or the subway Chuo line to Bentensho station. From there it is a five-minute bus trip by regular city bus from the station. In addition you can take

city bus No 53 from Osaka station or bus No 60 from Namba station to 'Benten-futo' stop.

Tempozan pier is most easily reached by Chuo-sen subway line. The terminus, Osaka-ko station, is a three-minute walk from the pier. In addition to the subway, buses No 53 and 88 from Osaka station, No 60 from Namba station and No 107 from Tenmabashi go to Tempozan terminal.

Osaka Nanko can be reached easily by taking Yotsuhashi-sen subway line to its terminus, Suminoe-Koen, then taking a bus from there (15 minutes) to Osaka Nanko (the end of the line). There are also buses from Sumiyoshi-koen station of the Nankai-densha private railway line but it is advisable to check the frequency of these buses in advance.

Hitching Between Osaka and Kyoto, forget it. It takes too long to try to get a ride, and then you have to get into the city at the other end – take the train.

For hitching to more distant points, it is necessary to reach the Meishin Kosokudoro freeway (between Kobe and Nagoya) or the Chugoku Kosokudoro freeway from Osaka to the western end of Honshu. There is no simple way to get started as the interchanges are all to the north of Osaka and it is necessary to take a train or local road to the entrance, or start at an entrance in Osaka itself and try to get a car that will switch to the exact road you want to take. The latter requires a sign indicating where you want to go, as hitching is not allowed on the freewways themselves.

One entrance is close to Osaka station and leads onto the Osaka-Ikeda route, which leads to Toyonaka interchange (Meishin) and Ikeda interchange (Chugoku); the latter is near the interchange for Osaka Airport.

Somewhat to the northeast is another entrance to a local freeway (Kinki Freeway) that becomes the Chugoku expressway and intersects the Meishin at

Suita. The starting point is the Kadoma interchange, which is about one km from Kadoma station of the Keihan-Kyoto line. Ibaraki, on the Meishin expressway, is about two km from the Ibanaki JR station, and there may be a bus passing close to it.

Alternatively, you can use the slower national highways which switch from Route 1 (from Tokyo) to Route 2 (to Shimonoseki at the far west) in front of Osaka station. However, this is in the middle of Osaka, so hitching could be rather poor. If you are near the station, ask at the information office for a map and suggestions for getting a better starting point.

Getting Around

Airport Transport Buses that depart from the front of the airport terminal building are the most economical way to get in from the airport. The most useful destinations for most travellers are Shin-Osaka station (for Shinkansen trains), Osaka station (for most JR services, posted as Osaka-Umeda) and Namba, another station south of the city. There are also buses direct to Kyoto and Kobe. There are buses every 10 to 20 minutes to most destinations; the trip takes 20 minutes into Osaka and one hour to Kyoto.

Buses to the airport leave from several points in Osaka; one is in front of the Daimaru building, about three minutes walk to the right when leaving the front of Osaka station.

Subway & City Trains Osaka has six subway lines: Midosuji, Tanimachi, Yotsuhashi, Chuo, Sennichimae and Sakaisuji. All but the Chuo line run roughly north-south for much of their length, although Midosuji, Sennichimae and Tanimachi lines run east-west for part of their length. The Chuo line runs primarily east-west.

While the subway lines criss-cross the central part of the city, the JR Kanjo-sen loop line circles around the central district in both directions. The subway lines

intersect each other at many places, making transfer simple. They also cross the Kanjo line at several points, but there is not always a station near the intersection where you can transfer between JR and subway lines.

Separate tickets are required for JR and subway lines, and tickets must be kept and surrendered when leaving the system. A subway map in English is available at the information centre at Osaka station.

Bus A map of all city bus services in Osaka is available (Japanese only) at the small information office near the bus departure area in front of the station (to the left when leaving the station). Ask for a 'basu (bus) no chizu'.

Around Osaka

KOBE

Kobe is an international port of entry to Japan, mostly for cruise passengers, and is also an industrial and commercial city. In a reversal of the old saying, it is considered a nice place to live but you wouldn't want to visit there.

Mt Rokko provides a view over the city but there is relatively little else for a visitor. For this reason most of the following information refers to getting to the nearby cities of Kyoto, Nara and Himeji.

Visiting liners dock at Pier 4. From there a wide road (known among foreigners as the Bund) goes straight to Sannomiya station, effectively the main station of Kobe. Bus No 92 runs between the station and the port and taxis are also available.

Home Visit

A visit to a Japanese family (afternoon or evening) is an enjoyable experience and can be arranged by contacting the organisers: Sannomiya Kotsu Centre Building (tel 391-4753), 2F, near Sannomiya station; or through your hotel or shipping company.

Places to Stay

Kobe has many hotels. Feedback regarding the *Youth Hostel* has not been favourable so it might be preferable to stay in Kyoto or Osaka if space is available.

Places to Eat

Kobe is famous for a type of beef that takes the name of the city. It is reputed to be delicious and is very expensive; even more so than the already outrageous prices charged for beef of any kind in Japan. It is very fatty and might not appeal if you are accustomed to lean beef.

Getting There & Away

Train Kyoto, Osaka and Himeji can all be reached quickly and conveniently from Kobe. Even passengers on cruise liners could reach Kyoto for some sightseeing and be back at the ship the same day. An alternative is to leave the ship at Kobe and rejoin it at Yokohama, if the ship goes there next. All major train services in the region are detailed in the Kinki district

Getting Around section at the end of this chapter.

Shinkansen super-express trains use Shin-Kobe station, which nestles at the foot of the mountain that overshadows the city. This station can be reached from the main JR station, Sannomiya, in about 10 minutes by bus No 4 or by taxi. The extra speed of the train may be counterbalanced by the less convenient station for going to Osaka or Kyoto.

Regular JR services, including the speedy Shin-Kaisoku expresses, use Sannomiya; Kobe station is relatively unimportant. The main station of the Hankyu line (to Osaka and Kyoto) is Hankyu-Sannomiya. Similarly for the Hanshin line (to Osaka only), the main station is Hanshin-Sannomiya, terminating at Hanshin-Motomachi. All the Sannomiya stations are close to each other.

Ferry There are ferries between Kobe and Konoura, Tosa-Shimizu, Matsuyama, Imabari, Takamatsu, Tokushima, Niihima and Kawanoe on Shikoku; Oita, Kokura, Hyuga and Beppu on Kyushu; and Okinawa.

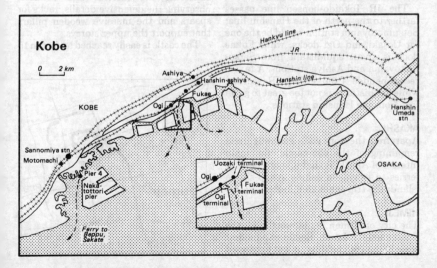

Services to the relatively close points on Shikoku are detailed in the relevant places on Shikoku.

Naka-Tottei pier is in Kobe harbour, in central Kobe, at the end of the Bund. The pier is easily identified by the red Port Tower. Boats to Okinawa leave from near the end of the pier; passenger ferries to Kyushu leave from the near end; car ferries to Kyushu leave from the middle.

The other ports (Ogi, Uosaki and Fukae) are collectively known as Higashi-Kobe-ko (East Kobe port). The map shows their relative locations. Ogi and Uosaki are most conveniently reached from Ogi station of the Hanshin line; and Fukae from Fukae station of the same line. At Ogi station the docks are on the track-4 side of the station, on the far side of the expressway (Highway 43); there is a guide map at the station.

Express trains do not stop at these stations so it is necessary to take a local train from Kobe/Osaka, or an express from either city to Hanshin-Ashiya and change there to a local train. Trains from Osaka leave Hanshin-Umeda station. From Kobe they leave Hanshin-Sannomiya and Hanshin-Motomachi stations.

The JR Tokaido-honsen line passes farther to the north of the Hanshin line; Setsumotoyama station would be the one for Uosaki and Ogi docks, while Fukae dock is about equidistant from Setsu-motoyama and Ashiya stations. A taxi is recommended from either JR station, while the distance is not too great to go on foot from the Hanshin stations.

AKASHI

Apart from the stone walls and two turrets remaining of the old castle, the main interest of Akashi is that it is one port for ferries to Iwaya on nearby Awaji-shima island; the trip takes 25 minutes.

HIMEJI

The city of Himeji is noteworthy for the finest castle in Japan. Begun on a modest scale in the 16th century, it was expanded by later *daimyo* until it reached its present form in the early 1800s, and was restored to nearly original condition in the 1960s. It is on a hill not far from Himeji station and its white form can be seen soon after leaving the station's front exit.

Other lesser attractions of Himeji include the unusual cemetery of Nago-yama (15 minutes from the station by bus), and Enkyo Temple at the top of Shosha-san (eight km from the station). Access from Shosha station is by bus, then a cable car.

Hakuro-jo Castle

Hakuro-jo (White Egret Castle) is made up of 78 individual buildings, the main one standing five storeys high. It is a defensive castle despite its aesthetic appeal, approached by narrow paths that could be showered with arrows from slits in the walls.

In contrast, the upper part (which was unassailable) was designed for the best in gracious living, as defined by the tastes of the day; this can be seen in the delicate wood carving and bronze decorations around the rooms.

A couple of hours can easily be spent exploring the interior and exterior, observing the defensive details, racks for spears and the massive wooden pillars that support the upper storeys.

The castle is easily reached on foot in 15

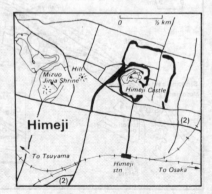

minutes from the station. The lighting for photos is most dramatic as the sun gets low in the sky. An interesting vantage point, for those determined enough and with a telephoto lens, is the top of the hill where Mizuo-jinja shrine stands.

Festivals

3 April: Rice Planting Festival at Hiromine-jinja.

17-18 April: Spring Festival at Hiromine-jinja.

14-15 October: Kenka-matsuri is held at Matsubara Hichiman-jinja (near Shirahama-no-miya station).

Places to Stay

There are many hotels and *ryokan* because Himeji is a major destination for Japanese sightseers as well. The *Youth Hostel* is rather dilapidated and the staff reportedly uncaring, so staying elsewhere might be preferable.

Getting There

Information on trains connecting Himeji with Kyoto, Osaka and Kobe is in the Getting Around section at the end of this chapter. Heading west you can use regular JR services (to Hiroshima, etc) as well as the super-express Shinkansen trains.

NORTH OF OSAKA
Expo 70 & Its Legacy

Osaka came to international attention by hosting the World Fair, Expo 70. The use of the structures as pavilions ended in September 1970 but some of them have been preserved and converted to other display purposes and the famed garden has survived.

Japanese Garden A garden incorporating the elements for which Japanese gardens have become famous – the placing of rocks, water, hills, trees and other shrubbery – was created for Expo 70 and is one of the most pleasant places to visit in Osaka.

National Museum of Ethnology This is on the old Expo grounds and has been rated as very worthwhile by all who have visited. Exhibits include items of daily use, plus video tapes of festivals, music, etc, from a large number of countries. Most interesting and exotic to the Japanese is Spanish flamenco.

Access to both the garden and museum is by bus from Ibaraki-shi station of the JR Tokaido line, or Ibaraki-shi station of the Hankyu Kyoto line. These stations are between Osaka and Kyoto (closer to the former) and can very easily be visited from Kyoto as a day trip.

Koriyama Honjin

This is in the same area as the Expo garden. During the Edo era (1603 to 1867) feudal lords were compelled to spend part of their time in Edo (Tokyo) as virtual hostages, so there was much movement of their parties to and from Edo.

To provide accommodation fit for people of such exalted rank, inns of the finest construction and facilities were set up along the route. Koriyama Honjin was one and it looks much as it did then. It is open for inspection and has many historical items on display. It is accessible from JR Ibaraki station.

Japanese Farmhouse Museum

This open-air museum (Nihon Minka Shuraku Hakubutsu-kan) is an interesting collection of 12 traditional thatched-roof farmhouses of the type once common in Japan but now quite rare. They were brought to Hattori Ryoichi Park and reassembled in a village-like arrangement.

The buildings house exhibits of traditional furniture and items used in daily life. There is an English-language pamphlet available.

Hattori Ryoichi is accessible from Sone station (before Toyonaka) on the Hankyu Takarazuka-sen line from Hankyu Umeda station, or from Ryokuchi-koen subway station. It is closed on Mondays.

SOUTH OF OSAKA

Sakai Nintoku Tomb Mound

The greatest tomb mound in Japan, covering a larger area than the Great Pyramid (about 460,000 square metres), is a short distance south of Osaka. The keyhole-shaped mound is 478 metres long, 300 metres wide at the flat end and as high as 35 metres. An immense amount of work went into its construction, involving the movement of 1.45 million cubic metres of earth. Three moats surround it.

After this description, it is only fair to say that, for most people, it is not worth the effort to go to see; from ground level it looks like little more than a broad ditch surrounding a low hill. There is a tall tower at its base that looks like an observatory, but it was closed when I visited.

The mound is more interesting for what it stands for than what it is physically. For several hundred years from the 5th century onwards, the Osaka area was the residence of the rulers of Japan who had the power and resources to build these tombs. One theory is that this was the eastern tip of a crescent of the same ethnic group that stretched to Kyushu and into part of Korea, and that the labourers who built the tomb were captives from wars on the Korean peninsula. This is only interesting speculation at this point but would explain how so many people could be assigned to non productive work.

The practice of building these mounds seems to have died out in the 7th century, possibly indicating a shift of power to a local clan.

Access is from Mozu station of the JR Hanwa-sen line (from Tenno-ji station).

Yoshimura-ke House

This is a large farmhouse built in the 17th century and preserved in excellent condition. It is accessible from Takawashi station of Kintetsu Minami Osaka-sen line, which leads to Yoshino.

Getting Around Kinki District

TRAIN

The Kinki district, particularly between Nagoya and Osaka, is intensively blanketed by railway services. Since there are many destinations of interest to foreign visitors, and many places can be visited on a day trip (such as Nara or Toba from Kyoto or Kyoto from Kobe), it is useful to have a general idea of the frequency of train services and the travel time between one place and another.

The following is a summary of the lines likely to be of most interest to visitors. There are others but they are of limited interest and are no use for inter-city travel, only for specific tourist destinations.

In the majority of cases, railway connections in the Kinki district are more convenient, faster and cheaper by private railways. JR services are mostly useful for travellers with a Japan Rail Pass.

Nagoya – Kyoto – Osaka – Kobe – Himeji

JR Shinkansen The fastest, most frequent and convenient service through these cities is the Shinkansen. Both Kodama and Hikari trains run between Nagoya and Osaka; the former make one extra stop (Gifu-Haneshima) and take 82 minutes over the distance – against 67 minutes for the Hikari. Charges are the same.

Beyond Osaka, trains are mostly Hikari, but there are several different services (some only stop at Himeji and some even bypass Kobe) so it is necessary to check in advance to be sure of getting the right train beyond Osaka.

The time and fare chart shows Hikari services that stop at all these cities. Trains are very frequent – usually eight or more per hour through Nagoya.

JR Tokaido Line & Sanyo Line The former is the main JR line from Tokyo to Osaka; the latter from Osaka to Okayama, and both were the principal lines until the Shinkansen was built.

Between Nagoya and Kyoto/Osaka there are only three direct expresses a day (just under two hours); for all the other trains (about 17 a day) it is necessary to change at Maibara, sometimes at Ogaki as well. This way the Nagoya – Kyoto trip can take 2½ hours with optimum connections if the trains are all locals; or 15 minutes less if one gets a Nagoya – Maibara express.

From Osaka/Kyoto to Nagoya there is a similar number of trains also with changes at Maibara or Ogaki.

Alternative JR Service There is another way from Nagoya to Kyoto/Osaka that might be of use to some travellers. From Nagoya, the trip begins by Kansai Honsen (Kansai main line) which passes through Nara en route to Osaka (14 a day), changing first at Kaneyama after about 1¼ hours, going to Tsuge (about 35 minutes), then at Tsuge to the Kusatsu line to Kusatsu (45 minutes), then to the Tokaido line to Kyoto (25 minutes). About eight trains a day go direct from Tsuge to Kyoto without the need to change at Kusatsu. Depending on the connections, the trip can take 3½ to 4½ hours. The only exception is a single express between Nagoya and Kyoto that takes about three hours. There are about 20 sets of trains through the day in each direction that you can use for this route.

Nagoya – Kyoto

Kintetsu The Kinki Nippon (Kintetsu) line offers a convenient service between Nagoya and Kyoto by a transfer at Yamato-Yagi between the Kyoto – Ise line and the Nagoya – Osaka line (both described later). Total travel time between Nagoya and Kyoto is about 2¾ hours and costs about Y2600.

JR Another route to Kyoto from Nagoya is via JR to Nara, then to Kyoto.

Nagoya – Osaka

Kintetsu The only direct service between these two cities is operated by the Kintetsu private railway. Every day on the hour, between 8 am and 7 pm, a train of the 'non-stop *tokkyu*' service leaves Kintetsu-Nagoya and Kintetsu-Namba (Osaka) stations arriving at the other station 2¼ hours later. The fare is Y2590, including the express surcharge.

Every hour on the half hour, from 7.30 am to 7.30 pm (from Nagoya) or 8.30 pm (from Osaka), there are similar expresses that make a few intermediate stops and take an extra 13 minutes. These are the trains to take for destinations between the cities, such as changing to go to Kyoto or Nara or to visit Iga-Ueno. The fare is the same as for the non-stop express.

It is also possible to travel more cheaply between Nagoya and Osaka by non-express Kintetsu trains (same tracks) by using the Nagoya – Yamada, and Yamada – Osaka lines, with a change at Ise-Nakagawa. Time on the trains is 3½ hours plus the wait for the connecting train. You could also go from one city to Ise/Toba for sightseeing and then proceed to the other city by this route. Refer to the later section on services to Ise for more details.

JR There are no direct JR Nagoya – Osaka trains; it is necessary to change trains at Nara. Refer to the sections Nagoya – Nara, and Nara – Osaka. There is normally a train at Nara for the transfer, so the wait is not more than a couple of minutes.

Nagoya – Nara

Kintetsu The quickest service from Nagoya to Nara is the Kintetsu Nagoya – Osaka line from Nagoya to Yamato-Yagi (just under two hours), changing there to the Kintetsu Kyoto – Ise line to Yamato-Saidaiji (20 minutes), and then taking the Osaka – Nara line to Nara (five minutes). As described before, trains are scheduled for a minimum wait at Yamato-Yagi (about two minutes); and Nara – Yamato-

Saidaiji trains run every five to 15 minutes.

JR There are two expresses per day (about 2½ hours), one of which runs direct between the two cities, while the other requires a change of train at Kameyama. This change is required for all regular trains (12 a day); the delay at Kameyama for regular trains varies from three to 35 minutes. The trip usually takes 3½ hours.

Nagoya – Ise/Toba
Kintetsu The Kintetsu line offers convenient service between Nagoya (Kintetsu-Nagoya station) and Ise, Toba and Kashikojima (on the Shima-hanto peninsula). In both directions there are *kyuko* expresses every five to 30 minutes and *futsu* (regular) trains every 15 to 30 minutes; plus about 32 *tokkyu* special expresses (the fastest) daily. *Tokkyu* trains take about 1½ hours from Nagoya to Ise (Y1610), and 1¾ hours from Nagoya to Toba (Y1810), while ordinary *kyuko* and *junkyu* expresses take about 15 minutes longer and cost Y910 (Nagoya – Ise).

The less expensive *kyuko* and *junkyu* trains can be used for travel between Nagoya and Osaka by taking a Nagoya – Ise train to Ise-Nakagawa and changing to an Ise – Osaka line train. This is slower than the *tokkyu* Nagoya – Osaka trains (about three hours) but is cheaper. The route can also be used for a visit to Ise/Toba en route between the two large cities.

JR JR services are much less convenient, requiring a minimum of one change of train. Five expresses run directly from Nagoya through to Taki, where a change must be made to a different train to Ise, Toba, etc. The expresses to Taki take from 1½ to two hours; and the local trains that connect with them take about 20 minutes to Ise and 50 minutes to Toba (depending on whether a change at Ise is required).

Other than the expresses, no other trains leave from Nagoya; it is necessary

to first go to Yokkaichi, change to a train going to Tsu, change again to a Shingu-bound train and take it as a far as Taki, then change one last time to the local train to Ise and Toba. Nagoya – Yokkaichi takes about 45 minutes, Yokkaichi – Tsu about 45 minutes, and Tsu – Yaki about an hour. This routing is obviously only of interest to holders of a Japan Rail Pass.

Nagoya – Kii-hanto Peninsula – Osaka
A JR line runs around the periphery of the Kii-hanto peninsula. The links of this route are Nagoya (Yokkaichi) – Shingu – Wakayama – Osaka.

Nara – Osaka
Kintetsu There are about 13 daily *tokkyu* expresses between Kintetsu-Nara and Kintetsu-Namba (Osaka) stations taking about 35 minutes (Y660), plus slower (five to 10 minutes longer) semi-expresses every five to 15 minutes through the day (Y360).

JR There are nearly 90 trains a day between Nara and Osaka (each direction) via two routes. Trains of the Kansai-honsen line take 49 minutes to each of the terminus stations in Osaka; Osaka station (in the north of the city, 27 a day) and Minato-machi station (in the south of the city, 31 a day).

Trains of the Kata-machi-sen line take 51 minutes (30 a day) and also terminate at Minato-machi station. The fare for both is Y570.

Nara – Ise/Toba Area
Kintetsu There are no direct services from Nara but the trip can be made very conveniently by taking a local train from Kintetsu-Nara station to Yamato-Saidaiji (five minutes) and catching a Kyoto – Ise *tokkyu* train (described later); they leave Yamato-Saidaiji station 30 minutes after the times listed for leaving Kyoto.

JR It is necessary to take the Kansai-honsen line (Nagoya bound) as far as Kameyama (about two hours), transfer to a Shingu-bound train as far as Taki, then take an Ise-bound train from there. There are generally connecting trains at Kameyama and Taki for minimum wait, but these should be checked in advance.

Kyoto – Nara

Kintetsu The fastest Kyoto – Nara services are the 26 daily Kintetsu *tokkyu* expresses that run between Kyoto and Kintetsu-Nara stations with only a single stop (at Yamato-Saidaiji). Most leave every 30 to 60 minutes, on the hour or half-hour, although there are also some jokers in the pack at odd times. The earliest is 6.22 am from Nara, 8 am from Kyoto. Travel time is 33 minutes and the fare is Y670.

Other expresses with the same fare but a few minutes slower and requiring a change at Yamato-Saidaiji are the Kyoto – Ise *tokkyu* expresses (detailed later) and *tokkyu* expresses bound for Kashihara-jingu-mae; these generally leave Kyoto on the quarter-hour and three-quarter-hour, respectively, through the day. Travel time to Yamato-Saidaiji is about 30 minutes; from there, Kintetsu-Nara station is only a five-minute ride away.

Through the day at 10 to 30-minute intervals there are many *kyuko* expresses (somewhat slower) and *futsu* (local) trains that take 39 to 54 minutes but cost only Y370. With these it is generally necessary to change trains at Yamato-Saidaiji.

For the journey from Nara to Kyoto, the reverse trains can be used, so if there is no convenient train listed for Kyoto, you can take any train (generally for Osaka) and transfer at Yamato-Saidaiji to the first train passing through to Kyoto.

JR Through the day there are about 24 trains running direct between Kyoto and Nara. One of these is an express train, taking 51 minutes; the rest are locals that take 68 minutes. The regular trains cost Y570; while there is a surcharge for the express.

Kyoto – Ise/Toba/Shima-hanto Peninsula

Kintetsu The most convenient and fastest service between Kyoto and the Ise/Toba area is the Kintetsu *tokkyu* expresses that leave Kyoto hourly on the quarter-hour from 7.15 am to 6.15 pm, all of which run to Kashikojima (Shima-hanto peninsula) except the last two which terminate at Toba. In the opposite direction there are trains every hour between 8.20 am and 6.20 pm, plus one train from Ise at 8.14 am. The fare from Kyoto to Ise is Y2220, from Kyoto to Toba is Y2410, and from Kyoto to Kashikojima is Y2700.

Less expensive but longer and more troublesome is to take a local train to Yamato-Saidaiji (35 to 50 minutes), change to a train bound for Kashihara-jingu-mae and take it as far as Yamato-Yagi (about 30 minutes), then change to the Osaka – Yamada line to one stop beyond Ise (1 hour 40 minutes). Waits between trains are variable and should be checked in advance.

JR To use JR trains to the Ise/Toba area, a train from Kyoto bound for Nara can be used to connect with a train originating in Nara that will lead to the Ise area. As detailed in the section Nara – Ise, this trip requires more than one change of train. The quickest connection to the Nara – Ise train is generally made at Kizu, one stop out of Nara. Many trains from Kyoto do not reach Nara in time for the earliest connection with a train to the Ise area.

Kyoto – Osaka/Kobe

The least expensive way to travel between Kyoto and Osaka is on one of two private lines, Hankyu and Keihan. The fastest and most direct is by JR. To Kobe, the less expensive Hankyu line may be used with a transfer at Osaka.

Hankyu *Kyuko* expresses of the Hankyu ('Osaka – Kyoto') line take 46 minutes, *tokkyu* expresses a little less, and ordinary (*futsu*) trains take 64 minutes between the two cities. Trains of the various services are interspersed throughout the day and can be identified on the timetable on the platforms by colour code: white on solid red for *tokkyu* (four per hour), red in a red box is the next fastest, red for the next, and black for *futsu*.

The four stations in Kyoto of the Hankyu line are conveniently located underground along Shijo-dori, and the line functions as an east-west subway line along this street, connecting with the north-south subway line at Karasuma station, although separate fares are charged.

At Osaka, the terminus is Hankyu-Umeda, very close to JR Osaka station, at the north of the city. The fare is Y280.

The Hankyu line can also be used for convenient transport to and from Kobe by taking it as far as Juso, one station from Osaka terminus (Hankyu-Umeda), and transferring to the Hankyu-Kobe line. (This line is detailed in the section Osaka – Kobe.)

Keihan Trains of the Keihan ('Kyoto – Osaka') line take longer than those of the Hankyu line and the main Kyoto station (Keihan-Sanjo) is less conveniently located a few blocks east of Karasuma-dori, the main street of Kyoto. Trains of the Keihan line also go to Otsu, to the east.

The Osaka terminus is Yodoyabashi, somewhat closer to the centre of Osaka and the line intersects the JR Osaka loop line at Kyobashi. There is no convenient transfer to a Kobe-bound train. The fare is Y280.

JR Trains of the JR line run a considerable distance beyond Kyoto and Osaka in each direction, so the Kyoto – Osaka segment of the JR service is covered in the following section.

Kusatsu – Kyoto – Osaka – Kobe – Himeji
In addition to the Shinkansen trains which pass through this area several times an hour, there are regular trains that

normally stop at every station, plus an express service (the Shin-Kaisoku) that stops only at the cities listed in the heading, plus one other. Although the Shin-Kaisoku is a *tokkyu* express, there is no surcharge over the regular fare so its price is reasonable and it is faster than any of the competing private lines.

The extremities of the Shin-Kaisoku are Kusatsu (east of Kyoto) and Himeji (west of Kobe), although not all trains serve all cities.

West from Kyoto: Trains leave Kyoto station every 15 minutes between 9.15 am and 4.30 pm and take 29 minutes to reach Osaka, 55 minutes to Kobe (Sannomiya and Kobe stations), 1 hour 23 minutes to Akashi and 1 hour 45 minutes to Himeji. Trains leaving on the quarter hour and three-quarter-hour from 10.15 am to 3.45 pm go through to Himeji, while those on the hour go only to Akashi.

West from Osaka: West-bound trains leave Osaka station (platform 5 and 6) 30 minutes after the times listed for departure from Kyoto.

East from Osaka: At 9.10 and 9.39 am and every 15 minutes on the quarter-hour from 10 am to 4.45 pm, a Shin-Kaisiku train leaves Osaka station (platforms 7 and 8) for Kyoto and arrives (non-stop) 29 minutes later.

Some trains continue east from Kyoto as far as Kusatsu (25 minutes). From Osaka, between 10.45 am and 3.45 pm the trains on the three-quarter-hour, plus those at 9.39 am, 3.15 and 4.15 pm, continue to Kusatsu.

East from Himeji: Trains from Himeji are scheduled so they leave Osaka on an exact hour or half hour (except 12 noon).

In addition many *futsu* trains that stop at every station also make the run, continuing beyond in both directions, to Okayama (west of Himeji) and to Maibara and Nagoya (east of Kyoto).

Osaka – Ise/Toba
Kintetsu From 6.50 am to 7.10 pm there is a

tokkyu express train leaving Kami-honmachi station at 10 to and 10 after the hour for Ise (1¾ hours), Uji-Yamada (1 hour 50 minutes) and Toba (just over two hours). The '10 to' trains go through to Kashikojima (2½ hours). The last of these trains from Kami-honmachi is at 7.50 pm.

There are also slightly faster trains leaving at 20 past the hour from 7.20 am to 4.20 pm that skip Ise but stop at the other three stations. The fares are: Ise Y1890, Toba 1280 and Kashikojima Y2470.

As well as the expresses, there are cheaper local trains at five to 20-minute intervals through the day from Kami-honmachi. The fastest of these (*tokkyu*) takes just over two hours to Ise and costs Y1160.

JR The situation for using JR from Osaka to Ise/Toba is the same as that from Kyoto to Ise/Toba – you go to Nara first then through a succession of train changes from there.

Kyoto – Osaka – Kobe/Himeji

In addition to the JR Shinkansesn, Shin-Kaisoku and regular services already described there are also two private lines that can be used between Kyoto, Osaka and Kobe, and one on to Himeji.

Hankyu The Hankyu-Kobe line runs from Hankyu-Umeda station (near Osaka station) to Hankyu-Sannomiya (central Kobe). There are expresses and local trains every 10 minutes (the latter takes about 40 minutes) and the fare is Y280.

Juso, one stop out of Umeda, is the transfer point between the Kobe line and the Kyoto line, so Hankyu trains can be used between Kyoto and Kobe.

Using a *kyuko* express from Kyoto to Juso (44 minutes) it should be possible to travel from Kyoto to Kobe in less than 1½ hours for just under Y500. The Hankyu line can also be used beyond Kobe to Himeji; this is detailed in the section Kobe – Himeji.

Hanshin Also giving Osaka – Kobe service is the Hanshin line from Hanshin-Umeda station (also close to Osaka station) to Hanshin-Sannomiya and Hanshin-Motomachi stations, both in central Kobe. The fare to both is Y210 and it takes about one hour to Sannomiya.

Osaka – Himeji

The alternative to the JR services detailed previously is the Hankyu line from Kobe. The first leg is Hankyu-Sannomiya to Nishi-Shiro (17 minutes, Y80), then the Sanjo-denki line to Dentetsu-Himeji station (one hour, Y560). Trains leave every 10 to 15 minutes.

LONG-DISTANCE BUSES

Virtually the only long-distance bus services in Japan run between Tokyo and Osaka, with the major stops at Nagoya and Kyoto. The buses run along the Tomei (Tokyo – Nagoya) and Meishin (Nagoya – Kobe) expressways. Buses do not go into the many cities along the road; they stop only at shelters by the expressway from where passengers can walk a short distance to transfer to local transport.

Buses run frequently through the day between Osaka/Kyoto and Nagoya, and between Nagoya and Tokyo. All passengers must change at Nagoya when travelling between Tokyo and Kyoto/Osaka during the day.

Buses that make every stop in the Nagoya – Kyoto run take nearly three hours, while the few super expresses take 2½ hours. Most buses stop at Kyoto; only seven a day go to Osaka and only one of these is an express. Travel time is about 3½ hours. Between Nagoya and Tokyo buses take about 6¼ hours. The fares are: Nagoya to Kyoto Y1800, Nagoya to Osaka Y2200, and Nagoya to Tokyo Y4500.

Every night, buses run non-stop Tokyo – Nagoya, Tokyo – Kyoto, and Tokyo – Osaka (both directions). They leave late enough and drive slowly enough that they reach their destination at a reasonable hour in the morning. Seats recline so sleeping is relatively easy and if you're lucky you can get a seat at the back where there is slightly more leg room. The advantages of taking the night bus are the saving of a night's accommodation and an enforced early start to the day's sightseeing.

The fare is reasonably low (same as for day service) but the buses are popular and heavily used so reservations are often a necessary evil, costing Y1500, which brings the fare close to two-thirds of the Shinkansen fare (Tokyo – Kyoto).

The departure-arrival times (reverse direction in parentheses) and fares are:

Tokyo – Nagoya: 11.20 pm-6.01 am (11.20 pm-6 am), Y4500

Tokyo – Kyoto: 11 pm-7.45 am (10 pm-6.43 am), Y6300

Tokyo – Osaka: 10.20 pm-7.40 am (10.40 pm-8.15 am), Y6700

Chugoku Highway Bus

The only other expressway bus runs 189 km westward from Osaka into the Chugoku region. Most go as far as Tsuyama, almost due north of Okayama and about mid way between the coasts.

Western Honshu

This section describes the region known as Chugoku ('Middle Country'), the western end of the main island of Honshu. The description begins from Himeji and follows a route along the south shore (San-yo *kaigan*), around the western end of the island, and back along the northern shore (San-in *kaigan*) almost to Kyoto.

The name Chugoku implies that this area was in the centre of Japanese civilisation in the past. Archaeological remains have been found near Okayama and other places, and the nation's most venerated ancient shrine site is at Izumo near Matsue on the San-in coast.

Himeji properly belongs in this region, but it is described in the Kinki chapter because it can easily be reached from Kyoto as a day trip, and is dealt with as part of the Kinki region.

The San-in coast is by far the more enjoyable for scenery and the lack of crowds and development. The route is excellent for cyclists as it is mostly flat, and road traffic is reasonable.

The San-yo coast is very heavily developed through to Hiroshima, and road traffic moves very slowly. However, it has more specific places to visit.

GETTING THERE & AWAY
Road
There are many major highways along the full length of both the San-yo and San-in coasts, with a network of roads joining them at a number of places across the island. The Chugoku expressway (Chugoku *kosokudoro*) runs through the middle from Osaka to Shimonoseki, at the west end; there it connects with the Kyushu expressway via the Kanmon-ohashi bridge. This is the route for hitch-hikers in a hurry, but the scenery is not memorable.

Further details on road conditions and a summary of attractions along the way are in the Getting There & Away section on Shimonoseki.

Ferry
In addition to road and rail connections between the Osaka area and places in western Honshu, there are also daily ferry connections from Osaka and Kobe to several points on Kyushu and Shikoku.

There are also numerous connections from points in the Chugoku region to Shikoku and Kyushu, and these are detailed in the relevant city section.

Okayama-ken

BIZEN
The city of Bizen is famous in Japan for the pottery known as Bizen-yaki. There are numerous potteries and kilns in and around the city. The pottery is of a very old (1200 years) and simple style, obtaining its characteristic finish and patterns from the firing rather than the glazing.

An interesting sidelight of the pottery craft is a reported reduction in the number of birds in the coastal area. So many pine trees have been cut down for kiln fuel that the roosts and sources of insects have been reduced.

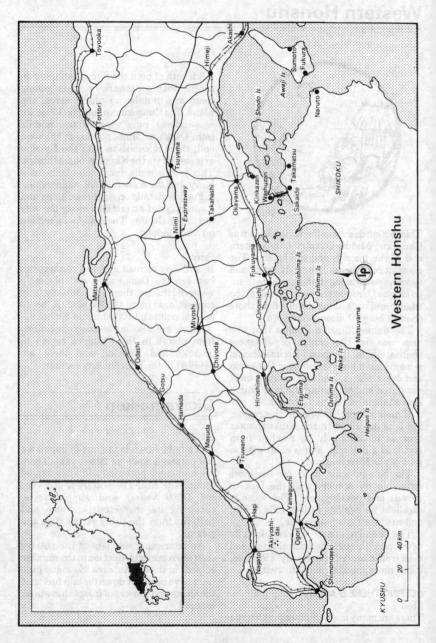

Western Honshu

SHIKOKU

KYUSHU

Toyooka
Tottori
Tsuyama
Himeji
Akashi
Sumoto
Fukura
Awaji Is
Shodo Is
Kinkazan
Washuzan
Takamatsu
Sakaide
Naruto
Expressway
Takahashi
Niimi
Okayama
Fukuyama
Onomichi
Omishima Is
Oshima Is
Matsue
Odashi
Miyoshi
Chiyoda
Hiroshima
Etajima Is
Oshima Is
Naka Is
Matsuyama
Gotsu
Hamada
Masuda
Tsuwano
Heigun Is
Akiyoshi-
dai
Hagi
Yamaguchi
Ogori
Nagato
Shimonoseki

0   20   40 km

Shizutani School

This historical school may not be recognisable as such to westerners. It dates from 1666 and resembles classical schools of China and Korea, and it was the first school in Japan for commoners.

The white-walled buildings are roofed with Bizen-ware tiles and are surrounded with a rock-covered earthen wall broken by small picturesque gates. It is at the foot of a tree-covered hill that is colourful in autumn. The appearance of the school is very uncommon in a Japanese setting.

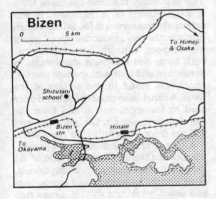

OKAYAMA

Okayama is the better known city of the pair Okayama-Kurashiki, but they can best be regarded as two parts of a whole. The city centres are only 16 km apart, so travel between them is convenient.

Koraku-en Park

Koraku-en park is the main attraction of Okayama and is one of the 'Big Three' gardens of Japan, as rated by the Japanese. The landscape garden was laid out more than 300 years ago and in places it has the features westerners associate with a Japanese garden – careful placement of rocks, water, miniature hills, etc – plus plots of blooms and a teahouse. However, I was rather disappointed by it as much of its expanse is open lawn similar to that

found in any western park. This is a novelty to the Japanese, where space is at such a premium, but not to westerners. To be sure, it is pretty, but do not expect too much of it. Near the garden is a museum (hakubutsu-kan).

A bus from Okayama station runs reasonably close to the garden; a taxi can also be used. The information centre at the station (well equipped with literature in English) can help you get the right bus.

Okayama-jo Castle

The original castle was built here in 1573 but was subsequently destroyed. The present concrete reconstruction preserves the external appearance and adds a traditional note to Koraku-en park, which it overlooks. It is black, in contrast with

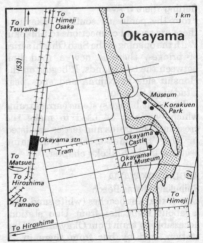

the white of the castle at Himeji (Japan's finest); its nickname, Ujo (crow), is a joke on the name of Himeji's pride, which translates as 'white egret'.

The castle is only a short distance from Koraku-en park and is accessible by a bridge across the river. Nearby is Okayama Bijutsukan (Art Museum).

Kinkozan Hill

An excursion by bus from Okayama passes by Kojima Bay to Kinkozan hill. The bay is not spectacular but is interesting for being the second largest man-made lake in the world. The biggest is in Holland.

From the top of Kinkozan hill (403 metres) you have one of the best views of the Inland Sea. Check at Okayama station for buses to Kinkozan.

Festivals

On the night of the first Saturday in February, Saidai-ji temple is the scene of an interesting festival when young men wearing loin cloths vie to grab and keep two sacred wands (*shingi*) that are thrown into their midst; the wands are supposed to bring lifelong happiness.

Getting There & Away

From the peninsula south of Okayama there are several connections to Shikoku. With the opening of the Seto Ohashi series of bridges, there is now a road link between the two islands. It begins on the Honshu side at Nijima and ends near Utadsu on Shikoku.

The same bridge systems carries trains which can also be used to make the crossing. The trains and ferries are listed in the Takamatsu and Marugame sections in the Shikoku chapter.

AROUND OKAYAMA
Shibukawa-hama Beach

One of the best beaches (white sand, etc) is about eight km from Uno station, accessible by train from Okayama to Uno station, and by bus from there in 25 minutes.

Tsuyama

Inland, due north of Okayama, lies Tsuyama. In cherry blossom season the site of the old castle (destroyed in 1873) is very beautiful as the grounds (now Kazukan-koen park) are planted with 8000 cherry trees.

Of interest at any time to historians is the site of a Yayoi-era (pre-Yamato Japanese civilisation) pit-dwelling that has been excavated.

Little is known of the people of that era but their pottery and the remnants of their dwellings of 2000 years ago have been found in many parts of Japan. About 2½ km northeast of Numa station, one Yayoi-type dwelling has been reconstructed and is open to the public.

KURASHIKI

This is possibly the most charming town in Japan (parts of it, at least). It was extremely prosperous in feudal days when rice from the very productive inland region was shipped through here. Merchants built large and elaborate storehouses of dark stone and contrasting white mortar, which still stand in one section of the town. A canal (also stone-walled and once used to transport rice to and from the storehouses) passes by the buildings, and willows droop gracefully over the water.

Although the architecture is Japanese, the mood of the area is almost that of old Europe. You can enjoy just walking around, absorbing the appearance and atmosphere and possibly taking a short rickshaw ride along the narrow streets. I first saw the area late in the afternoon when the sun was low, and was captivated, but I could never quite capture that mood again. May every visitor have such an opportunity. The area is not large, so a stroll of half an hour or so down the back streets will probably be enough before returning to the attractions along the canal.

Information

The city has an information office near the Ohara Museum. If you are beginning your travels in Tokyo, you should pick up a copy of the information sheet on Kurashiki at the TIC.

The Warehouses

Several of the *kura* (warehouses, hence the name Kurashiki) have been converted

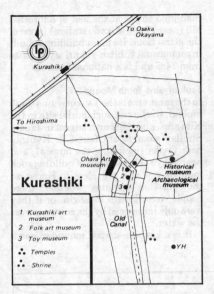

Kurashiki

1 Kurashiki art museum
2 Folk art museum
3 Toy museum
∴ Temples
∴ Shrine

into museums and are worth visiting. They are described in the order that they are encountered along the canal bank.

Toy Museum (Kyodo gangu-kan) This houses a collection of toys from all over Japan, including many types no longer used. They are interesting for the simplicity of their designs (using local materials).

Folk-craft Museum (Mingei-kan) Several adjoining *kura* have been combined so you can walk back and forth within them, up and down floors, while admiring a large collection of folk-craft and articles of daily utility made of indigenous materials. Most are of Japanese origin but enough pieces have been brought from other countries and cultures to stress the similarities and individualities. It is closed on Mondays.

Kurashiki Art Museum (Bijutsu-kan) This museum houses mostly European art,

including some ancient Mediterranean works.

Kurashiki Archaeological Museum (Koko-kan) Many relics excavated in the region are on display here to show the cultures that have flourished around Kurashiki and Okayama since ancient times, particularly the Kibi culture that survived into the 5th century; it is known for a number of tomb mounds in the vicinity of the city. Closed Mondays.

Ohara Art Museum (Ohara Bijutsu-kan) No, not founded by an errant Irishman, but by a wealthy Japanese textile manufacturer, Magosaburo Ohara, who collected western art.

To house his collection, he constructed a large Greek-style building complete with columns. The collection is interesting but not exciting, at least for those who have had access to the great western museums.

In the grounds behind this building are other museums housing contemporary Japanese art, pottery, Chinese art and other assorted collections. Some regard these as more interesting than the main museum.

Kurashiki Historical Museum (Rekishi-kan) This museum is apart from the others and can be reached in 10 to 15 minutes on foot.

Ivy Square
Built as a textile factory soon after the Meiji restoration in 1868, this ivy-covered red-brick complex has been converted into a cluster of tourist attractions. It is of greatest interest to the Japanese (to whom such a brick structure is exotic) but there is a small museum of the Kurashiki textile industry (which may interest foreign visitors) plus restaurants, coffee houses, an open square and a hotel.

Places to Stay
In addition to the hotel in Ivy Square,

there are many hotels and *ryokan* of various price ranges, as well as a pleasant hill-top *Youth Hostel*.

Assistance in finding a room is available at the information office in the railway station.

Getting There & Away

Kurashiki is accessible by Shinkansen via Shin-Kurashiki station, but the connections make it simpler to transfer from Okayama station (also on the Shinkansen), which allows a short visit to Okayama as well.

AROUND KURASHIKI

Just north of Kurashiki is the Kibi plain, which was settled long before recorded history; many historic and prehistoric remains are found in the area. Kibitsu-

hiko-jinja shrine at the foot of a forested hill (near Bizen-Mikado station) is one of the attractions. Its main building is built in an unusual Kibitsu-zukuri style, dates from 1425 and is a national treasure.

Tsukuriyama Tomb Mound

In the same area is the Tsukuriyama tomb mound, the largest such burial site in the Kibi area, and the fourth largest in Japan. Similar mounds are found in Kyushu, near Osaka (including the largest), and near Tokyo. The practice of building such mounds was also prevalent in Korea, so the question remains whether these people were Korean in origin, or if they were only influenced by the culture across the water.

It is a keyhole-shaped mound of earth

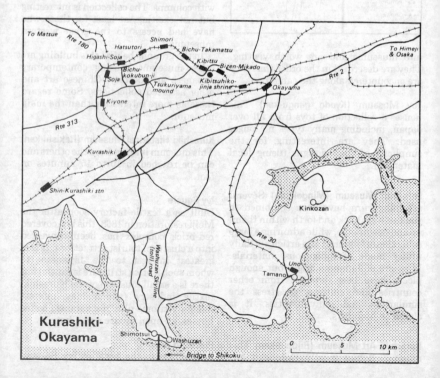

Kurashiki-Okayama

350 metres long, 238 metres wide at the greatest point, and 25 metres high. It is of limited interest to most people, however, because it simply looks like any other hill, even though it is man made; its significance is what makes it interesting.

Another attraction in the same area is Bichu-Kokubunji temple. It has a picturesque five-storey pagoda. To reach these attractions make inquires locally.

WASHUZAN

An excellent view over the Inland Sea (Seto Nai-Kai) is available at Washuzan, almost due south of Kurashiki. Buses run many times a day from Kurashiki station, taking about 80 minutes. Buses also run regularly from Okayama station (90 minutes), so you can make a looping trip from one city to the other. There is a bit of a climb from the bus stop, so be prepared with walking shoes.

Places to Stay

There is a *Youth Hostel* near Washuzan.

Getting There & Away

A regular boat service runs between nearby Shimotsui and Marugame on Shikoku. See the Marugame section for detail.

FUKUYAMA

This industrial city is of little interest, although it has a 1966 reproduction of its historic castle. It is best known for the nearby town of Tomo-no-ura, which is the port for Fukuyama and is regarded as one of the most picturesque places in the Inland Sea area, and in fact the whole of Japan. The town of Tomo-no-ura overlooks the islands of Sensui, Benten and Kogo.

Abuto-Kannon Temple

This temple to the Goddess of Mercy is built on a cape less than 30 metres above the water and is noted for its superb view over the water. It is only four km from Tomo-no-ura and is accessible from there by bus or boat, or from Fukuyama by bus to Abuto- guchi, and then a 20-minute walk.

Getting There & Away

There is a regular boat service between Fukuyama (Higashi-Fukuyama port) and Tadotsu and Takamatsu on Shikoku. (Details are in the sections on those places.)

ONOMICHI

One of the best views of the Inland Sea may be had from the heights of Senko-ji temple. It is accessible in 20 minutes by direct bus, or by bus (five minutes) to Nagaeguchi, then by cable car to the top. The park at the top is noted for cherry blossoms in season, and picturesque rocks.

The city was not touched by WW II so many older houses and buildings have survived. A walk around may provide some of the mood of olden times. The city is noted for a number of temples including Jodo-ji, Saigo-ji, Saikoku-ji and Tennei-ji, although there are many others.

A map of the city, showing the temples, is available at the station and can be used as a guide while strolling around.

Mukai-shima Island

Not far from Onomichi, and accessible by a bridge, Mukai-shima island has an observation post (*tempodai*) that gives an excellent view of the Inland Sea and Onomichi.

Getting There & Away

There is a regular boat service between Onomichi and Matsuyama and Imabari on Shikoku, the latter offering a service to Omishima island as well. Details are given in the sections on those places.

IKUCHI-JIMA ISLAND

The industrial city of Mihara is the gateway to the island of Ikuchi-jima, 12 km to the south of Onomichi. Setoda, on Ikuchi-jima, is noted for its interesting Kosan-ji temple.

Dating from 1946, the temple has several buildings modelled on those of famous temples elsewhere in Japan (such as the Hall of Dreams in Nara) as well as a collection of cultural and religious objects. It is regarded as rather kitschy, so don't make a special trip just to see it.

Getting There & Away

Access is by ferry (50 minutes) or fast boat (20 minutes) from Mihara to Setoda; the temple is about 10 minutes on foot east of the dock.

There is a regular boat service between Mihara and Matsuyama and Imabari on Shikoku. Details are given in the sections on those places. The terminal is close to the station.

TAISHAKU-KYO GORGE

This scenic gorge stretches about 20 km upstream from Taishaku-mura village along the Taishaku River. About 2.4 km from the village is Oni-wa-iwaya (Demon Cave), known for its stalactites. Further along there are two natural rock bridges. The gorge is in one part of Hiba-Taishaku Quasi National Park.

Other attractions of the region include mountain, marsh and forest views. Taishaku-mura can be reached by bus in about one hour from Bingo-Shobara station.

MIYOSHI AREA

The inland areas of Chugoku have not gained a great name for tourist attractions

but the scenery along the expressway from Miyoshi to Osaka is enjoyable.

Ukai (cormorant fishing) is carried out in June, July and August near the junction of three rivers, not far from Nishi-Miyoshi station.

TAKEHARA

There is a regular boat service between Takehara and Imabari and Namikata on Shikoku, the former offering service en route to Omishima island.

KURE

Along the coast east of Hiroshima is the ship-building centre of Kure. During WW II, the giant battleship *Yamato* was built here. The largest of its day, carrying 18-inch guns, it was sunk by US aircraft without contributing to the Japanese war effort.

In post-war days Kure has produced many of the world's super-tankers that would dwarf the *Yamato*. If you want to visit the shipyards, inquire in advance; the city has no other attractions – it's just a typical industrial port city.

Getting There & Away

There are regular boat services between Kure and Matsuyama on Shikoku, and between Niigata and Imabari on Shikoku.

NIKYU GORGE

About 15 km northeast of Kure lies this scenic gorge, most noted for many waterfalls and Jacob's wells. It can be reached by bus from Kure in 40 minutes.

Hiroshima-ken

HIROSHIMA

The city of Hiroshima is known to the inhabitants of every western country because of an instant in 1945 when it was destroyed by an atom bomb. For this reason large numbers of tourists visit the city during a stay in Japan, but be warned that there is relatively little in Hiroshima city itself, as it is first and foremost an industrial city, which is why it was chosen as a target in the first place.

It is built on the flat estuary of the Ota River and has little natural beauty, although this is more than offset by the beauties of nearby Itsukushima Island (also called Miyajima). However, the relics and exhibits related to the A-bomb do make Hiroshima a recommended destination – if for no other reason than to make everyone aware of the true horrors of nuclear warfare.

The bomb exploded almost directly over the Industrial Promotion Hall, formerly an architecturally noteworthy structure. It is the only ruined building still allowed to stand, its dome the symbol of the destruction. It is easily reached from Hiroshima station by a tram No 2 or 6, or bus No 3.

Information

There is an information centre in front of the station that supplies a good map and brochure in English. They should also be able to help with tram information, etc, but don't expect proficiency in English.

Travellers starting from Tokyo can pick up information at the TIC there, including a printed pamphlet (MG-19).

Peace Memorial Museum

The area around the Industrial Promotion Hall has been made into Peace Park (Heiwa-koen) with a peaceful canal (row boats for rent), greenery, etc. From the dome it is an easy and pleasant walk through the park to the Peace Memorial Museum, a broad, low building standing on pillars; along the way one passes the saddle-shaped cenotaph.

Every visitor to Japan should try to visit the museum, or its equivalent in Nagasaki – though this one is possibly better. Its purpose is to show the effects of the bomb on Hiroshima, and to serve as a warning to national leaders about the

horrors of such weapons. It should be kept in mind that the terrific destruction was done by a bomb equivalent to about 20,000 tonnes of TNT; the average nuclear weapon in the world today is equivalent to 2000 Hiroshima bombs.

The museum has film showings (in English) at 10 and 11.25 am, and at 12.50, 2.15 and 3.40 pm, as well as a film of Hiroshima in wartime (in Japanese only) every hour from 9.30 am to 3.30 pm. There are signposts in the lobby.

Most visitors leave the museum in a sombre or depressed mood; it is a very sobering emotional experience, but one not to be missed. An excellent book showing the effects of the bombing is worth looking for; the title is simply *Hiroshima-Nagasaki*. Two Hiroshima bookstores which have sold the book in the past are Kinokuniya (Sogo Department Store, 6th floor), and Maruzen Department Store (3rd floor). The publishers are Hiroshima Heiwa Kaikan, 1-4-9, Shiba, Minato-ku, Tokyo.

Shukkei-en Garden

This landscape garden was originally

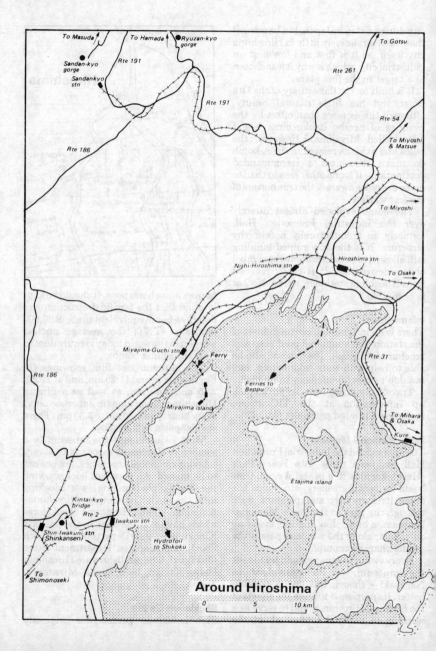

Around Hiroshima

To Masuda

To Hamada

Ryuzan-kyo gorge

To Gotsu

Sandan-kyo gorge

Sandankyo stn

Rte 191

Rte 261

Rte 191

Rte 54

Rte 186

To Miyoshi & Matsue

To Miyoshi

Nishi-Hiroshima stn

Hiroshima stn

To Osaka

Miyajima-Guchi stn

Ferry

Rte 31

Rte 186

Ferries to Beppu

Miyajima island

To Mihara & Osaka

Kure

Etajima island

Kintai-kyo bridge

Rte 2

Shin-Iwakuni stn (Shinkansen)

Iwakuni stn

Hydrofoil to Shikoku

To Shimonoseki

0   5   10 km

designed in 1620, though its form has been changed. It offers a pleasant respite from the busy city and is only about 700 metres from the station.

Hiroshima Castle

The original castle stood here from 1589 until it was destroyed by the bomb. It was rebuilt in concrete and its external appearance is a re-creation of the original. It is now a local museum and gives some idea of the appearance of old Hiroshima. The late afternoon offers the best light for photographs.

Sandan-kyo Gorge

A pleasant excursion from Hiroshima is Sandan-kyo gorge to the northwest. Its 16-km length, covered on foot, takes in a number of waterfalls and scenery ranging from pretty to spectacular. Access is by train to Sansan-kyo station (JR) or by bus, both from Hiroshima.

Places to Stay

There are many hotels, etc, in Hiroshima, as well as a *Youth Hostel*. The information centre may have directions on how to get to the youth hostel; if not, walk toward the post office (to the right at the front of the station), cross the street and turn right. A short distance along is a sign '50 metres to Hiroshima Youth Hostel bus stop'. More than one bus uses the same stop so ask the driver before boarding, and get off at Ushita-shin-machi or Ushita I-chome; signs from there are clear guides up the hill to the hostel. It is one of the best marked hostels in Japan, and is one of the more pleasant (apart from the 6.30 am reveille); it is also an excellent source of travel information.

Another accommodation centre is the World Friendship Association; the information centre at the station should be able to help.

Getting There & Away

Train Hiroshima is one of the major stops on the JR Shinkansen train that runs

between Tokyo and Hakata (Kyushu). Tokyo is about five hours away (depending on the number of stops made), while Kyoto is two to three hours away. There are also slower, less expensive JR services.

Ferry There is a daily overnight ferry service each way between Hiroshima and Beppu, making this a convenient and relatively inexpensive way of getting to Kyushu, saving the cost of one night's accommodation.

There are also regular boats (including speedy hydrofoils) between Hiroshima and Matsuyama and Imabari, both on Shikoku.

The dock area can be reached from Hiroshima station by tram or bus. The information centre can give assistance. There are also boats from nearby Iwakuni to Shikoku.

Hitching Hitching along the south coast is very slow and unpleasant, although unavoidable if you wish to go to Okayama, etc. Route 2 passes through the city and can be intercepted by a tram No 8 going south.

To use the Chugoku expressway to or from Shimonoseki (west) or Osaka/Kyoto (east), the most convenient interchange is Hiroshima-kita, about 25 km out of the city. From Hiroshima it can be reached by taking Route 54 to Kami-ga-hara, then going left about seven km. The interchange is close to the west (far) end of the tunnel. The interchange can also be reached from Aki-Imuro, which is a little more than an hour out of Hiroshima station (some trains begin only at Yokogawa station, through which all pass), but there are only about five trains a day. The interchange is about three km east of Aki-Imuro station.

Getting Around

Tram The simplest way to get around Hiroshima is by tram; one goes to the A-bomb dome, and you can return by the same route or walk along Peace Boulevard (Heiwa Dori) and across the river, returning to the station by another line.

The reason for the weird and wonderful variety in the colour scheme of the trams is that Hiroshima (which wisely kept its tram tracks) bought up trams from other cities as they phased out tram services, and they retain their original colours.

Bus There are buses to Hiroshima station from various parts of the city. The bus station is in the Sogo department store; it serves both city buses and those to other cities. Any red or orange bus goes to the station; red-and-white striped ones pass by the castle.

MIYAJIMA ISLAND

The major attraction of the Hiroshima area is Miyajima (Shrine Island), more correctly known as Itsukushima. Its best known feature is one of the most famous symbols of all Japan, the huge offshore *torii* gate that is seen in every travelogue and book on Japan.

The island is ranked traditionally as one of the three most beautiful sights in Japan (along with Matsushima, near Sendai, and Amanohashidate, on the north coast). There are many beautiful scenes on and around the island and a visit is sure to be enjoyed – for the famous shrine, the *torii*, a walk through the heavy woods, tame deer and other attractions. A half-day will take in a good number of the features of the island but an overnight stay would allow greater relaxation and time to absorb the mood.

Information

The ferry from Miyajima-guchi on the mainland takes 10 minutes for the trip to Miyajima-ko. In front of the building at the entrance to the dock is a large, three-dimensional information board for orientation. Most visitors set off immediately to the right, to the Itsukushima-jinja shrine.

Itsukushima-jinja Shrine

The shrine is unusual because the buildings are built on piles over the shallows at the water's edge and are joined by narrow galleries. One explanation for the unusual construction is that the island has been regarded as sacred from ancient times, and Taira Kiyomori had the shrine built in this way in the 12th century so that it could be approached by boat without setting foot on land. Earlier shrines had stood on the same spot since 593.

The principal buildings of Itsukushima Shrine are the *honden* (main hall), *heiden* (offering hall), *haiden* (hall of worship) and *haraiden* (purification hall). In the *Asazaya* (morning prayer room), dance costumes and masks are displayed. The public is allowed only as far as the outer sanctuary of the *honden*; all these buildings, plus the corridors, are ranked as national treasures.

The great *torii* gate in the water (accessible on foot at low tide for those who don't mind mud) dates from 1875 and is the largest wooden *torii* in Japan at 16.2 metres high and 23.3 metres wide. The large stone *torii* on the shore dates from 1905.

The first shrine structure seen when approaching from the ferry dock is Marodo-jinja, the largest shrine after Itsukushima-jinja itself.

Noh Theatre Most of the shrine buildings are of comparatively recent construction, but the Noh theatre dates from 1568 and was rebuilt in Edo times. It is the oldest Noh theatre in Japan, and one of the only stages in the world where the audience is unlikely to crowd around and block the view, especially at high tide.

Dances The shrine is noted for performances of *bugaku* and *kagura* dances on the *takabutai* stage at the end of the shrine nearest the channel; every brochure on Japan is likely to feature a photo of a masked dancer with the *torii* in the

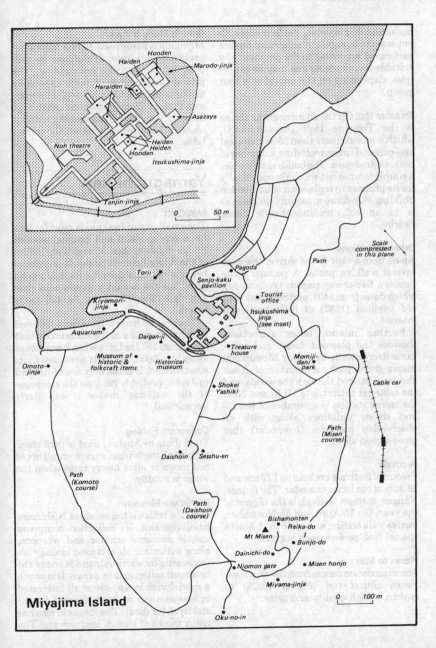

Miyajima Island

Torii

Kiyomori-jinja

Aquarium

Omoto-jinja

Museum of historic & folkcraft items

Daigan-ji

Historical museum

Senjo-kaku pavilion

Pagoda

Tourist office

Itsukushima jinja (see inset)

Treasure house

Momiji-dani park

Shokei Yashiki

Scale compressed in this plane

Path

Cable car

Path (Misen course)

Daishoin

Sesshu-en

Path (Komoto course)

Path (Daishoin course)

Bishamonten

Reika-do

Mt Misen

Bunjo-do

Dainichi-do

Misen honjo

Niomon gate

Miyama-jinja

Oku-no-in

0   100 m

Inset:

Honden

Haiden

Marodo-jinja

Haraiden

Asazaya

Noh theatre

Haiden Heiden

Honden

Itsukushima-jinja

Tenjin-jinja

0   50 m

background. However, performances do not seem to be regularly scheduled but are performed according to the payment of a suitable fee, so seeing one may be hit-or-miss, depending on the arrival of a tour group.

Treasure Hall On the shore near the shrine is the Treasure Hall (*homostu-kan*), which contains more than 3500 historical and cultural items including a number of national treasures. The building resembles a simple temple but was built specifically for its purpose to replace an older wooden building. A folklore museum (*mingeikan*) is in an old, traditional-style house nearby.

Other Attractions

Apart from a visit to the shrine, there are several walking paths. A popular route passes a five-storey pagoda (*goju-no-to*), which dates from 1407, and Senjokaku, an old pavilion (1587) of little particular interest.

Further inland, other attractions (besides the pleasant forest and semi-tame deer) await, including Momijidani maple-grove park, a number of lesser shrines scattered through the woods, and the cable car to the top of Mt Misen. Near the upper station is a number of temple and shrine buildings along with an observation platform (*tempodai*) that gives a good view.

Festivals

Colourful festivals are held on 17 June and 18 July of the lunar calendar. The former, Kangen-matsuri festival, is the biggest of the year. On 15 April and 15 November, monks walk on fire; and on 16 to 18 April a special Noh performance is given.

Places to Stay

Accommodation ranges from the *Miyajima Youth Hostel* (tel (08294) 40328) to *ryokan* of high quality and price.

Getting There & Away

Miyajima is easily reached (via Miyajima-guchi station) from Hiroshima by rail, both by JR and by private line. The private line is shown on maps as starting at Higashi-Hiroshima station. However, some trams from Hiroshima station go directly to Miyajima-guchi without transfer. Inquire locally about the correct tram.

Yamaguchi-ken

IWAKUNI

The small city of Iwakuni is most famous for a very graceful and unusual wooden bridge of five arches, Kintai-Kyo (Bridge of the Silver Brocade Sash). It is unusual because not only does the frame form an arch, but the actual walkway also rises and falls five times in its 193-metre length.

The present bridge dates from 1953 and is an exact replica of the historic one that stood from 1673 to 1950, when it was swept away by a flood. No nails were used in its construction. It is the only one of its kind in Japan, probably because the steepness of the walkway makes it so utterly impractical.

Cormorant Fishing

From June to August, *ukai* is performed nightly at the bridge, except on nights of full moon or after heavy rains when the water is muddy.

Nishimura Museum

Near the bridge is the excellent Nishimura hakubutsukan. Its collection comprises mostly *samurai* armour and weapons, along with other objects used in daily life (especially by warriors), and is one of the best such collections in Japan. It is worth a special visit by anyone at all interested in how *samurai* warriors dressed, fought and lived (or died). The museum also has many pieces of superb lacquerware. The collection was put together over a period of 45 years from all over Japan and was opened in 1963.

Shiroyama

On the top of Shiroyama, one of the hills overlooking the museum and bridge, is a novelty – a southern-European-style castle! A Japanese-style one stood here for the brief period from 1608 to 1615 before being torn down. The present building was constructed in 1960. Easiest access is by the cable car that rises from Kikko-en park (close to both the bridge and museum). All are easily reached from Iwakuni or Shin-Iwakuni (*shinkansen*) stations by bus.

Places to Eat

Because of the US military base near Iwakuni there are several restaurants and fast-food joints that serve American or pseudo-American food, which may be of interest to those suffering advanced junk-food withdrawal symptoms.

HOFU

Here is one of Japan's better-known shrines, Hofu-Tenmangu (Matsugasaki). The buildings are large, colourful and impressive.

YANAI

There is a regular boat service between Yanai and Matsuyama on Shikoku.

TOKUYAMA

There is a regular boat service between Tokuyama (Shinnanyo port) and Taketazu, on the Kunisaki peninsula of Kyushu.

OGORI

There are no notable tourist attractions at Ogori other than its summer steam-train excursions to and from Tsuwano.

YAMAGUCHI

Formerly a castle town, Yamaguchi reached its zenith in the 1500s and declined when the *daimyo* found himself on the losing side in the civil war. Relics from those days include Ruriko-ji temple (from the 14th century) and its five-storey pagoda, a landscape garden by the famous designer Sesshu, Joei-ji temple, and the (modern) cathedral that commemorates the time spent in Yamaguchi by St Francis Xavier in 1551.

CHOMON-KYO GORGE

About 20 km from Yamaguchi is the pretty Chomon-kyo gorge. It begins close to the station of the same name and extends for 12 km to Uzugahara. The Abu-kawa river has sculpted the rock into fanciful shapes, pools, falls and Jacob's wells.

AKIYOSHI

Clumps of limestone rocks dot this rolling tableland, looking like thousands of sheep or tombstones. Although the rocks look small from a distance, many are as tall as a man.

Akiyoshi-do Cave

Beneath the plateau is Akiyoshi-do, the largest cave in the Far East. It extends for several km and about one km is accessible to visitors. Electric lights and walkways make the expedition simple, and you pass typical features of limestone caves, such as stalagmites and stalactites and other fantastic forms that the limestone takes as it precipitates out of solution.

Well into the cave there is a lift that rises near Kurodani (Black Valley), which is among the rocks of the plateau. A path leads up to a lookout (*tempodai*) and a museum of specimens associated with the cave and plateau.

Buses run between the Kurodani area and the terminal near the entrance to the cave, so you can return to one entrance from the other by bus or retrace your steps through the cave.

Places to Stay

There is a large variety of accommodation (including a *Youth Hostel*) in the area,

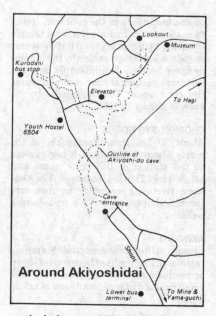

Around Akiyoshidai

particularly around Kurodani. There are places near the lower entrance as well.

Getting Around
There are buses throughout the day to and from Shimonoseki, Yamaguchi, Mine, and Ogori (south coast), and Higashi-Hagi (north coast).

SHIMONOSEKI
Shimonoseki (known to locals as 'Shimo') is at the far western end of Honshu and is important as a crossing point to Kyushu as well as an international port for the daily ferry service to and from Pusan, Korea. The name of the city has the well-earned meaning 'Lower Gate'.

Information
The Korean consulate, Kankoku ryojikan, is near the ferry dock. Visas can be obtained here the same day if you apply early in the morning, but more than one

traveller has reported rather brusque treatment.

Things to See
One of the major attractions of Shimonoseki is the large and colourful Akamon-jinja shrine. It is made of concrete, not wood, and is thus not really representative of Japan's best. It is named for its red gate of uncommon Chinese shape. There are many shrines in Japan that are more exciting. The shrine can be reached by the same bus that goes to the youth hostel.

Another attraction is a view over the Kanmon Strait from Hinoyama (Fire Mountain). Those staying at the youth hostel are only a couple of minutes walk away. It is also easy to reach from the city by bus, either the hourly one from stand No 3 to 'Koku-minshuku-sha-mae', which goes right up to and past the top station, or any bus going past 'Ropeway-mae', where you get off and either take the cable car or walk up the hill.

Along the way out you may see a sign pointing to the site of the battle of Dan-

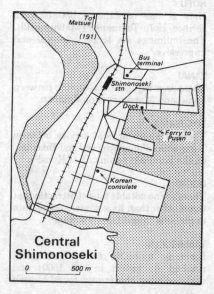

Central Shimonoseki

0   500 m

no-ura in 1185. Don't get out to look for anything, as most of the action took place in the water and whatever beach might have existed has disappeared under the tall pillars of the graceful Kanmon-ohashi suspension bridge.

Shimonoseki Aquarium

Shimo's aquarium is claimed to be the largest in the orient. It has a collection of some truly weird and wonderful creatures of the deep; dolphin and seal shows are part of the entertainment. The aquarium (*suizukukan*) is easily reached from Shimo station or by bus; the name of the bus stop is Suizuku-kan-mae.

Chofu

This is a separate town that is included as part of Shimo. Its claim to fame lies in a couple of streets with earth-walled *samurai*-style houses, and a few shrines and temples. It is an enjoyable walk for those with time to pass.

Places to Stay

Along with several hotels, etc, Shimo has the very pleasant *Hinoyama Youth Hostel* beautifully located overlooking the Kanmon Strait and the suspension bridge. It has one of the best vantage points in the city, with a view second only to that from the top of Hinoyama, 100 metres away. To get back to Shimo from the hostel, the choice is the cable car down to the road and a bus from there, or a 1.8-km walk (mostly downhill) to the Mukuno bus stop for a bus to the station. Recent reports have not been all that favourable about this place. Only a passport is required.

If *Hinoyama Youth Hostel* is full, there may be vacancies nearby at *Toyota Youth Hostel* (tel (08376) 6-8271) or *Akiyoshidai Youth Hostel* (tel (08376) 2-0341), or in northern Kyushu.

Getting There & Away

Train Regular JR services to points in Honshu and Kyushu leave from Shimon-

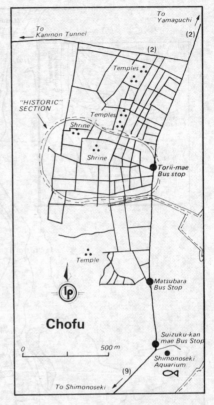

oseki station. The Shinkansen super-expresses (the fastest service to Hiroshima, Kyoto, Tokyo, etc) leave from Shin-Shimonoseki station, two stops away by local train and also accessible by bus from Shimo station; local trains are scheduled to reach Shin-Shimo station in time for each train.

There is a schedule of all services posted in Shimo station in adequate English, and staff at the information centre should be able to give basic information.

To cross to Kyushu, the simplest way is by train through the tunnel to Moji and Kitakyushu.

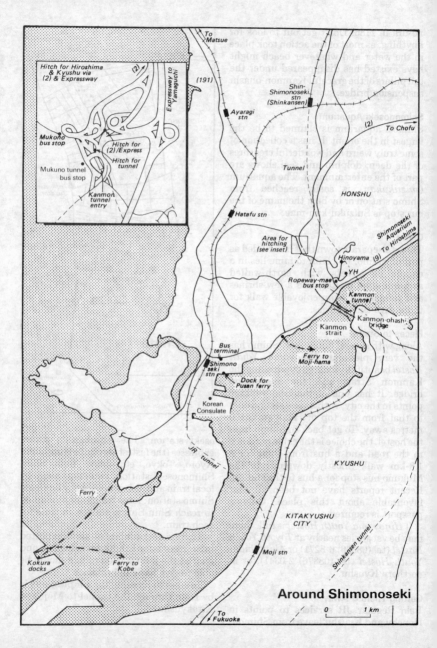

Around Shimonoseki

To Matsue

(191)

Ayaragi stn

Shin-Shimonoseki stn (Shinkansen)

(2)

To Chofu

Tunnel

HONSHU

Hatafu stn

Shimonoseki Aquarium

To Hiroshima

Area for hitching (see inset)

Hinoyama

(9)

YH

Ropeway-mae bus stop

Kanmon tunnel

Kanmon strait

Kanmon-ohashi bridge

Bus terminal

Shimonoseki stn

Ferry to Moji-hama

Dock for Pusan ferry

Korean Consulate

KYUSHU

JR tunnel

KITAKYUSHU CITY

Ferry

Moji stn

Shinkansen tunnel

Kokura docks

Ferry to Kobe

To Fukuoka

0   1 km

Inset:

Hitch for Hiroshima & Kyushu via (2) & Expressway

(2)

Expressway to Yamaguchi

Mukono bus stop

Hitch for (2)/Express

Hitch for tunnel

Mukuno tunnel bus stop

Kanmon tunnel entry

Top: Cherry blossoms and evergreens at Heian-jingu shrine, Kyoto (IMcQ)
Left: Entrance of Sanzen-in temple, Chara, near Kyoto (IMcQ)
Right: Kinkaku (Gold Pavilion) of Kinkaku-ji temple, Kyoto (IMcQ)

Top: Blood-red waters of Chi-no-ike jigoku, near Beppu, Kyushu (IMcQ)
Bottom: Carved stone Buddha heads, Usuki, Kyushu (IMcQ)

Ferry - To/From Korea The dock for the ferry from Korea is a 10-minute walk from Shimo station. There is a money changer in the ferry terminus; the rate is the same as that given at local banks.

There is a daily sailing in each direction by the Kampu ferry *Pukwan* between Shimonoseki and Pusan in Korea. It leaves from Shimo at 5 pm, and from Pusan at 6 pm. The lowest fare is Y9600 (less 20% with a student card) for an open *tatami* area; smaller open rooms and cabins with bunks are available at higher cost.

It is advisable to buy your ticket as early in the day as possible. By doing so, you get a reservation number that will save queuing near boarding time; try to get on board ship early to guarantee a place to lie at night.

Once under way, it is also advisable to go to sleep early, as fellow passengers have been known to be up at 3 am standing in line (noisily) even though disembarkation does not begin until 7 am; there is no need to rush as there is a separate immigration line for aliens.

One reason for getting in line early, however, is to try to observe the 'Passing of the Bribe' ceremony, when a group of women collectively give the Korean immigration and customs officials their stack of extension-paged passports, interleaved with US bank notes, for processing. This is so that they can get their refrigerators and other household appliances landed in Korea without hassles. They make the trip every day.

The Tokyo TIC has a hand-out sheet with up-to-date fares and sailings. Kampu office telephone numbers are Tokyo (03) 567-0971 and Shimo (0832) 666-8211.

For those arriving from Korea, the only problem is likely to be the immigration officials here, who have a reputation for being the most unpleasant and officious in Japan; passports are rigorously scrutinised and an entry stamp given as if it were a precious gift. Travellers re-entering Japan can expect to be questioned as to the purpose of entry. See the Visa section in the Facts for the Visitor chapter.

Ferry - Domestic A convenient way to get from Shimonoseki to points farther east on Honshu and to Shikoku is by overnight ferry from places in nearby northern Kyushu. Overnight ferries run from Kokura (part of Kitakyushu city) and nearby Shin Moji-ko to Kobe, Osaka, Sakai and Tokyo (all on Honshu), as well as to Matsuyama (on northwest Shikoku).

Further information on these ferries is given in the sections on Kokura and Shin Moji-ko. However, the ports of departure and destination cities change with annoying regularity so some of the routes described may have stopped, and others may have started. Learn how to use *Jikokuhyo* and inquire locally about available ferries.

From Shimonoseki (Karato district) there is a ferry crossing to Moji-ko (on the northeastern tip of Kyushu) every 30 minutes between 6.15 am and 10 pm (Y250). Moji-ko is near Moji city; Shin Moji-ko is some distance away.

Road By road eastward from Shimonoseki toward Osaka/Kyoto and Tokyo there are three main routes: north along the San-in coast (Route 191 out of Shimo), south along the San-yo coast (Route 2 out of Shimo), and the Chugoku expressway (*kosokudoro*).

The northern route has only a few specific places to visit, like Hagi and Matsue but it is one of the most pleasant areas in Japan to travel through for seascapes, peaceful landscapes of farms, mountains (generally low) and even sand dunes. The road is quite flat along the coast so it can be particularly recommended for cyclists; traffic is not too heavy either. At the end of the San-in region it is easy to get to Kyoto and other attractions of central Honshu, or you can take a ferry to Hokkaido.

The southern route is quite pleasant

and scenic as far as Hiroshima and has many hilly roads, large farmhouses and some interesting side trips. East of Hiroshima is heavily populated and industrialised and road traffic moves at snail's pace most of the way to Kyoto. However, the attractions of Okayama, Kurashiki and Himeji are on this road, and there are some views of the Inland Sea.

A 'compromise' route can be followed by travellers who do not have the option of going by one coast in one direction and returning via the other, and that is to cut across country one or more times using any of several road or rail links across the island. The width at this end of the island is approximately 70 to 110 km.

The quickest road route eastward is via the Chugoku expressway to Osaka; there it connects directly with the Meishin expressway past Kyoto to Nagoya, where you can continue (without stopping) via the Tomei expressway to Tokyo (and onward non-stop to the north of Tohoku). The scenery along the expressway is attractive but not outstanding. For hitch-hikers in a hurry it is the only way to go.

Hitching If you are heading east along the southern coast of Honshu, the road is labelled Route 9 but it runs only a few km before becoming Route 2, and doesn't resume a separate identity until Ogori, 60 km away. Route 2 to Osaka (where it ends) is more direct than Route 191, and takes in Hiroshima, Kirishima/Okayama and Himeji, but travellers should be aware that this road, along with Route 1 from Osaka to Tokyo, is one of the busiest in Japan and is almost one continuous urban area from Ogori to Tokyo.

Route 2 curves to meet the coast and generally runs parallel to it as far as Osaka, passing virtually the only non-built-up area of the entire road, with good views of countryside and farms. The expressway, on the other hand, saves time in terms of distance covered.

The Chugoku expressway runs from

Shimo east to Osaka. The expressway from Shimo also runs west to Kyushu across the graceful Kanmon-ohashi suspension bridge.

To hitch on the expressway or Route 2 toward Kyushu (via either bridge or tunnel), the best starting point is in a maze of interchanges – a map of which resembles the result of an explosion in a spaghetti factory. To reach it from Shimo station, take a bus from stand No 2, but be sure that it is not an express; the destination is Mukuno-tunnel, where you get off and continue walking in the same direction. This leads to a junction identified with direction signs to Kawatana (left) and Hiroshima/expressway/tunnel (right); follow the road to the right, and another set of signs comes into view. Traffic heading left to the expressway subsequently splits into streams going west to Kyushu and east toward Yamaguchi, while that to the right branches off either toward the tunnel to Kyushu or to Hiroshima.

Position yourself for the stream you want; there is one place that catches all traffic, but it is very busy so you must have a very large sign with the name of your destination in *kanji*, and there must be a clear place for a car to stop safely. It might be advisable to make a choice between trying for the expressway or Route 2 tunnel, as the approach road to each offers better stopping places than the point where they divide. If you want only the tunnel, it would be better to stand near the entrance (quite close to Mukuno bus stop).

For those people hitching to the Shimo area, a bus from Mukuno bus stop goes into the station, but quite infrequently during the day. If you are coming through the tunnel you should try to get out of the vehicle as soon as possible after clearing the tunnel exit. If crossing the bridge, get off at or before the Shimonoseki/Dannoura exit and scramble back to the road that leads back to the youth hostel.

SAN-IN COAST

The northern San-in coast is relatively undeveloped and is mostly lush green farms (in summer) and prosperous-looking farm houses, and there's coastal scenery as well. It is a much more pleasant area to travel through than the heavily industrialised southern coast although it has few specific attractions.

The area between Shimonoseki and Hagi was quite off the beaten track until comparatively recently. In the early '70s there were still many houses made of mud and wattle. Along the main road they have now all been replaced by wood or concrete buildings with aluminium doors and windows – vastly more practical and comfortable, but yet another vanished Japanese tradition.

There are several picturesque fishing villages along the way and many views of the sea.

NAGATO

Off the end of Omi-shima island, near Nagato-shi city, is a picturesque promontory of rocks, including twin pillars that jut more than 40 metres straight out of the sea. Access is by bus, and a cruise around the island is available.

The caves of Akiyoshi (described earlier) are accessible from Nagato. You can go by train to Mine and to Akiyoshi by bus, then carry on from there to Hagi (north coast) or Mine, Yamaguchi, etc, on the south coast.

HAGI

The city of Hagi is a very popular holiday destination for the Japanese, partly for what there is to see, but also for its historical associations, particularly those leading to the Meiji restoration. The latter is invisible to foreigners of course, so the importance of Hagi is less for non-Japanese. However, there are historic areas and it can be worth a look around.

The attractions of Hagi result from its having been the castle town of the Mori clan. The castle stood from 1604 to 1871,

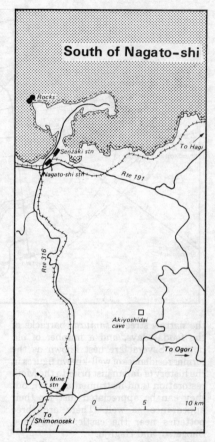

South of Nagato-shi

when it was torn down – unfortunately, because the remaining walls and moats are quite picturesque.

Visitors will be most interested in the castle fortifications, the grounds (which now make up Shizuki-koen park, and house its historical museum as well as a shrine) and a lovely beach. Hagi is built on the delta of several rivers.

The nearby attractions, good for an hour or two of exploration on foot or by bicycle (available at the youth hostel across the road from the castle), include

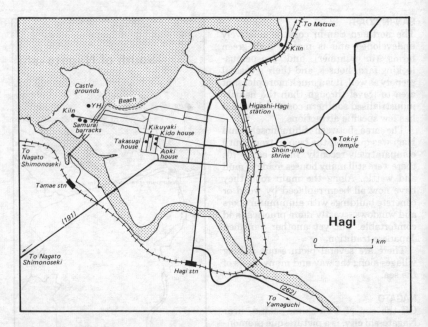

the narrow streets, *samurai* barracks of the feudal days, and a number of old houses. Several are best known as the former residences of well-known figures in the history of Japan just prior to the Meiji restoration (and instrumental in it), but they can be appreciated just for their appearance as well. There are three potteries near the castle: Shiroyama, Shogetsu, and Hagi-jo.

The castle area is closest to Tamae station, one stop beyond Hagi station. Buses are also available, the closest stop being Shizuku-bashi.

East from Hagi to Tottori the coast is pleasant with a succession of towns and cities, some fishing villages, and many farms. It is one of the better areas for observing unpolluted rural Japan. Foreigners are quite rare, so the people are even nicer than usual.

Shoin-jinja Shrine

Another area of touristic interest centres around Shoin-jinja shrine. In the grounds is a building that served as the village school where local hero Shoin Yoshida taught; he was loyal to the emperor and was executed by the Tokugawa government.

Near Shoin-jinja is Toko-ji temple, the family temple of the Mori family and famous for 494 stone lanterns erected by their subordinates over several generations. The Shoin-jinja shrine area is easily reached by bus from Higashi-Hagi station (Nakano-kuru stop).

Myojin-ike Lake

Built as a retreat by the Mori, this lake outside the city is connected to the ocean and follows its tides.

Potteries

There are four potteries in the vicinity of Shoin-jinja shrine: Miwa, Shodo, Renzokan and Hosen.

Other Attractions

Of lesser interest is a pretty little shrine to the right of the road when going into Hagi from Hagi station. I was interested in a stone turtle statue bearing a commemorative stone on its back, a common sight in Korea but almost unknown in Japan. It may have some relationship to the Korean potters who were brought here in the early 1600s by the Tokugawa following an invasion of Korea, or it may indicate earlier ties with that country. The latter is logical in view of the short distance across the water to Korea, and it is known that this area was settled in very early times by people from Korea.

Places to Stay

There are numerous hotels, *ryokan*, etc, in Hagi, as well as a *Youth Hostel* near the castle. Across the street from it is a Koku-minshu-kusha.

Shimane-ken

MASUDA

In the somewhat industrial city of Masuda the attractions are Manpukuji and Iko-ji temples, both of which have noted landscape gardens.

From Masuda, Route 9 and the train run southwest to Yamaguchi via Tsuwano, while Route 191 and rail continue west along the coast to Hagi and Shimonoseki at the western tip of Kyushu.

TSUWANO

The old castle town of Tsuwano has long been known for carp, and recently for steam as well. The former come in a variety of beautiful colours, number in the tens of thousands, and measure up to a metre in length. They are found in ponds of most business establishments, hotels, etc, and even in the channels passing beside the road in the Tonomachi district of the town.

Inari-jinja shrine is the best known shrine in Tsuwano, and is noted for its huge, bright orange *torii* gate. Near the shrine is a museum (Kyodo-kan) of historical items.

The other reason for fame is that Tsuwano is the northeast terminus of a steam train run from Ogori (Yamaguchi-ken), one of only two such runs surviving in Japan. Further details are given in the section on rail transport in the Getting Around chapter.

MT SANBE

The next major attraction is inland from Odashi. The mountain can be climbed easily in an hour from Sanbe-onsen (hot-spring resort), which is accessible by bus (12 per day) from Oda. Nearby is a large lava field and a lake, Ukinu-no-ike.

Easily reached from the area is the Dangyo-kei ravine that stretches four km along the Yagami-kawa river. The ravine is six km from Imbara, on the railway line passing close to Sanbe-onsen; a bus runs toward the ravine from Imbara.

MATSUE

Picturesquely located between a lake (Shinji) and a lagoon (Naka-umi), the city of Matsue is the proud owner of one of the few original castles surviving in Japan, a small but attractive structure dating from 1611.

Near the castle is *bukei yashiki*, an old *samurai* residence that has been well preserved; it is open to the public. Nearby is the former residence of Lafcadio Hearn, an English writer who lived in Matsue during the 1890s and wrote a number of books about the Japan of that day, most of which are still readily available as reprints. Close to his old house is Yakumo-kinenkan, a museum of manuscripts and other memorabilia.

Festivals

Festivals are held in the first half of April (Castle Festival), and the last third of July (Matsue-odori dance and fireworks

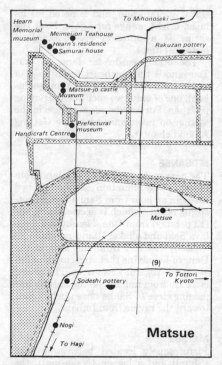

display); there is also the summer festival of Tenmangu jinja shrine.

On 16 August (Toro-nagashi), many paper lanterns on tiny boats are released on Shinji-ko lake. In the middle of the month is the *Obon* festival, and Takeuchi-jinja shrine festival is at the end. There are also various festivals on 3, 5 and 6 November.

AROUND MATSUE

Kaga

There is a stretch of picturesque coast at Kaga, north of Matsue. The most interesting part is the cave Kagano-kukedo, which is entered by boat; the opening is small but the interior is large. Access is by bus from Matsue, taking a little over an hour.

Fudoki Hill

The Matsue area was one of the regions settled before the Yamato conquest of the Japanese islands. There is an archaeological site of an ancient village to the south of Matsue at Fudoki-no-oka, with a museum displaying artefacts of this old civilisation. Inquire locally for information on how to get to the museum.

Hirata

Between Matsue-onsen and Izumo is Hirata, where Gakuen-ji temple is noted for the brilliant autumn colours of trees in its grounds.

Izumo-taisha Shrine

Not far from Matsue is the oldest Shinto shrine in Japan, Izumo, which ranks only behind the grand shrines of Ise in importance. It is most easily reached from Matsue by the Ichihata private railway line; the 40-km trip takes less than an hour, and 21 trains a day run from Matsue-onsen to Izumo-taisha-mae station. You can also go by JR, transferring at Izumo-shi (city) to Taisha. In either case, turn right when leaving the station of either line and walk up the hill. If travelling by the private line note the tall trees grown as windbreaks on the windswept flat peninsula.

It is typical of shrines in Japan that although the site is ancient, the buildings are comparatively recent, dating from 1874 (the main shrine from 1744). They are built in the oldest style of architecture known in Japan and are quite imposing. The grounds are covered with tall old trees and the shrine is backdropped by Yakumo hill. There is a museum in the grounds.

This area was one of the earliest settled by the post-Yayoi people. It is probable that they came from nearby Korea, although their ancestry is not known with any certainty. There is strong evidence that the present Japanese are descendants of settlers from Korea.

By the old (lunar) calendar, the month of October was the time when all the Shinto gods met at Izumo, so the month was

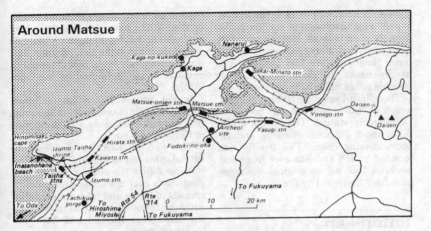

known in the Izumo area as Kamiarizuki (month with gods) and as Kaminazuki (month without gods) everywhere else in Japan.

Festivals Annual festivals at Izumo-taisha shrine are on 14-16 May, 11-17 October (lunar calendar) and 22-23 November. October is also very popular for weddings at Izumo, so it should be possible to see gorgeous bridal kimonos against the backdrop of the shrine.

Tachikue-kyo Gorge

Near Izumo-shi is the pretty one-km-long Tachikue-kyo gorge, formed of cliffs, picturesquely eroded rock and basalt columns. It is easily reached from Izumi-shi station by train to Tachikue-kyo station in 30 minutes.

Inasano-hama Beach

This is a beach close to Izumo-taisha shrine, about two km from the stations; swimming is good.

About 6½ km northwest of the beach is Cape Hinomisaki, site of ancient Hino-misaki shrine and a lighthouse, and with very pretty coastal scenery. Buses run to both the beach and the cape (35 minutes to the latter from the station).

Oki Islands

These islands, almost due north of Matsue, are known for their high steep cliffs and generally wild scenery. Access is by boat from near Matsue (Sakaiminato and Nanarui) to Saigocho on the main island.

Places to Stay There are two *Youth Hostels* on Dogo-shima, and one each on the three lesser islands.

Mt Daisen

Mt Daisen is interesting because although

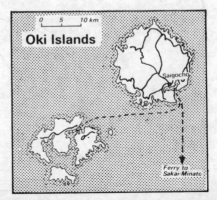

it presents a conical face from the west, it is seen as a succession of smaller peaks from the north or south. It may be climbed quite easily and offers a good view over the coast (including the Oki Islands) and nearby peaks. In clear weather it is possible to see Shikoku to the south.

The climb begins at Daisen Temple, which is easily reached by bus from Daisenguchi station. The 5½-km climb takes about 3½ hours going up and 1½ hours coming down. The temple was founded in 718 and was once huge and powerful, but all its original buildings have been destroyed by fire.

Tottori-ken

TOTTORI

The best-known place along the San-in coast is the extensive area of sand dunes at Tottori; it is two km wide and 16 km long. The dunes have a stark beauty all their own, their broad flanks rippled by the wind. Even though there are usually hundreds of sightseers on the dunes at any one time, they are swallowed in its expanse, and the energetic can walk beyond the area usually tromped by the hordes. In the heat of the summer it is advisable to have a canteen of water or some soft drinks as the air is very dry. The dunes are slightly to the east of town; the entrance is easily reached by bus from Tottori.

In the city of Tottori itself, Tottori Mingei-hakubutsukan (Folk Art Museum) may be of interest, along with the garden of Kannon-in temple.

The San-in coast is considered to extend as far east as Amino. The road and rail line follow the coast closely, giving good views over the sea to contrast with spreads of farms and inland mountains. Although there is no particular attraction, the areas near Kasumi and Yoroi are highly regarded.

TOYOOKA

In the vicinity of this small city (pronounced 'Toyo-oka') are the well-known basalt caves of Gembudo. Unlike limestone caves, these were not formed by water erosion that dissolved the rock, but by a lava flow that cooled on the surface. Some liquid lava underneath escaped, leaving caves or tunnels within the solid mass.

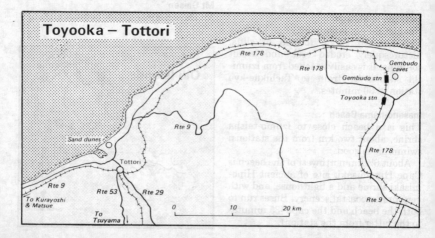

Toyooka – Tottori

Rte 178 · Rte 178 · Gembudo caves · Gembudo stn · Toyooka stn · Rte 9 · Sand dunes · Tottori · Rte 9 · Rte 53 · Rte 29 · Rte 178 · Rte 9 · To Kurayoshi & Matsue · To Tsuyama · 0 · 10 · 20 km

Visible inside the caves are pillars six to nine metres in height, of five, six, seven and eight faces, some parallel, others growing at odd angles. There are five caves or grottoes, 23 to 30 metres or so in depth. They are not far from Gembudo station, 5.3 km out of Toyooka.

AMANOHASHIDATE

About 30 km west of Maizuru and almost due north of Kobe lies one of the Japanese 'Big Three' scenic places, traditionally regarded as having the finest views in Japan. The other two are Matsushima near Sendai and Miyajima near Hiroshima.

The cause of this excitement is a sand bar that stretches 3.6 km across peaceful Miyazu bay. It varies from 35 to 110 metres in width, and has many picturesque, twisted pine trees.

The best view is obtained from Kasamutsu Park to the northwest, accessible by cable car or from Ochitoge pass on a local road to Tango-Omiya. The former can be reached by bus to Ichinomiya from Amanohashidate station (15 minutes), or by ferry from Amanohashidate or Miyazu (15 and 25 minutes respectively). The traditional way to look at the scene is by bending over and looking at it through your legs!

It should be noted that the scenery is in fact not terribly spectacular and the modern generation of Japanese do not fall into raptures at the sight. It's worth a look if you are passing through, but not worth a special trip.

OKU-TANGO PENINSULA

A route taken by few travellers leads around the Oku-tango (or Yosa) peninsula, which begins at Amanohashidate. The very picturesque fishing village of Ine is about 20 km from Miyazu. It is built right to the water's edge around a semicircular bay, with the back part of the houses on stilts over the water.

WAKASA BAY

This area is north of Kyoto. Tsuruga, like Maizuru, is a port for ferries to Hokkaido.

Travelling along Route 27, or by rail along the coast between Tsuruga and Maizuru, you can see the Mikata Five Lakes. They can all be viewed from the top of Baijo Hill, near Lake Suigetsu.

Obama

The city of Obama is noted for Wakasa lacquerware. There are several old temples in the city; to a foreigner, probably Mantokuji and its landscaped garden would be of greatest interest. A cruise boat from Obama takes in the nearby scenic Sotomo coast.

Wakasa-Takahama

Another good view is available at Wakasa-Takahama, especially at Shiroyama-koen park, 1.6 km from the station. Stretching for two km northwest of the city are the Otomi cliffs, rising almost vertically in places, sometimes to more than 250 metres. Boat cruises lasting about two hours are available from Takahama.

Maizuru

This is an industrial city of no touristic interest but it is the port of departure for a ferry service to Otaru on Hokkaido (four boats a week).

The terminal is a short distance north of Nishi-Maizuru station. Details on another boat service to Otaru from Tsuruga is described in the section on Fukui-ken.

The Inland Sea

Seto Naikai, the Inland Sea, is one of those areas in Japan about which travel writers have traditionally written in superlatives. The fact is, that while there *are* many very lovely views around this body of water, it has changed greatly since it first came to the notice of western eyes.

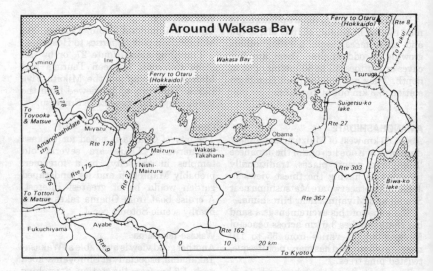

Many fishing villages have been replaced by modern industries – substituting 'progress' and pollution for idyllic scenes. The waters are filled with large numbers of ships and the peace and serenity of 20 to 30 years ago has gone. Anyone arriving with the expectation of charming views at every turn is doomed to disappointment, but time spent seeking out some or all of the places mentioned will be rewarded.

The book the *Inland Sea* by Japan expert Donald Richie, although in many ways a narrative of personal development and change, gives a good description of the area through the eyes of a Japanese-speaking foreigner. The book is beautifully illustrated, though it probably outdoes present reality.

Along the north shore of the sea, good views are available (from east to west) near Okayama/Kurashiki, Onomichi, Fukuyama, and Itsukushima (Miyajima, near Hiroshima), as well as at Shimonoseki, at the western end of the sea. The most beautiful maritime views are in the area bounded on the east by Shodo Island and on the west by Tono-no-ura (Honshu) and Tadotsu (Shikoku).

The best way to enjoy the mood of the Inland Sea (if you have time to spare) is to pick an island or two and spend some time there. Some have *Youth Hostels*, and an island of any size is sure to have a few *minshuku*; an isolated area is the best place to enjoy the homely pleasures of *minshuku* accommodation.

The islands described fall into three groups: Awaji-shima; Shodo-shima and nearby islands; and Innoshima and nearby islands.

Getting Around

In addition to the numerous shuttle ferries between Honshu and Shikoku that pass through various parts of the Inland Sea, the overnight ferry from Beppu to Kobe and Osaka (leaving Beppu at 9 pm) passes through some of the most scenic parts of the sea in the early morning. Because the sky is light as early as 4.30 am in the summer, early risers can have a couple of hours of sightseeing before the boat docks at Takamatsu at 7.30 am (and more after it leaves). It reaches Kobe at 11.50 am and Osaka at 1.10 pm. The boat that leaves Osaka at 9 pm and Kobe at 10.30 pm reaches Imabari at 5.40 am, so this trip would provide some views of the western part of the Inland Sea by daylight, although you would have passed through the best part before sunrise.

There are a number of ferries and hydrofoils across the Inland Sea between Honshu and Shikoku. Terminals are shown on the map and the frequency and travel time information is given in the places on Shikoku.

AWAJI-SHIMA ISLAND

This is the largest island in the Inland Sea and is one of the most densely populated islands in Japan. It is relatively flat and agricultural, holding no fantastic visual delights. It serves as a bridge between the Kobe area (via Akashi) and Shikoku.

Puppet Theatre

Awaji appears to be the home of the oldest puppet theatre in Japan, more ancient though less famous than the *bunraku* of

Osaka. Short performances (about 30 minutes) of puppet plays are given daily at Ningyo-za, the small puppet theatre by the ferry dock at Fukura, at 11 am between 1 March and 30 November. At other times you must be content with a look at the large number of puppets on display around the walls.

It was feared that the puppetry tradition would die out completely, as the 15 performers at Fukura are the only ones left on Awaji and their average age is close to 70. However, a renaissance seems to be in action, so there may be a return to the golden days of the start of the Meiji era when there were 48 theatres on Awaji-shima island.

Naruto Whirlpools

The whirlpools are almost next door to Fukura. They are at their mightiest at high and low tide, when the water swirls into or out of the Inland Sea through the narrow Naruto Strait between Awaji and

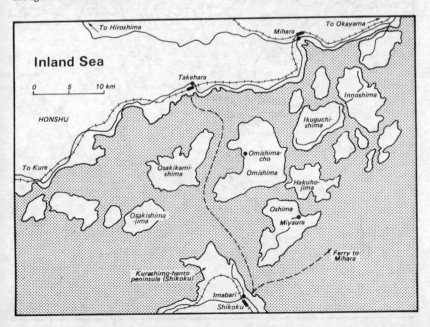

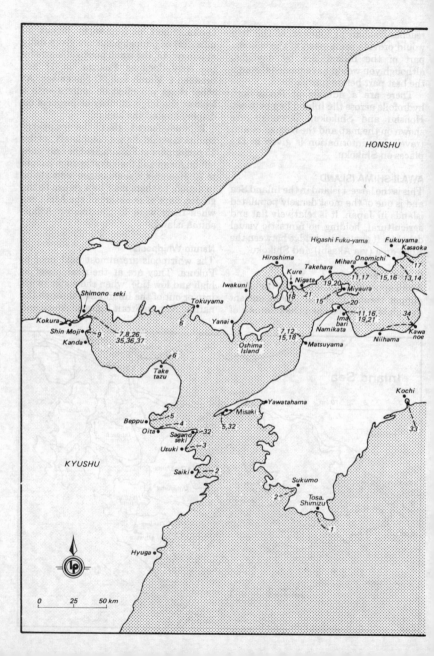

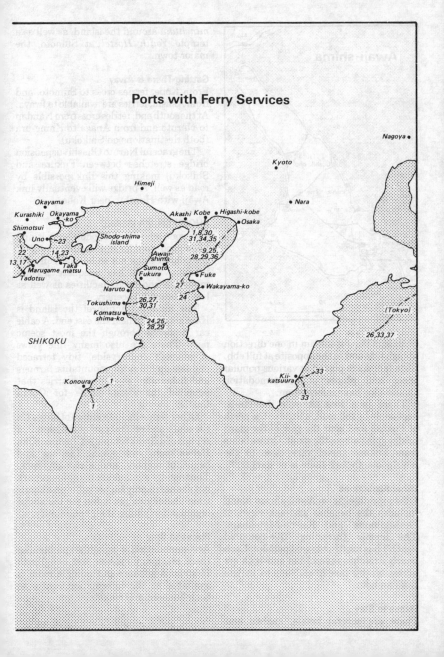

Ports with Ferry Services

Nagoya

Kyoto

Nara

Himeji

Okayama

Kurashiki

Okayama-ko

Akashi Kobe Higashi-kobe

Shimotsui

Osaka

Uno 23

Shodo-shima island

1,8,30
31,34,35

22

14,23

9,25
28,29,36

13,17

Taka

Awaji-shima

Marugame matsu

Sumoto
Fukura

Tadotsu

Fuke

Naruto

21 Wakayama-ko

24

Tokushima 26,27
30,31

Komatsu
shima-ko

(Tokyo)

24,25
28,29

26,33,37

SHIKOKU

Konoura 1

Kii-
katsuura 33

1

33

Shikoku. The rapids run in one direction at high tide and in the opposite at full ebb. Tide tables are posted at various popular spots and places of accommodation should also have information.

There is a lookout over the strait, accessible by toll road, a little to the north of Fukura and near the pier of the giant bridge going across the strait. Cruise boats from Fukura travel very close to the whirlpools, though there is no danger.

Other Attractions
Other sightseeing on Awaji-shima island includes the beaches and sea views of Goshikihama and Kei-no-Matsubara. The former (meaning 'five-coloured beach') has multi-coloured pebbles. Each beach stretches several km and both are accessible by bus from Sumoto in less than an hour.

Places to Stay
There are several hotels, *ryokan* and *minshuku* around the island, as well as a temple *Youth Hostel* at Sumoto, the major town.

Getting There & Away
From Kobe, ferries cross to Sumoto, and from Akashi, ferries are available to Iwaya. At the south end, ferries cross from Nandan to Naruto and from Anaga to Kame-ura (both destinations on Shikoku).

The graceful Naruto Ohashi suspension bridge stretches between Fukura and Shikoku, making this link possible by road as well. A bridge will eventually link Awaji with Honshu, near Kobe.

SHODO-SHIMA ISLAND
Everyone who visits Shodo-shima island has a good word for it. It is sufficiently off the beaten track not to be over-run with tourists, but it has adequate accommodation and travel facilities as well as lots of beautiful scenery.

The main attraction of the island is Kanka-kei gorge near the east end. A cable car descends through the most scenic part. There are also many fine views of unspoilt countryside, tidy terraced paddies up hill sides, mountains, farmers and fishermen, as well as quarries that supplied the giant stones for Osaka Castle.

Other sights include groves of olives (in the south and central part of the island), a replica of a Greek temple (at Tayo-no-Oka Heiwa-koen) overlooking the sea and beautiful scenery, and a monkey park. The friendly simians are in the lower park but are unfriendly higher up; even a short-time visitor can get a feel for the social organisation within their community.

Places to Stay
Accommodation is usually no problem as there are many *ryokan* and two *Youth Hostels*. Assistance in finding a room is available at the information centre at both Tonosho and Sakate.

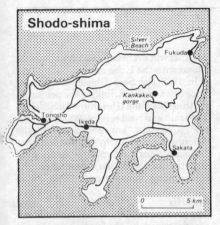

Shodo-shima

Silver Beach
Fukuda
Kankakei gorge
Tonosho
Ikeda
Sakata

0   5 km

Getting There & Away
Ferries connect the towns of Tonosho, Ikeda, Sakata and Fukudo (on Shodo) with Takamatsu, Ono, Okayama, Hinase, Himeji, Kobe and Osaka. Check the schedules in *Jikokuhyo*, or get help at an information centre or travel agency.

Getting Around
Getting around Shodo is no problem as buses run regularly – both special and sightseeing coaches, and scheduled public transport. The usual starting point is Tonosho but tour buses also leave from Sakata and possibly from other ports served by ferries. Generally it seems there is a tour bus waiting for each ferry arrival.

More than one person has liked the relaxed pace of Shodo life and stayed for several days. You can get a good idea of its attractions by taking a bus tour on arrival, then exploring by public bus afterward.

OTHER ISLANDS
From Shodo-shima island you can island-

hop via Toyo-shima to Uno, near Okayama. Other pleasant, really off-the-beaten-track islands (some of them listed here) are between Imabari (Shikoku) and Mihara (Honshu) and are accessible (along with nearby islands) from both places. Anyone really interested in this type of exploring might try to obtain an old copy of Nancy Phelan's book *A Pillow of Grass*.

Ikuguchi-jima Island
The island offers views of orange groves, shrines, temples, and, most importantly, has an atmosphere of rural Japan.

Places to Stay Besides the *Youth Hostel* overlooking a quiet village, there are also *ryokan* and *minshuku*.

Innoshima Island
This island is also worth a visit but has no youth hostel, however Ikuguchi Island is close by.

Omishima Island
Fifteen km off the north coast of the Kurushima-hanto peninsula, Omishima is noted for the Oyamazumi-jinja shrine, dedicated to the guardian gods of sailors. In historic times it was visited by many warriors off to battle, and a large amount of the finest armour was donated in supplication for good fortune in battle. As a result, 80% of all the armour in Japan that has survived and been given the rating 'national treasure' or 'important cultural property' belongs to this shrine. Most of it is on display, unlike at other museums which show only a small sample of their collections. The shrine is near Miyaura, the town where the ferries dock.

Shikoku

Shikoku is the fourth main island of the Japanese group. It is generally rural and gets left by most travellers as a place to see if time permits; not an unrealistic evaluation. There is, however, a couple of unique attractions.

On Shikoku you are almost sure to see large numbers of people dressed in white, making pilgrimages to the 88 temples related to the priest Kobo-Daishi. It should not be difficult to locate the temples as they are marked by road signs (in Japanese only). As places of interest to foreigners, however, none is really outstanding.

Apart from scenery, the most noteworthy place on Shikoku is Ritsurin-koen garden in Takamatsu, one of the finest gardens in Japan.

GETTING THERE & AWAY

There is a great variety of ship services to and from Honshu and Kyushu; connections are described in the text. There are also air services from the principal cities in each of the four prefectures that give Shikoku its name of Four Districts.

In 1985 the graceful 1629-metre-long Naruto Ohashi suspension bridge between Awaji-shima island and Naruto, across the Naruto Strait, was opened. It is the longest suspension bridge in the orient.

Another will eventually link Awaji-shima island with the Kobe area.

In 1988 the Seto Ohashi complex of bridges was opened, linking the peninsula south of Okayama (Honshu) with Shikoku. The train and road services which use this bridge system are described in the Takamatsu and nearby Utadsu sections.

Another such complex is under construction in the Mihara area where the Inland Sea is narrowest.

NARUTO

The great whirlpools of the Naruto Strait are described in the section on Awaji-shima island. From the Shikoku side, an excellent view is available from Naruto Park on Oge-shima island (eight km northeast of Naruto city); buses run from Naruto station. The park is also accessible from Awaji-shima island by ferry from Anaga (a little north of Fukura), and there is also a ferry service from Fukura.

TOKUSHIMA

This city is known for a crazy dance, puppets and a fine garden. One of the most famous festivals in Japan is the Awa-odori (15 to 18 August) when large numbers of celebrants dressed in traditional costume dance in the city streets through much of the night.

Puppet Theatre

Along with Awaji-shima island and Osaka, Tokushima has a tradition of puppet theatre. Performances are usually given by farmers, so they are more likely to be seen after harvest time and before planting; make inquiries locally.

Tokushima Park

This park contains a garden that was part of the mansion associated with Tokushima Castle (now ruined) and dates from 1586. It is a landscape garden typical of the

Momoyama period. The park is 400 metres east of the station.

Other Attractions

East from Tokushima you can go to Anabuki station and then take a bus (15 minutes) northeast to see an interesting natural phenomenon; pillars of earth have been formed by erosion and stand 12 to 18 metres high. They are similar to the Hoodoos in Alberta (Canada) and other formations in the Tyrol.

South from Tokushima lies Anan, beside Tachibana Bay. It offers a good view of many islands and is compared by locals to the famous Matsushima (near Sendai), although the slightest resemblance of anything in any way to a more famous sight in Japan receives similar comparisons.

From a point one km south of Mugi, Yasakahama beach stretches for about 10 km.

Getting There & Away

The ferry between Tokyo and Kokura (Kyushu) every two days stops at Tokushima en route each way.

Locally, boats run from Tokushima to various docks in Osaka, Kobe (including a hydrofoil), Wakayama-ko, and Fuke-ko (near Wakayama). The boats are too numerous to list here, and the schedules (and ports) change from year to year, but typical times are two hours from Osaka by passenger boat (Y4400) and 3½ hours (Y1920) by car ferry. From Kobe, the hydrofoil takes two hours (Y4400), the ferry 190 minutes (Y1920). For up-to-date information, consult *Jikokohyu* or an information office.

To Komatsushima There are many boats throughout the day between Komatsushima-ko and Wakayama-ko, and a couple to Osaka.

From Komatsushima you can continue down to Cape Muroto at the far southeast tip of the island.

To Konoura The daily boat between Kobe and Tosa-Shimizu (southwest Shikoku) stops en route both ways at Konoura, but the arrival time from Kobe is awkward.

TAKAMATSU

Probably the most enjoyable city on Shikoku, Takamatsu features one of the finest gardens in Japan as well as a number of other attractions.

Ritsurin-koen Garden

This garden is superior (in my eyes) to at least two of the 'Big Three' gardens – those at Mito and Okayama – and at least the equal of Kenroku-en in Kanazawa. It is built around an interconnected series of ponds and affords a variety of views, taking advantage of a large hill and natural forests in its plan. It dates from the mid 1600s.

A folk-craft museum in the park features an excellent collection of hand-crafted utensils, etc. It has two sections; one for Shikoku crafts, the other for those from other regions of the country.

The garden is easily reached by tram; the stop is Ritsurin-koen.

Takamatsu-jo Castle

Most of the castle has been destroyed but the remaining walls, three turrets and one original gate are quite picturesque. It is close to Takamatsu station and pier and is thus easy to reach. The site is now called Tamamo-koen park.

Yashima

Technically this is an island because a narrow channel surrounds it, but it appears to be a high hill (292 metres) on the east of the city. Historically it is famous for a battle, one of a seemingly endless number throughout western Japan between the Taira and Minamoto in the late 1100s which the Taira usually lost.

The top of the hill is accessible directly by bus from the station or by tram and cable car to the south peak. At the top, Yashima-ji temple has a display of relics

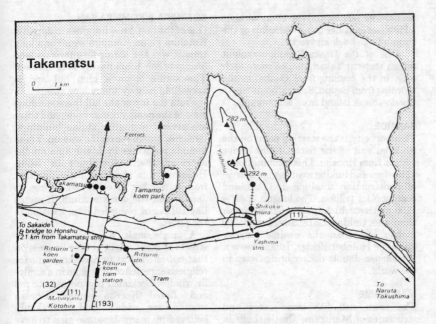

from the battles, while the north peak offers a good view over the Inland Sea.

Shikoku-mura

This is a collection of typical, traditional buildings from various locations around the island and includes a vine suspension bridge of the type once common in isolated valleys. It is interesting if you have not visited such a village elsewhere, but could be a bit of a let down if you have already been to Takayama.

Megishima Island

This tiny island (eight km in circumference) is famous in Japan through the children's story of Momotaro, a boy who cleaned out a pack of demons. It offers a good view of the Inland Sea, is only four km from the city and is easily reached by ferry.

Places to Stay

There are two *Youth Hostels* at Takamatsu, as well as *ryokan*, *minshuku* and hotels.

Getting There & Away

The situation up to late 1987 was that Takamatsu was linked with Kobe and Osaka by boat. The fastest were hydrofoils, two and three per day taking two and 2½ hours respectively, while the regular boats (one or two per day) took about 5½ hours from Osaka, an hour less from Kobe (same boat).

Between Takamatsu and Uno (near Okayama) three lines have operated ferries with departures at 20, 30 and 40-minute intervals throughout much of the day, the crossing taking 60 to 75 minutes and costing Y370.

However, all these boats are now complemented by road and rail services following the opening of the giant Seto Ohashi bridge system in April 1988. The Shikoku end begins at Sakaide, which is only about 20 km from Takamatsu. Since JR trains now run across the bridge, anyone using a Japan Rail Pass can go to Shikoku by train rather than having to bother with ferries, and travellers without a Pass can consider using train, bus or the thumb to go back and forth.

One of the Osaka-Beppu overnight ferries stops at Takamatsu en route each way, in the evening from Osaka, in the morning from Beppu. Several boats run to Shodo-shima island from Matsuyama.

SAKAIDE

This port city is the starting point on the Shikoku end of the Seto Ohashi bridge system from Honshu. This combination of 11 bridges and linking roadway is a marvel of construction totalling 13.1 km and costing Y1.1 trillion. The longest span is 1100 metres, which is 180 metres shorter than the Golden Gate bridge and 300 metres less than the world's longest, Britain's Humber Bridge. It is, however, the longest double-decker bridge span in the world.

MARUGAME

The town still has some gates and structures of Marugame Castle (built in 1597) remaining. The castle is about one km south of the station.

Getting There & Away

Between Marugame and Shimotsui (near Kurashiki) there are nearly 20 ferry crossings daily in each direction (Y850, 70 minutes). Between Marugame and Fukuyama there are four daily crossings each way (Y3100, 70 minutes).

TADOTSU

Tadotsu is interesting in *sakura* time when 10,000 trees in Toryo-koen park (1½ km west of the station) are in bloom. The same park gives a good view over the sea, and there is a good beach nearby.

Getting There & Away

Between Tadotsu and Fukuyama there are 15 boat crossings a day in each direction (Y1300, 1¾ hours).

KOTOHIRA & KOMPIRA-SAN

One of the best-known shrines in Japan is Kotohira-gu on Kompira-san. For a long time it was the shrine for mariners who brought their boats nearby to be blessed. The shrine is on a high hill and is accessible only by a very long climb.

From the top of the hill there is a good view of the nearby countryside, and there are several attractive shrine buildings, lanterns, etc, to see on the way up. These include paintings by Maruyama on the doors of the Shoin (built in 1659). However, this shrine is little different from a number of other old shrines in Japan, and the one-km climb (it seems like 10) is not rewarded in proportion to the effort.

A single male wandering the back streets at night might get the impression that not all visitors to Kotohira come for religious experience. A woman in a dimly-lit window beckoned conspiringly to me and offered 'Korean women'. Korean women are widely and mistakenly believed by many Japanese men to have no morals.

Places to Stay

Of interest to anyone wanting to sample gracious *ryokan* living is a small cluster of high-class (and price) inns at the foot of the hill where the path, and rows of souvenir stands, begins. Several of the *ryokan* have very ornate carved wooden panels, intimate gardens and other 'typical' Japanalia, that are in fact not often seen. Of minor interest is an old-style bridge with a decorative roof, just a little to the south.

Getting There & Away

Kotohira is easily reached from Takamatsu by Takamatsu-Kotohira Dentetsu railway (the same line that can be taken from Takamatsu station to Ritsurin), or by bus, both taking about an hour.

KANONJI

An unusual sight here, visible from

Kotohiki-koen park (1½ km north of Kanonji station), is Zenigata, the huge outline of an ancient square-holed coin with four *kanji* characters. It is made of a series of trenches in the ground and is 345 metres wide. It dates from the Kan-ei era (1624 to 1644) and is explained by one source as having been made by the people as a reminder to their feudal lord that they would be careful not to waste money. In view of the heavy taxes of those days, it was more likely a reminder to the lord not to waste *their* money. A good view of the Inland Sea is available from Kotohiki Hachiman shrine.

KAWANOE

From here you can go east via Route 192 to Awa-Ikeda, to travel south by the (recommended) route described later. There is also a ferry service to Kobe.

NIIHAMA

There is a regular ferry service between Niihama/Kawanoe and Kobe (Higashi-Kobe, Aoki port); one by day, one by night. Both boats from Kobe go first to Kawanoe, then to Niihama; 7½ and 9¾ hours respectively. The fare is the same to both places. In the return direction the day boat leaves Niihama, then goes to Kawanoe, while the night boat takes the opposite course before going to Kobe.

You can also travel west from here, but the north coast is more industrialised and of little interest.

AWA-IKEDA TO KOCHI

South of Kompira-san lies some lovely inland mountain and valley scenery. The starting point is Awa-Ikeda, not far south of Kompira. Road and rail continue through the valley of the Yoshino River, passing the biggest gorge in Shikoku, which is particularly noteworthy for a 7½-km stretch that includes two picturesque rock formations (Koboke and Oboke). There is a JR station near each, both of which are accessible by train or bus from Awa-Ikeda station. From a point two km

north of Oboke, a boat is available for a descent of the river (30 to 40 minutes), ending about 3½ km from Koboke station. A toll road links Oboke to Iyadani-kei gorge.

Iyadani-kei Gorge

This is a very lovely valley rather off the beaten track. The gorge extends from a point near Iyaguchi for about 45 km to Sugeoi. After only a few km a toll road branches west to rejoin Route 32. A short distance past the junction is the 45-metre-long Iya-no-kazura-bashi bridge, the last surviving original vine suspension bridge of the type once common in the region. This type of bridge had the advantage of being easily cut to block the ingress of the invaders. The bridge is of the same type as the one at Shikoku-mura in Takamatsu. There is a fee for crossing, and the keeper becomes angry if you even set foot on it without paying.

The inhabitants of the valley are believed to be descendants of the Taira who survived the defeat at Yashima and retreated here, much as other Taira descendants are found in the Shirakawago area of Gifu-ken.

There are several buses daily running through the very pretty valley to Sugeoi. Beyond that the bus continues almost in a circle north to Sadamitsu station, an area where a foreigner is definitely a rarity. From there it would be simple to return to Awa-Ikeda. Alternatively, you can back-track to the toll road and out to Oboke to take the boat ride, or just continue south toward Kochi.

Jofuki-ji Temple

On the way to Kochi, Toyonaga station is the landmark for Jofuki-ji temple. Not a famous sight, it is a temple Youth Hostel (No 7404; tel (0887) 74-0301). The young priest speaks good English, is very friendly, well-travelled and happy to introduce guests to Zen, including meditation.

Travellers have been known to stay here

for weeks and it's easy to understand why – the surroundings are peaceful and beautiful. The temple is high on the side of the valley among tall trees and is 1.7 km from the station; ask for directions on arrival.

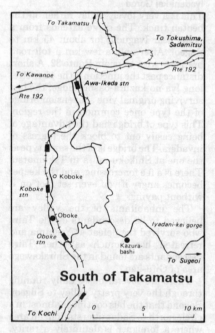

South of Takamatsu

Buraku-ji Temple
One km north of Otaguchi station, this temple is noted for the architecture of its main hall, Yakushido, which was built in 1151. It is a national treasure and a good example of Fujiwara architecture (897 to 1192).

Ryugado Cave
Discovered in 1931, this cave contained clay dishes of a prehistoric people. It features stalagmites and stalactites and other sights of a typical limestone cave. It is accessible in 20 minutes by bus from Tosa-Yamada station.

Oshino
The Kochi area is noted historically for the raising of roosters with incredible tail plumage, sometimes more than six metres in length. The village of Oshino is the traditional centre of this activity, which is said to be a fading interest.

Oshino is a district in the city of Nangoku, accessible from Gomen station. Local inquiries in the city (or possibly in Kochi) are required to track down these birds.

KOCHI
The main attraction of Kochi is its five-storey castle. The present buildings date from 1748. It gives an open view of the city and surrounding hills which are only of limited interest.

Getting There & Away
There is a daily overnight ferry in each

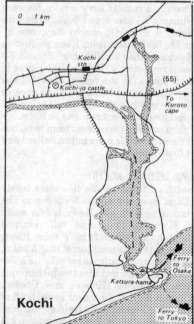

Kochi

direction between Kochi and Osaka, and every second day between Kochi and Tokyo. The latter stops at Kii-Katsuura (each direction) on the Kii-hanto peninsula south of Osaka and Nagoya.

CAPE MUROTO

From Kochi you can make a side-trip to Cape Muroto in the southeast (also accessible from Tokushima). The five-km tip is known for its lighthouse and generally wild atmosphere. About 10 buses a day run to the cape from Kochi or nearby Harimaya-bashi. Close to the tip is Higashi-dera temple, which is also a *Youth Hostel.*

KATSURAHAMA BEACH

Some 13 km southeast of Kochi, this beach offers white sand, good swimming and scenic rock formations. It is accessible in 35 minutes by bus from Kochi station. Collectors of seashells will find a wide variety of beautiful specimens on sale at very reasonable prices.

INO

This is a town noted for producing handmade paper. It may be possible to arrange to watch the process. Inquire locally for directions. The town is the last stop of the Kochi tram system.

ASHIZURI-MISAKI CAPE

The beauties of this cape and the surrounding area are reached from Tosa-Shimizu. Three roads, each with their own bus service, run to the tip. The coastal road is adventurously narrow, while the central (toll) road – the Ashizuri Skyline – passes over the central ridge, skirting 433-metre Shiraou-san. The name Ashizuri translates as 'leg grazing', quite possibly a reference to the narrowness of the paths of olden times.

Attractions of the tip are the wildness, the lighthouse, and Kongo-fuku-ji temple, which is close enough to the sea for you to hear the crash of the surf. Today's temple dates back 300 years but there has been

one on the site for more than 1100 years. The vegetation verges on tropical, with palms and banyan trees, and there are coral reefs to contrast with granite cliffs.

Tosa-Shimizu

There is a daily boat between Tosa-Shimizu and Kobe, stopping en route (both ways) at Konoura on the southeast coast of Shikoku.

MINOKOSHI AREA

Continuing west from Tosa-Shimizu takes you to the coastal area of Minokoshi, which contains some of the most beautiful views of all. Glass-bottom boats can be hired to see the colourful fish of the coral reefs.

Beside the road are eroded limestone cliffs of wondrous shapes, which lead up to another strange rock formation at Tatsukushi. Tatsukushi means 'dragon skewers', a name taken from the number of slim cylinders of stone.

The Hall of Shells

At Tatsukushi town there is a very interesting museum that displays nothing but seashells – about 50,000 of them – including many rare and beautiful types. The building is modern and the displays are well planned. Many typhoons pass through this area and stir up the sea bottom, bringing large numbers of sea shells onto the shore.

NORTH FROM MINOKOSHI

The coast north from the Minokoshi area is also very scenic, although of the rias type (submerged fingers of land). There are views of the sea and the coast to the west, orange groves and other greenery to the east – sometimes in both directions when the road goes a little inland.

Sukumo

Ferries run between Sukumo and Saiki (Kyushu) usually six times a day (three hours, Y1600 minimum).

UWAJIMA

Uwajima has several attractions. Places of interest include Uwajima Castle (dating from 1665) and Atago-koen park on a hill high enough to give a good view of the city and sea. The impressions of this city and the entire coast is of unusually lush foliage. There is a fine landscape garden, Tensha-en ('Heavenly Forgiveness Garden'), two km south of the city.

Those with an interest in WW II might like to look for the remains of the Shiden-kai fighter aircraft that was raised from the bottom of Kure Bay in 1979, where it had lain since being shot down in July 1945. It is believed to be the only one of its type in Japan.

Bull Fights

Uwajima is famous for its *togyu* bull fights. These are not the kind that pit matador against animal with the result of hundreds of kg of beef, but are contests between two animals that lock horns and try to push the other backwards. Generally there is a fight every month but, with the exception of Wareisai summer festival (23-24 July), dates vary from year to year.

Information offices such as the TIC in Tokyo or Kyoto, as well as travel agencies, should be able to provide details. Ehime-ken also maintains an office in Tokyo and other large cities, so a friend can phone in Japanese for up-to-date information. The fights are held at Togyu-jo at the foot of Tenman-yama, a 30-minute walk from Uwajima station.

Getting There & Away

There is one ferry daily each way to Beppu (3¼ hours, about Y5500).

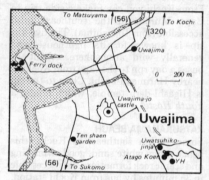

OZU

There is *ukai* (cormorant fishing) on the river at Ozu from 1 June to 20 September.

YAWATAHAMA

The hill sides behind this port city are noted for the scenic appearance of their terraces as well as the many orange groves. Kinzan Shusseki temple, at the top of Kinzan, gives an excellent view of the Inland Sea and as far away as Kyushu.

Getting There & Away

Yawatahama is a convenient port for ferries to Usuki and Beppu, both in Kyushu. There are five boats in each direction for Beppu (three hours, about Y5100), and up to nine a day each way for Usuki (three hours, Y1270).

SADAMISAKI CAPE

This cape, more than 50 km long, projects toward Kyushu. Reports indicate, however, that there is nothing of exceptional interest there.

Misaki
There are three ferries a day in each direction between Misaki and Saganoseki on Kyushu (70 minutes, Y400).

MATSUYAMA
The main attraction in Matsuyama is Matsuyama-jo castle. It is a three-storey building dating from 1602 and is one of the best-preserved castles in Japan. It also functions as a museum. It is atop Shiroyama hill, which is accessible by climbing or by cable car (gondola) from the east side (remote from the station).

Dogo-onsen
Matsuyama is famous among the Japanese for its nearby hot-spring resort, Dogo-onsen, which is known for the traditional architecture of its municipal bath-house (Shinrokaku) and the variety of waters available there. However, Japanese sources continually over stress hot springs

in tourist literature, so this one will be of limited interest to most foreign visitors.

Ishite Temple Near the hot spring, this is the only temple of note in the area. It dates back to 1318 and illustrates the Kamakura style of architecture.

Getting There & Away
Matsuyama is connected by a number of ferries to ports on Honshu and Kyushu. Overnight ferries between Beppu (Kyushu) and Osaka, and between Oita (Kyushu) and Kobe, stop at Matsuyama.

In addition, there are numerous ferries to nearby points on Honshu. Between Hiroshima and Matsuyama there are more than 25 daily crossings each way, typically 17 hydrofoils using Matsuyama kanko-ko port (one hour, Y3600), and 10 conventional ferries that go to both Matsuyama kanko-ko port (2¾ hours,

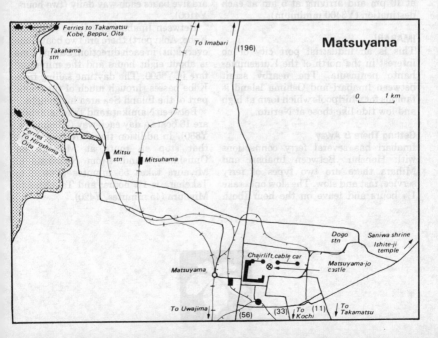

Y1800) and Mitsuhama port (three hours, Y1800).

Between Yanai and Mitsuhama there are also hydrofoils (seven daily, one hour, Y4950) and ferries (22 daily, 2½ hours, Y1950 hours).

Between Iwakuni and Mitsuhama there are six daily ferries, three direct (2½ hours, Y1950) and three that stop at Inoda on Oshima (2¾ hours, Y1950).

Between Mihara and Matsuyama kanko-ko there are up to nine hydrofoil crossings daily in each direction (140 minutes, Y4800).

There are 16 daily crossings in each direction between Kure and Horie-ko port (two hours, Y1200).

Between Matsuyama and Onomichi there are five hydrofoil crossings per day (85 minutes, Y4800).

Between Kokura (northern Kyushu) and Matsuyama kanko-ko there is one overnight ferry in each direction departing at 10 pm and arriving at 5 am at each destination (Y3400 minimum).

IMABARI

This is an industrial port city of no interest in the north of the Kurashima-hanto peninsula. The nearby strait between Imabari and Oshima Island is famous for whirlpools which form at high and low tide like those at Naruto.

Getting There & Away

Imabari has several ferry connections with Honshu. Between Imabari and Mihara there are two types of ferry service, fast and slow. The slow ones take 1¾ hours and leave on the hour (both directions) throughout most of the day; the fare is Y1270. The fast boats also run throughout the day but don't have such evenly spaced departures. They take one hour and cost Y2880.

There are two different services between Imabari and Onomichi, with differing patterns of stops at islands en route. There is a total of about 14 boats daily each way, taking 1½ hours between the two end points (Y3180).

Between Imabari and Takehara there are three boats a day each way. With a stop at Miyaura (Omishima island) en route, the trip takes one hour (Y2320). To Miyaura from Imabari takes 40 minutes. The same company operates up to 12 boats a day between Imabari and Miyaura (1¾ hours, Y700).

Between Imabari and Nigata (not Niigata!) there are four high-speed boats daily each way (1½ hours, Y2980).

Between Imabari and Hiroshima there are five boats each way daily (two hours, Y4100).

Between Imabari and Kobe (Higashi-Kobe, Aoki) port there are two boats (one overnight) in each direction. Sailing time is about eight hours and the minimum fare is Y3500. The daytime sailing from Kobe passes through much of the scenic part of the Inland Sea area in daylight.

Between Namikata and Takehara there are 16 boats a day each way (70 minutes, Y860). In addition there are four a day that stop en route at Miyaura on Omishima island. From Namikata to Miyaura takes 55 minutes (Y640); to Takehara is 1¾ hours; and Takehara to Miyaura (45 minutes, Y420).

Kyushu

Kyushu, the southernmost of the four main islands of Japan, is regarded as the cradle of Japanese civilisation and has many places of interest.

It was from here that the Yamato tribe (probably of continental origin) spread to the Kobe/Osaka/Ise area before subjugating the peoples already occupying other parts of the country. However, because these events date from about 600 BC, only archaeological remains are left, and these are mostly in the Usuki and Miyazaki areas.

Kyushu has also been substantially influenced by Chinese and Korean civilisations because it is the part of Japan closest to those countries.

The main attractions of Kyushu are Mt Aso, the Yamanami Highway, Kagoshima/Sakurajima, Kirishima, various islands off the coasts, some interesting hot-springs temples, shrines, Nagasaki, the anti-Mongol wall, and many gardens. The people of Kyushu also have a reputation for being more friendly than in most parts of Japan (although there can be no complaints about the people elsewhere!).

Even if you have studied Japanese and speak it well, you can expect great difficulties in speaking to people in Kyushu, especially around Kagoshima, as the local dialect is quite different from standard Japanese. The old dialect of Kagoshima, Satsuma-ben, is now spoken only by the older generation and is totally incomprehensible even to other Japanese.

The story given (and apparently believed by most Japanese) is that a local feudal lord commanded that the people change their way of speaking so that spies from Honshu could be detected. But as any school teacher can certify, correcting even one grammatical error like 'I seen' can be a hopeless task, so this explanation can be taken *cum grano salis*.

The most likely answer is that the accent is a carry-over from languages spoken by early inhabitants from other areas, such as neighbouring Korea, in the same way that accents in England reflect intonations brought by the various tribes and groups from the continent. The dialect of Okinawa, for example, only a relatively short distance to the south, is virtually a separate language.

GETTING THERE & AWAY
Air

There are airports at or near the major cities of Hakata (Fukuoka), Nagasaki, Kumamoto, Kagoshima, Miyasaki, and Oita/Beppu, in addition to those on several small islands off the north and northwest coasts. Access information is given in the individual city Getting There sections.

Road

The city of Kitakyushu is joined by road and rail tunnel to Shimonoseki, at the southern end of Honshu. Both of these are described in the section Shimonoseki.

Ferry

There are numerous boat and ferry connections to Kyushu from both Honshu and Shikoku. The following are all the services:

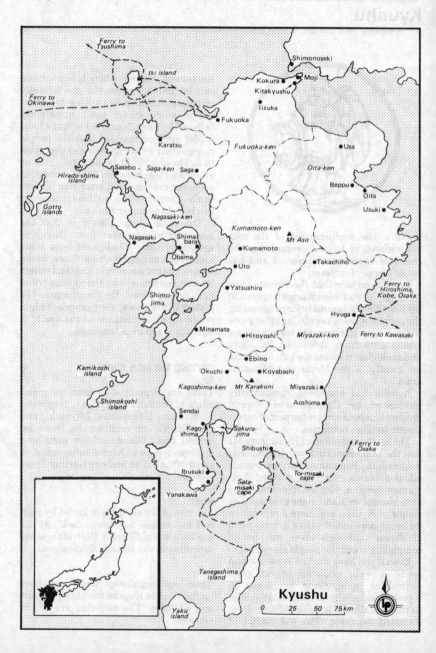

Kyushu

0   25   50   75 km

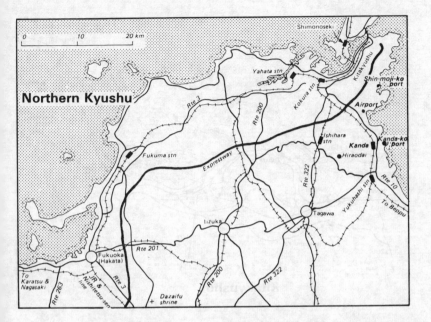

Northern Kyushu

Taketazu to: Tokuyama (western Honshu)
Beppu to: Hiroshima, Takamatsu (Shikoku),
   Matsuyama (Shikoku), Kobe, Osaka,
   Uwajima (Shikoku), Hachiman-hama
   (Shikoku), Misaki (Shikoku)
Oita to: Kobe, Matsuyama (Shikoku)
Saganoseki to: Misaki (Shikoku)
Usuki to: Hachiman-hama (Shikoku)
Saiki to: Sukumo (Shikoku), Hachiman-hama
   (Shikoku)
Hyuga to: Kawasaki (near Tokyo), Kobe,
   Osaka
Shibushi to: Osaka, Tokyo, Naha (Okinawa)
Kagoshima to: Osaka, Naha (Okinawa)
Hakata to: Naha (Okinawa)
Kokura to: Tokushima (Shikoku), Tokyo,
   Kobe
Moji to: Osaka

For services between Kyushu and Honshu,
the description is given in the section
covering the port on Honshu or Kyushu.

For services between Kyushu and
Shikoku, details are given in the Shikoku
section.

Fukuoka-ken

KITAKYUSHU

After crossing from Shimonoseki (on
western Honshu) to Kyushu, the first city
encountered is Kitakyushu, 'North
Kyushu city', a composite of five formerly
separate cities (Moji, Kokura, Tobata,
Yahata and Wakamatsu) that stretches a
considerable distance along the north-
eastern coast of the island.

Few people will want to visit this city for
its tourist attractions, unless of course you
are enamoured of steel mills, smoke
stacks and other appurtenances of a
modern industrial city. Fortunately, it is
the only major city of this kind in Kyushu;
most of the island is still green and natural
attractions abound. It has been pushing for
development in producing semiconductor
products and has achieved about 40% of
present Japanese production, so Kyushu
has been nicknamed 'Silicon Island'.

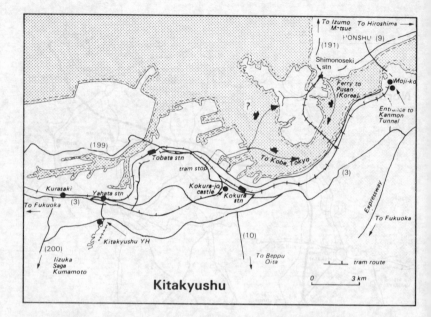

Kitakyushu

(map labels: To Izumo M~tsue, To Hiroshima, HONSHU (9), (191), Shimonoseki stn, Ferry to Pusan (Korea), Moji-ko, Entrance to Kanmon Tunnel, (199), Tobata stn, tram stop, To Kobe, Tokyo, (3), Kurasaki, Yahata stn, Kokura-jo castle, Kokura stn, To Fukuoka, (3), Expressway, To Fukuoka, Kitakyushu YH, (200), Iizuka Saga Kumamoto, (10), To Beppu Oita, tram route, 0 3 km)

If you do have a reason for staying in the area, there are some places worth visiting. About 500 metres west of Kokura station there is a reconstruction of parts of the once-great Kokura-jo castle. The original was destroyed in 1866 during the fighting that attended the Meiji restoration.

Places to Stay

In addition to the usual hotels and *ryokan* there is also the nice *Kitakyushu Youth Hostel* (tel (093) 681-8142), which has good views. It is accessible from Yahata station.

Getting There & Away

Train The simplest way of getting to and from Shimonoseki, on the other side of the Kanmon Strait, is by JR train (which goes through a tunnel). Any of the several stations on the Kyushu side can be used as the starting point, such as Moji, Kokura etc. Moji is the first after exiting the tunnel.

Ferry There are convenient connections to Tokyo, Kobe, Matsuyama (Shikoku) and the Osaka area by ferries leaving from two ports in the Kitakyushu area.

From Kokura (one of the cities making up Kitakyushu) there are nightly boats to Sakai (south of Osaka) and Matsuyama, and three per day to Kobe, plus one every second day to Tokyo. From Shin Moji-ko there are two boats per day to Osaka. All of these boats leave in the afternoon or evening, arriving the next morning, except the ones to Tokyo as it is considerably further.

Kokura-ko harbour dock is not far from Kokura station; there should be a bus. There is likely to be a bus from JR Moji station to Shin Moji-ko, but it will be necessary to check on the spot.

Hitching Hitching from central Kitakyushu to the other side is not exactly simple, as the city is the seventh largest in Japan and is very spread out. To get to Honshu, I would recommend taking the train across and following the instructions in the Shimonoseki section for hitching from there.

Similarly, it is simpler to take a train or a bus some distance out of Kitakyushu before trying to hitch to other places in Kyushu. For the adventurous who would nevertheless like to try to hitch out of Kitakyushu, the entrance to the Kanmon tunnel for cars (where it should be possible to get a lift to either Shimonoseki or into Kyushu) is not far from Moji station (the final stop of the tram line that passes through the city) or JR Moji-ko station.

As for the expressway across Kanmon-ohashi bridge and on to Hiroshima, Osaka and Tokyo or through Kyushu to Kumamoto, etc, the nearest interchange is some distance from the centre of the city and quite difficult to reach; local help would be required to find out how to get to it.

AROUND KITAKYUSHU
Hiraodai
An unusual geological feature that makes a pleasant excursion and hike in the open countryside (a rarity close to cities in most of Japan) is Hiraodai. This is a rolling plateau covered by weathered and rounded outcroppings of limestone, many taller than a person; this is known as a karst tableland. A similar sight can be seen at Akiyoshidai in Yamaguchi-ken on Honshu. At the east end of Hiraodai lies the limestone grotto of Sembetsu.

Hiraodai can be reached most easily by JR (or Route 322) from Kokura to Ishihara, from where a local road leading to Yukuhashi passes Hiraodai. There might be direct bus transport from Kokura; make inquiries at the station.

FUKUOKA (HAKATA)
The largest city of Kyushu, Fukuoka has a limited number of attractions worth

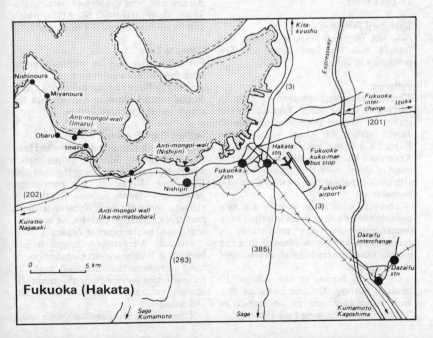

Fukuoka (Hakata)

looking at. It is also an international port of entry.

Information

If setting out from Hakata station, first stop at the Travel Centre and pick up a copy of their map of the Fukuoka area. Everything is marked in both Japanese and English, so it can be useful for finding your way almost anywhere. There are other information centres in the same station but they don't have much useful info, so be sure to get the right one.

There is a Korean consulate in Fukuoka, making it a convenient place to obtain a visa.

If you need film, Doi camera shop, near the station, has good prices.

Sumiyoshi-jinja Shrine

This shrine, less than one km from Hakata station, has buildings dating from 400 years ago. Its annual festival is held on 12-14 October.

Shofuku-ji Temple

Also not far from Hakata station, this temple was the first centre of Zen teachings in Japan.

Potteries

There are several pottery centres in northern Kyushu. Some, if not all, are the legacy of Korean potters who came to Japan about 200 years ago. Within Fukuoka are the well-known towns of Agano and Koishiwara; less famous is the town of Onta, near Koishiwara, the last village of Japanese potters who work as a cooperative.

There is usually no pottery for sale because the climbing kilns are fired only occasionally and the production is generally spoken for in advance, but the methods used are traditional, as is some of the equipment.

Of the 14 houses in the village, 10 produce pottery. On the Fukuoka city map is another pottery, indicated as 'Takatori Kiln (Famous Folk Pottery)'.

Festival

10-12 July: This is the time of the *Daiko* drum matsuri festival, when over 100 floats carrying drums and drummers parade through the city. Japanese drumming is both complex and unexpectedly primitive, so such a festival is interesting.

Places to Stay

There are many hotels, business hotels and *ryokan* in Fukuoka, as well as in nearby hot-spring resorts. Assistance is available at the information centre at Hakata station.

Daizaifu Youth Hostel (tel (092) 922-8749) is a temple and these are usually the best hostels in Japan, but it has only 24 beds. It is close to Dazaifu jinja shrine, one of the major places to see in Fukuoka.

Other hostels in the area include the 90-bed *Yakiyama-kogen Youth Hostel* (tel (0948) 22-6385), which is about half way to Kitakyushu, and the 96-bed *Kitakyushu Youth Hostel* (tel (093) 681-8142), which can be reached from JR Yahata station.

Places to Eat

For those who may be suffering acute junk-food withdrawal symptoms, there is a *Shakey's Pizza Parlour* in Fukuoka. It is in the central business district; ask for directions at the travel centre.

Getting There & Away

Air Fukuoka is connected by air with Hong Kong, Honolulu, Manila, Taipei, Seoul and Pusan – the latter being the cheapest flight from Korea. It is a convenient gateway to Japan because it allows a circular route through Kyushu without backtracking before carrying on east and northward to the heart of Japan.

Fukuoka Airport is a delight to use because it is only a short distance out of town and connections are easily made by frequent bus service from the main JR station (which is called Hakata, not Fukuoka).

There is only one drawback with using

Fukuoka and that is that budget travellers, especially those who have been in and out of Japan on a regular basis (as if working illegally and prolonging their stay in this manner), may have a rougher time here than at the larger, more cosmopolitan ports of entry.

For those who are entitled to a 90-day period-of-stay by bilateral agreement, the bad news is that the officials here, like those at Shimonoseki, have been very reluctant to grant it and one is often forced to accept a much less desirable 60-day 'tourist' status.

Train Hakata is the western terminus of the Shinkansen, and the trip to or from Tokyo takes less than seven hours by the fastest trains.

SOUTH OF FUKUOKA
Dazaifu-Temmangu Shrine
Less than an hour south of Fukuoka by train is the famous shrine Dazaifu-Temmangu, one of the highest ranking shrines in Japan. The grounds and picturesque bright orange buildings (dating from 1590) are attractive and include an arched stone bridge. From the 7th to the 14th century, Dazaifu was the residence of the Kyushu governor. The shrine's annual festival takes place on 23-25 September and features a procession.

Close to Dazaifu-jinja are Komyo-ji and Kanzeon-ji temples, as well as the Fukuoka-ken Rekishi Hakubutsukan (historical museum). Komyo-ji has a very pretty Zen-style garden. Kanzeon-ji has a number of valued Buddhist images on display.

Getting There & Away The shrine is easily reached by the Nishitetsu line, leaving from Nishitetsu-Fukuoka station, first to Nishitetsu-Futsukaichi (12 minutes by *kyuko* express), where it is necessary to change trains and go two stops to Dazaifu station. From there the shrine is about 500 metres away.

If you are beginning at Hakata station it is simpler to go by JR to Kokutetsu-Futsukaichi station, then take a bus to the other station, Nishitetsu-Futsukaichi. These buses run every 10 minutes. Dazaifu Youth Hostel is near the shrine.

Kurume
If you are interested in pottery, it is worth visiting the kilns and potters in the towns of Koishiwara, Hoju and Ichinose, all in the vicinity of Kurume.

Harazura & Hita
Two hot-spring resort towns, Harazura (in southern Fukuoka-ken) and Hita (just across the boundary in Oita-ken) feature *ukai* (cormorant fishing) on the nearby river; the dates are May to September in Harazuru, and until the end of October in Hita.

WEST OF FUKUOKA
The major route west from Fukuoka takes you along the coast toward Nagasaki.

Anti-Mongol Wall
To combine a swim on a white-sand beach with a bit of history, visit the remnants of the 20-km wall built around Hakata Bay to prevent the landing of the Mongol hordes in 1281. Kublai Khan made one try to invade in 1274, but was beaten off.

A defensive wall was built over the following years, but it was feared that the next wave of invaders would nevertheless overpower the defenders. However, a typhoon sank the Mongol fleet, thus saving the Japanese the need to use the wall. This was the last attempted invasion until 1945, which explains the great shock felt at the end of WW II. Because this wind saved Japan, it was named *Kamikaze* (Wind of the Gods), a word revived in the last war, but with less effective results.

Only traces of these walls (originally three metres high) remain. Near Imazu, one stretch of 100 metres or so has been excavated from the sand. Once you see this remnant (still nearly two metres

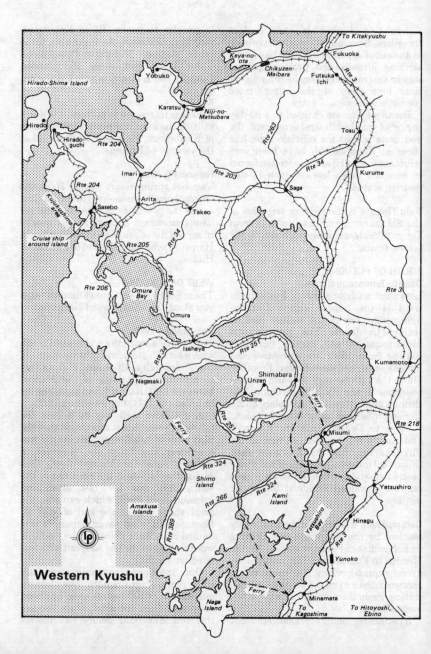

Western Kyushu

high), you realise that the traces of rocks, just below the sand through the groves of picturesque twisted pine trees near the shore, are the top of the wall. From here it is only a short walk to the beach.

Getting There & Away To take the bus from Hakata station, ask for the Nishi-no-ura yuki bus, which probably leaves from gate No 3 on the 2nd floor. The location is shown on the handout map in Japanese as well as English. The wall is marked as 'Genko Fort', but ask for 'boheki', which is its local name. The bus trip takes about two hours.

GENKAI PARK
The anti-Mongol wall at Imazu, and others (shown on the handout map, but said to be in much poorer condition), are part of Genkai Quasi-National Park that extends about 90 km along the north coast of Kyushu into Saga-ken. Other features are more white sand beaches and more groves of gnarled pine trees, the best-known of which is at Niji-no-matsubara.

Keya-no-Ota
The main attraction of the park is 'the Great Cave of Keya', a rocky promontory at the western end of Itoshima-hanto peninsula. It juts 60 metres out of the sea and is formed by groups of parallel columns of basalt projecting at different angles (probably created as lava cooled in a large mass and formed giant crystals). The sea has eroded a cave nine metres high and 18 metres wide that extends more than 50 metres into the rock. Like most attractions in Japan it has many tourists and tour buses.

Keya-no-Ota can be reached by bus from either Chikuzen-Maibara station (40 minutes) or directly from Hakata station (95 minutes).

Saga-ken

KARATSU, IMARI & ARITA
These are the three famous pottery towns in Saga-ken. The pottery is noted for its very colourful glazes and is considered more artistic than that from the kilns of Seto (near Nagoya in central Honshu). You can get to the Imari potteries in 15 minutes by bus from Imari station, passing through pretty countryside with thatched-roof houses.

Festival
3-5 November: Giant floats of papier-mâché figures are drawn through the streets of Karatsu.

ISLANDS OFF THE NORTHWEST COAST
There are three large islands off the northwest coast of Kyushu: Iki-shima, Tsushima and Hirado-shima. While none has any particular sightseeing attractions, nearly all are relatively isolated and visited by only a few foreigners. The people are therefore 'unspoilt' and friendly, though even less able to communicate with outsiders than most Japanese, as they have still less incentive to learn foreign languages, and their dialects are usually incomprehensible even to other Japanese.

Iki-shima and Tsushima are both accessible from Saga-ken and Fukuoka-ken. For up-to-date information on transport to these two islands, as well as scheduled services to a number of smaller islands not mentioned here, consult the *Jikokuhyo*.

Iki-shima Island
This island is recommended for cyclists as there is flat terrain and beautiful beaches; the island is small and the sea always close.

Places to Stay There are several campsites and a *ryokan*.

Getting There & Away There are four boats a day, between Iki and Yobuko on the tip of the peninsula near Karatsu, which take just over an hour, as well as others from Hakata (2½ hours). There are also three flights a day from Fukuoka.

Tsushima Island

Very close to Korea, this island is much larger and more rugged than Iki, and you will need a bus or car for transport. One traveller reported several quizzings by police during his visit, because foreigners are very rare and there is a lot of drug smuggling from Korea. Just prior to his arrival a smuggler had been killed by police bullets, so the authorities were edgy.

Places to Stay In addition to *ryokan*, there are two *youth hostels* on the island (one a temple) and a Kokuminshuku.

Getting There & Away There is a boat service to Kokura as well as to Iki. There are also four daily flights to and from Fukuoka.

Hirado-shima Island

At the north of Nagasaki-ken is Hirado-shima island, accessible by bridge from Hirado-guchi (JR station). The island is hilly with many high cliffs.

Kujukushima Islands

Between Hirado-shima island and Sasebo (on the coast of Nagasaki-ken) is Kujukushima ('99 islands'), in fact a group of about 170 islets.

A cruise boat makes two trips daily from Sasebo (Kashi-mae pier).

Goto-shima Islands

This is the name of five islands west of Kujukushima. Like other islands in the area, they are mostly agricultural and fishing communities. The coast is rugged.

Getting There & Away Access is by boat from Nagasaki, Sasebo, and other centres, as well as by air from Fukuoka.

Nagasaki-ken

NAGASAKI

So much has been written about Nagasaki that it is difficult for another travel writer to try to follow suit. However, although I enjoyed my visit to Nagasaki, I would not claim that it is the one and only place in Kyushu (or in Japan for that matter) to visit, as implied by some writers who have gone before. It certainly has several attractions, but reality should temper enthusiasm. It definitely lacks the 'haunting beauty' and 'fatal charm' gushed by one writer.

Nagasaki has an interesting history and has long flourished as a port. During the period when Japan was closed to the outside world (the early 1600s to 1867), Nagasaki was virtually the only gateway open for trade. Formerly a point of contact with the Asian continent, it became the entry point for western knowledge (mainly via the Dutch) and religion (Roman Catholicism).

Nagasaki gained some fame through Puccini's *Madame Butterfly* but it might never have become so well known if it had not been the second city to be A-bombed, having been picked as a target because of the huge Mitsubishi shipyards across the harbour from the city.

Information

There is an information office at Nagasaki station where maps and tourist literature in English are available. The Nagasaki Tourist Centre is on the 2nd floor of the building opposite the station.

Things to See

The following route covers all the major places of interest. It is based on the tram routes, beginning and ending at the Dejima Pier/Nagasaki station area.

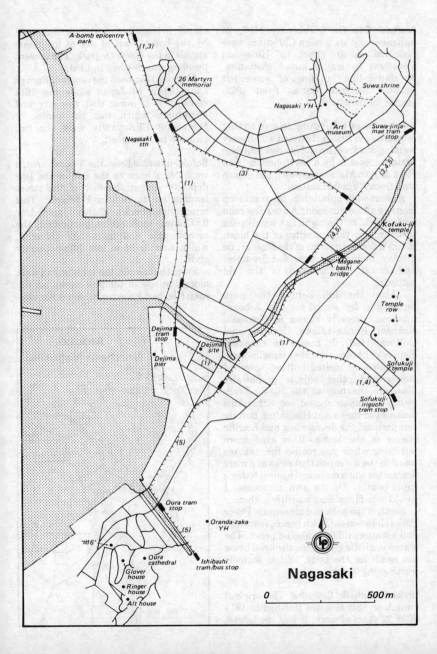

Nagasaki

0   500 m

Martyrs' Site On 5 February 1597, 20 Japanese and six foreign Christians were crucified in an effort by Hideyoshi Toyotomi to stamp out Christianity. A church-like building of somewhat unusual features (dating from 1962) stands on the site.

A-bomb Relics Everything related to that fateful day in 1945 is clustered within easy walking distance. From Nagasaki station, easiest access is by a north-bound tram No 1 or 3 to Matsuyama-cho, the eighth stop from Nagasaki station.

A short walk uphill from the tram stop leads to the main road. Across the road and a little to the right is a small park which marks the epicentre of the blast. Relics showing the force of the blast are on display, including a crumpled fire-tower and a bit of the wall of the old cathedral.

Atop the hill behind the park (accessible by stairs) is the A-bomb museum, properly known as Nagasaki Kokusai Bunka-kaikan (International Cultural Hall). It houses an excellent display of photos and other remains from the explosion; melted bottles, scorched stones and other objects graphically illustrate the fury of the blast. Every visitor to Japan should see either this museum or the one at Hiroshima to fully comprehend the devastating and horrific effects of the bomb. It is even more terrifying when you realise the damage was done by a weapon that rates as a mere firecracker when measured against today's super-bombs. Of the two museums, I would rate Hiroshima's a little higher.

North of the park and museum is Peace Park (Heiwa-koen), with ponds, fountains and a statue said to symbolise peace. The statue is a little grotesque, the head being too small for the body, and is scarcely worth going to see.

Urakami Catholic Cathedral The original church on this site was finished in 1914 after 32 years of work. It was the largest church in the orient until it was destroyed by the bomb. Part of one of its pillars stands in the epicentre park. The present building was finished in 1959.

Nagasaki has been the centre of Roman Catholicism in Japan since the 16th century; it is ironic that this city and Hiroshima which was the centre of Protestant Christianity were the two cities to be A-bombed.

Sofuku-ji Temple From the A-bomb area, a tram No 1 back to the end of the line deposits you at the foot of the street leading up to Sofuku-ji temple. This temple dates back to 1629 and is noted for its Chinese architecture, particularly the second gate and main hall (Hondo), which were built in late Ming-dynasty style.

From the temple, the athletic can walk along the row of temples shown on the map (the best known of which is Kofuku-

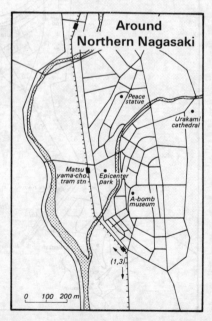

Around Northern Nagasaki

ji) via Megane-bashi bridge to Suwa-jinja shrine. An alternative route is tram No 4 to Suwa-jinja-mae.

Megane-bashi Bridge 'Spectacles Bridge' has two steep arches, and when the river level is high enough the reflection forms two ovals that look like eyeglasses. The original bridge was built in 1634 with the help of Chinese Buddhist priests but was swept away in a flood caused by a typhoon in 1983. The bridge was rebuilt in three months in its original form.

Suwa-jinja Shrine Although there is no particular 'sight' here, the buildings are attractive and typical of large shrines throughout Japan. There is a good view over the city from the hill on which Suwa-jinja stands. The grounds are heavily wooded and offer an escape from city buildings. Okunchi is the shrine's annual festival (7-9 October), and its dragon dance dates from the days of trade with China.

Glover House From the shrine area, tram No 5 (south-bound) leads to Glover House. Get off at the first stop after the tram turns left to run beside a canal. A nearby bridge leads to the house.

One of the best-known landmarks of Nagasaki, Glover House is a large English-style mansion that was the home of a remarkable Englishman named (what else?) Glover. He supervised the construction of railways and the opening of mines, and introduced a tremendous amount of modern technology to Japan after it was opened to the world in the latter part of the 19th century.

The house has a lovely garden, and the view from the porch out over the harbour is probably the finest in the city. The interior of the house is well preserved. Attesting to the numbers of visitors is an outdoor escalator that lifts people up the hill on which the house is perched.

In the grounds, observe (for humour's sake) the statue of Madame Butterfly.

Whether there ever was such a person is not really known but there is certainly no connection with this house. However, local tourist authorities are pushing the story for all it's worth.

Nearby are three other houses of the same era, two of which are also known for their former residents, Alt and Ringer. The third house (No 16) has considerable quantities of Victorian bric-a-brac. In the bottom of the building is a museum of portable shrines, costumes and a dragon – all of which are carried in the annual Okunchi festival. A videotape shows scenes from the celebrations.

Oura Tenshu-do Catholic Cathedral This is the oldest Gothic-style structure in Japan, dating from 1865. It was built in memory of the 26 Christian martyrs. A museum (*shiryokan*) in front of the cathedral has exhibits showing the history of the persecution of the Christians under the Tokugawa.

From this area, tram No 5 returns to Dejima Pier area.

Koshibyo-tojinkan This building is in very traditional Chinese style with red pillars and walls, and a yellow roof with dragons cavorting on the peaks. The original temple, built by the many Chinese merchants once in the city, was destroyed by the A-bomb. The present structure is now a museum of traditional Chinese art.

Dejima Pier The pier where visiting cruise ships dock is named after Dejima Island, a small body of land to which Dutch traders were restricted during the closed years when Japan's only connection with the rest of the world was through Nagasaki. The island no longer exists, as the harbour was filled in to make the pier, and the dock area is now further out than the island used to be. A garden and reproduction of an old warehouse now stand on the site of the former island.

Nagasaki Aquarium There is an aquarium about 12 km from the city; access is by bus or taxi from Nagasaki station.

Prins Willem In mid-1984 it was announced by the tourist firm Nagasaki Dutch Village that they had ordered a full-scale exact replica of the Dutch warship *Prins Willem* which was launched in 1650. It is like the ships which sailed between the Netherlands and Asia at that time – sea trade which brought great riches and power to the small European country. It is planned that the ship will serve as a seafaring museum and be moored in Omura Bay.

Views of the City The best view of the city is from the top of Mt Inasa (332 metres). A cable-car runs to the top from a point about one km from Nagasaki station. The view at night is especially attractive, somewhat resembling Hong Kong, although the lights are neither as numerous nor as bright.

Places to Stay
As can be expected at a very popular destination for domestic travel there is plenty of accommodation available, with many hotels and *ryokan* clustered around the station.

As in any city of reasonable size in Japan, assistance in finding a place to stay can be obtained from the station or the tourist centre.

There are three youth hostels: two are in town, the third is quite far away. *Nagasaki-kenritsu Youth Hostel* (tel (0958) 23-5032) is a 12-minute walk from Nagasaki station. Go up to the end of the little street opposite the station, then turn right and cross seven intersections of various sizes. It is a little to the left from there.

Nagasaki Oranda-zaka Youth Hostel (tel (0958) 22-2730) is farther away, and can be reached by taking a No 1 tram. Staff at the information office could help.

Getting There & Away
Air Nagasaki has an air link with Shanghai, a city with which it has historic trade ties, and it also has flights to several other places within Japan.

The airport is 10 minutes from Omura station by bus and 90 minutes from Nagasaki by bus.

Train Nagasaki is served by JR lines.

Bus Inter-city buses leave from the terminal across from Nagasaki station.

Hitching If you are travelling by thumb, you will find it simplest to take a train or bus to Isahaya and start hitching from there.

Getting Around
The easiest way to get around the city is by tram, as the five lines pass near all points of interest and are clearly numbered. The lines and their turning points are shown on the map.

City buses cover much more extensive routes but they are difficult to use because they are identified only in Japanese.

NAGASAKI TO KUMAMOTO
From Nagasaki, one of the most popular routes is via Obama and Unzen to Shimabara, from where frequent ferries ply to and from Misumi on the Uto Peninsula. From Misumi it is only a short distance north to Kumamoto. The route south from Uto leads to Kagoshima.

Unzen
In the days of the British empire, Unzen was a favourite resort for colonial officials and old China hands (breeds now vanished). There are still some attractions, though most travellers stop only for a look around before continuing.

Unzen has golf courses and other recreational facilities, but its *raison d'être* is the hot-spring waters. These boil up – violently in places – in a steaming and desolate, but colourful, area near town.

The waters are conducted to the various hotels for the baths. The claims of curative properties would get hotels in plenty of hot water of another kind if made in countries with strong consumer-protection laws. During the days of Christian persecution, these boiling waters were put to another use – disposing of those who refused to renounce their faith.

Another attraction of Unzen is the Roman Catholic church, a Y130-million, brick-clad building which is a bit of a curiosity as there were only eight known catholics in the area when it was built in 1982. This anomaly makes a little more sense with the knowledge that the area's relics, remains and evidence of the exotic Christian history and tradition constitute one of the mainstays of what had been a declining tourist industry.

A toll road loops up between Nodake and Myoken mountains. The view from the road itself is not spectacular, but from the top cable-car station there is a beautiful view of the ocean and offshore islands. Wildflowers are pretty in spring and summer, while leaves are the attraction in autumn. The youth hostel at Unzen is unusually large.

Shimabara

Another place of interest is Shimabara, with its reconstructed castle. The original was destroyed in 1637 in an episode during the government's effort to eradicate Christianity. About 30,000 of the faithful captured the castle but it was later retaken by the authorities and the defenders were slaughtered.

The castle was ruined at that time but the large reproduction, built in 1964, recreates the beautiful appearance of the white original and serves as a museum. Among the exhibits are *fumi-e* ('trampling images'), images of Christian significance upon which people had to tread in order to prove that they were not Christians. The castle is about 400 metres west of the station. Ferries to Misumi are frequent.

Misumi

From Misumi it is 27 km to the main north-south road (Route 3) at Uto, from where it is only 15 km to Kumamoto. An alternative is a visit to the Amakusa Islands.

Kumamoto-ken

KUMAMOTO

Kumamoto is the third largest city on Kyushu and was one of the major military centres of Japan until the last century. It is best described as rather provincial; although it has modern buildings, shops, etc, it is not a metropolis.

Some sections of the city are delightfully seedy and are worth seeing for that reason before they are conquered by the aluminium-and-glass invasion that has transformed the traditional appearance of nearly all Japan.

The two major attractions of Kumamoto are Suizenji-koen garden and Kumamoto-jo castle, plus a shrine or two.

Information

A small handout map with tram lines and major sightseeing spots is available at the station. It has sufficient English to be useful.

Suizenji-koen Park

This is a very attractive landscape garden, larger than most in Japan. I would rate it ahead of two of the 'Big Three' gardens, behind only Kenroku-en in Kanazawa. The hills and water have been arranged to resemble famous natural features, such as Mt Fuji and Biwa-ko lake, and there is a teahouse identical in every feature to one of the most famous of such buildings in Kyoto. The garden dates from 1632, so it is much older than the more celebrated ones mentioned. It was part of a villa of the Hosokawa clan, who once commanded the region.

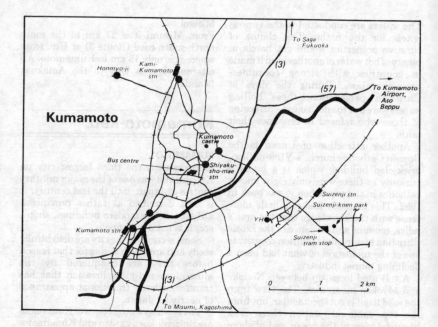

The park is easily reached by tram from Kumamoto station; the stop is Suizenji.

Kumamoto-jo Castle

Kumamoto was once one of the principal castle towns of Japan, ranking only behind Osaka and Nagoya. The original castle was finished in 1607 and stood until 1867, when most of it was burned in a siege during the civil war period at the time of the Meiji restoration.

In 1960 the structure was reproduced in concrete and now houses a good museum. I usually play down such reproductions for their lack of authenticity but this one is so large and set in such attractive surroundings of tall trees and stone walls that it is worth at least a look if you are passing through.

The castle is easily reached on foot or by tram from the station; the stop is 'Shi-yaku-sho mae' (town hall).

Other Attractions

Other attractions that can be singled out are Hommyo-ji temple and Tatsuta-koen park. The latter houses a folk-art museum (mingei hakubutsukan) as well as an attractive garden and teahouse from 350 years ago.

Indefinable attractions include several streets of shops that appear to have survived from pre-war times and preserve the appearance of the Japan of those days. The buildings are all wood, with features such as sliding wooden doors and small glass panes, and canopies that overhang and shelter the sidewalk.

The other intangible feature of the city is an impression of 'raunchiness'. This is the only city in Japan where I encountered a 'pink-light' area. Along a riverside road I passed several small buildings, the open doorway of each illuminated by a single pink fluorescent tube. Inside could be seen a small bar in one room and a bed in the adjacent one; there was a woman standing near the doorway. Yes, Kumamoto is a little out of the ordinary.

Festivals

15 September: At Fujisaki Hachi-mangu shrine there is an annual procession of 'warriors' on horseback, who wear ancient armour to escort three portable shrines.

Places to Stay

There are several hotels, *minshuku*, etc, in Kumamoto. Assistance in finding a room can be obtained at information centres at the airport, station or travel agencies.

There are also two youth hostels: *Suizenji Youth Hostel* (No 8406, tel (0963) 71-9193), accessible in 25 minutes by tram from the station, and *Kumamoto-Shiritsu Youth Hostel* (No 8408, tel (0963) 52-2441), a municipal hostel that is more difficult to reach.

Hostels in the Mt Aso area can be considered as alternatives because of the short travelling time from Kumamoto (100 minutes by train).

Getting There & Away

Air In recent times Kumamoto has joined the list of international ports of entry for air travellers. Although the connections are limited to Seoul, it is a step forward and offers an alternative to, say, Fukuoka.

The airport is near the road/rail route to Mt Aso, so on arrival you have the option of taking the bus into Kumamoto or proceeding directly to the Aso area. From the airport there is a possibility of a direct bus service to Aso, or it might be necessary to go to Higo-Otsu station and take a train or bus from there.

Mt Aso Region

Aso-zan (Mt Aso)

The present Aso-zan sits in the midst of the largest volcanic crater on earth, and is still fuming after 30 million years of activity. Several routes go to the top if you have your own vehicle, but for most travellers the simplest way is by bus from either Aso JR station (seven per day; Y530) to the west entrance (Kako-nishi), or from Miyaji JR station (seven per day; Y270) to the east side (Kako-higashi). At one time there was a bus connection at the top between west and east entrances, but this has been suspended. There are also a couple of daily buses to the west side directly from Kumamoto, and a couple more from nearby Akamizu.

The west route goes to the west side of the crater (Kako-nishi). Complete bus schedules are printed in *Jikokuhyo*.

En route to the western peak the road twists and turns up the flank of the mountain passing Aso Youth Hostel (1½ km from Aso station, a 15 minute walk).

At the lush meadows you may see Japanese tourists jumping out of their cars to photograph an exotic species of animal life – the cow. Clearly visible in the green fields are fingers of lava from prehistoric volcanic flows. The road also passes nearby to a quite smallish cone,

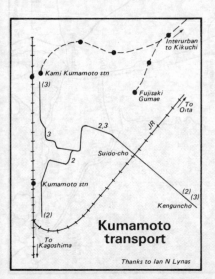

Kumamoto transport

Thanks to Ian N Lynas

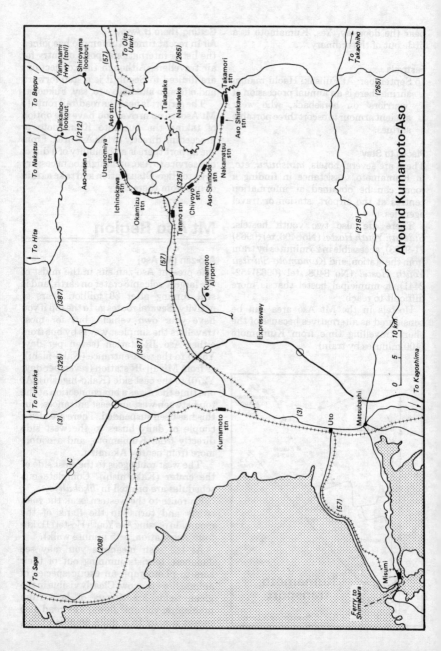

Around Kumamoto-Aso

Komezuka, an afterthought from a later mini eruption.

Eventually the road reaches the flattened top of Aso-zan. From the first lookout near the crest of the road, you can finally see (on a clear day, at least) the enormity of the crater. The cliffs several km away are in fact the walls of the original hole. Its dimensions are given variously as 23 or 32 km north-south, 16 km east-west, and 80 or 128 km in circumference. Any way you measure it, it's huge, and the mind boggles at the amount of energy released from this place. Although the volcano has been active for about 30 million years, the present form probably dates back little more than 120 millennia.

The road circles around a lake before reaching the base station of the Kako-nishi cable car (four minutes to the top). A toll road also goes the short distance to the top, and you can also walk. The view from the top is one of great desolation, mostly black ash thrown out over the centuries. A path leads to the very rim of the main crater (no guard rail – caution!) in the side of Nakadake, on the far side of which can be seen layers of ash and lava – mostly black, but with colourful streaks of dark red. In its own sombre way it is very picturesque.

Far below, down in the deep black cavity, steam billows forth continuously, sometimes diminishing only to burst forth in greater volume. Is it safe? Generally, yes, as a constant watch is kept and visitors are barred from the rim area when it is active. However, in September 1979, while access was barred, a particularly violent explosion hurled head-sized rocks nearly a km away into an area thought safe, killing three sightseers. Prior to this, the last eruption had been in November 1977. These eruptions explain the presence of the numerous concrete domes near the rim, built in 1958 as emergency shelters after an unexpected eruption killed 12 people.

Views of Aso-zan Another good overall view of the crater can be had from Takadake ('High Peak'), an easy hike to the east from the upper station at Kako-higashi.

There are also two places on the northern rim that offer excellent views of the present mountain and the valley floor with its patchwork of small fields. One is Daikanbo, a little distance above Aso-onsen (also known as Uchinomaki-onsen) and accessible from Uchinomaki station. The other is Shiroyama-tempodai, at the rim of the old crater where the Yamanami Highway climbs out of the valley – the view from almost any point here is memorable.

Miyaji

A short distance from Miyaji station lies Aso-jinja shrine. This is one of those attractions that can be described as 'nice if you haven't seen one before'. There are some attractive carvings on the buildings.

Yamanami Highway

Aso is on the highway that links Beppu with Nagasaki. Between Aso and Beppu this road traverses some of the nicest countryside in Kyushu, and some of the most unusual in Japan. It is a rolling highland plateau that passes a number of mountain peaks, like Kuju-san at 1788 metres the highest in Kyushu.

The overall effect is memorable in all seasons; in spring it is made colourful by wildflowers; in summer it is a lush green; and the autumn has its own beauty, for even though all is reduced to shades of brown, the tall pampas grass moves gracefully with the wind.

There are several buses each day that make the run between Aso and Beppu along the Yamanami Highway. Depending on the number of stops, the trip takes three to four hours. An alternative route northward from Aso (for those in a rush) is via Hita, but the attractions of the Yamanami Highway make it preferable.

From Aso, another route goes southeast

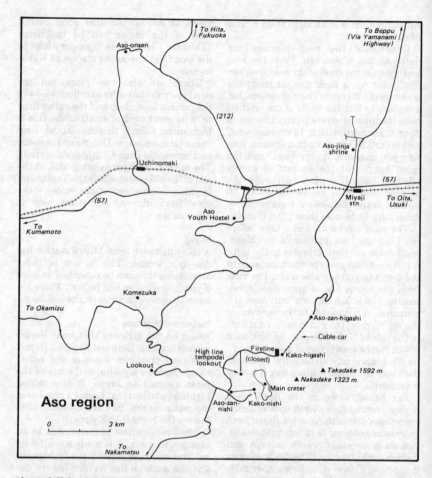

Aso region

through Takachiho Gorge, a very pleasant place to visit. Like Beppu, however, it is in Miyazaki-ken and is described in that section.

Places to Stay

In addition to hotels, *ryokan* and *minshuku*, there are three youth hostels around the base of the mountain. I stayed at *Aso Youth Hostel* (No 8402, tel (09673) 4-0804) and found it pleasant. It can be

reached by the bus to Kako-nishi and is a 15-minute walk from Aso station.

The other hostels are *Aso YMCA Camp Youth Hostel* (tel (09673) 5-0124) and *Murataya-Ryokan* (tel (09676) 2-0066), though one traveller gave a low rating to this last place.

KUMAMOTO TO KAGOSHIMA
Yatsushiro

This is an industrial city of little interest except for pottery addicts; it is the place of origin for Koda-yaki (or Yatsushiro-yaki) pottery, carrying on a tradition started by Korean potters who came here in the 16th century.

In late August and early September, strange lights can be seen in the sea late at night. Known as *shiranui*, it is caused by phosphorescence from a kind of marine life.

Hinagu

The view from the shore near this hot-spring resort is regarded as particularly appealing, taking in the Amakusa Islands and the bay in front of them.

Minamata

This is another industrial city of no touristic merit but it was brought to world attention in the early 1970s because of the illness caused by mercury poisoning, now known as Minamata disease.

Yunoko

The swimming is regarded as particularly good here.

Hitoyoshi

People travelling from the Kumamoto area bound for Kagoshima could do far worse than to turn inland at Yatsushiro and travel through the pretty, wooded valley to Hitoyoshi by rail or road (Route 219). The Kuma River, flowing through the valley, is intensely green.

At Hitoyoshi, both rail and road turn southward; the road (Route 221) to Ebino and Kobayashi, rail to Yoshimatsu and Kagoshima. A branch from Yoshimatsu goes to Ebino and Kobayashi.

From Hitoyoshi, you can shoot the rapids in a 2½-hour trip on the Kuma River for 18 km to Osakahama. The starting point is 1½ km southeast of Hitoyoshi station, opposite the grounds of the former Hitoyoshi-jo castle. The rapids are rated among the three swiftest in Japan, but there is no risk involved.

Kobayashi

This is one entry point for a trip through the very scenic Kirishima National Park. Several buses a day leave for Ebino-kogen, the changing point for the most scenic parts. (This same trip can be made in reverse from Kagoshima.) There are also buses to Kobayashi from Miyazaki many times a day. The trip takes 1½ to two hours.

Kagoshima-ken

KIRISHIMA AREA

The Kirishima area is very scenic and well known for the two peaks, Karakuni-dake (1700 metres) and Takachiho-no-mine (1574 metres) which are 16 km apart; between them stand 21 lesser peaks. Easily visible from the Kirishima Skyline toll road (along which the bus passes) are colourful caldera lakes, craters and other evidence of volcanic activity. It is unusual scenery and is definitely worth seeing.

Ebino-kogen

From Kobayashi, the local road passes under the freeway, twists along to the entrance of the toll road, then twists a great deal more up to Ebino-kogen (Ebino highland plateau). This is the terminus of the bus and the transfer point for another bus bound for Kagoshima.

At Ebino-kogen there are three small lakes, or rather 'ponds'. They are quite round volcano calderas of different colours, including one of the most intense green I have ever encountered. (Use a polarising filter to photograph them, otherwise reflection from the water will wash out the colour.) There are several paths to follow for different views. Karakuni-dake is visible from here as well.

From Ebino-kogen south along the toll road to Shinyu-onsen, various views of Karakuni-dake unfold to the east. A short distance later is Onami-ike, a caldera lake

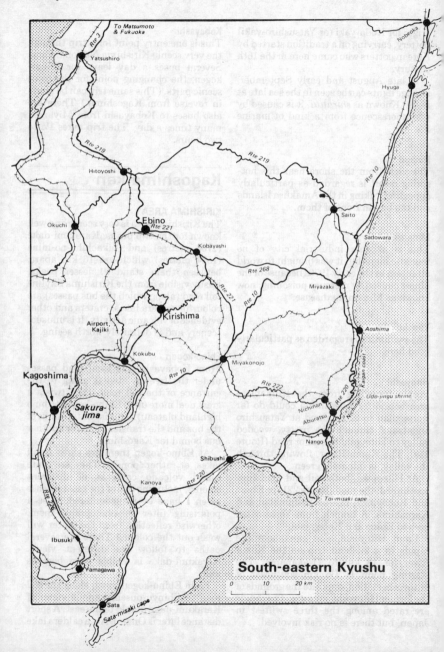

South-eastern Kyushu

0   10   20 km

even more circular than the others mentioned. (Shinsho lookout gives a good view.) Here and there along the road steam pours out of the ground, sometimes beside the road, or even through the cracks in the pavement – evidence of the geothermal activity underfoot.

A road to the east at the junction of the toll roads (Shinyu-onsen) leads to Takachiho-kawara. From here there is a good view of Takachiho-no-mine, an ugly, scenic, active volcano. Its rim is red-brown, heat-discoloured rock; the conical top vanished in prehistoric eruptions. The gaping crater, backdropped by yet more craters and peaks, gives an other-worldly look to the area. Takachiho-kawara is the starting point for hiking to the picturesque cratered cone.

Kirishima

Kirishima-jingu shrine (in Kirishima town, which is 15 minutes from the JR Kirishima-jingu station) is colourful, has wood carvings and is set amidst tall cedars.

Places to Stay There is a *Youth Hostel* in the town as well as *ryokan* and hotels.

Getting There & Away There are several bus services through the Ebino – Kirishima area. The main routes are: Miyazaki – Kobayashi (two bus routes, the cheaper goes from Miyazaki station); Kobayashi – Ebino-kogen/Hayashida-onsen; Ebino-kogen/Hayashida-onsen – Kirishima-jingu – Nishi-Kagoshima.

A map in *Jikokuhyo* shows a bus route past Takachiho-kawara, but although the schedules show no stop, it would seem that service is available; check locally.

KAGOSHIMA

The largest city in southern Kyushu, Kagoshima has an international airport, as well as a seaport for regular boats to and from Okinawa and other southern islands. It is also a stop-over point for some cruise ships.

There are some things to see in Kagoshima itself, and enough attractions nearby that two or three days can be profitably spent looking around.

Kagoshima is one of the few cities in the world where an umbrella is useful, rain or shine. The reason is Kagoshima's most spectacular sight – the massive smoking cone of Sakurajima, across the harbour. Sakurajima has an awesome history of eruptions, and its south peak is still active, regularly spewing fine black ash into the air. With an unfavourable wind it blows over Kagoshima and covers the streets with a thin layer, or drifts into shallow piles. A good view of Sakurajima may be had from the top of Shiroyama, the hill behind the city. Bus No 25 runs close to the top, and you can also walk up from Shiroyama tram stop. The park was formerly the site of a castle.

The main attractions of the city are a little to the north and are associated (like most history of Kagoshima up to the time of the Meiji restoration in 1868) with the Shimazu family, who controlled the area

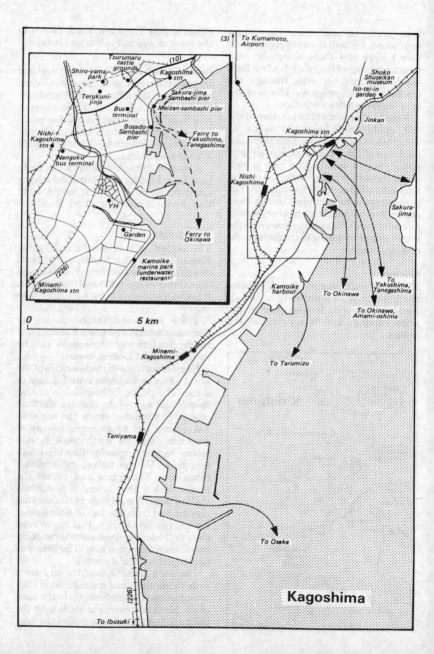

To Kumamoto,
Airport
(3)
(10)

Tsurumaru
castle
grounds
Shiro-yama
park
Kagoshima
stn
Terukuni-
jinja
Sakura-jima
Sambashi pier
Bus
terminal
Meizan-sambashi pier
Bosado-
Sambashi
pier
Nishi-
Kagoshima
stn
Ferry to
Yakushima,
Tanegashima
Nangoku
bus terminal
YH
Ferry to
Okinawa
Garden
(226)
Minami-
Kagoshima stn
Kamoike
marine park
(underwater
restaurant)

Shoko
Shuseikan
museum
Iso-tei-in
garden

Kagoshima stn
Jinkan

Nishi
Kagoshima

Sakura-
jima

Kamoike
harbour

To
Yakushima,
Tanegashima
To Okinawa
To Okinawa,
Amami-oshima

0   5 km

Minami-
Kagoshima

To Tarumizu

Taniyama

To Osaka

Kagoshima

(226)
To Ibusuki

for only five years short of seven centuries.

Information

There is an excellent information centre at Nishi-Kagoshima station (which is the main JR station). The office keeps long hours (6 am to 10 pm), has literature in English and can give any information required for further travel connections, access to boat docks for Okinawa, etc.

Home visit At the information centre at Nishi-Kagoshima station you can arrange a visit to a private home. Families who speak English or other foreign languages have been selected for this programme. Arrangements can also be made by phone (tel 24-1111).

Iso-tei-en

This is a large landscape garden over 300 years old, one of the nicest in Japan, employing ponds and plants in artistic arrangement. It stretches along the coast, overlooking the magnificence of Sakurajima and overlooked by nearby Isoyama (which has a cable car).

In the midst of the garden stands a 13-room villa (traditional Japanese style) and there is a good beach nearby. Iso-tei-en can be reached by city bus No 1 in 20 minutes.

Shoko-Shuseikan Museum

This building was formerly a factory, built in the second quarter of the 19th century by Nariakira Shimazu, an exceptionally enlightened *daimyo* of the area. He introduced his people to a number of western skills such as photography, telegraphy, cotton-spinning, glass and armaments making, etc. The museum displays items from 700 years of the Shimazu family, and is beside Iso-tei-en garden.

Ijinkan

A short distance back toward the city from the museum is Ijinkan ('foreigners residence'), built for overseas advisors in the last century. It is a large wooden house of distinctively foreign architecture (probably early Victorian) and is an anomaly in Japan, especially when contrasted with the lovely and traditional villa in Iso-tei-en garden.

Other Attractions

Another lesser attraction of Kagoshima is the foundation stones and walls of the former Tsurumaru castle. The north-bound tram passes it, and the closest stop is also the most convenient for walking up to Shiroyama ('Castle Mountain').

The castle was built in 1602 but was destroyed in the 1870s when local Satsuma rebels under Saigo opposed the Meiji restoration. There isn't space here to describe Saigo's activities, but his battle was futile and he committed *sepuku* (ritual suicide) in a cave near the castle. His name will be found in many places in Kagoshima, and Terukuni-jinja shrine at the foot of Shiroyama honours him.

There are three potteries in Kagoshima area: Satsuma Toki, Urushima-Togei and Chotaro-Yaki. You can arrange to visit them through the tourist office at the station.

Places to Stay

There are many hotels in Kagoshima and nearby resort towns like Ibusuki and the hot-spring town of Furusato. Help in finding a room can be obtained at Nishi-Kagoshima station.

There is a pleasant *Youth Hostel* in a large, old, semi-western style building in Kagoshima, the *Kagoshima-ken Fujinkaikan*, (tel (0992) 51-1087). It is easily reached from Nishi-Kagoshima station by tram No 1 (north-bound for Kagoshima station). One line branches off to the left after crossing a bridge; shortly afterward another branches off to the right. If your tram doesn't make this right turn, get off at the next stop and catch a tram No 1 going in the opposite direction; it will make the turn. Get off at the fourth stop after the turn, the second after crossing the large Takeno bridge. Buses No 16 and 25 also pass close by.

There are also hostels at Sakurajima across the harbour (*Sakurajima Youth Hostel*, tel (099293) 2150), at Ibusuki (*Ibusuki Youth Hostel*, tel (09932) 2-2758) and another is the *Tamaya Youth Hostel* (tel (09932) 2-3553).

Getting There & Around

Air Kagoshima is linked with Hong Kong, Guam and Nauru (South Pacific) by regular flights. This makes it a convenient port of entry for travellers from those areas who wish to start their Japan travels in the south.

The airport is north of the city and is reached easily by bus. Departures are every 20 minutes, and the trip takes about an hour. If you want to make your way immediately to the Kirishima area, try to get to Kajiki station, from where seven trains a day run directly to Kirishima-jingu station. Information can be obtained at the airport about schedules.

Airport buses make more than one stop in Kagoshima; the best place to get off is Nishi-Kagoshima station (West Kagoshima), which is close to the post office and the central business district.

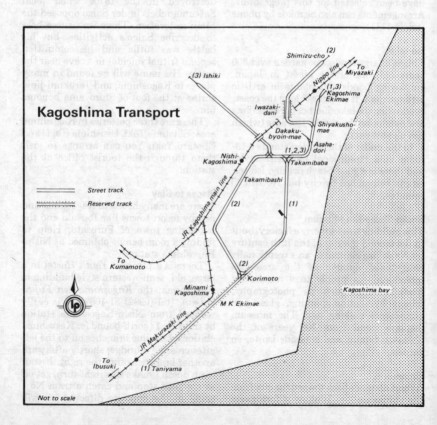

Kagoshima Transport

Street track
Reserved track

Not to scale

Ferry From late July to late August there is a boat every day or two to Osaka. During the rest of the year the boat goes to and from Shibushi, which is accessible by ferry to the Sakurajima side and bus from there, or train to Nishi-Miyakonojo and bus from there. There is also a service every second day to Okinawa.

Ferries to Sakurajima leave the Kagoshima side regularly; the dock (Sakurajima-sambashi) is close to Kagoshima station.

SAKURAJIMA

The cone of Sakurajima dominates the Kagoshima skyline. The city is sometimes compared with Naples, and this is one time that the comparison is not far-fetched (as it often is elsewhere in Japan).

Sakurajima was an island until 1914, when an immense eruption poured out an estimated 3000 million tons of lava and ash, and bridged the gap to the mainland on the side facing away from Kagoshima. The peninsula is virtually one lava-and-ash field, and it is interesting to spend some time looking around the huge and jagged masses of ugly but fascinating black rock. You can take a sightseeing bus from the Sakurajima ferry dock; the trip takes 1¾ hours. The lava field begins about 10 minutes walk away from the dock.

Only Minami-dake (south peak) is still active; it occasionally ejects rock, so climbing is prohibited. Large clouds of smoke and fine ash are also common.

One of the interesting sights on the island is the *torii* gate of a shrine at Kurokami. It was once four metres tall, but the eruption buried so much of it that only the top metre still shows above the ground.

There is a lava observatory (*tempodai*) on the south side of the island, giving a good view of the great lava expanse hurled out during the 20 or so known eruptions during recorded history. On the peninsula are farms that produce the largest

radishes in the world – some 50 cm in diameter and 45 kg in weight!

Other attractions include the Tropical Plants Botanical Garden, and nearby Kamoike Marine Park with its underwater restaurant.

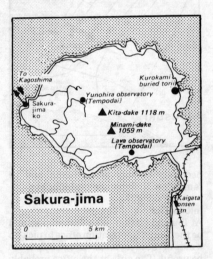

Map: Sakura-jima. To Kagoshima. Sakura-jima ko. Yunohira observatory (Tempodai). Kurokami buried torii. Kita-dake 1118 m. Minami-dake 1059 m. Lava observatory (Tempodai). Kaigata onsen tn. 0 — 5 km.

CHIRAN

This little town, a bit over an hour from Kagoshima by bus, preserves one corner much as it was two centuries ago. Several *samurai* houses are open to the public and are worth visiting to see the lovely gardens and large residences of this formerly privileged class.

Getting There & Away

Buses to Chiran leave Kagoshima from Yama-gataya bus terminal (Yamagataya department store) and there are 11 trips daily in each direction.

IBUSUKI

About an hour south of Kagoshima by train or bus (from Nishi-Kagoshima station), Ibusuki is a pleasant hot-spring resort town. Unlike most such towns, this one can be readily enjoyed by westerners as well as Japanese, because it isn't

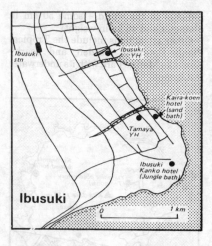

Ibusuki

necessary to stay at a *ryokan* and be familiar with Japanese customs, etc.

Information

At Ibusuki station, your first stop should be the tourist information office to pick up a map of the area; it has enough English to be useful. The girls at the office probably won't speak English but they are friendly and helpful.

Sand Bath (Sunamushi)

One of the most enjoyably unusual sensations of Japan is to be buried up to the neck in hot sand. This is possible where a hot spring surfaces near a beach, permeating the sand and heating it to a high but still bearable temperature.

Go to the Kairo-kuen Hotel and ask for a *sunamushi*; you'll be directed to a small area on the beach behind the hotel next to the sea-wall, where the attendant will dig a hole and bury you. The experience is wonderfully relaxing, probably better left for the end of a day's explorations lest all your energy be sapped at the start!

Jungle Bath (Junguro-furo)

After lying in the sand, move down the road a km or so to the huge Ibusuki Kanko

Hotel, a very popular destination for Japanese honeymooners and recommended to anyone travelling on a non-budget basis. Its facilities are quite luxurious and on a grand scale.

The Jungle Bath is a building the size of an aircraft hangar, to the left of the main hotel building. It contains over 15 pools of hot-spring water of different temperatures, size, shape and mineral content. Luxuriant growths of tropical plants decorate the room. Depending on the season it may be crowded or you may have the place almost to yourself. The sensation of luxuriating in the various pools is marvellous.

Mixed bathing used to be the practice here until recent years but the shy younger generation, and active peepers among the male contingent, has brought about a division of the facilities. The place is definitely worth the Y500 or so. The baths are open from 7 am to 1 am.

There is also a sand bath adjacent to the pools, but it is indoors and the water is piped, so the *sunamushi* at the beach is more authentic.

Kaimon-dake

Another attraction of the Ibusuki area is the graceful conical shape of Kaimon-dake mountain. Buses run from Yamagawa (near the Kanko Hotel) past the mountain to Makurazaki; from there buses run to Kagoshima via Chiran, making it possible to follow a circular route around the south of the peninsula. Kaimon-dake can be climbed in about two hours, starting from Kaimon-dake bus stop.

Another nearby feature is the round caldera lake, Ikeda-ko, and projecting to the southwest of the peninsula is the spit Nagasaki-bana (Long Cape Harbour), which offers an excellent view of Kaimon-dake and the sea.

Places to Eat

For the day's nibbles you could try to find the *Lotteria* coffee shop near the station; a shop in the building sells a variety of *tempura*, good for a picnic lunch.

Getting Around

Bus Tours Several bus tours begin at Ibusuki station and make sightseeing in the area very easy. All but one begin in the morning; some return to Ibusuki, and some terminate in Kagoshima. The basic tours take in Kaimon-dake mountain and Ikeda-ko lake; others take in destinations such as Ibusuki Skyline Highway, Chiran and Sakurajima, while others cross the bay and travel to Sata-misaki cape, ending at Kagoshima.

Information on these tours, and others beginning at Kagoshima, is available from the information centres at Nishi-Kagoshima or Ibusuki stations.

SATA-MISAKI CAPE

Sata-Misaki, across Kagoshima Bay, is the southernmost point of the main islands of Japan. Rugged rocks projecting out of the sea, blue water, and the first lighthouse in the country (built under the supervision of an Englishman soon after the country was opened to foreigners) are the attractions.

The area is a park with lush semitropical vegetation. The cape can be reached easily by tour bus from Nishi-Kagoshima station or by ferry and bus from the Ibusuki area. The ferry crosses from Yamagawa to Sata.

Miyazaki-ken

TOI-MISAKI CAPE

This is another scenic cape, northeast of Sata-misaki cape, famed for small herds of wild horses that are allowed to roam free. It is most easily reached by bus from Aburatsu or Miyazaki; a sightseeing bus travels from the latter along the picturesque Nichinan-kaigan coast.

NICHINAN-KAIGAN COAST

This is a very pretty stretch of coast extending about 100 km from Shibushi Bay to Miyazaki city. It has been compared with the Amalfi coast of Italy, and one cyclist friend said he was tempted to turn around and return the way he had come because he found it so good. Because the climate is so mild, semitropical plants, such as palms, flourish.

Along the way is Udo-jingu shrine, perched on cliffs at the edge of the sea, partly in a cave.

Aoshima Island

Aoshima is a small island connected to the mainland by a causeway. It is covered with betel-nut palms, and the surrounding beach has many tiny sea shells mixed with the sand. It is famous for the Ogres' Washboard, formed over the ages when sedimentary rock became up-ended and eroded to form a series of parallel ridges of rock a metre or so apart. It is quite interesting at low tide.

There is good swimming at Aoshima. Other places to visit are the Cactus Park (with a reputed million plants) and the Subtropical Plant Garden.

Places to Stay Because it is a popular tourist destination, there are many hotels, etc. There is also a *Youth Hostel* close by.

MIYAZAKI

The city of Miyazaki sits in the middle of the area that was the centre of early Japanese civilisation (as we know it). Because this period predates written history, much of its story is mythical and no structures survive. However, some interesting remains have been excavated and are worth visiting. The name Miyazaki means 'shrine promontory'.

Heiwadai-koen Park

The city of Miyazaki is quite ordinary but you can spend your time profitably by visiting Heiwadai-koen park. Heiwa means 'peace', so it is somewhat ironic that the 36-metre tower was built in 1940.

The tower is of little interest unless you look for the marker on the path leading to the main staircase, stand there, and clap your hands. The result will be a strange groaning echo. The main attraction of the park, other than the many flowers that bloom during the first five months, is Haniwa-niwa.

Haniwa-niwa

Haniwa are charming and attractive clay figures that have been excavated from the many burial mounds found in the vicinity. Reproductions of many of these have been artistically located around the park, surrounded by flowers, under shrubs and beside trees. Most of the

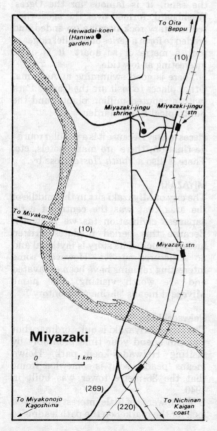

figures are about a metre high so the details of their charming and humorous expressions are clearly discernible. There are knights with horses, court ladies, even a vacant-faced village idiot – I found it an excellent introduction to archaeology.

Miniature reproductions of many of the figures are on sale at the administrative building near the garden. They can also be bought in Tokyo and other centres, but finding them elsewhere can be a problem if you don't have time to look around, and the selection may not be as great.

Miyazaki-jingu Shrine

The first emperor of Japan is said to have been Jimmu, a man known more from myths than actual fact. He is believed to have been the ruler of this area of Kyushu about 600 BC; his descendants (the Yamato tribe) went on to conquer all of Japan, thus determining its culture. He is enshrined in Miyazaki-jingu, and in the grounds there is a museum of items excavated from nearby tombs.

Both Heiwadai and Miyazaki-jingu are accessible from Miyazaki station by bus; the first station north of Miyazaki (called Miyazaki-jingu) is also close to the shrine.

Saitobaru

The early settlers of this area brought with them the practice of building tomb mounds (*kofun*), which was carried on into at least the 7th century – culminating in the largest at Sakai, near Osaka. Similar mound-building customs existed in Korea, especially in the Kyongju area, not too far from the coast facing Japan. It would seem likely that the origin of the early settlers was Korea, but debates among scholars still continue.

Other evidence suggesting continental ties are *haniwa* funerary clay figures of horses and horsemen found in the tombs; horses were not known in Japan until the 3rd century AD. The figures were buried with important people, in place of live humans, as was the practice in China.

This is intended as an introduction to Saitobaru, where about 300 tomb mounds dot the flat countryside. They will probably be of limited interest to most visitors because they are little more than grassy mounds of earth. Some are only a metre or so in height, others are large enough to be mistaken for hills; they will be of greater interest to archaeologists.

Items excavated from the tombs *are* interesting, and are displayed at the museums in Saito and at Miyazaki-jingu; the figures at Haniwa-niwa are reproductions of funerary items from this area.

The tomb area is close to Saito on Route 219, which leads to Hitoyoshi; the closest railway station is Tsuki, reached by branching off the main line at Sadowara.

HYUGA
The city of Hyuga is not especially interesting but ferries connect it with Kobe, Osaka and Kawasaki (near Tokyo).

TAKACHIHO-KYO GORGE
Inland from Nobeoka by road (Route 218) or JR, or southeast from the Mt Aso area by Routes 325 or 265 and 218, is the lovely Takachiho-kyo gorge. The cliffs are formed by columnar basalt, lava that has cooled into parallel pillars of rock up to 80 metres high. The green water of the Gokase River passes through the narrow valley, and waterfalls splash down here and there.

Also of interest is Takachiho-jinja shrine. This sacred site is said to be the 'Cradle of Japan', so the shrine is quite important. Of special interest is the sacred dance, Iwato Kagura, which is performed every day.

Places to Stay
In addition to other accommodation in the area, there are three *youth hostels*. One traveller had nothing but the highest praise for the food at *Yamatoya Youth Hostel*; however I tried three times to obtain accommodation there without success.

Oita-ken

SAIKI
There is a regular boat service between Saiki and Sukumo on Shikoku. Details are given in the Sukumo section.

USUKI AREA
The attraction of the Usuki area is a number of statues of Buddha dating from the 10th and 12th centuries. The most artistic and numerous of these are near Usuki; several are largely intact, while elsewhere only the heads have survived (but these heads are well formed and some of the original colouring remains).

The Usuki images, Seki-butsu, are displayed in a small ravine not far from Kami-Usuki station (JR). A good descriptive pamphlet in English is given out when you enter.

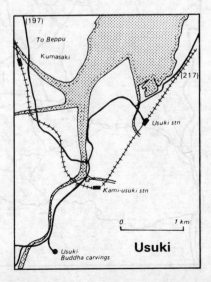

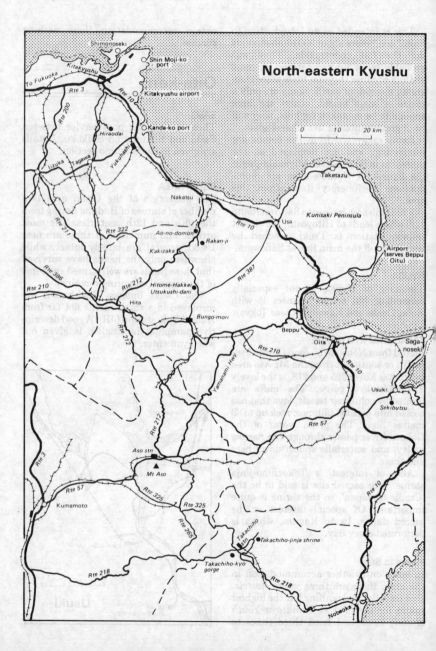

North-eastern Kyushu

0   10   20 km

Other rock sculptures are scattered through the valleys of the Oita and Ono rivers at Motomachi, Takase, Sugao, Ogata and Fukoji, as well as on the Kunisake Peninsula to the north. Motomachi has some of the best preserved images; those at Magari are badly weathered, and those at Takase are so-so.

Saganoseki

There is a ferry service between Saganoseki and Misaki on Shikoku. Details are given in the Misaki section.

Takeda

Ogata and Fukoji are quite close to Takeda (Bungo-Takeda station) where Oka-jo castle once stood. The castle was destroyed in the late 19th century and only its foundation stones and walls still stand, rising high up a hill side. It inspired the very famous composition Kojo-no-tsuki ('Moon over Castle Ruins'), a hauntingly beautiful piece of music, especially when played on the intended *koto* and *shakuhachi* instruments. Its composer, Rentaro Taki, was influenced by western music, so western ears will find it very pleasing. A record including this composition makes a good souvenir of Japan. Also in this area is Harajiki-yaki waterfall.

OITA

There is a daily overnight ferry service each way between Oita and Kobe, with a stop at Matsuyama (Shikoku).

BEPPU

Beppu is one of the best-known hot-spring resorts in Japan, ideal for sybaritic delights and interesting sightseeing. There are eight 'towns' with hot-springs within the bounds of Beppu; the total water outflow exceeds 100 million litres per day.

Information

There is an information centre at the station that gives out maps and other literature, some in English. As usual with Japanese maps, some may only have a superficial resemblance to true scale and actual locations.

The Hells (Jigoku)

For those not particularly interested in hot-spring bathing, there is another attraction – the *jigoku* or 'hells'. In several places around the city, boiling subterranean water comes to the surface, sometimes violently, sometimes quietly but colourfully – would you believe a pond of naturally red water? Other malevolent emanations include geysers and dark, malodorous, bubbling mud pools.

The hells are in two areas of Beppu. Several are clustered close together at Kannawa, about six km from Beppu station, and the other two are a couple of km farther away. The first cluster can be reached from Beppu station by bus No 16, 17, 24, 25 or 27; get off at Kannawa.

A ticket for entry to most of the nine hells is available for the price of five. (Actually, only about five of them are really worth visiting.) The following list describes the hells from west to east, and then the separate ones.

Hon Bozu Jigoku Not included on the multiple ticket, and some distance up a long hill (accessible from Hon Bozu bus stop, the second after Kannawa), this hell features a number of grey mud pools that plurp and plop in a humorous manner. Recommended more to those who will not have any other opportunity to see such boiling mud.

Umi Jigoku *Umi* means sea, and the water here is a very picturesque green. It is hot enough to boil eggs, as demonstrated by a basket of them suspended in the water. Around the grounds are *torii* gates. There is a second pond, also green, but cooler.

Yama Jigoku This is of minimal proportions, and wild animals on display are the so-called attraction. Their living conditions

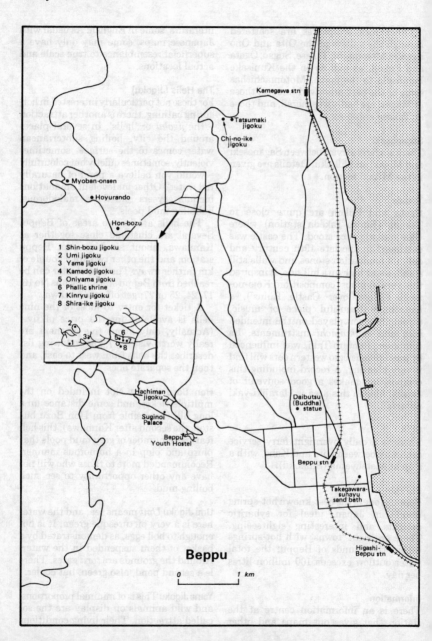

Kamegawa stn

Tatsumaki
jigoku

Chi-no-ike
jigoku

Myoban-onsen

Hoyurando

Hon-bozu

1 Shin-bozu jigoku
2 Umi jigoku
3 Yama jigoku
4 Kamado jigoku
5 Oniyama jigoku
6 Phallic shrine
7 Kinryu jigoku
8 Shira-ike jigoku

2
3
4
6
5
7
8
1

Hachiman
jigoku

Suginoi
Palace

Beppu
Youth Hostel

Beppu stn

Daibutsu
(Buddha)
statue

Takegawara-
sunayu
sand bath

Beppu

0   ___   1 km

Higashi-
Beppu stn

demonstrate an unfortunate Japanese trait of not caring for the comfort of animals. Not recommended.

Garden The garden on the corner between the hells is pleasant, but not particularly noteworthy. Admittance is separate.

Oniyama Jigoku The hell content here is negligible; the attraction is a number of crocodiles.

Phallic Shrine Amidst the hells is this unusual 'museum', which houses a sizeable collection of carved phalluses and other erotica (appropriate for a hot-spring town, where these sum up a major industry). For those with an earthy sense of humour and Y1500, recommendable; for those easily shocked, to be avoided. It can be recognised by the Indian sculptures in metal.

Kinryu Jigoku The name means 'golden dragon'. There is nothing to see except clouds of steam and gaudy, faded Buddhist images. A waste of time.

Shiroike Jigoku The attraction is a cloudy-white pond and several small aquaria of fish not native to Japan, including large ungainly pirarucu from the Amazon. The pond is similar to that at Hoyurando (described later) but of minor interest. The name, by the way, means 'white pond'.

Kamado Jigoku One of the main attractions here is the noise, as steam jets non-stop out of the ground with a great roar. Also interesting is red-brown bubbling mud. If one dares to believe signs, the precipitated minerals on sale are good for the following collection of ailments: 'chronic mascular rheumatism, mascular rigidity, neuralgia, arthritis, gout, swelling of gland and syphilis, anaemia, weakness after illness, chronic gastroenteric catarrhs and fatigue, evidation after getting a wind, haemorrhoids, scabies, honeycomb ringworm, scaly tetter, moist tetter, leucodermia and other chronic skin diseases and ulcers'.

Chi-no-ike Jigoku The name means 'blood hell' and comes from the surprising red of the water (due to ferrous oxide); for this it is worth seeing. To reach this and the following *jigoku*, it is necessary to take a bus or taxi to Chinoike stop. The two hells are a short walk back up the hill.

Tatsumaki Jigoku This is the only geyser of the Beppu hells. The name means 'waterspout hell' and it erupts frequently enough to be worth waiting for.

Tsurumi Jigoku Not on the regular route, this *jigoku* is close to the Suginoi Hotel. It also has a number of Buddha statues, said to be 'in good taste'.

Takasagi-yama Mountain
One of the other sightseeing targets, this mountain is known for its semiwild monkeys (tame enough to have no fear of humans, but wild enough not to trust). The mountain is most easily reached by bus from Beppu station; ask at the information centre for directions.

Daibutsu
This large concrete figure of Buddha is a rather unusual sight in Beppu; it is mostly of curiosity value. Unlike the usual benevolent visage, this Buddha scowls and looks generally unpleasant. Mixed into the concrete are the ashes of thousands of cremated Buddhists.

Hoyurando Hot-spring Baths
The best (perhaps only) outdoor hot-spring pools around Beppu are at Hoyurando, a hotel-style resort; the name translates as either 'Recreation land' or 'Recuperation land'. Behind the hotel building are two sulphurous, bluish-white, outdoor pools. Bathing is mixed but there are segregated pools inside the buildings.

To use the baths, you enter the hotel lobby, pay the fee, then leave by the rear and follow the long covered walkway downhill to the baths. After disrobing and washing, you then enter the chosen bath or pool. The outdoor pools are most enjoyable in warm, sunny weather, although the warm water guarantees comfort in any season while submerged. There are also two kinds of mud baths.

Behind the hotel and to the left is the source of the hot water, marked by the bright colours of chemicals precipitated from the subterranean water as it cools.

Hoyurando is a couple of km beyond the *jigoku* of the Kannawa area, on the road that forks off to the right. There is a bus service (en route to Ajimu); the stop is Hoyurando. On the way the bus passes through another of the eight active hot-spring areas, Myoban. Numbers of little tent-like grass huts have been built over the sources of undergound steam and heat to form natural steam baths.

Suginoi Hotel

The huge Suginoi Hotel can be recommended for its annexe, Suginoi Palace. Along with arcade games, it has a large stage with a nightly production of a play, mini-circus or other act. In the same complex are two gigantic bath rooms, both the size of an aircraft hangar, one each for men and women.

In each are several pools of different size and temperature; from two-people size to gigantic, from frigid to *very* hot. Decorations on the men's side include a waterfall, a slide, *torii* gate and a Chinese-style temple with heated marble floor. The ladies' side has a large and benevolent Buddha and equally lush greenery.

Oishi-so Bath

This smaller scale bath is open to the public. It has tastefully decorated pools, with rock walls and floors. The Oishi-so bath is a short distance down from the cluster of *jigoku* on the main road and it

also offers accommodation. A sand bath is included in the amenities.

Hot Sand Baths

Another activity to enjoy in Beppu is a sand bath, where you can be buried to the neck in naturally hot, steaming sand. Public sand baths (*suna*) are found both on the beach and indoors at Takegawara. The latter is a large, old, wooden building where you pay at the entrance, put your clothes in a locker, rinse at the small concrete tub, pick up your towel (or one of the many lying around), and follow one of the ladies to the hole she has dug for you in the sand. Lie down, put the towel where it will do the most good, and relax while she piles hot sand over your body. A feeling of infinite relaxation will overtake you as the warmth permeates. When your time is up, rinse off the sand, soap, rinse again and it's all over. Take your own soap and towel. Definitely worthwhile and it costs only a few hundred yen.

It's quite common to have your picture taken in the sand bath; preset your camera, and use sign language to explain to the 'burier' what you want. It is best to keep your camera in a plastic bag until it is time to take the picture, otherwise the lens will steam up.

There is also an open-air sand bath on the beach near Kamegawa station; ask for *sunayu*.

Places to Stay

In addition to countless hotels, *ryokan* and *minshuku*, there is also the *Beppu Youth Hostel*. The information centre should have instructions on how to get there. It is very close to the Suginoi Hotel.

Getting There & Away

In addition to train services and flights from nearby Oita Airport (which is actually north of Beppu, on the Kunisaki Peninsula), there are also ferries to points on Shikoku. The dock is 10 minutes from the station by bus. There are regular overnight ferries between Beppu and Hiroshima, Kobe and Osaka, as well as between nearby Oita and Kobe (stopping at Matsuyama en route).

Some of the boats to Kobe and Osaka stop at ports in Shikoku en route, and the last boat of the evening passes through much of the most scenic part of the Inland Sea in daylight.

YUFUIN-ONSEN

This is another hot-spring resort town, not too far from Beppu. Accommodation is about Y10,000 a night, so is not for budget travellers, but if you are not worried about money you could enjoy staying at one of the thatched-roof farmhouses that serve as inns.

The town reputedly has the only free public bath in Japan. The setting is very scenic, with a mountain in the background. It can be reached by bus directly from Beppu or indirectly via Oita by train.

YAMANAMI HIGHWAY

Beppu is the eastern terminus of this highway that crosses Kyushu via Mt Aso and Kumamoto, ending in Nagasaki. It passes through some of the prettiest countryside in Kyushu and can be recommended. In the past there have been buses that made the trip directly. It is likely that there is still such a connection, so inquire locally.

USA

To the north of Beppu lies the shrine city of Usa. The bright orange shrine buildings are decorated with carvings; the style of the buildings is of the Heian era (1000 to 1100) but the shrine was founded earlier (725). The hill on which the shrine is built is an old burial mound.

Usa was once the political, economic and cultural centre of Kyushu. At one time there were 65 temples in the area, but through the years they have disappeared – only the carved Buddha heads and tombstones scattered around nearby Kunisaki-hanto peninsula testify to its former importance and strong Buddhist influence.

A story, probably doubtful, reported that interest in Usa picked up in the immediate post-war occupation period because of companies who wanted to be able to mark their manufactures 'Made in USA'.

Kunisaki Peninsula

There are nine ferries a day in each direction between Taketazu (Kunisaki Peninsula) and Tokuyama (western Honshu). Sailings are scheduled 24 hours a day (Y300, two hours).

YABAKEI GORGE

There is attractive scenery along the Yamakuni-kawa river in Yabakei gorge. It is pleasant rather than spectacular, as the cliffs on either side of the river are often too far apart and do not soar skyward as do those of some other gorges in Japan.

The gorge is easily seen by bus from Nakatsu. The starting point of the main gorge is near Ao-no-Domon, about 16 km out of Nakatsu, and continues for about 10 km to Kakizaka. Apart from the main gorge (Hon-Yabakei), there are several gorges that branch off from it, the most attractive of which is Shin-Yabakei ('deep Yabakei'), beginning at Kakizaka.

The main attractions begin about eight km into the valley, and include Hitome-Hakkei ('one look – eight views') and Utsukushi-dani ('beautiful valley'). However, despite the fame and reputation of the valley, I was somewhat underwhelmed, and would suggest it mostly for those with a little extra time.

Getting There & Away

From Nakatsu station, buses run at least as far as Kakizaka (23 a day); of these, three a day turn and go through Shin-Yabakei (with another four a day that originate at Kakizaka) as far as Bungo-Mori (on Route 210 and JR).

There are six buses a day returning from Bungo-mori to Kakizaka and a much greater number from there back to Nakatsu (or on to Hita), so a one-day excursion out of Nakatsu is possible.

MOJI

There are two daily boats between Moji (Shin Moji-ko port) and Osaka, both leaving late in the afternoon. This is a way to cover a long distance while saving a night's accommodation charge.

Information for getting to the dock is given in the Kitakyushu section.

Southern Islands

There are two chains of islands to the south of the main islands of Japan: the Nansei-shoto group, stretching south and east from southern Kyushu; and the Ogasawara-shoto group (the Bonin islands) more-or-less due south of Tokyo and a continuation of the Izu Seven Islands.

Nansei-shoto Islands

South of Kyushu and stretching to Taiwan are the Nansei (southwest) Islands. Some are mere atolls while others support sizeable populations. As far south as Yoron-to is Kagoshima-ken, while Okinawa and all the islands south of it make up Okinawa-ken.

Close to Kagoshima are Tanegashima and Yakushima, and further south is the Amami-shoto group (which includes Amami-oshima, Tokuno-shima, Okino-erabu-jima and Yoron-to).

Further south again is the Ryukyu group (made up of Okinawa and the islands around it), the Saki group (around Miyako) and the Yaeyama group (Ishigaki, Iriomote and Yonaguni). All offer a semitropical flavour not found in the main islands of Japan.

The culture of the Nansei Islands is basically Japanese, but there is also a Chinese element. The islands closest to Kagoshima were most strongly influenced by the Satsuma culture of the Kagoshima area, while the islands closest to Taiwan had the greatest Chinese influence. The unfortunate islanders had the misfortune of being squeezed between two powers and had to pay tribute to both, causing much misery in olden times.

Until quite recently there was a distinct Okinawan language, related to Japanese but quite incomprehensible to main-island Japanese, even to those of the Satsuma area. The dialect in common use is still incomprehensible.

Many place names use unique local pronunciation of *kanji*; these are used in this book as much as possible and may differ from other sources that use standard Japanese (but incorrect) pronunciation.

Snake Warning
Nearly all islands except Miyako are inhabited by a venomous snake – the *habu*. Every year about 300 people are bitten, four or five of whom die. Prompt medical treatment from special clinics keeps the toll this low.

The snakes are nocturnal so be especially careful at night. Carry a bright light (which they dislike) and make lots of noise. Walking heavily is effective because, although snakes are deaf, they can feel the vibrations. They are always found in pineapple plantations.

Getting There & Away
Air There are air services to Tanegashima, Yakushima, Amami-oshima, Kikai-jima, Tokuno-jima, Kume-jima, Kita Daito-jima, Minami Daito-jima, Miyako-jima, Shimoji-jima, Tarama-to, Ishigaki-jima, Yonaguni-jima and Hateruma-to.

Ferry There are boat services from Tokyo, Osaka/Kobe, Hakata, Fukuoka (northern

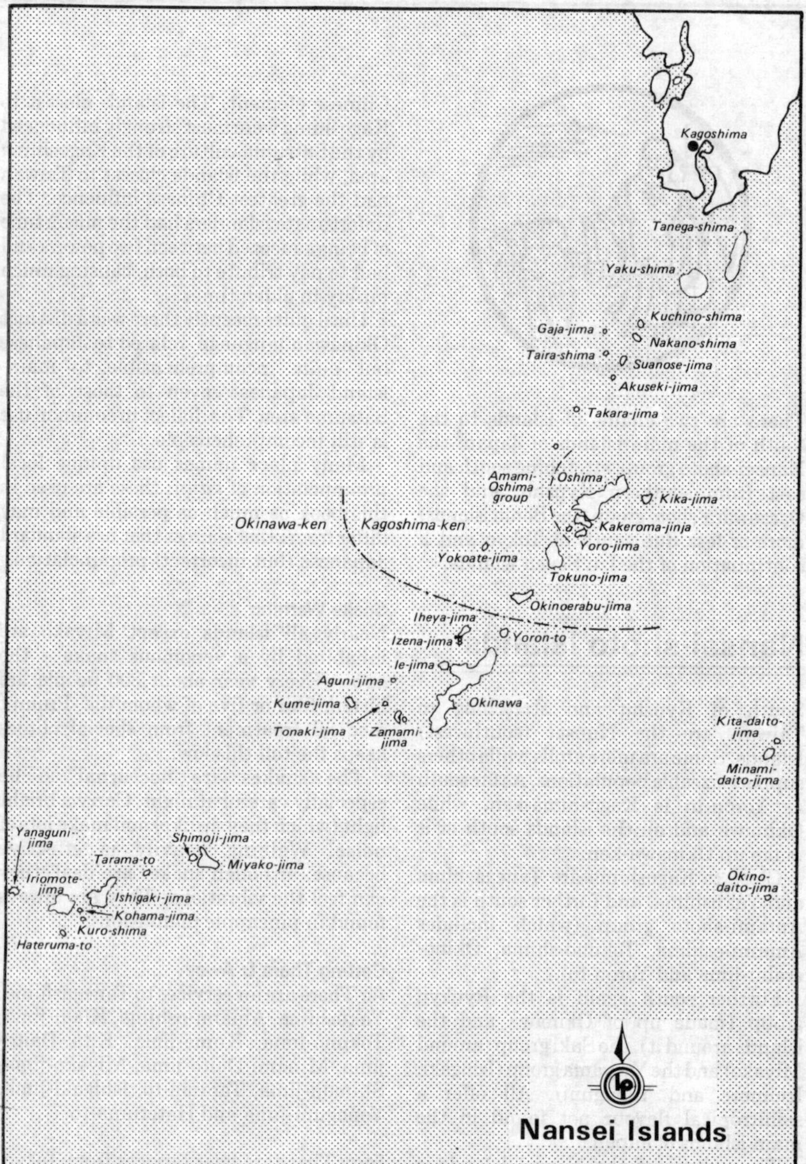

Kagoshima

Tanega-shima

Yaku-shima

Kuchino-shima

Gaja-jima

Nakano-shima

Taira-shima

Suanose-jima

Akuseki-jima

Takara-jima

Amami-Oshima group

Oshima

Kika-jima

Okinawa-ken

Kagoshima-ken

Kakeroma-jinja

Yoro-jima

Yokoate-jima

Tokuno-jima

Okinoerabu-jima

Iheya-jima

Izena-jima

Yoron-to

Ie-jima

Aguni-jima

Kume-jima

Okinawa

Kita-daito-jima

Tonaki-jima

Zamami-jima

Minami-daito-jima

Yanaguni-jima

Shimoji-jima

Iriomote-jima

Tarama-to

Miyako-jima

Ishigaki-jima

Kohama-jima

Kuro-shima

Okino-daito-jima

Hateruma-to

Nansei Islands

Kyushu) and Kagoshima (southern Kyushu) to Naha on Okinawa. Many of these ships stop at some of the smaller islands between Kagoshima and Okinawa (the Amami-shoto group of islands, a group beginning just north of Okinawa), and there are separate services from Kagoshima to just this group as well as to the two closer islands of Tanegashima and Yakushima.

TANEGASHIMA ISLAND

There is no special attraction on Tanegashima other than its relative remoteness; the island is flat and agricultural. There are campsites, and a bus service runs several times a day between the north and south. The main city and boat landing point is Nishino-omote.

Getting There & Away

Both this island and Yakushima are close to southern Kyushu and are easily reached by boat (two or more sailings a day to each island), or by air from Kagoshima.

YAKUSHIMA ISLAND

Whereas Tanegashima is quite flat, Yakushima has the highest mountain in Kyushu, Miyano-ura-dake (1935 metres), plus a number of lesser peaks. The island is well-known for huge centuries-old cedar trees (*yaku-sugi*).

Boats from Kagoshima dock at Miyano-ura, and there are several buses daily

covering three-quarters of the distance around the island.

AMAMI-SHOTO ISLANDS

The Amami group comprises the main islands of Amami-oshima, Kikai-jima, Tokuno-shima, Okino-erabu-jima and Yoron-to. While there are no single attractions (these islands are also basically agricultural, producing semitropical crops such as bananas, pineapples, sugar, etc), there are many good beaches for relaxation.

The scenery of Amami-oshima and the other islands is beautiful. There is a bus service through Amami, or you can rent a bicycle or motorcycle. Camping is good. In contrast with the emerald colour of the coral sea around Okinawa, the water here is deep blue.

OKINAWA ISLAND

The largest of the southwest islands is

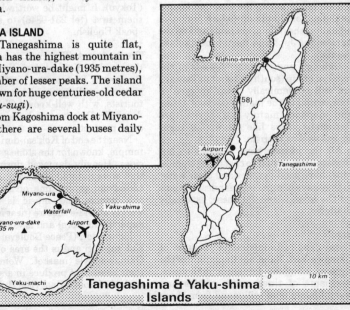

Tanegashima & Yaku-shima Islands

Okinawa. From the 14th to the 19th century, this was a nominally independent kingdom with its own language and culture. Both were related to Japanese but there was a strong Chinese influence. The rulers of both Japan and China maintained suzerainty of the islands, and the people were kept poor by having to provide tribute to both governments.

In the last century the Japanese connection became dominant, but the people have generally been regarded as somewhat second-class citizens. After WW II the American military occupation continued, making travel there difficult until 1972 when it reverted to Japanese control.

During the war the Japanese military treated the Okinawans much like subject peoples, and a very large number of civilians were killed during the invasion (many murdered by the mainland Japanese). For this reason there is still much resentment toward both the mainland and toward the emperor, so schools refuse to sing the song that is used as the national anthem (which is not, in actuality, the official anthem) and refuse to raise the Japanese flag at most school events.

Okinawa and the other islands of the Ryukyu group (south and west to Taiwan) are still economically disadvantaged in comparison to the main islands of Japan and depend mainly on agriculture (especially crops like pineapple, sugar etc) as well as tourism.

All the islands have a warm to hot climate, very similar to that of the tropics. Most have good beaches and clear water so they have become popular destinations for the main-island Japanese, especially in winter.

Naha

Today the administrative centre of Okinawa-ken, Naha was the capital of the Ryukyu kingdom for about 400 years. Remnants of three major castles and several lesser ones still stand from those days, along with some historic gates and other relics of Ryukyu design. Although the design of some of these structures appears Chinese, the architecture is an authentically Ryukyuan style that evolved through the centuries.

Information A good first stop is the tourist information office, on the city side of the harbour and river near the end of Meiji-bashi bridge. It is near the bus terminal and can be recognised by its red roof-tiles. Staff there can provide ample information for getting around and can also make hotel bookings.

Additional information on Okinawa is available from the TIC in Tokyo, including the booklet *Okinawa Japan* and the photocopied sheets *How to Get to Keelung* (No 20) and *Okinawa* (No 54) which give updated information on ships to Naha, hotels, etc.

Information can also be obtained from the Okinawa-ken office in the Kokusai-kanko-kaikan building in Marunouchi (Tokyo). It might be worthwhile ringing them first (tel 231-0848) to see if they speak English.

The Boulevards The main area of Naha is the 1.6-km Kok'sai-dori (International Boulevard). It has several large department stores as well many shops catering for tourists, with well-known Okinawa products like Bingata textiles, and shell and coral products.

Near the end of Kok'sai-dori is Sogen-ji temple, known for the stone gates on two sides. Heavily damaged during WW II, they were restored afterward. A uniquely Okinawan programme of classical and folk dances and music is performed weekly at Oki-e theatre (near Mitsukoshi department store) and is worth seeing.

Heiwa-dori (Peace Boulevard) runs off Kok'sai-dori and is the area of a typical Okinawa-style market. Women sit by their baskets of produce in a scene more typical of South-East Asia than Japan.

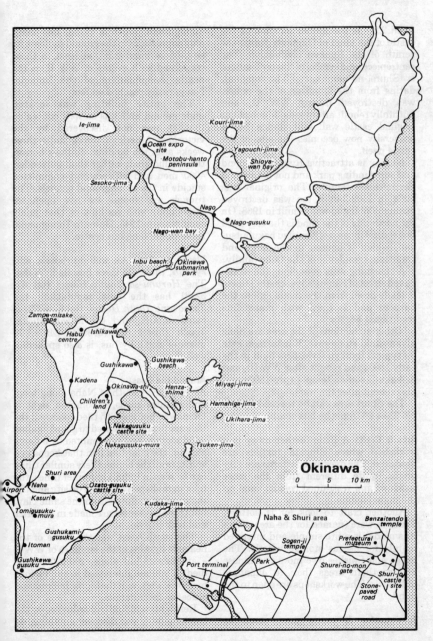

Okinawa

0   5   10 km

Naha & Shuri area

Shuri This is the former location of the castle of the kings of Okinawa during the zenith of the Ryukyu civilisation. The centrepiece, and symbol of this civilisation, is Shurei-no-mon gate. The original, dating from the founding of the castle, was destroyed during WW II, and faithfully rebuilt afterwards. Much of the original castle wall still stands but a university now occupies the site of the castle itself.

Nearby is attractive Ryutan-ike pond and surrounding park and not far away is Benzaitendo temple. The original was built in 1502 but it too was destroyed during WW II and was rebuilt in 1968. On the north side of the pond is the very good prefectural museum, Kenritsu hakubutsu-kan, which is housed in the large and traditional residence of the Osho family.

A charming walk goes along the stone-paved street of Kinjo ('silver castle') town. It leads down from the castle site to the harbour and is lined with many fine traditional houses.

Other attractions of the area are Sone hiyan-utaki stone gate, Kankaimon gate (of typical Ryukyu style, first built in the early 1500s and rebuilt after WW II), and Enkaku-ji somon temple (pre-1500s and also rebuilt after the war).

The Shuri area can be reached by bus No 25 or 26 from the bus centre.

Arts & Crafts A little further away is a workshop where Bingata textiles are produced. The dyes and patterns are very bright, quite different from the more subdued and restrained colours used on the main islands.

Another craft to look for is pottery. Tsuboya ware (named for the area where it is made) is quite simple and intended mainly for use as storage vessels. The forms and finishes owe more to Chinese and southern areas than to Japanese influences. The workshops are open to the public.

Tomigusuku A castle once stood at Tomigusuku, south of Naha, but today only depressions in the ground indicate its site. More interesting, at least to those concerned with events of WW II, is the nearby headquarters of the Imperial Navy, easily reached on foot.

The entire building was located underground and was so well concealed that it was not discovered by the victorious American forces until three weeks after the landing. To their horror, they found that, rather than surrender, 4000 men and officers had committed suicide in the underground tunnels. The tunnels and rooms are now open for inspection, with no hint of that grisly occurrence in 1945. Buses to Tomigusuku leave from Naha bus centre.

Places to Stay As well as hotels and *ryokan*, there are three hostels in Naha. The *Harumi-so Youth Hostel* (tel 67-3218) has the best reputation; the *Tamazano Youth Hostel* (tel 67-5377) is rated as OK, and the *Maeda-Misaki Youth Hostel* (tel (098964) 2497), 70 minutes north by bus, is also spoken of well.

Around the Coast
As you travel south of Naha along town and country roads, a common sight is Okinawan houses with tiled roofs. All the tiles are firmly cemented to guard against wind storms, and surmounted by a fierce *shiisaa*, the guardian lion that keeps evil spirits from the house. (Very similar tiling can be seen in India.) In former times, the tiles were shaped and fired on site and the *shiisaa* was sculpted from the same clay, but these days most are made in factories and lack individuality.

The south coast was the scene of the heaviest fighting of the landings of WW II – at Mabuni hill alone, 200,000 people died. If you are interested in the various memorial sites, visit the tourist information office for more details.

Residents still find live ordnance on the battlefields. If you discover anything, do not touch it; notify the police or contact the USAF Kadena base.

Gyokusendo This is a limestone cave with a claimed 460,000 stalactites and other limestone configurations, many of which have interesting and lovely colours. About 800 metres of the cave is open for inspection.

Kasuri If you are interested in weaving, visit the village of Kasuri (comprising Kiyan, Motobo and Teruya) where the hand-woven, vegetable-dyed Kasuri fabrics (mostly silk) are made.

Coastal Views Continuing around the south coast and up the east, you are constantly in view of the deep-emerald sea. Along this coast and others you are likely to see uniquely Okinawan tombs – large structures with a surrounding semicircular wall, set into hillsides overlooking the coast. There is nothing like them elsewhere in Japan.

Nakagusuku Castle Site This is possibly the finest of such sites on Okinawa; the length and height of the remaining walls and three citadels give a good idea of the scale of the former buildings. From the ramparts you can see the Pacific Ocean in one direction and the East China Sea in the other. It is close to Nakagusuku-mura ('Central Castle Village').

Nakumuru House (Nakumuru-ke) In the same area as Nakagusuku castle, this is probably the finest residence on Okinawa. It was built in the mid-1700s by a wealthy farmer, and the five structures embody the best of traditional Okinawan building and decorative techniques.

Okinawa City

Much of this city is aimed at providing recreation for the US airmen of nearby Kadena Air Force Base. With its many clubs and bars, it bears little resemblance to anything typically Okinawan or Japanese (other than an ability to make money). The mood is American, or at least the Japanese impression of American.

Of great interest to the Japanese is Plaza House shopping centre, complete with large car park (an unaffordable luxury in most of Japan because of land costs). The Tuttle Bookshop stocks a large number of books on Okinawa.

Okinawa Children's Land (Kodomo-no-Kuni)
Southeast of the city, this aquarium raises more than 60 kinds of reptiles, and has exhibitions of more than 200 kinds of tropical freshwater fish.

Municipal Colosseum At Gushikawa, near Children's Land, this is the venue of Sunday bull fights. These are not like the Spanish variety, but are 'bull *sumo*', each bull trying to force the opponent out of the ring by locking horns and pushing. Similar fights are found on several other islands of Japan and as far south as Indonesia.

Southeast Botanical Garden This garden has a large variety and huge number of tropical plants, 600 kinds of flowers and 200 types of tropical fruit trees intended to emphasise the island's near-tropical climate. A small lake and boats are also attractive.

Hedo-misaki Cape
The view from this, the northern tip of Okinawa, is very pretty. On a clear day you can see Yoron Island on the horizon. The view is definitely worth the trip, passing a number of attractive villages along the way.

West Coast
Much of the west coast has been set aside as Okinawa Coast Quasi-National Park, which takes in the area from Hedo-misaki cape to the northern side of Motobu-hanto peninsula, and resumes from the south side of the peninsula almost an equal distance to Zampa-misaki. The main

attraction is the view of the coast and the beautiful colours of the water.

Motobu-hanto Peninsula

At the northeast neck of the peninsula, there is a beautiful view overlooking Yagachi and Okubo islands.

In 1975 a mini World Expo was held near the northwest tip of the peninsula, based on the theme of using oceans. Although the exhibition lasted only six months, sufficient attractions have been carried over or added to give you an enjoyable day's outing.

The Okinawa Village Pavilion demonstrates the old culture of Okinawa and has examples of houses in both traditional and modern styles. The Oceanic Culture Pavilion shows the rich variety of cultures found among the races and ethnic groups of the South Pacific.

On the same site is the largest aquarium in the world, featuring three display areas that show tropical, ocean and deep-sea fish as well as a number of performing dolphins (at Okichan Theatre).

Floating City is a science-fiction writer's delight – a large steel multi-columned structure in the water that supposedly represents the way we will live in the future (with appropriate phrases such as 'new era', 'producing harmony between science and nature', etc). It's interesting, but not to be taken seriously. All attractions are closed on Mondays.

At the northern end of the site is the graceful arc of beautiful Expo beach.

Accommodation in the vicinity of the Expo site is generally expensive. Okinawa Resort Station is a resort village for young people, and uses retired JNR sleeping cars for accommodation. They had to be brought to Okinawa, along with a retired steam engine, as there are no railways on the island.

Nago

At the southern neck of the peninsula, Nago was little damaged during WW II so you can still see several houses in the traditional Okinawan style. There are also tall, 300-year old *gajyumaru* trees on the southeast approaches to the city.

In late January and early February the cherry blossoms are beautiful on the site of former Nago-gusuku castle, reached via a long stone staircase. At the top, you can enjoy an excellent view of the surrounding sea and land.

Okinawa Marine Park A long walkway extends beyond the shallows of a reef here to a column with underwater windows so visitors may look out from beneath sea-level. Depending on conditions, the number of fish in view may be rather limited; visitors generally tend to visit Ocean Expo instead.

In addition to the 'reverse aquarium' where fish can come to look at people, there is a museum showing many of the sea shells found around the island. Glass-bottomed boats may be rented as well.

A short distance to the south are three fine beaches, the first of which is Inbu Beach.

Habu Centre Here you can see the venomous *habu* snake in perfect safety. A feature is a fight between a *habu* and a mongoose; the agile animal wins about 99% of the time, particularly because the nocturnal snake is at a disadvantage. The fights are staged relatively frequently, probably a reflection of the plentiful snake supply. Recent research has shown that mature snakes can survive two to three years without any food whatsoever.

Places to Stay In addition to several hotels of good quality, there are also many *ryokan*. Bookings may be made at the information centre.

There are three youth hostels: *Naha Youth Hostel* (tel (0988) 57-0073), *Naha Harumi-so Youth Hostel* (tel 67-3218, 67-4422) and *Tamazono-so Youth Hostel* (tel 67-5377).

There is one other youth hostel on Okinawa; it is *Maeda-so Youth Hostel*

(tel (09896) 4-2497), not far from the *habu* centre.

Getting There & Away

Air There are flights between Naha and Seoul, Taipei, Manila, Hong Kong, Guam, Saipan and Nauru.

There are also domestic flights from Sendai, Tokyo, Osaka, Nagoya, Fukuoka, Nagasaki, Kumamoto, Kagoshima, Miyazaki, and the more important small Nansei Islands nearby. Nearly all the main small islands are accessible by air.)

Ferry Arimura Sangyo shipping company operates a weekly boat to Taiwan, alternating between Keelung and Kaohshung in northern Taiwan. The ship leaves Naha at 7 pm Friday and reaches Keelung at about 5 pm Saturday. En route it stops at Ishigaki Island from 7 to 9.20 am on Saturday. It leaves Keelung on Monday at 8 am and sails direct to Naha, arriving on Tuesday at 7.20 am. The lowest fare (shared, open *tatami*-mat area) is Y15,600 to Keelung, Y18,000 to Kaohshung. Reservations are recommended. The phone numbers of Arimura Sangyo offices are: Tokyo (03) 562-2091, Osaka (06) 531-9271 and Naha (0988) 68-2191.

There are domestic boat services to Naha from Tokyo, Osaka/Kobe, Hakata (Fukuoka) and Kagoshima. Because several of these stop at islands between Kagoshima and Naha, island hopping is feasible.

Getting Around

There are several bus tours (in Japanese only) to different destinations on Okinawa lasting 4½ to 9½ hours. There are also many local buses for the adventurous.

OTHER RYUKYU ISLANDS
Ie-jima Island

Off the Motobu-hanto peninsula, Ie-jima island is easily traversed in a short time. There are many lovely views of the deep-blue sea. The Travel Village (on the side nearest Okinawa) is especially aimed at young travellers.

Minni-jima Island

This island is claimed to have the most beautiful sunsets in Okinawa.

Kohama-jima Island

Once bypassed by tourists, Kohama now has full-scale recreational facilities (Japanese-style) and is attracting more visitors to its fine beaches of white sand and the coral reefs offshore.

Kudaka-jima Island

The 'Island of the Gods', just off Okinawa, is quite sacred to Okinawans. There are many burials here and funerary practices in the past were rather unusual. Many bodies were exposed to the elements in special places, and only after decomposition were the bones cleaned and buried.

Especially on Kudaka, but true everywhere on Okinawa, foreigners are ill-advised to enter cemeteries. It upsets many of the local people, who believe that the presence of an outsider (especially a foreigner) will disturb the spirits of the dead, with bad results for the living. It is worth reading up in advance of a visit to Kudaka to avoid misunderstanding. The Tuttle bookstore in Naha has books on the subject.

Other Islands

Other islands that may be visited from Okinawa are Iheya, Izena, Kerama (a group of about 20) and Kume. Information on how to get there can be obtained at the information centre or from travel agents.

MIYAKO-JIMA ISLAND

There are many beautiful views on Miyako-jima, as well as fine beaches. Miyako-jima island was not damaged during WW II so its appearance is more traditional than Okinawa. Most houses are surrounded by walls of coral as protection against the frequent typhoons. Unfortunately it can be a little difficult to actually see the houses because a screen of wood and rock blocks the view through the gateway. Its purpose is to keep out evil spirits, believed able to hop only in straight lines. Such superstitions are still strong and a talisman will often be seen on a wall opposite the road that ends at a T-junction.

Miyako-jima island is at least as interesting for culture as its basically agricultural landscapes. It is one of the few islands free of the deadly *habu* snake.

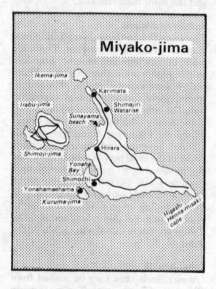

Ohonoyama-mura

Miyako Tropical Botanical Garden near here occupies 226 hectares of land and boasts 40,000 trees and more than 1200 kinds of flowering plants from Central and South America, Africa and the Philippines.

The 'poll stone' near Ohonoyama is a relic of harsh times in the past, when the islanders were little more than slaves, being taxed by both Chinese and Satsuma authorities. A person was compelled to pay taxes when his or her height equalled

that of this stone. Its name is Jintozeizeki or Bubakariisu, depending on the dialect.

Yonahamae Beach

Four km of white sand stretch along the shore and the blue waters offer excellent swimming.

Sunayama (Sand Mountain) Beach

Swimming is also good here, and nearby Miyako-jinja shrine is worth a visit.

Agari-henna Misaki Cape

The view over the sea here is beautiful. Cliffs drop to the sea, rocks jut above its surface and, with the exception of a solitary lighthouse, there are no nearby buildings to interfere with the wild atmosphere.

Jofu Fabric

A common sight following the rainy season is great lengths of yarn draped over any available support to dry in the sun after dyeing. It is then woven into Jofu fabric, a well-known product of the island and historically an item used in payment of taxes.

Places to Stay

There are several *minshuku* near the harbour. A good one is Ueno-so.

Getting There & Away

Ferry In addition to regular air services, there are scheduled boats between Okinawa (Naha) and Ishigaki. Two lines operate the ships and they largely complement each other. There is a Naha – Miyako boat every one to four days, and an Ishigaki – Miyako boat every two to seven days. In addition to these, there are some sailings that skip Miyako, cutting a few hours off the trip between Naha and Ishigaki.

Ships from Naha that make the stop depart at 6 or 8 pm (depending on the line), and depart Ishigaki at 11 am for both lines. Sailing times are: Naha – Miyako 13½ to 14½ hours, Naha – Ishigaki (non-stop) 13 to 14 hours, Miyako – Ishigaki 5½ hours, Ishigaki – Miyako eight hours, Ishigaki – Naha (non-stop) 12 to 14 hours, Miyako – Naha 12½ to 13 hours.

Getting Around
The best way to get around is by bicycle or motorcycle rented from one of the shops near the harbour of the main city, Hirara.

YAEYAMA ISLANDS
The Yaeyama group of islands extends from Ishigaki to Yonaguni in a south-westerly arc.

Ishigaki-jima Island
The most important of the group, Ishigaki-jima island is famed for its many beautiful beaches. The main city and port is Ishigaki.

Miyara Dunchi This is the house of a noble of the old Ryukyu kingdom, which dates from 1819. It follows the plan of houses for people of equal rank that were built around the castle at Shuri on Okinawa. Here it is unique and is the island's most valued cultural asset. It may be described as a *samurai* house, but there were no true *samurai* in this region. It houses a small museum of the period and is also noted for its garden and stone wall.

Yaeyama Shiritsu Museum Exhibits relating to the culture of the Yaeyama islands are on display at this very interesting museum. Labels, unfortunately, are only in Japanese, but most displays can be understood.

Chorin-ji Temple This temple has some beautiful old Buddhist sculptures.

Chinese Cemetery The very Chinese-looking monument here commemorates 128 Chinese who were killed in a fight on a British ship in the last century, and is

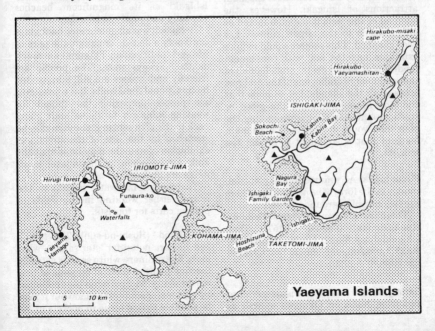

Yaeyama Islands

considered a general monument to peace.

Kabira-wan Bay Most visitors consider this the most beautiful place on the island. Pearls are cultivated here and are of an unusual (and thus very costly) black hue. They take the name of the island group, Yaeyama. The bay can be reached by bus.

Beaches Most visitors will want to enjoy the fine beaches of Ishigaki; equipment for both skindiving and scuba are available for rent. Since there are many types of incredible and beautiful tropical fish in the waters around this (and all the other) islands, diving can be recommended. Water-skiing and fishing are other potential activities.

At the moment there are still good coral reefs around much of the island, with the usual complement of colourful fish, clear water, etc; they have been one of the main attractions of Ishigaki. However, the survival of the reefs is not guaranteed as an extension to the airport runway has been planned. This project would require extension into the sea, with consequent landfill that would destroy much or all of the reefs near Shiraho, one of the best reef areas of all the islands. Let us hope that common sense overcomes the greed or political ambition that is promoting the plan that would destroy one of the main features that is supposed to attract the tourists.

Places to Stay Accommodation is plentiful, mostly in the form of *minshuku*, but there are two camping grounds as well.

There are three youth hostels: *Yashima Ryokan* (tel (09808) 2-3157), *Trek Ishigaki-Jima Youth Hostel* (tel (09808) 6-8257) and *Ishigaki-shi-tei Youth Hostel* (tel (09808) 2-2720).

Getting There & Away There is air service to and from Naha on Okinawa as well as to Yonaguni, Tarama, and Hateruma islands.

Nearby Taketomi can be reached by ferry in about 20 minutes (Y300, eight trips a day) and Iriomote is accessible by regular boat or hovercraft.

There is a regular Naha – Miyako – Ishigaki (and return) boat service, and the weekly boat to Taiwan from Naha also stops at Ishigaki, but only on the outward journey.

Getting Around Bicycles, motorcycles and cars can be rented from several shops near the centre of town (even by bicycle it is possible to see the island in a day). There is also a bus service.

Taketomi-jima Island

Just a short distance west of Ishigaki, tiny Taketomi (11 km in circumference) can be explored easily in a day by bicycle (available near the boat dock). The island is very popular with day-trippers from Ishigaki as its magnificent beaches virtually surround the island.

Because it was an untouristed backwater until only a decade or so ago, the pace of life and traditions on Taketomi are much as they always were. The people are friendly and houses are still surrounded by traditional coral walls. It is common to see people preparing the thread for weaving *minsaori* fabric, a craft going back to the 17th century; the yarn may be stretched by the side of the street. An exhibition of weaving may be seen at the Folk Art Museum in the village; small items are on sale.

There are some water buffalo on the island, either working in the fields or pulling carts for tourists.

Star Sand (Hoshi-no-sun) *Taketomi's* beaches are noted for 'star sand' – what looks like ordinary white sand is actually the five-pointed skeletal remains of tiny sea creatures. Most of it has been collected by visitors (or souvenir sellers) but it may be possible to find some in pockets in the coral, particularly on the south side of the island. The sand is stirred up from the depths by storms and washed ashore, so the supply is renewed periodically. (Not generally known is that this sand is found on all the Yaeyama islands.) If you find some, remember the motto: 'Take a little and it will bring lots of happiness; take a lot and it will bring little happiness'. Leave some for the next person.

Places to Stay There are *minshuku*, a *Youth Hostel* and *Takana Ryokan* (tel (09808) 5-2151) in Taketomi.

Iriomote Island

More than 80% of this island (plus nearby Kohama, Taketomi, Kuroshima and Aragusuku islands) forms Iriomote National Park, habitat of the primitive Triomote wild cat. Thought to have remained unchanged in five to 10 million years, this 'living fossil' is the size of a domestic cat and nocturnal, so it is seldom seen, even by residents. It is believed there are only 30 to 40 still living.

Star-sand is also found on the island but you are not allowed to collect it because Iriomote is a national park. The island also has *habu* snakes, so take care.

Ura-uchi-kawa River The best single excursion on the island is up the Ura-uchi-kawa river. Beginning at the mouth of the river, the boat usually carries about 12 people. There is no trouble making up a party because many day-trippers cross from Ishigaki. After half an hour or so, you disembark and walk for about 40 minutes through canopied near-jungle to two pretty waterfalls, Mariyudo and Kampira. The first has three drops totalling 33 metres, ending in a deep pool; the latter is a long incline with numerous Jacob's wells.

Skindiving As on many of the other islands, skindiving in the colourful coral

beds among equally colourful fish is to be recommended. A barrier reef surrounds the island.

Places to Stay There are several *minshuku* as well as two *Youth Hostels* at Funaurako. Of the hostels, *Irumote-so Youth Hostel* is the better and has pleasant staff and a nice view over the countryside.

Getting There & Around The boat, and possibly a hydrofoil, from Ishigaki (60 to 90 minutes) docks at Ohara, from where a bus leaves soon afterward for the other side of the island and the trip up the Ura-uchi-kawa river. You can rent bicycles and motorcycles at a shop two minutes from Irumote-so Youth Hostel.

Yonaguni-jima Island

This is the westernmost part of Japan, and on a clear day you can see Taiwan from Irizaki (West Cape). The main attraction is scenery, beaches, warm water, and the largest moths in the world. There is a beautiful view from the top of the 231-metre-hill overlooking the village of Sonae.

Kubura-wari One curiosity is this natural hole in the ground near Kubura. Legend has it that anyone able to jump over it won't have to pay taxes and will have a long life, and women will give birth easily. It is wide enough that few are known to test the legend. It is surrounded by interesting rock formations and is behind Kubura school.

Places to Stay There are only *minshuku*, no youth hostels.

Getting Around Bicycles and motorcycles may be rented for convenient transport.

Hateruma-jima Island

This small island is the southernmost part of Japan and is a pleasant place to visit. One good place to stay is a room adjacent to the Ishino-ume Restaurant.

Ogasawara-shoto Islands

South of the Izu islands is another group, the Ogasawara-shoto islands. These are part of the Tokyo-to administrative district and extend to latitudes as far south as Okinawa.

The islands are ideal for really getting away from it all; access is only by ship from Tokyo (generally twice a week), and they are beyond TV and regular radio range. The climate is semitropical (slightly cooler than Okinawa), small palm trees grow, and there are frequent rain showers. While the Izu islands offer a good weekend excursion for swimming and meeting other people, the Ogasawara-shoto islands are better for quiet exploration and adventure.

The main islands are named after family members, such as Chichi-jima (father), Haha-jima (mother), and Ani-jima (elder brother). The first two are the main islands; Ani is a small island just north of Chichi-jima. Muko-jima is a cluster of small islands to the north.

To the south are the Kazan (Volcano) islands, which include Io-jima (better known in English as Iwo-jima), famed as a battle site in WW II and memorialised in the photo of Marines raising the US flag atop 185-metre Suribachi-san (a posed shot, by the way).

Tourists are not allowed on Io-jima because large areas still have live ordnance from the fighting, and the remains of many Japanese soldiers lie entombed in the caves where they died. Only Chichi and Haha are regularly populated.

CHICHI-JIMA ISLAND

This, the largest island, has peaks up to 600 metres, and also has beaches and good swimming. It is small enough to walk across in two hours, or around in a day; roads are good, and there is a bus service. Bougainvillea and hibiscus give a tropical air.

There are three beaches, one of which is sandy, while another has some coral. Skindiving can be recommended at many places around the island, especially between Chichi-jima and Ani-jima because of the many fantastically coloured tropical fish; they are not afraid of people, and come close. There are also turtles and rays. Scuba and less complex diving equipment is available for hire. You can also rent a boat and circle the island, stopping to dive where desired. It is reminiscent of Australia's Great Barrier Reef. Throwing bread on the water from shore results in 'instant fish'. The water is a darker blue than that of the Okinawa area and is not as clear.

On the west side, the rusting hull of a small ship is a relic of the war. There are also caves around the shore that were used for defence purposes; some are now used by fishermen for storage, and others are blocked by gates.

There are *minshuku* on the island but they tend to be crowded and generally do not serve meals so you have to eat at restaurants or buy food at a local store. The few shops close by 6.30 pm; the hottest nightspot, a coffee shop, is closed by 10 pm.

Because the island was under US control for a long time, many people can communicate in English and there are several US-style buildings, a curiosity to the Japanese.

Getting There & Away

Access is from Tokyo to Futami-ura. There are one or two sailings a week in each direction (depending on season); the trip takes a little over a day. Further information is available at the Tourist Information Center, Tokyo.

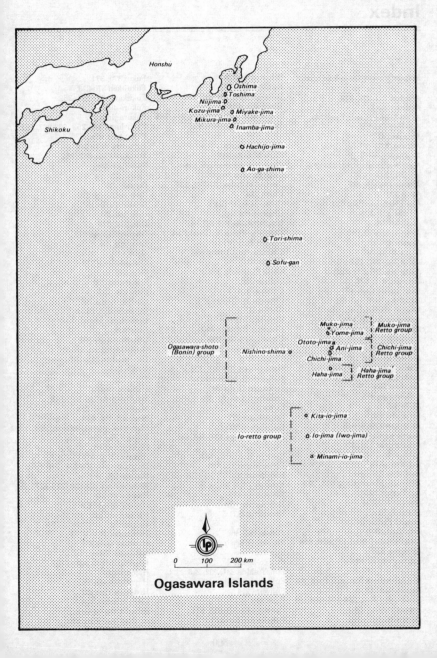

Ogasawara Islands

Index

Map references are in **bold** type.

MAPS

Temperature

To convert °C to °F multiply by 1.8 and add 32

To convert °F to °C subtract 32 and multiply by · 55

Length, Distance & Area

	multiply by
inches to centimetres	2.54
centimetres to inches	0.39
feet to metres	0.30
metres to feet	3.28
yards to metres	0.91
metres to yards	1.09
miles to kilometres	1.61
kilometres to miles	0.62
acres to hectares	0.40
hectares to acres	2.47

Weight

	multiply by
ounces to grams	28.35
grams to ounces	0.035
pounds to kilograms	0.45
kilograms to pounds	2.21
British tons to kilograms	1016
US tons to kilograms	907

A British ton is 2240 lbs, a US ton is 2000 lbs

Volume

	multiply by
Imperial gallons to litres	4.55
litres to imperial gallons	0.22
US gallons to litres	3.79
litres to US gallons	0.26

5 imperial gallons equals 6 US gallons
a litre is slightly more than a US quart, slightly less
than a British one

	°C	°F
	50	122
	45	113
	40	104
	35	95
	30	86
	25	75
	20	68
	15	59
	10	50
	5	41
	0	32

Dear traveller

Prices go up, good places go bad, bad places go bankrupt ... and every guide book is inevitably outdated in places. Fortunately, many travellers write to us about their experiences, telling us when things have changed. If we reprint a book between editions, we try to include as much of this information as possible in a Stop Press section. Most of this information has not been verified by our own writers.

We really enjoy hearing from people out on the road, and apart from guaranteeing that others will benefit from your good and bad experiences, we're prepared to bribe you with the offer of a free book for sending us substantial useful information.

Thank you to everyone who has written, and to those who haven't, I hope you do find this book useful – and that you let us know when it isn't.

Tony Wheeler

Japan grieved in 1989 after the death of Emperor Hirohito. His son Akihito has become the new emperor. Japan's ruling LDP party has lost prestige due to scandals involving its top politicians, which brought down two Prime Ministers in one year. Elections for the House of Representatives were held in February 1990 and, despite all the scandals, the LDP won again.

In Tokyo, there is a new type of accommodation, capsule rooms, which are cheap alternatives for those too drunk or tired to look for a 'real' place to stay. They are basically holes in the wall that measure about 180 cm in length, big enough for one person to lie down in – so long as they don't try to roll over! Capsule rooms contain a bed, a radio alarm, a miniature television and a telephone. They cost the equivalent of UK£14 per night, making them one of the cheapest types of accommodation in Japan.

Money & Costs

Currently, the official exchange rate is around US$1 to ¥148.26. As expected, the economy is doing quite well and inflation is expected to remain at around 1.5%.

Photography

It is difficult to buy 126 film for an instamatic camera. You are much better off buying a new camera, duty free, that takes 135 film. One traveller wrote that he was lucky enough to obtain some 126 film from a special Kodak booth at the Yokatopia Asia-Pacific Expo in Yukuoka. The only other places he saw some 126 film was in Kyoto and Matsumato.

Telephone

For information concerning international calls dial 0057 anywhere in Japan. Collect calls to Switzerland are not possible due to the fact that there is no agreement between NTT (Japan) and PTT (Switzerland). There are reduced tariffs (20% off) and discount tariffs (40% off). Discount hours start at 11 pm and end at 5 am. Check reduced and discount tariff times yourself. If there is no yellow or green international telephone you can use a private telephone and the operator can give you the price of the telephone call.

Getting Around

The best way to get from Bihoro to Akan-ko is with the sightseeing bus. It stops at the Bihoro Pass, Sunayu, on the shores of Lake Kutcharo, Io-san, Kawayu-ansen, Mashu-ko, and Sakadai lookout. Even JR Railpass holders should travel this way as local buses will cost as much and are not convenient. The time you'll save will make up for the cost of the bus.

If you are travelling from Akan-ko to Kushiro you should note that one of the morning buses has a scheduled stop at the sanctuary for White Cranes at Isuruoka. The same bus also stops at Kushiro Airport, so it's a popular way to enter or leave Hokkaido.

Getting There

There is only one boat to the USSR and the cheapest fare is ¥62,600 one way and ¥122,400 return. When you get off the boat, you can't stay overnight at Nakhodka because it's off-limits to foreigners! I think you'd get a better deal if you slept on the train to Moscow or Leningrad, but that's not cheap either. The current one-way train fare is ¥122,000 from Yokohama in Japan to Helsinki in Finland.

Travellers' Tips & Comments

Bread crusts, *pan no mimi* or *hashi*, are either amazingly cheap or free. *Mr Donuts* has American coffee at a cost of ¥200 for a bottomless cup – a bargain! The 3% consumption tax means most things are more expensive now.

Two national holidays have changed: 29 April is now a Green Day and Emperor's Birthday is on 23 December.

Liz Youman

Guides to North-East Asia

China – a travel survival kit
Travelling on your own in China can be exciting and rewarding; it can also be exhausting and frustrating – getting a seat on a train or finding a cheap bed in a hotel isn't always easy. But it can be done and this detailed and comprehensive book tells you how.

Hong, Kong Macau & Canton – a travel survival kit
Essential information on Hong Kong, one of the world's most energetic capitalist states; Macau, a fascinating mixture of Portugal and Las Vegas; and Canton, the gateway to China.

Taiwan – a travel survival kit
This guide takes you from modern cities to traditional villages. If you are interested in the hustle and bustle of business in Taipei you will find this guide invaluable – so will travellers who are looking for mountain hikes and Taoist temples.

Korea – a travel survival kit
Though overshadowed by the might of China and Japan, Korea has a proud and independent culture. Vistors can immerse themselves in seoul or get away to spectacular mountains and untouched villages.

North-East Asia on a shoestring
Shoestring guides give essential information for low-budget travel in an extended region. This book includes up-to-date information on six unique states: China, Hong Kong, Japan, Korea, Macau, and Taiwan.

Tibet – a travel survival kit
After centuries of isolation, this extraordinary region is now open to individual travellers. This comprehensive guidebook has concise background information, and all the facts on how to get around, where to stay, where to eat, what to see . . . and more.

Also available:
Japanese phrasebook (1989), *Korean* phrasebook, *Chinese* phrasebook, and *Tibet* phrasebook.

Lonely Planet Guidebooks

Lonely Planet guidebooks cover virtually every accessible part of Asia as well as Australia, the Pacific, Central and South America, Africa, the Middle East and parts of North America. There are four main series: 'travel survival kits', covering a single country for a range of budgets; 'shoestring' guides with compact information for low-budget travel in a major region; trekking guides; and 'phrasebooks'.

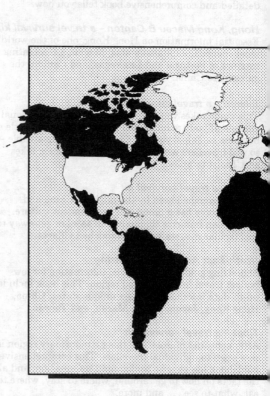

Australia & the Pacific
Australia
Bushwalking in Australia
Papua New Guinea
Papua New Guinea phrasebook
New Zealand
Tramping in New Zealand
Rarotonga & the Cook Islands
Solomon Islands
Tahiti & French Polynesia
Fiji
Micronesia
Tonga
Samoa

South-East Asia
South-East Asia on a shoestring
Malaysia, Singapore & Brunei
Indonesia
Bali & Lombok
Indonesia phrasebook
Burma
Burmese phrasebook
Thailand
Thai phrasebook
Philippines
Pilipino phrasebook

North-East Asia
North-East Asia on a shoestring
China
China phrasebook
Tibet
Tibet phrasebook
Japan
Japanese phrasebook
Korea
Korean phrasebook
Hong Kong, Macau & Canton
Taiwan

West Asia
West Asia on a shoestring
Trekking in Turkey
Turkey
Turkish phrasebook

Indian Ocean
Madagascar & Comoros
Maldives & Islands of the East Indian Ocean
Mauritius, Réunion & Seychelles

Mail Order

Lonely Planet guidebooks are distributed worldwide and are sold by good bookshops everywhere. They are also available by mail order from Lonely Planet, so if you have difficulty finding a title please write to us. US and Canadian residents should write to Embarcadero West, 112 Linden St, Oakland CA 94607, USA and residents of other countries to PO Box 617, Hawthorn, Victoria 3122, Australia.

Lonely Planet

Lonely Planet published its first book in 1973. Tony and Maureen Wheeler had made a lengthy overland trip from England to Australia and, in response to numerous 'how do you do it?' questions, Tony wrote and they published *Across Asia on the Cheap*. It became an instant local best-seller and inspired thoughts of a second travel guide. A year and a half in South-East Asia resulted in their second book, *South-East Asia on a Shoestring*, which they put together in a backstreet Chinese hotel in Singapore in 1975. The 'yellow book', as it quickly became known, soon became *the* guide to the region and has gone through five editions, always with its familiar yellow cover.

Soon other writers came to them with ideas for similar books – books that went off the beaten track with an adventurous approach to travel, books that 'assumed you knew how to get your luggage off the carousel,' as one reviewer put it. Lonely Planet grew from a kitchen table operation to a spare room and then to its own office. Its international reputation began to grow as the Lonely Planet logo began to appear in more and more countries. In 1982 *India – a travel survival kit* won the Thomas Cook award for the best guidebook of the year.

These days there are over 70 Lonely Planet titles. Over 40 people work at our office in Melbourne, Australia and another half dozen at our US office in Oakland, California.

At first Lonely Planet specialised in the Asia region but these days we are also developing major ranges of guidebooks to the Pacific region, to South America and to Africa. The list of walking guides is growing and Lonely Planet now has a unique series of phrasebooks to 'unusual' languages. The emphasis continues to be on travel for travellers and Tony and Maureen still manage to fit in a number of trips each year and play a very active part in the writing and updating of Lonely Planet's guides.

Keeping guidebooks up to date is a constant battle which requires an ear to the ground and lots of walking, but technology also plays its part. All Lonely Planet guidebooks are now stored and updated on computer, and some authors even take lap-top computers into the field. Lonely Planet is also using computers to draw maps and eventually many of the maps will be stored on disk.

The people at Lonely Planet strongly feel that travellers can make a positive contribution to the countries they visit both by better appreciation of cultures and by the money they spend. In addition the company tries to make a direct contribution to the countries and regions it covers. Since 1986 a percentage of the income from each book has gone to aid groups and associations. This has included donations to famine relief in Africa, to aid projects in India, to agricultural projects in Central America, to Greenpeace's efforts to halt French nuclear testing in the Pacific and to Amnesty International. In 1989 $41,000 was donated by Lonely Planet to these projects.